The Psychoanalytic Study of the Child

VOLUME III/IV

INTERNATIONAL UNIVERSITIES PRESS, INC.

NEW YORK   NEW YORK

Manufactured in the United States of America

The Psychoanalytic Study of the Child

VOLUME III/IV

CONTENTS

NOTES ON THE THEORY OF AGGRESSION

By HEINZ HARTMANN, M.D., ERNST KRIS, Ph.D., and RUDOLPH M. LOEWENSTEIN, M.D. (New York)

I. *Introduction*

The concern with problems of aggression crystallized only gradually in Freud's thinking, but once it had taken root, the delay seemed to him hardly comprehensible (1932). Freud made his own "resistance" responsible for that retardation; however, it seems preferable to consider some of the steps that led him to the final formulation of his views.

The age-old religious tradition that abounds with references to the dichotomy of love and hate seems not to have determined his interest before he had established his own approach; nor did he seek stimulation in Nietzsche's revelatory writings. He relied mainly on his own tools, on the constant interaction of clinical data and theoretical assumptions. Most of Freud's formulations on the problem of aggression are intimately linked to that period in his writings, approximately from 1911 to 1926, in which he reformulated in several steps his basic hypotheses.

Freud's points of departure were his earlier findings and hypotheses regarding the nature of instinctual drives. In his first theoretical formulations on this subject (*Three Contributions to the Theory of Sex*, 1905), his attention centered on the development of sexuality and on the vicissitudes of psychic energy attached to the sexual impulse, i. e., on the vicissitudes of libido. Impulses of an aggressive nature—manifestations of destructiveness or cruelty—were treated as components of sexuality as "an admixture to it, a propensity to subdue, the biological significance of which lies in the necessity for overcoming the resistance of the sexual object by actions other than courting" (p. 22). Aggressive impulses were thus considered as derivatives of a drive for sexual mastery (Bemaechtigungstrieb).[1] This assumption was not modified for a decade, a period during which clinical data on the importance of aggressive impulses during the various phases of libidinal development gradu-

---

1. Here as in the following we substitute "drive" or "instinctual drive" for the word instinct, used in most English translations of Freud's writings and in psychoanalytic writings in general. Some reasons for this substitution will be discussed later.

9

ally became familiar, mainly through publications of Freud and Abraham. But while Freud had stated in 1905 that the analysis of the drive for mastery had "not yet been successfully established" he assumed ten years later ("Instincts and Their Vicissitudes") that the drive for mastery was, in conjunction with other drives serving self-preservation, part of the ego drives; aggressive impulses were "amongst their essential constituents" (Bibring).

The further clarification of Freud's structural concepts, the ego, the id, and the superego, made this assumption questionable. The ego, i. e., the psychic organization oriented toward the external world, in control of syntheses of conflicts, and of motility, perception, and thought, could no longer be assumed to be equipped with drives of its own, especially since drives were conceived as the general motor power, linked to the vital substructure of personality, the id. (Bibring; Lowenstein; Hartmann, 1948). At the same time a number of clinical observations suggested that the assumption according to which aggressive impulses were only part of a drive to mastery, was no longer satisfactory. It seemed appropriate to distinguish between various types of mastery, some of which were in part correlated to various functions of the ego; others appeared as manifestations rather than as source of aggression and it thus also seemed appropriate to assume that the aggressive impulses were manifestations of an independent, primary (innate) aggressive or destructive drive.

It is difficult to overestimate the stimulating effect that this theory excercised when it was first formulated. Familiar clinical phenomena suddenly appeared in a new light. The influence of the new point of view extended to all areas of psychoanalytic work, even to the therapeutic technique and proved to be especially fruitful in the study of psychoses and other regressive phenomena, and of problems of infancy and childhood.

The close link between Freud's reformulation of his hypotheses concerning the psychic apparatus and its structure and his assumptions concerning the existence of two primary drives, of a libidinal and of an aggressive nature has not always been clearly recognized. This is undoubtedly due to the fact that Freud combined two steps in his formulation: While he put forward his new assumptions on psychic structure and the existence of two primary drives, he also inquired into the biological meaning of the latter, linking them to strivings toward life and death.

We do not propose to discuss the reasons that suggested to Freud this extension of his hypothesis, or to discuss the value that the assumptions concerning "Life and Death Instincts" may have for the unification of psychoanalytic propositions. We feel that at least a part of the considerations, on which Freud bases his speculation in his monograph "Beyond the Pleasure Principle" refer to questions to be discussed and probably to be decided within biology proper, possibly with the help of experimental biologists. Moreover it seems that the very area of problems that to our mind should become part and parcel of inquiries of biologists in the narrower sense of the word has little immediate bearing on the problems to be discussed in this paper. Assumptions concerning the existence of drives toward life or death at present facilitate neither the "fitting together" of existent propositions, nor the formulation of new ones, at least if one limits oneself, as we do, to hypotheses that can now or in the foreseeable future be checked against empirical evidence, against data of clinical observation, developmental studies, or experimentation in normal or abnormal psychology. We therefore do not enter into a discussion of Freud's biological speculation, and all that will be said concerning the nature of aggressive drives is independent of Freud's hypothesis, according to which manifestations of aggressions directed against the world without are externalizations of the "death instinct".

A somewhat different position has been adopted by a number of psychoanalysts, for instance, by Fenichel in his "General Theory of Neuroses". With him and some other authors one might speak of a kind of genuine discomfort in the face of Freud's far-reaching constructions, especially where they concern the "death instinct". This discomfort has, it seems, extended from the area of biological speculation to that of psychological theory. The authors who feel ill at ease with Freud's speculative extension of his views tend to discard also assumptions concerning the existence of a primary drive toward aggression or destruction. We, however, consider this assumption of immediate relevance in the formulation of psychoanalytic propositions. Those, on the other hand, who apply Freud's views concerning Eros and Thanatos literally to the analysis of psychological phenomena tend to introduce biological speculation at a point in their hypothesis where it has not yet a place; they therefore tend to omit a detailed discussion of the consequences arising for psychoanalytic theory from the assumption of a primary aggressive propensity in man.

Such a discussion is the purpose of this paper. We aim at clarifying some of the implications for psychoanalysis derived from this assumption. We do not aim at a simplification of our theoretical constructs, however loudly that demand may be voiced in many quarters. We are not deterred by the fact that some of our deliberations may seem to increase the complexity of psychoanalytic thinking as long as they are likely to explain a number of concrete phenomena less well accounted for by other assumptions. As in previous papers we are not interested in theoretical clarification for its own sake. We aim at linking psychoanalytic theory closer to empirical findings in order to facilitate a future validation or falsification of propositions.

In presenting our views we shall largely rely on a comparison between libido and aggression, first because more attention has been given to problems of libidinal than to problems of aggressive involvements and second because for an adequate understanding of several problems to be discussed, general assumptions on the nature of instinctual drives have to be taken into account.

The comparison of libido and aggression begins with problems of terminology: we contrast sexual impulses in the broad sense defined by Freud with aggressive impulses; but while we designate the energy ascribed to sexual impulses as libido, we do not choose to adopt a similar term for the energy of aggressive impulses, though two such terms (mortido, destrudo) have been suggested;[2] we refer to this energy as "aggression". The context will, we hope, make clear where we speak of aggression as a drive and where we speak of it as the energy of this drive.

II. *Structural Concepts and Instinctual Drives*

In stressing the importance that the introduction of structural concepts had in the development of Freud's views, we implied the existence of a more general interdependence in psychoanalytic theory, i. e., between structural concepts and assumptions on the nature of instinctual drives in general. This interdependence has been discussed by Hartmann (1939, 1948) in various papers during the last decade. Those of his views that have a special bearing on our subsequent discussion are here briefly summarized.

Since we have become used to thinking of the psychic apparatus in terms of three structural organizations, the id, the ego, and the superego, it has become possible to differentiate between "instinct" as it is used generally in psychology, and especially in animal psychology, and "instinctual drive", by which we have come to refer to "Trieb" as used by Freud. This distinction is the more desirable since English translations of Freud's writings originally rendered *Trieb* as *instinct*, and while some critics had early pointed to possible misunderstandings (Mitchell, 1928), the usage has survived until recently,[3] not without giving rise to various uncertainties. However, this distinction between "drive" and "instinct" not only eliminates a terminological confusion; it also permits a differentiation of concepts which in essential points clarifies Freud's views and resolves contradiction in psychoanalytic theory.

2. See Federn, Weiss.
3. See, for a critical point of view, Jones, Fenichel.

While the term "instinct" as used in animal psychology is not always strictly defined, and controversy as to some of the properties of instinctive behavior has continued to inspire a considerable body of research during the last decades, the difference between "instinct" and "instinctual drive" can be illustrated by the use of pointed formulations: for example, from a comparison of conditions existing in lower animals and in adult man. A first approach may be made from the fact that while the structural organization is maximal in man, it is minimal in lower animals; hence the differentiation of id and ego functions, all-important in man, plays no or no relevant part in animals. In man the ego mediates between the instinctual drive and the environment. Its organization guarantees adjustment. Whereas the drive cannot reach its goal without the ego's intervention, the instinct can do so by itself; or, to quote Murphy, in man intelligence substitutes for instinct.

Since the formation of the ego can in part be described as a learning process—which supplements the growth of the apparatus of the ego—one might say that in man the gratification of demands stemming from instinctual drives is guaranteed by learning. Instincts can lead to gratification with a minimum of or no learning.

The formulation of such antitheses implies the existence of a large number of intermediary stages between the suggested extremes, covering the range from various animal species up to higher apes, where conditions prevail that in many respects resemble those existing in man. According to Yerkes' observations, cohabitation and nursing with chimpanzees are essentially facilitated by some sort of learning process.

For our purposes it is not necessary to enumerate all the comparisons between "instinct" and "drive", but only to note that "instinct" in the ideal case guarantees the survival of the individual, at least in lower animals, while in man the guarantee of survival rests with the ego. We no longer assume the existence of an independent "instinct of self-preservation" or drive for survival but stress amongst factors contributing to survival the functions of the ego, which in order to assure the individual's safety, reacts to a large set of signals derived in part from the physiological apparatus, uses all available human equipment from the reflex organization to the most highly differentiated processes involved in reality testing, and coordinates these varied means and functions (Hartmann, 1939, 1948).

The sharper distinction between "instinct" and "drive" and particularly the assumption that self-preservation is to be considered not as the manifestation of an "instinct" or an "ego drive" but as one of the regular functions of the ego as a circumscribed system, seems to clarify current problems in psychoanalytic theory. In the following we shall refer to at least one important consequence of this clarification. We speak of clarification rather than of modification since none of the Freudian concepts is essentially redefined: rather have the contradictions been eliminated that arose during the development of psychoanalytic theory; they have, as it were, been "synchronized". The fact however, that Freud's structural concepts and his assumptions concerning instinctual drives can be more firmly linked to each other without essential re-definition is not due to a fortunate accident, nor to a generous interpretation, which we attach to Freud's concepts. It is rather due to the nature of the development of Freud's thought, a development that in many respects can be adequately described as a gradual unfolding.

In Freud's earliest attempts to theorize on the nature of the psychic apparatus, the continuation of his earliest interest in the anatomy of the central nervous system, which he relinquished only reluctantly and with considerable hesitation, we find assumptions concerning psychic structure. In one of his earliest theoretical essays—an attempt to survey the total field of psychology and psychopathology, written in 1895 but not destined for publication—he developed the construct of the "ego"; he then still sought to express psychological findings in neuro-physiological terms. Though Freud did not pursue these attempts the structural approach survived in his published work, initially, as the opposition of repressing agent and repressed impulse, or as "function of the censor". When the gradual development of therapeutic technique (especially the analysis of resistance, and various clinical observations—the study of psychoses and of neurotic patients in whose treatment unconscious guilt feelings seemed to limit the scope of therapy) again suggested to Freud the usefulness of structural concepts, he could draw on an old set of assumptions, and revive certain hypotheses, tentatively formulated 20 or 30 years earlier.

Similarly Freud's views on the nature of instinctual drives have their roots in the expectations with which he started his work in psychopathology. His hypotheses arose out of two sources: out of early assumptions concerning a dynamic factor in mental functions of any kind, and out of clinical observations concerning the part played by sexuality in the etiology of neuroses. Dynamic assumptions were current amongst neuro-physiologists, when Freud worked in this field. His special contribution consisted in the formulation of a general principle concerning the regulation of this energy. He thought it followed a principle of "constancy" (1892), according to which nervous energy tension in the central nervous system would tend to return to an established level: it is this theory which, based on Freud's and Breuer's formulation and expanded in their *Studies in Hysteria* later found entrance into psychoanalytic thought as the "pleasure" and still later as the "nirvana principle".

The application of dynamic principles proved fruitful when, as a result of his clinical findings, Freud turned his attention to problems of sexuality. In assuming that a specific kind of energy was part of the sexual drive he could describe manifestations of sexuality in many disguises. He was first enabled to describe the pregenital stages of libidinal organizations, and thus to include modes of behavior that had previously never been brought into relation to sexuality as its components or derivatives. Moreover, he was enabled to abstract from a simple stimulus-reflex pattern that a behavioristic approach might have suggested. Assumptions concerning the transformation and the vicissitudes of libido that "act as a constant force" (1915) became one of the main operational tools in psychoanalysis. The psychoanalytic concept of instinctual drive as a source of such a constant force transcends, at present, any definite link to physiological processes, to subjective experience, or to data obtainable from the behavioristic approach. However, the concept of instinctual drive includes all these aspects (Hartmann, 1948).

Instinctual drives in this sense have been studied by Freud in their relation to objects, to the self, and as to their modification in neutralized psychic energy. Neutral energy, which Freud occasionally identified as sublimated or desexualized libido, is assumed to provide the cathexes of the ego and partly of the superego; it accounts for a large number of psychic activities both in the individual's relation to his environment and within ego and superego. Equally familiar are Freud's assumptions as to the possible and partial re-tranformation of neutral energy into a form closer to the original instinctual drive. Assumptions concerning neutral energy permit a particularly clear presentation of some of the ego functions previously explained by independent ego drives.[4] At this point, however, a new complexity must be introduced in what might have seemed to be a simplified theory.

We have in this section purposely omitted reference to the existence of two instinctual drives, of libido *and* aggression. We now must add that neutral energy vested in ego and superego may stem from and may be re-transformed into either libido or aggression.

III. *Libido and Aggression*

Classification of phenomena as "sexual" or "aggressive" is in psychoanalysis based on descriptive and genetic criteria. The uncertainties

4. Psychic energy is here considered only in relation to instinctual drives. We do not discuss the problem of other, non-instinctual, sources of psychic energy.

that arise if only descriptive criteria are used are well-known[5] and are at least partly due to the fusion of libido and aggression. The genetic criteria, elaborated in psychoanalysis in some detail, reduce the area of uncertainty but confront us with further questions as to the essential similarities and differences of the two drives. We may compare libido and aggression according to the four characteristics enumerated by Freud as essential for the description of any drive: *impetus, source, aim, and object.* Differences may be pointed out between *source, aim, and object;* but a strict parallel is evident in regard to *impetus* of libido and aggression.

"By the impetus of a drive[6] we understand its motor element, the amount of force or the measure of demand upon energy which it represents. The characteristic of impulsion is common to all drives, it is in fact the very essence of them. Every drive is a form of activity; if we speak of passive drives, we can only mean those with a passive aim" (Freud, 1915).

Though this was written at a time when Freud was thinking only of libidinal drives, it is clearly valid for aggression also. Freud's remarks about activity draw our attention, however, to a number of complexities in terminology.

We shall distinguish three meanings of "activity" as used in psychoanalysis, mainly by pointing out its various forms of opposite meanings: First: activity may be considered a general property of all psychic processes. The opposite of activity in this general sense is inactivity. Though in psychoanalysis the origins of activity in this general sense have mainly been studied in relation to instinctual drives, we have to consider whether the scope of investigation should not be widened. Activity in this general sense may also be rooted in the proclivity of the congenital equipment of man, which co-determines later manifestations of the ego as well as of the id.[7] Second: "activity" and "passivity" are used in reference to opposite aims of a drive. Third: "actively" loving is differentiated from "passively" being loved.

We do not here discuss to what extent, empirically, the predominance of active or passive aims correlates positively to the active or passive varieties of object love. We only briefly mention that in sexual life the man may be passive in the sense that he desires predominantly to be loved, but active in his sexual behavior.

Though activity in the general sense is a characteristic of all psychic events, activity of all kinds is, as we shall see later, likely to offer oppor-

5. According to Bernfeld a special viewpoint, the "physiognomic", frequently supplies the basis for classification. See also Loewenstein.

6. *Drive* has been substituted for *instinct.*

7. For recent research on the congenital equipment in relation to activity patterns see Bender, Kaiser and Schilder; Fries and Levi.

tunities for the discharge of aggression. We do not forget that on the other hand, the very absence of activity may express aggression in one of its forms. In the case of aggression it is often difficult to distinguish between the above defined second and third meanings of "activity". "Active" aggression refers to the wish to harm, to master, or to destroy an object; passivity refers to the wish to be mastered, harmed, or destroyed. This wish, however, is accessible to observation, usually as a result of masochistic strivings, i. e., it presupposes some degree of fusion of libido and aggression.

A more detailed discussion of aim and object in relation to instinctual drives may be prefaced by some remarks on the source and nature of discharge. Freud studied the assumed biochemical sources of libido particularly in relation to development of the erotogenous zones. No similar hypothesis has been offered regarding aggression.[8] The preferred relationship that Freud (1915) noticed between the skeletal musculature and aggression does refer to the problem of discharge; however, both libidinal and aggressive tensions may be discharged by motor activity.

The discharge of libidinal tensions frequently follows specific time curves, best known from the study of orgasm. The discharge of aggressive tension is less clearly structured. Some observations suggest that a time element plays its part; they indicate, for instance, that in preparing for aggressive discharges a phenomenon corresponding to "forepleasure", or to tension-increase occurs and that definite feelings of saturation or satisfaction accompany and follow the completion of the aggressive act.[9] Naturally this does not take account of the reactions of other psychic systems to this completion, i. e., for instance, of the guilt feeling that may ensue. The question here is only whether and to what extent the various stages of discharge of aggression are related to the pleasure —unpleasure continuum; also, to what extent the discharge of aggression is dependent on special curves of discharge, pertaining to stages of libidinal development in general, especially during the pregenital phases (Brunswick). It seems that certain manifestations of sexuality as well as certain types of outbursts of rage follow patterns of discharge specifically related to the oral and anal phases of pregenital development; as far as curves of rage-discharge are concerned the imprint of anality seems to be particularly lasting and regularly observable. Moreover we

8. For one type of hypothesis see Simmel, who, however, considers aggression part of the self-preservatory "instinct".

9. Freud raised the question "whether satisfaction of purely destructive instinctual impulses can be felt as pleasure," and considered also the possibility that pleasure in aggresive action may be due to narcissistic components. We here assume, however, that aggressive discharge per se may be experienced as pleasurable.

assume that certain disturbances in the expected discharge of libido are due to the fact that the discharge of libido and aggression is frequently accomplished in the same act. While such a simultaneous or fused discharge must in many instances be considered normal, a quantitative increase of aggression simultaneously to be discharged may contribute to the deviation of the discharge process from the "libido curve" (Abraham).

Any manifestation of an instinctual drive can be viewed in terms of mounting and decreasing tension, and certain manifestations can be exhaustively described in these terms. This is true particularly of phenomena of infancy in which the importance of motor discharge has repeatedly been stressed. In other cases, in those mostly discussed in psychoanalysis, discharge can be studied only if we take into account the differentiation imposed by the existence of definite aims and object relationships.

The variety of aims of the sexual impulses are well known. The aims of aggression are generally considered to be less diversified. In this sense one is wont to contrast the plasticity of libido to the rigidity of aggression. We should like to supplement this traditional view by an alternative: it seems that the plasticity of aggression manifests itself in the control of the body, in the control of reality and in the formation of psychic structure, areas that will in part be later discussed in greater detail.

What should we assume the aims of aggression to be? It has been said that they consist in total destruction of objects, animate or inanimate, and that all attempts to be "satisfied with less", with battle with or domination of the object, or with its disappearance imply restrictions of the original aims. It seems that at the present stage in the development of psychoanalytic hypotheses the question as to the specific aims of the aggressive drive cannot be answered; nor is a definite answer essential. However, it seems possible to distinguish between degrees of discharge of aggressive tension. The aims of aggression could then be classified according to the degree of discharge they allow for and according to the means utilized in discharge.

In emphasizing the relation of instinctual drive to discharge of energy, the similarities and differences of aim inhibition with libido and with aggression become evident. Libidinal impulses may be aim-inhibited under two conditions: the inhibition may be temporary, may induce an accessory and preparatory stage of impulse completion; or it may substitute for the uninhibited action. In the first case discharge is delayed but under certain conditions mounting pleasure is experienced;

in the second case, in which behavior is permanently aim-inhibited, there occurs, in addition to the damming up of libido, substitute-formation or sublimation.

As far as ego and superego impose modifications on both instinctual drives, conditions with libido and aggression tend to be similar. In the case of aggression, however, modification of aims is imposed by an additional reason of particular and paramount importance: The unmodified aggressive impulse threatens the existence of the object and the investment of the object with libido acts as its protection. Through a simultaneous cathexis with libido the aims of aggression are modified. This modification may be brought about in two different ways: by the mere coexistence of two investments, leading to the prevalence of libido over aggression; and by the fusion of both instinctual drives. In discussing types of ambivalence we will later refer to this difference. The fact, however, that the ultimate aims of aggression are more frequently modified by libido than those of libido by aggression may well be thought to be connected with the genetic importance of the love object for the survival of the individual.

In rounding off our discussion it seems appropriate to enumerate four types of conflict through which the aims of aggression are modified. 1) Aggression and libido may be involved in conflict when the cathexis of both drives is vested in the same object (instinctual conflict). 2) The reaction of the object to attempts at completion of aggressive acts may endanger the individual (conflict with reality). 3) This danger may be anticipated by the ego, which is in part already identified with the object, and the ego might be opposed to the completion of aggressive acts (structural conflict, involving the ego). 4) The conflict may involve moral values (structural conflict, involving the superego).

The character and impact of these conflicts is well-known from psychoanalytic clinic. This is not the place to concern ourselves with them nor with the mechanisms of defense usually mobilized to resolve the danger situations alluded to; nor about that specific vicissitude of aggression (internalization) which is used in the formation and functioning of the superego. We merely point to the probability that some mechanisms of defense may be more efficient in dealing with libidinal, and others with aggressive impulses; and we wish at least to mention what Freud (1930) considers a "possible formulation" for the case of repression: that libidinal elements are transformed into symptoms and aggressive components into guilt feelings.

Here we select four types of processes which *modify* the impact of aggression. This modification is achieved: 1) by displacement of aggression to other objects; 2) by restriction of the aims of the aggressive impulses; 3) by sublimation of aggressive energy; and 4) through the influences of libido mentioned above; one of these influences operating as "fusion". These processes are frequently interdependent; in clinical observation they cannot always be separated. Parallel modifications of libidinal impulses are well known. However, their relevance is greater where aggression is concerned, since the "full" discharge of aggressive energy would endanger the objects, whereas the full discharge of libido, however dangerous it may be, does not threaten the existence of the object itself.

Displacement of cathexis is, one might say, the simplest of the four processes. The object, Freud said, "is the most variable thing about a drive and is not originally connected with it but becomes attached to it only in consequence of being peculiarly fitted to provide satisfaction" (1915). The role of displacement of libido and its vicissitudes have been much discussed in psychoanalysis; less data have been accumulated in relation to aggression. Of all processes discussed here, it is the one that does not of necessity limit the discharge of aggression itself; full discharge is not excluded, if the substitute object is conveniently chosen, particularly if it is inanimate. It is here that both reality and structural organizations are to be taken into account. They determine occasions, intensity and forms of aggressive action and organize the hierarchy of motivation.

The problem of "man in search of a target" is familiar not only from clinical observations, from the daily life of the child, but—as Freud had seen—from the vicissitudes of our social organization itself: One might say that social conflict is exploited by the manipulation of masses to provide the individual group member with an enemy whom he eagerly accepts as target of aggression, thus using social tension for the displacement of individual tension (Freud, 1928; Bibring).

Since often the ultimate aims of aggression cannot be reached, modification of aggression must be largely entrusted to the other methods enumerated above. Little is known about the conditions of fusion and diffusion of aggression and libido, and no new theoretical problems seem to arise in relation to the restriction of aims of aggression. However, it seems necessary to discuss briefly the sublimation of aggressive energy.

Here we touch upon a gap in Freud's presentation (Kardiner, Menninger, Bergler, Lampl-de Groot, Hartmann). He introduced the idea of sublimation of libido, i. e., of a transformation of libido in neutralized energy, which contributes to the constitution of permanent object relations and to the forming of a psychic structure; then, as soon as psychic structure exists, this energy is at the disposal of the ego and superego;

but Freud did not in sufficient detail elaborate the implications of the idea of the neutralization of aggressive energy.[10]

We are inclined to consider the contribution of neutralized aggressive energy to the equipment of ego and superego to be at least as important as that of libido. Aggression is dangerous because it involves the individual in conflicts that are difficult if not impossible to solve, since they threaten the very object on whom man depends; but in a sublimated form aggressive energy can be integrated into the structure of ego and superego. Libido, on the other hand, can be fully discharged and can therefore be linked more closely to the object.

We should like to go one step further: the formation of a permanent object relation is, as has been shown elsewhere, dependent on the capacity of the individual to bear frustration; no permanent object relation, or no true constitution of a love object could be achieved without this capacity. We now add another condition: Such permanent object relation is also dependent on the sublimation of aggression. And if we here return to the concept of fusion of instincts it seems suggestive to assume that partial neutralization of drive energy establishes favorable conditions for the fusion of (residual) libido and especially of (residual) aggression.

The assumption regarding the sublimation of aggressive energy also sheds new light on one of the central problems of Freud's theory of aggression, i. e., the problem of self-destruction. If in order to divert aggression from another object the self is adopted as substitute object, the safety of the individual may be threatened. "A person in a fit of rage often demonstrates the transition from the checking of aggression to self-destructiveness by turning his aggressiveness against himself: he tears his hair or beats his face with his fists—treatment which he would evidently have preferred to apply to someone else" (Freud, 1939, p. 33).

But this simple example is part of a more far-reaching, if speculative consideration. Aggression in the form of self-destructiveness constitutes a serious threat for the individual's survival, ". . . it at length succeeds in doing this individual to death" (1939).[11] Freud here implicitly refers to his speculation on the death instinct. An impressive array of clinical studies published since 1939 tends to confirm the validity of his con-

10. Freud (1923) assumed that neutral energy originates only in libido. However, he also assumed that this neutral energy could reinforce both aggressive and libidinal impulses.

11. See also Freud (1932, p. 136): "It would seem that aggression, when it is impeded, entails serious injury, and that we have to destroy other things and other people in order not to destroy ourselves, in order to protect ourselves from tendencies to self-destruction."

siderations: studies of various psychosomatic conditions seem to con-
verge in the finding that internalized aggression plays a relevant role
in the etiology of illness.

However clinically important the assumptions concerning the internalization of aggression are, we cannot, in establishing general
hypotheses on the vicissitudes of aggression, be satisfied with the dichotomy of self-destructive and externalized aggression. Not all internalized
aggression leads the way to destruction of the self, no more than all
internalized libidinal energy leads necessarily to self-infatuation. Freud
was used to comparing the relation between narcissism and object-love
to that between self-destruction and destruction of the object. This
analogy might have contributed to his assumption of self-destruction as
of the primary form of aggression, to be compared to primary narcissism.
However, he omitted to extend the parallel to other aspects which are
relevant for the context of this paper. He neglected to take account of
the fact that he had established a more complex concept of narcissism,
which includes not only "self-love" but also other cathexes of the self; one
of the forms of these cathexes is the cathexis of the ego with neutralized
libido. Similarly we assume the existence of a neutralized "de-aggres-
sivized" psychic energy, that does not lead to self-destruction but supplies ego and superego[12] with motor power and equips particularly the
ego for its function in action. On the basis of this assumption we may
venture to say that if in the balance between libido and aggression
a shift toward aggression takes place, such shift need not necessarily interfere with the individual's emotional stability.

We have said that the ego helps to modify aggression by directing
it to substitute objects, by restriction and by sublimation. On the
other hand, it is well known that internalization of aggression is an
essential condition for the formation of the superego, and that once
the superego is formed, modified aggression is used by the superego in
its relation to the ego. But what appears as displacement, restriction, or
sublimation, considered in relation to the id and to discharge of aggressive energy, is, if we take into account the total personality and its position in social reality, a most important prerequisite of mental integration
and of mastery of the environment.

The relation of aggression to the ego-organization is not exhausted
with these remarks. It is specific in various other ways. Aggression is
closely linked to the apparatus of the ego, specifically to the muscular
apparatus, the function of which is, as indicated above, more essential
for the discharge of aggressive than of libidinal tension. Once the ego

12. For differences, see below.

exists as a functioning organization the relation between aggression and the skeletal musculature implies a particularly close tie between the ego and aggression since this organization normally controls motility.

Musculature and motility, apparatuses for the discharge of aggression, contribute decisively to the differentiation between self and environment and, through action, to the differentiation of the environment itself. The environment in turn invites action and determines specific areas of action; it thus offers opportunities for the discharge of particular modes of aggression and their individual modifications.[13]

The methods to be used in action develop *pari passu* with the apparatus of the ego, and the general scope of ego functions. Where aggression is involved means and ends are more highly differentiated than where libido is involved. The variety in the relation of means and ends as far as aggression is concerned can be considered a counterpart to the variety in the aims of sexuality.

These means and ends comprehend a development that has led from the use of the body itself to its extensions by the tools of modern technology and to the "conquest of nature". It seems that their importance led Freud to retain the assumption concerning the identity of ego drives and aggression, even at a time when his definition of the structural organization already implied that the controls of means and ends are to be considered as important functions of the ego as a system.

Objective danger is one situation that allows for and invites the discharge of aggression. The two responses to it, fight and flight, both call for motor discharge but only fight implies also the direct discharge of aggression. Hence objective danger is less likely to lead to pathological responses if adequate aggressive reaction remains possible. If passivity is enforced, the probability of pathological responses increases.

A clinical example may illustrate these conditions:

"A young man in his early twenties, Jewish, intellectual, whose interest in modern psychology was the conscious reason for his wish to be analyzed, suffered from a severe anxiety neurosis. The anxiety attacks reached considerable intensity. They were related to situations in which unconscious passive-homosexual tendencies predominated. The center of the apprehension was the situation of being overpowered: former Gentile playmates and friends in the neighborhood were the preferred objects of the fearful fantasies. The case was analyzed in Vienna. When Hitler came to power in March 1938 the fantasies of the patient suddenly met with supporting conditions in the environment. The objects of these fantasies had gained the power which in his imagination he previously had attributed to them. One day he was confronted with a gang of young Nazis. A street fight ensued. He was a young man of athletic appearance, who had repeatedly been encouraged to train

13. For cultural modifications see f. i. Bovet, Elias.

as an amateur boxer. His neurosis, however, had prevented him from availing himself of these opportunities. In the brawl mentioned he did well indeed. Impressed by his courageous initiative, his violent and skillful defense, the gang did not try to prevent his retreat. Since their code of behavior had not yet been corrupted by National Socialist education, they also refrained from subsequent retribution.

The young man was seen shortly after the encounter. He described how he felt anxiety rising when he met the gang on a narrow street. In his own words: "I switched to action" (Kris, 1944).

In an objective danger situation discharge of aggressive energy is normal and physiologically pre-formed; sexualization of objective danger situations leads to pathology (masochism). Since we consider objective danger situations as a prototype of all danger situations this difference in the relation of the two instinctual drives to objective danger may have far-reaching consequences for a general theory of neuroses (Hartmann).

Aggressive energy not discharged in fight may be internalized. It may be used as cathexis of the superego and be the source of guilt feelings; internalization may also lead to neutralization of aggressive energy in the ego without interfering with the integrity of the individual; if it is internalized (in the ego) without neutralization the incentive to some kind of self-destruction may exist.[14] It will be important to clarify in the future the conditions under which these different solutions occur. While much seems to depend on the nature of the reality situation, particularly on the gravity of the danger, and on vicissitudes of the aggressive drive in the individual's previous life, a decisive part is played by the structure of the ego and superego. Tentatively we are inclined to assume that the capacity to neutralize large quantities of aggression may constitute one of the criteria of "ego strength" or of the high capacity of the ego for integration. Alternatively, the internalization of non-neutralized aggressive energy in the ego may be the hallmark of a weak, or eventually of a masochistic, ego.

These various outcomes can be exemplified in one particular type of danger situation: the position of the defeated toward the victor. The defeated might wait for the opportunity to defeat in turn the victor. In that case one cannot even speak of internalization but of suspension of the aggressive response. The neutralization of the internalized aggressive energy might lead to a modification of the superego demands: victory or aggression might be devaluated, and a moral victory over the physical victor might be ultimately achieved. Or, the defeated might feel guilty for the defeat. Internalization without neutralization leads to some kind of self-destructive attitude. If the latter is libidinized, the attitude of the defeated will be that of pleasurable submission, or what could be called the mentality of the slave; the defeated will renounce

14. See Weiss for a further reaching hypothesis on the origin of trauma.

his superego for the superego of his master. Then we can speak of masochism of the ego in relation to the superego. It might safely be presumed that the latter situation occurs when in childhood, before the formation of the superego, a strong passive attachment to the father prevailed which becomes the pattern of the relation of the ego to the superego. Alternatively, if a strong superego has been formed, guilt feelings will dominate the picture.

IV. *The Genetic Aspect*

We have hitherto attempted to discuss the properties of aggressive and libidinal impulses without explicit reference to the problems of personality development; so intricate is the relation of dynamic and genetic assumptions in psychoanalysis that such independent discussion proved difficult. We frequently found it necessary either to imply reference to genetic propositions or to interrupt our discussion at a point where it was leading into the developmental area. In the following we shall make our references explicit, enlarge our discussions, and attempt to investigate the relation of both aggressive and libidinal drives to some critical problems especially of early childhood; however, we shall not be able to adhere strictly to chronological sequences but shall rather use problems of a genetic order as a framework for discussion.

We start from the assumption of the existence of an undifferentiated phase of psychic structure.[15] During this phase manifestations of both libido and aggression are frequently indistinguishable or difficult to distinguish. However, observation of the neonate and infant invariably enables us to differentiate between manifestations of pleasure and unpleasure of various degrees. These manifestations are part of a set-up in which gradually the differentiation between self and non-self takes place. According to Freud's assumptions (1915) it seems likely that at an early stage this process of differentiation is linked to the perception of pleasure and unpleasure; and that there is a tendency to relate unpleasure to "outside of self" and pleasure to "self".

This assumption would permit us to gain some further insight into earliest stages in the economy of aggression. We observe in infants the avoidance of external stimuli and assume that this avoidance indicates pain or unpleasure. Later manifestations of aggression may then draw upon this mechanism.[16] During the undifferentiated phase one might assume aggression (and libido) to be centered in the self.

15. Hartmann (1939); Hartmann, Kris, Loewenstein (1946). See also Fenichel.
16. Defense against external stimuli is known to be the model of defense against internal stimuli. Hence we may here be faced with one of the roots of later defense mechanisms, operating also against internal danger. It would be suggestive to consider in the future in greater detail the particular rôle aggression seems to play in the functioning of defense mechanisms (Hartmann). Somewhat similar ideas were presented by M. Brierley in a paper published after the completion of the present article.

The motor discharges we observe and which we are used to considering as aggressive discharges are during this phase of infant development not directed against an organized world. At the present stage of our knowledge we are unable to decide whether, during this phase, acts of actual or "true" self-destruction occur, or whether the observed destructive actions of the infant—such as self-infliction of damage, f. i., by scratching —can be explained by assuming that the distinction between self and external world is not yet possible; and that unpleasure or pain are not yet recognized as signals warning of danger, because of the incomplete awareness of the bodily self as represented in the image of the body. And yet it might not be an unjustified extrapolation from analytic material to assume that self-destructive tendencies exist even at an early age.

In both cases,—i. e., whether we are justified in speaking of earliest self-destructive tendencies (Riviere), or whether we assume that in an earliest phase we are faced with indiscriminate discharges of quantities of aggression—it seems likely that the localization of unpleasure outside the body itself invites the cathexis of the source of unpleasure with aggression. This process will recur throughout the course of life, and plays an important part in our subsequent considerations on the economy of aggression.[17] Such cathexis then channelizes aggression away from the self and protects the self. However, as said above, this view is fully valid only under conditions of little differentiation in the psychic apparatus, i. e., as long as neutralization of aggressive energy through the ego and the superego has not yet taken place.

Freud (1914) partly explains the development from narcissism to the libidinal cathexis of the outside world by assuming that the damming up of narcissistic libido in the self, if it exceeds a certain degree, is experienced as unpleasure. We think that an analogous hypothesis as to aggression is even more plausible.

The process here described may be considered as a first source of what in a subsequent stage of development becomes the "bad object". The corresponding process, the linking of pleasure to a source outside the self and the cathexis of this source with libido is responsible for what in a subsequent stage of development becomes the "good object".[18]

In speaking of a subsequent phase of development we try to compress a complex state of affairs. Every step in the formation of the object corresponds to a phase in psychic differentiation. That differentiation

17. We stress here only one aspect of the economic importance of external sources of unpleasure and do not discuss the "need for unpleasure", as discussed traditionally in connection with masochism.

18. These terms and similar considerations are familiar from the work of Melanie Klein. They are here used in a different theoretical context.

itself is determined by the maturation of the apparatus, which later come under the control of the ego, and by the experiences that structure the psychic apparatus. Hence both processes, differentiation of psychic structure and relation of the self to external objects are interdependent; the nature of this interdependence can be characterized as dialectical.

The economic function of the external source of unpleasurable feelings is however not exhausted in pointing to its function as catalyst, i. e. to the discharge of otherwise self-destructive energy, aroused by the existence of this external source. It seems unavoidable to assume that the very fact of discharge of aggressive tension is pleasurable. Thus, looked at from one angle, what has started as a process of localizing the source of unpleasure in the outside world and of linking this unpleasure to an object, reveals itself as a roundabout way leading to a partial pleasure-gain: pleasure in aggressive discharges. The conflict arising here with those tendecies that try to preserve the object, has been briefly mentioned above.

The realization that the discharge of aggression and the destruction of objects may be considered pleasurable per se, permits clearly to state our views on the aim of sadistic impulses; they have to be differentiated from other aggressive tendencies directed against objects. The additional element that characterizes sadistic aims is a specific kind of pleasure; pleasure not at the discharge of aggression and at destruction only, but additional pleasure at the infliction of pain, at the suffering or humiliation of others. Sadism therefore can be viewed only in the context of an already developed and complex object relation. If one frequently speaks of the greater "cruelty" of man, as compared to animals, one thinks mainly of sadistic phenomena. However, it is also true that structural differentiation in man, with the subsequent development of aggression as a drive (distinguishable from the instincts of animals), implies a considerable widening of the scope of aggression beyond the limits of immediate self-preservation.

There seems little doubt that in observing the child's relation to his mother the transition from the discharge of aggression in a general sense to that specific kind of discharge which we here consider as sadistic can actually be studied. Similar observations would equally well permit a differentiation between aggression turned against the self and masochism. Both with sadism and masochism the new aims of the impulses are dependent on the fusion of aggression and libido.

We now seem prepared to approach one type of conflict that arises in earliest childhood: the conflict *with the object* (conflict with reality). This type of conflict has up to this point only briefly been mentioned. We spoke of *conflict concerning the object* due to the opposition of aggressive and libidinous strivings (instinctual conflicts) but did not discuss what influence the reactions manifested by the object are bound to have.[19]

The discussion of conflict *with* the object introduces the psychological reality in which the child lives and develops; object here naturally, at least as far as the early phases of development are concerned, means mainly mother or mother substitutes. In a more general sense, however, it introduces the rôle played by the continuum of indulgence and deprivation to which the child is exposed. This contact with his environment imposes upon the child unavoidable deprivations—if no other, the one which is most closely linked to the formation of the ego: the child has to learn to postpone immediate gratification, in order not to lose the favor of the mother; it has to learn to wait. According to an early hypothesis of Freud (1917) deprivations instigate aggressive response and those who rely on this part of Freud's work in contradistinction to his later propositions seem to assume that aggression in man arises as a consequence to the deprivational experiences to which he is exposed. While the relevance of these experiences for the economy of aggression is undoubted and unparalleled, a number of problems are not elucidated by it. The vicissitudes of aggression resemble those of sexuality to such a degree that the assumption of a constant driving power comparable to that of libido seems appropriate. To judge from the development of our clinical insight during the last two decades it seems that Freud's revised theory of aggression facilitated the process of further "fact finding" in clinical work (Hartmann, 1948). This does not eliminate in any way the relevance of the relationship of aggression to deprivation, a field to which learning theory has devoted special attention.[20]

However, it seems that from the vantage point of the assumptions we here pursue, new light can be shed on the relation of deprivation and aggression. A uniform response can, at least theoretically, be differentiated and a number of specific dynamic situations can be distinguished from one another.

19. Our discussion is even here by necessity sketchy since we decided to avoid the discussion of structural conflicts and the problems connected with the mechanisms of defense. No other way seemed possible without rendering this presentation even more involved.

20. In its most recent formulations this hypothesis no longer assumes "a universal causal relation between frustration and aggression," (Dollard, et al, 1939) but rather that "frustration produces instigation to a number of different types of response one of which is the instigation of some form of aggression" (Miller, et al, 1941). Moreover "it is not certain how early in the infancy of the individual the frustration-aggression hypothesis is applicable and no assumptions are made as to whether the frustration-aggression is of innate or of learned origin."

It might here be appropriate to point out that Mowrer and Kluckhohn (p. 112) who discuss the concept of aggression in terms of an older and a more recent theory of Freud's identify the latter with the theory of the death instinct and omit reference to the assumption of an independent primary aggression.

Our starting point is an unavoidable terminological clarification, necessitated by the fact that most authors were not prepared consistently to operate with the concept of an instinctual drive. *Deprivation* designates a number of situations: If in any specific situation the discharge of libido is made difficult or impossible we speak of deprivation of libido; if the discharge of aggression is made difficult or impossible, we speak of deprivation of aggression. Similarly we specify any other need or tension, of a physiological nature, that remains ungratified or undischarged; to these latter situations we shall refer only in passing.[21]

For the purpose of illustration we select as a model the feeding situation; deprivation in our example consists in the withholding of food. The need for food is related to and its intake is regulated by physiological mechanisms. The food intake permits gratification of libidinal needs,[22] both through zonal pleasure and—possibly at a somewhat later stage—through the libidinal significance of the incorporation of the "source" of satisfaction; giving of food means at this stage also giving of love. At the same time we are aware that the biting of food, its disappearance, its incorporation, affords aggressive satisfactions early in development. The significance of both these processes is evidenced by much clinical material in psychoanalysis.

The reaction of the infant may therefore be related to three different kinds of deprivation; for reasons of simplicity we start with the last enumerated component: the absence of food deprives the child of the opportunity to discharge aggressive tension in its incorporation; the aggression the child displays may as far as this deprivation is concerned be a displacement; aggression has chosen another pathway of discharge. In so far as the child has been deprived of libidinal gratification, libido has been blocked; i. e., its discharge has become impossible. That the child substitutes discharge of aggression for that of libido may be explained in two ways, first, by the assumption of a vicarious excitation, second by the traditional "frustration-aggression hypothesis". The first explanation takes into account the possibility that, if the libidinal tension is increased by non-gratification, this increase may imply also a heightening of aggressive tension. If the discharge of libido is blocked while that of aggression remains possible through displacement the observer may gain the impression of a substitution, that is he may feel that an agressive reaction has taken place in response to a libidinal deprivation. We have also to take into account that according to our previous deductions the absence of gratification and of a gratifying object is experienced in terms of "unpleasure outside" and also used to free the self from aggressive tension by discharge.

21. In contrast to this frequently one refers to "frustrated needs," without taking into account the drives from which the needs arise.
22. For experimental work in this area see D. Levy, 1934.

The second explanation refers to Freud's original assumption on the relation of frustration and aggression, according to which aggression is called into being as a true reaction to deprivation.

As a further subsidiary explanation it also may be mentioned that in cases of instinctual deprivation of any kind the mounting tension may be experienced as danger, first because of the ego's "hostility to instinct" (Anna Freud), second because of fear of punishment.

Little can be said about the third component of deprivation, the mounting physiological tension, since we do not know how "hunger and thirst" per se contribute to the increase of aggression apart from the fact that physiological deprivations imply deprivation of libidinal and aggressive needs.

While in current observation data on modes of gratification are rapidly accumulating, data on the modality of restraint are comparatively scarce. The complexity of the problem area upon which we here touch is great and challenging. We only can comment on three points, that seem to be clarified by the theoretical assumption to which we try rigorously to adhere: First, it has frequently been noted that any interruption of activity, at least in the child, is likely to evoke an aggressive response; that in other words non-completion of actions specifically affects aggression. If we assume that neutralized aggression supplies the ego with essential parts of its energy discharged in action, we find it easily understandable that at any point act interruption is likely to mobilize aggression of the child, that the child without outlet tends to turn naughty.[23] In many instances such behavioral changes may be described as regressive.

Second, its has been pointed out (Greenacre, Kris 1949) that such aggressive response to interruption in the child—and naturally also in the adult, though to a lesser degree—is more intense, when the interference was in itself an expression of aggression. This, too, we find understandable: The love object that interferes with activity *and* does so in an aggressive response to interruption in the child—and naturally also in the all disguises—becomes doubly bad; and as a "bad object" is exercises an appeal to aggression, attracts it, thus inviting aggressive behavior. In making this point we refer only to reality-aspects of the situation without considering the equally important and partly equally typical ways in which the meaning of such reality situations is modified through the child's instinctual needs and his fantasy life.

Our third comment takes us far afield. We have dealt with interruption of activity as an instigation to aggression, and we said that the

23. One might at this point also refer to observations Levy and Buxbaum have made. While Levy pointed out that early interruption of activity in an initial stage were less likely to be followed by outburst of aggression, Buxbaum's observations seem to indicate that the chance of aggressive response to the interruption of activity is greatest when this interruption occurs during a period in which the activity is being learned. We find this plausible, since we might assume that during practice the cathexis is most intense. We are naturally aware of the fact that other factors co-determine the intensity of the child's reaction.

fact that one kind of discharge of aggressive energy has become impossible, may well account for the specificity of the response. From these detailed problems we now turn to the more general, to the response of the object to aggression.

At first one might feel inclined to assume that that response will be counter-aggression, increase of restraint or punishment of some kind. But a closer examination reveals a very great complexity indeed.

If we turn to problems of child development parental response will tend to vary considerably according to the stage of libidinal and ego development of the child, according to the manifestations of aggression, according to the individual pre-dispositions of the parents but also according to prevailing social norms. Anna Freud (1947) has recently pointed to the part that in England class mores play, that tend to inhibit manifestations of aggressions more sharply under certain class conditions than under others and similarly anthropologists have occasionally produced data that have a bearing on this problem. We feel that we cannot here enter into the area of this discussion, but rather should like to focus our attention on one kind of response to aggression not infrequently encountered at present, since we may, from this instance, derive further clarification.

Let us envisage a child at that stage of development when his aggressive behavior is already clearly addressed to an object. The child then expects the object's response. That response might be of many kinds; it may be anger, physical reactions of the attacked, it might be and frequently is an invitation to restraint by the object. When the child has reached the stage, in which he is himself dissatisfied with his aggressive outbursts, when his ego, or later his superego, already disapprove of aggression turned outward, the outburst solicits limitation from the parent as a help in solving the internal conflict. If in this constellation the response to aggression is not the expected one, if the aggressor is disarmed by indifference, kindness or love, aggression has been frustrated. It seems that this type of frustration particularly favors one solution of the conflict, the internalization of aggression. This internalization in turn may contribute to an increase of guilt feelings and be related either to a rigorous superego or to a masochistic ego.

After this deviation we now return to our original purpose; it was our plan to discuss the interplay of aggression and libido during critical phases of child development. We take our lead from the child's relation to the love object. We are interested to establish what problems arise in the economy of aggression when the child becomes able to form a lasting object relationship.

We said that the formation of a lasting object relationship depends on a partial neutralization of libido. From the viewpoint of the present discussion we added that the formation of a lasting object relationship not only depends on the fact that libidinal impulses must be inhibited and residual libido neutralized; we assume that similar requirements exist in the economy of aggression. Discharge of aggressive energy is limited and residual aggressive energy is neutralized.

Other interdependences concern the relation of libido and aggression to each other. As long as no constant object relation existed we could speak of an oscillation between attitudes related to "objects" that were "kept apart".

There are transitional stages, in which the older type of oscillation and the attempt at permanent object relationship are in conflict with each other and when rapid oscillation between aggressive and libidinal strivings directed against one object becomes observable; but ultimately the restriction of aggression and the neutralization of aggressive energy must occur.

When finally the constant object relationship has been established, and when the fear of losing the love object is replaced by the fear of losing love, then this conflict appears in a new form. The behavior of the child early in his second year of life toward his mother, to whom he clings tenaciously, whom he tortures by his demands, that appear concomitantly to rise with his anxiety, may well be accounted for as a reflection of the battle between aggression and libido.[24]

The transition from the stage in which fear of losing the object dominates the child's life to the stage in which the fear of losing love predominates does not only make it essential that both libidinal and aggressive energies should be neutralized; also their expression is "socialized". As an example we may refer to some of the expressions of aggression during the pressure of the anal phase, when spite and obstinacy, the refusal to give, and, closer to the function of the anal zone itself, the opposition of expulsion and retention have become expressions of aggression; expressions that are undoubtedly fused with libido, meant to engage struggle or controversy with the object but probably less often definitely intended as full attack against its existence, than on previous stages.

During the second and third year of life the child's ego development not only proceeds with great rapidity, but his independence in motility and thought, in the creation of an inner world, gives new scope to discharge of his aggression in the control of reality. Apart from the one predominant fear of losing the parents' love the child is adventurous and bold. In his activities neutralized aggression is set to work; it can now be displaced to objects in reality where conquest, domination and even destruction are ego-syntonic.

The phallic phase and the oedipus complex give rise to new and specific problems in the economy of aggression. Through the amount

---

24. In speaking of ambivalence one refers in psychoanalysis to a specific degree of fusion of drives, but also to the fact that attitudes of love and hate are simultaneously directed toward the same object. Here only the second type is being discussed.

of aggression vested into the rival parent the previously established short-lived balance is disturbed. New dangers and new concomitant anxieties invade the child's life. The limitations imposed upon the child's aggression necessitate new processes of dealing with it. This leads to somewhat different results than those achieved when the transformation of aggression was meant to equip only the ego with neutralized energy. One might say the process of neutralization as far as the superego is concerned is not as complete: the energy vested into the superego retains very definite characteristics of the original instinctual drive.

It is essential here to keep certain obvious distinctions in mind. Many important ego functions immediately inhibit gratification of instinctual needs but secondarily the ego can be put into the service of aggression and indicate the way to aggressive action against the outside world. In contradistinction superego functions aim at control of both id and ego functions. The superego is specifically suppressive. While the ego is oriented toward reality, and modifies instinctual drives normally also in respect to their compatibility with reality, the functions of the superego retain in part the original characteristics of the drive from which they derive their energy, in directing that energy against the ego.

Naturally it is not meant that during the oedipal phase only the superego develops; the increasing scope of ego functions, especially the widening of ego functions of an autonomous nature, in the sphere free from conflict (Hartmann, 1939), the increased scope of the child's activities during latency, its motor and intellectual skill offer to aggression opportunities for energy discharge with limited aims.

At this point it seems necessary once more to return to the comparison of the development of libido and of aggression. We have in our previous discussion mentioned but not sufficiently stressed one of the essential differences, that any survey of genetic conditions is likely to put into a full light. Briefly stated the difference may be characterized by saying that libidinal gratification is partly zone specific, while aggressive gratification is not zone specific. Libido is specifically related to certain organ zones as sources of stimulation and of discharge; aggression also has a specific relation to certain organs, f. i., to the mouth, to the hands, or the arms, but these organs do not appear as sources of stimulation; as far as aggression is concerned they function as instruments of discharge. However, it seems that in the same way as libidinal cathexis follows in many instances the pathways established by physiological processes, so aggressive cathexis follows the pathways of certain phases of physiological maturation and also of the stages of libidinal development.

During the oral, anal and phallic phases of libidinal development integration of the drives remains incomplete. It is only the development of the object relation during latency and prepuberty and the maturation of the new modes of discharge provided by the genital organization that allow for what might be considered as optimal integration of the discharge of both drives (Freud). This integration then leads to a diminished proclivity toward ambivalence. Little is known about the influence of later (post-genital) stages of development on the economy of aggression. There seems to be agreement only on one point: post-climacteric character changes tend to reactivate modes of ambivalence and other manifestations of aggression known from the study of pre-genital phases of personality development. However, the structure of the ego and the superego in the aged account for fundamental differences.

BIBLIOGRAPHY

1. Abraham, K. 1927. "Ejaculatio Praecox", *Selected Papers*.
2. Bender, L., Keiser, S., and Schilder, P. 1936. "Studies in Aggressiveness", *Genetic Psychol. Mon.*, XVIII.
3. Bergler, E. 1945. "On a Five-layer Structure in Sublimation", *Psa. Quart.*, XIV.
4. Bernfeld, S. 1935. "Ueber die Einteilung der Triebe", *Imago*, XXI.
5. Bibring, E. 1941. "The Development and Problems of the Theory of Instincts", *Internat. J. Psa.*, XXI.
6. Bovet, P. 1923. *The Fighting Instinct*.
7. Brierley, M. 1947. "Notes on Psycho-analysis and Integrative Living", *Int. J. Psa.*, XVIII.
8. Brunswick, R. M. "The Pre-Oedipal Phase of Libido Development", *Psa. Quart.*, 1940.
9. Buxbaum, E. 1947. "Activity and Aggression", *Am. J. Orthopsychiat.*, XI.
10. Dollard, J., Doob, L., Miller, N. E., Mowrer, O. H., Sears, R. R., 1939. *Frustration and Aggression*.
11. Elias, H. 1939. *Ueber den Prozess der Zivilisation*, I (See pp. 263 ff., Ueber die Verwandlung der Angriffslust).
12. Federn, P. 1936. "Zur Unterscheidung des gesunden und kranken Narzissmus", *Imago*, XXII.
13. Fenichel, O. 1945. *The Psychoanalytic Theory of Neurosis*.
14. Freud, A. 1936. *The Ego and the Mechanisms of Defence*.
15. Freud, A. 1947. "Emotion and Instinctual Development", in T. W. B. Ellis, *Child Health and Development*.
16. Freud, S. 1892. Footnotes in: *Poliklinische Vorträge* by J. M. Charcot, I. Bd. Schuljahr 1887-8.

17. Freud, S. 1892. Brief an Josef Breuer, *Gesammelte Werke*, chronologisch geordnet, XVII, 5-6.

18. Freud, S. 1895. "Entwurf einer allgemeinen Psychologie", Sigmund Freud: *Aus den Anfängen der Psychoanalyse, Abhandlungen und Entwürfe aus den Jahren 1887—1902 und Briefe an Wilhelm Fliess*, ed. by A. Freud and E. Kris, in press.

19. Freud, S. 1895. *Studies in Hysteria* (with J. Breuer).

20. Freud, S. 1905. *Three Contributions to the Theory of Sex.*

21. Freud, S. 1914. "On Narcissism: an Introduction", *Coll. Papers*, IV.

22. Freud, S. 1915. "Instincts and their Vicissitudes", *ibid.*, IV.

23. Freud, S. 1917. *A General Introduction to Psychoanalysis.*

24. Freud, S. 1920. *Beyond the Pleasure Principle.*

25. Freud, S. 1923. *The Ego and the Id.*

26. Freud, S. 1930. *Civilization and its Discontents.*

27. Freud, S. 1932. *New Introductory Lectures on Psychoanalysis.*

28. Freud, S. 1937. "Analysis Terminable and Interminable", *Internat. J. Psa.*, XVIII.

29. Freud, S. 1940. "An Outline of Psychoanalysis", *ibid.*, XXI.

30. Fries, M. E. and Levi, B. 1938. "Interrelated Factors in Development, A Study of Pregnancy, Labor, Delivery, Lying-in Period and Childhood", *Am. J. Orthopsychiat.*, VIII.

31. Greenacre, P. 1944. "Infants' Reactions to Restraint. Problems in the Fate of Infantile Aggression", *Am. J. Orthopsychiat.*, XIV.

32. Hartmann, H. 1939. "Ich-Psychologie und Anpassungsproblem", *Internat. Ztsch. f. Psa.*, XXIV.

33. Hartmann, H., Kris, E., and Loewenstein, R. 1946. "Comments on the Formation of Psychic Structure", *this Annual*, II.

34. Hartmann, H. 1948. "Comments on the Psychoanalytic Theory of Instinctual Drives", *Psa. Quart.*, XVII.

35. Jones, E. 1946. "A Valedictory Address", *Internat. J. Psa.*, XXVII.

36. Kardiner, A. 1933. "The Bio-Analysis of the Epileptic Reaction", *Psa. Quart.*, II.

37. Keiser, S. See Bender, L.

38. Klein, M. 1932. *The Psychoanalysis of Children.*

39. Kris, E. 1944. "Danger and Morale", *Am. J. Orthopsychiat.*, X.

40. Kris, E. 1949. "Roots of Hostility and Prejudice." In: Family in a Democratic Society. *Anniversary Papers of the C. C. S. of New York.*

41. Lampl-de Groot, J. 1947. "Development of the Ego and Superego", *Internat. J. Psa.*, XXVIII.

42. Levy, D. M. 1934. "Experiments on the Sucking Reflex and Social Behavior of Dogs", *Am. J. Orthopsychiat.* IV.

43. Loewenstein, R. 1940. "Von den vitalen oder somatischen Trieben", *Internat. Zeit. f. Psa. und Imago*, XXV.

44. Menninger, K. A. 1942. *Love against Hate.*

45. Miller, N. E., with Sears, R. R., Mowrer, O. H., Doob, L. W. and
     Dollard, J. 1941. "The Frustration-Aggression Hypothesis", *Psy-
     chol. Rev.*, XVIII.

46. Mitchell, W. 1928. *The Psychology of Medicine.*

47. Mowrer, O. H. and Kluckhohn, C. 1944. "Dynamic Theory of Per-
     sonality", in *Personality and the Behavior Disorders*, I. ed. J. McV.
     Hunt.

48. Murphy, G. 1945. "The Freeing of Intelligence", *Psychol. Bull.*, 42.

49. Riviere, J. 1936. "On the Genesis of Psychical Conflict in Earliest
     Infancy", *Internat. J. Psa.*, XVII.

50. Schilder, P. See Bender, L.

51. Simmel, E. 1944. "Self-Preservation and the Death Instinct", *Psa.
     Quart.*, XIII.

52. Weiss, E. 1935. "Todestrieb und Masochismus", *Imago*, XXI.

53. Yerkes, R. M. 1943. *Chimpanzees, a Laboratory Colony.*

AGGRESSION IN RELATION TO EMOTIONAL DEVELOPMENT; NORMAL AND PATHOLOGICAL [1]

By ANNA FREUD (London)

INTRODUCTION

I shall try as my contribution to this symposium on aggression, to outline in general the contribution made by Freudian psychoanalysis to the subject. I may find it impossible to do so without committing grave errors of omission and misrepresentation. If this happens, I should like you to ascribe the defects to the difficulty of dealing with a wide and complicated problem in the prescribed quarter of an hour rather than to any tendencies I may have towards systematisation and over-simplification.

The role of the instincts in shaping the personality

The main changes brought about in child psychology by the investigations of psychoanalysis concern the re-orientation with regard to the role of the instinctive urges in the development of the individual. In pre-analytic psychology, childhood was regarded as a more or less peaceful period of progressive growth and development in which the instinctive urges, where they appeared, played the role of disturbing elements. Analytic psychology, on the other hand, ascribes to the innate instincts the main role in shaping the personality. It is the claim of the instinctive urges on the mind which results in the development of new functions, the so-called ego functions. The main task of the ego functions is seen in the attempt to reconcile the demand for gratification made by the instinctive urges with the conditions existing in the child's environment. When these external conditions permit satisfaction of an instinctive wish which has arisen, the ego merely plays its part in helping to guide the instinct towards the desired aim. When the demands made by the environment clash with the claim of the instincts, the ego is faced with a problem and has to find a solution. It may decide to

1. Read at a meeting of the Royal Society of Medicine, Section of Psychiatry, London, Dec. 9, 1947.

disregard what happens in the outside world (a mental process which we call denial) or to disregard the claims of the inner world (the mental process which we call repression). The ego may choose to act either in submission to the environment and oppose the instinct (parents will then say that the child is "good", obedient) or to submit to the claims of the instinct and revolt against the outer world (to be "bad", naughty, disobedient). The ego may also have to choose between claims arising from two rival instinctive urges or between representatives of his instincts and his own ideals. In all these cases the ego is faced by dangers (of painful tension from within, threat of injury, punishment, loss of love from without) and reacts to them with outbreaks of anxiety.

This never-ending series of inner conflicts serves as a constant stimulus towards higher development of mental functioning and finally determines the shape of the child's personality. What we call character formation is, roughly speaking, the whole set of attitudes habitually adopted by an individual ego for the solution of these conflicts: the choice of which instinctive urges to help towards satisfaction, which to oppose, and what methods to adopt in its defence against the threats represented by a powerful outer world as well as a powerful inner world.

Sex and aggression as the two main forces

Psychoanalytic theory groups the whole range of instinctive urges under two headings: sex and aggression; those included under sex serving the purposes of preservation, propagation and unification of life; those included under aggression serving the opposite aim of undoing connections and destroying life.

The psychoanalytic theory of sex

The essential contribution made by psychoanalysis to the knowledge of the sex instinct is the discovery of the diffuse sources of sexual excitation which exist from birth onward in various parts of the body and give rise to the pregenital sex urges of infantile life. According to the origin of these component instincts (the skin, the mucous membranes of the mouth and anus, the penis) we differentiate between an oral, anal and phallic sex organisation of childhood in which satisfaction is sought, either on the body itself or by contact with the love objects in the environment. Normally, these infantile sex elements, so far as they do not undergo far-reaching transformations under the influence of the ego, contribute certain non-genital admixtures to adult genital sexuality (kissing, touching, looking); in abnormal cases one of the infantile component instincts may dominate adult sex life as a so-called perversion (fellatio, cunilingus, scoptophilia, exhibitionism, etc. etc.).

Infantile sexuality is, thus, not only shown to exist, but to be of a purely perverse nature. This latter element of perversity made it more difficult for it to be accepted as a normal, healthy, regular and necessary occurrence. Even today there are certain authors who—though otherwise adopting the principles of analytic psychology—will suggest ways and means of upbringing which promise to do away with one or the other of the component sex urges (the sucking impulses of the infant, the anal interests of the toddler, phallic masturbation) as if these were unwelcome and abnormal occurrences produced by adverse environmental conditions.

On the other hand, ample evidence of the existence and the manifestations of the various component instincts has been provided over the last 20 or 30 years by authors all over the world on the basis of direct observation of young children under a large variety of external conditions (normal, happy or unhappy, home life, group life, institutional life).

The psychoanalytic theory of aggression

The aggressive character of the infantile sex urges from the beginning did not escape notice, of course. It was at first attributed to the crude nature of infantile sexuality itself, later on recognised as the expression of the second group of instincts—the destructive urges.

Aggression, destruction, their expressions and their development are as much in the centre of interest for dynamic psychology now as the development of the sexual function was at the beginning of the century.

AGGRESSIVE URGES DIRECTED AGAINST THE CHILD'S OWN BODY

In very early phases aggressive energy may find outlets on the child's own body, just as sexual energy (libido) may find outlets in auto-erotic activities. Instances of this are the so-called head-knocking activities of infants, a self-destructive equivalent of the auto-erotic rhythmical activity of rocking. Head-knocking occurs more rarely than rocking, is on the verge of abnormal behaviour and may sometimes result in real injury. The same is true for the rather infrequent self-destructive activity of hair-pulling in infants and young children.

I refer in this connection to Dr. W. Hoffer's contribution "Hand, Mouth and Ego Integration"[2] and to other unpublished papers by the

2. *This volume*, p. 49.

same author. In discussing the case of a mentally defective infant girl who grievously injured her arms and hands by biting, while she was unable to chew food, Hoffer illustrates the following point: while, in the first year, sucking the thumb or any other part of the hand is a normal autoerotic expression, biting as a self-destructive activity is abnormal, only to be found in defective or psychotic children. From this stage of development onward it is essential for the child's normality that the aggressive urges should be directed away from the child's own body to the animate or inanimate objects in the environment.

At a later stage aggression will normally be used again in a self-destructive manner. But it will then be invested in the superego and directed against the ego itself, not against the body.

Aggressive Urges Directed Toward the Object World

In the child's relations with the object world, erotic and destructive elements are so intimately bound up with each other that it is difficult to determine in any given reaction what has been contributed to it by either set of instincts. In each of the successive phases of pregenital development the aggressive energy is an indispensable admixture to the sexual (libidinal) urge. The pictures of childhood behaviour with which we are familiar invariably include both elements. We find it natural that the young infant's first emotional attachment, in the beginning to the mother's breast, later to the mother's person, shows the same characteristic qualities of aggressive, insatiable greed that we know from his attitude to food. In the oral stage the infant destroys what he appropriates (sucks the object dry, tries to take everything into himself). On the next, the anal level, the fusion between erotic and aggressive tendencies is obvious even to the unskilled observer. Whoever has dealt with toddlers knows the peculiarly clinging, possessive, tormenting, exhausting kind of love which they have for their mothers, an exacting relationship which drives many young mothers to the point of despair. We know, further, that the originally sexual inquisitiveness of children destroys the inanimate objects towards which it is directed; that loved toys are, normally, maltreated toys; that pet animals have to be rescued from the aggression which invariably accompanies the love showered on them by their childish owners. We understand that on these pregenital stages it is not hate but aggressive love which threatens to destroy its object.

During the phallic sex organization, the mixtures between sex and aggression are of a more adult nature. Boys on this level of development dominate but also protect their mothers, or other love objects. Where the aggressive element is linked with the exhibitionistic tendencies, the combined aim is to impress and thereby to subdue the love object.

IMPORTANCE OF THE QUANTITATIVE FACTOR

This fusion of sexual and aggressive urges is normal and typical. Variation in the quantities of energy contributed from the two groups of instinctive tendencies account for a wide range of individual differences. A larger amount of aggression contributed to the child's behaviour on the anal level creates the picture of a sadistic perversion; a decrease in the aggressive addition to behaviour on the phallic level makes for shyness, lack of masculine behaviour. So far as the upbringing of children is concerned, these quantitative fluctuations account for the difference between manageable and unmanageable, "good" and "bad" children. Most of these variations are within the range of normality.

Pathological aggressiveness in children

In recent years special interest has been directed towards certain states of pathological aggressiveness of young children, occasional in family life, but mostly of children who are either orphaned or who grow up in broken homes, under war conditions, with a series of changing foster-parents, in residential institutions, in camps, etc. Though not mentally deficient, they possess the uncontrollable, apparently senseless destructive attitudes of defectives. They show either pleasure in, or complete indifference towards damage done by them to things, or towards suffering caused by them to people. They wreck their toys, their clothes, their furniture, are cruel to small animals, hurtful to younger children, defiant or indifferent toward adults. Their handling is a baffling problem for the educator, the explanation of their state a challenge to child psychology.

Closer observation shows that the pathological factor in these cases is not to be found in the aggressive tendencies themselves, but in a lack of fusion between them and libidinal (erotic) urges. The pathological factor is found in the realm of erotic, emotional development which has been held up through adverse external or internal conditions, such as absence of love objects, lack of emotional response from the adult environment, breaking of emotional ties as soon as they are formed, deficiency of emotional development for innate reasons. Owing to the defects on the emotional side, the aggressive urges are not brought into fusion and thereby bound and partially neutralized, but remain free and seek expression in life in the form of pure, unadulterated, independent destructiveness.

Efforts to control these pathological states of infantile aggressiveness by force, and efforts, with all the means used in upbringing, to urge the child to control his destructiveness are bound to fail. The appropriate therapy has to be directed to the neglected, defective side, i. e., the emotional libidinal development. Where it is possible to help the child's arrested or otherwise disturbed libidinal impulses to become more normal, the fusion between erotic and destructive impulses will follow automatically, and aggression will be brought under the beneficent influence of the erotic urges.

Life and death instincts

I have not, in the short time at my disposal, discussed the theory of the dualism between life and death instincts which forms the background of the concepts I have used. My reason is that on this particular occasion we are concerned with circumscribed psychological problems rather than with more far-reaching biological speculations.

AGGRESSION [1]

By BEATA RANK (Boston)[2]

Observations of a group of seriously disturbed atypical young children at The James Jackson Putnam Children's Center which we have recently described (3,4), illustrate the great importance of the emotional climate of the mother-child relationship within which the infant experiences his early gratifications and, later, increasing deprivations and frustrations. Deprivation is necessary, we said—following the statement of Hartmann, Kris, and Loewenstein (1)—for the development of the ego, for the differentiation of self and the outside world. However, every transition from indulgence to deprivation brings tension, which is tolerated only when the child feels secure, confident that indulgence will again follow deprivation. As the child learns to distinguish between himself and the mother, he develops understanding for her communications. The detailed processes of this understanding are unknown; hence we speak of the quasi-mystical union of mother and child, of the dynamic unit that mother and child represent. When the mother herself is a poorly organized personality, narcissistic and immature, though not infrequently extremely conscientious and eager to become a mother, the child's ego has a very precarious existence. It remains largely undeveloped and hence is not capable of organizing and controlling drives (libidinal and aggressive). In the case of our atypical children we speak of a fragmented ego[3] because it has no unity and represents an unintegrated conglomeration of various segments or fragments of the successive stages of development. The frailty and ineffectiveness of such an ego is responsible for the fact that these children with atypical or arrested development have a very low threshold of tolerance for frustration which, in turn, produces constant tension and/or anxiety. The tension and/or anxiety finds its primary expression in a motor-expressive discharge. We agree with Mahler's concept presented at this Round

---

1. Presented at the Annual Meeting of the American Psychiatric Association in Washington, D. C., May 18, 1948, Round Table Discussion.

2. Co-Director, The James Jackson Putnam Children's Center, Boston.

3. A special paper devoted to the elaboration of our new concept of the "fragmented ego" is soon to be published.

Table (2) that the "affectomotor phenomena appear to be expressions of rage and thus may be regarded as the precursors of aggression" but think that it is not always pure rage, but rather tension or anxiety with or without rage. For example, the tantrum-like reaction to interruption of children deeply absorbed in fantasy-life seems to us to be one of panic rather than rage, as if the child felt threatened by annihilation. (See the case of Peter M. (3)).

Many of these children with atypical development are in a constant frenzy expressed by explosive motor discharge because they are so easily frustrated from within or without. However, aggressive-destructive behavior directed toward people or objects is rarely observed. It is only when treatment has progressed sufficiently so that ego functioning and reality recognition are strengthened that the *diffuse* explosive motor discharge is gradually abandoned and the child reacts to fear and frustration with more or less goal-directed aggressive and destructive behavior. In other words, only when the child's relationships with others are sufficiently developed do such outbursts assume the form of hostility toward the frustrating person or object.

The case of Anne G.[4] illustrates this progression during treatment from the early form of motor-explosive reaction to the later direct aggressive-destructive behavior.

Anne G., a little girl of nearly 7, our patient for the past 3 years, and one of a group of seriously disturbed, atypical young children, suffers from involuntary rage-like outbursts. She had a markedly passive infancy except for a period of one day or so at 6 months when she was abruptly weaned in the midst of a severe reaction to immunization injections, when she cried continuously and was very restless.

During the first year of our treatment when Anne was 4 she displayed at home and at the Center violent outbursts of shrill screaming with stamping of her feet and hitting out of her hands. These episodes often occurred when any action was required of her, whether imposed from within or without, when she seemed to find herself overwhelmed by diffuse, almost simultaneous contradictory feelings or desires. Similar attacks took place whenever there was a change in her routine or environment. Her face would contort, her feet stamp, her hands strike out as she shrieked: "You don't want it," alternating with, "You do want it," "You don't want to do it," "You want to do it," or "Why did he come?" in a loud, anxious voice that echoed throughout the building. If a new child rushed into the nursery, if her mother took a new route to the Center or if the therapist sat in a different chair, her magic control seemed to be threatened. The maintenance of an extremely rigid routine with an anticipation of what was to come was her principal defense against such panic. Occasionally Anne allowed herself to be comforted; more often the outburst went on for some time, while no one except possibly her teacher or therapist could make contact with her.

4. We have utilized here the notes of one of our co-workers, Dr. Eveoleen Rexford, who is in charge of the treatment of both Anne G. and Ronny K., mentioned below.

With the slow growth of her rudimentary relationships and some maturing of her ego functions, Anne's diffuse infantile expressions of frustration and anxiety gave way to more focused attacks involving definite hostility to the frustrating person, mostly the mother. She directly attacked her mother, biting, scratching, and trying to choke her. Her fear of complete abandonment by the mother made even the threat of a brief separation traumatic for her, and her anxiety was discharged in this attacking, aggressive behavior.

During the past year Anne has had fewer outbursts of any kind. However, even today as she sits reading in her school, she bursts out for several minutes at any interruption, screaming repeatedly: "Why did he come in?" or "Why did you talk?" or "Why is that noise?", unable to tolerate interference with the completion of her activity without registering her protest of frustration and anger.

In contrast to Anne G., Ronny K., now 5 years old, presents a picture of an extremely destructive and aggressive youngster. We assume that, though severely handicapped and anxious, he reached a stage of development of differentiation between self and the outside world and was able to conceive of hostility and direct his aggression to people and objects outside of himself.[5]

He came to us 2 years ago because his mother could not handle him and was convinced he had something wrong with his brain. He was so overactive and destructive that it was difficult to judge whether he was feebleminded, as she feared. He made frequent, lightning attacks upon persons and objects and these were dangerous and impossible to forestall. The mother told us that he had something wrong with his eyes but glasses would not help and she thought his poor vision was responsible for some of his behavior. We learned from his ophthalmologist that Ronny has a congenital choreo-retinitis which leaves him about 15 per cent vision and unfortunately affects principally the macular areas. His visual handicaps and behavior had been discussed freely and punitively in his presence, and it was not difficult to understand why one of his most frequent methods of attack was to pull glasses off and hurl them upon the floor or to thrust his fingers hard into someone's eyes. In addition, in the nursery school he made vicious, apparently unprovoked attacks upon the children, striking them over the head with heavy blocks or a metal truck. For many months an adult had to hover over him constantly to protect the others and to protect him from their retaliation. He became the prototype of the bad boy for many boys and girls who had played with him or near him.

During the first year of treatment, we found that his teacher and his therapist could establish warm relationships with him, that he could in the setting of warmth and understanding learn to engage in constructive activities and diminish his active and aggressive behavior. The outbursts began to occur more often when he was frustrated in trying to carry out some specific act, in trying to crayon, for example, or to

5. The specific factors which contribute to the given ego-structure cannot be dealt with in this paper, which reproduces only our contribution to the Round Table Discussion, and which had to remain necessarily brief. We hope in a subsequent publication to do justice to this problem.

build a block house like another child's. Although he has learned to
utilize more skillfully the peripheral vision he has, Ronny remains very
handicapped; and the frustration he suffers continually is quite obvious.

We discovered during the course of our work with the mother that
she is an infantile, very demanding, and punishing woman who is in
marked conflict over Ronny's handicap and his behavior and has subjected him to violent physical attacks. She has been able to make only
limited progress in restraining her hostility and in treating him with
some understanding. A recent outburst of violent aggressive and destructive behavior illustrates the anxiety and frustration which engender
Ronny's extreme outbursts.

Ronny's eyes were to be examined under anesthesia, and we had
requested that the mother give us ample time to prepare him for such
a traumatic experience. It is characteristic of the mother's behavior
that she called to announce that she had that morning started administering the drops and that Ronny would be examined the next day. She
added that he was wild but that he had to overcome these foolish fears.
She was persuaded to bring Ronny in so that the therapist could talk
with him; and we saw a frantic, aggressive little boy, running around
hitting other children, smashing any objects he could reach, and begging
for something he could break. The teacher reported to the therapist
that Ronny behaved just as he had 2 years ago and that it seemed impossible to reach him in his anxiety and fury.

Ronny did not appear to recognize the therapist, but his pupils
were so dilated that he obviously could see little. He clutched the
therapist's hand, jumped, giggled, and then began to kick her, hitting,
scratching, and biting. Once in the therapy room, Ronny made a quick
tour, sweeping all objects he could reach to the floor, jumping on them,
and screaming for more to break. When the therapist tried to pick him
up, he fought as if in absolute terror, perspiration broke out on his
forehead, and he began to moan. He seemed unable to listen to the
interpretation of his anxieties and the remarks about the drops and the
examination but ran bumping into chairs and toys, kicking, smashing,
and yelling. When the therapist chanced to say that she had had drops
in her eyes and that drops made everything look foggy, he stopped,
turned toward her, and said wonderingly: "Ronny can't see. Everything
is foggy for Ronny, too. He had drops." Although he insisted then on
returning to the nursery school room, the therapist was able to talk
with him on the way, reassuring him that the fogginess from the drops
would go away, that the doctors would not hurt his eyes tomorrow, that
they wanted to help him see better, etc. It was possible to refer briefly
to previous discussions about his eyes and his anxieties in regard to them.
After a few minutes in the nursery school room, his anxieties overwhelmed him; and he became again a tornado of destruction, crying
for more and more to break.

There is no doubt that seen from the outside Ronny fits the description of a very aggressive and destructive child. Ronny's outbursts seem
to us to stem from the continual frustration and anxiety he suffers, first
in regard to his poor eyesight and second in regard to his domineering

and frightening mother. The aggressive pattern which was his response to all situations the first year we knew him could be considerably altered when he established confident relationships with his teacher and the therapist and when his mother mitigated to a slight extent her exceedingly restraining and punitive handling of him. The fear of annihilation under which he lived kept him in constant anxiety, and his identification with his hostile and aggressive mother helped crystallize a pattern of responding to all experiences with aggressive and destructive behavior; this pattern was partially broken as we helped him meet his anxieties. The birth of a brother during our second year of treatment led Ronny to substitute more passive and feminine patterns in apparent identification with the mother, who softened in her care of the normal little baby. After a few months, however, Ronny's anxiety over the mother's open favoritism for the baby and her hostile treatment of his rivalry grew overwhelming, and he reverted more and more to a consistent pattern of aggressive and destructive behavior. It was in such a setting that the eye examination was carried out, and the outbursts described above occurred in response.

In conclusion: The above examples have been given to support our thesis that we do not conceive of aggression as an *unmodifiable innate* force of destruction. We surmise that aggressive behavior means adaptation to the surrounding reality, hence is a part of ego-organization. We have attempted to demonstrate that it is precisely the structure of the ego which defines the ways in which one expresses the reactions to inner or outer frustration.

Case I (Anne G.) illustrates our theory that where the ego is undeveloped, "fragmented", and hence without the capacity either to establish a clear distinction between the self and the outside world, or to organize the drives, the reaction to constant frustration has to remain *self bound* and can only be expressed by the explosive, diffuse outburst of rage-like tension. As Anne's ego gained sufficient strength through the establishment of an object relationship, even though a rudimentary one, her anxiety and hostility could then be expressed in a goal-directed attack, chiefly on the mother.

Case II (Ronny K.) in contrast, serves as an example of the direct aggressive-destructive behavior to objects and people, established as a response to continuous frustration and anxiety (because of his organic defect and his demanding mother). But Ronny's ego had already reached the stage of distinction between the self and the surrounding reality, and of an identification with the aggressive mother, which was a further step in development. We have pointed out how this pattern became gradually modified in a setting of a more positive confident relationship: in the Center with his teacher and therapist, at home with his mother who was able to mitigate her attitudes. However, the change did not remain permanent but was in turn subject to an immediate reversal once the conditions of the original anxiety-creating situations were again re-established.

In brief, our clinical observations indicate how the vicissitudes of aggression and its forms of expression depend on the relationship between the frustrating and frustrated forces. By providing an emotional climate favorable to the development of an ego which has the capacity to organize and to control drives, we may be able to modify or even eliminate the destructive element of aggression.

BIBLIOGRAPHY

1. Hartmann, H., Kris, E., and Loewenstein, R. "Comments on the Formation of Psychic Structure", *this Annual*, II, 1946.
2. Mahler, M. S. "Aggression", Contribution to Round Table Discussion, Am. Psychiat. Assoc., May 18, 1948.
3. Putnam, M. C. et al. "Case Study of an Atypical Two-and-a-half-year-old", *Am. J. Orthopsychiat.*, XVIII, 1948.
4. Rank, B. "Adaptation of the Psychoanalytic Technique for the Treatment of Young Children with Atypical Development", *ibid.*, in press.

MOUTH, HAND AND EGO-INTEGRATION [1]

By WILLIE HOFFER, M.D., Ph.D., LRCP. (London)

What Bertram D. Lewin recently called Oral Psychology is a complex subject, encompassing not only the familiar aspects of the oral drive in infancy and its vicissitudes in later life but also such remote aspects as oral eroticism and skin sensitivity (Fenichel, 1942), hypnagogic phenomena in states of fever (Isakower, 1938), the structure of delusions and finally a detail in the psychology of dreams, called the dream screen.

While one has to acknowledge the fact, that the work of psychoanalysts is not lacking in hard research and ingenious imagination, one still wonders whether its tentative and experimental character is sufficiently recognised, and whether generalisation will not come about before the comparative slowness of analytic practice has permitted the full re-examination and final assessment of innovations.

In his admirable study "Sleep, the Mouth and the Dream Screen", Bertram D. Lewin (1946) puts forward the view that in the sleeper's mind the psychic residue (unconscious memory) of his mother's breast is represented as a dream screen, on which the dreamer projects his dreams. He also thinks that, when falling asleep and regressing into an objectless, fetal state we pass through an early oral stage of mental organization. On this he throws a powerful light.

The difficulties which psychoanalysts have been facing when discussing mental processes of early infancy are caused by the absence of the familiar functions of an ego and superego, which through speech and other external indications reveal the psychic reality underlying human activities. The instincts themselves cannot be studied directly, they "are superb in their indefiniteness" and "we are never certain that we are seeing them clearly" (Freud, 1933).

Much, if not everything, therefore, depends on the detection of those early functions which either germinate from an inborn ego core (Jeanne Lampl-de Groot, 1947) or present themselves as the first results

---

1. Read at the Conference of European Psychoanalysts at Amsterdam, Holland, Spring, 1947. The time allowed was 20 minutes.

of the differentiation from the id. They belong to the no man's land
between biology and psychology, which Freud called "Biological Psychology". From the exploration of these early stages of mental life we have
to learn that the ego as a contour is inherited and its differentiation
from the id is phylogenetically outlined.

In the following investigation I shall enlarge on the idea that the
differentiation of the ego from the id (Hartmann, Kris, Loewenstein,
1946) shows itself on the infant's body-surface when, in the service of
the oral partial instinct and for the sake of autoerotic pleasure, two sensations, an oral one and a tactile one, are aroused simultaneously by
finger-sucking. Such a situation does not usually arise before the 12th
week when, quite intentionally and no longer reflexively, the hand is put
into the mouth in order to relieve oral tension.

In general psychology the function of the hand has mainly been
studied as that of an organ which grasps. I am not suggesting that
before this grasping function manifests itself, the hand is merely an
attachment to the mouth, but that from intra-uterine life onward it
becomes closely allied to the mouth for the sake of relieving tension and
within this alliance leads to the first achievement of the primitive ego.
From now on the hand cannot relinquish the function of relieving
tension and in this way it becomes the most useful and versatile servant
of the ego.

Having in mind these far-reaching implications of infantile finger-
sucking I now suggest the following of a systematic line of presentation.

The observations to which I shall refer are partly taken from the
writings of Gesell and Ilg, mainly from their book on the feeding behaviour of infants (1937), and partly from observations of my own which
I was privileged to make at the Hampstead (War) Nurseries with the
active support of Anna Freud and Dorothy Burlingham and their co-
workers (Burlingham and Freud, 1943; Anna Freud, 1946 and 1947).

According to Gesell the hand to mouth response is anticipated
in utero. Preyer, more than fifty years ago, stated that a fetus introduces
its fingers into the mouth and thus elicits the first sensation of touch
on its own body.

How do the hand or fingers reach the mouth in the fetus or newborn child? In fetal life the fist is brought into contact with the sensitive oral zone because the posture of the fetus adjusts itself to the con-
cavity of the uterus in such a way that the hand or fist is nearest to the
chin and mouth. Touching the face elicits in the fetus and newborn

infant the sucking reflex. Until the second quarter of the first year sucking depends entirely on touch and afterwards it will in addition be initiated by the sight of the breast or bottle (Gesell and Ilg, l. c.).

Does the infant show any preference for the breast or bottle in contrast to the hand during the first twelve weeks? This question must be answered in the negative. It is at first neither breast, bottle, nor hand, but only the touching of the oral zone which elicits sucking movements. Sometimes, Gesell states, it is necessary to hold the hands down or the fingers and the nipple would be sucked together. Approximately from the twelfth week onward the infant shows progressively greater and greater preference either for breast (bottle) or hand. The hand serves the need for oral pleasure (sucking) only, breast and bottle serve the need for both sucking and food. From the twelfth week onward the hand helps in the feeding process by being placed half open on the breast or bottle. From 16 weeks on a more definite grasping response may occur when the infant on seeing the bottle grasps it as it is brought to the mouth. During the feeding his hands are placed more firmly around the bottle or on the breast.

If we turn now to the Hampstead Nurseries infants, the most striking fact in their sucking behaviour was the directness and resolution with which from the twelfth week on the infant made the fingers approach and enter the mouth. This could be observed at any time during waking hours; it was of course more accentuated before and immediately after feeding. The hand may be introduced by the shortest route or by a wide circle of the arm while the eyes may follow the movements of the hand. At that age I could seldom observe vigorous sucking movements when the fingers entered the mouth, which was quite in contrast to the response when the bottle was brought to the mouth. The finger-sucking is mainly a rhythmic, intensive and pleasurable sucking. Length of duration seems to be more important than intensity. It may stop for a shorter or longer period while the hand with fingers bent hangs on the mandible. This indicates irritation of the gums due to teething.

Bertie, a boy of 16 weeks, is an experienced finger-sucker who suspends his ring finger in his mouth by bending the three remaining fingers and pressing them like a scaffolding towards the lower lip, thus preventing the hand from sliding into the mouth. One cannot overlook the high degree of adaptation the infant achieves in easing the oral tension. It is the hand which skillfully adapts itself to the needs of the oral zone, its shape and volume are changed from the fist to one small finger according to the need for stimulation. Finger or fist can penetrate deeply or slightly into the mouth, it can be directed toward the outer or the inner structures of the mouth. The versatility of the hand in the sucking process allows of originality and the elaboration of individual pleasure patterns in great numbers. Regarding Bertie's scaffolding, however, I have one reservation to make. Bertie was breastfed for the first seven weeks while he was still at home. It may be that a tactile sensation was aroused on his chin or lower lip by his mother's hand holding the nipple in his mouth. The position of his fingers while finger-sucking might therefore also be interpreted as a voluntary reproduction of an epidermic stimulation which he felt when sucking at the breast.

Another example of a genuine and self-directed hand to mouth movement was observed in Tom, when 16 weeks old. He had never been breastfed, but had been brought up with the bottle in a most satisfactory way. Filmed when sucking his thumb he revealed an unusual effort and exertion for a 16-week-old child. Tom held his arms slightly bent in front of the face, the fingers were stretched and those of the left hand tried to grasp the right thumb with a pincer movement. While both hands tried to get closer to each other with jerky movements, Tom's mouth was kept open, he made an effort as if he were trying to lift his head from the pillow, and his lips sucked in air like a turbine. When he succeeded in catching the thumb and introducing it into the mouth the left hand then was held over the mouth, locking it and preventing the right hand from sliding out again. Or if it did slide out, the left hand quickly pushed it back again and the thumb was pushed far back toward the palate, accompanied by quite intensive sucking. No other form of oral greed in connection with food was observed in Tom.

In the case of Bertie, we said that his hand achieved a high degree of adaptation for sucking, for increasing and probably varying the autoerotic pleasure. In Tom's case both hands (and arms) operate together. One hand, though with the greatest difficulties, grasps the other, as some weeks later it grasps inanimate objects.

Gesell and Ilg (1942) say of the 16-week-old baby that he brings his fingers together over his chest, and engages them in a mutual fingering play. His fingers finger his fingers! Thus he himself touches and is being touched simultaneously. This double touch is a lesson in self-discovery. He comes to appreciate what his fingers are; and that objects are something different (p. 101). In Gesell's view the eyes lead and the hands follow. This applies to a baby learning to control the outer world; it does not apply to the baby learning to know its own body. He learns it by touching one hand with the other and by touching his mouth.

The association of hand and mouth may become so close that it can temporarily interfere with the feeding process and the feeding function of the mouth. The infant may either insist on sucking his fingers at the same time as he is being fed, or refuse to be fed at all because of its wish to suck his fingers only. While Gesell records this observation as if it were an accidental interference with the feeding process caused by the hand, our Hampstead Nurseries film leads us to interpret this behavior as a *competition* between the feeding process and finger-sucking.

The necessity of holding the hands down to prevent fingers and breast (or bottle or spoon) from being sucked at the same time, as Gesell states, has probably obscured this competitive behavior on the part of the infant. Winnicott (1945), however, mentions that "some babies put a finger in the mouth while sucking the breast, thus (in a way) holding on to self-created reality while using external reality." This behavior could quite frequently be observed in infants from about the 14th week onward. In one case the infant adds his thumb to the bottle in the mouth and insists on its remaining there while he is fed; in another case he tolerates the bottle well without interfering by finger-sucking but starts to introduce the finger immediately when fed spinach with a spoon.

Looking for an explanation of this behavior, we cannot prove that the competition with the fingers aims at prevention of feeding. Not in all cases was the bottle or spoon rejected while the finger was added. This can mean that the child while being fed did not experience the expected or accustomed oral stimulation in the feeding act itself, and reverted to the accustomed autoerotic stimulation of the oral zone by finger-sucking. This shows the infant's preference for the repetition of the known and experienced gratification. The negative reaction to abrupt changes of stimulus and the importance of acquired habits of keeping sensory stimulation within certain limits, high or low, as the case may be, has perhaps not been taken into account sufficiently in child psychology. The troublesome fussing of the infant, when put to the breast, described by Gesell and Ilg (1937) and Middlemore (1941) may justifiably be viewed as the infant's dislike of a too abrupt change from a low to a high level of stimulation or the reverse.

The competition may persevere for some weeks. The range of activities widens rapidly during the second and third quarters of the first year, and no longer shows an exclusive preference for the oral zone. I am inclined to believe that the hands, after being libidinized during the intensive sucking period, now function more independently of the oral zone and are more under the influence of the eyes, playing the part of an intermediary between eyes and mouth. They have developed from instruments serving as a means for discharging tension into tools which control the outer world. They have at this stage become a most active extension of the growing ego.

When studying early ego functions we have to take into account that the customary feeding methods very early deny the infant the pleasurable use of his hands when he is being fed. The newborn child needs to be fed actively, the breast or bottle has to enter the mouth, the hand is still unable to help or to participate in the feeding process. It does not provide food, it provides oral pleasure. The more breast and bottle are superseded by semi-solid and solid food, the more important do mug, spoon and hand become as instruments. Instead of the accustomed soft nipple, which remains in the mouth, the hard spoon or mug touches or enters it—with increasing frequency—leaving it after a very short interval to be refilled and put back again. The accustomed feeding method consists in feeding by the bottle, mug and spoon until the baby has gained full control of his movements so that he can feed himself, which usually starts during the second year. Modern feeding methods, as practised in the Hampstead Nurseries, allowed the child to feed himself before the end of the first year. The transition is a gradual one, from spoon feeding out of a bowl by the adult to the next stage when the infant grasps the spoon and follows the movement to the mouth. It often happens, of course, that the infant puts his hands into the bowl and splashes the food, but as soon as he develops enough skill he directs his hands from the bowl to mouth, and feeding entirely by his own hands has begun. This leads finally to self-feeding by spoon. This self-feeding training coincides with the oral-sadistic stage, the stage of teething and biting.

Surprisingly enough it very rarely happens that a child bites his own hand, though he may quite often fail to keep balance and may drop the food just as the fingers have been put into the mouth. Contrary to expectation the infant shows a high degree of self-regard for his hands and will not go further than chewing his fingers occasionally. Although bodily injury is only too frequent at this stage—if the child is given a fair opportunity to move about—the teeth are very rarely the cause of self-injury, although licking and biting are practiced on toys and on the cot. We might say that the child that likes himself will not bite himself. It is the first triumph of primitive narcissism over a partial instinct like the oral-sadistic instinct, and the child achieves this without being protected by his mother. This does not apply in the same degree to the infant's food, at this age. Sometimes there is some oral-sadistic handling of the food but one wonders what are the motives which make the infant treat his food and his hands with care and regard, at any rate for some months, until the anal-sadistic stage has been fully reached. In the control of oral-sadism toward solid food, paradoxical as it may sound, the infant has taken his first step toward the acquisition of eating manners by imposing on himself the first restrictions in handling the food, for instance by biting it slowly and into tiny bits. Semi-solid food is devoured, the hand being used merely as a shovel.

Simultaneously with the appearance of the teeth and of biting the functions of the arms and hands develop far beyond the original hand-mouth relationship. We have said that at first hand and mouth convey the primal sensation of self. Then the hand associates itself with the eyes and other sense-organs, particularly with the sense of equilibrium, in which the infant's arms and hands are of great importance. During the short quadrupedal phase of motor development the child's hands are more frequently in contact with the ground than ever before or after. The innate urge to put the hands up to the face consequently leads to a stimulation of the olfactory system as well.

Considering also the fact that the infant places everything that is within reach into his mouth with the help of his hands, the accumulation of experience as a result of the mouth and hand relationship by the end of the first year seems to be rather rich and promising. We can therefore safely assume, that when entering the second year the infant has built up an oral-tactile concept of his own body and the world around him and regulates to a certain extent by this means his erotic and aggressive (active) drives.

BIBLIOGRAPHY

Fenichel, O. 1942. "Symposium on Neurotic Disturbances of Sleep", *Internat. J. Psa,* XXIII.

Freud, A. and Burlingham, D. T. 1943. *Infants Without Families,* Allen & Unwin and Internat. Univ. Press.

Freud, A. 1946. "The Psychoanalytic Study of Infantile Feeding Disturbances", *this Annual,* II.

Freud, A. 1947. "The Establishment of Feeding Habits", in Ellis, R. B., *Child Health and Development,* Churchill.

Freud, S. 1933. *New Introductory Lectures on Psychoanalysis,* Hogarth Press and Norton.

Gesell, A. and Ilg, F. L. 1937. *Feeding Behavior of Infants,* Lippincott.

Gesell, A. and Ilg, F. L. 1942. *Infant and Child in the Culture of Today,* Harper.

Hartmann, H., Kris, E., and Loewenstein, R. 1946. "Comments on the Formation of Psychic Structure", *this Annual,* II.

Isakower, O. 1938. "A Contribution to the Pathopsychology of Phenomena Associated with Falling Asleep", *Internat. J. Psa.,* XIX.

Lampl-de Groot, J. 1947. "On the Development of the Ego and Super-Ego", *ibid.,* XXVIII.

Lewin, B. 1946. "Sleep, the Mouth and the Dream Screen", *Psa. Quar.*, XV.

Middlemore, M. P. 1941. *The Nursing Couple,* Hamish Hamilton Medical Books, London.

Preyer, W. 1895. *Die Seele des Kindes,* Th. Grieben Verlag, Leipzig. (*The Mind of the Child,* Appleton).

Winnicott, D. W. 1945. "Primitive Emotional Development", *Internat. J. Psa.*, XXVI.

THE RELATIONSHIP OF TWINS TO EACH OTHER

By DOROTHY T. BURLINGHAM (London)

It has been the purpose of my two former papers "The Fantasy of Having a Twin" (1) and "Twins, Environmental Influences on Development" (2), to show how outside influences play a part in forming the characters of twins and the relationship of twins to each other. The mother's attitude to the twins; the brothers' and sisters' reaction to this twin relationship; the particular behavior of all the various persons who come in contact with twins; all these have a direct influence. The fantasy of having a twin, common to many people and formed to counteract the disappointments of real relationships, also has, in all probability, a subtle and indirect but still effective influence on twins. A study of the relationship of twins to each other is only valuable where there is a full awareness of these other environmental and related factors. Otherwise it would be impossible to discern and distinguish the various components which make up the emotional life of twins and the emotional relationship of twins to each other.

Four sets of twins and one set of triplets were in the Hampstead Nursery during the war and were observed over periods of 1 to 4 years. The observations reported here were made on three pairs of children admitted in infancy.

Identical Twins	Non-identical Twins, Triplets	Age at Arrival	Length of Stay
Bill, Bert		4 months	3 years, 3 months
	Iris, Louise	1½ years	1 year, 1 month
Jessie, Bessie		4 months	4 years, 3 months
Mary, Madge		3 years, 7 months	2 years, 11 months
	Rolland, Jill,[1] Molly	3 weeks	2 years, 7 months

1. Rolland and Jill, two of the triplets, came directly from the hospital to the nursery when they were 3 weeks old and remained until they were 2 years, 7 months. The third triplet came later and was abnormal, and therefore is not included in these observations.

The material gathered from such a small number of twins cannot give any definite information about twins in general. It can only be a study of these particular twins. However it may suggest avenues for discussion and lead to further investigations on twins.

First notice taken of the twin

Each twin and each triplet who came to the nursery as a baby was put into a separate bassinet. Each child was then placed next to his or her twin; the triplets also had a place to themselves. When changed, the twins often were on the dressing table at the same time, but did not take the slightest noticeable interest in each other. When at 4 months they outgrew their baskets, they were put in adjacent cots from which they could easily see each other. They were often put in the same cot for short periods of time.

Rolland and Jill: during the 5th and 6th month, Rolland and Jill were observed looking at each other. If they got into each other's path of vision, each one would look at the other and away again. At 7 months, Rolland used to stare at Jill when she cried. It was not until the next month that they appeared to take any real notice of each other.
Bill and Bert: Bert began to smile at Bill at 7 months, but Bill did not respond. At 8 months, when they were put in the same cot, Bert would fall asleep immediately and Bill would then try to scratch him. At other times, Bill would disturb Bert so much that they had to be separated.
Jessie and Bessie: It was still later before Jessie and Bessie seemed aware of each other. At 8 months, Jessie stretched her hand into Bessie's cot, Bessie did the same to Jessie a month later, but it was not until the 10th month that Jessie used to watch Bessie, while Bessie still took no notice of Jessie.

During this whole period from 5 months on, all these babies showed their growing attachment to their mother and the nurse who cared for them.

At 4 months, it was possible to tell if Rolland's nurse was in the room with him from the way he cooed and "talked" to her. At 5 months, both Rolland and Jill seemed to recognise the various people who handled them; at 8 months, they showed interest in everything that went on in the room.
From 7 months, both Bill and Bert responded to their mother when she visited them several times a week. They were friendly toward her as they were toward the nurses who handled them. At 12 months, they were always excited and disturbed when the mother left after visiting them.
Jessie's and Bessie's mother at first saw the twins daily; later she worked in the nursery, and was frequently with them during the day. At 4 months, Jessie smiled at her and seemed to enjoy her visits; at 7 months, both had contact with her. At 9 months, Bessie stretched out

her arms to be picked up. At 12 months, Jessie smiled happily when her mother entered the room, while Bessie trembled with excitement.

From 8 months all these children responded when they were spoken to and played with by members of the staff whom they knew. They all watched closely and intensely everything that their mother or their special nurse did when she was within sight or hearing.

Competition for attention

At about 10 months, when the mother or nurse paid attention to one of the twins the other took notice and later tried to get her attention for himself. When she picked up or fed one of them, the other sometimes stared or became unhappy. It was only at this stage of development that the twin who was not picked up or fed first showed that it objected to being the one who was left behind. This may be the origin of the competition between the twins expressed later by the refrain, "Me too," "Me first," "Only me." Often, however, the two children in a pair of twins may behave very differently. One may be indifferent when left behind, while the other may scream desperately in the same situation. Moreover, one may object several months before the other does.

With the two non-identical triplets, Rolland and Jill, Rolland at 11 months cried when Jill was picked up to be changed or to be fed, Jill remained indifferent. At 12 months, Rolland banged his head when he was not fed first; only at 15 months did Jill get into tempers when Rolland was fed first. They showed these reactions when other children were handled or fed, but not to the same degree. This may have been because their cots were next to each other and because the triplets were brought more together by the outside world.

In the case of the identical twins, Bill and Bert, at 10 months, Bert was upset when Bill was fed first, but Bill was indifferent. At 14 months both showed that they minded when the other was favoured. Bert cried while Bill was fed and Bill rocked in his cot as he watched his brother being fed by his mother.

The greatest amount of emotional reaction was observed in the feeding situation.

Jessie and Bessie: Bessie simply refused to be fed second. The mother had made up her mind always to be fair to the twins and always to treat them alike. But when Jessie was picked up first Bessie would scream and get into such a state that the mother was forced to pick her up. Jessie made no fuss when she was not taken but waited patiently until Bessie was finished. At 12 months, Jessie cried quietly when Bessie was picked up first. At 13 months, they would sit at a table opposite each other and the mother would then take her place between them. The mother had to feed Bessie twice as quickly because each time she picked up the spoon to feed Jessie, Bessie would start screaming.

Jessie was forced to wait while the mother tried to satisfy Bessie by pushing two spoonfuls into her mouth for every one she gave Jessie.

Bill and Bert: Much the same happened in the feeding situations of Bill and Bert. At 16 months, when a nurse fed the twins sitting at the table between them, Bill got furious when Bert was offered a spoonful of food although he was given more spoonfuls. Bert, on the contrary, would wait patiently and watch Bill while he was fed.

Bessie and Bill were the lively ones of these two pairs of twins and they were more greedy as well, which may have caused their greater impatience at this age. At 17 months, Bill and Bert were able to feed themselves and sat at little individual tables for their meals; when Bill noticed that a nurse was feeding his brother he would throw his plate on the floor in a fury. It was evident in this instance that it was not greed which produced this reaction in Bill but anger that his brother was getting attention from the nurse and he was not.

In all these instances the twin, who loudly objected that his mate is getting attention or something that he himself is not getting at the moment, shows that he wishes to take the place of the other twin and receive what the other is getting.

Activity and passivity in pairs of twins

These dominant characteristics in one of a pair of twins tend to produce an active twin and a passive one. This can be very easily observed at the toddler age, when the main occupation of children is to be on the move, to take things and to push things about. When a toddler finds himself with another child of the same age he will pull the other's hair, push him, hit him, pinch him or bite him. What generally happens with a pair of twins in this period is that one of the twins is the more vigorous, and he will bite, push, pull or snatch things away from his weaker twin. The weaker one, as is usual with children of this age when attacked, will just cry over the hurt he has received, will in no way try to defend himself, but will behave in a completely passive way.

Rolland and Jill: Although Rolland started out as the heavier child and even sat and stood first, Jill at the toddler age was the more energetic and aggressive one. At 14 months, she took away Rolland's toys, and he would just look bewildered and grumble. A month later Rolland would try to keep hold of the things Jill was snatching away from him. At 17 months, she attacked him fiercely and continuously, and as he still only cried helplessly and grumbled, they often had to be separated. Jill maintained her domination over him during this whole period.

Bill and Bert: Bill showed greater activity then Bert and was first to crawl and stand. At 8 months, he already took things from his brother; at 12 months, he was not only taking things away from Bert but would throw him over and sit on him, while Bert would simply cry helplessly. At 13 months, Bert could sometimes keep a toy. At 15 months, they would bite each other but Bill attacked much oftener and more fiercely so that Bert often had to be protected from him.

Bessie and Jessie: Bessie had always weighed less and been more temperamental, Jessie had been more placid. At 13 months, Bessie was bullying Jessie, she would take her toys, and pull her hair. Jessie would try to avoid Bessie by getting down to the other end of the cot. At 14 months, Bessie found great pleasure in teasing Jessie and the more she succeeded in making her unhappy, the more she would tease her. An example: they would both get biscuits. Jessie would eat hers quickly. Bessie would nibble at hers very slowly watching Jessie's longing eyes. She would break off and offer her little bits and, as Jessie would reach out to take them, she would pull her hand back quickly, and smile with glee when Jessie cried. But at 15 months, Jessie began to assert herself and even bite Bessie. At 17 months, Jessie was hitting back and even attacking Bessie. At about this time they were separated for a short time because Bessie had whooping-cough more severely than Jessie and in addition had had many weeks of diarrhea. Whether this had weakened Bessie and given Jessie the chance to stand up for her own rights is hard to say. But it was from this time that Jessie became the active twin and Bessie the passive one. At 19 months, Jessie was taking everything from Bessie, pulling her hair and hitting her. Bessie just suffered these attacks and then some time later would attack Jessie. Bessie would cry bitterly when Jessie hit her and tried her best to avoid her. Jessie now began to tease Bessie in her turn very much as Bessie had done 5 months earlier. They might, for instance, be fighting for a toy. Jessie would get it, and put it on the table with a very innocent expression. When Bessie tried to take it she snatched it away and laughed at her.

The passive twins showed that they were not necessarily content with their subordinate roles. It was forced upon them as a result of various conditions, such as the greater strength, the greater activity, or the more passionate nature of the other. But if for some reason the greater strength or activity of the active twin was reduced, the passive twin would immediately take advantage of the situation. This was most clearly seen in the case of Bessie and Jessie, when Jessie took the lead the moment she was able to do so. Bert, because of his more gentle nature, was never able to get the upper hand over the very aggressive Bill, although he tried from time to time to hold on to his possessions when Bill wanted them and even to attack him occasionally; but in the end he always got the worst of the struggle. He then became completely passive again.

Competition in achievements

It was possible to observe that the twins, at an early age, were aware of the differences in their achievements. The less advanced of the twins noticed that the other was able to crawl, kneel and stand while he himself was only able to lie or sit, and was upset as he watched these activities of the other.

As already mentioned, Jill was at 14 months more active at taking things from Rolland, but was not able to stand, as he was. During this period Rolland and another child were observed standing near Jill while she made repeated efforts to get up too. She kept falling back and was very unhappy about it. At last in her efforts she knocked down one of the two children and she was obviously delighted that the child was no longer standing.

At 11 months, Bill could crawl and kneel but Bert could not. He would watch Bill and get very cross. This situation was even more marked when Bill could stand and he was unable to. Bert was definitely unhappy and would cry desperately as he watched him.

Younger children will try to imitate the achievements of older brothers and sisters if the difference in age is not too great or if, as at the toddler age, the difference in ability is not so great that it discourages imitation. With twins the development of both is on the same level, they both want to sit, crawl and walk. The slower twin sees the other doing just what he himself wants to do and is trying to do. This forces the less active child to compete with the active one at a much earlier age than is usual in children. The competitive situation will again be increased through the relationship to the mother or nurse. The spontaneous admiration they receive from the mother for each new accomplishment causes pleasure. The more backward child not only observes the achievement of his twin but also the expression of pleasure that the mother shows.

Copying each other

Imitating another child or person is a normal expression of a certain stage of development, beginning approximately at 9 months.

The twins began to imitate each other some time later. If one of the twins did something that interested the other twin, the other copied him.

At 12 months, Jill noticed that Rolland was drinking out of a mug. She picked up her mug and drank too.

At 12 months, Bert shook his head, Bill copied him. At 13 months, Bert noticed that Bill was singing, he sang too.

At 15 months, when Jessie dropped her spoon Bessie dropped hers.

When the twins were potted, Bert banged his feet on the floor. Bill copied him. This was something that most of the children used to do, one of the children would start and the others followed suit.

This imitation of each other became especially pronounced in two pairs of twins, Bill and Bert and Jessie and Bessie. The copying developed into an expression of their closer relationship. With Bill and

Bert it took the form of a mutual game. One had pleasure in observing the other doing what he was doing, the other had pleasure in copying. Jessie's and Bessie's competition with one another developed in each the wish to do what the other was able to do.

Copying in the form of a game

Copying in the form of a game was not only observed between Bill and Bert but between other children in the nursery.

At 12 months, Rolland used to watch Jill with amusement when she spat. Spitting for her had for some months been a pleasurable occupation. At 13 months, Rolland leaned over his cot and copied Jill as she spat; both were delighted.

It appeared that it was Bert who started the copying games with Bill. At 14 months, he clapped his hands and Bill did the same; he banged bricks on the table, Bill followed suit. These acts were always accompanied by laughter from both children. Soon it was impossible to tell who copied whom. At 14 months, both twins were lying in their cots on their backs. One would start to shout and kick and the other would watch him and laugh, then the other would take his turn to shout and kick and the first one would watch and laugh. The twins provoked each other to join in these games. One would kneel suddenly and laugh, the other would then do the same and laugh too. Or from a sitting position, one would throw himself onto his back, looking at the other twin, and immediately the other would copy him. Laughter was an essential element in these games. Both twins tried to find new ways of entertaining the other. It was Bill who started grimacing, making sudden jerky clownish movements, jumping from one foot to the other, standing up and throwing himself down, making funny noises and laughing uproariously. Bert would imitate him. Bill would get himself and Bert more and more excited until the game was like an orgy. Bert at 16 months used these copying games not only to get momentary pleasure but to distract Bill.

Bert watched Bill screaming. He went up to him and clapped his hands; Bill stopped crying, copied him and began to laugh.

Bert with his quieter ways used the games with a purpose in mind. Bill was carried away by his inner excitement which was increased by the games. In spite of the fact that it was Bert who started these games in the first place, it appeared even here that because of his greater vitality Bill was able to gain the lead over Bert, just as he had by his aggressive ways. Bert could not resist Bill's passionate, provoking behaviour.

These games which started at 13 months as fairly simple bodily movements developed with increasing complexity as one idea was added to another.

At 21 months, the twins would crawl on their knees each holding a doll in his arms; first they would copy each other crawling through the room and then go round in circles, one following the other.

At 21 months they sat together near the garden gate, playing with tins. Bert drank out of his tin, so did Bill. Bert offered a drink to Bill and Bill to Bert, then both banged their backs against the gate. They started drinking out of their tins again and the game was repeated as before while the twins shook with laughter. The game came to an abrupt end when Bill suddenly bit Bert who then cried and went away.

At 2 years, 5 months, when they played on the slide they invented many ways of getting off the slide, copying each other.

The other children of the nursery would often watch Bill and Bert, laugh at them and with them, and sometimes would try to join in the game; but the twins paid little attention to them; they preferred to amuse and excite each other. (There was one exception to this, when the twins were separated. They then chose other partners and tried to start these same games with them.)

On an observer these games made a curious impression since the likeness of the twins was greatly increased by their similar behaviour. Bill and Bert were not only alike in appearance, and in their actions. They even took the same positions in periods of rest. From the moment they arrived in the nursery at 4 months, they were the mirror image of each other. When they lay in their baskets, Bill on his right side, Bert on his left, Bill sucked his right thumb and Bert his left. At 17 months, they still sucked these same thumbs and when they masturbated they did so with the hand opposite from that which they used for sucking.

As they grew older they were often found asleep in exactly the same position on their stomachs, Bert's head turned to the right, Bill's to the left, or lying on their backs, eyes covered with one arm. They would sit on the floor opposite each other with one leg tucked under their bodies; they would stand in their cots, one arm hanging over the edge of the bar, the other in exactly the same position. At 14 months, their movements were absolutely alike when they crawled. At 15 months, they would rock in the same rhythm, holding on to the bars of their cots at the same height, head bent in the same way, their mouths usually open. At 15 months, they pushed their cars at the same time, with absolutely the same movement and with the same expression. At 17 and 19 months, they would start rocking at the same moment and in the same rhythm.

They also had the same physical marks, birthmarks over the forehead and eyes (more distinct in Bill than in Bert); the marks disappeared in both at about 7 months. They often had the same infectious diseases at the same time, which was not surprising since they were always together, but Bert generally more severely than Bill. But at 8 months, each had a blister on his chin, developed one day apart; and both developed hydrocele at 14 months, Bill's on the right side and much more pronounced than Bert's, which was on the left side and of a more bluish colour. These disappeared at about the same time and reappeared again several times, always together; Bert's always less distinct than Bill's, disappearing completely a few weeks befor Bill's, when they were 18 months.

How much the constitutional identity of these twins influenced them to imitate each other in postures and movements and later in the games they thought out for each other is hard to say. Of the three pairs of identical twins in the nursery they were the most alike in looks and behaviour. They were backward in development, erratic and unable to make normal contacts with adults and with children. They became more and more uncontrollable and stopped developing normally. When they were absorbed in one of their games of imitation, it was impossible for the mother or nurse to get their attention or influence them in any way. Wild movements about the room, aggressive actions against adults, children, and each other were generally the result of these games. Bill was more aggressive, more uncontrollable, and less able to be influenced than Bert. Bert was not able to cope with Bill's aggressive actions, he became afraid of him and in the last months at the nursery it was felt best to separate them.

The relationship between the twins expressed in these copying games did not further their development. On the contrary, it seemed to hinder them from making normal contacts with each other, or with other people. It was felt that if the twins had been brought up without each other, Bert would have been able to develop normally. The influence that Bill exerted on him made it impossible for Bert's ego to develop as it might if he had not been carried away by Bill's dominant, domineering and erratic nature. Bill, if brought up without his twin, would not have had the added thrill of observing the reactions he created in Bert and would have lacked the enjoyment of watching Bert, which obviously gave him sensations of excitement. The double pleasure created in this way absorbed them and prevented them from achieving the development normal for their age.

Copying because of dependence

Jessie and Bessie were very different from Bill and Bert. They went through the various phases of development without any special difficulties. However, their development did show differences. They did imitate each other, and each had original ideas which the other found interesting and copied. The imitating brought them into a closer relationship, but their behaviour even while they imitated each other followed different patterns and their individualities became more rather than less marked.

Up to about 2 years they imitated each other in much the same manner. When one did something interesting the other wanted to do it too; when one demanded admiration the other asked for it also.

At 19 months, when Jessie heard that Bessie asked for her dog, she asked for hers, too.

When Bessie saw that Jessie was undressing, she undressed too.

At 23 months, Bessie was ill in the night; the next morning the nurse looked into her throat. Jessie, who was sitting next to Bessie, pointed to her throat and said "Me, me."

Jessie quite openly expressed her wish to copy Bessie and to compete with her.

At 2 years, 5 months, when both the twins were on their beds for their afternoon naps, Jessie jumped up and down on her bed; Bessie copied her. Then Bessie lay down with her legs in the air and waved her arms, singing "My mummy, no sleeping." Jessie watched her for a minute, said "Me too, Bessie," and then copied Bessie's movements.

At 2 years, 3 months, the twins were clean, with occasional lapses. They had a curious habit for about a week: after their lunch they sat on their pots next to each other; after a while they got up, looked at their achievements and exchanged pots. On two consecutive days Bessie had had a motion and Jessie not. On the third day both said "finished", and got up. They looked into their respective pots. Bessie had had a motion. When Jessie saw it she said, "And me big job," and sat down again with immediate result.

Jessie was a good sleeper but Bessie had a sleeping disturbance and waked and cried in the night. The nurse would come to her and cover her up. On such occasions Jessie (23 months), without opening her eyes and without giving any sign of being awake, would say, "Me too."

At about 2 years it became noticeable that Bessie was copying Jessie more and more and in an intense and compulsive manner. Whatever Jessie did, she had to do it too. If Jessie got on a chair to get something down from a shelf, Bessie would get up on a chair too, although she had nothing to get down. When Jessie played she was a dog, Bessie would stop whatever she was doing and be a dog too. The senselessness of these actions became very marked. Whenever she copied, there was no obvious purpose other than to copy, no real interest in the activity she imitated. She copied Jessie only because Jessie was the object of her attention, and she did it even when the result conflicted with her own desires.

At 20 months, when Jessie stopped eating, Bessie stopped. When Jessie asked for a second course, Bessie, although her plate was still full, asked for one too. When Jessie went on the pot she followed suit, although she might have been on it only a few minutes before.

At 2 years, 7 months, when Jessie was given a top shelter bed, into which she had to climb by means of a ladder, Bessie, who had a lower bed, also used the ladder to get to her bed. None of the other children did this.

At 3 years, when Jessie wet herself because she could not undo her panties quickly enough, Bessie was discovered to be wet too. She explained "Jessie been wet."

At 3 years, 6 months, the twins had been washing. Jessie was carrying a bowl with the washing in it. She put it down to pull up her knickers which were coming down. When Bessie saw this, she did the same although her knickers were quite in order.

Jessie never imitated Bessie in this compulsive way but continued to copy her only whenever she thought Bessie was having an advantage over her. The intention of her imitation was always obvious.

Bessie had always shown a special interest in men. Whenever visiting fathers or workmen came to the nursery, she would get very excited, run to them, climb on their laps and in this way provoked a lot of attention. Jessie, on the other hand, did not behave differently toward men from the way she behaved to other visitors. But when she saw that Bessie was getting attention by her behavior she climbed on the visitor's lap too.

At 3 years, 5 months, Bessie fell down and hurt herself on a walk; her nurse offered to hold her hand. Jessie was greatly annoyed and as the nurse also held the hand of another child she had to walk alone. A few minutes later she fell down and would not get up until the nurse helped her. Then Jessie quickly got hold of the hand Bessie had held.

In spite of Bessie's dependence on Jessie, she was not without independent ideas. It was she who started dancing to the gramophone at 25 months and Jessie who copied her. Bessie started climbing on the jungle gym first, Jessie following her there too. But at the same time she was more dependent on Jessie and needed her support and example.

At 22 months, when Bessie was in strange surroundings, she followed Jessie about, never leaving her side and doing exactly what she did. In this way she got the security she needed. At 25 months, they were on the street for the first time with their mother. Jessie was interested in this new experience and poked her head into everything, Bessie did the same, but only because Jessie was the leader. Alone she would not have had the courage to be so enterprising.

Both children were delighted when they got new dresses on their second birthday. Jessie expressed her pleasure and said "Look, look." Then Bessie said the same, but not spontaneously. She forced herself to ask for admiration because Jessie did.

At 25 months, Jessie loved to play with Olga, an older child. They played mother and child. Bessie joined in the game but only because Jessie was playing. Bessie remained playing just as long as Jessie did, but she gave the impression that she would have been quite ready to stop earlier.

The fear of being left out, left behind, appeared to be the incentive of Bessie's imitation on these occasions.

At 2 years, 6 months, the twins were always on their pots at the same time because Bessie interrupted whatever she was doing when Jessie went on her pot. When Jessie was in bed in the nursery because of a slight indisposition and asked for her pot, Bessie went to the lavatory while Jessie was on her pot in her bed. When Bessie was finished and came back she found Jessie still sitting on her pot. Bessie immediately turned around, fetched her pot and sat down on it again, next to Jessie's bed.

Bessie could concentrate much longer on an occupation than Jessie. At the Montessori Kindergarten class that they both attended, Jessie continually changed from one occupation to the other. Bessie always chose the same material as Jessie and, in spite of being engrossed in a newly-chosen piece of work, she would leave whatever she was doing as soon as she saw that Jessie had given up one piece of work for another, and she would again choose the same as Jessie. Jessie acted in this manner because of her lack of concentration and resulting restlessness, Bessie dragged herself away from interests because of her concentration on Jessie's every move.

Jessie, through her imitation of Bessie, added to her achievements and where she competed with her was always stimulated. Bessie also increased her accomplishments in this way, but on the other hand she imitated Jessie to give herself needed security and confidence. Her senseless dependence developed because of her fear of being left behind or left out. (It was extraordinary that there never was a sign from either twin of annoyance when they copied each other. Jessie never seemed to mind Bessie's dependence; though she often appeared quite indifferent to it.) Bessie's dependence prevented her from following up her own intentions or carrying out her creative ideas. She had to concentrate on Jessie to know what she was doing, and in doing so gave up her own thoughts and actions and adopted Jessie's. Separated from Jessie, she would probably have been able to develop her own personality, which showed her to be active and original in many ways, and to have great powers of concentration. In imitating Jessie she tried to take over her personality. As a result she often appeared at this age to be sad, shy, sulky, stubborn, slow, retreating and inhibited. Jessie, on the contrary, was bright, lively, friendly, outgoing, restless and lacking in concentration. Bessie's imitation of Jessie, caused by her dependent attitude, did not make the twins more similar. On the contrary, it made them more unlike, whereas Jessie's imitation of Bessie created whenever it happened an appearance of great similarity.

Copying of feeding habits

When the twins behaved alike it was often very difficult to see whether one of them first copied the other and then both took over the same behaviour, or whether they reacted similarly to the same situation. In their attitude towards food they often appeared to have the same reactions.

At 14 months, when the children were transferred from the baby room to the toddler department they both refused to eat bread and butter although they were quite accustomed to it in the baby room.

It is likely that both children felt strange in the new surroundings. One probably expressed her dislike by refusing the bread and butter and the other, in the same mood, followed suit.

At 19 months, both were given bread which they broke up into little bits and threw on the floor. At another time at the same age they threw sandwiches on the floor after taking a bite. With both the pleasure in throwing seems to have been greater than their appetites during this period.

At 2 years, 1 month, both were fond of peas; both liked gravy especially and repeatedly asked for more; both said they liked their food wet.

Between 2 years, 1 month, and 2 years, 3 months, they went through a phase of being very greedy. They could not wait until their plates were set before them; they ate a few spoonfuls voraciously, and then ran to the trolley where the food was served and asked for more. If attempts were made to make them first finish what was left on their plates they flew into a temper.

The greed was not only a sign of hunger but rather an expression of another emotion which they showed in this way—a need for more of something else that they were missing, probably a longing for their mother. At this stage of development it is very usual for children to refuse food or to be greedy when they are emotionally upset in some way. It may have been that they were both dissatisfied or that one twin was able to express her dissatisfaction in this way, and that the other took over this emotional reaction which most probably fitted into her own feeling of discontent as well.

At 2 years, 3 months, although the twins ate everything, even new dishes, they both refused semolina pudding. They seemed disgusted with it. At 2 years, 3 months, Bessie refused cheese; Jessie immediately pushed her plate away.

In the first example it seemed that the twins reacted toward the pudding in the same way. In the second Jessie took over the dislike which Bessie showed.

At 2 years, 4 months, they would hardly eat any vegetables except carrots, although they had until then eaten them with pleasure.

At 2 years, 6 months, they both, for no obvious reason, had temper tantrums just when the food was brought into the room. After these violent scenes both were less keen on their food.

At another time Bessie, for no obvious reason, refused to eat her dinner. Jessie, who had been enjoying hers, stopped at once and from then on both refused potatoes for a fortnight; then one day both started eating them again.

At 3 years, 8 months, they again had a period when neither ate any potatoes.

There are several possible explanations for this behaviour of the twins. It is well known that children, if not interfered with, will have preferences for certain foods and dislike of others. These fads may last one day or several weeks. It is possible that the twins were at that time developing such food fads. Bessie's dependence on Jessie may have resulted in their both liking or disliking certain foods at the same time. But it seems more likely that they used their food to express some common dissatisfaction and discontent which possibly had reference to their emotional relationships with the parents or parent-substitutes. The violent outbreaks in behaviour when the food was brought in was most strongly expressed by Jessie. As both children had, probably, the same emotional desires and needs, and therefore the same disappointments, expression of discontent about food by one of them called forth an immediate response in the other by a contagion of feelings.

Contagion of feelings

Contagion of feelings was observed in many situations. With Jessie and Bessie, when one showed a strong emotion the other caught it and expressed it in identical behaviour.

Fear:

When the twins were 2 years, 3 months, they were given their baths in the big bathtub. One day Bessie showed great fear and refused to sit down in it. She quieted down only when taken out of the bath and put in a little bathtub instead. Jessie, who was not at all frightened at first, as soon as Bessie had been taken out of the big bath showed fear and insisted on being bathed in the little bathtub also.

Up to 2 years, 3 months, the twins had shown no fear. Then one day they suddenly showed fear of animals, fear of ducks and sheep on the Heath.

It was difficult to see which twin was afraid first; the emotions seemed to be expressed simultaneously.

Anger:

At 20 months, Jessie showed off her new dress, Bessie copied her. Jessie was furious when her dress was taken off. Bessie would not have objected when hers was removed but when she saw that Jessie was furious she was furious too.

Sensitiveness:

At 2 years, 3 months, Bessie and Jessie were awakened from their afternoon nap by another child. All three began pushing their beds about and playing. When told to get back to bed Jessie settled down and would have gone off to sleep; but Bessie, who was very sensitive to disapproval, began to howl. When she was taken out of the bedroom, Jessie started to howl too. She then joined Bessie. They were given toys to play with but both continued to cry for half-an-hour.

Jessie had joined in Bessie's crying only after the latter had been taken out of the room. Though she had not been sensitive to the original reproof, at this stage she took over Bessie's feelings. She then behaved in the same way as Bessie, crying and refusing to play.

Longing for their mother:

At 22 months, Bessie had difficulty in going to sleep but she did not call for her mother unless Jessie did. When she heard Jessie calling she joined in at once; she got up and stood near the door calling "Mummy". (Bessie may have thought that if Jessie called the mother, the mother might come to Jessie and she, Bessie would be the one left out.)

At 20 months, when Bessie realised that her mother was leaving the room, she rushed to the door shouting "Mummy", and got into a temper. When Jessie, who was not upset when her mother left, saw Bessie's reaction, she cried and got into a temper too. (Jessie imitated Bessie so as not to be left behind in case Bessie's fuss proved successful.)

The similar reaction in the twins occurred because one feared that the other was getting an advantage.

Dissatisfaction and revolt:

At 22 months, Bessie and Jessie were on a walk with their mother. During the walk Bessie asked to be carried. The mother refused. Bessie sat down on the street, Jessie followed her example. They both refused to walk and remained sitting on the pavement. The mother could not move them from the spot until someone came and helped her carry them home. In the nursery both children continued to scream for half-an-hour.

Bessie here showed a dissatisfaction which she expressed in tiredness and a wish to be carried by her mother. Jessie, seeing Bessie's behaviour, immediately behaved in the same way. She felt the intensity of Bessie's emotion and became dissatisfied too, not with Bessie for spoiling the walk, but with her mother. She then took up Bessie's manner of showing dissatisfaction, and both revolted together, refusing to get up and trying to force the mother to carry them. Individually they each wanted to be carried and Jessie feared that only Bessie might succeed.

At 2 years, 1 month, both children behaved very similarly towards their mother; they showed pleasure when she appeared, took possession of her and made innumerable demands. They watched her jealously and did not accept the slightest refusal without getting cross and aggressive. It is clear that during this period the twins were going through a violent emotional experience with their mother. Their own personal demands for attention and love increased their jealousy of each other. Their powers of observation were taxed to the utmost to watch for any sign of affection from their mother. At the same time each was well aware that her twin was also demanding and hoping for the sign of love.

A recognition of this need to resolve the jealous tension and find some sort of equilibrium between their loyalty to each other and their loyalty to their parents may in fact be crucial to an understanding of twin development.

Provoking behaviour:

At 2 years, 7 months, they seemed especially possessive and angry with their mother. Together one morning they deliberately did everything to annoy her. They refused to wear the frocks she had prepared for them, they insisted on wearing rubber boots instead of their usual shoes, they kept on making demands and when refused, threw themselves on the floor. They insisted on having another child's new slippers on the breakfast table, their own shoes under the table, and on sitting on special chairs. They took turns making demands; each cooperating with her twin every time, insisting that the demands be carried out, and behaving in a similar manner.

In other words, they behaved as a well-organised team, each in perfect agreement regarding the demands of the other, and regarding the manner of enforcing the acceptance of these demands. The contagion of feelings between the twins prompted them to cooperate in order to accomplish a common purpose, in this case, to provoke their mother because she had dissatisfied them.

BIBLIOGRAPHY

1. Burlingham, D. T. "The Fantasy of Having a Twin", this Annual, I, 1945.

2. Burlingham, D. T. "Twins, Environmental Influences on Development", this Annual, II, 1946.

A CONTRIBUTION TO THE STUDY OF
SCREEN MEMORIES

By PHYLLIS GREENACRE, M.D. (New York) [1]

In an early paper (6), Freud described screen memories as any childhood memories which are retained into adult life. These isolated islands of recollection were found on analysis to mark the location of and to represent the lost continents of childhood experience. Among these memories some were noted as having special characteristics of brightness or intensity which generally contrasted with their relatively indifferent, innocuous, or patently distorted content. They were not only predominantly visual, but Freud further noted that, in contrast to memories from later periods of life, the rememberer was detached and seemed to watch himself as a child performer. Such memories seemed to be screen memories par excellence. In this early paper the mechanisms of repression and displacement were especially noted and screen memories were likened to slips of the tongue or of behavior, and the other psychopathological phenomena of everyday life. In his book of this title (7) Freud developed the concept of screen memories further and attempted to classify them somewhat formally as retroactive or regressive, interposing, or contiguous memories according to the time relationship between the retained memory and the events which it was concealing. This classification has not proved especially useful as screen memories are found to draw their strength from or "feed on" (to use Fenichel's hunger analogy) events which have happened both before and after their occurrence. It is probable that they may even be molded somewhat and get new increments in the course of years.

In later papers (8, 9), Freud stated that screen memories could be treated in ways similar to dreams and like them were products in which repression, displacement, condensation, symbolization and secondary elaboration might all participate.

The relation of screen memories and especially of the screening process to precipitating traumata in traumatic neuroses has been dealt

1. From the New York Hospital, and the Department of Psychiatry, Cornell University Medical College, New York.

with by Fenichel (3) and Glover (10). Fenichel further discussed their
relation to déjà vu experiences, the traumatic experiences to which
perversions are often erroneously attributed, and to pseudologia phantastica (5). H. Deutsch has described the latter also (1) and has also
pointed out that hysterical fugues are sometimes reactivated screen
memories (2).

Fenichel especially has dealt systematically with the economics of
the screen memory (3). He emphasized that it results from a struggle
between denial and memory in which a substitute for the memory of
the disturbing experience is seized upon and is utilized as a kind of
compromise; and that the gradual development of the ego with an
increasingly strong sense of reality weakens the tendency to deny. He
further considered that this struggle would naturally be greater if it
arose in the immediate setting of already established anxiety. This state
of affairs might even create a kind of hunger for screen experience
which would facilitate the use of old (remembered), symbolic or even
contiguous experiences as screens for the repressed experiences, this
hunger being felt as a compulsion to remember or to test the memory
(4). It is possible that the appearance in dreams of special phrases or
sentences is a phenomenon also of this order.

In a recent paper on visual stimulation and stress in the course of
superego development, I was concerned with certain problems which
encroached upon the screen memory from a different angle (11). The
suggestion was there made that intense and shocking experiences of
early childhood, especially those which involved strong visual stimulation, resulted in a reinforcement of some visual components in the
superego formation, which might be reactivated later in life in similar
situations of stress, and could be regularly observed in the course of
analyses of such patients. I was impressed with the observations of
E. Kris that these light effects—halo or aurora—might be related to the
peculiar peripheral luminosity and general intensity of screen memories.
It is the purpose of this paper to examine this situation more carefully
and then to consider a special form of screen memory in which there is
an intensity of stubborn persistence but without brightness, and in
which the content appears factually disturbing and very little elaborated.
In the most extreme of such cases the memory appears as an insistent
unpleasant scene which is told readily by the patient, a marked degree
of isolation being achieved by an almost complete withdrawal of affect.
In my experience such memories are related to the central theme of the
neurosis, are rigidly defended throughout, resist analysis directly, and
connections are made by the patient only toward the very end of the
analysis.

A careful scrutiny of the structure of a number of screen memories has led to the conclusion that the special intensity and visual quality depends upon pressures of varying degrees from five different inter-related sources: (a) The strength of the sense of reality dependent on the stage of the ego development: The stronger the ego and the firmer the sense of reality, the better can the young individual tolerate frustration and anxiety and the less need he has for the compromise involved in displacement and screening. (b) The intensity of the disturbing experience which provokes the screening. The more severe the experience, the greater is the aggression aroused, sometimes with accompanying erotization. This severity or intensity may itself cause an overflow in the form of secondary visual excitement even when the primary trauma has not been visual as in the case of the severest pain, concussion or other physical distress. In general, however, psychic traumata of childhood do involve vision directly in greater proportion than in adult years. The severity or shock character of traumata with accompanying visual stimulation may contribute directly to the bright edge and vividness of the screen memory through the process of displacement.

This may be observed *in statu nascendi* even in adult life. In extremely frightening experiences the person often finds himself noticing and stressing some inconsequential detail of the scene which seems inexplicably vivid and sticks in his memory afterward even when the central horrifying part of the experience is not forgotten. The mechanism is much the same as in the screen memory—a deflection of focus from an intolerable horror to something which is reassuringly innocuous and familiar. Analysis to be sure often reveals that the very detail selected is itself a screen for some earlier frightening or guilty experience, the emotion of which has been reactivated by the new trauma. For example:

A young man surprised a marauder as he opened the door of his home one night. He believed the man was armed but was not sure whether or not he actually saw a pistol. He was shocked by the experience, and was surprised to find his attention fixed on the door knob which shone in the light of the nearby street light rather than on the man and the question of whether or not he had a gun. The door knob was the vivid spot in his memory both immediately afterward and long after. Analysis showed that the deflection of focus to the door knob served to temper his anxiety at the time. Back of this however lay much earlier experiences of peeping through the nearly shut door of the bathroom to watch his parents at the toilet and of attempting to look through the keyhole to verify suspicions of their activities in the bedroom.

Anyone who has examined witnesses to some shocking event will recognize how unreliable are their observations, and especially how irrelevant and peripheral details may be stressed and even invented with a persistent and even annoying circumstantiality.

Katherine Mansfield's story "The Fly" (14) is a succinct account of such a horror fantasy, showing this mechanism: An older man in a moment of competitive exultation in life is suddenly reminded of the death of his son in battle. Attempting to conjure up the memory of the boy in a kind of orgy of guilty grief, he finds his attention wandering instead to a fly which has been caught in an ink well and is attempting to free itself. He watches and experiments in its struggle. With its death, he is seized by a "grinding feeling of wretchedness" which frightens him. A moment later he calls for fresh ink and blotter and suddenly wonders what he has been thinking about.

(c) The stage of libido development of the child and the degree of general erotic arousal at the time with resultant frustration and anxiety. Thus the utilization of a traumatic experience or event may be markedly different depending on whether it occurs in the oedipal phase or during the latency period, i. e., whether in the ascendency or relative quiescence of erotic feeling and interest. This certainly is but a restatement with a different emphasis of Fenichel's observation about the hungry condition and quantivalence for screen experience of certain infantile states of mind. It is obvious too that not only the stage of libido development but the specific concatenation of recent experience of the child may determine his point of saturation for frustration and anxiety after which he must resort to displacement and denial as defensive measures.

(d) The genetic stage of the superego development, corresponding in a general way but not always proportionately with the ego development, but also influenced by the special vicissitudes of the individual superego formation and its interrelation with other components of the ego. This is so much discussed in my paper on vision and superego that it is unnecessary to repeat it here. It seems, however, that the detached onlooker quality characteristic of the typical screen memory may be due not only to the paralysis and temporary depersonalization caused by fright or panic and carried over to the substitute remembered experience, but further and perhaps chiefly to the arousal of the superego functions whose force influences decisively the need to deny and the feeling of general intensity, and which are represented by an actual watchfulness in the screen memory.

(e) The form and degree of sado-masochistic character structure which has already been built up in the person at the time of the event (s) for which the screen memory is substituted. It is to be expected that where there is no severe degree of sado-masochistic character structure, simple, pleasant or tepid events may be used as the screen, whereas in severely morbid personalities really traumatic events may be seized upon as representations of the earliest anxious fantasies or experiences of the child and may be used variously as justification, verification or gratification. This has been presented by Fenichel in his discussion of traumatic

experiences which act as screens in traumatic neuroses (3) and in perversions such as voyeurism and fetishism. He emphasized that the way
in which a traumatic experience is incorporated into the psychic life
and into the memory of the person depends upon the intensity of the
unconscious readiness to develop anxieties and on the past ways in
which persons have learned to deal with anxieties; that where there is
already a strong sado-masochistic character, a new trauma may be felt
as a gratification. He mentioned especially people who habitually involve themselves in thrilling temptations to Fate and feel some sort of
satisfaction when their latent fantasies come true. An extension of this
is the situation in which the trauma is not provoked but is a true accident of Fate and is accepted by the sado-masochistically impaired person
as a magic fulfillment of his punishment desires. Fate in this way is the
successor of the parents who have often held a prolonged Olympian sway
in the childhoods of these patients. All this will be discussed in relation
to the clinical material of this paper having to do with the special type
of screen memory which I have already described, i. e., one in which the
content appears traumatic and unelaborated, factual and isolated,
has persistence rather than brightness, and is stubbornly resistant to
analysis.

Case Report:

An unmarried medical nurse of 35 came to analysis because of
certain instinctual temptations toward both men and women which she
could neither accept nor reject and which consequently threw her into
a state of arousal, frustration, guilt and anger, reaching the proportions
of a severe panic. She said at once that her sexual interest and enlighten-
ment had been extraordinarily delayed and that only during the past
3 to 4 years had she been aware of any erotic feelings since which she
had become involved in a series of singularly disturbed and rather
adolescent attachments to both men and women. Although she was an
unusually able and intelligent woman she saw nothing odd in this
delayed development, regarding it as part of her upbringing and general
background. This was the more striking since she came from a rather
normal appearing family with both parents still living, and her description of the family life was of warm-hearted energetic people in a
modest semi-rural community. She insisted that she had had neither
interest in nor knowledge of sexual matters until toward the end of her
nurses' training. She even believed that she had never seen male genitals
until she was in training when the experience was forced upon her in
the course of her regular duties. When I indicated that this was unusual
especially as the family had lived in small quarters and that anyway
there was the probability of some observations at summer camps and
bathing beaches where she went every summer, she protested that I did
not really understand her background and how protected she had been.
On the fifth day of the analysis, after saying that when she was

quite grown-up she had asked her mother some facts about her own birth and that her mother had replied by asking *her* facts about obstetrics, she told me that at 8 or 9 she had gotten up in the night, had passed her parents' bedroom where a low light was burning and had observed them having intercourse. She could not say whether she had understood the scene at the time or when she had come to realize its nature. She did not even know whether or not their bodies were uncovered. Still the scene had a dreary clarity in her mind and she recalled especially that her father's face looked cruel and unattractive although he was a very good-looking man. Later in the analysis when the scene came back to her as it did rarely, she would repeat it as she had originally, in a dry factual way as though she were including it conscientiously as part of the anamnesis, but she could neither elaborate it nor discuss it. Her attitude at most was that it had occurred, that it might have given her an unfortunate impression of her father and of sexuality, but there the story ended. This attitude persisted throughout the greater part of her analysis even after she had brought out many memories which gradually came back spontaneously, involving awareness of a neighbor boy's genitals at 4, sex play with a girl cousin her own age at around 6, and a wealth of other reminiscences of curiosity indulged in with other children involving farm animals, of mutual masturbation and experimentation followed by profound guilt feelings. Still the patient could not say more about this primal scene experience at 8–9.

About 2 weeks after the beginning of the analysis the patient had a dream, reported as follows:

> "You were saying to me, 'You have been at this for 4 months and are not getting anywhere.' The idea was that since the therapy was not working, I was to bathe all over in Saline, then soap and leave a coating of soap on."

In association she said that whereas the Saline felt and seemed clean, a coating of soap was a spurious cleanliness, really a nasty disagreeable mess. The 4 months she attributed to the fact that she had been a little over 3 months with another analyst and this plus the time with me would approximate 4 months. She had feared that the other analyst disdained her and questioned whether she was analyzable. She felt that the analysis with me would have to bring out a mess or turn into one. She began also to project on to me some of her guilt feelings of uncleanliness, saying that she felt that I too disapproved of her and at other times making indirect criticisms of me and of my office. She could bring out these latter only with the greatest difficulty and on several occasions rushed impetuously from the analytic hour rather than say anything which conceivably could offend me. In other respects, however, she was not at all an ingratiating or subservient person and did not show any positive need to please.

The extremeness of the patient's defenses as well as the shape and consistency of the experience defended was forecast by the third week of the analysis when she brought a dream:

> "I was going in and out of places in Rockland County with the question whether I should stay and work there. I was trying to decide about it."

On the same day she brought me a sonnet written some years earlier, of which I quote a part:

"I built a wall of thoughts in even row
Like bricks they were to be, so firm and strong
Protecting me from laughter and mad song
And echoes of a fear that would not go.

*　*　*

Now bricks have crumbled and the scattered dust
Is scuffed by hurried steps of passers-by
And I shall learn because I know I must
I too can roam the world with courage high,
Build fair castles, place a firmer trust
In golden spires that pierce the sky."

Here clearly the first stanza indicated the rock-like wall of defense which was to characterize her analysis throughout, while the last stanza showed the direction of hope for a favorable outcome.

Several months later she presented a dream which proved to be a remarkable condensed version of her very severe neurosis:

"You were hypnotizing me. I was in another room than this, but lying down. A young girl in her late teens or early twenties put a whisky bottle on my chest. I realized you were hypnotizing me. As part of the process you made faces. Finally I just gave in. Next I was on my way home and dropped this bottle and broke it. It seemed then as though I had bought it."

At this time, the patient remarked that she very much disliked having to speak about me or see me even in a dream and that always in dreams about me somebody was interfering. Here however the whisky bottle seemed a part of the treatment and had to do with the hypnosis against which she seemed to struggle futilely. She further associated the whisky with her first homesexual contact, in which she had climbed a mountain with her friend, been caught in a rain storm and on returning to the hotel had taken whisky and gone to bed to avert a cold; with the croup of her early years, and with breath-holding which she resorted to in anger at 4—5, reaching a point of panic and fear of losing consciousness. This was coincident with another kind of withholding, namely constipation as a spite against her mother. The making faces was related vaguely to a period of severe neurosis at 7—8 when she suffered obsessive thoughts of guilt toward her mother, necessitating endless trivial confessions, and at the same time had a facial tic with wrinkling of the nose and shrugging of the shoulders. She had recovered from—built a stone wall (of her poem) against—this neurosis on being forcibly returned to school at 8. About this event there was another screen memory—a recollection of herself clinging to the newel post screaming and resisting frantically while her parents cajoled, then forced her to release her grip and go back to school after an absence of several months due to her neurotic fears.

Only toward the end of the analysis when the patient could not be kept from some rather dangerous acting-out, could these dreams or the full significance of the original screen memory be understood. One more episode during treatment is an interesting link. Fairly late in the analysis, she reacted with extreme anger and panic when a friend of hers referred to me in a mixture of derogation and appreciation as "a reliable old percheron", with the manifest reference to my size and durability—that of a good reliable work horse. The patient considered this an extreme insult, abused her friend, and forbade her to speak in such a fashion again. Mentioning it with hesitant humor to me during the analytic hour, she could at first make no associations, then thought of the painting by Rosa Bonheur, with horses' rumps in the foreground, then of another early screen memory of laughing uncontrollably at 5—6 when a fat aunt laced her corset and "her buttocks looked so funny." She next thought of the farm of another aunt where there were work horses, and skipping over the thought of a schizophrenic cousin who lived on this farm and had the same name as her father, she suddenly said, "I think of father showing me things I wasn't supposed to know about. I don't remember what. I think I would get close to father then and get frightened." Her next thought was of a charming baby she had seen in the clinic that morning. The probable pun on the word percheron (perch-on-her) did not occur to her even when she spoke of watching in the chicken yard and wondering what the roosters did to the hens.

To go back to the original screen memory, the drearily clear yet not very specific primal scene observed at the age of 8, many of the components of which must be evident from the dream material already given. The patient slept in her parents' room until 4 (cf. the 4 months in the first dream). During this period she had croup rather severely. After she was removed to another room, the croup was better, but she reacted to this expulsion with angry breath-holding to the point of fading consciousness, constipation and smearing, for which she was condemned and punished by being made to sit incommunicado in a chair. She was passionately attached to her father until 6, a fact which she had completely denied at the beginning of the analysis. At that age she suffered a severe sexual trauma in seeing some man exposed and masturbating. From the analytic material it seemed probable that this was the schizophrenic cousin who had the same name as her father, or a foreign handy man who worked around her father's place of business. Both figures appeared frequently fused with that of the father, and it seemed clear that she projected on to her father her reaction to this experience and to an even more severe sexual trauma of attempted rape, to which she was seduced by being given money. She had actually a ruptured hymen which was first discovered in her early twenties and which she unconsciously understood in attributing it to having ridden horseback too vigorously. In her official memory at the beginning of the analysis, this rape experience appeared only projected as a memory that her mother had had a severe operation for gall stones and hysterectomy when the patient was 6. The mother did actually have such an operation when the patient was 10, and this situation must have been projected backward some time after that. The identification with the mother in the primal scene experiences before the age of 4, with pressure on the chest during croup attacks, was now turned around and her own castrating experience of rape was put on the mother in a backward displacement of memory, not finally accomplished until the pre-puberty period. Reality was in this way utilized as the basis of projection, which was the patient's mechanism of choice. There was some evidence that before she found the satisfying reality of the mother's operation she used various fantasies of medical procedures, gleaned from a chum who was the daughter of the neighborhood doctor.

Practically all of these elements are represented in the third dream. The hypnotizing refers to giving in to the analytic procedure, to the fading-out sensations of the croup and of the breath-holding (and probably at a deeper level, to nursing). The whisky bottle is another version of this, as in states of extreme depression the patient would drink to produce the effect of obliteration. But the whisky bottle is peculiarly condensing symbol, not only representing nursing, and taking an anesthetic, but also being a bisexual symbol. Its breaking meant both castration and rape, which she had brought on herself by "giving in" for the sake of the bribe. The "girl in her late teens or early twenties" was of the age at which the patient discovered the rupture of her hymen and so the repressed rape trauma was unconsciously reactivated and redefended. This girl probably also represented my daughter with whom the patient made a jealous hostile identification. The fact that I was making faces, immediately associated with her own facial tic, returns however to the screen memory with which she had begun the analysis, the memory of her parents having intercourse and her father's unattractively contorted face.

It has now become clear that the screen memory held many of the elements which were seen in their dispersed forms in her dreams and symptoms. Although the memory appeared so simple and unmodified, critical review brings up two probable discrepancies. It is unlikely that the door would have been left open, especially if a light were left on. One suspects then that the little girl at least opened the door, and felt somewhat guilty at her own intrusion. The other incongruity is that the father seemed to be on top of the mother, yet in some way she had the impression of seeing his face. This would certainly be unlikely if not actually impossible. It seems likely therefore that this screen memory is really combined with early memories from before the age of 4, in which mother and father appeared more fused and interchangeable. There comes next the question whether the child of 8 saw the mother's face (as I was making faces at her in the dream) or whether she saw very little but on coming to the door of the room, realized what was occurring, and that this in itself was enough to re-instate unconsciously the old primal scene experiences. Certainly there was a displacement from genitals to face. This was apparent in her occasional laments during the analysis when she felt sexually frustrated and would feel like drinking: "I can't stand a world with people who are just eyes and noses to me." Again it is noteworthy that she used reality as the basis of displacement, i.e. that the faces may have looked flushed and passionate during intercourse, but that to this is referred the observation of genital changes. It seemed too, that this was even more determined by the experience at 6 when she saw the seminal fluid of the masturbating man (the soap coating of the second dream) and experienced the rape with obviously a fantasy of pregnancy following. This latter was repeated later in life with a 9-months amenorrhea following an appendix operation.

The question may well be asked whether the screen experience at 8 occurred at all at that time or whether it too was a displacement from an earlier to a later time. This cannot be absolutely settled. The patient believed that there was some definite experience then, most likely that she did go to the parents' room and was aware of something. The utilization of this disturbing screen memory as a defense and as a peculiarly stubborn one fits in with her general methods of defense, viz., withdrawal of affect and displacement of disturbing events onto quite similar real ones in which she is less or not at all involved.

If this screen memory is scrutinized in the light of the five forces which have been designated as lending pressure and intensity to such memories, it will be noted that this patient had a *strong ego* development. She was well loved by both parents and seems to have been a happy child up to the age of 4. There was, evidently, an over-stimulation both erotically and aggressively by the primal scenes up to her expulsion from the parents' room at 4. She was well-endowed intellectually and learned readily, except for telling time and arithmetic both of which seemed connected with severe toilet training problems at 3. Then her aggression took the form of both constipation and smearing. She took on the punishments of the parents, the father who stormed, and the mother who put her on a chair and did not speak to her. She stormed and then built a wall (of bricks or rock) around this, and at disturbing periods in her analysis would retreat into a really stony silence and almost immobility.

The traumatic *experiences were unusually severe,* the sight of the man masturbating and the experience of rape, both occurring with men who were associated to an unusual degree with her father. It is probable that this patient was really a very seductive little girl, who was predisposed by long exposure to sexual scenes and that she cooperated in the instigation of these experiences. At the beginning of her analysis she always spoke of herself as having been so awkward she was almost deformed as a child. Later she said she thought some change had come over her at 4 to 5, and still later showed me pictures of herself as a very merry young child, but with a solemn lack-lustre look at about 7.

The traumatic experiences occurred at 5 to 6, coincident with and probably under the influence of the oedipus arousal, that *most susceptible of all periods of infantile libidinal development.* The struggle with overly severe toilet training and with her aroused aggression seemed to have formed the beginnings of a severe conscience, and the traumatic intensity of the oedipal struggle intensified this enormously. So far all of the factors mentioned would tend to produce unusually severe repressing forces and one might expect almost blazingly intense screen memories, if any. Actually the child went into a very severe depressive obsessional neurosis, with phobias and frequently reiterated confessions of guilt, to an extent that hospitalization was considered. The end of this was marked by a sudden wave of repression and a flight into intellectualization and physical overactivity, somewhat comparable to defenses frequent in adolescence. The neurosis became encapsulated, behind her wall of rock. The brightness which is missing from the screen memory appears however in the "fair castles... and golden spires that pierce the sky" in the latter part of her poem. As for the screen memory itself, of the drearily clear primal scene witnessed at 8, it was chosen at a time when the patient was already in a stage of intense repression and in the latency period as well. It was largely fortuitous (i. e. with less guilt), and fitted almost exactly the original traumata from which the oedipal ones had developed. It was, indeed, a snug and effective cover. The patient here used reality to cover reality, and the screen memory served in part as a reality testing, in part—as a most effective projection. This reminds one that a frank confession often deflects suspicion. Jones (12) in an early paper. "Persons in Dreams Disguised as Themselves", describes a similar phenomenon in dreams.

As to the *sado-masochistic* character structure in this patient, it is true that there were evidences of a considerable sado-masochistic reinforcement. This was of a special type, however, in that she had used external reality and ego gratifications as her main defenses against her instinctual conflicts. The result was a seemingly productive and too energetic young woman who burdened herself too much but generally succeeded. Only in certain work relationships with men did the full force of the self-destructive combination of competitiveness and need for punishment show up clearly in her daily work. She was quite different from the sado-masochistic type who retreats from reality and uses a traumatic screen memory in repeated self-stimulation and acting out with a constant infiltration of masochistic fantasy into daily activity.

One more question presents itself. It is obvious that screen memories and dreams have very much in common. Yet in general the screen memory is isolated, bright-edged, whereas the dream does not have so clear a periphery, and, as Lewin (13) has shown, may have curled edges that roll under or back. I believe that this difference is on a rather simple basis. According to Lewin the deepest dream screen is the breast and the nursing experience. Here the mouth rather than the eye is the primary receptive organ. The dream occurs during sleep and has as its base the earliest twilight and sleepy states at the end of feeding. The screen memory on the other hand arises in consciousness and seeming alertness, utilizing experiences then in which vision has the primary role and is generally reinforced by the all-seeing function of the superego.

BIBLIOGRAPHY

1. Deutsch, H. "Ueber die pathologische Luege (Pseudologia phantastica)", *Internat. Zeit. f. Psa.*, VIII, 1922.
2. Deutsch, H. *Psychoanalysis of the Neuroses,* Hogarth, 1933.
3. Fenichel, O. "Zur oekonomischen Funktion der Deckerinnerungen", *Internat. Zeit. f. Psa.*, XIII, 1927.
4. Fenichel, O. "The Inner Injunction to Make a Mental Note", *Internat. J. Psa.*, X, 1929, p. 447.
5. Fenichel, O. "Zur Oekonomik der Pseudologia Phantastica", *Internat. Zeit. f. Psa.*, XXIV, 1939.
6. Freud, S. "Ueber Deckerinnerungen", *Ges. Schriften*, I, pp. 465-488; also *Monatsschrift f. Psych. u. Neur.*, 1899.
7. Freud, S. *Psychopathology of Everyday Life,* Macmillan, 1914, Chap. II.
8. Freud, S. "Recollection, Repetition, and Working Through", *Coll. Papers*, II, p. 368.
9. Freud. S. "A Childhood Recollection from *Dichtung und Wahrheit*", *ibid.*, IV, p. 359.
10. Glover, E. "The Screening Function of Traumatic Memories", *Internat. Zeit. f. Psa.*, X, 1929, pp. 90-93.
11. Greenacre, P. "Vision, Headache, and the Halo", *Psa. Quart.*, XVI, 1947, p. 177.
12. Jones, E. *Papers on Psychoanalysis,* Bailliere, Tindall & Cox, 1938, p. 299.
13. Lewin, B. D. "Sleep, the Mouth, and the Dream Screen", *Psa. Quart.* XV, 1946, p. 419.
14. Mansfield, K. *The Dove's Nest and Other Stories,* Knopf, 1930, p. 74.

AUTOEROTISM

SOME EMPIRICAL FINDINGS AND HYPOTHESES ON THREE OF ITS
MANIFESTATIONS IN THE FIRST YEAR OF LIFE.[1]

By RENÉ A. SPITZ, M.D. (New York)

with the collaboration of KATHERINE M. WOLF, Ph.D. (New York)

I. *Introduction*

A behavioristic investigation of autoerotism in the first year of life is
confronted by various obstacles. The first of these is the definition of our
term. We shall use it in the sense in which it was used by Freud
(5, p. 865): [2]

"These manifestations of sexual impulses can be recognized from the
beginning, but at first they are not yet directed at any outer object.
Each individual component of the sexual impulse works for a gain in
pleasure and finds its gratification in its own body."

On the basis of this definition of autoerotism we propose to investigate some autoerotic activities that occur during the first year of life.

One of the difficulties in such an investigation is that of observing
a relevant number of cases over sufficiently long periods. A really unim-
peachable study would have to offer continuous 24-hour observation of
the infant during the whole of the first year of life. For obvious reasons
this is hardly feasible.

Another difficulty lies in the abundance of phenomena to be
studied. Activities of the oral zone in infancy would require a whole
monograph; one sector of these activities, thumbsucking, has formed
the base of the well-known monograph of Lindner (8) and of numerous
later publications.

The detailed investigation of the oral autoerotic activities would
indubitably yield some interesting facts. We have however, for practical

1. Extensive bibliographical research has been undertaken in connection with
this article and the whole literature on autoerotism during the first years of life published in psychiatric, psychoanalytic, pediatric and pedagogic fields has been investigated. We have collected about 300 items. They will be set up in a separate
survey and will be published in the near future. Space does not permit their publication here.

2. See also Freud (4).

reasons,[3] excluded them from the present study, limiting ourselves to a detailed investigation of the following three autoerotic activities:

1.   The well-known "rocking" of infants during their first year.
2.   Genital play.[4]
3.   Fecal games.[4]

Like sucking, these three activities are characterized by their rhythmicity, their character of self-stimulation, and the fact that the child appears to derive some sort of pleasure while performing them (4).

Thus what we have set out to do in our present paper will be more in the nature of a description than in the nature of classification; it will be an attempt at illustration and our interpretations will be tentative.

3. The objection may be raised that it is not possible to discuss autoerotism in infancy intelligently without using oral autoerotism as the basis of our observations and discussions, as a frame of reference, so to say. For by definition infancy is the oral phase. The reasons why we have not done this are mainly of a practical nature. While the three autoerotic activities observed by us are amenable to direct observation, much of the oral activity is not. That oral activity takes place in the first year of life is a statement of the obvious. It is not so with the other autoerotic activities we have observed. We would therefore have to use a completely different approach to be able to make any statements about oral activity, namely an experimental approach in which the oral activity would be modified either in the sense of its being artificially increased or in the sense of its being artificially decreased. Either would present great difficulties in regard to the policies of the institutions involved, as well as to the attitudes of the parents and nursing personnel. Sucking frustration experiments can be performed on dogs, as D. Levy has done. One is loath to perform them on infants. Furthermore, 24-hour observation would become necessary, and this, with our observational setup, is unfeasible. It is also a problem, even with a 24-hour observational program, how much of the oral activity should be considered as autoerotic; how to differentiate between oral activity which is gratified during the feeding procedure and therefore does not require autoerotic gratification, and how much is not.

We have therefore, very much against our wishes, been forced to neglect the oral autoerotic activities, though we possess extensive observations on the oral behavior of the infants discussed by us. We have limited ourselves to three autoerotic activities and consider our approach justified for the following reasons:

a) We have observed the incidence of each of these activities. The comparison of these incidences has given us certain information of their relative frequency, information which we consider instructive independent of whether other autoerotic activities, even those as important as the oral ones, are present or not.

b) In comparing this incidence with the one environmental variable established by us, namely the mother-child relation, certain regularities have become apparent. These regularities have a significance of their own. This significance is independent of the answer to the question whether oral autoerotism is co-variant with, or varies independently of the regularities found by us.

The final verification or modification of the theoretical assumptions made on the strength of the regularities observed by us will depend on future findings on oral activities made under similar conditions.

4. It should perhaps be stressed that we do not use the term anal play because we have not been able to observe any instance of active tactile approach to the anal region at this period of life, whereas we have been able to observe a significant number of cases in which feces of the children became their favorite and preferred play object. We also use the term "genital play" instead of "masturbation". As will become evident below, we consider masturbation too specific a term for the activities observed at this age level.

If certain regularities do appear in the course of this procedure we will consider them in the nature of approximations; an orientation, as it were, within the map of the ontogenesis of sexuality.

II. *Sample and Method*

The main body of our investigation was conducted in an institution on a total of 196 infants.

Table I

Total Sample Nursery

	Male	Female	Total
White	56	65	121
Colored	32	32	64
Mixed	7	4	11
Total	95	101	196

Of these 26 have not yet reached the age at which according to our observations autoerotic activities usually begin nor did they show any tendency toward such activities at the time. We have therefore excluded them and bring the results of our observations on the remaining 170, as shown in Table II.

Table II

Children of Nursery observed for
Autoerotism

	Male	Female	Total
White	50	56	106
Colored	35	29	64
Total	85	85	170

The institution in question is a penal institution[5] in which the infants observed by us were raised from birth to the end of their first year by their own mothers under the supervision of personnel experienced in child care. The hygienic and environmental conditions of the institution were satisfactory, as witnessed by the fact that no child

5. For a detailed description of this institution, under the name of "Nursery", see Spitz (11).

died during the 4 years in which we made observations in the institution and that serious diseases did not occur during this time (12).
This is a finding which is quite exceptional for any institution
housing children during their first year of life; it is actually much more
favorable than the mortality rate during the first year of life for the
United States as a whole, where during the same years it was 40.7 per
thousand in 1943 and 39.4 per thousand in 1944. This represents an
average for the country as a whole. In the state where the institution
is located the death rate is somewhat below the average of the U. S.,
namely 32.8 per thousand (16).

As in all our investigations, the unselected total sample of the
children present in the institution was observed by us and used for our
study. Each child was observed at weekly intervals for 4 hours per week,
over a period of 1 year or more, averaging over 200 hours of observation
per child. This method of observation will surely miss many instances
of autoerotic activities of these children. Therefore our figures on the
absence of such activities cannot be regarded as conclusive. We, nevertheless, believe that the method will yield a sufficiently informative cross-
section of the more striking items of behavior. We believe that with this
method we have been able to achieve some insight into the incidence of
the three above named autoerotic activities, into their frequency and
into their phenomenology. Actually the observation of the latter gave
us the possibility to distinguish the three classes we mentioned, the rocking,
the genital play and the fecal play.

We conducted regular weekly interviews with the nursing personnel
as well as with the mothers of the children. Rorschach tests were
administered to approximately 30 per cent of the mothers.

Simultaneously we investigated the emotional climate of each child
studied and we attempted to correlate the children's emotional background to their observable autoerotic behavior.

The total study up to the present day has been running for close
to 4 years.

III. Results

We wish to stress that the results obtained in the present study are
limited to the age group represented by our sample, i. e., from birth to
15 months. Our conclusions therefore apply to the first year of life and
to the first year only. Any comparisons with phenomena observed at a
more advanced age can only be misleading.

We found that from the point of view of autoerotic activities these
infants could be divided into 4 groups (if we neglect oral activity):

1) Those children whose autoerotic activity consisted predominantly of rocking,

2) those whose autoerotic activity consisted predominantly of genital play,

3) those whose autoerotic activity consisted predominantly of fecal play,

4) and finally those in whom none of these activities was ever observed by us.

A. Incidence

Out of 170 children autoerotic activities of at least one of above three types were observed in 104 up to the time of this writing. Rocking was observed in 87 children. Genital play was observed in 21 children. Fecal play was observed in 16 children. These figures overlap to a certain extent because more than one autoerotic activity was observed in certain children.

These figures in themselves do not tell us very much if we accept the finding that *in this environment* both genital play and fecal play appear to be rarer during the first year of life than we had been led to expect by scattered remarks in the literature.

The sex distribution and the race distribution of autoerotic activities can be seen from Table III:

Table III [6]

Race and Sex Distribution of Autoerotic Activities in Nursery

	Male	Female
White	76%	45%
Colored	63%	62%

A sex difference in autoerotic activities with a predominance in the males appears in the white group. No such differences were observed in the colored group.

Differences between the races appear ambiguous. We do not believe that the numbers involved are large enough to justify any conclusions from these results.

B. Distribution

The distribution of the autoerotic activities is shown in Table IV, in which genital play and rocking are illustrated. We did not include fecal play because of the comparatively small numbers involved.

6. Our sample was not evenly matched in regard to either race or sex. Instead of the number of subjects involved we have therefore given the percentage of these subjects in relation to the population of our sample.

Table IV

Relation between Genital Play and Rocking

	Rocking	No rocking	Total
Genital Play	7	14	21
No Genital Play	80	69	149
Total	87	83	170

It appears that it is infrequent that both genital play and rocking should be present in the same child. We shall discuss later the conclusions that we believe can be drawn from this incompatibility.

The age distribution also presents some points of interest. First, that of genital play:

Chart I

GENITAL PLAY: AGE DISTRIBUTION

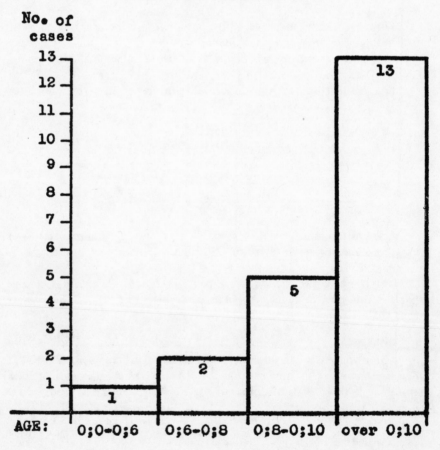

From this chart it appears that a certain level of general development is a prerequisite for the appearance of genital play. That is not unexpected. After all, directed activity and a certain capacity for adequate handling of objects as well as a certain discriminatory perception, are prerequisites for such play.[7]

The more significant distribution, however, is seen in Chart II, in which we compare the age distribution of rocking and genital activity.

Chart   II

AGE DISTRIBUTION OF ROCKING AND GENITAL PLAY

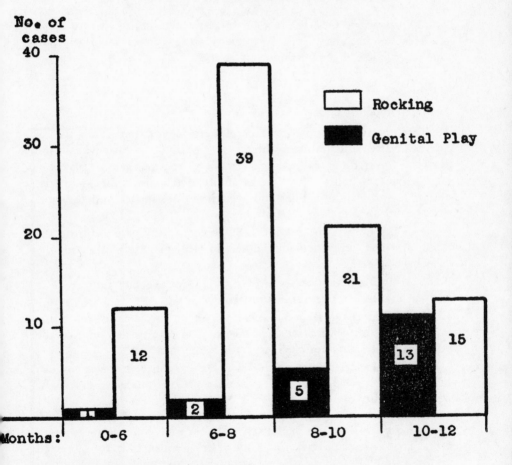

7. In the literature on infantile autoerotic activities collected by us references to exact age of the inception of genital play are almost absent. The only exact reference which coincides with our observations is that of Lauretta Bender (2) who states that genital play starts between the 8th and 9th month with normal children.

Chart II shows that the rocking activities reach their maximum at an age at which genital activity is the rare exception and that from there on they successively decrease until the end of the first year. In both charts it is not the incidence of the activity itself that is shown, but its inception, that is, the age at which the activity was first observed in a given child. We have no factual data for the explanation of the inverse course of these two activities. It suggests, however, the assumption that genital play is a more mature activity of the infant than rocking and that in this capacity genital play will progressively increase with the progressing age, whereas the more archaic rocking will decrease with maturation.

This assumption suggests some further questions. They are of an etiological nature and therefore cannot be answered by a mere behavioristic observation of the phenomenon itself.

C. Etiology

1) Methodological Consideration

Our observations up to this point have yielded figures on the incidence and age distribution of three groups of autoerotic behavior in the first year (excluding oral activities), namely: rocking, genital play and fecal play. Our figures have further shown that some of these activities appear to inhibit the manifestations of the others in one and the same child. We will therefore ask ourselves:

1. Why do certain children indulge in rocking games during the first year, others in genital play, others in fecal play, and others finally in none of these?

2. Why does the presence of certain of these activities seem to exclude indulgence in the remaining ones?

In attempting to find the answer to these questions we shall first have to investigate the etiological factors operative in determining the selection of one autoerotic activity rather than another.

The etiological factors which can be distinguished in this group can be divided into hereditary, congenital, and environmental ones. As regards heredity, at present no reliable criteria are available. Actually we have the impression that in the case of such gross phenomena with which we are dealing here hereditary differences may not be very significant. That at least has been our conclusion in an investigation directed at the differentiation of the developmental quotients in our group according to white and colored race, where the results during the first year show such minimal differences between the developmental quotients, such small fluctuations between the two developmental curves, as to lack any kind of significance. We were able to demonstrate that such differences at best can only represent a fraction of the difference provoked by the environment, as demonstrated by a second curve in the same investigation (14).

This finding regarding racial differences applies also to the congenital factor. It may be added that in our population there were no gross findings of congenital disfunctions demonstrated either by the medical examination at birth, nor by results of the test examinations beginning with the second week after birth.

This leaves us with the environmental factor as the decisive one. In infancy and particularly in a nursery setting environment is restricted and elements easily analyzable. In our case certain factors were uniform for all the subjects involved. They were: food, housing, clothing, hygiene, cots, toys and the daily routine.

There remains one possible environmental variable, the human element. This variable, however, is also that which represents, at this age at least, the highest emotional valence, one might nearly say: the only emotional valence. The variable "human element" will at the same time provide us with information about the role and significance of emotions as a factor in autoerotic activity—as could be expected by anybody familiar with psychoanalytic propositions.

The human element and its emotional corollary is provided in the first year of life by the mother, a term by which we mean both the child's actual mother and/or any other person of either sex who may take the place of the child's physical mother during a significant period of time. Our variable therefore will consist in the difference of the attitudes of the mothers of the children in question, in the differences in their behavior toward their children. These differences will be predicated upon the varying personalities of these mothers.

This analysis suggests our next step, namely that of correlating the variable we have found, the mother-child relationship, with our other findings in regard to autoerotism. But, while our findings in regard to all other elements of the child's environment were lacking in variety, we discovered that the variable which we are investigating now presents us with a diversity which appears to offer well-nigh insurmountable obstacles to classification. The mothers of these children vary widely in their personality, in their intellect, in their emotional attitude toward sex, toward each other, toward authority and toward their children. Some of them are of low intelligence and good-natured, many of them have an infantile personality, others again are more on the psychopathic side with manifest aggressions. There are a few borderline cases, some are even definitely psychotic, though not disturbed. There are a number of prostitutes on one hand and quite a few small town girls who had the bad luck to be caught.

As heterogeneous material as the above does not lend itself readily to the establishment of a leading hypothesis. For the purpose of establishing a leading hypothesis one would normally choose the performing of a series of controlled experiments in which certain variables would be held constant and only one permitted to vary. Such experiments are unfeasible in our case; but it is at least possible for us to choose groups in which within the group itself most of the factors are relatively homogeneous and their variations not too significant; and to isolate one factor as a variable in which quantitative variations of a rough and ready kind can be ascertained. The factor in question is the intensity of the mother-child relationship. For this purpose it appears advisable to approach our problem from two opposite poles and to try to find one environment in which the mother-child relationship is at its lowest, and to oppose to it a second environment where the mother-child relationship can be expected to be at its optimum. The diversity presented in the picture of "Nursery" would thus be reduced to a minimum —since it cannot be completely eliminated. It is of course not easy to find a group of children whose environmental beckground on one hand, whose relationship to their mothers on the other, is sufficiently homogeneous. Certain environmental situations, however, make a rough approximation of such a desideratum feasible.

Once such environments can be found we will be in the position to compare the autoerotic activities of the groups with each other.

For our first environment we have chosen a group of 17 children raised in white collar worker private homes where close personal exploration of the child and the parents convinced us that the mother-child relationship was either an exceptionally good one, or that at least efforts were being made to achieve this. This environment we have considered as offering optimal relations from the point of view of maximal intensity.

It was easier to find the second environment, the one in which mother-child relations were non-existent. For this purpose we chose Institution II, a Foundling Home situated in another country in which the children were raised without their mothers, and by an insufficient number of nurses; officially one nurse cared for 8 children; in practice one nurse took care of 10 to 12, thus providing the child with one tenth of the attention a mother normally gives her offspring and with even less love. As regards food, housing, clothing, hygiene, the conditions were comparable to those encountered in "Nursery".[8]

8. For detailed description of the institution under the name of Foundling Home, see Spitz (11).

2) The etiological factor responsible for the incidence

The findings made in these two environments are distinctly startling. In the case of the children reared in private families we found that of 17 children 16 manifested genital play within the first year, at ages which were on the average two months earlier than those observed in Nursery. Only in one child was rocking observed exclusively.

In Foundling Home, where emotional relations were completely absent, we observed 61 children in their first 18 months. Of these, only one (CC 62, age 1; 1+10) [9] manifested any genital play. As far as rocking is concerned: it was observed in 2 of the children *after* the first year (CC 41, age 1; 3+10, and CC 45, age 1; 1+12) and in two children before the first year (CC 11, age 0; 10+1, and CC 58, age 0; 11+3). There was very little thumbsucking. The only other activity which—by any stretch of imagination—can be called "autoerotic" were shaking movements of the nature of spasmus nutans as described by Moro (9).

Our findings in these three different environments are illustrated in Chart III. (following page)

They can be summarized as follows:

Environment 1: 17 children (Private families, excellent mother-child relations):
autoerotic activities were observed in all,
rocking in 1 case,
genital play in 16 cases.

Environment 2: 170 children (Nursery, mother-child relations varying from emotionally very good to emotionally very bad) :
no autoerotic activity was observed in 65 cases,
rocking in 87 cases,
genital play in 21 cases,
fecal play in 16 cases.

Environment 3: 61 children (Complete absence of emotional relations):
Practically no autoerotic activities.

We are forced to conclude that:

1. Autoerotic activity appears to be covariant with the pattern of emotional relations between mother and child, since when these emotional relations are absent, no autoerotic activities are observable. Where mother-child relations are at their maximum all subjects produce autoerotic activities.

9. The designations CC, P, N, etc. refer to individual cases in the several environments.

Chart III

AUTOEROTIC ACTIVITIES IN THREE ENVIRONMENTS

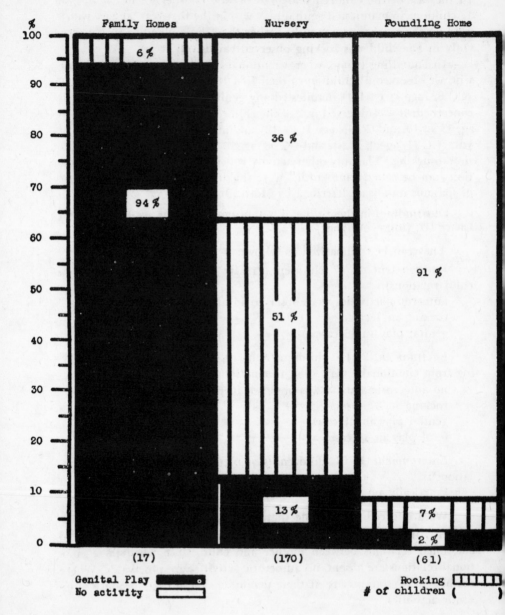

Genital Play ▮
No activity ▯

Rocking ▯▯▯▯▯
# of children (   )

2. The closer the mother-child relation of the particular given environment, the more infants we find manifesting genital play in the first year of life. This finding is confirmed by a case published by Emmy Sylvester (15).

3) Etiological factors in different types of autoerotic activity

a) Genital play

Our leading hypothesis thus appears established: the presence of mother-child interrelation is a necessary prerequisite for the appearance of autoerotism in the first year of life. A further qualification of the leading hypothesis from the same table follows: it appears that the amount of genital play varies with varying mother-child relations, a statement which will not surprise psychoanalysts. It is therefore incumbent upon us to examine more closely the elements constituting what we up to here have called mother-child relation, as well as its variations in the different environments studied by us.

In investigating the mother-child relationship we have to realize that in this relation, barring severe sickness of the child, there is only one partner who can take the initiative or be active in any way: the mother. It is she therefore who determines the nature of the relationship. Consequently we will have to visualize the relationship from the angle of the mother. Before doing this, however, we will again consider our three environments:

Foundling Home: no mother-child relation, no genital play; D.Q. (Developmental Quotient) progressively dropping down to level of imbecility.[10]

Nursery: mother-child relation shifting from extreme closeness to extreme rejection. Moderate percentage (13 percent) of genital play, fairly good average of D. Q. (107) of the second half of the first year.[10]

Private families: extreme closeness of mother-child relation, genital activity 94 percent, average D.Q. 135.[10]

The co-variance between closeness of mother-child relation, genital activity and developmental level is striking.

At this point an examination of the term "closeness" imposes itself. For physical closeness of the mothers to their children in Nursery is at least as great as that of the mothers in private homes.[11] The problem

10. For exact comparison of the D. Q. figures see Chart IV, page 103.
11. It is this physical closeness, this luxuriation of a great variation of emotional interchange between the mothers and the children which we stressed in a previous study (11). There we contrasted the overprotection in Nursery (pp. 70-71) with the complete libidinal impoverishment and lack of contact observed in Foundling Home. A differentiated analysis of the mothers' personalities was not significant for the purpose of that study. We pointed at the probable role of these factors (Footnote 10, p. 65), though at the time we were not yet in the position to be more specific in our statements, as we had not yet collected sufficient data on the personalities of the mothers.

arises: since it is the mother's personality which determines the mother-
child relationship, how does the emotional personality of the mothers
in Nursery differ from that of the mothers in private homes?

There appear to be two main differences, the one based on social
background and social adaptation, the other on problems of emotional
balance.

The mothers in Nursery came there because of a failure in social
adaptation. In a large percentage of the cases this maladaptation is not
severe, consisting mainly in sexual indiscretion at the wrong age. (Compared to the figures of the Kinsey report on present day morality in
private families, extramarital intercourse of females of the average age
of 20 does not impress us as differing fundamentally from the general
attitude toward sex.) Thus the background of the mothers of children
in private homes contains emotional factors which are potentially similar
to those of the mothers in Nursery. We suspect that the difference
between the mothers in this institution and other mothers of an urban
background is one based on cultural attitudes of their immediate environment and on the diversities of their economic status. Such differences in themselves seem insufficient to warrant the assumption of
basic dissimilarities in the emotional attitude of the two groups of mothers
to their children. However, in Nursery, motherhood has been penalized
by social disapproval going to the point of internment (which inevitably
will elicit feelings of resentment and guilt) and involving a separation
of the mother from the father of her child.

This brings us to the other main difference between the mothers of
private children and the mothers in Nursery: the mothers of private
children have a sexual partner, their husband; the mothers in Nursery
have none.[12]

This difference has far-reaching psychological consequences from
the dynamic and economic point of view. In the private homes the
mother is able to discharge a goodly part of her instinctual drives, both
libidinal and aggressive, on the marriage partner and does so not only
in a particularly effective manner in the course of normal sexual activity, but, as we know, through the exchanges of everyday life. Apart
from this it will be comparatively easy for a woman with a husband,
particularly during the lying-in period, to direct any additional hostile
tendencies which her baby might provoke to a concerned and, in this
situation, generally particularly considerate partner.

12. We may disregard the frequently observed condition in private families, that
when a mother was unresponsive to her child, the father would often manifest a
strikingly loving, one might say "motherly", attitude and thus offer compensation.
That probably is a factor of chance which in the institution might also be manifested
through the interest taken by somebody besides the mother.

Not so in the institution. In Nursery the mothers have no adequate and accepted outlet for their libidinal or their aggressive drives; they are separated from their husbands and therefore the only possible outlet for the libidinal drive are relations of a homosexual nature with the other inmates. Such relations are discouraged and as far as possible frustrated. In a large percentage of the cases the mothers in question would not even be capable of indulging in such relations because of their personality structure. In those cases where homosexual contacts were possible we found the libidinal balance of the mothers in question so seriously upset in consequence as to make their relations with their children abnormal, to say the least. As for the aggressive drives, they have to be repressed when directed to the authorities of Nursery and they find their outlet partly in quarrels with other mothers, partly in modified relations with the children.

It can be seen from these considerations that the role of the father for normal relations between mother and child is an extremely significant and important one. This is an assumption which had been made frequently in psychoanalytic literature regarding disturbances of the pre-school child, school-child and adolescent. To my knowledge it was not made yet regarding infants in the first year of life.

We must argue from this that the concept of "close" mother-child relationship should be qualified. It appears that in this relationship "closeness" alone is not the determining criterium, but that balance, a modicum of instinctual equilibrium, is a further prerequisite. It is imperative for the mother to be able to discharge her instinctual drives, particularly the aggressive ones, without involving her child.

Where those drives do not find an adequate discharge, where they are dammed up and finally are discharged on the child, overprotection or hostility to the child results. Mostly, however, the two alternate in violent ups and downs.

The modification in autoerotic activity to which such violent extremes lead is the subject of a later chapter of this study. As we have shown above, violent unchecked emotions in respect to the child are absent in those cases in which genital play develops already during the first year of life. In these cases we have therefore a "close" mother-child relationship in which a relatively consistent attitude prevails which does not show the extremes of libidinal neediness or of aggressive hostility.

It follows from this statement that we consider a "close and balanced" mother-child relationship an important prerequisite for the development of genital play during the first year of life. This statement should not be confused with the assumption frequently made in the literature[13] that genital play is induced by a maternal approach equivalent to a genital seduction. Hygiene and the washing of the genital parts, cleanliness in connection with evacuation, inappropriate caresses on the part of the mother, are again and again mentioned as probable cause of genital play in early infancy. We do not share this opinion, we definitely believe that the factor responsible is not only a local physical one but an emotional one. After all, not only do we have a large number of children in Nursery who never were observed to indulge in any kind of autoerotic activity, but we also observed *rocking only* in 80 cases; all of these children, who did not indulge in any genital play, were also exposed to the same kind of "genital seduction" in matters of hygiene— the washing of genitalia, cleanliness in regard to evacuation, etc.—as were those children who did indulge in the genital play.

Striking evidence that the physical and local seduction by the mother in the close mother-child relationship need not lead to genital play, was provided by our observation of actual cases of genital stimulation which did not lead to genital play at all, let alone to excessive masturbation, but to psychiatric conditions of a quite different nature. We will present two unequivocal cases from our material: One that of a medical treatment of the female genital at an early age, the other that of deliberate genital seduction during a large part of the first year of life.

Case N 18:
This child was infected with gonorrhoea and subjected to local treatment during her first 2 months. Nevertheless during the whole subsequent year in which we observed this child she was never seen to indulge in genital play. On the other hand she was probably the most persistent rocker in our experience, she rocked with such violence that one would hear her from several wards and corridors away.

Case N 3:
Beginning at 4 months and up to 11 months the mother (latent manic depressive) regularly performed cunilingus on the child: she was repeatedly observed doing so by reliable witnesses. In this child also no genital play developed. Instead the child developed excessive thumbsucking, from the 4th month on. At 9 months thumbsucking was replaced by excessive fecal play which reached its climax at 1 year and 1 month. Every time the child was observed she was found sitting in her cot with a dreamy absent-minded expression, collecting feces from her diaper and alternatingly putting the excrement in her mouth or throwing it out of her cot, frequently vomiting the eaten excrement.

The two cases in question lead us to assume that genital seduction in the first year of life is not responded to by genital activity. The response appears to be rather one which is appropriate to the phase of the sexual

13. Already in 1912 this assumption was rejected by Federn (3) who in his theoretical point of view anticipates a number of our empirical findings.

organization in which the child happens to be at the time of the genital stimulation. In the case of the first child we have extremely early genital stimulation through the local therapy for gonorrhoea. The resulting response is of the nature of diffuse muscle activity corresponding to the early level of the organization of this child's personality, namely the level of primary narcissism.

In the case of the second child the response to consistent genital stimulation up to the 11th month again is one that is manifested in the age adequate sector of sexual development, namely in the oral sector from the 4th to the 9th month and in the anal sector at the end of the first year. In other terms: we believe that the early genital stimulation of Case N 18 resulted in rocking, whereas the genital seduction of Case N 3, taking place in the transition from the oral to the anal stage, resulted first in excessive thumbsucking and later in coprophagia.

Of course we are aware that beyond this gross difference in the age level at which the local genital stimulation took place there also were significant differences in the personalities of the mothers of the two children. The role which the personality of the mother plays in the development of rocking and fecal play will be the subject of a later chapter.

There is further evidence that genital stimulation in itself is not sufficient to provoke genital play. It so happens that at certain periods in the institution in which these children were observed eczema was rampant. In addition to the children suffering from eczema we also observed a small number of children (5 in all) suffering from various other itching skin conditions like impetigo, rash, etc. As the skin irritation would cover many of these children from head to foot, including the region around the genitals, the theory of genital masturbation in infants being provoked by local stimulation like oxiuris, eczema, etc., would lead one to assume that all the children suffering from eczema would have also manifested genital play. Obviously the number of our cases is not large enough to establish significant correlations. Nevertheless, as far as it goes, our material shows that eczema and genital play are independent of each other.

Table V
Relation between Eczema and Genital Play in Nursery

	Eczema	No eczema	Total
Genital Play	3	18	21
No Genital Play	21	128	149
Total	24	146	170

The stimulation itself, be it of a general nature like eczema, or of a local circumscribed nature directed at the sexual organ itself, as in the two cases mentioned by us, does not appear to be that factor which elicits genital play in the first year of life.

Thus we have at present no adequate explanation why a "close" mother-child relation, without particular genital stimulation, should result in genital play when local stimulation does not. We have only tentative observations to offer to guide us if we want to formulate a hypothesis.

The observations in question are of a physiognomical and behavioristic nature. We have recorded them with the help of motion pictures made from the subjects during their autoerotic activities. From the beginning it has struck us that there was a wide difference in the physiognomical expression which accompanies the three autoerotic activities investigated.

While in the case of rocking, whether supine, knee-elbow, or standing, the children's expression was one which could go to the point of orgiastic delight, while in fecal play and coprophagia the expression was one of dreamy withdrawal, of a turning inward, going to the point of depressive daze and psychotic suspicion—we saw nothing of the kind in any of the children we observed during their genital play. Here we saw regularly a facial expression which might go from indifference to alert attention or to friendly sociability.

In other words: the children in question did not seem to be emotionally more involved when playing with their genital than when playing with any other part of their body, their feet, ears, etc. In some of these children it is quite instructive to compare the facial expression during genital play with the infinitely more absorbed and orgiastic expression manifested during ingestion of food, be that at the breast or with a spoon from a plate.

We suspect that genital play in the first year of life has the significance of one of the many normal bodily activities and games of the infant. However, normal activities develop equally in all sectors only when the emotional climate is adequate, when the relations between the child and its mother are satisfactory. As soon as they become unsatisfactory an imbalance is manifested in some of the sectors of bodily and mental development, some activities being retarded or arrested, others unduly facilitated. It would seem that genital play, possibly because it has relatively little specificity in this phase of infantile sexuality, is one of the earliest victims of unsatisfactory mother-child relations.

The third co-variant mentioned, the developmental quotient achieved in the three environments, supports this hypothesis. It is vividly

illustrated by the following chart showing the variations of the average
D.Q.'s of the three environments throughout the first year of life.

Chart IV
DEVELOPMENT QUOTIENTS
IN
FAMILY HOMES, NURSERY, FOUNDLING HOME
ACCORDING TO AGE IN THE COURSE OF THE FIRST YEAR OF LIFE

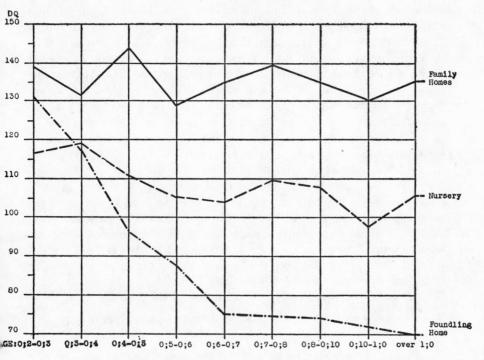

It might be concluded from this that the genital play is nothing but
a part of the whole developmental pattern during the first year of life;
that therefore a high D.Q. will involve the early appearance of genital
play just as it involves the early appearance of other motor and play
activities also.

We prefer to assume that both autoerotic activity and the D.Q. itself
are but the manifestations of a more basic factor, namely of the
mother-child interrelation. Where this interrelation is at its best, genital
play will be general in the first year of life and general development will
surpass the average. Where this interrelation is absent, genital play will
be missing and general development will drop far below the average
and deteriorate progressively.

The next chapters will deal with those cases which fall between the two extremes, complete absence and optimal presence of mother-child interrelations.

b) Rocking

The mother's personality

As indicated above, rocking is one of the autoerotic activities found in those children where the mother-child relation is neither completely absent nor of the really well balanced, close type. However, the mother-child interrelation which obtains in these intermediate cases no longer lends itself to such large generalizations as were possible in the case of complete absence of autoerotic activity or even in the case of genital play. We are therefore compelled to narrow down our field of investigation. We can no longer make a simple sweeping generalization, all-inclusive for the whole group but will have to inspect every single individual within the group. Regrettably enough this was not evident at the beginning of our study and we therefore have only been able to get detailed data on one-quarter of the individuals involved. As shown in Table IV, we have a total of 80 children in our group which manifested rocking exclusively. The mothers of 20 of these were given a battery of psychological tests: the Rorschach, the Szondi, the modified Stanford Binet, the Pass-A-long, the Minkus, etc., and a personal interview.[14] Obviously, the findings cannot be considered conclusive for the whole group. They are, however, consistent with our personal impressions of the mothers: and since the findings within the 25 per cent closely investigated by us have been unusually consistent, we consider them fairly indicative of what to expect in the rest of the group.

Of the 20 mothers so tested we have found that 17 have a psychological structure which shows striking similarities, as follows:

1) The general level of maturity of the mothers residing in Nursery is definitely below average. However, the 17 in question are unusually infantile even for this environment. This is expressed not so much in their intellectual level; it is more closely expressed in the incapacity to plan, as evidenced in a number of tests. It is further manifested in the Rorschach, by something which gives the appearance of a defectiveness in the elaboration of defense mechanisms, particularly sublimation.

2) The 17 mothers in question are definitely extrovert personalities with a readiness to intensive positive contact. They show definitely alloplastic tendencies; this agrees well not only with their extrovert

14. Results are being organized for publication in an article on delinquent mothers.

attitude, but also with their infantilism, which is in definite contrast to the autoplastic tendencies found in neurotics.

3) All 17 lack the faculty to control their aggression and present both in the tests and in our observations frequent outbursts of negative emotion, of violent hostility.

Accordingly these mothers who are subject to the emotions governing them at any given moment and who do not have the foresight (lack of planning, infantilism) to measure the consequences of their behavior, are unusually inconsistent in their approach to their environment. As already mentioned, their babies are of necessity the main outlets for their labile emotions. Consequently their babies will be exposed alternately to intense outbursts of love and equally intense outbursts of hostility and rage. This is the parental relationship described by Wilhelm Reich (10) in his study of the impulsive character. We shall discuss why in our opinion the children of such mothers develop rocking as their only autoerotic activity in the first year of life.

The rocking child's personality

The similarity of the rocking children's personalities is perhaps even more impressive than that of their mothers. In contrast to the mothers, where as yet we have detailed personality evaluations and test protocols in only 25 per cent of the cases, we are thoroughly informed on the large majority of the children observed by us; each of these children was tested at regular intervals and closely observed once a week during one year. It is by the objective data of the testing procedure, quite apart from any personal impression gained through observation, that the conviction was forced upon us that rocking children show a characteristic personality structure all of their own. No such uniformity is demonstrable in the children who do not rock.

To explain this statement it becomes necessary to give a brief summary of the developmental profile method used in the Hetzer-Wolf Tests. These tests investigate with the help of standardized items (10 per month of age) 6 sectors of the personality: Body Mastery, Social Adaptation, Memory plus Imitation, Manipulative Ability, and Intelligence. In the profile the ordinate represents the Developmental Age achieved in the different sectors. (Illustrations on following pages.)

The points reached at a given age level in the different sectors are connected. To the expert the structure of the resulting profile reveals, beyond individual personality constellations, typical developmental and characterological patterns.

The striking finding is that rocking children regardless of their general level of development show two characteristic low points of the profile in two-thirds of the cases. These low points may represent ab-

SAMPLE OF AVERAGE SLIGHTLY ADVANCED CHILD'S PROFILE IN THE FIFTH MONTH
Case P 9, white, male, 0; 4+15

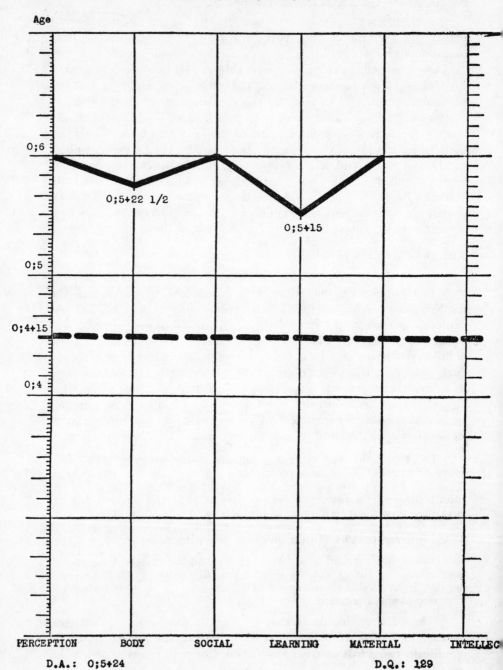

D.A.: 0;5+24   D.Q.: 129

TYPICAL PROFILE OF CHILD RETARDED IN SOCIAL AND MANIPULATIVE SECTORS
Case N 16, white, male, 0; 10+17

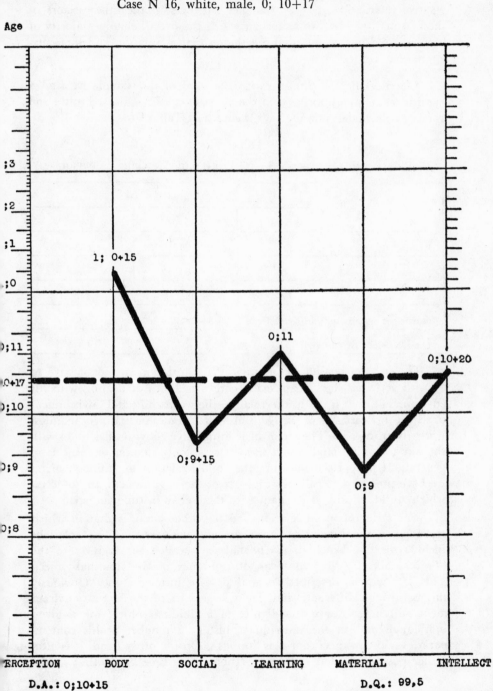

Age

1; 0+15

0;11

0;10+20

0;9+15

0;9

PERCEPTION   BODY   SOCIAL   LEARNING   MATERIAL   INTELLECT

D.A.: 0;10+15   D.Q.: 99,5

solute retardation in respect to the chronological age of the infant, or
relative retardation in regard to performances in the other sectors of
the personality. The two sectors in which the overwhelming majority of
rocking children are retarded are their social adaptation and their manipulative ability.

On checking this finding with the total of our sample we find a
significant relationship between the above-described —S —M Profile and
rocking behavior in infants. This is shown in Table VI.

Table VI

Relationship between —S —M Profile and Rocking Behavior

	Profile:		
	—S —M	No —S —M	Total
Rocking	49	28	77
No Rocking	4	60	64
Total	53	88	141
Insufficient records indicating tendency to "—S —M Profile"			29
Total Number of Children			170

The two personality sectors in which retardation is evident have to
do with activities that measure the child's methods of dealing with his
environment, that is, with interrelations between child and environment
in which the initiative of the child himself becomes increasingly manifest
with advancing age. The sector of manipulative activities has to do with
the way the child handles and masters toys, tools, inanimated objects in
general. It purports to measure the child's relation to "things", or, as
we have preferred to call this category of the environment, to "objects"
which are identical and constant with themselves in time and space.

The sector of social relations, on the other hand, is that in which
relations to the human environment are evidenced. These relations
include the one which in psychoanalysis is called the relation to the
libidinal object. We also speak of constancy of the libidinal object.
This constancy is described in analysis as a historical one. Obviously
this is a rough differentiation; for a large part of the human environment will never attain the dignity of a libidinal object for a given
individual; and in the individual's history a number of his contemporaries will run their course as "things". On the other hand, it is altogether possible (and it regularly occurs at one time or another in the

development of the individual) that an inanimate object is by a particular constellation of events enabled to fulfill needs which correspond to the drive structure directed toward the libidinal object.

The consistent retardation of the majority of rocking infants in the sectors of "things" and libidinal objects is a measurable proof of these infants' disturbance in the field of object relations in general. For we find it permissible to assume from unpublished observations of K. M. Wolf that libidinal object relations have to be firmly established to enable infants to form relations with inanimate objects.

Our attention is aroused by the fact that in both sectors it is the relation to environmental objects that is disturbed. Of course, from the point of view of dynamic psychology, we usually consider the relation to libidinal objects as the only one worthy of attention. We are apt to take the relations to things as granted and as of subordinate importance— and so they are. But our finding in the case of infants is a reminder that the world of the psyche is one and indivisible. So that we cannot encounter a disturbance of one sector of the objectal relations without its involving a disturbance of the relations to all other objects, be they even as insignificant as a toy. The disturbance with which we are confronted in the case of the children whose main autoerotic activity consists in rocking is one of complete incapacity to form object relations.

We will ask ourselves now whether this finding sheds any light on the form of autoerotic activity selected among the many possible ones by these children. We believe that a tentative proposition is justified. If we pass in review the different forms of autoerotic activity available to the infant during its first year, such as thumbsucking, playing with the lips, playing with the ears, nose, hair, certain privileged limbs, playing with the genital, or playing with feces, we realize that each of these forms involves an "object" and necessitates cathecting an object representation. The cathexis is of a secondary narcissistic nature, but nevertheless distinguishes the particular "object" of autoerotic activity from the rest of the body.

The only autoerotic activity which does not require such a privileged "object" is rocking. For in rocking the whole body of the infant is subjected to the autoerotic stimulation. The activity is an objectless one — or rather the object activated is the object of the primary narcissistic drive.

With this proposition we have postulated a parallel to the "impulsive personality" described by Reich (10). In Reich's "impulsive personality" the alternation of extreme permissiveness and extreme hostility on the part of the parents resulted in a personality which is incapable of introjecting a consistent parental imago and as a result of this incapacity cannot develop a normally functioning superego. As a result of this the relations of such impulsive personalities to their environment are as variable and unpredictable as were the original imagines and no object relation is possible, only the acting out of impulses preponderant at any given time, regardless of consequences.

In the case of our infants it is not a question of introjecting parental imagines for the purpose of forming a superego. It is the question of forming the memory traces of an object constant in time and space and consistent with itself. In our proposition the primal object is the libidinal object which forms the pattern for all later object relations. As this object, the mother, is so contradictory that it does not lend itself to the formation of an object which can remain identical with itself in space and time—nor is it sufficiently consistent to remain genetically identical with itself because of the vagaries, ups and downs, in its emotional temperature,—the formation of the primal object relation pattern becomes impossible. Consequently the formation of all later object relations, even with the non-libidinal objects, with things, will be impaired through the inadequacy of the original experience. It is the original experience with the libidinal object which creates an expectancy pattern. Where that is lacking each single object will have to be approached as an experiment, as an adventure, and as a peril.

Rocking as a dominant autoerotic activity in the first year thus appears as the symptom of the arrest of object relations of every kind, resulting from the inconsistency of the environment's emotional interchange with the child. As such it is to be considered as a pathological sign when it is the exclusive autoerotic activity of the infant and not replaced by more normal ones. Nevertheless it does imply the presence of emotional interchange, be it ever so unsatisfactory and it is a manifestation of the original drive. This places it in stark contrast to the complete absence of all autoerotic manifestations we have observed in cases of extreme emotional starvation in Foundling Home.

Another aspect of rocking which corroborates our assumptions is that this is one of the few autoerotic activities at this age in which the child frequently manifests a wild delight, an orgiastic pleasure. The fractioning of the libidinal drives in the different subordinate modes of discharge which one witnesses in genital play, and play activity of all kinds, does not take place in rocking. Here the drive in its totality is directed toward the narcissistic object, the role of which thus becomes comparable to the role of the genital at a much later stage, when the primacy of the genital concentrates upon itself the energy obtained from the partial drives. In the same manner the energy from the different sectors of the infantile personality is concentrated in rocking upon the narcissistic object — of course the concentration in the case of the genital is a genuine one, whereas the concentration in the case of rocking is simply due to the fact that a division of the drive components has not taken place (i. e., that the drive components have not been allocated to their appropriate sectors).

To summarize: Inconsistent, contradictory behavior of the mother makes the establishment of the adequate object relations impossible and arrests the child at the level of primary narcissistic discharge of its libidinal drive in the form of rocking.

c) Fecal Play

In discussing this, the last of the 3 autoerotic activities observed, we are obliged to change somewhat our presentation. While in the case of genital play and in that of rocking a few words were sufficient to describe the activities in question which are familiar to all observers in the field such is not the case with fecal play. We shall therefore begin by defining and describing it.

Fecal play in the course of the first year of life is not frequently seen. In the comparatively large number of children (384) observed by us we have not found it in more than 16 cases, all of them in the institution we have called Nursery. As regards onset, the earliest age for which we have it recorded is 8 months and 3 days. The vast majority of our cases fall between 10 and 14 months. In 11 out of these 16 cases the fecal play culminated in coprophagia. We will therefore speak interchangeably of coprophagia or of fecal play. Though the fecal play itself was prolonged and contained many varieties, we had the impression that all this playing was but a preliminary to the final aim of putting the feces in the mouth and, in a number of cases, swallowing it. In those cases in which coprophagia was not observed it may well have occurred during our absence. Therefore we came to the conclusion that fecal play during the first year of life is intimately connected with oral ingestion.

It is a handicap of this presentation that the behavior cannot be shown in the form of the motion pictures we have made of our observations. We must perforce give as close a description as we can from the protocol of one of our cases:

Case N 117 1; 1+26 female, white

"In standing position when approached by observer offers her hands filled with feces which she tries to put into observer's mouth. She is not unfriendly, reciprocates play and smiles.

When observer withdraws to a distance she sits down, an abstracted expression on her face. The expression is not really depressive. She takes a pellet of feces, rolls it between her thumb and index, then smears it over the sheet and over her legs. She takes another one, manipulates it, passes it from one hand to the other. She uses large walnut size gobs for manipulation. From these she forms pea-size pellets which she puts into her mouth at rare intervals, chewing them. As she does not spit them out they are probably swallowed. The abstracted expression of her face deepens and she passes an audible fecal movement. She lifts her skirt, looks at the full diaper, her face lightens with pleasure while she listens to the flatus she is passing. Except when listening to the flatus she vocalizes a lot.

When the fecal provisions in her hand are exhausted, she begins to manipulate the full diaper with one hand, lifting her skirt with the other and looking at her manipulations. Now she bends forward, seizes the full wet diaper between her teeth and alternately chews and sucks the urine soaked fecal mass through the diaper. From time to time she sticks two fingers sideways into the diaper, picks out some feces, forms a pellet and slips it into her mouth.

This play was observed for 1 hour and 20 minutes. The observer's presence did not disturb her, on the contrary: she related her play to him in a flirtatious, smiling, laughing, vocalizing, contact creating manner, without any apprehension, from time to time offering feces to the observer."

This protocol is presented because of its completeness; it contains approximately all the behavior patterns of the coprophagic child.

However, not all coprophagic children show each of these behavior patterns; neither the offering of feces to the observer which we have observed in three instances, nor the contact seeking, the smile and the laughter can be seen in all the cases. On the other hand the forming of pellets and eating them is a characteristic of the typical coprophagic child. Only one child (Case N 60), though he smeared feces just like the others, did not form pellets but stuck large pieces of feces into his mouth. This child was mentally deficient.

Our previous findings in the case of complete absence of all auto-erotic activities, our findings on children showing genital play, and on those showing rocking, have led us to expect that a specific form of auto-erotic activity implies a concomitant specific form of mother-child relation. We found this expectation fully justified when we investigated the mother-child relationship of the coprophagic children.

The mother's personality

We have already previously stressed the variability of the personalities of the mothers in Nursery, but also the fact that psychoses and psychotic trends are relatively rare. It came as a surprise to find that the bulk of the psychoses which came to our attention in this environment was concentrated in the group of those mothers whose children manifested fecal play. Eleven out of the 16 mothers showed the clinical symptoms of depression, reactive or otherwise; two of them were paranoiac. Of the remaining three, one was very severely disturbed, but no diagnosis was made; on two we have no information. The picture is still more striking when we compare the incidence of depression in the mothers of the group showing fecal play with that of the mothers of the other children, as shown in Table VII.

Table   VII

Relation between the Mother's Depression and the Child's
Fecal Play

Child	Mothers		
	Depression	No depression	Total
Fecal Play	11	5	16
No Fecal Play	5	132	137
Total	16	137	153

The correlation between depressive mothers and children with fecal play is significantly positive in spite of the small sample.

A closer study of these depressive mothers reveals further meaningful details. In the first place we have found that 11 of our 16 cases (70 per cent) in accordance with their diagnosis, showed definite intermittent changes of the mothers' behavior toward their children. The duration of these changes varied from a minimum of 2 to a maximum of 6 months. In the cases where shorter periods occurred we could observe such swings up to 4 times in the course of one year. As for their character, the swings varied from extreme hostility with rejection to extreme compensation of this hostility in the form of "over-solicitousness".

We have put the term "over-solicitousness" in quotations for a good reason. In a high number of our coprophagic cases, our protocols reveal that remarks to the effect that the mother is tender or loving to her baby are qualified by the statement that this love has some exaggerated traits. We find, for instance, a hungry fascinated incapacity of the mother to tear herself away from the child. Or we find a statement of a mother that she "cannot look at other children, only at her own". Or such a mother may dislike the other children to the point where she not only neglects them, but does them actual harm. The rejecting or hostile behavior is, in its way, just as peculiar. Overt rejection usually takes the form of a mother declaring that she does not want her child, and offering it for adoption. However, these overt rejections are in the minority; equally infrequent are overt hostile statements of mothers about their children, like that of a mother who "hates her child to be called 'darling' ".

Whatever the overt manifestation of feeling, we found unconscious hostile behavior in all our cases. A suprisingly large number of the coprophagic children (6) have suffered injury at the hands of their mothers. They suffer burns; they are scalded; one swallows an open safety pin; one is dropped on his head; one is nearly drowned during bathing,—we got the impression that without the attentive supervision of the staff few of these children would survive. It is worth mentioning in this connection that the only 2 cases of actual genital seduction of children by their own mothers which have come to our notice are to be found in this particular group of depressive mothers.

The "love" period is mostly manifested (7 cases) in the beginning of the baby's life and the hostility comes later. But in 5 cases the obverse holds good. In 4 cases our records are incomplete in this respect.

The child's personality

The children who manifest coprophagia show also a definite character structure. Of the 16 coprophagic children 10 are depressive.[15]

Table VIII shows the relations of these figures to each other.

Table VIII

Relation between the Child's Depression and the Child's Fecal Play

	Child		
	Severe depression	No depression	Total
Fecal Play	10	6	16
No Fecal Play	24	115	139
Total	34	121	155

15. For the criteria of depression in the first year of life we refer to our previous publication (13). For the sake of simplification we shall in the following speak of depressive children. The concept of psychiatric disturbance in infancy is so recent that adequate differentiation of syndromes has hardly begun. We have been able to differentiate such syndromes as hospitalism, marasmus, and depression. In the above quoted article we have already hinted that the anaclitic depression syndrome probably shows certain subdivisions, one of which we have qualified as "mild depression". We believe that in the coprophagic cases another of these syndromes will in due time become discernible, for, though these children may present many of the signs and symptoms of the anaclitic depression. a certain percentage of them show striking physiognomical differences. While the facial expression of children suffering from anaclitic depression is actually comparable to that of a grown-up suffering from severe reactive depression, more than half of the coprophagic children showed a facial expression which resembled far more that of paranoiac suspicion or that of catatonic daze. Furthermore the basic phenomenological difference between the anaclitic depressive and the present category lies in the coprophagia. For children with anaclitic depression present oral symptoms, if any, mostly *after* they have come out of their depression. Coprophagic children on the other hand, though frequently depressive, manifest their oral symptoms *during* this depressive state.

Coprophagia is not limited, however, to the depressive episode of the child. We observed also after the depressive episode the following phenomenological differences: These children tried to feed their feces to any person available, be that another child or be that the observer. We could observe this behavior in three of our 16 coprophagic children. These subjects showed a smiling expression during their fecal play and took up smiling contact with the observer.

The dynamic effect of the mother-child relationship

The picture presented by the mothers of these coprophagic children is that of a personality with a deep-seated ambivalence. Periodically the superego has the upper hand, the hostile components are repressed, the presenting picture is that of a self-sacrificing, self-debasing mother, who envelops her child with her love. Such a mother may for instance pester the observer consistently during this period with her worries about her child, particularly during the first months, when they frequently assume that the child is deaf or blind. Or in another case the mother said: "My baby is so little, (at the time it was one year old) I am afraid to hurt it." Or again in another case a naive observer, a nurse, remarked about a mother: "She is defiant, like a lioness with her cub."

In the case of the 11 mothers with periodical changes these "love" periods lasted for an appreciable time, never less than two months. After that they would be replaced by a swing to the opposite attitude, to overt hostility or to overt manifestation of unconscious hostility. In all cases such hostile periods again lasted for an appreciable time, again not less than two months.

Thus the child is confronted with a libidinal object which presents one consistently maintained attitude during a period which appears to be sufficiently long to permit the forming of object relations. When this period is at its end the object of these object relations becomes the opposite of what it was before. But then again it remains consistently the same for a sufficiently long time to permit on the one hand the formation of new object relations, on the other the formation of a compensation reaction to the loss of the previously established object. It is of this compensatory reaction that we will speak further on.[16]

Prior to that, however, we wish to compare the dynamic picture of the mothers of the rocking children to that of the mothers of the coprophagic children. In the case of the rocking children we had stressed the inconsistency of the love object, of the mother. We mentioned that

16. Such a picture has been assumed by Rado. (Rado, S., Das Problem der Melancholie, *Int. Zsch. f. Psa.*, XIII, 1927, pp. 449ff.) He extrapolated from adult analysis and postulated the presence of a "bad mother" as distinct from a "good mother", at the age of early ego-ideal formation.

they expose their children alternately to intense outbursts of love and equally intense outbursts of rage. But it would be an error to confound this picture with the periodicity observed in the mothers of the coprophagic children. The infantile personality of the mothers of the rocking children does not permit a consistent attitude lasting for days, let alone months. Their tantrums alternate with kissing jags within the hour and at no time is their behavior predictable from the point of view of the child. Its libidinal object alternates so rapidly between the opposite poles and passes so rapidly through every point of the compass of emotions that all attempts at forming an object relation must fail.

It is interesting to note that the correlation between genital play and rocking on one hand, genital play and coprophagia on the other offers support to our proposition. We have called rocking the most archaic of our three activities, with only thumbsucking going back possibly to an earlier level. Rocking is preobjectal. Its object is a primary narcissistic one and therefore it is observed in a number of cases before the appearance of genital play as a simple infantile form of autoerotic behavior without any pathology attached to it. It becomes pathological only when it persists throughout the whole of the first year. When it does that it excludes in the large majority of cases the coexistence of genital play, understandably so, as genital play presupposes a certain level of object relation. This mutual exclusiveness is evident in Table IV (p. 90).

Fecal play on the other hand consists in the actual manipulation of an object. Therefore it presupposes object relations of a sort, even though they may be pathological ones. It is noteworthy that in 5 out of our 16 cases of fecal play genital play was also observed. Furthermore, in most of these cases genital play appeared before coprophagia, thus implying the presence of object relations, which later were disturbed. One might say that in these cases the subsequent fecal play appears as a distortion of the original object relations.

However, this does not provide us as yet with an explanation why fecal play and particularly coprophagia is chosen by these children. We believe that such an explanation involves speculative assumptions, a step we are hesitant to take. We offer a hypothesis on the question therefore with diffidence, as a working hypothesis, and feel ready to renounce it if a better one can be found.

Our hypothesis is in the first place based on the assumption of the oral introjection postulated for depression by Freud (6, p. 160) and Abraham (1). This oral introjection in the depressed person is of course unconscious. But its manifestations are perceptible enough to the observer. The devouring oral attitude of the mothers in question was evident, going to the point of cunilingus. Our proposition therefore is

that the children identified with the unconscious tendencies manifested
by their mothers. This identification led the children to the oral introjection of their object. It took place as a result of the change in the
personality of the original love object, which was thus lost to the
children. As this loss, or one of these losses, coincides with the end of
the first year—in our opinion the transition to the anal phase—the object
which becomes available at this point is the fecal object. Of course the
fecal object becomes an object only at the moment when it is discovered
in the diaper. Whether the deep absorption of the infant's face during
the expulsion of its feces at this age denotes its perception of the excrement as an object or only its perception of the anal stimulation; and
whether the following expression of gratification, when expulsion has
been completed, is amenable to an interpretation; whether this interpretation can be expressed in the terms of the fecal mass becoming an object
already during the expulsion and whether therefore the expulsion is experienced as a repetition of the loss of the libidinal object—that we are not
prepared to say. However, when the expulsion has been completed and
the visibly pleasurable sensations of the child have been savored and
come to their end (that is, half a minute later), a new act begins. The
child turns again to the outside world. In many cases he sits up, looks
around, discovers the diaper and visibly interested, reaches for the fecal
mass. At this point the fecal mass in the diaper has become an object,
and a libidinally cathected one. Witness the way these children handle
the feces-filled diaper and how they rapidly proceed either to put the
whole diaper with the fecal mass in their mouth and chew it, notwithstanding the acrobatic contortions necessary for this; or, in the other
case, take out a piece of the mass and go through the procedure already
described in our case history. At this point the object has become one
which is introjected. It is an open question whether we should think of
this introjection in terms of a part-object.

   This hypothesis is not quite as speculative as it would appear. The
question of the child's identifying itself with the mother's unconscious
wishes is not at all problematic at this age. As published elsewhere (13)
the ego of the infant in the first year is rudimentary and is only able to
subsist thanks to the circumstance that it is supplemented by the
mother's personality. As a result of this circumstance which we have
described as the "mother-child dual" [17] most of the infant's functions
take place in closest concomitance and interaction with the mother's
actions and attitudes, either as their prolongation, or as their origin, or
paralleling them all along the way. Such a function will of course

---

17. A similar concept of the unity between mother and child, object and the
precursor of the ego, was described by Ernst Paul Hoffman (7) and called "Zwei-
einigkeit" (7, p. 367).

amount to something which (if we wish at this early age to avoid the term of identification which implies a specific mechanism) could be called a practical identity, a lack of differentiation between ego and environment. If we add to this that at this period, conscious and unconscious, ego and id are not yet delimited in the infant, it is easy to imagine the infant enacting unconscious attitudes of the mother.

There is some support for this assumption in our figures also. Not only do 11 of the 16 mothers of the coprophagic children suffer from depression, but 2 of the 5 remaining mothers show similar periodic changes in their attitudes to their children, bringing this relationship up to the impressive total of 13 out of 16. Furthermore we find that out of a total of 11 of these mothers who were depressive, 8 have children who had also manifest depressions. This should not be taken as an indication of heredity.

Thus our assumption would be that coprophagia as autoerotic activity in the first year of life is co-variant with depression in the mother. The effective factors in the mother's depression are two: its periodical nature and its unconscious oral introjective tendencies. In the child we find three factors: 1) the compliance of the child's structural level for the purpose of identification with the mother's trends, 2) the child's reaction to the loss of its libidinal object, a dynamic compliance, 3) the phase compliance or genetic compliance of the child's being situated at the transitional period from the oral to the anal phase.

IV. *Theoretical Conclusions*

If we consider now the three autoerotic activities we have observed and discussed, we find that they represent stages of object relations. The nature of the objectal relations is the determinant of the particular autoerotic activity chosen. The nature of the object relation also is expressed by the form the autoerotic activity takes.

From this point of view our presentation should in reality have started with rocking. Here the nature of the object relation was the most primitive one, a primary narcissistic relation, or to be more exact, a regression to the primary narcissistic stage. It is caused by a maternal personality which does not permit the formation of any object relation whatsoever. The form it takes is a non-objectal activity of the libidinal drive.

The coprophagic activity is on another level. Here we have a real object relation, though a distorted one, to a part-object. The formation of the object relation is made possible by a consistent attitude of the mother lasting for an appreciable time. The distortion of the object relation is caused by a change in the mother's personality which change in its turn is maintained for an appreciable period. The object centers upon itself the aggressive and the libidinal drives.

In genital play the object relations are satisfactory and remain attached to the libidinal object, thanks to its consistent facilitation of such object relations. Here the autoerotic activity remains within the framework of the whole of the objectal activities of the child and is a subordinate activity of minor importance.

V. Summary

A group of 170 children was observed during their first year of life for the incidence of three autoerotic activities, genital play, rocking and fecal play. The mother-child relations were established as the variable among the environmental factors which could affect this group. Two control groups were used in which the variable was kept as constant as possible: one group of family children with optimal mother-child relations and one group of institutionalized children where mother-child relations were so to say absent.

It was found that autoerotic activities are a function of the object relations prevailing during the first year of life. They are absent when object relations are absent; when object relations are so constantly contradictory that object formation is made impossible, rocking results. When object relations change in an intermittent manner fecal play results. When object relations are "normal", genital play results.

The dynamics of these different object relations were investigated and discussed.

BIBLIOGRAPHY

1. Abraham, K. "A Short Study of the Development of the Libido Viewed in the Light of Mental Disorders", *Selected Papers*, Hogarth, 1942, 435 ff.
2. Bender, L. "Mental Hygiene and the Child," *Am. J. Orthopsychiat.*, 1939, IX, 574—580.
3. Federn, P. *"Die Onanie."* 14 *Beiträge zu einer Diskussion der Wiener Psychoanalytischen Vereinigung*, I. F. Bergmann, 1912.
4. Freud, S. *Three Contributions to the Theory of Sex*, Nerv. Ment. Dis. Mon., 7, 1930.
5. Freud, S. "Totem und Taboo", *Basic Works of Sigmund Freud*, ed. A. A. Brill, Modern Library, 1938.
6. Freud, S. "Mourning and Melancholia", *Coll. Papers*, IV, 160.
7. Hoffman, E. P. "Projektion und Ichentwicklung", *Int. Zeit. f. Psa.*, XXI, 3, 1937.

8. Lindner, S. "Das Saugen an den Fingern, Lippen, etc. bei den Kindern", *Zeit. f. Psa. Päd.*, VIII, 1934.

9. Moro, E. "Das erste Trimenon", *München. med. Wchnschr.*, 1918, 65, 1147—1150.

10. Reich, W. *Der triebhafte Charakter*, Internat. Psa. Verlag, 1925.

11. Spitz, R. A. "Hospitalism", *this Annual*, I, 1945.

12. Spitz, R. A. "Hospitalism. A Follow Up", *this Annual*, II, 1946.

13. Spitz, R. A. "Anaclitic Depression", *ibid.*, II, 1946.

14. Spitz, R. A. and Wolf, Katherine M. "Environment vs. Race", *Archives of Neurol. and Psychiat.*, 57, No. 1, 1947.

15. Sylvester, E. "Pathogenic Influence of Maternal Attitudes in the Neonatal Period", *Problems of Early Infancy*, Publication of Josiah Macy, Jr. Foundation, Trans. First Conf., March, 1947, p. 67.

16. Wolff, G. "Maternal and Infant Mortality in 1944", *U. S. Children's Bur. Stat. Series No. 1*, Fed. Sec. Agency. Soc. Sec. Admin., U. S. Children's Bureau.

THE REACTION OF INFANTS TO STRESS

A Report of Clinical Observations

By MARY LEITCH, M.D. and SIBYLLE ESCALONA, Ph.D. (Topeka) [1]

The Theoretical Framework

The construction of a systematically consistent and specific theory of personality development based upon psychoanalytic knowledge has met with considerable difficulty. Freud's formulations concerning the phases of psychosexual development, concerning the establishment of the reality principle, and concerning a host of related aspects of normal development, form the structural nucleus for any dynamic understanding of developmental processes. Yet as Hartmann, Kris and Loewenstein (8) have called to our attention, there exists a need for greater conceptual clarity in psychoanalytic theory, especially in regard to genetic aspects. As psychoanalytic theory becomes integrated with all other scientific knowledge, they pointed out, a more precise and less anthropomorphic definition of concepts becomes expedient. They proposed that psychic structures be defined in terms of their functions, and that they be regarded as dynamically interrelated systems rather than as entities.

The attempt to act on this suggestion proves difficult as soon as one departs form the level of abstract theory and deals with actual behavioral phenomena of the infancy period. There is, as yet, a wide gap between concepts such as "primary narcissism" or "oral aggression" and what we see when regarding a squirming, smiling, babbling, sucking and crying baby. The obstacles to a conceptual treatment of infant behavior do not primarily arise from the nature of psychoanalytic concepts or the systematic inadequacies of their definitions. The greater difficulty lies in the relative lack of information regarding the phenomenology of infant behavior. Psychoanalytic concepts in regard to personality functioning in maturity derive their sharpness and specific meaning in large measure from the imposing array of factual observation and case material in which they are embedded. The main con-

1. From the Menninger Foundation.

tribution of the "Psychopathology of Everyday Life" for instance, was not to advance new insights but to demonstrate the generality of principles and mechanisms, thus helping to break down the barrier between "pathology" and "normalcy", which proved an essential step for a meaningful comprehension of psychic experience.

A similarly close familiarity with the raw data of our science is conspicuously lacking in regard to the first two years of life. This is true in spite of the fact that growth and development have received intensive study during the last two decades. The systematic study of early developmental processes was carried on primarily with an academic rather than a clinical orientation. This is true even in the case of medical men, for which the monumental work of Arnold Gesell may serve as an example. Almost without exception factual studies of infant development used a normative approach. Interest was focused on those observable aspects of the developmental process which occur with great statistical frequency and regularity. Thus we know the "average age" at which the "average child" chosen from a "representative sample" of the population may be expected to smile, to sit without support, to grasp an object or to recognize a picture. Such normative standards have proved their value for the detection of deviates and for other clinical purposes—they have done but little to increase a dynamic understanding of the behavior of the young child.

In order to consolidate and extend our understanding of the psychodynamics of normal development, it will be necessary to undertake the systematic and painstaking observation of what infants actually do.[2] We need to know the behavior repertoire of infants at different developmental levels, we need to know the way in which environmental circumstances or somatic processes may alter behavior and, last but not least, individual differences in the behavior of infants require careful attention. Such observation, in order to be useful, cannot be a mechanical recording of overt behavior in arbitrary "standard" situations. Rather, it needs to be guided by selective principles of relevance to fundamental psychodynamic hypotheses. In other words, the observations themselves, not their implications or derivatives, must lend themselves to conceptualization. Among the characteristics of a "good concept" in science those of generality and of systematic relatedness to other concepts on the same level of abstraction are of outstanding importance. Yet another attribute is that the concept should bear a precise relationship to observable and communicable facts, i. e., it should be subject to "operational definition".

2. The recent work by Spitz, Ribble, Fries, Hendricks and other psychoanalytic investigators is representative of a felt need to integrate our basic theoretical concepts with observable aspects of infantile experience.

In this publication we have chosen to describe certain clinical observations of infant behavior in terms of one concept borrowed from general dynamic theory and relevant to several important psychoanalytic hypotheses. The concept is that of *tension*. On the basis of the observations to be reported we arrived at the tentative assumption that behavior observed at times when young infants are experiencing stress, deprivation or frustration may often be understood in one of several ways: (1) the infant's behavior is of a kind which may be regarded as a direct manifestation of the presence of increased tension in the organism; (2) a profound disturbance of functioning can occur—especially when stress is severe or has operated over prolonged periods of time—which may reflect the response of the organism to having been in a state of excessive tension over an appreciable period of time; (3) some of the behavior shown by children who have experienced severe traumata may also be regarded as a defense against the disruptive effects of a heightened tension level within the organism.

A precise theoretical definition of tension as applied to the state of the infant would be premature. For purposes of this discussion the following may suffice: with Freud we assume that instinctual needs are present at birth and seek gratification, that delay of such gratification causes a state of tension which, if sufficiently severe, causes discomfort or displeasure. It is further assumed, in accordance with established psychodynamic principles, that the infant organism (like all other organisms) maintains a relative equilibrium of forces and that the disruption of this equilibrium through stimulation of any kind results in an increase of tension, however temporary. In keeping with the principle of homeostasis this state of excitation leads to alterations in functioning which tend to re-establish a state of equilibrium whenever a disruption of the existing balance of forces has occurred.[3]

Dynamic psychology has used the concept of tension in this sense, and experimental evidence is available to show how tension systems may be created and how a heightened state of tension alters many aspects of psychological functioning (1,10). Certain general effects of tension states have consistently been encountered. Since they are precisely of the kind we observed in infants under stress situations we shall briefly refer to them.

According to the work of Kurt Lewin and his associates, increased tension produces numerous behavioral changes which may be considered

3. This is, by definition, a property of all tension systems as postulated in the mathematical science of mechanics. It is in part for this reason, namely the conceptual equivalence of tension as used in physics and the other dynamic sciences, and as it can be used in psychology, that we choose this particular term.

a primitivization or a de-differentiation of functioning. This manifests itself, among others,[4] in the following forms:

(1) The variety of activity decreases, i. e., the person engages in a fewer number of different activities.

(2) Behavior becomes less organized, or organized at a lesser level of complexity and integration.

(3) The relative autonomy of various systems within the person may decrease or disappear, i. e., changes relating to one system may bring about a change in functioning in entirely different systems due to a spreading of tension.

(4) Perception and apperception of the environment is dictated by inner needs, wishes, fears, etc., to a higher degree than is usually the case. This implies that behavior becomes less "realistic" or less adaptive.

(5) The "economy of action" breaks down, so that unnecessary or purposeless action may take place.

(6) Greater sensitivity is present, at least in certain respects, so that minor events which would usually not be disturbing are reacted to more strongly than under ordinary circumstances.

It should be mentioned that not all of these alterations in functioning necessarily occur when a person is under tension. Which aspects of functioning are most affected appears to depend on the characteristics of the person, the nature of the situation, and the severity of the tension state.

In describing our case material we have chosen to regard as tension manifestations all those observable alterations in the infant's functioning which fall under one or several of the categories stated. Since in infants somatic and psychic processes are interwoven even more closely than is the case at higher levels of maturity, we have included somatic manifestations such as heightened muscle-tonus or shallow and belabored respiration. These may, in fact, be considered as falling under category (3), since they demonstrate a lack of such autonomy which a given system (respiratory or neuromuscular) may have attained previously.

The Clinical Situation

Since our discussion is based upon observations made under rather narrowly circumscribed conditions it is necessary to state briefly the manner in which they were obtained. During the last 4 years the Children's Division of The Menninger Foundation has rendered psychological clinical services to the agency in charge of child placement and adoption

4. Certain of these tension manifestations are observable only in older children and adults, as they occur in areas which have not yet been developed in infants and they are omitted from this enumeration.

in the State of Kansas.[5] The service consists of psychological testing of infants, augmented by observational procedures devised by the writers, and by interviews with boarding-home mothers who care for the infants under the supervision of the agency. Ordinarily infants are referred before they are 3 months of age (usually during the second month of life) and are seen again 1 to 2 months later. Whenever so recommended, which has occurred in approximately one-third of the cases, infants were seen on several more occasions for further psychological study until a definite recommendation could be made. Thus, a total of 112 infants have been examined 1 or 2 times, 14 infants were examined 3 to 5 times, and 2 infants were seen on more than 5 occasions before they reached the age of 12 months. The observations to be reported, therefore, are based upon a total of 214 psychological examinations conducted under comparable circumstances.

As a group, these children differ in several respects from the normal population. The large majority were born out of wedlock, and all came under the care of the agency because the mothers were unable or unwilling to assume responsibility for them. In regard to socio-economic status and perhaps in regard to hereditary background, these infants are somewhat inferior to the general population.

In many respects, however, the experience of these children closely parallels accepted standards in our culture. Some are removed from the hospital between the ages of 6 and 10 days, and subsequently live in boarding-homes where, under the supervision of agency workers, they are cared for by experienced mothers. Others are born in the Florence Crittenden Home[6] where they frequently remain until the age of 4 to 7 weeks before removal to boarding-homes. The agency in question is aware of the emotional needs of infants and boarding-homes are selected and supervised with this in mind. The mothers are encouraged to devote considerable personal attention to the babies in their care, and the number of young infants placed in any one home is kept small. The fact that our group of babies compared favorably with average standards of developmental progress, as measured by psychological tests, may be taken as evidence to show that, by and large, these infants were not exposed to traumata sufficiently severe to interfere with adequate growth and development during the early months of life at least.

The Behavioral Manifestations of Tension

If one applies the criteria for the existence of a heightened state of tension which we have previously listed, and assumes that a stress situation exists whenever alterations in the infant's functioning meet these criteria, it becomes necessary to broaden the concept of what constitutes stress beyond ordinary usage. Recognized traumatic conditions, such as grossly inadequate mothering, loss of the mother, severe restriction of

5. The Kansas Children's Service League has appreciated and shared our research interest in the problems of infant psychology. The unfailing courtesy and cooperation of its staff members is gratefully acknowledged.
6. The Florence Crittenden Homes are private charitable institutions for the care of unmarried mothers.

movement, premature habit training, etc., may indeed result in behavior disturbances characterized by excessive tension. In addition, however, tension manifestations of the same kind and nearly the same intensity may occur temporarily, in response to an immediate situation. To illustrate: the infant is hungry but food is not forthcoming; he is in pain for which insufficient relief can be given; he is sleepy but instead of being allowed his customary nap he is taken to the doctor for an examination. One can surmise that the situations just enumerated result predominantly in displeasure. However, clinical observations lead us to believe that pleasurable experience too may result in a disturbance of equilibrium and be accompanied by an increase in the momentary state of tension.

This view of the matter is indeed suggested by Freud in *Beyond the Pleasure Principle,* where he states:

"We have decided to consider pleasure and pain in relation to the quantity of excitation present in the psychic life—and not confined in any way—along such lines that 'pain' corresponds with an increase and pleasure with a decrease in this quantity. We do not thereby commit ourselves to a simple relationship between the strength of the feelings and the changes corresponding with them, least of all, judging from psycho-physiological experiences, to any view of a direct proportion existing between them . . ."

The existence of stress, therefore, is not necessarily attended by or equivalent to pure displeasure. The following observation may serve as an example:

During the process of psychological testing a well functioning, somewhat sensitive infant, 4 months of age, was presented with a number of toys one at a time. With the appearance of each new toy he became increasingly pleased and excited. Gradually, along with indications of mounting pleasure and excitement, tension became manifest. There was an increase in generalized, non-purposive and uncoordinated movement, his vocalizations became less differentiated though they continued to be expressive of pleasurable affect, and his rate of respiration increased markedly. It is probable that had stimulation been continued the degree of tension would have reached an intolerable point and his apparent pleasure would have been replaced by displeasure. As a matter of fact, we have occasionally observed the sudden change from apparent pleasure to apparent displeasure as infants became overly stimulated.

To pursue the above example we should like to point out that presentation with an increasing number of toys results in pleasurable excitement in some infants only; others will regard the same number with equanimity while still others will lose interest after the first few. The manifold ways in which infants respond to this one aspect of the testing situation points to a factor of prime importance, that of individual differences. While it is patent that there are a limited number of stress situations (those intimately associated with fundamental biological needs) common to most infants, the variety of specific conditions which constitute stress for individual infants is almost innumerable. Striking differences are also noted in the apparent degree to which the equilibrium of individual infants may be disturbed by a common stress situation. Some of the infants in our group apparently did not object to remaining wet or soiled for prolonged periods of time, seeming oblivious to this kind of alteration in their physical environment; some habitually began to cry as elimination occurred and became increasingly tense till diapered, the remainder fell somewhere between these two extremes in the apparent degree of discomfort experienced. Certain of them became tense only when wet or only when soiled while others seemed to experience being wet as a stress only under certain circumstances; for example, one infant cried immediately when she urinated while in her crib but if the act occurred while she was being held she seemed perfectly content and cried only if she was put down to be diapered. In regard to satisfaction of hunger we encountered infants who were made very tense by the slightest delay in gratification. In contrast to these were others who seemed to experience a much lesser degree of discomfort.[7] Yet others could be temporarily appeased by a substitute gratification such as thumbsucking or being picked up and held. Wide individual differences existed also in the type and degree of physical contact with the mother which seemed necessary in order for the infant to maintain a state of equilibrium. These differences could not always be related to the mother's way of handling the child or to her capacity for mothering. Often they seemed to depend on specific individual needs of the child for a certain type of handling. Whereas some babies were made tense by being held closely, apparently experiencing this as unpleasurable restraint, others seemed to find a good deal of close contact necessary for their well-being. Certain babies were made tense by any but the gentlest handling, while others could be handled quite roughly without being disquieted. In numerous instances the infants seemed to be most contented when left in their cribs a greater part of the time, tending to become tense whenever picked up or handled. Needless to say, we are here referring to individual differences encountered among infants of the same age.

The variety of conditions under which tension manifestations were observed in our group of infants was very great. The following stimulating situations are among those we noted. They are described in order to convey a feeling for the type of stimuli apparently important for young infants: a sudden approach by strangers and/or the mother; direct regard; noises of varying intensity and type; specific colors, especially

7. It could be argued that in the latter group the hunger sensations were not so severe as in the former and therefore the stress not so severe.

if worn by a person coming into contact with the child; loud voices or certain tones of voice; contact with particular persons whereas most persons were readily accepted; being held in positions which other infants of like age accept with pleasure; etc., etc. Thus it would seem that whether or not a particular situation is experienced as stress is partially dependent on the makeup of the individual infant.

It is not intended to imply that manifestations of tension are per se a reflection of the adjustment status of the infant. Every infant encounters stress situations and responds with increased tension. It is true that if the tension manifestations are severe and unremitting the infant may come to be regarded as maladjusted. Nonetheless a large group of well functioning babies will be seen to include not only those who occasionally show mild to moderate degrees of tension but also those (often a sensitive, well-endowed type of child) whose daily experience includes many situations resulting in stress and temporary tension states. Characteristic of these well-functioning infants is their ability to recover quickly from tension once their need is met or the stimulus is removed. Hence, while the existence of stress situations is often associated with maladjustment, it cannot be said that there is a direct relationship between them.

In many instances we have been unable to speculate as to the possible reasons for the extraordinary variability in regard to the kind of situation that may be experienced as stress by different infants and in regard to the individual differences which exist in the manner in which tension is shown. In fact, we have seen infants who displayed characteristics of functioning clearly related to an unusually high state of tension where these manifestations did not appear to be related primarily to changes in the external environment. We are referring to hyperactive infants who may show excessive physical activity even during sleep, to infants who are irritable, overly sensitive or show chronic high muscle-tonus resulting in hypoactivity and a kind of muscular rigidity. Nevertheless, our observations have led us to speculate that the particular way or ways in which tension is manifested is likely to bear a relationship to the following factors, among others:

The modes of expression available to an immature organism: it is our impression that, in general, tension is reflected in disturbances in physiological functioning more readily by infants than by adults. During the first year gastro-intestinal upsets, rapid changes in skin color, alterations in respiratory rate and rhythm, and rapid alterations in temperature are frequently encountered as a part of the total response to stress situations. With increasing age and possibly due to the relative increase in autonomy of functioning of the various organs, and the greater stability of the organism as a whole, disturbances in physiological functioning are seen less frequently. Inversely, developmental limitations prevent the infant organism from producing some of the tension manifestations which are seen at older age levels. For instance, infants cannot manifest tenseness by an increased rapidity of speech nor by restless locomotion.

Certain modes of expressing tension appear to be characteristic of individual organisms. Although any one infant is likely to display a variety of tension manifestations in different areas of functioning, one particular type of response to a stress situation may occur with such frequency that it can be said to be characteristic of the individual. For example, some infants characteristically respond with visible circulatory changes, some with altered respiration, some with an increase in muscle-tonus, and some with an increase in generalized activity. Our observations have not been sufficiently detailed to permit fruit ful speculation concerning the genesis of these apparent predispositions, nor their implications for future personality development.

In some cases at least, the specific nature of the stress situation appears to be a determining factor. If a stress situation impinges directly on a certain physiological function, disturbances in that function may be the main indicators of the resulting tension.

For example, a 2-months-old infant received abundant loving care from a mother who was tolerant and flexible with one exception; she insisted on forcefully administering spoon feedings of semi - solids despite the baby's lack of willingness to accept this. Forced feedings always precipitated rigidity of the whole body, apparently in an attempt to resist the procedure, and were invariably followed by rapid, nervous burping, spitting up and at times vomiting. In all other situations except feeding this infant was relaxed and normally responsive.

We have speculated that the specific nature of the stress situation is likely to have a different significance at different developmental levels. If a disturbance is present which primarily interferes with oral activities (for instance thrush), this may be experienced as a more severe stress in an infant below the age of 6 months than at a later age.[8]

The duration and severity of stress is a crucial factor and merits more detailed discussion. If a well - functioning infant organism is subjected to momentary stress, such manifestations of tension as appear tend to subside quickly once the stimulus is removed. This phenomenon can perhaps best be studied in a clinical testing situation where it

8. This consideration could well be elaborated in terms of Erik Erikson's concept of the coexistence of "organism processes" and "social processes" which postulates that whether or not a given event is experienced as traumatic by a given child at a given time depends upon whether or not the event bears a significant relationship to dominant organismic needs at that time.

is possible to observe the infant's reaction to a variety of stresses such as sudden loud noises, being presented with a task which is attractive to the infant yet which he is not able to master, presentation with an increasing number of toys, removal of toys from his grasp, brief delay in giving the bottle or the breast when the infant is hungry, brief attack of digestive distress, a heightened state of irritability subsequent to inoculations, etc. Under such conditions some of the following tension signs appear with great frequency: tense body posture, body posture less mature than that usually assumed by the infant, increase in muscle-tonus, arching of the back, significant increase or decrease in physical activity, sudden flexion or extension of extremities, breath holding, rapid, shallow respirations, respiratory arrhythmia, nervous cough, failure to attend to object stimulation, turning to the mother, clinging to the mother, frightened withdrawal from the examiner, avid thumbsucking, mouthing movements, crying, anxious facial expression, pallor, flushing, skin blotches, rapid changes in skin color, temporary lack of the capacity for coordinated movements, temporary loss of the ability to use different objects in a discriminatory fashion, etc. Often several of these signs appear at the same time, and the organism may be temporarily rendered unable to adapt to the situation at hand. However, as stated above, the recovery tends to be rapid and mothers are likely to report that while the infant occasionally shows momentary disturbances in the home he functions adequately the greater part of the time.

If an infant encounters an unusual number of stresses, or if the stress is prolonged and severe (for example, persistent forced feeding, prolonged physical illness, loss of accustomed mother figure), the clinical picture is different. Some of the signs of tension mentioned above, such as excessive muscle-tonus or hyperactivity may be observed throughout the entire examinational period. In addition, tension manifestations may appear with comparatively little provocation, and the infant may experience great difficulty in recovering from both fatigue and tension. Apparently the continued existence of stress and the consequent increase in the level of tension renders the organism more vulnerable. Usually, in addition to the type of observation made during the examination, the mother reports that the baby is characteristically "nervous" or "tense" and presents problems such as repeated spitting up or vomiting, greedy appetite, resistence to routine, diarrhea or constipation, failure to gain in spite of adequate food intake, continual thumbsucking, frequent crying, respiratory difficulties, skin rashes, marked circulatory changes, undue fearfulness of strangers, etc.

Occasionally we have encountered yet more severe indications of disturbance in young infants. These may include severe head banging, hair pulling, pulling at and digging the nails into parts of the body, moaning while rocking and holding the hands before the eyes, withdrawal from stimuli ordinarily tolerated, lethargy, apparent absence of tension (or even animation) under circumstances expected to provoke it, retarded or uneven development, and a complete lack of pleasure in developmental achievement. Some of these phenomena such as moaning and rocking can be regarded as more or less direct manifestations of tension. However, a different explanation must be sought for lethargy and an apparent complete lack of excitability and tension. Possibly these symptoms occur when the tension becomes so intolerable that the organism becomes completely fatigued or paralyzed. Or the infant may resort to a kind of withdrawal as a mode of protection against further tension arousing stimuli.[9] Lack of pleasure in developmental achievement (for example, in learning to stand, walk or master the use of a toy) and/or retardation in development likewise seem to indicate a serious far-reaching disruption of the normal functioning of the organism.

As to the type of stress producing such profound disturbances, Spitz has described the syndrome of anaclitic depression which embraces some of the symptoms we observed, and which is precipitated in institutionalized children by prolonged separation from a loving mother beginning between the 6th and 8th months. In the cases under our observation the etiology has unfortunately been obscure. While the infants were separated from their own mothers at a few weeks of age, they were provided with continuous and special loving care by mother-substitutes.[10]

In some instances there has been a question of organic damage though its presence was not definitely established.

This was the state of affairs in the case of an infant who at an early age showed signs of acute disturbance. At the ages of 5—7 months, when approached, looked at, spoken to in an ordinary tone of voice or shown toys, he moaned, rocked back and forth, buried his head in his arms and covered his eyes with his hands. Yet, when this baby was unaware of being observed, he played with objects in a normal manner, and his motility was of the type expected of an infant at his age level. While neurological examination was negative, a decided hemorrhagic tendency as well as a brief period of attacks resembling petit mal seizures and disturbances in motor development suggested the possibility of intra-cranial hemorrhage or other cerebral defect. Oddly enough, mental development proceeded at an approximately normal rate throughout the first year and well into the second.

It is conceivable that organic damage itself might result in disturbances of the level of tension either by acting as an irritative focus and/or

9. It could be speculated that infants of the quiet "activity pattern" type described by Margaret Fries are more prone to this type of reaction.
10. Special attentiveness from boarding-home mothers whom we knew to be maternal and successful with children was arranged for in these cases in an effort to improve the child's condition.

because the defective nervous system offers inadequate protection against external stimuli. In our cases we had to conclude that the infant was characterized by some inherent weakness or vulnerability, the nature of which was not at all clear to us but which resulted in a lessened tolerance for the ordinary stresses of daily life.

We should like to mention one additional effect of the presence of severe or prolonged tension. Among our group of infants it was noted that where tension manifestations were severe or maintained for a prolonged period of time, psychological test findings were characterized by more extensive scatter than is ordinarily seen. That is, the infant's behavior was characteristically much more mature in some areas of functioning than in others so that failures occurred on test items corresponding to average standards for infants of a lesser age, and at the same time test items corresponding to average standards for relatively older children were achieved.[11] We have speculated that prolonged or severe tension states may interfere with orderly developmental progress, causing in some instances unusual alertness and sensitivity in some areas but interfering with adequate integration of functioning.

Case Illustrations

In the following we describe, in somewhat greater detail, 5 cases demonstrating tension manifestations in response to a variety of stress situations. It is recognized that in some instances (especially cases C and D), it may be questioned whether physiological disturbance—which we have regarded as a stress—arose on the basis of a heightened state of tension, or whether it was the rather causative agent producing tension. In the instances to be reported, the physiological disturbances arose at a time when the infants were not exposed to any environmental changes, nor were we able to detect any other factors which could account for a change in the child's adjustment status. The circumstances under which physiological disfunctioning may arise on the basis of excessive tension, (as we believe occurred in case E), and the circumstances under which a disturbance in physiological functioning gives rise to excessive tension can be sharply delineated only after a great many more systematic observations (probably in the form of longitudinal studies) have been accumulated.

It may be well to preface the case reports by a brief statement regarding the formal aspects of the examination. Two psychological tests

11. A wide scatter involving mainly age levels above the child's chronological age and accompanied by very few failures below the child's chronological age has seemed to us to be indicative of superior endowment rather than of developmental disturbance.

were administered to each infant on each occasion: the Gesell Developmental Schedules and the Cattell Infant Intelligence Test. The Gesell Schedules yield separate ratings for four different aspects of development. These are: (1) Motor, which refers to neuro-muscular strength and maturity; (2) Adaptive, which refers to discriminatory perception and response to external objects and to other aspects of functioning considerd to be most closely related to intelligence proper; (3) Language, which refers to all manner of vocalizations as well as to other means of communication between the infant and other persons; and (4) Personal - Social, which refers to the relative maturity in the expression of affective states and to social responsiveness generally. Our primary emphasis has not been on the quantitative ratings of predicted intelligence status, but upon the qualitative aspects of the child's performance. Particular interest attaches to the extent of "scatter". As already stated, we have gained the impression that excessively wide scatter reflects imperfect integration of total functioning, and may suggest the presence of a developmental disturbance.

Infant A

We were interested in the instances where a child's tenseness appears to be directly related to the tenseness of an adult. Certain infants, apparently, are especially sensitive to tension states in adults with whom they are in direct contact (3). The manifestations of tenseness are no different from those described in other connections, but one example will be given to illustrate what is meant.

A, whose birth and history were normal, was referred to us at the age of 17 weeks. As he was brought into the office he seemed noticeably irritable and complaintive, and quite tense muscularly. His toes and fingers were curled or fanning, his breathing was irregular and belabored, he moved in a jerky manner and seemed generally uncomfortable as well as unresponsive. This irritability seemed only to increase with the boarding - home mother's attempts to soothe him. She held him close to her body, grasped him tightly, spoke to him with considerable intensity though lovingly and changed his position in her arms frequently—to no avail. The boarding-home mother reported that infant A was among the most tense in her experience, and that he especially seemed to become stiff when she picked him up, bathed him, or attempted to interest him in play with toys. She thought his behavior in the office, as described above, characteristic of him and stated that she found him to be most comfortable when placed in his crib and left to his own devices. It was noted that she held him rather awkwardly, and her general manner lacked calmness and suggested the presence of tension. The examiner took the infant in her arms and within less than a minute his behavior had altered considerably. He ceased crying and whimpering, breathing became somewhat more even, he began to show an interest in objects surrounding him, and the excessive curling and fanning of the toes disappeared. Once infant A was apparently comfortable and definitely responsive he was returned to the boarding-home mother and again he stiffened, looked at stimulus objects briefly or not at all, and soon resumed crying. Thereupon the examiner again held the child and, in fact, several more trials showed that A could be tested only when not held by the boarding-home mother. The latter spontaneously stated that she had not seen this infant as interested in his surroundings, or as relaxed, on any previous occasion except when lying in his crib. (It may be of some interest that, throughout the years, general irritability, frequent crying and minor feeding disturbances occurred more frequently with infants under the care of this particular boarding-home mother than with the infants in the charge of most other boarding-homes under the supervision of the same agency.)

Infant B

The following case illustrates our observation that stimuli evoking pleasurable excitement may arouse tension, that if the stimulation is continued tension eventually results in pleasure giving way to displeasure, and that tension having reached this degree interferes with responses at an optimal level of functioning.

Infant B was referred to us at the age of 10 weeks to determine the advisability of adoptive placement. Birth history was normal. When 10 days old he was placed in a boarding-home where he received a good deal of cuddling and kissing to which he responded with obvious pleasure. Always he seemed to want a good deal of attention and cried when it was not immediately forthcoming. For some time, although he accepted feedings eagerly, he tended to be uncomfortable after them, spit up, and also had frequent bowel movements. By the 8th week, after several formula changes, the severity of the diarrhea had diminished markedly and he was much less fussy. Weight gain was consistently satisfactory.

When tested at 13 weeks he received developmental ratings just a little above average, although there was a slight lag in the adaptive area. He tended to startle at even very small noises but otherwise showed few signs of tension. Responsiveness to both people and objects was satisfactory. Characteristically, he tended to respond to each object immediately upon presentation, not showing the delay frequently observed in very young babies. Seen again at 17 weeks, his tendency to have loose stools had completely disappeared and he seldom spit up. Formal testing now showed that his development had proceeded at a considerably accelerated pace, his achievement in most areas resembling that of the infant 5 to 7 weeks older than he. He was especially mature in the adaptive area where he had formerly shown a mild retardation. His activity, which was moderate in amount, was of a somewhat more mature type than would be expected. Social stimulation resulted in considerable increase in activity. Again his responses to toys were always immediate. He reached for, grasped and vigorously manipulated them with evident pleasure. As the test proceeded and he was presented with more and more toys he appeared increasingly pleased and excited. However, at the same time his facial expression reflected a marked degree of tension and his movements were of less mature type. Finally his excitement reached such a pitch that, when the last few toys were presented, he showed frantic excitement and an over-all increase in activity, crying and waving his arms about. Random movements became so predominant that he was no longer able to really get at the toy. Fatigue was now marked. It should be stated that it was our impression that the boarding - home mother took such pride in his rapid development as to perhaps drive him to behavior more mature than he might develop spontaneously and thus to over-stimulate him. For instance, she had already placed him in a highchair and also encouraged him to "walk".

In regard to the discrepancy between the developmental ratings received on the 1st and 2nd test, it is believed that the relatively slow rate of development first seen with a lag in the adaptive area reflected the after-affects of the early prolonged gastro-intestinal difficulties. It could be speculated that his tendency to become readily over - stimulated at the time of the 2nd test was yet another after - effect of the early illness, still finding expression in a relatively labile equilibrium. Again the boarding - home mother's tendency to over - stimulate him may have left him more vulnerable to a type of stress (repeated object stimulation) better tolerated by many other infants of his age.

Infant C

In C, who was ordinarily a relaxed child, increased activity, heightened muscle-tonus, jerkiness of movement, crying, failure to attend, fatigue and increased readiness to startle, all appeared rapidly with the onset of gastro - intestinal distress and resulted in a temporary severe disturbance of functioning.

Infant C was first seen by us at 8 weeks of age on a research basis. Her parents had separated before her birth and she received an extra special amount of loving care from her mother who, because of a severe facial disfigurement and psychological peculiarities, led a lonely, isolated life. Except for minor transient "kidney trouble" immediately following birth and a brief bout of diarrhea at 4 weeks of age, health history was normal till 3 or 4 days preceding the psychological examination. At that time C again became ill with diarrhea, having as many as 17 bowel movements a day. She was exceedingly fussy and could be comforted only by being held. The morning of the examination she seemed very much better. When first observed she appeared comfortable and was alert, regarding the various persons in the room and also objects presented to her. For some time she "played" contentedly in the crib, kicking gently, waving her arms about and vocalizing softly. It was our impression that she was of the quiet activity type and this was confirmed by the mother's report. Muscle - tonus was only moderately firm. When picked up she cuddled and relaxed completely. Few startle responses were observed. This happy state of affairs was brought to an abrupt ending when she suddenly began to strain and whimper and within the next half-hour she produced 4 liquid bowel movements. During this time she appeared to be in acute distress, whimpering and writhing about continuously. Movements of the arms and legs, formerly smooth, became jerky. She now startled frequently to even very minor noises. A number of times she arched her back or held her legs extended rigidly. Muscle - tonus was tight. When picked up she stiffened and was completely unable to relax. Following the cessation of bowel movements she continued hyperactive although she appeared exceedingly fatigued. Her attention could not be gained for more than a split second at a time and it was necessary to discontinue attempts at testing.

Seen 8 days later, the mother told that the diarrhea had disappeared the night following the examination. Since that time stools had been of normal frequency and consistency. During the entire observational period C now appeared healthy and content. She again relaxed completely when held. Attention and response to both objects and persons was completely satisfactory for her age. She seldom startled. Muscle - tonus was rather low. She was not particularly active. Formal test achievements showed average developmental progress which had proceeded evenly in the various areas.

On can speculate that C, who was relaxed and functioned well when first seen after several days of the diarrhea and who, 8 days after the illness, showed absolutely no after - effects, was an infant with a relatively high degree of tolerance for severe stress or, at any rate, for stress of this particular kind.

Infant D

This case illustrates the occurrence of tension manifestations, and a mild developmental disturbance, occurring subsequent to physical illness of a minor sort. In this instance, we knew the baby before the physical difficulty arose, shortly after it was apparently overcome, and subsequently.

D was a full-term baby; delivery was normal; neither the history nor medical examination revealed any atypical features. He was examined for the first time at the age of 11 weeks. Tests and observations alike indicated an infant who functioned normally in all areas; his responsiveness to persons seemed relatively more advanced than any other aspect of development. It was noted that he engaged in sucking movements and "bubble-blowing" more frequently than is the case with most infants, and the boarding - home mother observed that sucking movements were as frequent and intense after feedings as prior to them.

D was referred again at the age of 20 weeks. He was then considered to be in good health although he had been "having a little difficulty with diarrhea for the last few weeks". It was also reported that he was uncomfortable after feedings, sometimes crying and squirming so that it was necessary to hold him for prolonged periods of time. Minor sleeping disturbances were present; he awakened at night and cried but could usually be soothed by means of patting or rocking within a period of 10 minutes or so. These disturbances subsequent to feedings and during sleep developed while he suffered from diarrhea but persisted subsequently up to the time of the 20 - weeks test. While responsive and interested on the whole, this baby now exhibited some behavior suggesting the presence of tension strong enough to interfere with optimal functioning. At various times during the psychological examination, usually after having been stimulated rather intensively with a number of toys or by special approaches, he showed a marked increase in physical activity. In contrast to his motility most of the time, at such times he showed entirely uncoordinated jerky movements which were followed by a general stiffening of the body and by a trembling of the limbs. It is of interest that D could be made to relax if he was picked up and held and fondled. It was also noted that he startled easily at sudden noises even if these were of minor intensity. (At 11 weeks of age, when this might be expected behavior, startle responses had not been observed). Formal test findings showed a mild but definite retardation in all areas of development except that of social responsiveness. In view of the fact that D had not seemed unusually tense before, and had made average developmental progress previously, it was thought that increased tension and hence, a mild disturbance in developmental progress, had occurred in association with the diarrhea and its after-effects. He was observed again at the age of 31 weeks at which time he again showed average developmental progress though social responsiveness remained slightly more mature than other aspects of behavior. In marked contrast to the previous test observations, he displayed entirely normal types of behavior. Though very much interested in both objects and persons, and responsive to them, he did not become over - stimulated, motility remained coordinated to the degree appropriate for his age, and he showed no special alertness to noises or to any other type of stimulus. The internal history indicated that there had been no recurrence of the diarrhea, nor any other illness. Both the sleep disturbance and the irritability subsequent to feedings had disappeared entirely. D was seen again at the age of 24 months, at which time he again presented the picture of a healthy normally developed child. His intelligence functioning still fell in the average range and he seemed, if anything, more stable than most children of the same age.

Infant E

Lastly, we present the case of a well - developed, healthy infant who, subsequent to a major trauma, displayed not only signs of a greatly heightened tension level, but also the phenomenon of regression in one area of instinctual gratification.

E is one of the babies in our group who were tested serially throughout the first year of life, beginning at the age of 10 weeks. He lived with his natural parents and received competent and affectionate care in a stable family throughout his life. With the exception of a brief period of colic in infancy, and an occasional bout of diarrhea, his physical health has been excellent. When he was examined at the ages of 10 weeks, 18 weeks, 24 weeks, 30 weeks, 35 weeks and 41 weeks respectively, he always presented himself as a moderately active, alert, well - integrated baby. Consistently, on psychological tests, he showed very little scatter. In other words, his behavior was about equally mature in all areas of functioning. From our observation, and from fairly detailed observations related by the mother, the impression was received that E was a rather excitable child, that is, one who responded to marked changes in daily routine, to new persons and to new situations, etc. , with increased activity and generally in a vigorous manner. Such periods of heightened activity and responsiveness were typically followed by fatigue; he usually appeared able to relax completely and make a good recovery from such fatigue. As appears to be the case with many infants, his oral behavior was seen to change from predominantly mouthing movements and sucking during the first 3 months, through a period during which he tended to approach objects with his mouth (rather than reaching for them with his hands and bringing them to his mouth) approximately during the 5th and 6th months. When seen at the age of 35 weeks this behavior had given way to a type of behavior often seen in infants 7 months and above, namely, he reached for objects with his hands, brought them to his mouth and bit them. At the time of this examination, test findings indicated that E performed exactly in accordance with average standards for his age except in regard to motor development which was somewhat advanced. He was then described as an active but not overly active infant who demonstrated the capacity to relax, particularly when held and fondled. He was very friendly with the examiner though relatively more responsive to the mother. He gave the impression of being an outgoing child; in describing him the examiner stated "he hits out at the world in delight as well as in anger".

When E was seen again for psychological examination at the age of 45 weeks his behavior was of a very different nature and the test results were markedly different from any obtained either previously or, as it turned out, subsequently. His behavior while under our observation on this occasion was of the kind described previously as characteristic of a heightened state of tension. He clung to the mother and cried when the examiner addressed him or when he found himself looking at her. It required a full 20 minutes to establish rapport sufficiently good to enable the child to accept toys from the examiner and to use them. His attention span, whether for activities suggested by the examiner or self-initiated ones, was exceedingly short whereas before it had always been good. He became irritable and angry at the slightest difficulty and, when angry, screamed loudly and displayed entirely aimless and at times uncoordinated movements involving the entire body and particularly the arms. For instance, when presented with a small pellet, and encountering difficulty in picking it up with his fingers, he cried loudly, waved his arms and banged the table forcefully, arched his back and altogether presented the picture of a very much younger infant in a state of rage. Yet his affective state was decidedly labile, he fluctuated from extreme anger of the kind described to apparent keen enjoyment, to apprehensiveness and to a state of whining, complaintive irritability in rapid alternation. Occasionally, especially at times when his facial expression and demeanor suggested the presence of anxiety, he brought objects to his mouth and sucked them or merely held them in his mouth but was not observed to bite them.

From the mother it was learned that E had been given a small-pox vaccination 5 days prior to the day of the psychological examination. The reaction had been severe and was accompanied by a high fever of short duration. Subsequently, that is when the fever disappeared on the second day, he showed marked behavior changes. In contrast to his usual manner he became very fussy about food, rejecting many items and being quite unstable in his likes and dislikes even during the same meal. Whereas for the last 2 months he had shown much more interest in solid foods than in the bottle, he now seemed to really enjoy and want only the bottle. Furthermore, whereas just before the vaccination and for several weeks, he had shown a great deal of biting behavior, this disappeared entirely and was replaced by a prominent tendency to either suck objects or hold them in his mouth without chewing. His demands on the mother's attention had become more intense and insistent; she particularly complained that he seemed incapable of standing even the slightest delay; "He just goes to pieces when he has to wait." Also he experienced marked sleeping difficulties; he cried as soon as he was put to bed (this had not been a problem before) and continued to scream for prolonged periods of time in spite of being given a bottle and in spite of the mother's patient attempts to soothe him by talking to him, patting, holding him, rocking him, etc. He was greatly disturbed by approaches from unfamiliar persons, often crying at sight of them unless held securely in his mother's arms. Generally his irritability and the lability of his mood were more pronounced when away from home than in the home, something that had not been observed in E before.

The formal test findings also, for the first and only time in the case of this child, suggested some disturbance in functioning. Scatter was extensive in that at the age of 45 weeks his behavior in terms of standards of maturity simultaneously was on the level of a 32 and 36 weeks old in some respects and on the level of a 48 weeks old in other respects. When seen again at the age of 56 weeks and subsequently at 14, 16, and 17 months, no behavior of the type described was noted. The test picture had returned to one suggesting a uniform rate of development and good integration. The mother reported a marked improvement in his behavior beginning about 2 weeks after the vaccination, and after a month's interval had elapsed she felt E had regained his former stability and adaptability. At some time during the 3rd week after the vaccination he changed again from sucking objects or holding them in his mouth to biting them. However, he continued to remain more eager for his bottle than he had been before the vaccination for a period of several months. It may also be mentioned that, as he returned to the biting behavior, this type of oral activity seemed to become especially prominent so that for some time almost everything he touched was brought to the mouth and bitten.

These observations have seemed of interest to us because they exemplify behavioral changes which can be understood as a primitivization of behavior persisting for several weeks after a major trauma. These were: heightened irritability, affective lability, loss in attention span, in frustration tolerance, and in neuromuscular coordination (especially in regard to fine movements) and disturbances in perceiving unfamiliar persons and at a change in surroundings. The specific changes observed in the nature of his oral activity may be regarded not so much as a manifestation of an existing tension state (although it may have been that) but perhaps as a temporary regression to less mature modes of instinctual gratification. If this change from the biting phase

to the sucking phase is considered a regression, the regression probably
served as a defense against an intolerably high state of tension engen-
dered by the severe disruption of the homeostatic state through the
vaccination.

Summary

Adequate conceptual treatment of infant behavior requires not only
suitable concepts but also factual knowledge of the behavior character-
izing the infancy period. As a step in this direction, an attempt was made
to describe certain clinical observations of infants in terms of one concept, that of changes in the level of tension. The criteria of a heightened
state of tension developed by Lewin and his associates were found applicable to the behavior of infants under stress. Changes were observed in
the following areas of functioning: posture, motility, amount of activity,
readiness to startle, respiration, circulation, purposive use of objects,
social responsiveness and attention span. Those aspects of functioning
most affected appeared to depend on the characteristics of the infant, the
nature of the stress and the severity of the tension state. Extraordinary
variability in the kind of situation which aroused tension in different
infants was noted. Case material was described to illustrate these points.

BIBLIOGRAPHY

1. Barker, R., Dembo, T., and Lewin, K. *Frustration and Regression:
   An Experiment with Young Children,* Univ. Ia. Stud. Child Welf.,
   1, 18, 1941.
2. Cattell, P., *The Measurement of Intelligence of Infants and Young
   Children,* The Psychological Corporation, New York, 1940.
3. Erikson, E. H. "Problems of Infancy and Early Childhood", *The
   Cyclopedia of Medicine, Surgery and Specialties,* F. A. Davis Co.,
   1940.
4. Escalona, S., "Feeding Disturbances in Very Young Children",
   Am. J. Orthopsychiat., XV, 1945.
5. Fenichel, O. *The Psychoanalytic Theory of Neurosis,* Norton, 1945.
6. Freud, S. *Beyond the Pleasure Principle,* Hogarth, 1933.
7. Fries, M. "Psychosomatic Relations Between Mother and Infant",
   Psychosom. Med., VI, 2, 1946.
8. Gesell, A. and Amatruda, C. S. *Developmental Diagnosis,* Hoeber,
   New York, 1947.
9. Hartmann, H., Kris, E., and Loewenstein, R. "Comments on the
   Formation of Psychic Structure", *this Annual,* II, 1946.
10. Hendrick, I., "Instinct and the Ego During Infancy", *Psa. Quart.,*
    XI, 1942.
11. Lewin, K. *A Dynamic Theory of Personality,* McGraw-Hill, 1935.
12. Ribble, M. *The Rights of Infants,* Columbia Univ. Press, 1944.
13. Ribble, M. "Disorganizing Factors of Infant Personality", *Am. J.
    Psychiat.,* XCVIII, 1941-42.
14. Spitz, R. "Anaclitic Depression", *this Annual,* II, 1946.

DREAMS IN CHILDREN OF PRESCHOOL AGE [1]

By J. LOUISE DESPERT, M.D. (New York) [2]

I. *Introduction*

The present study forms a part of a series of investigations conducted at the Payne Whitney Nursery School since 1937, in an attempt to gain an understanding of the personality development of normal preschool children. The method of approach used to collect data has been described in previous articles (18, 19). In general, it can be stated that this method makes available systematically collected data which may be analyzed at any time, both for their qualitative and quantitative meanings. This particular point needs to be emphasized, especially in relation to the collecting of dreams in young children, since a good deal of the controversy reported in the fields of psychology and psychopathology over the concept of young children's dreams relates to the methods of approach more than to the material itself.

There is growing evidence among child psychologists that all forms of mentation bear a direct relationship to the behavior of the child; that a constant interrelation and interplay exist between any human experience, and the function and patterns of behavior. At the present time it seems that one aspect of mental experience, the dream, has not yet been sufficiently and systematically studied; nor has the role that dreams play as an expression, and in the development of the personality of the young child. It is the purpose of this study to analyze a series of dreams collected in 39 children of preschool age, and attempt to define the meaning and function of dreams in the feeling and thinking experiences of young children.

1. The author wishes to acknowledge the assistance of Rita Turchioe, Ph.D., in the preparation of this manuscript. She also wishes to thank the Nursery School staff for their valued cooperation through the years: Florence Eaton, Margaret Fitchen, directors; Eleanor Lewis, Helen Ratushny, nurses; Josephine Williams, Rachel Mayo, Bertha Kozick, Elinor Conly, Sylvia Dudley, teachers.

2. From The New York Hospital and the Department of Psychiatry, Cornell University Medical College, New York.

II. Survey of the literature

There is a wealth of material in the literature of dreams which is rapidly increasing; but the literature has been, to a very large extent, concerned with dreams of adults or children over 5 years of age. Students of child psychology are divided regarding the function that dreams play in the life of the child; and in consequence, there are many theories formulated relating to this point. It could be said that there are as many concepts of the nature of dreams as there are schools of child psychology.

While the problem is a good deal more complex than such arbitrary division would imply, for purposes of convenience it is possible to divide the methods of approach into two large groups: 1) a qualitative dynamic interpretation of data on a few single cases, and 2) a quantitative evaluation of material collected on a large number of children. In the first case, one or a few children were selected, but no attempt was made systematically to collect data; rather, the object was to understand the psychodynamics of the dreams of the individual child, and to utilize such understanding to study or alter the personality adjustment of the individual child. On the other hand, quantitative studies emphasized the statistical treatment of the data obtained from large groups of children, and systematic categorizations obtained. There was an attempt to classify subject matter, age levels, social factors, and other isolated items; but dynamic and longitudinal studies, as well as investigations of the individual child's deeper emotional life, were lacking.

In reviewing the literature, the material will be presented under three headings: 1) Theories of Children's Dreams, 2) Qualitative Studies, 3) Quantitative Studies. It is acknowledged that such a classification is arbitrary, and that there is some overlapping; however, for purposes of convenience and clarification, this division is maintained.

1. Theories of Children's Dreams

While the literature on dreams in general is extensive and complex, and includes formulations of concepts about children's dreams through retrospective analysis, formulations drawn from systematic studies of actual children's dreams are considerably less in number. The outstanding theories are associated with the names of Freud, Jung, Piaget, Griffiths, Wickes, and other students of child psychology.

Freud (27) maintains that children's dreams differ from the dreams of adults in that they are fulfillment of simple, unrepressed wishes.

"The dreams of little children are often simple fulfillments of wishes, and for this reason are, as compared with the dreams of adults, by no means interesting. They present no problem to be solved, but they are invaluable as affording proof that the dream, in its inmost essence, is the fulfillment of a wish . . ."

However, Freud states in a footnote that sometimes the dreams of adults are often of a simple nature:

"It should be mentioned that young children often have more complex and obscure dreams, while, on the other hand, adults, in certain circumstances, often have dreams of a simple and infantile character. How rich in unsuspected content the dreams of children no more than four or five years of age may be is shown by the examples in my 'Analyse der Phobie eines fünfjährigen Knaben' (Jahrbuch von Bleuler-Freud, vol. i, 1909), and Jung's 'Über Konflikte der kindlichen Seele' (vol. ii, 1910)."

In the main, Freud looks upon the child's dream as one in which the manifest and latent contents are the same, and principally differs from that of the adult by plainly representing the fulfillment of an ungratified desire.

While the analyses of adults' dreams in the writings of Freud include a large number of childhood dreams reconstructed, recalled, or relived by the patients and are, therefore, subject to retrospective falsifications, it is interesting to note that a comparatively small percentage of Freud's total writings is devoted to the problem of actual children's dreams. As is well known, Freud was the first to bring out the importance of the dream as material for analysis in the resolving of neuroses. Still more significantly, he emphasized the role of the dream as a major part of the total human experience; with the advent of this recognition, the dream gained admission into psychological studies.

In his analysis of a phobia in a 5-year-old boy (26), Freud introduced several symbols which were later to be widely recognized as significant in the dream life of the child.

Many child psychologists have accepted Freud's concepts of children's dreams in their entirety, and have formulated theories which can be considered only slight modifications of Freud's own. For instance, Thom (62) points out that children's dreams are frequently the overt expression of ungratified wishes. He describes such dreams as being highly pleasurable; so that there is a tendency for the child to delight in describing them, and to even talk of his dreams as actual experiences. Jones (40) follows Freud closely: To him, the unfulfilled desire is the main content of children's dreams, and this desire has not undergone repression. Anna Freud (25) states that many of the children's dreams are rather simple of interpretation because of the lack of complex symbols; however, some of them do not appear as simple as would be implied by Freud. For Coriat (16, 17), the latent content of children's dreams is synonymous with manifest content. He follows Freud in asserting that children's dreams are, in their essence, fulfillment of a wish.

A similar stand is taken by Wickes (65), who holds that children's dreams are simple and contain very few complex details; "They have often a naivete in a way in which they hand out a secret." Children's dreams are reported as being characteristically vivid and simple, and projecting the child's daytime problems in the child's unconscious.

Gutheil (32) carefully reviews the various psychological schools in relation to dream interpretation. In the case of children's dreams, his stand is that they are "in most cases, qualified for analytical interpretation. We can see in children's dreams their emotions of jealousy, love, ambition, a feeling of inferiority, and so on, in full bloom." A footnote indicates, however, that the interpretation should not be given to the child as is the case with the adult. To Gutheil, the dream serves as an index of the child's conflicts, and as an aid in orientation of the therapy. He also reports that death wishes toward relatives are often activated by the death of close relatives; and that children's dreams frequently reveal death wishes, owing to their incomplete comprehension of the actual reality of death which, to them, is only being absent.

While acknowledging the element of wish fulfillment in children's dreams, many authors point out that some other factors are in operation; however, there is much divergence as to the identity of these factors and the role they play in the dreams. Melanie Klein (44) postulates that besides wishes, which are always present, there are also expressed guilt feelings related to these wishes. This sense of guilt originates in the superego and, even in the most manifest of wishes, is a latent expression.

Grotjahn reports that dreams occur in the first year of life; and that before the age of 5, children generally are not able to report reliably their dream experiences. In his "Dream Observations in a Two-year, four-months-old Baby," (31) he emphasizes that although children's dreams contain elements of wish fulfillment they are, nevertheless, not completely without problems. He further states that "... in children, play, fantasies and dreams are very closely related to each other, and that what in an adult would be called hallucinations may be called vivid visual imaginations, very characteristic of infant thinking, and if such fantasied, hallucinatory form of memory is observed in a sleeping child it may be called a dream."

The child's mode of thinking is closely linked with the nature of dreams in the explanation offered by Jung (41):

"... the state of infantile thinking in the child's psychic life, as well as in dreams, is nothing but a re-echo of the prehistoric and the ancient."

It is not clear on what basis—clinical or purely hypothetical—but Jung's formulation is that the cosmic dream is commonly found in childhood, and characteristic of children's thinking: "The naive man of antiquity saw in the sun the great Father of the heaven and the earth, and in the moon the fruitful good Mother... Thus arose an idea of the universe which was not only very far from reality, but was one which corresponded wholly to subjective phantasies. We know, from our own experience, this state of mind. It is an infantile stage. To a child the moon is a man or a face or a shepherd of the stars... As we learn through Freud, the dream shows a similar type... The Dream, according to this conception might also be described as *the substitute of the infantile scene, changed through transference into the recent scene.*

"The infantile scene cannot carry through its revival; it must be satisfied with its return as a dream. From this conception of the historical side of regression, it follows consequently that the modes of conclusion of the dream, in so far as one may speak of them, must show at the same time an analogous and infantile character. This is truly the case, as experience has abundantly shown, so that today every one who is familiar with the subject of dream analysis confirms Freud's proposition that *dreams are a piece of the conquered life of the childish soul.* Inasmuch as the childish psychic life is undeniably of an archaic type, this characteristic belongs to the dream in quite an unusual degree." (41)

Piaget explains dreams in terms of the thought processes of the child, which he has studied extensively. He states (55) that young children identify thought with their dreams. He cites several examples of children who believed that thought and dreams have an identical origin. "In considering the origin of the dream we found two types of answer co-existing in the majority of children. First are those who offer no real explanation or whose explanations are simply elaborated from their ideas on the substance of the dream. For example, a child will say the dream 'comes from the room', all of which statements amount to much the same."

Reality for the child is so colored by his subjective experiences that such mental activities as dreams and thought are believed by him to originate in external objects. In compliance with this hypothesis of child's thinking, Piaget describes three stages of the origin of dreams: First, the child conceives of his dreams as pictures of air or light which appear before his eyes from the external world, so that anyone can see the dream come and go. At a later stage, the dream is thought to originate from an internal object such as the head or the stomach before it appears in the outside environment. At the last stage, the dream is believed to originate first in the eye and then in the head.

Piaget has been more interested in the meaning of the dream to the child, and in the origin and nature of the dream as conceived by the child rather than in the subject matter of the dream, and its significance in the emotional life of the child.

In her extensive study on the imagination of 5-year-old children, Griffiths (30) offers an interesting theory regarding the part which imagination plays in the child's thinking. Like other investigators she notes that the dreams of 5-year-olds are often of a simple nature, with little or no disguise of the dream motivation. She makes a unique contribution in that, prior to Grotjahn, she demonstrates that a similar pattern shapes the dreams, images, play activities, and ideas of the children studied. Even in the dream itself there is seen, according to her, a development of a theme throughout the series of dreams collected from the same child.

For Griffiths, the dream is the lowest level at which thought functions. It is dynamic in that it reflects present experience in its content, and expresses problems to be solved in the future—problems which are at first shaped by fantasies, and later incorporated in deliberate thought and direct action. As a postulate of the function of the child's dream in thinking, she evolves the hypothesis of different levels of thought. In adult life they can often be distinguished; the direct energy consuming type of thinking, and the more or less unconscious type of thought. The latter type is valuable, in that it frequently helps in bringing about the solution of a problem which could not have been achieved by the direct, logical thinking alone.

Owing to the limited amount of mental energy which any individual has at his disposal at any one time, the amount of concentrated attention involved in thinking processes varies from a high degree of concentration and awareness to the lowest degree possible. This would be even more so in the case of the child, where there would be not only less energy available than in the case of an adult, but also less experience in the use of this limited energy. Griffiths further observes that in the young child, there are more periods during which concentration is low and there is a continual shifting from one level to the other. It is in the dream that the attention is most dispersed, but the mind is active nevertheless. The daydream and the imaginative daytime activities of the children are intermediate between the dream where the lowest degree of attention obtains, and the logical and direct thinking where the contact with reality and consciousness is highest and the concentration is greatest. She points out that so much of the child's activities are of the fantasy type, that it is the characteristic mode of thinking for the child.

Griffiths also points out that the various stages of thinking cannot be separated in reality but that they operate in an interrelated way, one reacting upon the other. The nature of the fantasies is such that they are not altogether undirected, but rather governed by laws which direct the flow of imaginative thought in an unconscious way; and the origin of such thought may be found in deep, underlying emotional factors.

Other hypotheses regarding children's dreams are based on systematic investigations, among which are found the studies of Jersild (37), and Jersild, Markey and Jersild (38). The latter authors have analyzed findings obtained by interview and questionnaire methods, and they conclude that the dream content of the children studied is related to the children's everyday waking life. Moreover, children's dreams seem to be closely allied with their fears, as these authors have found that the children formulated the same themes in reporting their fears and their dreams.

Foster and Anderson (24), in their study of unpleasant dreams of children, agree with Jersild, Markey and Jersild by emphasizing that the experiences of the preceding day have a determining influence in shaping the type of dream experience. The contents of the dreams come most often from such experiences, especially those which are exciting or emotionally colored. According to these authors, this element of excitation and emotional tension could account for the vivid re-experiencing in the dream of past events which have taken place long ago in the child's life.

The significance of the child's everyday experiences was recognized by Blanchard (10) as an explanation for the motivation of children's dreams. However, the author points out that the method used in the study of motivation dealt with manifest content only. The latter point is of special importance, since the majority of the children studied were between six and eighteen years of age. Wish fulfillment does not seem to be so universal as reported in the studies of Freud and his followers, and sex does not appear openly in the motivation of the dreams; however, the author points out that this may be due to the deficiency of the method which did not analyze the latent content of the dream. There is a close relation between the motives, as obtained through two different sources: the child's own associations, and the information obtained by means of social histories and psychiatric studies.

Kimmins (42) held that the child at 5 still confuses dreaming with waking fantasy elements, that excerpts of conscious waking life are transplanted to the unconscious dream life. The dreams of young children studied were vivid and seemed very real, lacking in the characteristics of fantasy and unreality, and the dreams were frequently reported as actual happenings. The author pointed out that a certain characteristic of a constant nature was easily recognized in a series of dreams of the same child, regardless of the seemingly diversified details which each dream might have contained. This qualifying characteristic can be used as an indication of the child's chief interest, and can also afford a means for probing the child's mental life.

It is maintained by Kimmins that the dream may suggest the presence of repressed material in the unconscious. This concept was also formulated by Willoughby (67) who finds that some dreams function as a means of releasing the libido, and that the tension of fixated affect is abreacted through the dream.

In reference to this function of the dream and its relation to the mechanism of repression, Anderson (3) comments on a nightmare experienced by a girl of 2 years, 8 months, who had an intense fear of black dogs. His explanation is that the nightmare functioned as an outlet for an inhibited emotional response of the preceding day. With inhibitions released during sleep, the emotional response reappeared and its intensity was such that the child awakened from her sleep in terror. Anderson further defines the nightmare as a means of reconditioning the child to an original fear of dogs. The restimulation of the fear by the dream was of such intensity that the fear reaction lingered for a period of several months.

It is important to emphasize that apart from the few actual dreams of children under 5 (3, 10, 26, 31), the formulation of concepts on dreams was made from analyses of dreams in adults and older children.

2. Qualitative Studies

In surveying the literature on children's dreams, it is found that a large number of child psychology studies include reports on dreams of one child or a very small number of children, which are given as illustrations and exemplifications of the authors' psychological theories. These authors kept rather detailed notes of a biographical nature on their own children; or, in some cases, on an individual child with whom the author had some contact. Thus, Preyer (57) reported on his own son; Stern (60), on his three children; and Freud (27), on his own and several other children.

Preyer (57) in his studies of children's fears reports on the case of his 4-year-old son who had a marked fear of pigs, a fear which he carried over into his dreams. At night, he would frequently cry out in fear that the pig would bite him. The dreams seemed so vivid to the child that he behaved as if the animal was actually there, and could not be convinced that it was not. Previously, this child had an intense fear of dogs from which he was beginning to recover; and the author emphasized that the child had never been bitten by a dog, neither had he seen another child bitten so far as could be determined.

From the observations on his own children, Stern (60) concludes that the phenomenon of dreaming goes back to the child's first year, since about this time an infant may give indications that he is dreaming when he screams and makes significant movements. He points out, however, that the child very seldom reports his dreams verbally before the 5th year, since he has difficulty in distinguishing between reality and dream before that age. He considers the experiences of the previous day as probably the most important factors affecting the nature of the dream, and gives examples to support this theory; but he does not adduce any hypothesis with regard to the function and significance of the dream.

Freud cites some dreams of his own children, and of children with whom he was well-acquainted, in support of his theory that little children's dreams are nothing more than simple wish fulfillments. In his *Interpretation of Dreams* (27) he presents two dreams of his daughter's at the respective ages of 8½ and 3¼, both of which the child related to him. There is also a report on an observed dream of his daughter's at 19 months. Four other dreams are reported, the children being: Freud's 8-year-old son, his 22-months-old nephew, a 5¼-year-old boy, and an 8-year-old girl. All of these dreams were selected as illustrations of the wish fulfillment character of each, as well as the relative simplicity of the symbolic expression embodied in them. A dream of Freud's nephew, little Herman, under 2 years old (about cherries) is recalled (27).

Von Hug-Hellmuth (64) observes that the infant dreams during the first year of life, as demonstrated by the occurrence of well-defined movements and smiles or loud laughter which are observed in sleeping infants. One such dream is reported by the author about a little girl just under 1 year of age, who had been in the country spending most of the day splashing in the water. The following night, she was observed to make identical splashing movements in her sleep.

Anderson (3) reports on a little girl who at 1 year, 9 months, developed a fear of dogs. The fear was focused particularly on black Scotch terriers, or dogs of similar small size. The author believes that it was originally a black terrier that had precipitated the fear. After the family moved to the city, the child did not come in contact with Scotch terriers, and showed no fear reaction to dogs or other animals. Approximately a year later, when the child was 2 years, 8 months, a black Scotch terrier jumped and snapped at the child who, at the time, did not show any indication of excitement. However, on the following night, the child had a night terror in which she cried out in her sleep: "Mamma, I don't like little black dogs." Following this night terror, the child again evinced a fear of dogs which lasted 3½ years.

Anderson uses this example to point out that the night terror had the effect of reconditioning the fear reaction. He looks upon the dream as a delayed response to the restimulation; thus, acting as a factor in the reconditioning process. That the dream acted as a means of releasing the inhibited emotional response is in agreement with the Freudian concepts of inhibition, repression, and release of affect in dreams of adults.

Frances Wickes devotes the last two chapters of her book, *The Inner World of Childhood* (65), to the dreams of children. They are respectively entitled: "Dreams", and "A Correlation of Dream and Phantasy Material". In accordance with her general approach to the study of children's problems, she finds a close relation between the problems of the parents, and their expression in the emotional life and activities of the children. She expresses some concern about "the danger of turning the interest of the child back into the realm of the unconscious" by investigating children's dreams along scientific lines. In the child, unlike the adult, too great a self-consciousness may develop as a result of emphasis on his fantasy life. The dreams reported by Wickes are, for the most part, reconstructed childhood dreams from older children or adolescent patients. Some, however, are actual dreams of relatively young children; such as, the cases of a 10-year-old girl, an 8-year-old girl, a 12-year-old boy, a 7-year-old boy, a 6-year-old girl, a 9-year-old girl, and a 13-year-old girl. In the majority of cases, however, actual dreams of children are referred to—not by sex and age—but under the general heading of "the child"; and children under 5 years of age are not mentioned.

Wickes reports a frequent occurrence of "fear" and "cruelty" symbols in children's dreams; and contrary to the observation of Jung (41), she finds that dreams with cosmic symbols are not common. However, she reports that in children as well as in adults, the dream may contain "important messages from the collective unconscious", and cites several examples of symbols of "fate" in the dreams of children over 8 years of age. She emphasizes the carefully-guarded secret character of these dreams. Illustrations of content as found in children's dreams include the following: a great beast, a huge fish, a snake, a lobster which "grew and grew", a sleek gray cat, bears, apes, worms, dismembering animals, knocked out teeth, a tidal wave, a big black hole "that grew bigger and bigger", a devil, and people characterized by a variety of distorted features, such as: a woman "who had the feet of a man", tall women, "taller than the houses and taller than the trees...", etc.

In the final chapter, Wickes establishes a close correlation between the material of dream and fantasy in the child, and indicates that the dream material often reveals a conflict and gives a "glimpse of the way in which the underground forces are at work undermining the life of conscious adaptation". The dream material is also taken by the author as an index of possible dangers attached to repression in the conscious life, or as an index of the need for changes in the psychological approach to a child's problem. The dreams of a 10-year-old girl are cited and brought in comparison with her written compositions. The correlation between the two tpyes of material may be one of analogy, or of contrast.

For Wickes, analytical procedure is very different than that used with the adult, in that the symbolism of dreams is for the most part left untouched, since it is her feeling that such symbolism is beyond the range of the child's apprehension. Nevertheless, dreams are used by Wickes as material for psychoanalytical treatment of children's neurotic difficulties.

Anna Freud and Melanie Klein use children's dreams for the same purpose, but their approach is different from that of Wickes. Anna Freud (25) analyzes the dreams and daydreams of several children, ranging from 6 to 11 years. The dream content is treated very much as would dream content in adults:

"... in dream interpretation we have a field in which nothing new is to be learned by the application of adult to child analysis. The child dreams neither more nor less than the adult in analysis; as in everyone, the clarity or incomprehensibility of the dream content depends upon the strength of the resistance. The dreams of children are certainly easier to interpret, even if in the analysis they are not always as simple as the examples given in *The Interpretation of Dreams* (Freud)."

Melanie Klein (44) uses play technique in the treatment of children's neuroses. Several dreams of young neurotic children are discussed. According to this author, neurotic children unable to tolerate reality, however denying it, project the frustrations which arise out of the oedipus situation into dreams and daydreams, the analyses of which serve both to reveal the conflict and help to resolve it. Since her purpose in the analysis of the dream is primarily a therapeutic one, a systematic collecting of data on young children's dreams does not attain. She indicates that the approach in child analysis must be different from that of the analysis of adults; and points out that there is a close relation between dreams, daydreams, and the fantasies in the play activities of young children. Indeed, the dream often repeats the material of fantasy: "Very often children will express in their play the same thing that they have just been telling us in a dream, or will bring associations to a dream in the play which succeeds it. For play is the child's most important medium of expression." Commenting on the significance of several dreams in young children, Klein states in a footnote:

"My analysis of very young children's dreams in general has shown me that in them, no less than in play, there are always present not only wishes but counter-tendencies coming from the superego, and that even in the simplest wish-dreams the sense of guilt is operative in a latent way." (44)

Isaac's conception of dreams in young children is best presented in her condensed statement: "The child dreams of fierce animals eating him up, of giants and ogres, of huge engines running over him, and does not himself know that the fear of his father's punishments and his mother's anger is hidden behind these pictures." (35) She links all fears of biting animals with the child's own biting impulses at the mother's breast, and reports an observation of a boy of fourteen months who woke up in "frantic fear" that a white rabbit was going to bite him. She reports that these night terrors are common during the second and third year, but may also be noted earlier.

Observations on the dream made by Piaget (55, 56) are incidental to his studies on the thought function in children. His reports are concerned with isolated examples; dynamic motivation, age references, and other behavioristic data are lacking.

Grotjahn (31) reports on several dreams observed in a baby of 2 years, 4 months. These dreams seem to have been stimulated by events of the previous day, which had incited "... strong and strange emotions which he (the child) could not work through during the excitement and rapidity of reality and which consequently he had to repeat and work through more completely in his dreams."

Rivers (58) had previously expressed a similar conception with regard to the function of dreams of adults; namely, that of serving to resolve a conflict.

As is evident from the brief presentation of literature given above, qualitative studies have been based on a few instances of actual dreams of one or several children whose biographical backgrounds, although not reported, were well known to the authors. As a rule, the findings were generalized and served as the basis for broad formulations about the function and significance of dreaming in children. Furthermore, the interest in children's dreams were incidental to the more general interest in, and formulation of dream concepts as applied to adults.

3. Quantitative Studies

In attempting to investigate some of the problems which could not be considered in qualitative studies, several writers have collected data on a large number of children by means of slightly varying methods, all of which had a common statistical denominator. In this group, the more representative studies are those of Kimmins (42), Blanchard (10), Jersild, Markey and Jersild (38), Foster and Anderson (24), and Griffiths (30).

Kimmins, as Chief Inspector of Schools in 1920, collected the dreams of 5,600 children, ranging in age from 5 to 16. The youngest group consisted of 150 children of 5, 6, and 7 years. The dreams of the younger children were related individually to "skilled observers", while observations in the older children were recorded in response to the request: Write a true and full account of the last dream you can remember; state your age; and also say about how long ago you had the dream you have described. The children attended grade schools, industrial schools, and schools for the blind and deaf. Kimmins reported that children delight in telling about their dreams; that the type of dream differs from year to year; that the majority of children's dreams are of the wish fulfillment type, but that there are some which cannot be included in the category; and finally, that the maximum number of dreams are noted at the 12-, 13-year-old level. Further observations were to the effect that the younger children's dreams are much simpler than those of the older ones; also, that the children's physical health, as well as the events of the previous day, influenced the dream experienced by the child.

Blanchard (10) in 1926 reported on a study, the object of which was to determine the content and motivation of dreams in 230 of the 300 children under 18 years of age admitted at a child guidance clinic. All had been in need of diagnosis and treatment. The data were obtained from a single clinical interview in each case. There is noted a slightly greater frequency of dreams, as reported by children over 6. Statistically, the difference is considered significant; but the author feels that while children over 6 tended to report more dreams than children under that age, it is possible that if another method had been used—which did not rely so much on verbal expression—the difference might not have been found. There was no significant difference with regard to the relation between mental age and frequency of dream. This is in contrast to a report by Jersild, Markey and Jersild (38) that children of an I. Q. of over 120 appeared to have fewer dreams than children of a lower I. Q.

Reporting on the subject matter of 315 dreams of the 189 dreamers who gave positive answers, Blanchard emphasizes that dreams about parents are the most frequent. The death wish toward the parents, which is given a significant place in psychoanalytical writings, appears only in 4 of the 48 parent dreams, although 8 more dreams which reported the parents as "gone away" may also be considered in this group. The usual dream picture of the parents places them in a pleasant role.

Next to the parents, animals are the most frequent subjects. The animals are all contemporaneous, the most popular being lions, tigers, bears, apes and snakes. Many of the children traced their dreams to some unpleasant experience with an animal, or to thrilling situations in movies or stories. The large majority of animal dreams were those in which a definite fear element was present.

The subject matter of dreams was analyzed in relation to the chronological age and mental age of the dreamer, and very little significant differences were found when the test of validity was applied. However, there was a relative decrease in "parent" dreams in the period from 6 to 14. There was also an increase in play as subject matter between the ages of 6 and 16, which might be considered significant; but "the only figures which withstand the test sufficiently to seem of almost certain significance are those showing an increase in dreams of death between 6 and 14 years of age".

The largest number of dreams expressed wishes or fears, with a slight predominance of wish fulfillment. Sex did not appear openly in the subject matter of the dreams, but the finding is interpreted as probably reflecting the deficiency of the method for analyzing latent dream content.

Jersild, Markey and Jersild (38) conducted a systematic study of children's dreams as part of a study of the fears, wishes, likes, dislikes, pleasant, and unpleasant memories in children. Their subjects were 400 children, 25 boys and 25 girls at each level, from 5 to 13 years of age. The interview method was applied, with questions relating specifically to the subject of dreams. According to the authors, dreams appeared "to cover nearly all the events which occur to individuals during their waking moments". The element of wish fulfillment, while closely related to the waking life of the child, is not very prominent and it would be

"justifiable to say that dreams are a reflection of children's fears since a large number of dreams contain the same themes that children report when they tell about their fears. The dreams, for example, concerning supernatural creatures, mysterious events, or of dreams dealing with physical danger, activities of feared criminals, robbers, kidnappers, and the like, and concerning misfortune befalling self and others, constitute a decidedly large proportion of the dreams reported by children in answer to an unqualified question on dreams."

The "good" dreams dealt chiefly with finding, acquiring, receiving toys, food, clothes, money and pets (18.6 per cent) and with amusements, travel and play (18.6 per cent). There were also children who reported they had had no "good" dreams or could not remember any (16 per cent). The "bad" dreams dealt mostly with physical injury, falling, being chased, kidnapped, and with fires and supernatural creatures. Only 10.2 per cent of the children said they had had no "bad" dreams or could not remember them. Recurrent dreams which were recorded fell into the following categories: unpleasant dreams 163, pleasant 67, and uncertain 28, which indicates a large predominance of unpleasant dreams as recurrent.

There was no significant age difference in the relative frequency of pleasant and unpleasant dreams. There was a slight predominance of dreams about magical happenings and the presence of supernatural beings, ghosts and bogeys, in the youngest group. However, the general similarities of dreams reported by younger and older children is more noteworthy than the differences. The youngest children more frequently reported that they had no "bad" dreams or could not remember any: 19.9 per cent at the 5-6 year old level, and 7.9 per cent at the 11-12 year level.

There were no marked differences in regard to sex of the child, and differences in mental age were present only in relation to pleasant dreams; that is to say, children with an I. Q. of 120 and above reported less pleasant dreams than the other two groups with I. Q. of 80—99 and 100—119, in which there was an equal frequency of unpleasant dreams in the more intelligent group.

The majority of the children said that they had good dreams more frequently than bad, but this claim seems to be in contradiction with other statements made by the children. Actually, when asked to report dreams (unqualified), the children described a greater number of unpleasant than pleasant dreams. The authors set forth the explanation that possibly pleasant dreams are forgotten more readily than unpleasant ones, and also that the extreme vividness in which night terrors and nightmares appear may be an important factor in eliciting future recall. They point out, however, that further research is necessary for a complete understanding of this problem.

Foster and Anderson (24) conducted a study on unpleasant dreams, using 519 children between the ages of 1 and 12 inclusive (81 children in the 1-4 age level). Each morning, during a period of 7 consecutive days, the parents answered a set of questions about possible unpleasant dreams experienced by the children during each preceding night. Some data pertaining to the family set up and sleeping conditions were also collected.

In the 1-4 age group, 43 per cent of the children are reported to have had bad dreams. However, the criterion used as evidence of bad dreams is questionable, since the majority of the children considered as having had bad dreams were so considered because of a positive answer to the first question: "Did you hear the child cry or moan during the night?" Variations in terms of age levels are reported as significant, and the tables show the frequency of unpleasant dreams to diminish with the increase in age.

The authors found no relation between the number of siblings and the presence or absence of unpleasant dreams. On the other hand, they established a relationship between sleeping conditions and frequency of unpleasant dreams; children sleeping in a bed or in a room alone did not experience as many unpleasant dreams as others. They also report that the health of the child is a significant factor, in that children who had been ill within the 6 months prior to the investigation showed a greater frequency of unpleasant dreams. The type of illness is also commented upon, the authors suggesting that nose and throat difficulties were predominantly responsible. As to the possible factors affecting the appearance of the dreams, the events of the previous day were considered important, especially when these experiences were "exciting or emotionally toned".

A final observation is to the effect that "almost no recurrent dreams of the type that has been emphasized so much in the literature were reported. This may indicate that in young children, dreams, like waking mental states, have relatively less organizations than in older persons."

III. *Clinical data*

1. Collecting Data: Method and Comments

The records of 43 consecutive children, of 2 to 5 years of age, admitted at the Payne Whitney School were studied; and all the material relating to their dreams was analyzed. One hundred ninety dreams experienced and related by 39 children were compiled. In the records of several of the children, no material could be accepted as dreams, although some fantasies might have been related to their dreams. No material was entered as dream unless it could be ascertained that it was an actual dream experience of the child. A great many more dreams of young children, which bring additional evidence to the observations reported here, have come to the attention of the writer, but the difficulties of analyzing and integrating the total records of the children observed since 1937 compelled the writer to limit the number of cases used in this series.

There were three distinct sources for obtaining the data: individual play sessions, daily behavior notes, and reports from home. It is a common observation that young children seldom report their dreams spontaneously. It is also noted that they often respond to a direct question about their dreams by answering: "I forget," "I don't know," "I don't dream," or "I don't remember." On the other hand, under certain circumstances. they readily recount their dreams and freely elaborate upon them, as in the following illustrations:

When asked "Do these people dream?" (referring to the dolls), a 4-year-old girl stated: "Oh no, they don't go to sleep . . . they don't sleep." ("And what about you? Do you dream?") "Oh, I dream a little bit, but I don't dream very often." ("What do you dream when you dream a little bit?") "I dream about bad dreams . . . I dream about the bad witch, I dream about the wolf and the tiger, and I dream about everything like that."

The following excerpt from a play session (21) presents a slight variation in technique. The child was "pretending" that he and the physician were respectively the father and mother of two children (dolls); he was dramatizing many details of his home life, when the physician introduced the subject of the children's dreams ("... Say, do they dream ... these children?") "You ask them!" ("All right. Then I'll ask and then you answer ... you see? Tommy (name the boy had given to the boy doll) do you dream?" (laughing voice) "No." ("Oh, you don't dream, Tommy? I see. Do you have nice dreams or bad dreams?") *"He does—I dream but..."* ("Oh, you dream! What do you dream?") (Knocks of dolls) ("What do you dream?") *"I'm not gonna tell you what they dream. That means they don't dream."* (Knocks of dolls) ("Oh, that's right—he wasn't answering. But you say you dream. Are they good dreams or bad dreams that you dream?") (not audible) ("Oh, but you said you dream, before. Didn't you?"). (knocks) "What" ("What are the dreams that YOU have?") "Tommy?" (Are they nice dreams or bad dreams?") (knocks of dolls) *"Tommy has bad dreams."* ("Oh, Tommy has bad dreams. I wonder what kind of bad dreams they are?") "Ask him." As can be seen, the child was at first resistive to reporting his dreams, but the short excerpt of conversation reproduced here became the introduction to elaborating on his own dreams.

During an individual play session, a child may be play-acting a family scene with the dolls in the role of the members of the family. The same child who might have said, "I don't know," will respond actively to the question, "Do *they* dream?" when the question applies to the dolls. It could be taken for granted that when the child brings dream material, presumably related to these dolls, he uses his own dream material. Repeated experience and observation have shown that this is so. However, additional evidence is provided by the child himself; having started with the dreams of the members of the family (his own), the child leads spontaneously to his own dreams or, interchangeably, talks about his dreams and the dreams of the dolls in the roles assigned by him. This is a process of "facilitation" commonly observed in the play of young children. Furthermore, a check is made on the experience by asking the child *when* the experience was taking place, what he was doing while having this experience, and how does he know that it was a dream? To these questions, he usually answers relevantly that the dream took place at night while he was asleep and that when he woke up, "it wasn't there" or the experience had ceased.

As regards the daily behavior records, a child frequently brings up fantasy material which might be interpreted as dream, but this is not entered as a dream experience if it does not comply with the requirements outlined above. On the other hand, a child may refer to a dream he has had because another child in the group has referred to his own. The reading of a story may start off spontaneous accounts of dream experiences. For instance, a teacher was reading a story about a boy flying a plane, and which turned out to be a dream. When the latter statement was read, a girl of 4 years, 9 months, volunteered: "I dreamed a witch killed me, then another witch killed him and made me alive." There was no question that this was a dream experience; especially as, in this case, it had been both reported by the child and observed by the parents that witches appeared in her nightmares, as some of the figures involved.

Similarly, reports from home were carefully checked; not only as to the information given, but also against a knowledge of the child's dream experience known through other channels. This careful checking on the sources of information, as well as on the actual emotional experience of the child, is imperative since children pass so readily from dream to fantasy material in their verbal accounts and play activities. The fact that these three categories of experiences (dream, fantasy and play) are so closely related, and interchangeably expressed, does not preclude their clear demarcation in the mind of the child.

Sometimes, with no apparent stimulus, a child may report a dream; as when a boy 4 years, 5 months, turned suddenly to his companion at lunch time and asked, "Do you have things in your room at night? Do you have things that will bite you?" The question went unanswered; but the statement about the dream tallied with checked reports by the same child on his dreams of wolves, birds, snakes, alligators, and "fishes" which might or actually did bite or eat him up.

Although a total number of 190 dreams were collected on 39 children, and an effort was made to classify these dreams from the point of view of content, the study is by no means a statistical one. The numbers are too small, and the method of collecting data did not in any way conform with the requirements of a statistical approach. As can be seen from this brief presentation, there was considerable flexibility as to the sources of material, the one rigid requirement being: to be included as dream, the material was subjected to definite criteria. Thus, some "night terrors" were reported by the parents which could not be entered as dream material, because the dream content could not be ascertained. It is also obvious that under such circumstances, while content could be analyzed, observations on relative frequency could not be considered reliable.

2. Clinical Findings

There were considerable variations in the number of dreams which were collected on individual children: from no dream on 12 children (one record considered incomplete) to a maximum of 30 on 1 child. While no attempt was made to establish a relation between frequency of dreams and anxiety in young children, since the findings on frequency could not be considered statistically reliable, an observation was made to the effect that while all children who had frequent dreams were among anxious children—with the exception of one—it was not conversely true that anxious children necessarily reported dreams to any degree of frequency. The one exception was that of a 4½-year-old girl who was imaginative and apparently non-anxious, but presented transitory difficulties in adjustment at school 3 years after her discharge from Payne Whitney Nursery School. The content of her play activities was predominantly made up of oral sado-masochistic fantasies (for instance, of animals biting her or others); and she was a nail-biter. The lack of relationship between frequency of reported dreams and anxiety, however, is only apparent for it obviously refers to degrees of repression and inhibition. As a rule, the anxious children, whose records contained little or no evidence of dream material, were also inhibited in their fantasy expression as well as in their play expression, either within the group or in individual play sessions.

Dreams were more readily collected from play sessions than from any other form of records. The closer the child was to the 5-year level, the easier it was to obtain verbalization; and also to ascertain the demarcation between dream, fantasy, and realistic accounts of play activities. The younger the child, that is to say, the closer the child was to the 2-year-old level, the less verbalization was possible. However, this was not necessarily a hindrance in obtaining dream material; for while the 2-year-old may be unable to give a relevant account of his dreams by means of words, he is often able to dramatize dream content and clearly indicate that such action took place during the night while he was sleeping. For instance, in individual play sessions a little girl of 2 threw on the floor several times the baby doll, which she called by the name of a recently born baby brother, with marked emotional display and screaming. Whenever asked when these things happened, she would put her head on the doll pillow, close her eyes and say, "Sleep." Coincidentally, reports from home indicated great agitation and screaming during her sleep. ("No! Go away!...") (also the baby's name). As is usually the case, her fantasies as well as her play activities carried the same theme of hostile attitude and wish for destruction of the baby brother.

From the point of view of content, the dreams were classified under three headings: human beings, animals, and inanimate objects. This classification, established for purposes of convenience, is avowedly arbitrary; and there is considerable overlapping: one dream may include one or several of the categories, the dominant motive being the determinant factor for classification. Thus, it was noted that in the total number of 39 children with complete records, there were 75 dreams with human beings as predominant motives (43 from home reports and daily behavior records, and 32 from individual play sessions); 55 with animals (35 from home reports and daily behavior records, and 20 from individual play sessions); and finally, 60 dreams with inanimate objects (29 from home reports and daily behavior records, and 31 from individual play sessions).

Human motives were, in part, represented by parents in benevolent roles; such as saving the child from a painful situation, or providing him with some form of satisfaction, predominantly oral. Following are illustrations of these two trends:

A girl of 3 years, 10 months, recounted an anxiety dream in which a lion appeared in the room to eat her up. A policeman came and scolded her, and finally "My mother came in and put me right in the other room." ("Why did your mommy put you in the other room?") " 'Cause, 'cause, 'cause, 'cause the lion didn't like me, so that's why she did it." The home report indicates that the child had screamed that night, and that the mother had taken her to her bed.

A girl of 4 years, 9 months, gave the following dream: "Once I dreamed my daddy had a birthday cake, and it was covered with ice cream, and I ate it." It is significant that parents do not appear directly in hostile, aggressive or destructive roles. This, however, is obviously the effect of repression; since in the course of fantasying, elaborating, associating or play acting, children very often link the parents in the dreams with fearful animals, about which more will be reported later.

A boy of 4 years, 6 months, who in his daily behavior was mildly inhibited and insecure, reported dreams in which "big bad bears" ate him up; and immediately dramatized the bear as doing the destructive things that he, himself as the father, was engaged in doing in the play session. The identification was clear, and was later confirmed by his spontaneous defensive statement that it wasn't the father who did all these things but the bear. Elsewhere in his record there are numerous identifications of the father with powerful destructive animals, bears recurring frequently in this role; and hostility toward the father, who was estranged from his family, was frequently expressed.

People, exclusive of parents, were most frequently placed in fearful roles; and in several cases, it was also made spontaneously clear by the child that animals were identified with people. For instance, a boy of 5 years, 2 months, had been in the habit of asking at bed time that the light be left on in his room, and that someone be nearby. Once when his teacher was visiting and he was being put to bed, his mother reported on the boy's "bad mannils" which frightened him. When his teacher asked if they were animals, he answered, "No, people." When she asked if they were as big as she was, he shouted, "No, as big as this house!" He further commented that they were "all black". This illustration is fairly representative of the role taken by people in children's dreams; they are frequently destructive, superhuman in size and power, and sometimes supernatural. In the latter category belong ghosts and witches which appear in the third and fourth year, especially if the child has become acquainted with fairy tales, in his contact with older children or adults. It is a matter of speculation what form their dreams would take if 3-, 4-, and 5-year-olds were completely cut off from folklore and fairy tale stories. Undoubtedly, some other forms would serve the same purpose. It is apparent that the affective structure is the same, whether animals (realistic or otherwise) or supernatural beings are involved.

A girl of 4 years, 11 months, when asked about her dreams, stated: "I dream only the kind of dreams that I hate ... oh, the bad old things ... I don't know ... I said they were bad old things ... they just do everything ... things that make people die ... I dream about an old woman sticking people's eyes ... with an umbrella ... I can't think of any good dreams." During a later play session, she indicated that she had a "nice dream" on the previous night; however, this dream was almost identical with an anxiety dream which she had reported earlier about Snow White and the poisonous apple. On this date, when stamping the dream as "nice", she specified: "I like the happy part ... it's the part when the dwarfs went and Snow White slept on the dwarf's bed."

A girl of 4 years, 8 months, referring to the dolls, reported: "They dream BAD dreams ... they just dream BAD dreams." ("About what?") "Oh, they dream people are killing them, and you know ... they're killing them, and there's a war and they have to get cut ..." ("They dream all that? And what do you dream?") "I just dream things in my bed at night ... One day, I dreamed this thing was killing me, you know ..."

While a mere enumeration of human subjects does not necessarily represent a true and inclusive picture, it may serve to illustrate the variety of motives found in young children's dreams:

A girl of 3 years, 10 months, reported in her dreams: bad men, Santa Claus, policemen, a witch policeman, and a "witch bride". A boy of 4 years, 6 months, related dreams about a doctor in a destructive role, an older boy (unrelated to him) also in a destructive role, and Santa Claus. A boy of 3 years, 3 months, gave the following human motives: a giant, a clown, a cannibal, all in destructive roles (eating and biting); God playing a part in a simple wish fulfillment dream; his father being eaten by a cannibal in one dream, and in another, having his leg eaten by the cannibal. (The mother had a similar fate in one dream.)

Another illustration is that of a girl of 4 years, 6 months: She dreamed about "my new baby ... not the one that was killed." (She had a newborn baby sister); also of the baby being fed by the mother; of "two men with wooden heads" whom she feared because of their "funny faces" and from whom she hid behind her father; she also dreamed of Santa Claus in a simple wish fulfillment dream.

Animals as motives in young children's dreams are almost always sadistic and often totally destructive. They have characteristics which are of great significance, in that while they may vary in size and shape, their activities are identical; they bite and devour the child; and they often chase him, whether as a preliminary to final destruction or as an unique goal. The records are replete with such examples, and several typical dreams are quoted for purposes of illustration.

A boy of 4 years, 5 months, at first denied that he had any dreams, called the boy doll by another name than his own, and proceeded to tell about the dreams of this boy doll. "He dreams of foxes and bears and lions... he just dreams about them but they never come in." He described these dreams as "bad dreams", and the activities of the animals as "they eat Tommy up". It is interesting that at first he had even denied that Tommy or the other dolls dreamed, stating emphatically, "I'm not gonna tell you what they dream... that means they don't dream." Shortly after, he spontaneouly said, "Tommy has bad dreams," and asked the physician to question Tommy directly about his dreams, which brought the answers reported above.

The following dream of a boy of 4 years, 7 months, is given in detail because it illustrates the method of approach in obtaining dream material as well as the interplay between actual dream material, reality testing, and awareness of the dream as a dream experience. In this case, the dream was brought spontaneously by the boy in the midst of his playing with the boy and girl dolls. Thus, he began: "One time when I was sleeping, I saw... (lowers his voice)... a sly old fox. It was real." ("A sly old fox?") "A sly old fox, and a seal too." ("And a seal?") "Yes... (with an excited voice)... yes, and when... when... when the seal come down, came down, he didn't bite me. When the fox came down, he bi... he bi... he didn't bite me. He said 'I'm going to eat you up.'" ("He did?") "I said 'I'll...,' I said 'I'll... I'll shoot you with my gun.'" ("When was that?") "It was a long time." ("Was it in the night, or during the day? When was it?") "It was in the night, during the night." ("During the night?") "Yeah." ("Were you sleeping or were you awake?") "I was sleeping." ("Was it a dream, or was it just thinking?") "... It was real." (The child obviously means that it was real *in the dream.*) ("Oh, it was real—I see.") "... And the boards on the top of the... the *boards* on the ceiling... the BOARDS..." ("What kind of boards?") "Just real... just make-believe ones." (As later ascertained, he was referring to beams at the ceiling of his room, which were "real" in his dream.) ("Make-believe ones?") "Yes, but when morning came... when morning came, there wasn't any boards." (The child gave the above account with an expression of intense anxiety.) ("When morning came, there wasn't any boards? How do you explain that?") "'Cause there wasn't any... 'cause there wasn't any. See?" ("You mean in your room?") "Yes, my room... really, in my room." ("And was that something you dreamed, or something that happened?") "It was a real one." (i. e., a real fox) ("How did you know that?") "'Cause I saw it." ("Oh, you saw it?") (with an excited voice:) "I saw it come down, and it... and it... and it talked." ("It talked?

How did it talk?") (excited voice:) "It said ... it said ... 'gr ...' for the talk ..."

Following is an enumeration of the animals reported in the dreams of a girl of 3 years, 10 months: 8 dreams of wolves; 2 dreams of a wild beast (without further clarification); and single dreams of a bear, lion, cow, police dog, rabbit, duck, monkey, elephant, and tiger; and one of "wolfers and things." The animals in the dreams of a boy of 4 years, 5 months, were: circus animals, wild animals, wild cat, lion, elephant, monkey, tiger, and a "fox head" (all motives appearing in single, non-recurring dreams.) A boy of 3 years, 1 month, reported (also in single dreams) : horses, a cat, a lion, mice.

Animals appearing frequently in other records are: dogs, horses, elephants, tigers, lions, wolves, "big bad wolves," "moisters (monsters) like bad wolves," fish and alligators. Snakes appear infrequently (single instances in the records of 2 boys and 2 girls, four-year-olds) ; and animals which also appeared only once were: mice, a beetle, lobster, seal, an ant-eater, and "dead octopuses."

In the dreams of a girl of 2 years, 8 months, there frequently appeared an owl which frightened her. The owl threatened to bite and eat her. The child, however, referred to this bird by its French name "hibou". It neatly illustrates how a child's anxiety is expressed through forms provided by his environment. This child's nurse was a middle-aged woman of French provincial origin, who was deeply imbued with the superstitions and folklore of her childhood. To her, the owl was a messenger of death, and she had carried this connotation to the child. This nurse was threatening and punitive in her handling of the child and, at the same time, intensely possessive of her. Other animals appeared in this little girl's dreams, some of them in the French language as well as with the specific superstitions arising from French provincial folklore. It was so with frogs, doves and fish. The mention of "hibou", doves, and frogs is unique in this series, but recurs frequently in the dreams of this child.

Inanimate objects in children's dreams are found in the background of human and animal activities, but they also appear as active agents. Water plays an important role; especially in the bed-wetters who frequently dream of rivers or water in other forms, such as rain, invading their room or their bed.

A boy of 3 years, 6 months, woke up one morning after having wet his bed, as was frequently the case, and proceeded to paint a picture which he brought to school. This activity, as later ascertained, had been stimulated by a dream which had awakened him. While the dream structure was relatively simple, he elaborated on a number of details in his picture. There were "trees", one of which turned out to be "an elephant"; then "a nice duck", and "some funny ducks" swimming in the "rain that's already come down," while other spots of color indicated "the rain coming down." The association with the bed wetting was made spontaneously by the child, when he identified the paint and the "rain" on his pajamas.

No fire dream was reported by any of the children, although many in the group were bed wetters. Other inanimate objects mentioned were: umbrellas which were used "to poke the eyes", houses, blood and parts of the body.

In this connection, it is interesting to note the change in the dreams of a boy, who was observed from 3 years, 7 months, to 5 years, 4 months, and was seen again at 10½ years when he had developed a delinquency problem (stealing fairly large sums of money, lying, etc.) and was doing poor work at school. While at the Payne Whitney Nursery School, he was wetting his bed almost nightly, and the reported dreams were predominantly of drowning and being eaten by fish. When seen at 10½ (the bed-wetting had then ceased) he reported terrifying dreams in which men from Mars pursued him with "queer things... They had electrical spears and electrical guns on their fingers—so when they pushed their thumb down, they put electrical shocks into anything they want" (fear of passive homosexual wishes).

A girl, who was at the Payne Whitney Nursery School from 2 years, 10 months, to 4 years, 5 months, and was seen again at 10 years, was also a bed wetter through her stay at the nursery school. Reported dreams were frequently about the river flooding her room and her bed; this theme appeared frequently with minor variations. When seen at 10 years for minor social adjustment difficulties (no enuresis), she reported a recurrent anxiety dream in which the barn of the family's country home was burning; this had been activated by a fire at her boarding school.

A boy of 8½ years (not included in the Payne Whitney Nursery School series) was brought to treatment with the presenting complaint of bed-wetting, but was also found to be a very anxious and asocial child. He reported nightmares in which fire, as the destructive agent, played an important part; he also reported earlier dreams of drowning. It would seem, therefore, that in the dreams of these bed-wetters, water and fire appear in a definite sequence.

An important characteristic of young children's dreams is their simplicity. Even when the child, in his excitement, seems to be giving a wealth of details, actually it is noted that the details are repetitions, with only minor modifications, of the essential structure. The dream of a boy 4 years, 7 months, reported above, illustrates this point. The structure of the dream itself was extremely simple; an animal ("a sly old fox") threatened to bite him and made appropriate sounds; the set-up was his room, with ceiling beams called "boards"; the action, direct, uncomplicated, took place in a set-up of minimal complexity.

Cosmic dreams are extremely rare in the series of children's dreams collected from this 2-to 5-year-old group; in three different dreams there is a brief reference to "the sky", "angels in the sky", and "the moon".

An interesting aspect of the dream life of the young child is what has been referred to, in previous publications, as *segregation of emotional experiences*. Seldom does a child report spontaneously on his dreams. Even when in the midst of experiencing a nightmare he may acknowledge the "bad dream" experience and even refer to the subject, he generally refrains from giving details, and may have "forgotten" his dream in the morning.

This is clearly brought out in the "sly old fox" dream of the boy of 4 years, 7 months, reported above. Several days prior to the recounting of his dream to the physician, the child had become restless and anxious at bedtime; he was reluctant to be left alone in his room and found many reasons to detain his mother who had become somewhat impatient: "I don't know what's come over Tommy lately—he used to sleep so well." She described the specific demands that the boy put upon her; she was to check on the ceiling to see if there was anything there, look behind the window draperies, and then set them in a certain way. This ritualistic behavior was unintelligible to the mother since the child had not indicated any fears, and had not, at any time, told his mother of his dreams. This is a general phenomenon which cannot be overemphasized, especially since so little is understood about it.

An anxious, verbal girl of 4 years, 11 months, has given a possible clue to the clarification of this segregation. Her record includes 30 dreams, most of them expressing anxiety such as monsters cutting her in pieces, eating her up, etc. Furthermore, she was a bed-wetter and reported many dreams of water—a river for the most part—invading her room and her bed. Actually, she frequently got up during the night and tried to get into her mother's bed. Once, when she reported to the writer going to her mother's bed to escape from the "monsters", she was asked: "Did you tell mommy you were scared of the monsters?" and she answered emphatically: "No—I never!" When asked "Why not?" she answered in a whisper: "I don't want her to know such a terrible thing." ("You don't? Why?") " 'Cause I just don't want her to know." (Ambivalence toward mother.)

This tendency toward segregation is a general phenomenon. The child's unreadiness to tell his parents about his dreams has been mentioned, but this is also present in a variety of situations, and the explanation for it is not always clear. For instance, a child may have elaborated freely on a dream in the course of an individual play session; yet, at some later time (either at a later session or at the end of the same session and with the same observer), he may give some indication of having "forgotten" the material previously brought out. Indeed, he may become annoyed when reminded of his earlier statements, and may even deny the whole incident as ever having been brought up by him. It would appear that the need for emotional expression and repression varies considerably in terms of time, persons, and circumstances.

While the 3-, 4-, and 5-year-olds frequently report dreams of specific animals eating them, etc., the very young child may report the fear of being eaten, etc., without mentioning a specific agent. There are several instances of 2-year-olds who, when questioned about their dreams, stated: "Chase me"... "Bite me"... "Eat me up." What they report is a frightful experience occurring during their sleep, but there is no further indication of the "how" or "who" involved in this experience. Similar statements were reported to have been made at night when they had awakened in terror. Another verbal expression tied up with nightmares of these young children is: "Hold me," which probably represents a "fear" of falling.

As indicated above, no systematic record of frequency could be made under the conditions of this study. The parents were not asked specifically to report all the dreams of their children, although they usually included such reports under the heading of *SLEEP* in the daily Home Report. However, since time relations are always indicated and the total records include reports on physical illness, it is possible to check on the relation, if any, between the occurrence of dreams and physical illness. This seems a rather important point to establish, in view of observations reported in the literature. For instance, Foster and Anderson (24), in their investigations of unpleasant dreams in a large number of children, have concluded that children who had been ill (referring particularly to upper respiratory infections) within the 6 months prior to the investigation showed a greater frequency of unpleasant dreams. The selection of such a long span of time seems arbitrary, but especially so as applied to the preschool age level. An analysis of the total records of the children in this series does not bring supportive evidence to the reported relation between physical illness and increased frequency of unpleasant dreams. Since young children seldom report their dreams spontaneously, and also since the dreams which are reported by the parents are likely to be those associated with restlessness, outcries, and other signs observable by the adult, it is very likely that more dreams were reported during a period of illness, although this would not necessarily mean an actual increase in "unpleasant dream" frequency. In contrast to the periods when a child is well, he is likely to be more closely watched during sleep when he is ill. In the present series, dreams are not reported more frequently by the parents during the children's illnesses. However, another factor needs to be considered; namely, the psychosomatic expression of anxiety as represented in particular by the tendency of some anxious and insecure children to have upper respiratory infections (20).

Another finding which is at variance with observations in the literature (3, 24, 31, 38), is the lack of relation between the dream content and the actual traumatic experiences of the child. One need only point to the type of animals which are most commonly present in the anxiety dreams of the child to note the contradiction embodied in this statement. These are not domestic animals about whom the child could have had first-hand knowledge and contact in his home life; most of them are animals with which he is not actually acquainted except through occasional visits at the zoo, and through fairy tales or the fantasies of other children and adults.

Observations were made before, during, and after traumatic episodes experienced by children of the group. The cases of two children are cited, as they bear on the point:

A boy, who was observed from 1 year, 10 months, to 4 years, 8 months, came very close to death by drowning during a summer vacation when his parents were away for the day, and he was rescued by a large dog who had been his play companion. He was resuscitated but severely shocked, and spent several days in a hospital. The reaction to this traumatic experience is of great significance: the dream content which was recorded before and after the episode did not show any conspicuous change; the drowning did not appear in any reported dream; neither did experiences associated with water symbolism, directly or indirectly. Approximately 10 months after the near-drowning experience, a spontaneous reference was made by the boy at the end of a morning spent on the roof, when the children as a group had played with water, running around naked and splashing under the hose, and he had gotten very wet. At lunch that morning, he said without apparent display of emotion, "You know, yesterday I got drowned. I drowned in the water, and my mommy saved me. She bumped me out of the water with her teeth. She bited me out of the water." A further brief reference was made 2 days later when the children as a group were speaking of their respective hospital experiences. The boy then volunteered, "I was in the hospital, too, when I drowned." The following summer, he showed a fear of water, but only for a brief period (importance of delayed reaction defense).

A 4-year-old girl was badly bitten by a dog on the forehead, cheeks, and scalp. The face injuries were cauterized but the scalp wounds had to be stitched, and the child was taken to the hospital and given an anesthetic. When she awoke from the anesthetic, her first question was, "Did daddy burn the hornet's nest?" (She had been stung twice by hornets earlier in the day.) Although the mother later reported a few nightmares of dogs "chasing her and biting off buttons" during the following period of several weeks (vacation), the child rarely mentioned the incident even to her parents. Following her return to school in the fall, approximately 2 months after the biting, there was never reported any mention of the traumatic incident although the whole staff was on the lookout for any significant reference. In individual play sessions, there was no change in the dream content; i. e., biting animals appeared, but this was at no time a dog. Throughout the whole school year the actual episode was never mentioned by the child, in spite of the fact that other children in her group occasionally brought up their own fear of dogs or their observations of dogs biting other children or their pets.

This child's reaction to a lively dog, which the mother of another child frequently brought to the school, was interesting. At first (shortly after the traumatic experience), she was cautious but tentatively patted the dog, and did not appear frightened; neither did she withdraw. (Several other children showed such an anxiety or withdrawal reaction.) In a very short while, she became friendly with this dog, although no special attempt had been made to encourage her in this direction. Approximately 6 weeks after her return to school, she was even seen copying the little girl owner of this dog in putting her hand between his jaws without display of fear. However, coincidentally, two significant developments took place; the child began to take home toys and other things which did not belong to her. (This alarmed the mother out of proportion and she referred to it as kleptomania.) The child also reacted excessively to the occasional biting of a boy in her group; at first shrinking from him and running in tears to her teacher, then taking herself to biting this boy and other children. The biting phase was short-lived and, incidentally, was as much a group manifestation as an expression of her own individual problem, but she reacted with marked anxiety when the boy of whom she was afraid began to bite himself. (An outcome of his own parents' prohibitions.) It must be added that her nurse, to whom she was strongly attached, was quite upset by the transitory biting phase at school, and made loud disparaging comments about it before the child.

While these two cases present dissimilarities, there is a tendency in both to repress the traumatic episode in the waking life, dream and fantasy medium. Since Freud, the significance of repression has been recognized in the development of neuroses, but its mode of operation and its bearing on normal emotional development is not as well-known.

The function of the dream as wish fulfillment is clearly brought out in some dreams experienced by children at the time coincident with the birth of a sibling. The dream then serves the purpose of expressing hostility and death wishes toward the unwelcome sibling without intolerable guilt feeling. The same theme is frequently noted in the dreams and fantasies of the child in his group or individual play.

An illustration is found in a case quoted above, when a child stated: "My new baby—not the one that was killed" (referring to fantasies and dreams of destruction). These dreams frequently appear also when a sibling is ill and the child fantasies the possibility of the sibling's death (death wish). A typical dream is that of a girl of 3 years, 3 months, whose younger brother was admitted to the hospital. She reported a dream in which she and her mother stopped at a red light, but her brother went on and "A truck squashed him."

Another wish-fulfillment dream, which is illustrative of positive love object relations, is found in the record of a boy of 4 years, 6 months. He was an only child; his parents were separated, and his father lived and worked in a town in the Middle West. This boy reported a dream in which he started out for his vacation at an eastern summer resort, and the train, instead of reaching the latter destination, arrived in the western city. Everytime he told of this dream, his expression was one of joyful surprise. He then added with a disappointed expression that at this point he woke up. In his play fantasies, this parental-reunion theme recurred frequently; the parents had to be together and he frequently locked the room to make sure that the father would not go out. He was also very emphatic that "the daddy and the mama have to go in the same bed." Furthermore, in accordance with a universal pattern for boys of that age range, he was frequently identified with the father.

Direct sexual references do not appear. Some productions, however, present devious references, and interpretations might be made on such a dream as the following:

A girl of 4 years, 9 months, elaborated on a dream about a man with a "made-up name" which she soon identified with her father: "He has a big nose... he always has blood coming out... and he always picks it... he put his hand right in the hole..." While this child had the habit of picking her nose, for which she was rather severely reprimanded by her parents—particularly her father—in the dream she defends herself against forbidden libidinal movements by projecting the activity on to her father. Similarly, aggression (castration) is projected in another dream about a boy in her group. "I dreamed someone pulled his finger off." Since young children occasionally refer to the genitals as finger or foot, the transfer is obvious. This little girl, incidentally, was an anxious child who was confused by rather conflicting attitudes of her parents toward sexual matters. Generally inhibited and with a rather strict disciplinarian approach, they made it a point of going about naked in their apartment in the early morning, as a concession to progressive attitudes on sex. It is highly probable that their own insecurity was reflected in the little girl's anxiety about sexual taboo, in addition to the universal pattern found at that age level.

A similar instance is found in the record of a boy of 3 years, 11 months, who reported several cannibal dreams. The dream reported here was experienced approximately 6 weeks after the birth of a younger sibling, and when the child was expressing a good deal of hostility toward the baby in fantasy and play activity. Although, at first, he was reported as being gentle and affectionate in his actual contact with the baby, (his aggression toward the baby was more directly expressed when the baby was a few months old) the dream was brought out in a play session when he elaborated on fantasies of the mother having to wear crutches. "She has a broken leg... some cannibal cut it off... He ate the daddy's foot too... A tiger came out and you know, I gave one a shot... I didn't shoot him (the cannibal)... You know where I shot him? (the tiger) I shot in his mouth syrup... with a syrup gun... I was dreaming that... at night..." There is no question that this account, which began as the expression of a fantasy, was in the last analysis a dream experience, since it was brought out several times directly as a dream, and complied with the criteria outlined above for the testing of the material as a dream experience. Incidentally, it illustrates the way in which dreams are frequently brought in by young children. The reverse is true, and an account of a dream may be a starting point for fantasy elaboration, but the demarcation between the two can generally be established with the proper technique.

During the latter part of his mother's pregnancy, this child had shown play activities which were definitely open incestuous wishes. Specifically, he would engage in excited dances with the large size mother doll which he called the "bad mother"; then he would throw the doll down and throw himself on top of the doll. He referred to these activities as dancing a jig. Several times, following these episodes, he had to void and defecate; and at one of these sessions, he moved his bowels twice. In his fantasies, the death wish toward the brother was clear: "He (the baby) never came back ... he got lost one day ..." and the father was also frequently "broken" or "smacked". The sum total of this picture indicates that the child was in the acute phase of an oedipal conflict, with all the classical features. It was then felt that the "conflict" was very freely expressed and that this would be satisfactorily resolved. At a recent check (at 10½ years of age), it was found that he had made a good adjustment, intellectually and socially.

Even from the brief sampling of reported dreams presented in this publication, it is evident that unpleasant dreams far outnumber pleasant dreams. The actual ratio of relative incidence may not be identical in *reported* dreams and in *experienced* dreams; it is possible that, as suggested by certain authors, the child recalls or more readily reports his dreams when they are unpleasant than when they are pleasant experiences. From the nature of the overwhelming number of reported anxiety dreams it seems evident, however, that dreaming for a young child serves primarily as an outlet and a means of expression for anxiety. It is also evident that the anxiety is related to the fear of being destroyed by oral incorporation, and chased for the latter or other purpose.

As regards the relation of intelligence to dream productivity, while the number of children is too small to draw definite conclusions, certain trends are noted. The 7 children who offered the largest number of dreams (8 to 30) functioned at a high intellectual level (I. Q. range from 118 to 157). However, in this series of 43 subjects there were children of equally high intellectual level who reported only a few dreams or none. On the other hand, the children with the lowest intellectual level in this series (I. Q. 100 to 110) were not among those who reported dreams freely. While there seems to be no definite relation between the two factors, it can be said that the children who dreamed more actively were not found in the group of lower intellectual level.

Recurrent dreams in the sense accepted in the literature were not found; i. e., there was no indication that a child experienced a dream in its exact reduplication over a period of time. The total dream records indicate that the dream structure for each child represented well-individualized themes; these themes tended to reappear in the dreams with slight variations, with the essential structure remaining the same. While such patterns cannot be called recurrent dreams, there is, nevertheless, a tendency toward repetition which bears a loose relation to the nature of recurrent dreams. As indicated from time to time in this publication, the theme for each child is found in the dreams, fantasies, and play activities of the individual, with variations pertaining to the specific medium of expression. In fact, it is in part the free-flowing of the symbolic forms from one medium to the other which has led to the often expressed belief that the child is unable to distinguish between his dreams and his fantasies.

In the case of 4 children in this series, who were later carefully investigated when they had developed difficulties of adjustment (4 to 6 years after they had left the school at the ages of 9 to 11), it was found that dream content shows marked changes in the course of development. This has been pointed out in relation to 2 bed-wetters referred to above (water-fire symbolism), but it was also true of the 4 children insofar as the total content of their dreams was concerned. Furthermore, they did not recall their earlier dreams, and when confronted with the early material, their reaction was either that the dreams were silly, or had not taken place. Even when the predominant affect of the dream (anxiety) presented similarities, the dream content in all 4 children had radically changed. This is not to imply that the earlier dreams were altogether repressed, but there seemed to be, at that later stage, no indication of their being at a level of consciousness which would make them readily available.

Needless to say, all observations about children's dreams reported in this study refer only to the manifest content of dreams and associations to these dreams spontaneously brought out by the children.

IV. *Discussion*

As already indicated, this series of 190 dreams collected from a group of 39 children, 2 to 5 years old, is not taken to represent an all inclusive picture of the dreams of all children. However, it can be assumed that it is fairly representative of dreams in that age group, especially if one considers that the means of collecting data were reasonably objective, and that a rather extensive knowledge of the total and dynamic picture of the child's emotional life was part of the data studied.

While it is widely recognized that a child dreams as early as the first year of his life, dream content can seldom be ascertained before his second year, coincidentally with the advent of verbal expression. Sleeplessness, restlessness, and outcries would not in themselves be sufficient evidence, as they might be only an expression of somatic discomfort; it is indeed likely that many such manifestations, also observed during the sleep of 2-year-old children, are free from meaningful and recoverable psychological content. Nevertheless, they may accompany subjective experiences which are identifiable as dreams.

The facial expression and muscular activities seem a more reliable index of the infant's psychic life during its sleep than vocal expression alone; from observations reported in the literature, it is known that dreams, for the infant, are sometimes mere reduplication of waking-hour activities which have been pleasurable to him, for instance nursing, as indicated by sucking movements and associated expression of satisfaction (smiling). Expressions of fear with correlated muscular patterns have also been reported during the second year.

A few references in the literature indicate that even animals dream, and the writer made such an observation. A cat was seen making masticatory and swallowing movements while sleeping, following which he awakened and went through the whole process of washing his face and paws; his facial expression was one of satisfaction akin to a "smile", and the sequence of events clearly indicated that he had "dreamed" about a non-existent meal which required the customary post-prandial routine.

In analyzing children's dreams in relation to the age of the subject, it is striking that the very young child (2-years-old in this series) mostly dreams of being bitten, devoured, and chased. These are the first dreams ascertainable from the child himself. What he experiences is an intense fear of being destroyed in a very specific way; he never reports, for instance, being hit, kicked, pinched, pushed, scratched, etc., all hostile manifestations which the child might have personally experienced. Furthermore, when later the agents of destruction or pursuit are named, it is clear that they are not within the realms of actual experience of the child, but are animistic and totemic. While there is a possibility of phylogenetic determination of totemic fears, it seems more likely that projection, which is historically one of the first mechanisms of defense used by the ego in the conflicts of the oral period determines the form of the threat pictured or experienced. There is no instance reported by any child of his having actually been devoured or totally destroyed in his dream, and the self-preservation instinct is always, in the end, successfully operative in dreams from which the child is not awakened in anxiety.

Melanie Klein (44) has given a provocative formulation of the dynamics of anxiety associated with oral incorporation fantasies in the young child, which also apply to the content of anxiety dreams.

"The anxiety evoked in the child by his destructive impulses takes effect, I think, in two ways. In the first place it makes him afraid of being exterminated himself by those very impulses, i. e., it relates to an internal instinctual danger; and in the second place it focuses his fears on his external object, against which his sadistic feelings are directed, as a source of danger. This fear of an object seems to have its earliest basis in external reality in the child's growing knowledge—a knowledge based on the development of his ego and a concomitant power of testing by reality—of his mother as someone who either gives or withholds gratification, and thus in his growing knowledge of the power of his object in relation to the satisfaction of his needs."

In the identification of powerful, destructive animals with the parents, it must be pointed out that the father is more frequently involved than the mother. In accordance with the thesis of oral incorporation projection this should be the reverse, since according to Melanie Klein the oral sadistic fantasies of the infant, which are at the basis of his fear of being devoured, are interpreted as the desire for "possession of the contents of his mother's breasts by sucking and scooping it out."

It is widely known that the mouth plays a preponderant role in the physiology and psychological economy of the infant. It is highly probable that, except for anal and skin reactions, all pleasurable and unpleasurable reactions of the infant are centered about the mouth, and that it is the first link to reality (through the mother) experienced by the infant. While Melanie Klein's formulation could well explain the fear of being "incorporated" by the child's own impulse to incorporate, through a mechanism of projection, this formulation could not apply to the anxiety associated with being "chased". Since this latter fear is expressed at least as often by the young child as the fear of being devoured, and obviously refers to other experiences and other dynamics, it is important to seek some interpretation for it. It appears that the excitement of "being chased" in the dream replaced the greater excitement of being threatened by one's own blocked instinctual drives. Reaction to a danger situation may bring about two solutions, fight and flight, as is now widely accepted. In the face of overwhelming danger, as would seem to be the case with threat of destruction, a feeling of total helplessness would of necessity lead to flight rather than fight. Muscular manifestations of this attempt to flight are seen in the increased muscular tonus, motor patterns of restlessness and agitation, and finally in outcries, all of which are usually observed in the anxiety dreams of young children. Indeed, these dreams often contain accounts of attempts to escape danger, not fight it, utilizing in dream and fantasy the same method of escape from an "internal danger" (libidinal frustration) as from an external one.

The sequence in which the patterns of anxiety chronologically unfold in the dreams of young children is highly significant. There is first the fear of being destroyed or chased; then unfamiliar, powerful, destructive animals are named; and finally, in response to actual traumatic experiences in the life of the child, the anxiety may be transferred to the animal which actually threatened or attacked the child, or to any painful event which actually took place. Incidentally, the latter transfer would explain the apparent contradiction found in the literature as regards the types of animals found in children's anxiety dreams. In the studies of Blanchard (10), and of Jersild, Markey and Jersild (38) it is reported that many of the children had traced their dreams to some unpleasant experience with an animal, or to the witnessing dramatic expressions in movies or stories; also, that they reflected the events of their waking life. If the children in these series (most of school age) had been studied during their early childhood years, it is highly probable that their anxiety expression would have followed a pattern similar to the one outlined in this publication.

Anxiety dreams of very young children are so closely related to the earliest manifestations of anxiety in the young child that they warrant careful, systematic investigation. Freud has referred to the process of birth as the first determinant and prototype of anxiety, and has likened this anxiety to the later developed castration anxiety which is at the basis of neurotic manifestations. The earliest anxiety manifestations appear long before the I — not I is established and any ego structure firmly defined. Of the total instinctual life of the infant, the self-preservation instinct alone seems involved and threatened in the earliest anxiety dreams recorded.

Another arresting finding in this series of dreams pertains to the earliest manifestations of anxiety in the young child that they warrant instance, that in the dreams parents appear in benevolent roles (there is not one instance of direct parental hostility toward the child); and also, that whenever hostile attitudes of the child toward the parent appear, they always do so in a disguised form. This is manifested as early as 2 years, and possibly earlier if content could be ascertained in the pre-verbal stage. The fact that parents do not appear in hostile roles, except in the identifications with powerful animals, is demonstrated through the innumerable associations readily made by the child between these destructive, powerful animals and the parents. The child, however, cannot tolerate such associations except in fantasy. This, incidentally, has probably been responsible for a good deal of the confusion pervading our knowledge of the early development of the sense of reality in the child. Another interesting aspect of repression is related to the early taboo of direct sex expression in dreams. While again, associations revealing such a taboo are readily brought out by the child in fantasy, direct references are conspicuously lacking in the dream content.

It is felt that, owing in part to the phenomenon of repression, only a very small portion of the total dream life of the child is recovered and even perhaps recoverable. The infant is closer to the unconscious state, as found during intra-uterine life, than at any other period of his life. In that state, racial symbols and expressions precede the individual consciousness, which is to develop gradually during the first years of life. The beginnings of individual consciousness are, of necessity, almost unknown and leave all possibilities open to speculation. Now and again, through the emergence in consciousness of dream material, it is possible to get a glimpse of the instinctual demands, satisfactions, frustrations and anxieties of the individual.

The dream obviously has also a protective function, and in this sense again, the repression mechanisms play a part. It serves as an outlet for the discharge of anxiety; also of aggressive impulses which would not be tolerated during the conscious state. This is emphatically brought out by the many instances found in the children's records about their unwillingness to bring out the dream material, and particularly their occasional denial that they had earlier brought out such material; this, at a time when it no longer serves a purpose of release. In the child, more so than in the adult, there is a flexibility of expression between levels of consciousness, which emphasizes this point. When the psychological economy does not warrant the bringing out of dream content in consciousness, the dream is totally repressed, or, in various instances, suppressed; in the latter case, one gets the impression of an element of deliberateness in the child's refusal to relive the experience which he has previously freely recounted.

The forms are influenced by the environment in which the child lives at the time he experienced the dream. When the 4½-year-old boy reported the "sly old fox" dream, he obviously revealed his acquaintance with fairy tales, since the expression "sly old fox" could come from no other source. The verbal framework, however, is relatively unessential, and it matters very little whether the animals portrayed in children's dreams are small or large animals, and whether biting is an intrinsic characteristic of the animals. For instance, when the 3-year-old girl feared that an owl would bite and destroy her, she obviously expressed only a fear of being bitten and destroyed, without any special consideration of the biting and destroying object.

The function of the dream which has been stressed in several psychological writings is the reliving of everyday life events. In the dreams studied by the writer, this function is not conspicuous when supercharged with affect. However, this is not to imply that everyday events are not relived by the child in the dream; it only states that there is more pressure on the part of the child to bring back to consciousness his anxiety dreams, than the reduplication of his everyday life happenings.

The wish-fulfillment function of the young child's dream has been pointed out recurrently in the clinical findings; two large categories of wishes are expressed: the simple wish-fulfillment dream which represents a desire for positive gratification, and the anxiety-charged dreams which indirectly express hostile impulses toward others, predominantly parents and siblings.

As seen from the clinical data, the child himself is never directly engaged in destructive activities in his dreams. True, among the records of several older children (4-, 5-year-olds) there are a few instances of direct aggressive expressions, but these are always *defensive*. This finding is rather puzzling in view of the fact that the dream provides an ideal medium for the expression of "forbidden" impulses. The exclusion of these manifestations reveals that some prohibitive agency must be operating in the unconscious. This is the more striking since coincidentally the child indulges in so many sadistic and destructive fantasies in his waking life (superego operative in sleep).

The analysis of the total records shows that dream symbols reflect and express the major and minor conflicts and problems of adjustment found in the conscious life of the child, and provide means of releasing the tensions associated with them. They also give valuable indications about the child's total emotional adjustment.

V. *Summary and conclusions*

A summary of the literature on dreams has been presented. The records of 43 consecutive children of 2 to 5 years of age, admitted at the Payne Whitney Nursery School, were studied and 190 dreams were collected and analyzed. The dreams were obtained from three different sources: individual play sessions, daily behavior notes, and reports from home. No material was included as dream until it had been subjected to rigid criteria. The total history of each child was well-known, with special reference to emotional adjustment. The method for obtaining dream material has been described, and the various techniques devised to overcome resistances have been illustrated.

It was found that there were considerable variations among the children in their wish and ability to report their dreams; and, on the whole, spontaneous expression was limited. Human beings and animals figured predominantly. The parents appeared in benevolent roles; but, on the other hand, were readily identified with powerful, destructive animals which threatened the child with total destruction. People other than parents were most frequently placed in fearful roles. While the animals which were engaged in biting and devouring were usually large and fearful, there were also smaller animals which engaged in the same activities, although biting was not necessarily an intrinsic characteristic of these animals. The dreams reported were predominantly anxiety dreams. Chronologically, the expression of anxiety appeared in the following sequence: the very young child (2-year-old) expressed a fear of being bitten, devoured and chased without naming the agent; later (3-, 4-, 5-year-old), devouring animals were identified. The earliest dreams of children represent a threat to the psychobiological unity of the individual. The dream life serves in bridging the racial and individual past to the present experience. It has also a protective function, and provides an outlet for the discharge of anxiety as well as of aggressive impulses, which could not be tolerated during the conscious state. Repression mechanisms are in evidence, with projection, identification, displacement, and denial predominant as the child's mechanisms of defense.

BIBLIOGRAPHY

1. Abraham, K. *Dreams and Myths,* Nerv. Ment. Dis. Pub. Co., 1913.

2. Adler, A. "On the Interpretation of Dreams", *Internat. J. Indiv. Psychol.,* II, 1936, 3—16.

3. Anderson, J. E. "Dream as a Reconditioning Process", *J. Abnorm. Soc. Psychol.,* XXII, 1926-27, 21—25.

4. Bagley, E. "Dreams during Emotional Stress", *J. Abnorm. Soc. Psychol.,* XXV, 1930, 289—292.

5. Bailey, M. E. "Midnight Thinking", *Scribner's Mag.,* 87, 1930, 611—620.

6. Barahal, H. S. "Dream Structure and Intellect", *Psychiat. Quar.,* X, 1936.

7. Baynes, H. G. "The Importance of Dream Analysis for Psychological Development", *Brit. J. Med. Psychol.,* XVI, 1936.

8. Berrien, F. K. "A Study of the Objective Dream Activity in Abnormal Children", *J. Abnorm. Soc. Psychol.,* XXX, 1935-36, 84—91.

9. Blacker, C. P. "A Patient's Dream as an Index to His Inner Life", *Guys' Hospital Reports,* 77, 1928, 219.

10. Blanchard, F. "Study of the Subject Matter and Motivation of Children's Dreams", *J. Abnorm. Soc. Psychol.,* XXI, 1926, 24—37.

11. Bodkin, A. M. "The Representation in Dream and Phantasy in Instinctive and Repressing Forces", *Brit. J. Med. Psychol.,* VII, 1927.

12. Bond, N. B. "The Psychology of Waking", *ibid.,* XXIV, 1929, 226.

13. Brill, A. A. *Psychoanalysis,* Saunders, 1922.

14. Burt, C. "Dreams and Day-dreams of a Delinquent Girl", *J. Exper. Ped.,* VI, 1921, 1—11, 66—74, 142—154, 212.

15. Cason, H. "The Night-Mare Dream", *Psychol. Mon.*, 46, 1935, 5.

16. Coriat, I. J. *The Meaning of Dreams*, Little Brown, 1905.

17. Coriat, I. J. "Some Hysterical Mechanisms in Children", *J. Abnorm. Soc. Psychol.*, IX, 1914, 2.

18. Despert, J. L. "A Method for the Study of Personality Reactions in Preschool Age Children by Means of Analysis of their Play", *Am. J. Psychol.*, IX, 1940, 17—29.

19. Despert, J. L. "Protocol of an Individual Play Session", *J. Nerv. Ment. Dis.*, XCVIII, 1943, 133—147.

20. Despert, J. L. "Emotional Factors in Some Young Children's Colds", *Med. Clinics No. Amer.* (New York Number), 603—14, May 1944.

21. Despert, J. L. "The Meaning of the Young Child's Play", *Nursery Ed. Digest*, III, 1945, 1—12.

22. Ferriere, A. "The Psychological Types Revealed by Dreams", *New Era*, VI, June, 1925, 88—90.

23. Fischer, E. von. *Kindertraum*, Julius Puttman Verlag, 1928.

24. Foster, J. C. and Anderson, J. E. "Unpleasant Dreams in Children", *Child Dev.*, VII, 1936, 77—84.

25. Freud, A. *Introduction to the Technique of Child Analysis*, Nerv. Ment. Dis. Mon., 48, 1928.

26. Freud, S. "The Analysis of a Phobia in a Five-Year-Old Boy", *Coll. Papers*, III (1909).

27. Freud, S. *The Interpretation of Dreams*, Macmillan, 1939.

28. Gordon, K. "Dreams of Orphaned Children", *J. Delinquency*, VIII, S-N 1923, 287—291.

29. Green, G. H. *The Day-Dream: A Study in Development*, Univ. London Press, 1923.

30. Griffiths, R. *A Study of Imagination in Early Childhood*, Kegan Paul, Trench, Trubner, 1935, 253—68.

31. Grotjahn, M. "Dream Observations in a Two-Year, four-months-old Baby", *Psa. Quar.*, VII, 1938, 507—513.

32. Gutheil, E. *The Language of the Dream*, Macmillan, 1939.

33. Herzberg, A. "Dreams and Character", *Character and Personality*, VIII, 1940, 323—324.

34. Hollingworth, H. *The Psychology of Thought*, Appleton, 1926.

35. Isaacs, S. *The Nursery Years*, Vanguard, 1938.

36. Isaacs, S. *Intellectual Growth in Young Children*, Routledge, 1945.

37. Jersild, A. *Child Psychology*, Prentice-Hall, 1940.

38. Jersild, Markey and Jersild. *Children's Fears, Dreams, Wishes, Day-dreams, and Likes*, Teachers College, 1933.

39. Jones, E. *On the Nightmare,* Woolf, 1931.

40. Jones, E. *Papers on Psychoanalysis,* Wm. Wood, 1938.

41. Jung, C. and Hinkle, B. *Psychology of the Unconscious,* Moffat, Ward Co., 1916.

42. Kimmins, C. W. *Children's Dreams,* Longman's Green, 1920.

43. Kimmins, C. W. *Children's Dreams, an Unexplored Land,* Allen & Unwin, 1937.

44. Klein, M. *The Psycho-Analysis of Children,* Woolf, 1937.

45. Leherer, L. "Children's Dreams", *Unsere Schule 3,* No. 4, 1933, 1–4.

46. MacKaye, D. L. "Recording Emotional Qualities", *Psychol. Clinic,* XVII, 1929, 234–248.

47. Matthew, A. V. "Dreams of Adolescence", *Progress of Ed.,* VIII, 1932, 15–21.

48. Meader, A. E. *The Dream Problem,* Nerv. Ment. Dis. Mon., 22, 1916.

49. Megroz, R. L. "Dreams in Childhood", *Contemp. Review,* 153, 1938, 458–465.

50. Megroz, R. L. *The Dream World: A Survey of the History and Mystery of Dreams,* Dutton, 1939, Chap. XVI.

51. Miles, M. B. "Banishing Bad Dreams", *Parents' Mag.,* XI, 1936, 83.

52. Pearson, G. *The Problem Pre-School Child,* Univ. Penn. Press, 1929.

53. Pearson, G. "Children's Dreams", in *The New Generation,* ed. by Calverton and Schmalhausen, Macauley, 1930.

54. Perez, B. *The First Three Years of Childhood,* Kellog, 1894.

55. Piaget, J. *The Child's Conception of the World,* Harcourt Brace, 1929.

56. Piaget, J. *The Child's Conception of Physical Causality,* Harcourt Brace, 1930.

57. Preyer, W. *The Mind of the Child, the Senses, and the Will,* Appleton, 1888.

58. Rivers, W. H. *Conflict and Dreams,* Harcourt Brace, 1923.

59. Seidler, R. "Children's Dreams", *Internat. J. Indiv. Psychol.,* II, 1936.

60. Stern, W. *The Psychology of Early Childhood,* Henry Holt, 1926.

61. Sully, J. *Studies of Childhood,* Longman's Green, 1903.

62. Thom, D. *Everyday Problems of the Everyday Child,* Appleton, 1928.

63. Varendonck, J. *The Psychology of Day-Dreams,* Allen & Unwin, 1921.

64. Von Hug-Hellmuth, H. *A Study of the Mental Life of the Child,* Nerv. Ment. Dis. Pub. Co., 1919.

65. Wickes, F. G. *The Inner World of Childhood,* Appleton-Century, 1940.

66. Wiggam, A. "A Contribution to the Data on Dream Psychology",
     Ped. Sem., XVI, 1909, 240—251.

67. Willoughby, R. R. "A Note on a Child's Dream", *J. Genet. Psychol.*
     XLII, 1933, 224—228.

68. Willoughby, R. R. "The Adaptive Aspect of Dreams", *J. Abnorm.*
     Soc. Psychol., XXIV, 1929, 104.

THE ANALYSIS OF A PHOBIC CHILD [1]

SOME PROBLEMS OF THEORY AND TECHNIQUE IN CHILD ANALYSIS

By BERTA BORNSTEIN (New York)

This paper attempts to clarify some theoretical and technical aspects of child analysis by correlating the course of treatment, the structure of the neurosis and the technique employed in the case of a phobic boy who was in analysis over a period of three years. The case was chosen for presentation:

(1) Because of the discrepancy between the clinical simplicity of the symptom and the complicated ego structure behind it;

(2) because of the unusual clearness with which the patient brought to the fore the variegated patterns of his libidinal demands;

(3) because of the patient's attempts at transitory solutions, oscillations between perversions and symptoms, and processes of new symptom formation;

(4) because the vicissitudes and stabilization of character traits could be clearly traced;

(5) and finally, because of the rare opportunity to witness during treatment the change from grappling with reality by means of pathological mechanisms, to dealing with reality in a relatively conflict-free fashion.

I

Frankie, a 5½-year-old boy of superior intelligence who was eager to learn, was brought into analysis because of a severe school phobia. He liked to play with other children and was friendly and amenable with them, but shy and withdrawn in the presence of any stranger. He became panic-stricken if his mother or nurse were out of sight. Even when left with his father in his own home, he was occasionally overwhelmed by attacks of anxiety. His phobic symptom had existed for more than 2 years.

---

1. From a series of lectures given at the Menninger Foundation, Topeka, September, 1947.

Frankie was the older of two children of intelligent middle class parents. His father was a kind man with slightly compulsive character traits. His relationship to the child was predominantly protective and had the character of friendly interest. However, he resented the tension which the child's neurotic behavior caused in the family. His reproaches were not openly directed against the boy, but against his wife whom he did not consider affectionate enough to the child. Moreover, he accused her of having surrendered Frankie's care to a nurse.

The mother reported that Frankie was a planned child, that her pregnancy had been uneventful, and that she had felt happy and contented in anticipating her first baby's arrival. The delivery was normal, the child healthy, yet the very first moment she held the baby in her arms, she had felt estranged from him. The little boy's crying had given her an uncanny and uneasy feeling. She felt quite different toward her second child, a girl.

She herself was an only daughter, between an older and a younger brother. Her own mother had not displayed any warmth toward her, but was preoccupied with the older boy. This brother was "selfish, undisciplined, queer, and insisted on obtaining whatever he craved;" she used the same words in describing her son Frankie. Just as she had lived in terror of her brother, she now lived in terror of her son. Yet, in spite of her determination not to repeat her mother's behavior, her own feeling of aloofness toward Frankie was an exact repetition of her mother's attitude toward her. She was completely unaware of the fact that her primary rejection of Frankie was her unconscious revenge on her brother; later, after Frankie's neurosis made her suffer, her identification with her mother made her devote herself exclusively to Frankie.[2] In the end, however, the child's phobic symptoms, which made her and the nurse his prisoners, discouraged her profoundly, and made her realize her defeat as a mother. Thus she became not only eager to seek therapeutic help for the child but was also ready to identify herself with the analyst. Actually, her relationship to her son changed radically during the course of the treatment.

Frankie's first disturbance, his constant screaming and crying as an infant, were incomprehensible to the mother. She was convinced that the child's reactions were caused by unsatisfactory feeding in the hospital. And it is a fact that as soon as the intervals between feeding periods were decreased, the screaming attacks became less violent and less frequent. He was a bottle-fed baby and was described as a greedy eater. Night feeding was continued for an unusually long time and when, at the age of 5½ months, the 2 a. m. feeding was stopped, the child again evidenced his discontent. For several months he continued to scream at this hour. It could not be ascertained whether the baby's crying and screaming spells were unusually violent or whether they seemed so because the parents were over-sensitive. As a matter of fact, the parents did not dare to fall asleep because of their anticipation of the baby's screaming.

---

2. She gained insight into the motivation of her attitude only during the course of the child's analysis. She then understood that her longing to find a protective substitute mother had resulted in her dependence on her son's nurse.

When Frankie was 2, it became especially difficult to put him to bed at night. Regularly, he screamed for an hour before he fell asleep, and also whenever he awoke during the night. A third screaming period occurred at the age of 4½ years and was stopped only after the nurse threatened to punish him. As we shall learn later, it was during this period that the child developed his unusually severe insomnia which subsided only in the last period of the analysis.

We were told that toilet training did not lead to any neurotic reaction. Bowel control was easily established at the age of 1. Bladder control at night was established at the age of 3. However, Frankie refused to use any bathroom outside of the home, but instead retained urine for hours.

His sister Mary was born when Frankie was 3 years and 3 months old. Upon the mother's return from the hospital he displayed marked anxiety. He grew more ill-tempered toward his mother and his coolness toward her increased to such an extent that she became disturbed and made conscious efforts to win the child's affection. Despite her strong urge to devote herself to her little daughter, she left the baby in the care of a second nurse while she and Frankie's nurse were at the boy's disposal. Thus she hoped to prevent any further cause for the boy's jealousy. Yet her concerned attention did not improve Frankie's relationship to her. He refused to let his mother touch him and reserved all the intimacies of his care for his nurse. His distrust of his mother, especially during illness, became so intense that he accepted neither medicine nor food from her. Nevertheless he insisted tyrannically on her presence at all times and had outbursts of wild aggression if she did not adhere meticulously to his demands. When she occasionally wanted to leave him, he became violent, panic-stricken, and clung to her desperately. But immediately after, when left alone with the nurse, his outburst subsided, and the tyrannical child became curiously submissive.

The mother had suffered considerably from Frankie's rejections. In his clinging attitude she began to see a sign of the child's love, and she was so deeply impressed by his fear and his need of her protection that she succumbed to his phobic arrangements.

The child's anxiety reached its first peak when he was brought to nursery school at the age of 3 years and 9 months. At that time, his sister's nurse had just left the home, and he had to share his own nurse with the baby. He went to school for only 2 days. Each time, he had to be taken home because of his wild attacks of fear and screaming, and nothing could make him return to school. A second attempt to send him to a different school was made when he was 4½. Although the mother not only accompanied him to school, but actually stayed in the classroom with him, his anxiety did not subside. After 2 weeks, this attempt also was given up.

At the time of the third attempt, the teacher noticed that Frankie observed the activities of other children with the greatest interest, that he wanted to join their play, but could not move from his mother's side. Only when he could believe his teacher's promise that his mother would not leave the room without his knowledge, was Frankie able to play with the other children. However, even then he periodically interrupted his play to check on his mother's presence. Because of the intensity and duration of the child's anxiety, analysis was advised by the school.

The analyst suggested that treatment be postponed until after a period of preparation for analysis in which the school was to co-operate with the analyst.[3] This pre-analytic phase was designed to create a conflict in the child between his symptom and reality (8). To be sure, Frankie was already suffering from an internal conflict as shown by his phobia. However, as long as his phobic demands were met, he was insulated against anxiety or its equivalent, and in this state there was no reason for him to want to overcome his phobia. By our pre-analytic scheme we hoped to produce in him insight into his need for help, without which no psychoanalytic treatment can make any progress.[4] Thus, as soon as the child showed signs of a firm positive attachment to the school, his teacher was to inform him that his mother could no longer be permitted to be present. When the child protested that he could not remain alone, he was to be told that there was a person, the analyst, who might be able to help him stay at school, and to withstand the pain of his mother's absence. This pre-analytic scheme worked just as we had planned. Frankie, conscious of his conflict and his desire for help, was brought to the analyst, who now could act as a mediator between him and the school. The analyst "persuaded" the school to extend the trial period, and to agree that his mother be permitted in the classroom. We also had to promise that his mother would be present during the analytic sessions. By this arrangement the analyst quickly became an important person for the child and the ground was prepared for a positive transference patterned after the child's relationship to his nurse—a relationship which at that time the analyst did not know in all its complexity.

The first period of Frankie's analysis was characterized by his desire for help. As long as he was in a state of anxiety, his understanding of analysis and his willingness to co-operate were remarkable.

His dramatic play during his first session led straight into his conflicts, just as in adult analysis the first dream often leads into the core of the patient's neurosis. His play revealed at once the experiences that had led to his phobia and thus betrayed the meaning of his symptom.

Frankie started his first session by building a hospital which was separated into a "lady department", a "baby department", and a "men's

3. The psychological insight of the school's authorities and teachers was of great help. Such co-operation with the analyst is not frequent and should be commended.

4. For a further discussion of the need for an introductory phase in child analysis, see Anna Freud (16).

department". In the lobby, a lonely boy of 4 was seated all by himself, on a chair placed in an elevated position. The child's father was upstairs visiting "a lady" who, he informed us, when questioned, "is sick or maybe she's got a baby, maybe—I don't know, never mind." He made the point that newborn babies and mothers were separated in this hospital. Casting himself in the roles of a doctor and a nurse, he attended to the babies in a loving way, fed and cleaned them. However, toward the end of the play, a fire broke out. All the babies were burnt to death and the boy in the lobby was also in danger. He wanted to run home, but remembered that nobody would be there. Subsequently he joined the fire department, but it was not quite clear as to whether the firemen had started the fire or put it out. Frankie announced: "Ladies, the babies are dead; maybe we can save you!" Actually only those lady patients who had no babies were rescued by him. The one whom he several times—by a slip of the tongue—had addressed as "Mommy", however, was killed in the fire. No particular attention was given to the men's department. Most of the men had died anyway.

This game, which was repeated in the analysis for many weeks, betrayed the intensity of the boy's fury against his mother and sister. He could not forgive his mother for her unfaithfulness. He took her going to the hospital as a desertion of him and a sign of her lack of love. She must suffer the same tortures which he had suffered when she left him. He said, as it were: "I don't love you either; I hate you, I don't need you, you may die in the hospital. If you hadn't had a baby I would love you."

The dramatization of this biographical episode of his relationship with his mother was expressed repeatedly in a later period of his analysis, when in his play he reversed the roles: it was he who did the abandoning. A little boy escaped with his nurse into foreign countries and the mother was unable to find him. She looked for him but was usually killed by an army of enemies while he watched the execution from a hidden place. Sometimes he and his nurse joined the enemy army, sometimes he returned with his nurse to live with his father, who minded the mother's loss as little as did the boy.[5]

Frankie, who so thoroughly punished his mother by the withdrawal of his love, naturally lived in continual fear of retaliation. He could not stay at home or go out without his mother because he needed the presence of just that person against whom his aggressive impulses were directed. The presence of the ambivalently loved person prevents the phobic from being overwhelmed by his forbidden impulses and assures him that his aggressive intentions have not come true. But while the unconscious hatred directed at the protecting person is usually difficult

5. For more about this interesting detail in Frankie's play, which reveals his relationship with his father, see below, p. 193.

to uncover in the analysis of adults, it was still very close to the surface in this 5½-year-old boy (10).

The following methods of technical approach might have been applied in the subsequent analytic period:

1) We might be tempted to interpret to the boy the various motivations for his aggression against his mother and the newborn baby as: (a) his revenge for her abandonment of him—an aggression which was close to his consciousness; (b) the desire to take his mother's place, which was repressed and indicated only by the loving way in which he took care of the babies when playing doctor and nurse, and by his peacefully living with his father after his mother had been killed; (c) his desire to kill his mother, which we might interpret, as Melanie Klein probably would, in terms of the child's original sadistic intentions to destroy the mother by disembowelment (30). (In the last period of his analysis these fantasies were openly expressed by the child.)

This approach, in which the ego is brusquely forced to face unconscious impulses, would result either in a quick suppression of the phobic symptom or in the strengthening of the phobia and of the resistance. The suppression of the symptom would make the patient temporarily independent of further analysis, but his ego, still in jeopardy from this suppression, would not have won the freedom which is essential for sound development. The strengthening of the phobia might lead to a stage in which the analyst himself would become an object of the phobia, preventing the continuation of the analysis.

2) By our participation in the play, we might refrain from any interpretation and thus, or actively, encourage the child to express his hostility in further play actions. This catharsis might soon lead to a diminishing of his phobia. The cathartic approach would mean, in terms of the id, a temporary discharge of tensions, but would leave the conflict between ego and id untouched. This would correspond to the pre-analytic procedure which Freud described in 1895 before he introduced the theory of psychodynamics. A return to such therapeutic procedures is encountered not infrequently at present.

3) We might devaluate the conflict by reassuring the child that such conflicts are frequent, natural, and understandable. This would mean a consolation and encouragement for the ego but would tend to scotomize the conflict instead of analyzing it (25).

4) The therapist might take a criticizing attitude, by appealing to the child's desire to grow up and not to indulge in such infantile phobic mechanisms (4). This approach, also directed to the child's ego, would

be an appeal to give in to superego and reality demands, and would amount to an overpowering of his ego.

Any of these four ways might be applied, depending on the therapist's aims and personality. They all might lead to a quick disappearance of the symptom.

In order to bring about an *ego change* we chose for interpretation from the different themes revealed in the child's play that element in which the patient represented his ego. It was evident to us that he himself was the lonely 4-year-old boy in the hospital game, although feelings of sadness and loneliness had not been mentioned by him in his play. On the contrary, in his game he demonstrated only the *defense* against loneliness and sadness.

By placing the little boy's chair in an elevated position he had reversed the reality situation, presenting himself as omnipotent and successful. Thus he became a person who actually knew what went on in the hospital, who directed the events, and who had no reason whatever to feel excluded and unhappy. The omnipotence, as well as the destruction of mother and infant, were used as defenses by which he denied the affect of sadness. But before the defense proper could be dealt with, it was necessary to have the child recognize and experience such affects.

We must remember that at the time of the analysis Frankie himself did not know anything of his sadness. This sadness had been the original response of the child's ego to an external occurrence of traumatic effect. It had existed only temporarily and was not particularly noticed by those about him. The patient had successfully concealed from himself the affect of sadness which evidently had been too painful for him to bear. He had replaced it by his aggressive and tyrannical demands to which he later reacted with his phobic symptoms. Both aggression and anxiety were the end-product of an initial sadness and without recapturing that initial affect so that the patient was aware of it, no real ego change could be brought about.

The warded-off affect is a barrier to a successful interpretation of the conflict and therefore must be made conscious before any further step can be taken, lest the ego be pushed into a course beyond its integrative power (15). Bringing an affect into consciousness furnishes an opportunity for the unravelling of both genetic and dynamic elements. The re-experiencing of the original affects provides the emotional ground for the subsequent interpretation of unconscious material and makes it possible for the child to deal with a conflict consciously (17). Our aim, of course, was to make him conscious of the fact that behind the sad-

ness, aggression and anxiety, there was an intense, unrewarded and repressed longing for the mother.[6]

In order to introduce this emotion into the child's consciousness
without arousing undue resistance, the loneliness of the little boy in
his game became the subject of our analytic work for several weeks. The
analyst expressed sympathy for the lonely child who is barred from his
mother's sickroom and who is too little to understand why his father
is admitted. Frankie responded to the analyst's sympathy with growing
sadness, which could be discerned only from his facial expression. The
analyst's sympathy made it possible for him to tolerate this affect.

Once he had been able to face his sadness, Frankie showed relatively
little resistance when his specific situation was examined. We asked
whether by any chance he was a child who had been left alone
while his mother was in the hospital. Or had someone taken care of
him during that difficult period? He turned to his mother with the
question: "Was I alone, Mommy?" and before she could answer, he told
about his father and his nurse's presence, adding that his nurse would
"never, never leave him alone".

By taking advantage of the variations of the hospital game slowly
introduced by the child, we were able to go into the details of his life
immediately before his sister's birth and again after the mother's return
from the hospital. We learned from him how strong his affection for
his nurse had been even before his sister's birth; that she had appeared
a far more reliable person than his mother, who frequently went out
and left him alone with the nurse. Gradually he remembered periods of
separation from his parents before the sister's birth. Once when his parents left for vacation he stayed at his grandparents' home with his
nurse.[7] One of his memories referred to his watching the departure of
his parents in a plane,[8] and his subsequent illness. He assured us that
the nurse never left his side while the parents were absent.

This ample material referring to abandonment corroborated the
appropriateness of selecting his sadness as the first content of our interpretation. To him, being sent to school was an aggravating repetition

6. It may appear that bringing an emotion to consciousness is a scanty result of
many weeks of analytic work. However, it is noteworthy that the uncovering of recent
emotions is often extremely painful for the child, more painful than the direct interpretation of deep unconscious content, which is frequently easily accepted by
children and taken as a permission to obtain instinctual gratification.

7. I shall not follow up this episode because analysis did not reveal that any
definite trauma occurred during this visit. However, incidental remarks and Frankie's
behavior toward his grandfather led me to assume that the patient experienced a
castration threat from his grandfather at that time. It would seem that this trauma
did not have any immediate pathological effect on the child. The analytic material
suggests that subsequent events led retroactively to a revival of that experience—a
delayed effect comparable to that which similar occurrences had on "Little Hans".

8. An interesting relationship seemed to connect this incident of the plane with
the later development of the child's neurosis, particularly as manifested in his elevator
phobia.

of former separations: it happened just after his sister's nurse had left and his own nurse and mother had to share in the care of the baby. Thus, he lost not only his mother but also his nurse "who would never, never leave me alone". *This repetition of the traumatic experience of being abandoned* brought about the climax of his anxiety.

In his play, and later, in direct memories, he revealed the specific contents of his fear. He was afraid that he might not be able to stop the school bus which brought the children home, that he might not recognize his own home, that he might never find his way home and, worst of all, even if these obstacles were overcome, the door of the school bus might not open and he would be trapped.

His school phobia and the mother's stay in the hospital were thus linked. His fear of not finding his way home corresponded to his unconscious, revengeful wish that his mother who had abandoned him would never return, an interpretation which was confirmed by many play actions and verbalizations.

The same aggression against the mother underlay his fear that he would not recognize his house. When the mother returned from the hospital, he, of course, recognized her, but behaved as if he could not acknowledge her to be his mother. The fear of being trapped, which later became an important overt factor in his neurosis, referred to his original death wish against the newborn baby. The one who was to be trapped was his little sister. In a later phase of his analysis he said: "If Mommy had not opened her belly, my sister would never have come out." (30) [9]

The feeling of jealousy toward the sister whose birth had caused him such suffering found almost no overt expression. Frankie had learned to spare himself jealousy by denying the baby's existence almost completely during her first two years of life. He ingeniously escaped the pain of jealousy by creating exactly the same feeling of frustration in his mother as that which was gnawing at him. He refused to accept any affection from her, while he encouraged the nurse to cuddle him in his mother's presence.

The contradiction in his attitude toward his mother was the next step in our own interpretation. He was shown the discrepancy between his inability to be without her and the rejecting way in which he treated her. Our interpretation suggested that he had exaggerated his affection to his nurse because he wanted to take revenge for the disappointments he had suffered at the hands of his mother. Throughout the months following this interpretation he told us that his nurse had forced him to obedience by threats. We understood that some of his criticisms

9. See also p. 207.

against his mother were based on the nurse's deprecating remarks. Moreover, he intimated that there were some secrets between him and the nurse which he was determined not to reveal, and about which we learned only after the nurse had left the home. "Only God knows about my secret," he used to say, "and even God may not know it."

By continually connecting his recent experiences and emotions to their genetic counterparts, his sadness and jealousy, the pathological tie to his nurse was loosened. The analysis of the triangular relation between the mother, the nurse, and himself enabled him to desist from arousing his mother's jealousy. Only now his own jealousy appeared in its proper place, openly directed against his little sister.

Once the hostility toward his mother was diminished, his relationship to her seemed greatly improved, and his repressed love came to the fore. With this resolution the manifest school phobia subsided. He was able both to stay in school and to attend his analytic sessions without his mother's presence. This situation continued even after the nurse left. He took her leaving without an unduly exaggerated reaction, dared to express his sadness, and remained free of fear. In spite of all these encouraging signs, his neurosis was by no means dissolved.

In describing the first phase of Frankie's treatment it appears that we dealt with what might be called the preoedipal constituent of his disorder. Although his hostility as well as the clinical symptom revolved exclusively around female persons, such as his mother and nurse, two circumstances make one hesitate to speak of this phase of Frankie's disorders as preoedipal. There were indications that he had entered the oedipal phase prior to the onset of his phobia, but that this oedipal phase was interrupted by the outbreak of his neurosis. Furthermore, as we shall see later, the nurse was partly a representative of the father.[10] This may be one reason why, in the clinical manifestation of his illness, so little material regarding his father came to the fore at this period.

Although Frankie's conquest of his aggressiveness toward his mother now made it possible for him to re-experience and to express his normal positive oedipal conflicts, he did so only in the analytic session. At home, the child's reaction to the father seemed to be emotionally neutral. He was, for instance, apparently unaffected by his father's frequent arrivals at and departures from home during war-time and even the analyst's reference to this failed to provoke any direct response. Only in his dramatic play and fantasy material did he reveal his hostility toward men. Innumerable play episodes also betrayed Frankie's interest in procreation and his urge to know "what was going on" between his parents.

10. See also pp. 210 ff.

In the most frequent of his play dramatizations, a father was absent and a mother was alone. Then an apparently friendly man, a butcher, a policeman, or a vegetable man (each impersonated by Frankie), came to dinner. The "friendly" visit always ended with an attack on the mother who was killed. The ending was always the same: the visitors were taken by the police and sentenced to death by the judge, both of whom were again personified by Frankie.

It was our next task to connect these fantasies with his actual experiences. This was achieved by confronting him with a paradox: his lack of emotion about his own father's coming and going, and the excitement the child showed in his play when visitors arrived. The mother had reported that prior to the outbreak of his neurosis, Frankie had shown signs of irritability toward visitors, especially toward his grandfather. This irritability was markedly increased when his phobic symptom disappeared. Neurotic anxiety was supplanted by the aggression against which the phobia had been mobilized in an earlier period.

It became evident that the image of the father had been split into two groups of substitutes: male relatives of his mother, of whom the most important was his grandfather, and various tradesmen and craftsmen who Frankie asserted were the nurse's intimates.[11]

In the course of discussing his irritation toward visitors, Frankie admitted that there was actually no reason for him to assume that visitors would attack his mother. Nevertheless, he felt that he had to guard her against threatening dangers, especially if she were out of his sight. "She might run away," he said. "She might be run over, or her car might break, or men might kill her in the subway." We finally understood that he was afraid that all of these dangers would lead to a second hospitalization, just as when his mother had had her baby.

The circle was closed. The danger which threatened the mother from relations with men would result in what was the gravest danger to him: the arrival of a new baby. He had to guard against a repetition of this traumatic experience.

It was this concern that was responsible for the insomnia which became acute at this point of his analysis. There had been previous occurrences of insomnia when he was 2½ and again when he was 4½. Now again it took him hours to fall asleep. He listened silently and anxiously to the noises at night. Whenever his parents spent an evening at home, he ran back and forth between the living room and his bedroom. He wanted to know, as he expressed it, what plans they were making. They might eat something special and he wanted to share it. Or someone might come and hurt his Mommy. Ideas about the problem of procreation filled the hours of his severe insomnia.

11. See footnote 7.

Our attempts to discover what Frankie thought about birth and procreation met only with resistance. Even with our help, he could not verbalize his sexual theories, but expressed them in further dramatizations. His games presented scenes of attack duplicating those which he undoubtedly assumed were taking place in his parents' bedroom. The role of the attacker soon aroused anxiety, and he shifted in his play to the role of an observer of the attacks.

When he began to present this new content, and for some time thereafter, he became quite excited. It is not easy to describe his complex emotional state at such moments. It was a mixture of rage and triumphant conquest, of irritability and anxiety. These emotions changed rapidly and erratically without any obvious reference to the content of the dramatic play characterized by overactivity. Gradually the character of his dramatizations changed: the wild emotions became pacified, the kinesthetic storm was subdued to meaningful gestures. One element which was already present in his wild performances became the predominant and all-important feature: a strong inclination to gain pleasure by use of his eyes. This voyeuristic element led him to a new impersonation, that of an omniscient God.

In his new role he made the analyst a frightened, sleeping child into whose ears God whispered dreams of wild colliding horses, of violent scenes in which "Daddy throws Mommy out of the window so that she has to go to the hospital for eighteen days." The "sleeping games" revealed his suspicions of something frightful happening between his father and mother during the night—something he would have liked to observe. As God, he had the right to see and watch everything. His new role of God provided him with greater power than he had previously enjoyed as attacker, judge, or policeman—roles in which he had experienced the triumph of the conqueror, but also suffered the pain of the conquered.

The dynamics of these games may be reconstructed as follows: when Frankie made the analyst act the part of a child whose dreams were supplied by God's whispers, he was revealing his reaction to the noises emanating from his parents' room. The child obviously completed visually what had been suggested audibly. He was unable to endure his own conception of what was taking place and tried to overcome this terror by putting himself in control of the events—by becoming God who can create dreams by his whisper.[12]

Later, however, when he realized that God was not only his own

12. His role of God might be construed as an identification with the sexual father, but this was only partly true. The identification with the father was, in this instance, a defense against a greater danger, the yielding to passivity. The basic identification was with the mother, whose sexual role Frankie really craved.

creation but a concept shared by others and that he could not rule "his" God to the extent necessary to be protected from anxiety, he replaced his fantasy of an omniscient God by an imaginary television apparatus which belonged exclusively to his fantasy and thus was completely at the disposal of his wishes and plans. ("God sees everything, but the television apparatus sees only if *I* turn it on.") The television apparatus brought the child closer to reality. When he was God, he made the analyst dream about those frightful scenes between his parents, while with the introduction of his imaginary television apparatus, he himself attempted to face those scenes. The analyst was made a co-observer of eating scenes in restaurants, for which Frankie provided the music (another auditory manifestation) while explaining the observed events to the analyst. He reassured the analyst many times that the observations were "make believe" and actually he never again reached the previously described state of excitement and anxiety. By means of his invention of the television apparatus, he removed himself not only from the scenes he imagined, but also from the feelings of desire and concomitant guilt which those scenes aroused.

It was noteworthy that with his exchange of the machine for God, the content of his problems was no longer expressed on the phallic level, but in oral terms. The aggressive element persisted, but apparently the content of his fantasies became more acceptable to his dawning conscience when expressed in the relative innocence of oral gratifications.

The following is one of the scenes observed through the apparatus: Father was in the restaurant and ordered the most delicious food for Mother from the restaurant owner. Then he had a secret talk with the owner. As soon as Mother had eaten, she collapsed and died; the food was poisoned. (In his thoughts, eating was linked with being impregnated, for which Frankie had not yet forgiven his mother, and for which he still punished her by death.) Father and the owner of the restaurant were unconcerned by her death; they continued their pleasant talk and play, shoving Mother under the table.[13] Some drawings of this time show God and God's wife feasting at a dinner table, disturbed by "little gnomes" who alternately attack God and his wife.

These games helped the investigation and understanding of a past period of his life: We had reason to assume that when he was 4½, his screaming attacks had reappeared as his reaction to audible primal scene

13. This scene is rich in its overdetermined factors; it permits the reconstruction of Frankie's oedipus complex. The element, "Mother is shoved under the table", refers to the child's resentment against his mother, who did not pay any attention to him when he, sitting under the table, tried to disturb his parents' meal. The next element, "Father and restaurant owner confer about the food for Mother (from which she dies)" is an indication of Frankie's wish to participate in his father's sexual activities. Frankie's position as restaurant owner was evident in many daydreams: he possessed "all the restaurants in New York". This detail makes us anticipate that Frankie's hostility toward his mother contained also some envy of her role as father's wife. Owner and father-Frankie and father do together what otherwise mother and father do. We shall see later how strong the child's desire was to take the passive role with the father.

experiences. His father once wrote us that in former times, "in his prankish days", he used to pinch his wife and throw her into the air, "all in fun and for exercise . . . , I can imagine what it must have seemed like to someone who heard it but did not see what actually happened." Frankie's running back and forth between his bedroom and the living room occurred in reaction to auditory stimuli and continued until his nurse quenched his active interest and nightly curiosity by a threatening and punishing attitude.

With the process of internalization of his conflicts the actually threatening nurse was replaced by imaginary objects, mainly wolves, who stood guard under his bed and kept him from getting up and investigating what might be happening in the parental bedroom.

These imaginary wolves under his bed were able, like the God he had played, to see what he did and to surmise his intentions. As soon as he put out hand or foot to go into his parents' bedroom,[14] the wolves would snap at him; "but they would let me go to the bathroom." For a protection from their attacks the boy armed himself with many weapons, preferably with a long stick, in order to beat the wolves down when they raised their heads. He maintained that they observed all his movements, and he in turn countered with an equally watchful attitude. His configuration of the wolves contained as elements the punitive and protective parent figures as well as his own impulses. The wolves punish his intentions and prevent their fulfillment. Their symbolic role as superego was strikingly confirmed in a drawing which Frankie called the WOLVES' STATUE. It showed an oversized wolf (in human form) with outstretched arms, floating above Frankie in his bed, under which a number of smaller-sized wolves (also in human form) were engaged in mysterious activities, obviously of a sexual nature. In his comments on this picture, Frankie said: "It shows what the wolves hope for, what they will look like some day."

The dread of wolves which had haunted the child for weeks finally led to the analysis of his castration fear. In his stories and in his play, the mother's attackers who previously had been punished by death, now were punished by almost undisguised castration. In his pictures he endowed God with monstrously elongated arms and legs, only to cut off these limbs with scissors. Immediately after such operation he tried to undo this symbolic act of castration by drawing innumerable new arms and legs. Frankie derived reassurance from the idea that destruction is not necessarily irrevocable and consequently dared to express the thoughts of castration without any symbolic disguise. Mother's attackers were imprisoned and he, as a doctor, subjected the prisoners to operations which usually threw him into a state of exaltation. Playing the doctor, he exclaimed: "Those criminals, they have to be operated on. Off with their wee-wees. It has to come off!" In his play he guarded himself

14. The element of uncovering the hands and feet is overdetermined and it is obviously a presentation of its opposite, i. e., a reverse of the original warning against touching his genital under the bedcover.

against any awareness of his fear by identifying himself with the person performing the act of castration. His fear of the anticipated retaliation found expression in his behavior toward his pediatrician. Frankie had always been a difficult patient, but during this period he absolutely refused to be examined, and assaulted the doctor by throwing blocks or potatoes which he carefully had stored under his bed for this purpose.

The emphasis in our interpretation was on Frankie's preoccupation with the mechanisms of undoing, and his identification with the aggressor. After this, we were able to approach the theme of his castration fear by confronting him with a comparison of his impersonation of a cruel doctor and the kind attitude of his own doctor; with the fearlessness of his prisoners in contrast to his own frightened aggressiveness toward his doctor.

In view of the anxiety which was kept in abeyance by his identification with a castrative figure, particular caution was necessary in the interpretation and dissolution of this identification. Abrupt release of such large quantities of anxiety would have produced a traumatic effect. Therefore it seemed indicated to decrease this defense only gradually. In a preparatory period of several weeks, we "amused" ourselves by imagining how frightened the brave prisoners of his fantasy would feel if *they* were suddenly exposed to the reality of a doctor's office. By our bantering his fantasy-prisoners, Frankie was enabled to take a more tolerant view of these frightening thoughts which he had formerly warded off by identification with the aggressor. Through this playful approach we prepared him for the fact that it was he himself who feared for his genitals, or at least that in the past he had once done so, even if the past were only ten minutes ago. Introducing *humor* (23) as a benign defense, we saved Frankie the full impact of the suffering which accompanies castration fear. He learned to understand that the wolves represented not only the prohibiting nurse and the father, but also himself with his strong voyeuristic and castrative impulses.

Although his masturbation was not yet approachable, the decrease of his castration fear enabled him to bring his sexual curiosity into the open and to ask the questions to which he had tried to find the answers by his compulsive running back and forth to his parents' room.

The material obtained from his play actions, in which men violently attack women, was interpreted to him in terms of his fantasies about intercourse. The treatment made it possible for him to re-enter the oedipal phase, and the father then acquired that emotional importance in the child's reality which was due him in terms of the oedipal relationship. Yet despite this progress, we did not expect his behavior in this new phase to be free of neurotic disturbances.

II

When, at the age of 6½, Frankie's wolf phobia had yielded to analysis, a break-through of uninhibited active phallic behavior occurred. He no longer contented himself with symbolic expressions, fantasies, and play actions as at the beginning of his analysis. Now he tried to carry out in reality all those actions against which he had previously protected himself by his phobia. Even God, and the television apparatus, by means of which he had satisfied his voyeuristic impulses, no longer sufficed for his needs. He began to gratify his sexual curiosity by directly questioning his parents and the analyst about intercourse.

He could not bring himself to accept the differences between the sexes. Although Frankie had many opportunities to convince himself in real life of their existence, in analysis he denied them with unusual firmness; even during the period when he made active investigations of his sister's body, he was not able to accept what he had seen. Finally, when he could no longer maintain this denial, he resorted to the theory that it was *only* his sister, and not other females, whose genital was mutilated. Hers had been, as he said, "pinched off" or "screwed off"—as a punishment. (Reasons for this punishment were not obtainable at this time.)

The obvious danger of castration emanating from his sister made her disgusting to him and made him shift his voyeurism toward adult women. Under the assumption that their genitalia might provide the reassuring sight of a penis, he lifted the maid's skirt, then tried stealthily to do the same with his mother and the analyst. When all his investigations could not confirm his fantasy that all human beings had a penis, he felt disquieted, repelled, and stopped his investigations altogether. And as always when his fear reached a climax, he stopped verbal communication in analysis, and replaced it by dramatic play. The traumatic experiences which had so intensified his castration fear were now elaborated in harmless play activities by means of which he achieved some mastery over these experiences and some lessening of his fears.

One of his favorite dramatizations during this period contained an allusion to his masturbation in connection with his castration anxiety. He repeated the following play endlessly: The parents are away. The children ruin pipes and electric appliances and accuse the dogs of having caused the damage. The plumber and the electrician are called in, but they cannot repair the damage. In rude words they warn the children against playing with material "which is not meant for playing", and threaten to kill the children if they disobey. Upon the mother's pleading, the plumber and electrician finally undertake the repair, but ask an exorbitant fee.

This game shows us with particular clarity the means of defense which predominated after Frankie's phobic mechanism—avoidance—had subsided. They are the mechanisms of denial, projection and undoing. He denies the trauma of irreparability, and thereby defies the analyst's statement that all women are born without a penis and must remain so. He projects onto the dogs his feeling of guilt for the forbidden masturbation. He represents as the *restorers* of masculinity those grown-ups (plumber, electrician, doctor and nurse) whom he fears as castrators. They undo the damage committed by the children as he himself undoes castration when he adds innumerable elongated arms and legs to his drawings of the God whose limbs he has just cut off.

And finally the defense by undoing and restoring was also evident in the role in which he cast his mother. She, whom Frankie had previously made responsible for all evil, now became the instrument for providing help. (This referred to Frankie's knowledge of his mother's role in reality.) He knew that it was she who had insisted on the nurse and the analysis for him; with the allusion to the plumber's exorbitant fee he indicated the hope that by means of bribery, the analyst, like the nurse, would help against the danger of castration.

Frankie demanded that the analyst be the threatening, merciless adult in his game. The analyst observed that the child reacted to her rendition of the role of the punitive adult with an increasing excitement which at least resembled the mounting tension of sexuality. Therefore the analyst only intermittently sustained the designed rôle of the merciless adult in the play, occasionally adding to the character of the cruel plumber and electrician the reassuring element that reality was not quite as punishing as Frankie obviously wanted it to be. As the analyst went through the motions of the plumber, she would mumble under her breath: "Wouldn't I be happy if I could fix not only broken pipes but everything that is broken in the world. Children would be less scared if that were true." Or, on another occasion, breaking through her role of the merciless electrician, the analyst would say, "All right, if that child insists on my telling him that the switches are beyond repair and he has to die for having broken them, I'll tell him so. But that's all nonsense. No person should say such a thing to a child. That's not the way to learn. After all, things can be touched without being spoiled."

Frankie reacted to our reassuring interpretation with an annoyance that revealed intense resistance. We came to understand that this resistance was aroused by our having thwarted an important dynamic function of his game, i. e. the discharge of tensions emanating from traumatic experiences which were related to his castration anxiety and its masochistic exploitation. The attempt to confront him with the unreality of his play confronted us instead with the fact that our step was premature.

The child's insistence on the repetitious game and on the analyst's role in it placed her in a serious predicament: Continuation of the game might have shown us what particular experience he was driven to repeat in his play; there was, however, the danger that the child would take our participation in his play as permission for further indulgence in masochistic pleasures, which might have facilitated a masochistic fixation. On the other hand, had we refused to continue this game altogether, the child might have taken our refusal for a moralistic condemnation which would have undermined his positive relationship to the analyst at this crucial moment; moreover, it would have induced him to conceal the material from the analyst and himself.

The alternative to a direct interpretation of the masochistic pleasure involved in the game also seemed contraindicated chiefly because experience in child analysis has shown that, by such direct interpretative reference to the child's play, it might easily lose its natural function of pleasure, communication, learning and sublimation (6, 35). It might become a stereotyped or sexualized activity which would interfere with or block further sublimation. Pathological attitudes should not be analyzed in reference to constructive, relatively conflict-free (28) activities, but, if possible, in manifestations such as dreams, slips, neurotic symptoms, and the like.

In Frankie's case, while noting the unconscious content of his play for further use, we first approached his ego reactions, namely his feelings of guilt. We did so not during the game but later, in a direct conversation, when the child was occupied with something emotionally neutral. We asked: "Who in your life has given you so many do's and don'ts? To some of them you don't stick at all, while you do stick to others and nothing can make you change your mind." Or else: "Who told you that it is such a crime to touch certain things, and who told you that punishment would follow the touching of things? Once you told me that you were sure that your little sister has lost her penis. What did she do to deserve it and who do you think was mean enough to punish her that way?"

If such questions are timed correctly, by which we mean, in moments of diminished tension, the patient will respond favorably. The favorable response will not necessarily consist of recollections or of an answer to the analyst's questions. If a child is only ready to tolerate what the analyst says without covering his ears, he shows that he is making the first step in acknowledging the existence of a problem. If a week later the same problem is approached, the child may be prepared to assimilate the question put to him. Unfortunately, such a slow pace is unavoidable in child analysis. Children are in much greater danger of being flooded by instinctual demands, and their fear of real external danger is much greater than that of adults. Therefore resistances are, if anything, stronger in children than in adults.

It took a long time before we succeeded in making Frankie aware of the connection between his masturbation and his feelings of guilt. The violence of his resistance made it clear that he was not yet capable of allowing the subject of masturbation to be discussed, or even of acknowledging it as a problem in his life. He stated that he had never masturbated. (His parents and nurse had actually never observed masturbatory activities.) He told us, however, about other children's negligible misdeeds in tones of great disapproval. While we would soon expose such a mechanism of projection to an adult, in child analysis we gladly encourage this indirect method. By discussing the problems of other children we are able to prepare our young patient for the acceptance of his own. It seemed to us significant progress—a step closer to reality—when Frankie projected his own misdeeds on other children, rather than on such fantasy figures as the dogs in the incident of the "spoiled pipes".

Children often omit from their analytic sessions all references to the external world. When this happens we must rely on the parents' reports. For this reason, and other well known ones (16) a continuous relationship with the parents is necessary. At the time we were skirting Frankie's problem of masturbation, the parents reported that he was sporadically showing unmanageable and quarrelsome behavior at home. After a long period of trial and error in the analysis it was understood that the periodic flare-ups were due to some notion he had about menstruation.[15]

Once again, Frankie was unable to verbalize this affect-laden material of his observations. Indeed, his fear at this time was so great that he could not even dramatize his experience in his play. He could express himself only in his paintings and drawings. They served him as *preparation for verbalizing* contents which he was not yet ready to communicate directly. As long as fear was overwhelming, his paintings were shapeless, as if under the dominance of the primary process. Any spot could mean anything, just as in the pictures of very young children. When the content had lost its terror it was represented in his drawings in a manner appropriate to his age.

Many sheets of paper were flooded with red paint or red ink. Finally, the analyst broke the sequence of silent sessions with an interpreta-

15. The child analyst who repeatedly observes such periodic flare-ups of aggression and sexual excitement is in a good position to confirm Daly's important findings about the "menstruation complex" (9).

tive question: "Frankie, your pictures are red as blood, and Mommy
tells me that you are unbearable at home. You quarrel with her and
all the other women. Even with your sister Mary. What has made you
so angry at women lately?"

To such questions Frankie responded either with violence or with
complete silence. He increased the speed with which he flooded
the paper and the carpet with red paint. The analyst continued: "I
wonder, Frankie, whether you haven't seen some blood at home, and
you didn't know where the blood came from, and you did not know
what had happened. Is it that what makes you so angry?"

In response to our interpretations, his bloody pictures gradually
assumed definite form. One of his pictures showed a toilet with blood
in it, another a naked man urinating into toilet, the red paint still
dominant. He explained: "Here you see a man's wee-wee and blood is
flowing all over the place." This picture showed that all previous
explanations regarding sex differences had been of no avail, but were
actually repudiated by him.

Another picture, called "Bleeding Bones", he explained with the
following story:

"Once there was a lady who had 100,000 bones. And the lady was
a very poor lady, and her bones fell off; they came off and she died very
soon. And this lady when she died, had 106 cuts which she had all
her life. But she only pretended to be dead. She was really wicked and
very horrible. She wanted to be wicked to everybody."

The analyst's interpretation now focused on the child's increased
aggression against women as a reaction to his observations. We realized
that since bleeding women aroused his fears and distrust, he retaliated
by attacking all the women in his house.

Learning from Frankie that he had actually seen blood not only in
the toilet, but also on his mother's bedsheet, we reminded him of his old
anxieties about the injuries he thought had threatened his mother from
men. And although all this had frightened him, we both already knew
that he himself would also have liked to do that which he thought his
father did, namely to hurt his mother; and the sight of blood on his
mother's sheet and in the toilet might have stirred up both his fears and
desires.

His aggression toward women was intensified by the rough and
threatening way in which women had reacted to his explorations and
attacks. Even his mother had reacted to one episode of his sadistic love
play by saying: "I'll break your neck!" The following song was a
direct reaction to such an episode: he accompanied the song in his own
way, by smashing a waste paper basket, reflecting both his own phallic
sadistic impulses and the destructive impulses aroused by women's actual
counterattacks:

> "Break the lady's head,
> break, break the lady's head,
> break it with a knife, a sword,
> throw her up and then fight high,

cut the foot half-way off
and then we take it up with God.
God will throw the bottle where a leg is.
He will throw it on you,
And the lady's head will be broken off."

Since both reality and the analyst's statements refuted his firm conviction that women had a penis, he shifted his curiosity and his attacks to their breasts, their buttocks, and their possessions. His father, aroused by the child's attacks, attempted to restrain him forcibly. Although the child rebelled and forbade his father's interference with, "Don't butt in when I fight with Mommy. I can do whatever I want. You are not the boss. I am not afraid of my wolves anymore," his phallic activity finally gave way because of the repeated rejection and punishment he suffered from both parents.

Whereas in his phallic phase women had been of importance to him and he had felt charmed by their beauty, in his anal-sadistic phase his attacks were directed indiscriminately toward both women and men. The goal of his attacks shifted from assaults on women for the purpose of penetration to that of eliciting an aggressive response from the person he attacked. With a provoking smile he tossed around his own toys and other people's belongings, threatened to smash plates, his mother's vases and furniture, and wanted to destroy his father's and the analyst's papers.

His sexual excitement was unmistakable when after such an attack, he laughingly shouted: "Don't grab me!" He continued such assaults until he had provoked a counterattack. Then, with glee in his eyes, and with arms outstretched, he shouted, "I surrender, I surrender." Once, when asked which he preferred, to attack or to *be* attacked, he answered seriously, "One wouldn't be fun without the other."

To our repeated interpretation that this behavior was caused by his misconception of adult love life, he finally confessed that the anticipated counterattack was his immediate goal. The provocative violence in his behavior served the purpose of gratifying his passive drives which could not yet be called masochistic; he did not desire punishment. Once when he received a slap, he exclaimed with surprise and indignation, "But that hurts! I don't want to be hurt!" During a discussion of punishment, he insisted that he did not want a painful spanking, but something he called "a love spank", or "a love pat".

The compulsiveness of his provocative behavior led us to suggest that he was probably acting out some past experience. After many long and difficult periods of resistance Frankie finally revealed the carefully guarded secret, the "something he would never tell the analyst"—a bedtime ritual in which the nurse had participated. When he was a good, obedient little boy, he was tucked in by her, turned around on his belly and patted on his buttocks as a reward.

It was a repetition of this gratification of his passive desire which he now sought from everyone.

III

So far, we have given the material in almost chronological sequence, in order to round out the clinical picture and to illustrate the actual course of the treatment. Such further chronological presentation of complex analytic material would leave the reader with a feeling of confusion. Therefore we shall now discuss two of Frankie's symptoms, without regard to the order of their appearance in the analysis: his retention of urine and his elevator phobia.

The retention of urine could be traced back to the age of 3, shortly after bladder control had been established. One of the stories in the first period of Frankie's analysis indicated that the act of urination was connected with threats of castration:

"Two giants once ate up a river, so each river said: 'Get bigger so that the giants won't be able to eat you up.' " A big river equals a big penis "which holds lots of water".

Frankie had confessed with shame that he refused to use strange bathrooms because he thought that they were inhabited by giants who might *bite* off one's penis. However, when the retention of urine became the subject of his analysis, he denied ever having had such a fear, and claimed that the analyst had invented it.

Previously we had learned about a number of his oral impregnation theories, among which the most prominent had been that a woman conceived by swallowing a man's penis or, as revealed in his restaurant games, by taking in poisoned food. Frankie's present impregnation fantasies still contained the element of poison but now poisoning was linked with urination: the drinking of wine led to impregnation. In analysis he squirted the analyst with his water pistol, aiming at her mouth, and shouting: "I'll poison you, I'll poison you. My arrows are poisoned with germs." Many times he slipped, and said "sperms" instead of "germs".

Here the analyst should have become aware that the sense of urgency which he betrayed in his actions indicated an attempt to demonstrate more than a mere theory, namely a past experience which he could not verbalize. Such emotional urgency appears to us as a clinical indication that we are dealing not with a fantasy but with a reality experience—and furthermore, an experience the impact of which probably came before verbalization was possible.

Frankie's play with the water pistol showed his masculine intention toward women. When we pointed out the contradiction in his behavior, namely his excessive retention of urine (at this time from eight to nine hours) and his pleasure in squirting water, he recalled that in the past he had gaily and wilfully urinated on the floor. His nurse had threatened and shamed him into obedience. He did not recognize that his prolonged retention of urine was his defiant revenge upon the nurse.

The retention of urine exemplified his conflict between active tendencies and passive desires and it was patterned after the conflict between him and the nurse when she was intolerant of his urethral eroticism. At first, Frankie's wilful urination had been the expression of his exhibitionistic masculine tendencies. The nurse grabbed him whenever she saw him prepare to urinate and carried him into the bathroom against his will. He recalled that soon after this the struggle with her became more pleasant than the intended urination. Therefore he often *pretended* to urinate into the corner of the living room in order to be picked up by her and carried to the toilet.

At the time of his analysis, there was no open manifestation of any desire to be carried. On the contrary, we knew from his parents' complaints that, even as a very young child, he had a marked objection to being touched, lifted, or carried about. In view of the fact that the child's later struggle was directed at preventing passive locomotion, we concluded that he had once experienced great pleasure from equilibrium sensations, and that this pleasure must subsequently have had undesirable consequences for him.

We assumed in our reconstruction that he had urinated while being carried by the nurse and that the loss of urine had added to the pleasure of passive locomotion. We further assumed that the nurse must have threatened or punished him for this, and that his retention of urine also was aimed at preventing a repetition of that experience. Her threats or punishment must have contributed to his later anxiety over the loss of urine.

We may then recapitulate the history of his urinary symptom as follows:

At first, acting as if he wanted to urinate in the living room was a means of forcing the nurse to carry him to the toilet and provided him with gratification through passive locomotion. Later, however, the retention of urine became an adequate defense both against losing control during passive locomotion, and against being touched. His panicky fear of being touched pointed to an originally pleasurable tactile experience. He recalled that he often refused to urinate in order to force the nurse to take out his penis.

We assume that the craving to be touched was not satisfied in the way he expected. He must have expected a gentle handling whereas the nurse, annoyed by his provocative behavior, was rough and may even have accompanied her actions with direct castration threats, an assumption supported by the previous story of the giants in the bathroom.

In another of his stories he further confirmed this reconstruction: "A king killed his mother when he was three years old. He wanted her to cut trees in his garden, a hundred thousand trees. And she should do it with her *hands*. But she was fresh, she dared to ask for an axe—therefore she must die."

He told this castration story after an episode at school when he refused to submit to a medical examination by the school physician, a woman. The only fear which he would admit was a dread of the smallness of the consultation room. He denied any fear that the doctor might harm him although he had reported only the day before that his school friends claimed this doctor "is used to cutting off wee-wees". "Anyhow," he continued, "I will not permit a ladydoctor to look at my penis."

We might add here what the child could not express: The smallness of the consultation room revived recollections of the bathroom in which the scenes with the nurse had taken place. It was as if he were saying by his refusal: "I am afraid that women in 'small rooms', even if only looking at my penis, might arouse my desires. Women are as fickle as my beloved nurse. When I wanted to have my penis touched she hurt it." Her hands, instead of giving pleasure, might perform castration with an axe as the mother did in the king's story. (The experience in the bathroom with his nurse had contributed to his claustrophobic ideas of being trapped in small rooms.)

His panicky fear of being touched was a defense against the desire to obtain this passive satisfaction. While at the beginning wilfully retaining urine was a means of obtaining the gratification of being touched, subsequently the retention of urine—which by now had become an established symptom—was a means for defense against this danger. Furthermore, his urinary inhibition guarded him against his masturbatory wishes. By not urinating he avoided both the temptation to touch and the act of touching. He had even learned to direct the stream of his urine without touching his penis.

Frankie had already indicated his fear of losing control in his first phobic attack at school when he was afraid that he would not be able to stop the bus and the car would pass his house. He projected onto the school bus his own fear of being overwhelmed by a tidal wave of anxiety, and of being helpless in its grip.

On his second and last schoolday in the first school he was brought home crying and inconsolable. In analysis he described his plight in the following words: "I was crying and crying, because I had no handkerchief." Again his complaint is against being overwhelmed—this time by crying which he could not stop. He rejected our suggestion that he might at that time have feared the loss of bladder control, but then volunteered the statement that he could not bear the smell of the toilet at school, that the cot on which he should have rested smelled of urine, and he insisted that the teacher had threatened to lock up bad children in the bathroom.

Such a stream of recollections is unusual in child analysis. Whenever it occurred in Frankie's case it was a precursor of therapeutic gain. Soon after this, the retention of urine was given up.

While the child's memories were concerned with tears, a more basic fear was concerned with the loss of urine, a striking example of the oft-claimed connection between urination and tears. We should like to note here that the fear of uncontrollable flowing of tears and of urine both correspond to the uncontrollable flow of neurotic anxiety (26).[16] The main complaint of phobic patients is the danger of being overwhelmed by an uncontrollable flow of anxiety.

We shall now present, in some detail, Frankie's elevator phobia, which was one of his most impressive symptoms since it was a compound of all the etiological factors involved in his neurosis. It contained his aggression against and identification with his father on the oedipal level; his aggression against and identification with his mother; his death wish against his sister and his desire to take her place, and finally it included his masturbation conflicts: the fear of erections, the fear of losing control over his own emotions and the fear of being lifted, all of which were components of the danger of castration.

The child summarized the dangers which the ride in the elevator involved as follows: "The elevator might crash down, or the door might not open, and I would be trapped."

We recall that when Frankie was 4½ he spent hours at night trying to get out of bed to observe his parents and his nurse. His nurse curbed this restlessness by threats. She said she would call the elevator man to teach him not to disturb people. The threat was effective, and the boy stayed in bed. Whenever he heard the sound of the elevator, he was terrified, expecting the man to come in and take him away. He wished that the elevator would crash with the operator. Then what he wanted to have happen to the dreaded elevator-man, by his familiar mechanism, recoiled against himself, and he feared that the elevator might crash down while he was in it. Here the factors of aggression and retaliation stemming from his oedipus complex are encountered again; the elevator man represented his father, a fact which Frankie himself recognized.

A fear concerning his mother was also involved in his elevator phobia. Here his memories led into a period of life before his sister was born. He was deeply moved when he recalled that his father used to greet his mother by lifting her "high, high up in the air ... I always thought, he'll suddenly throw her out of the window.[17] Daddy whirled

16. K. R. Eissler has suggested that the biological root of full-fledged phobic attacks is the sensation of the uncontrollable flow of urine.
17. The same element is present in the sleeping game. See p. 192.

Mommy around. I hate this if someone does it to me. It makes you feel crazy." Beneath the verbalized displeasure was longing and envy of the mother because of the pleasure he suspected she derived from being lifted up by the father. The idea that his father would throw his mother out of the window found its analogy in the fearful expectation that "the crazy elevator man" would lose control over the elevator, so that suddenly Frankie would find himself "deep down in the cellar under the building". He would encounter the same fate that he wished for his mother.

The following dream mirrors his desire for participation in the sexual excitement which he believed his mother experienced when his father playfully lifted her up.

"Some boy came to my house and we wanted to make a fire escape so that cars could go down one side and people could go down the other. The boy that I invited to my house—he fell down, way downstairs. Then the room starts to go down, the whole room, and Mommy tried to hold on and Mommy tried to keep up. And my sister fell into the business—into the room. *She* started to go down. Mommy did not fall down (Daddy helped to keep up things). I was falling down with the rest. Finally we all landed in the cellar." (Actually, the emphasis on "going down" was a representation of its opposite, being lifted up.[18])

This dream would seem to be a scarcely distorted representation of some experience of the primal scene, an experience which had been condensed with the frequently observed lifting scenes between his father and mother and both experiences must have impressed him with the idea that a unity existed between father and mother from which he felt excluded. In his dream, he tried to participate in this unity: "I was falling down with the rest. Finally we *all* landed in the cellar."

The elevator phobia revealed another element, one which was contained within the phobia. This was a claustrophobia which was the result of Frankie's desire for being carried in his mother's womb and his defense against it.

Being carried symbolized to the child a means of unification with the mother's body (28). The perfect way to insure himself against his

18. It might be of value to summarize what we learned through Frankie's preoccupation with equilibrium sensations and the feeling of being lifted. This preoccupation and the conflicts it aroused were the result of: (1) His pleasure as a young child, when his nurse lifted him, and the fear that her castration threats made him attach to the act of being lifted. This was tied up with his dread of an uncontrollable flow of urine—and of anxiety. (2) His fear and loneliness at the airport when his mother had been "lifted away" from him in the plane. Somehow, the child connected this flight with the later birth of his sister. It is actually a fact that the mother became pregnant during this trip with her husband. In other words, Frankie felt, "If one is lifted, one becomes pregnant. I would like to have a child, as my mother did. But being lifted, and being mother, means losing my penis. I want to be lifted, but I dare not pay the price for it." Naturally, Frankie did not reason out all of these factors in this manner. Our presentation is a reconstruction of the way he *felt*—his emotional, rather than intellectual, reasoning.

mother's desertion would be to be inside her body. He reflected this fantasy by stressing the great advantages the fetus has in being so closely united with the mother, or, as he expressed it, "in being tied to her". His desire for the womb was accompanied by a great fear of it. It was seen as a castrating organ, and was visualized as a "lion's mouth", and a "trap which can bite or pinch off an arm or a leg". He projected his own aggression upon the womb, especially when he realized with frustration that his little sister had enjoyed the unity with mother at a time he was already separated from her. In one analytic session, he told us that he had actually wished that his sister should be trapped in the mother's womb; in his own words, "If Mommy had not opened her belly, my sister would have never come out."

The wish for his sister's entrapment aroused a fear of retaliation, but this time from all small spaces, such as buses, bathrooms and elevators. Being trapped in the elevator was the punishment for the identical wish against the sister. We find in his claustrophobia a condensation of his identification with his sister, the aggression against her, and the ensuing danger to himself.

When he was confronted with the contradiction between his desire to be a fetus and his fear of being trapped in small places, he explained that the embryo did not mind the restriction in space since it participated passively in the mother's locomotion. These thoughts had found expression in the following questions in which the connection between passive locomotion and the flow of urine was again emphasized. "Does the child feel every little step of the mother or does only the mother feel the child kicking around?" And another time, "What does the mother say if the child wee-wees into her?"

In view of these questions his claustrophobia appears as a fabric in which activity and passivity are interwoven. This appears to us as a possible reflection of an early ego state in which activity and passivity had not yet found separate representation.

The movement of the elevator became for Frankie an important factor through its affinity to kinesthetic sensations. The ride in the elevator was dangerous because it aroused his sexual sensations. He projected his own sexual excitement onto the elevator man and assumed that the operator, aroused by passive locomotion, would lose control over the elevator. He would therefore be unable to stop the elevator which would either continue to move indefinitely up and down, or would crash down in a sudden fall. This explains why Frankie called every elevator man "crazy", and why he drew dozens of pictures of "crazy elevators" which rolled up and down and could not stop, so that "the passengers would become dizzy and crazy like being whirled around".

For Frankie the up and down movement of the elevator had gained another symbolic meaning. It was equal to an erection, an analogy which the child directly communicated, and which at long last made it possible for us to approach his problem of masturbation.

Several times during the course of his analysis he had made allusions to this problem, for instance when he feared the wolves would snap at his fingers and later, when he dramatized the game of "bad children" who spoil pipes and electric appliances, and even more openly, when we discussed his retention of urine. But our previous attmepts to interpret to him the connection of this material with his masturbation had been of no avail. The child assured us that masturbation had never occurred in his life. However, he finally admitted that he derived some pleasure from another activity. It consisted in the contraction of the pelvic muscles and Frankie told us that he indulged in it for hours. We consider these manipulations as a masturbatory equivalent.

Frankie could not recall ever having been reprimanded for masturbation or threatened with castration for it. He did remember, however, that the nurse had interfered with his sister's masturbation and that she had warned him that retaining urine might cause a poisoning of the blood. To our questions as to the character of the disease of blood poisoning, he responded without any hesitation: "Blood poisoning? You might lose a finger or a leg!" and the following associations showed that to him, blood poisoning meant bleeding like a woman, being castrated like his sister, losing control over one's own emotions—in short, "going crazy". Frankie's behavior was occasionally called "crazy" when he indulged in his outbreaks of uncontrollable wildness. Since he had occasionally experienced erections during such outbursts, he felt that there was a link between phallic sexuality and craziness. He told us that erections were once a desired experience, especially if they could be brought about indirectly. He admitted that he had sometimes consciously used retention of urine as a means of producing erections. Later he discovered accidentally that by contraction of the pelvic muscles he could likewise produce erections. However, at the height of his elevator phobia he complained he could not produce any erections despite conscious efforts to do so.

The hour long contractions of the pelvic muscles had either led to or were accompanied by painful spasms in the umbilical region. He called these sensations "wee-wee ache", and had always feared that these symptoms were proof that he had the dreaded disease of blood poisoning, especially since he had actually experienced pains when retaining urine for hours. These pains represented the hysterical nucleus which is regularly to be found at the root of an obsessional neurosis (21). When analyzing this symptom, the pains around the navel shifted to the penis where the sensations probably had their origin. By the displacement of the sensation from the penis to the navel, he utilized an existing identity between his sister and himself. The furrow of the navel appeared to him similar to the female genital, and while his castration fear still did not permit him to accept the female genital itself as the point of similarity, he proudly pointed out that he had a navel like his sister's, that in this respect he was like her. By accepting the fantasy of being similar to his sister—by being a girl—he achieved the escape from the dreaded castration by an external force. We remind the reader that Frankie had been convinced that his sister had been deprived of a penis because she, like the "bad children" in the plumber game, had spoiled her genital by touching it.

Frankie's pelvic contractions, his first obsessional symptom, were a defense against the temptation of manual masturbation. In contrast to adult compulsive patients in whom the secondary struggle against anal-sadistic impulses is in the foreground,[19] Frankie's first compulsive symptoms still showed their connection with masturbation in an undistorted way. His prohibition against touching referred directly and consciously to the genital. The curbed impulses for masturbatory satisfaction had produced a state of tension which contributed to his insomnia. He called this state, in which he lay awake for hours, "boredom in bed", and vainly attempted to distract and amuse himself with games. He crowded his bed with a variety of toys in order always to be sure of finding something to play with. Unfatigued, he manipulated his toy vehicles, cards, and toy money for hours. As soon as the analyst explained that his need for toys in bed was a means of assurance against the temptation to masturbate, he strengthened his defense by extending his taboo to the touching of his toys at night.[20] He now substituted thought operations for the handling of the toys, which originally had diverted him from manual masturbation. He learned to play all his card games in his "head only", and was proud of being able to count his money "even without money". The fantasies which accompanied his masturbatory equivalent emphasized likewise the taboo of touching. They were centered around the automatic working of imaginary machines. "I need not even press a button to make trains or my elevator move upward," he explained. He imagined a truck or train or a passenger car going over a bridge, or "up, up, up the hill" and "slowly, slowly, down". To our question as to how his penis behaved during these fantasies, he answered that he tried to direct the descent of vehicles carefully so that the erection would not subside too quickly. "It goes up and down again, just as I want, and I try not to let it drop."

The blocking of sexual satisfaction had resulted in an uncontrollable outbreak of sadism and aggression. While he refrained from using his hands for masturbation he could not refrain from grabbing, in an almost obsessional manner, whatever he could get hold of. He destroyed possessions of his own as well as those of adults. It may well be that the breaking of objects symbolized the destruction of his own genital were he to touch it (11). His obsessional symptoms were transitory, but his preoccupation with certain thought operations made us aware of a nascent compulsive character. A tendency to brood about problems of life and death and morals emerged while he still indulged in sadistic outbursts. All these uncontrollable sadistic acts were designed to provoke repercussions, which in their turn served to gratify his passive desires.

Eventually he started to masturbate and his confession of manual masturbation was made through his drawings. Silently he spent many

19 The conspicuous absence of anal material in this patient can be explained by the fact that a temporary compulsive neurosis *in statu nascendi* subsided quickly under analysis.

20. The other side of his taboo of touching was expressed in his worry lest other people touch his eating utensils. He developed a preoccupation with contagious diseases which might be contracted through touch.

hours drawing hands. At first his hands could not be recognized as such. Later he used the analyst's hands and his own to trace around, but often left out a finger, once more indicating the danger of "blood poisoning", "losing a finger or a leg". Eventually, when interpretation had diminished his anxiety so that he could verbalize his problem, he could draw whole figures with complete limbs without resorting to tracing. This sequence of drawings from shapeless to accurate representations shows how the lifting of anxiety promotes simultaneously both greater sexual freedom and sublimation.

IV

Until now our presentation of Frankie's case may have given the impression that we centered our analysis primarily around the unconscious content of the child's symptoms and ignored his actual life experiences. However, we omitted to stress those parts of his treatment which referred to his current life only because we wished not to distract the reader's attention from the formative process of Frankie's neurosis. In presenting these processes we have been forced to schematize and simplify some of them but we hope that the reader will recognize that the forces which are now to be described as a sequence, were often at work simultaneously.

In analyzing two of Frankie's symptoms—the retention of urine and the elevator phobia—we learned about certain behavior patterns. In the past, they had been mainly related to his nurse but now they were centered in his father and reflected his fight against his passive desires. His passivity determined much of the nature and structure of his problem.

His symptoms were the carriers of the past and represented his experiences with his nurse. The dawning character formation could be observed in changes of his behavior, which were related to his continuing impressions and experiences pertaining to his father. The progressive analysis of his symptoms freed energy for the development of his character. But the passive drives which he turned toward his father stimulated the ancient memories of past passive gratifications connected with his nurse.

We mentioned that she was partly a representative of the father. It would be more correct to say that for the child, the father was a representative of the nurse. In many respects the status of the nurse in the family, and her behavior, were confusing to the child, because they invclved functions usually associated with the father's rôle. To Frankie it was she who laid down the rules and regulations and the mother seemed to be almost as dependent on her guidance as he himself was. This was actually true in periods of the father's absence, and facilitated the fusion of the father's image with that of the nurse.

When the nurse left the house, Frankie tried to re-enact the bed ritual with his mother, who complied with his wishes for a while. After a few weeks, probably disturbed by the importance the patting ritual had acquired for him, his mother gradually dropped it. It was this satisfaction the frustrated child sought to obtain by his aggressive acts against women.

The women's reaction to his sadistic outbursts again made him retreat from them and turn to his father. For a short time his rôle toward his father was like the one he had had toward his nurse after she had frustrated his masculine impulses, and this made him resort to his infantile dependence, which the nurse had been willing to gratify. Frankie had gone through at least three phases of obedience. All of these three phases followed periods during which his active strivings had been frustrated. His obedience was always dictated by his desire to obtain passive gratification and all three phases were abruptly ended when his expectations were disappointed. First he behaved like an obedient child with his nurse, who gladly accepted that pattern since it eased her responsibility for the child's care; she was motherly and kind when he was ready to play the rôle of the dependent little boy, but was intolerant of his active self-assertions. Next he acted as his mother wanted him to. He expressed love for her and suppressed all the signs of anxiety for which she had previously reprimanded him. In the third phase, in his relationship to his father, he indulged in long discussions on philosophical subjects, ranging from the existence of God, to the justification of laws, political and racial problems and, above all, questions about life and death—again behaving in a way satisfying to his father.

This intellectual relationship provided some gratification to his passive desires. His intellectual growth during this period was marked but this desirable sublimation was soon disturbed. The profuse passive gratification which he saw his little sister enjoying became a direct and potent stimulus to his own cravings. The longing for passive physical contact made him keen and alert in his observations and he meticulously noted any passive gratifications his mother and sister received from his father. When he saw his father stroke his sister's hair, he became depressed and longed for similar gratifications.[21] In order to experience the pleasures of a baby, he regressed to a behavior even more infantile than his sister's. He insisted on being washed and dressed like an infant, demanding this "love service" from his father. Once when his family was in a hurry to go out with him, he suddenly undressed completely and insisted that they dress him.

During this passive period he wanted to take the role of the woman, which meant, in his terms, to possess everything a woman has, while ignor-

21. In his analytic sessions at this period, he cut off the hair of all dolls before he could express this longing. We assume that the child displayed here a delayed reaction of jealousy which would have been appropriate when mother and nurse took care of his sister as an infant. The jealousy was focused on the father, since the father was to him at this time the phallic representative of mother and nurse.

ing the difference in the sex organs. He said that he wanted breasts like his mother's, and silky hair like his sister's. He asked his father to rest in bed beside him and he spoke openly about his wish to give birth to children.

His conscious desire for feminine satisfaction and the idea of change of sex was expressed in his attitude toward injections. While formerly even the thought of an injection resulted in unmanageable resistance, he now suddenly craved injections. In one of his uncontrollable outbursts during his analytic sessions he shouted ecstatically while looking at a picture of a boy he had been painting, "Give him an injection, make him a girl, make him a girl!"

His persistent courtship of his father was partly successful. He managed to achieve some anal-passive gratification in various ways, such as having his father throw a ball against his buttocks and rubbing his buttocks against the father's knee. The anal gratification aroused genital sensations (erections had been observed on such occasions) and he then craved to have the genital region treated by his father in the same way that he had wanted the nurse to treat it. He induced his father to button his fly and the coyness he displayed on such occasions made the father recognize the child's attempt at seduction, and caused him to become reserved. Here the patient must have felt a disappointment similar to the one he had experienced at an earlier age when his nurse, and, later, his mother withdrew gratifications. Like the father, they probably did so because his insistence and the intensity of his desires alarmed them.

After Frankie failed to obtain gratification from his father, he concluded that his mother was granted those gratifications which his father denied him, because she had no penis. Therefore, since the fulfillment of his passive desires was not obtainable without the loss of his penis, Frankie's fears forced him away from his father.

Frankie's castration fears compelled him to make an attempt to achieve an independence commensurate with his age. On the one hand, he joined the older boys in their play, and roamed the street far beyond his permitted limits. On the other hand, in his fantasies his desire for the passive role still prevailed. His passive cravings had, however, undergone marked changes and now were no longer pleasurable, but aroused anxiety. The passivity, which up to then had been openly and fearlessly expressed, was worked into a fearful fantasy of being kidnapped by strangers. He was preoccupied with this fantasy for months. The image of men lifting him up and carrying him away contained derivatives of earlier observations when he had seen his father lifting his mother. His ambivalent desire to be lifted and carried was condensed into the kidnapper fantasy, similar to that described in the elevator phobia.

The essential feature of these new kidnapping fantasies was that they contained no open reference to genital or anal gratifications and that the *factor of passive locomotion was dominant.* As long as these fantasies were of moderate intensity, carrying two toy revolvers sufficed as a magic gesture to ward off anxiety. But whenever his repressed passive desires increased in intensity, the fantasy of being kidnapped lost its playful features, and he went into attacks of violent panic in which he was unable to distinguish between the world of fantasy and reality.

Such an attack of panic was once observed within the analytic hour. It followed his return from a vacation trip. On the train, he happened to hear that two criminals had broken out of jail, and were hiding somewhere in the country. His first response to the news was to refuse to see the analyst any more. The next day, against his will he was taken to her office by his father. As soon as he saw the analyst, he lost all control, burst into tears, and assaulted her. He made attempts to choke her, and threatened to burn down her country house. (He had frequently referred to this house as a "hideaway", or "witch place", and had jokingly called the analyst a kidnapper, who kept kidnapped children hidden under the house.) His panic subsided when the analyst interpreted that he suspected her of hiding escaped criminals in her "hideaway", in order to give him up to them.[22]

We must assume that the train ride had touched off his conflict about passive locomotion and increased his susceptibility to anxiety.[23] The news of the jailbreak, therefore, stimulated his fantasies about being kidnapped and he repeated in analysis the reactive panic he had experienced when his nurse had threatened to give him up to the police or the elevatorman.

It would seem therefore that behind his peremptory refusal to see the analyst there was an unconscious challenge to be kidnapped. Indeed he provoked his father to take him forcibly to the analyst, thus succeeding in making the father his kidnapper.

To avoid such states of panic which the intensity of his passive desires repeatedly brought about, Frankie was forced to evolve an entirely new attitude. He began to ignore reality. Signs of passivity were eradicated and were replaced by feelings of omnipotence. He gave his parents nonsensical orders and was greatly annoyed if they were not carried out; he struck his sister and parents for not obeying unspoken orders. His world was divided into two camps: rulers and slaves—and he belonged to the world of rulers and supermen, who were characterized by incredible cruelty. He demanded that his father read him books in

22. The following elements were involved in the transference: The child reacted to the interruption of the work as if the analyst had abandoned him although it was the child and not the analyst who went on vacation. This separation from the analyst had revived the trauma when his mother had left him and then returned with a baby. The analyst is also accused of having children who live under her house. The child is saying—as it were—the analyst, like the mother, is unfaithful. She had taken advantage of his absence to give birth to another child and will give him up to kidnappers.

23. Trains always seemed dangerous vehicles to him, for the travelers were at the mercy of the conductor, who could create deadly accidents at will. In his games Frankie dramatized the following scene: children are separated from their mothers during a train ride. German soldiers masked as friends enter the train, shoot the mothers and take the children prisoners. Frequently the father and conductor are killed either by the German army or by burglars, and the children are left to the robbers, who are cannibals and murderers.

the middle of the night, and insisted on being served steak at two o'clock in the morning. In his analytic hour, he threatened that those who did not obey his orders would be sent to jail. When asked whether this could ever happen to him, he assured the analyst that if committed to such an institution, he would always find means of escape. He said: "They couldn't get me in, even if they carried me,"—indicating again his wish for passive locomotion and the resulting fear.

The analyst suggested that he was identifying himself with his tough radio heroes and criminals in order to ward off his passive desires. This interpretation had a negative therapeutic result. He reacted to it by strengthening this particular defense. His demands became even more fantastic, and from time to time his behavior resembled that of a megalo-maniacal patient. He claimed that he was actually a king: "Even if you don't know it and if you don't believe it." The fantasies of omnipotence were extensive; he called the exalted role he played in the universe, King Boo-Boo.

King Boo-Boo is master over life and death. Anyone who disobeys his orders will die. King Boo-Boo's thoughts are sufficient to cause another person's death. Sometimes some of his victims die, although they do not know of their own death and pretend to be alive.

King Boo-Boo also has power in political matters. "The U.S.A. only thinks she is a democracy, whereas in reality he governs her as a king. His army is stronger than that of the U.S.A. and Russia together. He is more cruel than Hitler, but people are so afraid of him that they don't dare to hate him. His soldiers and slaves love him so much that they finally *want to do* whatever he wishes" (an obvious projection of Frankie's passivity). Once in an outburst of exaltation he screamed:

"All the people, they like me better than anyone else in the world. I am better and I can kill everyone I want. I can even kill President Truman, I'm tired of him. I'm rid of him. I am going to make a new war against America. I am the manager of the world. I see that it goes around quick enough. I'm the executive committee. 'Execute her! execute her!' I said." (This referred to his little sister whose picture he had just drawn and which, at this point, he began to cut up).

A few minutes after this outburst, he tried to be Frankie again, but could not endure this rôle. While he was casting our parts in play, he shouted: "I am the policeman, I am the delivery man, I am the truck man, I am all the men together in the whole world!" Frankie's earlier fantasies about God were the predecessors of his later King Boo-Boo imagery and had contained similar elements of cruelty. His role of the all-powerful served two purposes: it was a defense against the fulfillment of the wish for passive gratification, and, at the same time, it was a means of obtaining that very gratification.

His dictatorial behavior at home and his fantastic ignoring of reality took on such proportions that it became questionable whether he could remain in his usual environment. This acute situation threat-ened the continuation of his treatment and necessitated special measures. As a last resort we had to bring to the child's attention the serious con-sequences his behavior would entail.

It was necessary that he be told that his behavior had actually one aim: to be sent away. This would be the realization of the one thing he had dreaded most: to be separated from his parents. We should like to amplify on the session which followed, and which brought about the decisive change in Frankie's attitude.

The analyst found him in the waiting room, the paper basket on his head, hilariously throwing books and blocks at his mother. After much maneuvering the analyst got him into the office. When alone with him, she asked him what he *really* thought the effect of his actions would be. She conceded that he acted as if he were a great king and as if he expected complete submission from his environment. But she expressed her doubts that he himself really believed in the truth of these ideas. She called to his attention the fact that his behavior would not have the desired effect and that no matter what he did, nobody would accept him as a superman or as King Boo-Boo. Frankie replied quickly: "Oh, they will find out some day, and they will do what I want!" The analyst then suggested that Frankie might not even know exactly what it was he really wanted and that he would probably achieve just the opposite of what seemed desirable to him.

Referring to several incidents during the analytic sessions in which he had acted out his King Boo-Boo ideas, she told him that even her positive relationship to him was influenced by his "actions". "Even before you enter my office, I can't help thinking: 'For goodness sake, what will Frankie try to do today; what is he going to break and to destroy today?'" He interrupted quickly: "Oh, you shouldn't care. You get paid for that, even more than it costs."

He was then asked whether he knew what had brought about this change in his behavior; after all, there had been a time when he had cared quite a bit for people, and when he had wanted to be with his mother all the time. Frankie replied triumphantly: "So that's fine; now I am cured of my fears, and I don't want to be with Mommy."

The analyst did not agree with him as to his being cured. She thought that he was still very much afraid, just as scared as he was at the time when he did not want to come to his session because he believed the analyst was a kidnapper. Only now he tried to hide his fear even from himself. He had never let her tell him what she actually thought about his kidnapper fantasies and about King Boo-Boo. But now she was seriously worried about his behavior. Therefore, she must show him that his King Boo-Boo behavior would end in something of which she had always thought he was terribly afraid. She had understood only recently that he really wanted to be carried off by someone, to be lifted and taken away. Didn't he himself see that he was behaving now just as he had when he used to attack people and then scream with fear, "Don't grab me! I surrender, I surrender!" Perhaps he was again looking for the old excitement, always waiting to see whether people would not eventually do the very thing which he dreaded.

The analyst told him she was compelled to assume that he wanted to create a situation where his being sent away was the only possible outcome. She was reminded of his nurse's threats to have elevator men and policemen come up and take him away. Perhaps these thoughts had always been somewhat pleasurable to him, although he had been aware of *only his fears.*

The child listened calmly, although this was quite unusual in this period of unmanageable wildness. Eventually he asked seriously: "Where can you send me? My parents promised they would never send me to a camp or to a boarding school if I didn't want to go there. And you yourself told me that children cannot go to jail. And a reform school wouldn't even take me because I'm very good at school."

Thereupon the analyst told him about hospitals which specialized in treating children whose sickness led them to behave in unacceptable ways.[24] He interrupted: "But I'm not sick; I have no temperature." The analyst stated that people who seriously believed that the world was divided into two camps "of an almighty king and the rest slaves" are seriously ill, even without a temperature and belong into special hospitals. He replied: "But Hitler could do whatever he wanted. Only, if I had been Hitler, *I would not have killed myself. I would have waited until they come and do something to me.*" Suddenly realizing that the analyst referred to mental illness, he became quite frightened and asked, "Do you think I'm crazy? Do you think I belong in a crazy house?"

Without waiting for an answer, he wanted to know in detail how those hospitals were run, how children were kept there, whether they were visited by their parents, what kind of toys they had, whether they were permitted to have knives and blocks and whether they were analyzed there. Our answers obviously disappointed him; they did not fit into his picture of exciting fights between attendants and patients and between kidnappers and the kidnapped.

The psychodynamics of this analytic session brought about a decisive therapeutic gain which may be explained as follows:

1) The beginning of the analytic session permitted Frankie to re-experience and to act out the full grandeur of his world of fantasy. He had an opportunity to demonstrate his narcissistic omnipotence, his disdain for reality and his belief in the inferiority and weakness of the analyst.

2) The next analytic step was a thrust into his unconscious, and a demonstration that his unconscious aim was to enforce a separation from home. This was a contradiction of his omnipotence which even the almighty King Boo-Boo could not overlook.

3) He readily picked up the suggestion about enforcing a separation and revealed his unconscious desire by the great interest he showed in the place to which he would be sent. By asking one question after another, he began to consider the reality of what would happen if his unconscious desires were really fulfilled. This process then effected a valuation of what might have appeared in brilliant colors if left in terms

---

24. The particular technique used in this session was an emergency measure in a very crucial situation, and should not be viewed as a typical or terminal procedure.

of the unconscious. The ego discovered that fulfillment of these unconscious desires was drab and monotonous if carried out in reality. Thus, step by step, he gratified his wishes in his imagination and simultaneously learned that the price he would have to pay was not in proportion to the pleasures to be obtained.[25] The analyst succeeded in proving that this defense was not perfect but would lead finally to the victory of his passive desires by commitment to an institution. Only then did Frankie start to doubt the wisdom of carrying his King Boo-Boo fantasies into reality. It is of interest to note why our earlier interpretations of his feelings of omnipotence as a defense against passivity did not have the desired effect. As long as the analyst merely discussed his megalomaniacal behavior as a defense without interpreting in detail his unconscious desire, she was doing nothing to impede the use of this mechanism. If anything, her remarks only helped him to consolidate this defense.

The threat which the child felt in our discussion of "craziness" had contributed to the deflation of his kidnapper fantasy. The final devaluation of the kidnapper fantasy and of the defense of being King Boo-Boo came about after we succeeded in showing him how the warded-off desire for passive gratification was contained even in this very defense. In addition, it was designed to result in satisfaction which he might have missed as an infant. After all, we said, acting as an almighty king was indeed a repetition of infantile behavior. We referred in particular to those scenes in which he demanded food in the middle of the night and we compared his behavior to that of a hungry infant whose screaming usually brings the desired food.

Nothing in our interpretation caused Frankie more despair than the analogy between his temper tantrums when his wishes were not fulfilled and the attacks of screaming and fury which an infant shows when its hunger is not immediately satisfied. Here we touched on what we probably might consider his "primal trauma" in a period in which he, hungry for milk and affection, screamed for hours. This, as the reader will recall, had happened when night feeding was stopped at the age of 5 months.

In brief, in the following months we were able to discuss with Frankie's active participation his feeling of omnipotence and his belief in the omnipotence of his thoughts. In so doing we followed Ferenczi's

25. Two other factors may have contributed to the child's willingness to accept the interpretations of this decisive hour: The analyst had discussed with his parents the possible necessity of removing him from the family. The parents were depressed by the prospect and the patient had probably sensed their depression and the seriousness of the situation. The analyst, through her active interference, had again contributed to his identification of her with his image of the nurse who, like the analyst, had threatened him, but on the other hand, had also acted as his protector.

conception, presented in his paper, *Stages in the Development of the Sense of Reality* (13).

After our frequent interpretations of his feelings of omnipotence as derivatives of infantile behavior Frankie announced that he had something to tell us. He had a "remembering machine", a "projecting machine"—which he could turn backwards as far as he liked. In it he saw that the analyst's mother had killed the analyst at the command of King Boo-Boo, because she, the analyst—when a baby—had screamed so violently that she had disturbed the whole world. When our discussion led to the motives for his projecting his feelings of frustration and fear onto the analyst he gave way to a fit of rage and ran away from his analytic session. Pale and disturbed, he hid in the family car, and requested his mother to "throw the analyst out", or else he would smash the car. It took several hours to calm him. We had to discuss with him the fact that though he might not remember his infancy, he must have heard many comparisons of his own baby behavior with that of his sister, and he must have received the impression that his parents had never forgiven him his screaming at night. His sister had always been praised as a good, quiet baby which must have made him even more angry at her. Perhaps it was not only the analyst who should have been killed as a baby by her mother—maybe he had often wished the same would happen to his sister, so that his family could not rave about her. Finally we had to enlist his mother's help in reassuring him that in spite of her despair about his early screaming attacks, she now felt no resentment whatsoever toward him. Since her relationship to him had become genuinely warm, this reassurance was of therapeutic help.

The following months during which the child was able to work through the conflict about his passivity were a period of consolidation during which he was preparing himself for the termination of his analysis.

The prospect of ending the analysis revived for him the pain of separation from his mother at the time his sister was born. This prompted us to use these last months for further working through his relationship to his mother. During the weeks of our analytic interpretation of his early oral frustrations, his anger against her was reactivated and he demonstrated an unusually strong oral envy and aggression. Whenever he suspected that his mother preferred his sister to him, whenever she did anything for the little girl, he either gave vent to his fury against his mother and sister, as in earlier periods, or became depressed. The investigation of these moods produced a flood of material referring to early orality. We could witness the changes which his oral impulses underwent and how the freed energy was diverted for reaction formation and sublimation.[26]

Even when he was on the verge of giving up most of his megalomaniacal fantasies, he still used King Boo-Boo's "remembering machine" to deny his own past experiences of frustration, aggression and fear of retaliation. He first claimed that this machine did not remember what

26. When Frankie came into analysis he was a greedy child who devoured huge bags of "animal crackers" during his analytic hour and frequently asked for more food from the analyst. His orality was characterized by possessiveness and cruelty. God was drawn as a creature with a huge mouth, and he frequently described God's

had happened in his own life but knew exactly the analyst's misdeeds and *her* mother's rage. Under the cover of the remembering machine, and through the voice of King Boo-Boo he expressed his aggressive fantasies regarding his intrauterine existence.

For example, King Boo-Boo—in contrast to all other people—could remember when he, the King, was still an embryo "and ate up his mother from the inside and also any other children she wanted to have." Only gradually could King Boo-Boo's "remembering and projecting machine" be focused on Frankie's own childhood and on more than the intrauterine period. Presently we could ask him to focus it on the transference situation and on events which had recently occurred in his analysis.

He wanted to know exactly who would take his particular hour after he had finished his analysis, and it seemed to us an important step when Frankie could say laughingly, "I hope that you won't take a child younger than me." And only in those last months of analysis was it possible for Frankie to realize the twofold nature of his transference to the analyst. On the one hand, he repeated the dependence which originally he had developed toward his nurse, and, on the other, the aggression with which he reacted to any frustration caused by his mother.

Only now could he be shown, for instance, that his rage and his fear at the thought that the analyst would give him up to kidnappers was also based on his fear of abandonment. He feared that the analyst would turn away from him as he had withdrawn from his mother when she came home from the hospital.

An important and new therapeutic gain was achieved when Frankie realized that his megalomaniacal behavior and fantasies were a defense not only against his passive strivings (kidnapper fantasy) but also a protection against suffering and death. Though he had rejected God and life-after-death at an early age, he had felt in need of some substitute consolation. He had tried to gain this consolation by making himself believe that at least a creation of fantasy, King Boo-Boo, was endowed with

teeth in detail. Devouring was a frequent element in his dramatizations, and impregnation was linked with oral incorporation. Punishment was seen in oral terms. During his analytic hour, he often had fantasies of cutting his sister into pieces, cooking her and preparing "totem" meals. In the period of working through his oral aggressive fantasies an expression of oral sharing appeared. He bought candies with his own allowance and offered them generously to the analyst, her secretary and the patient whose session followed his. He made plans to give a present to his sister before his analysis was ended and in an especially generous mood wanted to invite her to share an analytic session with him.

His desire to devour huge quantities of food was sublimated into his interest in the origin and preparation of food. Food, the object of incorporation, became the subject of investigation and learning. At school he wrote a long paper about the food of Indian tribes in which there was no reference to taste or to the act of eating as such; his report was exclusively devoted to the technique of food preparation and the use of eating utensils. His oral possessiveness was not only sublimated into the sharing of food and theoretical food interests, but he discovered the institution of keepsakes. Keepsakes, not only for the child, but also for the adult, mean, "I do not devour you as a whole, but I take a little piece of you and let you live." Frankie's tendency to start a collection of keepsakes, such as the little toys and vases which he asked the analyst to give him, impressed her as a definite sign that his oral greediness had developed into a socially acceptable though still narcissistically colored attachment.

immortality. And when he was faced with the demand that he give up
even this buttressing fantasy he once more had resorted to phobic mechanisms, albeit this time only in his thoughts.

The following incident which occurred at a time when he was eager
to attend a day camp during the summer will illustrate this: Having
injured his leg, Frankie was worried that this injury might prevent him
from starting on time. So he mentally rehearsed his phobic mechanisms,
all the ways of avoiding a repetition of such accidents. He told his
sister that he would not leave the house so as not to hurt himself before
going to camp. To her response that she had once hurt herself in their
own house, he replied: "That's right, but I could just sit in my room
and I would not move at all." She, however, showed him that there still
could be dangers, since he might fall off his chair and hurt himself that
way. To this he retorted: "Well, I could stay in bed. I wouldn't even
dress, and then certainly nothing could happen to me." He was somewhat ashamed when reporting this plan to the analyst, adding: "That's
very stupid, I know. For instance, it would be dumb not to use the
subway because you might catch a cold from germs. I know that germs
are all over the world and I might get a cold anywhere." Then he said
triumphantly: "But it would not be stupid to stay away from school, or
from camp if the Mayor tells you to, because there is an epidemic of
infantile paralysis." Here for the first time Frankie took a reasonable
stand toward real dangers, which mirrored a significant and far-reaching
change in his superego formation. It may be worth while to review the
long road which had led to this achievement.

When Frankie entered his analysis, he was completely enslaved by
his symptoms. His preoccupation with his mother and with the need
for assurance that he could obtain gratification without endangering his
existence, resulted in a constriction of his ego. He had not accepted any
external ideals and there were hardly any indications of internal prohibitions. These are the signs of a severe lag in the formation of a superego.

During his oedipal phase, his fears were displaced from real objects
such as his mother, his nurse, and his father, to imaginary objects and
situations. The fears referring to his mother were shifted to "uncanny
places" in which there was danger of being trapped, such as bathrooms,
elevators and small consultation rooms. His fears referring to his father
were projected to imaginary objects like wolves from which he expected
retaliation for his aggressive impulses. As the reader will remember,
the resolving of those fears temporarily resulted in an eruption of instinctual impulses as, for instance, when he rejected his father's authority with the words, "I'm no longer afraid of my wolves, I can do whatever I want."

Considering what had caused the lag in superego formation, we
must refer to two factors. One is that his environment did not provide
him with a clear-cut frame of reference as to objects of identification.

For example, his mother acted like a child in relation to the nurse, and it was the nurse who exercised authority. Yet he sensed that the nurse took a secondary position whenever his father made his sporadic and brief appearances during wartime and that she was paid to take care of him. The second and more important factor was that this nurse combined her prohibitions with libidinal gratifications. Normally, as the oedipal phase ends, the prohibitions of the environment are internalized and accepted. The sexual demands are renounced and these prohibitions and the growing demands of reality are consolidated to form the core of the superego. In Frankie's case, however, his nurse's prohibitions were sexualized as soon as they were expressed and therefore instead of forming the basis of a superego, these sexualized prohibitions laid the foundation for a masochistic perversion.[27]

It was only after the nurse's departure that we could observe the first brief and unsuccessful attempts at building a superego. We refer to Frankie's interest in laws and regulations. At about that time he suggested to his family the founding of a "Club for Democracy and Being Good". He invented rules and punishments, but they were so exaggerated that no one could abide by them. The slightest infringement was punished by complete annihilation, such as being "stamped to death by an elephant" or "being tied to a lion's mouth".

27. Throughout Frankie's analysis we pursued the vicissitudes of his passive drives, hoping that our observations would permit us some general assertions with regard to the origin of passive homosexuality in boys, as well as of masochism. We must admit that his analysis did not offer sufficient material to draw final conclusions about either. Whether the activation of Frankie's brief perversion was accelerated by some prohibition by the patient's nurse or even caused by it, is not the point of our discussion in this context. Whatever the biological roots of Frankie's passivity, his turning toward his father as a love object was preceded by the traumatic rejection of his phallic activity by nurse and mother, the two most important feminine figures in his life. We have reason to believe that the rejection itself had been preceded by manipulation of the child's genitalia by the nurse. Whatever his biological readiness for this passive satisfaction, it is still important that he had been habitually passively gratified by his nurse. By tradition, by training, and because of convenience, it is certainly a temptation to settle the question of genesis by recourse to the biological explanation. However, the ascription to constitutional factors as an explanation serves to block rather than to help our understanding. It is permissible only after we have exhausted all other possibilities. We should rather focus on those environmental elements which seem to be unique in each case, elements which although apparently accidental, may contain the common factors in the development of passive homosexuality and masochism.

The present disagreement among analysts on this topic will yield to constructive discussion after more analytic material on children will have been collected and scrutinized. Although child analysis will not solve the problem of the biological components of passivity and masochism, it may help to clarify it by bringing to light in greater detail the environmental influences. Especially if the parents' personalities are well-known to the analyst, he may be able to make a fair appraisal of the extent to which the environment may have been conducive to favoring or blocking the behavior which the child shows. It will probably be easier to observe fine gradations and to weigh the relative influence of external and biological forces in the analysis of children than in that of adults.

Once he drew a diagram for his father, explaining to him the battles which it represented. It showed a head and in it two "control towers" of good and bad Frankies. The "control towers" were responsible for the outcome of those battles. He himself could not control these battles, since "there is no bone connecting my mouth with my head or the control tower". He added, however, that there might be a chance that his good part and the good control tower would win the battle if his father were ready to do exactly what Frankie wanted him to do. Here he showed again the pattern of libidinizing the fulfillment of a duty. But this fantasy also shows the dawning of internal demands, expressed in his wish that the forces of good should win, although this internal prohibiting agent is still feeble and impotent.

We must draw the reader's attention to one more factor of this child's superego pathology. It is most significant in the development of his psychic structure that his earlier internalized superego configuration—King Boo-Boo—was not felt as something separate from his ego. Most children who have created such a primary and tyrannical superego, let it modify their behavior. Their ego accepts the superego as a prohibitory influence. When Frankie first invented King Boo-Boo, his ego, on the contrary, sided with this figure, and derived from it, in so doing, the strength and permission to act out an unrestrained omnipotence. This omnipotence served as an aggrandizement of his ego which had been tortured, humiliated, and frightened throughout the years of his neurosis.

Once he could give up acting out his King Boo-Boo fantasies, he could transfer his omnipotence to others who represented his ego-ideals. He could accept his father as a strong and enviable figure without becoming passively dependent on him. He had given up his wish for physical gratifications and therefore his anxiety had vanished. He could now compete in healthy and constructive ways with people of his environment, such as his athletics teacher, whom he admired for his strength and his justice, and the camp director, whom he praised for his ability and experience. In short, he had accepted the fact that there were people from whom he, a little boy, could learn.

The material produced in the next to the last hour of his analysis illustrates his new-found capacities.

The first topic related to the termination of his analysis. He had difficulty in bringing up his impending separation from the analyst, although he was now able to speak about his past separation from his mother. Frankie's acknowledgment that he did not really want to part from his analyst for good came indirectly. He suggested that the present which was to be given to him at the end of his analysis should be postponed until Christmas, rationalizing that "by that time, those particular trains will be of a better make". The analyst admitted that she herself did not consider the analysis completely finished, but that she trusted his ability to get along without her and to come back whenever he might need help. Thereupon Frankie showed his readiness to depend on people in the outside world for protection by announcing with a solemn expression his decision to let King Boo-Boo die. "Do you know that King Boo-Boo will not live always? I've made up my mind. Tomorrow is the day he is going to be 100 years old, and before that, he is going to commit suicide. First, all other people will die; his soldiers have killed all the other people; and then all his soldiers will commit suicide because they know King Boo-Boo will die and they do not want to live without him."

We hinted that though his King Boo-Boo was to die, Frankie was still not willing to admit that death was something he could not control; otherwise, he would have allowed King Boo-Boo to die a natural death. Frankie understood. He laughed wholeheartedly.

During this conversation he was toasting a biscuit over a gas flame. The biscuit suddenly caught fire and flared up. Frankie let it drop to the floor. For a second his clothes were in danger of catching fire. He showed no panic, but did what he was told. Only his sudden pallor betrayed his justifiable fright. Suddenly he went to the window and asked the analyst: "Would you let me jump out of the window? I mean just jump to the next roof [a distance of about twelve yards]?" He tried to convince her that he could hold on to the telephone wire, and when told that the analyst would not let him jump, he asked: "Why not? Would you jump?" "No," was the reply, "I would be afraid of being killed." Frankie asked: "What would you like better—to die jumping down, or to be trapped here?" When the analyst answered that she would neither like to jump nor to be trapped, but that if there were a fire, she would obey the instructions of the fire department, and even jump if told to, he replied: "I think I would too, if I were told; but I would not do it gladly."

What Frankie needed in order to let King Boo-Boo die was the reassurance that not only he, a little boy, but every person is exposed to injuries, sickness and death, and that mastering reality is a difficult task for all of us.

In this significant hour we see recapitulated all the elements which we encountered in his first analytic session when he dramatized the lonely boy and the fire in the hospital. We could observe that the derivatives of his initial fears were firmly embedded in an adequate relationship to reality without eliciting fear, although the contents of his past conflicts were present to his mind.

A prognosis in child analysis is not easy. We are by no means sure that we have forestalled a later recurrence of Frankie's neurosis. But when he stood at the window, gauging the distance to the next roof, when at last fear, fantasy of omnipotence, and reality had become synthesized in one constructive act, when he was able to ask how we guard ourselves from danger,—when he could face danger without resorting to pathological anxiety or belief in magic and omnipotence,—then we knew that the secondary process had won a victory over the primary process. And this we thought, was the utmost a boy of 8½ can achieve—even with the help of child analysis.

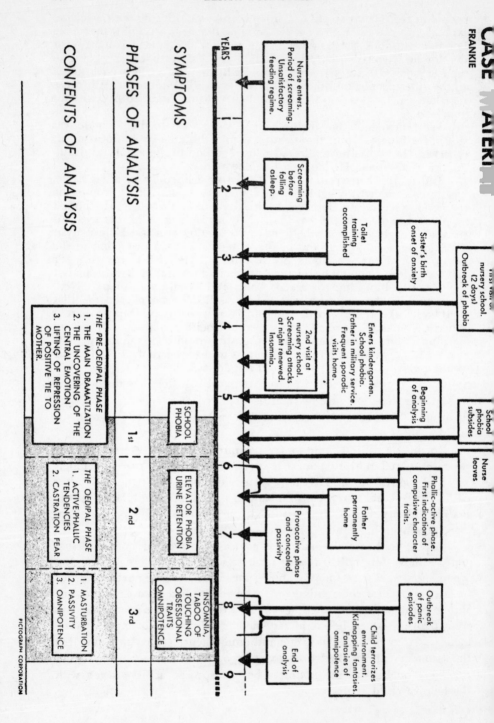

CASE MATERIAL

FRANKIE

SYMPTOMS

PHASES OF ANALYSIS

CONTENTS OF ANALYSIS

YEARS

Nurse enters. Period of screaming. Unsatisfactory feeding regime.

Screaming before falling asleep.

Toilet training accomplished

Sister's birth onset of anxiety

First visit at nursery school. (2 days) Outbreak of phobia

Enters kindergarten. School phobia. Father in military service. Frequent sporadic visits home.

2nd visit at nursery school. Screaming attacks at night renewed. Insomnia.

Beginning of analysis

School phobia subsides

Nurse leaves

Phallic-active phase. First indication of compulsive character traits.

Father permanently home

Provocative phase and concealed passivity

Outbreak of panic episodes

Child terrorizes environment. Kidnapping fantasies. Fantasies of omnipotence

End of analysis

SCHOOL PHOBIA

ELEVATOR PHOBIA URINE RETENTION

INSOMNIA, TABOO OF TOUCHING OBSESSIONAL TRAITS OMNIPOTENCE

1st

2nd

3rd

THE PRE-OEDIPAL PHASE
1. THE MAIN DRAMATIZATION
2. THE UNCOVERING OF THE CENTRAL EMOTION
3. LIFTING OF REPRESSION OF POSITIVE TIE TO MOTHER.

THE OEDIPAL PHASE
1. ACTIVE-PHALLIC TENDENCIES
2. CASTRATION FEAR

1. MASTURBATION
2. PASSIVITY
3. OMNIPOTENCE

PICTOGRAPH CORPORATION

BIBLIOGRAPHY

1. Abraham, K. "A Constitutional Basis of Locomotor Anxiety", *Selected Papers*, Hogarth, 1942.

2. Abraham, K. "Zur Psychogenese der Strassenangst im Kindesalter", *Klein. Beiträge z. Psa.* Internat. Psa. Verlag, Wien, 1921.

3. Alexander, F. and French, T. M. *Psychoanalytic Therapy*, Ronald Press, 1946.

4. Allen, F. *Psychotherapy with Children*, Norton, 1942.

5. Bonaparte, M. "Passivity, Masochism, and Frigidity", *Intern. J. Psa.*, XVI, 1935.

6. Bornstein, B. "Clinical Notes on Child Analysis", *this Annual*, I, 1945.

7. Brunswick, R. M. "The Preoedipal Phase of Libido Development", *Psa. Quar.*, IX, 1940.

8. Burlingham, D. T. "Probleme des psychoanalytischen Erziehers", *Zeit. f. psa. Paed.*, XI, 1937.

9. Daly, C. D. "The Role of Menstruation in Human Phylogenesis and Ontogenesis", *Internat. J. Psa.*, XXIV, 1944.

10. Deutsch, H. "The Genesis of Agoraphobia", *Internat. J. Psa.*, X, 1929.

11. Federn, P. "Beiträge zur Analyse des Sadismus und Masochismus", *Internat. Zeit. f. Psa.*, I, 1913, and II, 1914.

12. Fenichel, O. "Remarks on the Common Phobias", *Psa. Quar.*, XIII, 1944.

13. Ferenczi, S. "Stages in the Development of the Sense of Reality", *Contrib. to Psa.*, Badger, Boston, 1916.

14. French, T. M. "Some Psychoanalytic Applications of the Psychological Field Concept", *Psa. Quar.*, XI, 1942.

15. French, T. M. "Integration of Social Behavior", *ibid.*, XIV, 1945.

16. Freud, A. *The Psychoanalytical Treatment of Children*, Imago, 1946.

17. Freud, A. *The Ego and the Mechanisms of Defence*, Internat. Univ. Press, 1946.

18. Freud, S. "The Economic Problem in Masochism", *Coll. Papers*, II.

19. Freud, S. "Analysis of a Phobia in a Five-Year-Old Boy", *Coll. Papers*, II.

20. Freud, S. "Notes Upon a Case of Obsessional Neurosis", *ibid.*, III.

21. Freud, S. "From the History of an Infantile Neurosis", *ibid.*, III.

22. Freud, S. *The Problem of Anxiety*, Norton, 1936.

23. Freud, S. "Der Humor", *Ges. Schriften*, XI.

24. Fromm, E. *Escape from Freedom*, Farrar & Rinehart, 1941.

25. Gerard, M. W. "Alleviation of Rigid Standards", in Alexander, F. and French, T. M. *Psychoanalytic Therapy*, Ronald Press, 1946.
26. Greenacre, P. "The Predisposition to Anxiety", *Psa. Quar.*, X. 1941.
27. Greenacre, P. "Pathological Weeping", *ibid.*, XIV, 1945.
28. Hartmann, H. "Ich-Psychologie und Anpassungsproblem", *Internat. Ztschr. f. Psa.*, XXIV, 1939.
29. Hermann, I. "Sich Anklammern-Auf Suche gehen", *ibid.*, XXII, 1936.
30. Klein, Melanie, *Psychoanalysis of Children*. Hogarth, 1948.
31. Lampl-De Groot, J. "The Pre-oedipal Phase in the Development of the Male Child", *this Annual*, II, 1946.
32. Lewin, B. D. "Claustrophobia", *Psa. Quar.*, IV, 1935.
33. Loewenstein, R. "Phallic Passivity in Man", *Internat. J. Psa.*, XVI, 1935.
34. Menninger, K. A. *Man Against Himself*, Harcourt, 1938.
35. Rado, Sandor. Review of Anna Freud's *Einführung in die Technik der Kinderanalyse*, in *Zschr. f. Psa.*, XIV, 4, 1928.
36. Schilder, P. "The Relations between Clinging and Equilibrium", *Internat. J. Psa.*, XX, 1939.

ANALYSIS OF PSYCHOGENIC CONSTIPATION IN A TWO-YEAR-OLD CHILD [1]

By EDITHA STERBA, Ph.D. (Detroit)

Psychogenic constipation is a very frequent symptom in neuroses of childhood, and often a transient symptom during the normal process of toilet training. But it is seldom possible even in child analysis to penetrate to the first appearance of psychogenic constipation and to see the influence of toilet training in the genesis of the symptom. This is because the symptom often appears at a time when the child is not yet able to verbalize his feelings adequately and he therefore cannot subsequently produce memories of those experiences which might explain the details of the symptom formation.

The analytic study of little George's symptom presented an opportunity to observe psychogenic constipation almost *in statu nascendi* at such an early age that all contributing factors could be traced and the complex etiology of the symptom unravelled. George was 26½ months old when he was brought to me because of constipation which had lasted for several months, and which was clearly psychogenic.

He was an only child. Both parents were young, and were employed in business concerns; they were in modest but comfortable circumstances, and were greatly attached to their little boy, whom they tried to educate without prejudice. They made constant efforts to shield him from any unpleasant or frightening experience, gave him all possible freedom, and were never particularly severe, harsh, or unfriendly with him. They took pains to answer all his questions truthfully, kept nothing secret from him, and always tried to handle him as reasonably as possible.

George himself was a normally developed, perhaps somewhat delicate child. He was attractive, and had a particular charm which no adult could resist, so that wherever he went he immediately became the center of interest, and was spoiled by everyone. He was neither timid nor shy, nor on the other hand, was he bold or obtrusive. He was fully conscious of the effect he had upon others, and took the attention that came his way as a matter of course. He was wide-awake, observant, and intelligent for his age. His speech was already advanced. He wanted to know and to understand everything, and gave the general impression of a fully developed, independent little personality, who always knew exactly what he wanted. He had an apparently good relationship to his parents: he neither required too much affection, nor was he excessively dependent.

1. Reprinted from *Zeitschrift für psychoanalytische Pädagogik*, VIII, 1934.

The mother furnished me with a carefully kept diary, in which she had recorded the exact details of his early development. After a normal birth, his first suckling period had passed without any difficulties. When he was 3 weeks old, constipation, frequently observed among children who are breastfed, manifested itself, and upon the advice of the pediatrician George was given an enema almost daily until the end of the 4th month. During this time he never had a spontaneous bowel movement. At the end of the 4th month it was sufficient to insert the enema tube into his anus to cause him to move his bowels. When he was weaned, at 6 months, the constipation vanished immediately, and from then on his bowel movements were entirely normal.

When he was 9 months old, he was put on a potty. Six weeks later he defecated in it for the first time. Very soon after this the mother noticed that he always grumbled and whimpered when the potty with his excrement in it was carried out of the room.

At 13 months he refused absolutely to have his temperature taken rectally, but 6 months later he preferred to have it taken there, and as he then had an elevation in temperature for about two months, it was taken often. One can assume that the anal libido of this child was greatly stimulated, and that even if this had its basis in a strong constitutional anality, it was considerably increased by the constant use of enemas.

The actual toilet training was left to Mary, the nursemaid, since the mother worked and therefore had no time to do it herself. From what she was able to observe, the nursemaid seemed patient and not too severe in her demands. The mother did not attach particular importance to the toilet training, since it seemed to be taking a normal course. At 18 months George was almost completely trained. He never soiled himself, nor did he ever suffer from constipation; but although he never wet during the day, he still sometimes wet at night. In order to prevent the bed from getting wet, a diaper was put on him. The wetting at night lasted for several weeks after the child was completely trained in the daytime, and the mother felt that something was wrong. Upon the recommendation of an acquaintance, she came to my child guidance clinic for advice as to the quickest way of breaking the child of the habit of wetting himself at night. Since the diaper was put on only at night, when the child was undressed, I assumed that George understood this as a measure to stop him from touching his penis, and that the wetting was a substitute gratification for playing with it. I therefore adviced the mother to try leaving off the diaper. My assumption proved correct, because from the day they stopped putting a diaper on him he stayed dry at night. He even said very contentedly a few times in the evening, "George doesn't need a diaper anymore. He can touch his pee-pee (his name for his penis)."

During the first year George had shared his parents' bedroom, but as he woke up at night from time to time and seemed restless, he was given a room of his own, where he slept quietly, without any fear of being alone. At this time he showed no great dependence upon his parents, was not sad when they went away, but was usually friendly and happy with those around him.

When he was 16½ months old the mother first observed signs of anxiety. She was putting the child to bed one evening, when a friend of her husband came to visit. George who until this time had always been friendly with strangers, was suddenly terrified, showed great anxiety, and began to cry when his mother talked to the visitor. All her efforts to make him friendly toward the visitor had the opposite effect. He would not go to sleep alone afterward; he awoke during the night screaming, stood up in his bed, and when his mother came, clung to her and looked anxiously around the room. He refused to stay by himself. Inasmuch as, for several days after this, he would always start to cry when his mother had to go away and leave him, she again came to me for advice. I thought that George's anxiety was caused by a fear that the strange man would take his mother away from him. Perhaps something similar had happened with the nursemaid. I advised her to watch the nursemaid unobserved. The mother did discover that the maid met a man friend in the park, and quite naturally, while he was there, did not pay much attention to the child. These meetings had taken place several times, and the maid admitted that George had been very hostile toward and afraid of her friend. The meetings were stopped, and as a consequence the child's mind seemed to be quite at ease again. He no longer cried when the mother left him, and showed no more fear of strangers.

It was only during George's treatment that his mother recalled an incident that had occurred at this time, and that not only had a bearing on George's subsequent constipation, but was most certainly significant in relation to the appearance of his anxiety. Just before this anxiety appeared George had had a severe attack of diarrhea. Although he was already accustomed to the use of the potty, he naturally could not hold back his liquid stool. One day he soiled himself at least five times, and the nursemaid said sharply and irritably to the mother, "If he would just call me in time, and hold it back until I get into the room!" The mother paid no further attention to this remark, since Mary was otherwise always patient and never irritable when George dirtied himself. The anxiety of the child, as it manifested itself later in the treatment, was connected not only with the behavior of the nursemaid during his attack of diarrhea. He was obviously afraid that the mother as well as the nursemaid—whom he knew to be angry with him on account of his soiling himself—would go away with the strange man and that he would have to stay alone. He fled from the strict nursemaid to the mother, and therefore did not want his mother to go away and leave him alone with the maid.

The first signs of the psychogenic constipation were observed when George was 20 months old. From the time that he was weaned, that is, from the 6th month, he had never suffered from constipation. Since the mother was always at work, he had his bowel movements during her absence, and she had believed Mary's reports that things were all right, because the child was happy and well. During the summer vacation, when the mother was in closer contact with the child, she noticed that he refused to defecate in the presence of his father or her. He would use the potty only when he was alone with the nursemaid. At first the mother thought this a natural result of the nurse's supervision of his toilet habits, but after some time she noticed certain marked changes: George appeared to be anxious again; at night he begged to be tucked in tightly, so as to be warm. He would often stand alone in a corner of the room, very quiet and tense. He was afraid of sudden or strange noises. Thus, for example, he was frightened by the sound of a vacuum cleaner which he could hear being used in an apartment on the next floor, and could only be calmed when the cause of the noise was explained to him. He became particularly anxious when he thought he had been naughty, and it was often obvious that he felt guilty, although no severe demands had been made upon him.

Since the mother had observed that the nursemaid was no longer capable of answering all the questions of this intelligent child, she engaged a young nursery school teacher for a few hours a day, with the idea of gradually preparing George for separation from the nursemaid. Furthermore, it had seemed to her for some time that Mary, who had always loved and admired the little boy, had become on the one hand far too demonstrative and unrestrained in her affection for George, while on the other hand she was often unreasonably strict.

From the day that the nursery school teacher began to take care of George, it became quite clear that he was suffering from psychically conditioned constipation. The nursemaid had always reported that his bowel movements were regular and quite in order. However, now that he was no longer in her charge, he never had any regular movements, so that the mother had to assume that matters had not been quite in order, in spite of Mary's assertions to the contrary. He never asked for the potty of his own accord. If he were reminded to have a bowel movement, he had a thousand pretexts for postponing the matter for a whole day, and if finally forced to sit on the potty, he would sit there for a long time without doing anything. If he were strongly urged to defecate, he would scream continuously, "I don't want to press!" After he succeeded in this way in keeping back his stool for some days, he would lose all his appetite, would be pale and strained, and would hardly be able to eat at all. Laxatives were seldom effective, and if a suppository was used he knew how to expel it at once and yet retain his stool. Several times he was given enemas which he resisted with all his might. They were accompanied by temper tantrums and screaming. All educational efforts, such as the use of friendly persuasion, promises, and so on, even anger and punishment, were entirely without effect. Nor could the nursemaid exert any influence on him now that he was no longer entirely in her charge. In this period he never had a spontaneous bowel movement. Various diets prescribed by various doctors were unsuccessful, and matters went so far that George refused to eat stewed or fresh fruit, apparently realizing that an attempt was being made to influence his digestion in this way. He had never before caused any trouble about eating. Medical examinations given at this time to ascertain whether there were any organic reason for the constipation were completely negative.

About the time that George was 2 years old the mother once heard the nursemaid, who was playing with the child in the next room, say to him, "You must press me. You have to press me a little bit harder." She entered the room and saw that the girl was sitting with George pressed between her thighs and was kissing him violently. The child looked frightened and was struggling to get away from her. The mother, who had been displeased with the girl's exaggerated affection for the child for some time, and who suspected some connection between George's "I won't press," and the girl's demand, decided to dismiss the latter at once. She engaged an older maid who looked after the household in addition to taking care of George. Astonishingly enough, George, who had been with Mary over a year, showed no reaction to the separation, which he had neither expected nor understood. For the mother dismissed the girl so quickly that she did not even have time to tell him she was going away or to say goodbye to him. She was simply not there any more. He at once attached himself without any visible anxiety to the new maid who, as a matter of fact, very soon came to admire him as thoroughly as everyone else did who had anything to do with him, thereby contributing to and strengthening his narcissism.

After three weeks had passed without George's mentioning or asking about Mary, the mother one day heard him say softly, while playing, "Mary mustn't come back. Mary always gives George enemas." He then pushed a pencil into the hindquarters of a rubber cat and said, "George gives kitty an enema because he won't press. Kitty is naughty and can't go to the park." Since Mary had always said that in toilet training George she could get him to have a bowel movement at the time she wished, the mother assumed that by inserting the enema tube she had forced him to have a bowel movement when she wanted it. The little boy was apparently attempting to repeat a passive experience as an active one. On closer questioning, however, he would give no information and remained as uncommunicative as ever about Mary.

In spite of the constant struggles over his bowel movements, George's relationships to the adults in his surroundings did not become worse. He was as friendly and loving as ever toward his parents, although a little reserved. But he rejected the nursery school teacher who had been spending a few hours a day with him for several months, with the remark, "She mustn't come any more, because she wants me to make poo-poo (his word for his bowel movements)." Finally matters got so bad that he would have nothing to do with anyone in his environment whom he even suspected of trying to make him have a bowel movement. If he noticed no such intentions on the part of those around him, he again became loving and trustful.

On the whole George seemed to be freer from anxiety and less strained after Mary's departure. It was noticeable, too, that he masturbated more often and without embarrassment. He had done this previously when the diaper had been taken off, and the parents had never prevented nor intimidated him. But in spite of this he was frightened, obviously in connection with the threats Mary had made. He often said, "If George touches the stove, the coal man will come out and bite off my finger and nose. Mary said so." He also explained that a man could come out of a box or a store, and that he would bite too. His anxious looking at the door, his fear of strange noises and of the visit of the stranger must also be recognized as the expression of the same fear. Once when the father put on his pyjamas for him he said anxiously, "Mummy always leaves the lowest button open." This was true, although the father did not know it, and the child clearly wanted to be assured of his father's sanction of his masturbation.

His sexual interest at this time was primarily concentrated on everything that had an anal connection. Thus he once said to his father, "Daddy, take your clothes off. I want to see your naked behind." And another time he asked, "Mummy, has the mailman a behind too, and the policeman, and everybody?" Several times he made a curious request of his father. "Slide me along the ice on my behind, Daddy," he said. In this connection, it should be noted that George had often seen children of his own age naked, that his parents had never behaved prudishly with him, and that his questions about the body had always been answered truthfully. As for his pee-pee, which was what he called penis and urine, he showed no interest in it at all, and never asked any questions about it. However, he never spoke of his bowel movements either, but anxiously avoided all conversation on this subject, and, in spite of all efforts, no one in his environment was able to find out anything beyond the stereotyped remark, "I won't press." Only once did he betray to his mother how much and how highly he valued his excretions. He was given a big, long sausage-like red balloon. He became so excited about it that he hardly knew what to do, and cried out, "I'll make two little sausages on top of it." This was the only time that he spoke about his bowel movements. Obviously he was so delighted with the balloon because of its sausage-like shape, and regarded it as worthy of receiving what he otherwise so obstinately insisted on keeping for himself.

At this time, several clearly anal characteristics were to be observed in George, even by the adults in his surroundings. George was very precise in all his ways. In matters of routine he insisted that everything should happen in exactly the same sequence, and was most intent on cleanliness. One spot of dirt on his clothing or on the tablecloth would make him quite desperate. "Can it really be cleaned?" he would often ask me at the beginning of the treatment, if he saw that there were dirty footmarks from children's shoes on my carpet, or if he discovered a spot on his clothes. His feeling of guilt, if he made a spot, was, for so small a child, exaggerated and astonishing. It is unnecessary to say more about his obstinacy, since this is quite clearly represented in his main symptom. I should like to emphasize particularly how consistent this child was in his obstinate silence: for months he spoke not a word about bowel movements nor about Mary, who had so much to do with these, although, as was later proved, he thought uninterruptedly about both. He was also very greedy, would not give up any of his food if he were asked to do so, nor could anyone get him to give up a toy, even when he no longer used it or when it was broken. His fear of noises was particularly marked when he thought that he had messed up his room or that he had made something very dirty.

Since the constipation grew worse all the time, and since the pediatrician advised psychotherapeutic treatment, George, after a thorough physical examination to ascertain whether after all there might not be an organic reason for his symptom, was brought to me for treatment. The constipation was so bad that for about 4 months the child never had a bowel movement without a laxative. He consistently refused to defecate, and held back his stool so long that he could hardly walk, because the feces were sticking out of the anus. Even though those who cared for him made as little fuss as possible about this, it was only to be expected that after he had no bowel movement for two or three days their interest in the whole process could no longer be concealed. The particularly intelligent little boy did not fail to notice this, and it visibly increased his obstinacy. Once, when they took him to the potty to urinate at his own request he said, "I don't want to!" Then when they said that he did not have to he added triumphantly, "But I know that you'd like to have my pee-pee (his urine)." This happened several times while he was urinating, and the mother's fear that the keeping-back might extend to the urinating was certainly not unwarranted.

He came to me freely and willingly the first time. He had been told that he was going to visit a lady who wanted very much to meet him. He was, as always, friendly and trustful, and we got on very well together at once. He spoke very little in the first hour; he busied himself with arranging all the toys and animals I had prepared for him and noticed with disdain if a piece was missing from a toy, or if a toy was dirty or scratched. On the way home he asked his mother for exact information about me, and I repeat his questions here because they are so characteristic of the thoughts of this little 26½-months-old boy. "Where does Aunt Editha live? Who else is with her? Does the uncle live there too?" and so on. Before going to sleep in his room he called out my name several times. The mother asked him what he had said. "Nothing at all," he replied, "I'm just having fun." On the morning following his appointment with me he said to the father, whom until this time he had decidedly preferred to the mother, "Daddy, go away. I don't like you." This particularly impressed the parents, because he had never said anything like this before. He tried to conceal his relationship with me as much as possible, but it was just this new relationship which revealed for the first time that his attitude toward his parents was not so positive as had been assumed. In any case, as his behavior showed, he understood at once that his relationship with me was quite different from that with his parents, and that he had to a certain extent won me for an ally.

In the second hour he was much freer and more trustful. The little wooden dolls had already assumed roles in his play. He always made one shout, "Fix! Fix!," and laughed sheepishly each time because I did not understand this expression. After much urging on my part he explained, "Mary always said 'Fix' when she spanked me." ("Fix" was an abbreviation of the Viennese swear word, "Crucifix".) Since he was watching me anxiously to see if I would object to this word, I encouraged him to say "Fix" as many times as he wanted to. He then told me, "Mary often said, 'You'll see what'll happen,' and then she spanked George and I was frightened." Although I could well imagine why Mary had shouted "Fix" and had spanked him, I took care not to mention the forbidden subject, and it was remarkable how the child breathed more freely and felt relieved, as I sympathized with him over his fear of the spanking and let him see that I condemned the nursemaid's behavior. George kept drawing closer and closer to me and appeared to feel more and more relaxed. Finally, when he seemed to be quite sure that I would not talk about the prohibited subject of bowel movements, he

said, "I'll tell you some more about Mary." In this same hour he even
dared to give a spanking to Mummy and to Mary, but immediately
afterwards one could see how great his guilt feeling was. He did it once
or twice and then, terrified, said, "No, I mustn't do that! I must cry a
lot. I won't give them any more spankings." Other forms of aggression
came to light too. For instance, he tried to push my stove, to trample
on toys and to throw objects around, all actions for which the nursemaid would have given him a spanking. When he left me he was much
freer, and at home he became more aggressive. His obstinate reserve
also underwent a change. He shouted continuously, "Fix! Fix!", which
I had told him he could do. But the explanation for this which he gave
at home was most remarkable. When asked what this word meant he
would only repeat, "Fix means the poo-poo behind," thereby confirming
my conjecture as to the occasion on which the nursemaid had used the
word, "Crucifix", and had given him a spanking; and showing too how
this process continuously occupied his mind, although until now he had
been very clever in concealing it.

As George had again had no stool for two days, and, as was to be
expected, he gave no sign of alluding even distantly to this subject in
his games during the third hour, I tried to meet this difficulty in a form
which would give him no opportunity to make the usual refusal. Among
the playthings I had a round wooden box, which was filled with many
big wooden beads. While he was playing with the little dolls, I acted as
if I were sorting the beads. This naturally interested him. He wanted
to do it too, and was delighted with the "bally-game". Again and again
he shook the "ballies" out onto the couch and put them back into
the box again. The tirelessness with which he played this game, and
the happy screams with which this otherwise quiet child shook out the
beads gave me the idea of using this game to serve my own purposes.
I said to him, "I can do something much better with the ballies," took
the wooden beads from the box, emptied them quickly into the sleeve of
my blouse and let them fall back quickly into the wooden box. He
wanted to do the same thing at once. However, after the wooden beads
had with my help vanished into the sleeve of his sweater, he suddenly
became very pale, thoughtful, and silent, and said whimperingly, "I don't
want to take the ballies out." I reassured him at once, saying, "But you
can keep them. I know that you don't want to give them back because
you are afraid," and then reminded him of the spankings and threats
he had revealed (without mentioning his "I won't press," or his defecation). He kept the wooden beads in his sleeve for half an hour, then
said, "It scratches" and asked me to take them out, which I did. After
this game George's family noticed that for the first time he took some
interest in the process of his bowel movements. The observations that
he made on this day also confirmed, as did his behavior, that he had
understood the symbolic value of the game. At home, immediately after
his appointment, he asked a particularly beloved doll, "Have you done
poo-poo?" During his afternoon walk, when he saw some horse manure
in the street, he asked, "Who made that poo-poo?" Told, "A horsey,"
he said obstinately, "No, George did it." But when, on his return home,
he was asked to have a bowel movement, he said—and this was the first
time that he changed the form of his refusal, "I won't let the little

sausages out," and then continued happily with the same theme, "The little sausages are very nice. Aunt Editha has a potty." It was also observed that on this same day he kept butting his behind against various objects.

During the fourth hour there was again an animated game with the ballies. I would empty them quickly from my sleeve, while George would keep them inside his, always watching me expectantly. Although it had been three days since his last bowel movement, I naturally did not try to urge him to, but merely reminded him why he was afraid of letting the "ballies" come out, whereupon he behaved as though he had not heard me. Knowing that the sleeves of George's sweater were very tight about his wrists, and that it was very difficult for him to get the wooden beads out of his sleeve as quickly and as easily as I had, I went further: I looked at him with sympathetic pity and said, "I see, you can't let the ballies out. You're too little, and it's too hard for you." He hesitated thoughtfully, shook his arm carefully, and then anxiously stopped. When on that day they put him on the potty as usual, without saying anything, he said once or twice quite sadly, "Poor George can't do that." On being questioned by the nursery school teacher as to what he could not do, he replied, "Let the little sausages come out."

When he came to me for the fifth time, and I again quickly and skillfully let the wooden beads roll out of my sleeve, he watched me enviously for a little while, then tore the wooden box out of my hand, filled his sleeve with the beads and cried triumphantly, "I can do it too. I will make the ballies come out myself." He shook so long and so energetically that he really got the wooden beads to come out of his sleeve. Early in the morning of the next day he asked of his own accord to be put on the potty. The nursery teacher did as he wished at once, but he immediately wanted to stand up and said, "But I can't." I had expected this, and had told the nursery school teacher that when he stood up, she should simply let him stand there and say, "I have to go to the toilet myself just now." When she came back, after purposely having stayed away for a long time, the little boy had begun to defecate in his pants, was very anxious and asked, "Why didn't you come? I must do poo-poo quickly." He was put on the potty again and produced a large stool, for the first time in four days. It was also the first time since the departure of the nursemaid that he had done so spontaneously, and although the parents were very pleased, they concealed their feelings in accordance with my instructions, so that the whole incident appeared to George to have been ignored.

When he came to me on that afternoon he was very gay and good-humored, but did not say one word about what had happened, nor did he play with the wooden beads which he had always asked for at the beginning of the hour. I already knew what had happened, and had prepared some plasticene, which he had never seen before, and about which he was most enthusiastic. At first he hesitated, and would not touch it because of its suspicious brown color, but as he saw me busying myself with it, he began to play with it too, and said quite suddenly and irrelevantly, "Tomorrow morning at half-past ten I will— — —" He then interrupted himself, saw my questioning look, and said laughing, "Oh, it was just a joke." George was able to tell time roughly, and he knew that usually at ten-thirty in the morning he was supposed to have his bowel movement before going for his walk. "Tomorrow morning at half-past ten I will — — —" therefore meant, "Tomorrow morning at half-past ten I will have a bowel movement." But this remark was withdrawn at once when he dismissed it as a joke. He had, therefore, not only immediately understood the symbolic meaning of the plasticene, but also the significance of the gift I had wanted to make him in return for his giving up his stool. Immediately after he had said, "It was just a joke," he became frightened, obviously because of his refusal, looked apprehensively at my coal stove, and inquired several times whether I was sure that at home there was no little man who could creep out of the stove and bite something off him, if he turned on the water faucet after being forbidden to do so. Whereas earlier, as I have already mentioned, he had never said a word about his interest in anal matters, now, both in play and in conversation, he could not leave this theme. In the next hour he began at once to ask me to make him a little sausage, that is, feces out of plasticene. Then of course I had to make countless little sausages for him and, according to his instructions, throw them into an ash tray, which he called a potty. Gradually he began to take an active role in the game. I learned of some very important elements in his anxiety about bowel movements, and received confirmation of my assumptions about the processes that had occurred during the toilet training. George inquired once, "Does Aunt Editha do poo-poo every day?", and, as the answer was in the affirmative, he said, while we were playing and he was putting another plasticene sausage into the ash tray potty, "George is afraid of letting the sausages fall into the potty. It makes so much noise, and then it's gone." The mother's observation that at ten months he had already objected when one carried away his bowel movements in the potty now seemed to be explained. Also, he often talked about how he would never do poo-poo because he was too much afraid; he explained, "When George doesn't do poo-poo, Mary always gives him an enema." Although at this time I still did not know enough about his fear of losing his stool to interpret it to him, and could therefore only calm him superficially, he was always relieved for several days after such reassurance, and told me often, "Tomorrow I will go and do poo-poo." He kept to this promise for five days until a certain incident occurred, particulars of which I will give later. And he became more and more pleased over his accomplishment every time.

It was interesting to see that during the days when he had at last decided to give up his stools, he had displaced his keeping back to his urine. He said several times to his nursery school teacher while he was urinating, "I must put the pee-pee into my behind, because it belongs there." He would often put his hands into the potty, and stir the urine around. He said too, "I will do pee-pee in the water glass."

The game with the wooden beads changed very much in accordance with the circumstances. He would demand imperiously several times during his hour, "Give me the ballies." He would then quickly put them into his sleeve, shake them out rapidly all over the floor, trampling and dancing about on them and screaming triumphantly, "Now George can let out all the ballies very quickly alone. I was good. I did poo-poo." Immediately afterward he would squash and knead the plasticene and smear himself all over with it. He would become cross when I did not sufficiently admire how he shook out his beads and would say, "But you don't even notice how well I can do it already."

His interest in everything anal was still very much in the foreground of his treatment. He would often sing, "Poo-poo, Winter is through." He continually asked if Mummy and Daddy and everybody really did poo-poo. On one particular day when I had made something out of plasticene which he particularly liked, he said, "I will make a little sausage for you." When I replied that I did not need his little sausages, he was at first perplexed, but then said at once, "Oh well, for myself, then." Once when he was given some small sausages for supper he was delighted, and understood this as a return gift from his mother, "Mother dear, because I make such nice little sausages I get a good sausage for supper."

His curiosity, however, extended beyond stools, and he continually asked questions about everything that he saw in my room, until I finally asked him, "What is it that you really want to know?" He looked questioningly at me, and then said, pointing to the plasticene, "Make a woman." I modelled as well as I could a woman with a skirt. He immediately tore off the skirt and said, "Make the pee-pee." After I had added female genitals to the figure he looked at it very sharply, quickly tore off the arms and legs, then drew back, shocked, and in terror, grasped his penis. I had shortly before learned from the nursery school teacher that he had asked her to show him her pee-pee, which of course she refused to do, and that he had often tried to look under her skirt. Although prior to this he had often seen little girls naked, the game with the plasticene doll showed clearly that he had only now really grasped the difference between the sexes. And it was to be concluded from this game that he had thought that the female genitals resulted from tearing out the penis. After this scene had taken place with me, he often asked the nursery school teacher whether he could touch his pee-pee, whether everybody could do this, including his parents and me. His fear of losing this prized part of his body now became quite evident. He inquired anxiously of the nursery school teacher while he was urinating, "Are you going to bite it off?" And when the stove crackled during his hour he said, "Won't a man come out and bite my nose off? Mary said so."

Here I had an opportunity to show him a determinant of his fear of giving up his "little sausages". And although it was no easy matter for a two-year-old child to understand the interpretation that he had anxiety about the loss of his penis just as he had had about losing his stool, he did understand, as was shown by his answer, "Mary always said, 'If I give you an enema, I can take it away if I want to.'" In the course of the next two hours there were two opportunities to make this relationship particularly clear. As noted above, after having had bowel movements for five days, he suddenly again refused to defecate. He told me, "I didn't do poo-poo because Mummy scolded me. She said, 'You'll see what will happen.'" The situation with the mother had been the following: She had once told George, "If you don't do poo-poo, you'll get ill, and then you'll get a hard stomach, and then you'll see." The nursemaid had added, "Then they'll cut *open* your tummy." George, in telling it to me, said, "cut *off* my tummy". He was very frightened about this. He now remembered these words of his mother, because he had become very impudent and disobedient, and she had said to him, "Don't do that. You'll see what will happen if you disobey." He told me too that he had had a dream the same night, "Mary came back and hit me on the behind." Because his mother's words reminded him of the threat of his tummy's getting hard and being cut off, he would not give up his stool.

Before his next hour, on his way to me in the street-car, one of his fingers was pinched, although not badly, in a door. He was beside himself, screamed uninterruptedly, and had to be comforted and petted all through the hour. At home he declared, "I have no feet and no tummy," and insisted that they carry him about and treat him like a baby.

During the two weeks following his first five hours of treatment there was, in addition to all this, a marked return to behavior characteristic of the oral stage. He sucked his thumb a great deal and said quite spontaneously to the nursery school teacher, "Buy me a rubber nipple. I'll put it in my mouth and suck it and lie on the davenport. I want to be a baby." He began to take particular interest in the way his meals were placed on the table during the day, and although he had always been given good food, he now demanded quite exceptional dishes, about which he would talk for hours at a time, like an adult epicure. "Oh, how good! How wonderful that is! Ah, this tastes the best of all. I want to eat it forever."

The obstinacy George had shown earlier regarding the constipation was now transferred to other situations in his everyday life. He was immoderately stubborn about being washed, dressed, or going for a walk, and thus he was often unmanageable. He would break out into temper tantrums and yell endlessly, "I won't!" The origin of his temper tantrums was indicated clearly in one of his games. A small doll had to ride on a truck. She refused, and a long argument followed, with the doll screaming all the time, "I won't! I won't!" while George kept on urging her to ride. Finally he said soothingly to her, "You have to lie down and go to sleep now, and then you must do poo-poo. You have to do poo-poo, and even if you don't want to, you have to, just the same." But this refusal released even greater anxiety and guilt feeling. He became very frightened after this game, listened to every noise, did not want to leave me to go home and clung anxiously to me. I was able, therefore, to show him why he grew angry and obstinate when he was asked to do things which earlier he had agreed to do, and had done without the slightest difficulty.

After the discussion of his anxiety over the loss of his excrement, he had become more aggressive. Now this aggressiveness was intensified. From his games and from the information imparted to me by his family I could see that everything with which he had been threatened or forced, in short, everything that he had undergone passively he was now repeating actively in play. Thus he always wanted to bite off the nose of the nursery school teacher, to prick her eyes and ears, and then he would press her tightly to him, trying to hurt her, and say, "You must press. You have to press a little harder." These were the same words that the nursemaid had used when the mother caught her with the little boy squeezed tightly between her legs. He would march proudly around the room saying, "Just press. You only have to press." His visible joy in his own power when he was acting aggressively toward the nursery school teacher shows how very much George must have struggled inwardly not only against being made to press when he was supposed to have his bowel movement, but also against the enforced affection of the nurse-maid. He showed how much aggression he had repressed; and that as soon as she no longer had him entirely in her care, at least a part of his aggression was transferred to the obstinate keeping back of his stool. Although I had advised the adults in his environment to allow his aggressions to run their course freely at this time, it almost always happened that during his treatment with me, after particularly aggressive behavior he would produce exaggerated feelings of guilt, which he had not done after his attacks of stubbornness. For example, he once said, "I am going to be ill and have a hard tummy. My street car ought to be given away to a good child. I shouldn't have anything."

For three weeks, without the use of force, persuasion or laxatives, George had regular bowel movements. Then, because of a trip which I was obliged to take, treatment was interrupted for ten days. For the first four days his bowel movements were regular, then for three days he refused to defecate. On the third day, when his mother gave him an orange to eat, by chance she threw the pits into George's potty which was standing nearby. He noticed this at once, peered with much interest into the potty and asked her, "Is it very hard to make a little sausage on top of the seeds?" The mother understood this question at once, for I had told her a little about the treatment, and said she did not think he could manage it. Thereupon he became very angry, took down his pants and shouted, "I can do it." He sat down quickly and had a bowel movement without any difficulty.

Two days later, when the mother asked George to defecate, he said, "Put the seeds into the potty so that I can make a little sausage on top of them." The mother did not want this game to become a habit, and said that she had no seeds. He did not ask again, and began to play happily.

About an hour later he wanted to play cooking: "Cook myself something good," he said. The mother gave him some rice, which he emptied back and forth from one saucepan to another. Without recognizing the symbolic value of the grains of rice, but possibly with the unconscious intention of getting the little boy to have a bowel movement, the mother also gave him a tea strainer to play with. At once he tried to shake the grains of rice through the sieve. He made a great effort, while the mother said, "It won't go through, I'm sure." He then stood up at once and said emphatically, "Mummy, I want to do poo-poo." While he was defecating he looked disdainfully at the strainer and said to it, "That potty is stupid. It can't do poo-poo. I have already made a little sausage." The reason the constipation recurred during the interruption of the treatment was understood only in a much later part of the analysis, but from the results achieved both times by his mother, through the repetition of incidents similar to that of the "ballies" game in the analysis, it became clear that the regularity of his bowel movements was entirely bound up with his association with me.

The mother also told me that during this interruption of the analysis he often said challengingly, "I like Mary. She must come back.

I will write her a letter," although all that he had said about the nurse-maid would have contradicted such an attitude.

Although immediately after the resumption of the treatment he asked to be put on the potty daily and made no fuss at all, I learned nothing essentially new from him in this period with regard to the origin of his symptoms. He only played games connected with going to the toilet; all the dolls and animals had to go to the toilet and produced prodigious quantities of stool in the form of wooden beads, and so on, which he prepared and divided up with the greatest pleasure. It was very interesting to observe how in this game he demonstrated quite by himself the unconscious equivalence of money and feces. The stool was represented by means of every object possible, as I have already des-cribed, by wooden beads, checkers, little celluloid discs and the like. When once I gave him some little colored lozenges, in play he made a doll eat them up and then deposit them as stool, and then said, "I'll pick up these lovely ballies. I won't eat them so that they are made into poo-poo and come out from behind." He appeared at the next hour with the lozenges, which he had not eaten, but which he had carefully preserved, and said, "Give me something like the lozenges. Give me money, so that I can buy myself a balloon sausage," by which he meant a sausage-shaped balloon.

It was also clearly indicated during these hours that he identified himself entirely with his stool. For instance, he said to me one day, "I couldn't let the little sausages out today. I was so frightened. I dreamed that Mary was in the closet, and that she came out and scolded me." In the same hour he asked whether all little boys had pee-pees, and showed much fear of a little Minnie Mouse that I wanted to give him. "She will bite it off," he said tearfully. He felt that he had to keep his little sausages for himself, because obviously he was afraid that Mary would bite off his pee-pee. As a matter of fact, I had always presumed that during the severe toilet training the nursemaid had probably threatened him somewhat in this way: "If you don't do poo-poo or pee-pee at once, someone will come out of the closet and bite off your pee-pee." He appeared to be more relieved than ever before when I assured him again that no one would take his pee-pee away, even if he did poo-poo in his pants, or didn't do it at the right time. He cried out happily, "Even Daddy won't bite it off? Are you sure?"

That George was very narcissistic and valued his own little person very highly, has already been mentioned. At the slightest danger of injury to his person his anxiety about himself was expressed in his symptom. For instance, he once said suddenly, "I have a sore throat. That's why I can't let the little sausages out," or, "I'm cold, so I can't do poo-poo."

In the same way his theory of birth at this time was entirely anal. Although the mother and the nursery school teacher had answered all his questions as to the origin of children truthfully, he still maintained, "Aunt Editha says that children are in the tummy of the mother, and that they come out at the poo-poo place. They can't come out at the pee-pee place, because it's too little. But how do they get in? At the mouth?"

Since the constipation had entirely vanished, George seemed to be free from anxiety, and the treatment, during the last three weeks, had brought no new material regarding the formation of his symptom, I interrupted the treatment, but arranged with the parents that they should bring the little boy to me at the slightest indication of the reappearance of the symptom.

For six weeks all went well. I heard regularly from George and learned that during this time he had his bowel movements willingly and easily. In the meantime, however, the mother was having some difficulty with the older servant whom she had taken in Mary's place, and noticed that she spoiled George very much, admired him immoderately, overwhelmed him with affection, presents, and especially cooked dishes. And since, after the disappearance of his symptom, George had become very free and aggressive, there were many difficulties. Therefore the mother decided to send away this maid also. Being afraid that there might be a terrible scene, because the maid was so fond of the child, and being unable to remain at home herself, the mother sent the child to stay with her own mother for a while, and discharged the girl, who was disconsolate over the separation from the child and threatened to kill herself. Here again the same sequence was to be observed as after the departure of Mary. At home, he did not say a word about the maid, behaved as though her going away were the most natural thing in the world, and seemed very happy and cheerful. When he was brought to me, however, he showed immediately what mood he was in. He threw himself upon the couch, cried angrily and screamed, "I want to be alone. I don't need anyone. I don't want you either!" The affectionate understanding for his suffering which I showed without mentioning the girl at all, and my obvious taking of his side soon made him trustful again. "Please put the ballies in your sleeve and show me whether they come out," he begged. He was again very anxious. In the grandmother's house there had been many noises which were unknown and incomprehensible to him, and which had frightened him very much. "I will take my money and buy those people who make the noises a sausage balloon, and say to them, 'Take the sausage, but don't make any more noises, so that I don't get frightened.'" Here one sees how George hoped to propitiate the good will of the wicked people who wanted to do something to him, with the most valuable present that he knew of: he wanted to give them a sausage balloon, to be bought with his own money, that is, a symbol of his own little sausages. He was afraid again that they would threaten him for holding back his stool, but he was unable to give it up, as was soon evident.

In the next hour the maid, Lily, came to the fore. George assured me, "I am so angry because Mummy has sent me away from home." Since he always made up fantasies about people who were hidden in an apartment I asked the mother to take him home for one day so that he might be convinced that the girl had really gone, and that it was not just that the mother wanted to send him away from her. He was greatly relieved after this visit to his home and informed me sadly, "It was so nice with Lily. She had such a lovely dress." During this hour he went twice with me to the toilet, wanted to do poo-poo, then refused, was full of despair and indecision and said, "I want to do poo-

poo. No, I don't have to. I only go when I have to." This happened
again in the next hour. He screamed in his fear of falling into the
toilet, but in spite of this he would not use the potty, but only the
toilet. Since he was greatly excited, I wanted to break off this episode,
and tried to get him to come away from the toilet. He was then quite
beside himself, and yelled, "Leave me alone! You said I have to, and
I can't!" I need hardly mention that I had never said or demanded
anything of the kind. When we were back in the room of my office, he
suddenly went to my window, as though in a trance, and said ecstatically, "Look! How lovely! Lily is coming in through the window.
There she is! She's standing by the window." I was so impressed by
the reality with which he described this that I was silent. He looked at
me, and then said in his normal voice, "You are Lily."

With the explanation that he was angry with his mother because
she had taken Lily away from him, and that this was why he refused
to have a bowel movement, the chief part of his suffering from the
separation was overcome, and during the next hour he began to ask me,
just as any normal child would have done, about Lily's going away,
and where she was staying now. I answered everything truthfully, and
he was reassured. But he told me he was anxious about falling down
and being hurt. Then I reminded him of all that we had talked over,
about his fear of being injured and his not wanting to press, and
assured him that nobody wanted to hurt him, that his mother had not
taken it badly when he was angry with her, for sending him away, as
he had supposed. After he had asked again whether he might really
touch his pee-pee, he asked for the ballies, wanted to shake them out,
but said, pitying himself, "Poor George! The potty is too small for
me, the toilet is too big. I am big and I am not very big. I love Aunt
Editha and I don't love her, and I want to, and I don't want to."

He did not want to come to his next hour; when at last he did,
and I explained to him the cause of his ambivalent behavior, remind-
ing him of his anger toward his mother and of his anxiety, he was
suddenly able to let the wooden beads slide out, wanted to do it all
the time, was overjoyed and did not want to go away, but to stay with
me always. The following morning he asked for the potty of his own
accord. During the next hours he told me everything that had been
on his mind: how angry he had been with his mother, who had "taken
Lily away from him", as he said. However, he began to criticize the
girl for having gone away without saying goodbye, and remarked re-
gretfully several times, "But she could at least have waved to me."
Then he began to play at cooking for me, spoiling me very much, giving me plenty of very good things to eat. Thereby he acted the part
of the lost love object, the dismissed maid, toward me. I could tell by
this working through of the grief over Lily's departure that it, as well
as the resulting return of his symptom, was at an end. When he left
me he was happy and free from anxiety. His constipation was permanently removed this time.

To complete the analytic material, I should like to tell you of two
little episodes in George's life which occurred a long time after the
close of the treatment, and which appear to me to give distinct evidence
as to the origin of his symptom. George's tonsils had to be removed.

This was done under anesthesia and with the most careful approach. He apparently had no anxiety, and suffered no shock. However, several weeks before the operation, the date of which was not kept secret from him, he was observed to cover himself right up to his ears when he went to bed, and his sleep became restless. He also sucked his thumb a great deal during the daytime. He had a bowel movement only every third day, and said on one occasion, "It's so difficult. The poo-poo has to go first through the tonsil street." He was again afraid of harm being done to his person, and could therefore not let himself be separated from his feces. The operation itself he plainly experienced as castration. He informed me, during a few subsequent visits, "I dreamed of a bad man, who hit me on the cheeks, so that my teeth fell out." Another time, full of anxiety, he told me, "I dreamed that bad men did something to me. They wanted to cut off my nose and my pee-pee." That he experienced the operation not only as genital castration, but also as direct removal of his stool was shown by the following words, "The strange man put a little pillow in my mouth. It was very hard, and he pushed the poo-poo down with scissors, so that it came out behind. I don't understand how he did it." And another time, "It's hard for the poo-poo to come out. First it has to go down the tonsil street. The doctor took out my tonsils, but the street is still there." By this he meant his anxiety had remained, for he said, "I can only do poo-poo if the man who fixes children's tummies comes." Even at this time he still personified his bowel movements. "Tomorrow I'll do the rest of the man who's lying in the potty there." He was particularly friendly and affectionate toward his father at this time, because after all his bad experiences with strange men he did not want to annoy his father or make him angry. Once he showed passive surrender to his father, saying, "Daddy, bore something out of my behind." But he tried very bravely to get over these bad experiences himself and succeeded in a short time in freeing himself from his anxiety.

From the age of three, George attended a public nursery school, and there picked out the worst and naughtiest boy as his closest friend. He admired the wayward little urchin very much, copied all his bad manners and swear words, did not obey at all, and was very naughty and obstinate at home. When reprimanded, he would immediately cry out, "If you're angry with me I shall get frightened, and then I can't do poo-poo," trying in this way to defy the adults in his surroundings. Once, when he had been very naughty, refused to obey and had become more and more impudent, his father threatened to slap him. George said, "You fool, I'll just shit you away." The father was naturally not going to tolerate this, and there was a scene, after which George declared, "I won't be so naughty any more. I wanted to do it at the nursery school, but I'm not allowed to there." For a time he was again a little constipated and anxious. I let him come to me, and explained to him that he could not allow himself to be as naughty and rude as his friend, because he would then become so anxious that all the things which in his naughtiness he had threatened others with, would happen to him as a punishment. He was very contrite, understood at once, and said, "Johnny (the naughty friend) has a father and mother who aren't angry when he's naughty. They don't do anything to him, and then he isn't angry with himself either the way I am."

If we observe the libido structure of the patient at the beginning of the treatment, two factors appear most striking: first, the marked narcissism of this child, who was so attractive that he was admired and spoiled by everyone. The natural limitation of this self-love through the formation of object relationships was delayed and obstructed, because George was almost continually separated from his parents, who would have been the natural and appropriate recipients for such object relationships. Second, the behavior of the people in his environment, the perpetual admiration and spoiling, made it very difficult for him to progress from self-love to object-love, even prevented him from doing so. In his chief symptom, too, the constipation, narcissism played a predominant role. For this child, who was so fond of himself, would certainly not allow his right of decision with regard to his bowel movements to be denied him during the process of toilet training, and he charged this process with just as much narcissistic libido as he did everything else belonging to his own person. In the same way, his accentuated narcissism and the correspondingly slight object relationships hindered him from giving up this right of decision for the love of an educating person. So, too, the interest that the adults in his surroundings were obliged to show in his holding back his stools, the trouble that they had to take in order to get him to give up, were a continuous source of narcissistic gratification which, as his constipation increased, always afforded him an increase in pleasure.

It was quite in the normal course of libido development that at the beginning of the treatment we found George at the anal level, but, apart from his psychogenic constipation, there are some other indications which show that his anal eroticism, even before the appearance of his symptom, was unusually strong. We must assume that his slow bowel action as a suckling, which was partly due to a constitutional component, resulted in George's coming to know the pleasure brought about by constipation. His intestinal membrane, continually irritated through the organic slowness of the bowel action, was still further irritated by the countless enemas. His anal eroticism became quite apparent at the beginning of the toilet training. He objected when they carried away the potty with his stool in it, so that already at that time he disliked to "give up" his stool. Besides, the anal stimulus given by the enema tube during the suckling period, was reinforced by the frequent taking of his temperature rectally. The kind of gratification experienced by the insertion of the enema tube was such that the pleasure pre-formed by the lazy bowel action in holding back the content of the intestines was increased. So that we may assume that at the beginning of the toilet training the other form of anal gratification, pleasure in expelling the stool, meant far less to him.

I should like here to mention some more exact observations regarding the procedures of George's toilet training, because the manner of giving this education for cleanliness and the libido processes thereby set in motion are among the most important elements in the origin of constipation. If we imagine the effect of the toilet training on the libido economy of the child, we shall see that these demands for cleanliness mean for the child a double renunciation of satisfaction. On the one hand, we require him to have his bowel movement, not when it is convenient for him, but at the time desired by the educating person, that is, at the time the adult puts the child on the potty. Usually, at the beginning of the toilet training, one meets the child half-way, inasmuch as the latter is put on the potty as a matter of daily routine, and not forced immediately to yield all his rights regarding his own bowel movements. But the fact still remains that here for the first time the child must surrender a right which, up until now, he has enjoyed uncurtailed. We see here the first conflict between the demands that the pleasure-ego makes on the child, and the demands set up by the reality-ego of the adult. For the child, this demand signifies that he must renounce his pleasure in withholding his stool, because when the adult determines at what time the child shall have a bowel movement, the possibilities of gratification in withholding are substantially reduced. The second renunciation of gratification is that which the child obtains through touching, playing and smearing himself with the expelled stool. He no longer has the opportunity of lying in warm feces, nor of putting his hands into it, and so on.

Even if we can only infer the manner in which the nursemaid undertook the toilet training from the way George expressed himself during the treatment, we nevertheless know enough about this to understand the effect of these demands. Mary was impatient, which is to be concluded from her behavior when George had diarrhea, and her impatience was greatly increased when George, on account of his pleasure in "keeping back", resisted her demands. He was, besides, too small to incorporate these strict demands as quickly as the nursemaid desired. We also see from the guilt feeling that George always developed when, during the treatment, he had refused to have a bowel movement, with what severity and harshness Mary must have made her demands. We know that a child acquires his first feelings of guilt during the toilet training when he learns that he owes it to his surroundings to control his own excretory processes, that in giving up his stool and urine to a certain extent he pays off a debt. There are two ways to produce this feeling of having a debt to pay. One is through love for the educating person; the other is through coercion—by arousing the child's fear of the results of not giving up his excrements. When we recall George's description of how Mary so often gave him an enema to compel him to have a bowel movement, the whole series of threats she made, and the actual spanking she gave him, we are justified in our assumption that she forced George to have a bowel movement out of fear. The demands must have been worded thus: "You must give up your stool at once, when I want you to. You must press." And when the child did not comply at once, because he could not, severe punishment probably followed at once, in the form of spankings and enemas, by means of which what he had refused to give up was simply taken away from him. He was continually obliged to feel guilty. It was always being held up to him that his wanting to keep his stool was something so bad that it had to be punished immediately in the most severe way. His feelings of guilt were also increased by the fact that he had otherwise incorporated the demands of toilet training. It was only with the bowel movements that success had not been achieved.

We may assume that the toilet training was undertaken just as severely with the urination as with the defecation. One can also imagine the kinds of threats, certainly used unsparingly by the nursemaid, from George's anxiety about the little men who would come out of the boxes and shops and bite off his pee-pee, and also from his marked anxiety about the diapers he was made to wear when he wet the bed. Here too he reacted with obstinacy and urinated in the diaper, thus creating a substitute gratification for himself because, as he understood it, he had been forbidden to touch his pee-pee. And another circumstance must also have intensified his guilt feeling. Mary, who usually overwhelmed him with affection and proudly told the whole household everything he said, who was always telling him how clever and how attractive he was, would suddenly become severe, harsh, and impatient, so that George must have thought, "What I do must be very bad, if Mary, who otherwise loves me so much, is so strict with me now." Out of fear of the threats and punishments, but also out of fear of loss of the admirer who was doubly precious to him because of his threatened narcissism, George had, in the realm where he could, incorporated Mary's demands. In his despair over the smallest spot on his clothing, on the tablecloth, or on the carpet we recognize the severity of Mary's prohibition against soiling himself. In the same way this severity had increased his desire to withhold his stool. Out of fear of soiling his pants he would not defecate. We know already how afraid he was of soiling; and that he had not learned to control his bowel movements at all was shown in the treatment, not only the first time that he had a bowel movement after the treatment had begun, but also later when he soiled himself several times and no punitive observation was made. As to the effect of George's toilet training as a whole, not only did it fail entirely in its aim, but his constipation and his "I won't press," was actually produced by the severity of the toilet training. For, as he would not comply with Mary's severe demand because of his anal eroticism and his pleasure in "keeping back", and because he was completely at the mercy of her aggressions when, by means of an enema, she simply took the content of his bowels away from him, there was no course left to him but to transform his own aggression into obstinacy and to show that obstinacy as readily as possible. Thus, as soon as Mary no longer had him in her power, he refused entirely to have a bowel movement. From the strength of his obstinate "keeping back", which really extended to all anal objects, one can deduce the strength of his repressed aggressions.

If we now go into the question of the anxiety which played a highly important part in George's symptom, the very exact diary of the mother is of great help in enabling us to understand this anxiety as it existed before the beginning of the treatment. George's first manifestations of anxiety appeared during the toilet training when, at thirteen months, he anxiously resisted having his temperature taken rectally, no doubt because it reminded him of the many enforced enemas. Although he was accustomed to the enemas, which were given every time he refused to "press", he must early have regarded them as a seizure of the content of his bowels which he did not wish to give up. During the anal phase every child experiences the loss of his narcissistically charged stool as a kind of robbery, a sort of physical deprivation. How much the more would George feel this, since the content of his bowels was really taken away from him by enemas. Thus one can understand that this child, who as far as one could ascertain, had never been forbidden to masturbate, understood the putting on of the diaper as a prohibition to masturbate. Therefore the nursemaid's threats during the toilet training had a particularly intense effect upon George, as had her countless other threats that the coalman or somebody else would bite off his fingers or his nose, or that someone would cut off his tummy. Because of all this, George was quite ready to imagine that his father might bite off his pee-pee although the father had never threatened to do so, and up to that time had never been severe or angry with him.

When George manifested anxiety, as he did on the evening that a strange man came to visit his mother, this anxiety was not only about losing his mother because of the strange man, but also anxiety that the strange man might do the same things to him that Mary had threatened. When Mary, who was angry with him not only because he would not press, but also because of the diarrhea, was suddenly occupied with a strange man during the walk, and thereby withdrew attention and affection from George, he was justified in assuming that this man could rob him not only of a beloved object, but also of other valued objects. Here again it was his narcissism which made his anxiety that his dearly-loved body would be injured stronger than his fear of losing a loved object.

During the toilet training, George, with his great anxiety, was really quite forlorn and deserted: on the one hand there was Mary, his substitute mother, who almost daily took away violently the treasured content of his bowels, and on the other hand there were all the strange men who, he feared, would bite off his penis; since they had already taken away from him one beloved object, he imagined that they could rob him still further; which, according to his experiences in anal matters, was quite feasible. It is therefore comprehensible that it was not only out of obstinacy but also out of fear that he would not press. How enduring the effect of these early castration traumas must have been is made particularly evident by the things the child said at the time of his tonsillectomy.

Anxiety and obstinacy because of the loss of a loved person were both components which revived George's symptom. On the one hand, he was afraid, after the sudden departure of the second maid, that still more than the loved person could be torn away from him and so out of anxiety that his own person could be injured he kept back his stool. For this reason he was also afraid of falling and of hurting himself. On the other hand he identified with the love object his most highly valued "little sausages", introjected the lost object, and kept is, as it were, within himself, out of obstinacy. I should like here to emphasize the fact that in George's pain over the separation from the second maid a change was to be noticed in his object relationships. He had a decidedly positive relationship to Lily, whereas with Mary this could never be observed, inasmuch as his relationship to her consisted only in wanting to keep her admiration.

We also see in George that even the preliminary formation of the superego was influenced by his experiences during the toilet training. He himself had incorporated Mary's severe demands that he should not soil his pants, as we have seen by his anxiety about every spot of dirt and by his pedantic cleanliness. And when, later, he expected all aggression to be followed by severe punishment, the severity of his own conscience again corresponded to the severity of the toilet training demands.

I should like here to give a justification for the game with the wooden beads, the "ballies", which I inaugurated during the third hour. For this game was a most active intervention and did, to say the least, through its symbolic value and its intentional effect, force the analytic material in a certain desired direction. It may even have had a more decisive influence on the entire sequence of material which was yielded than we are able to estimate. Though the severity of the symptom and the obstinacy of this patient, the dissolution of which by the usual analytic methods would have required a very long time, justified an attempt at acceleration of the treatment, still these facts might not be sufficient to justify the introduction of this game. I think, however, that the essential nature of this game justifies its introduction. In it I tried to approach George's symptom through his narcissism, endeavoring in a deliberate fashion to displace his ambition from keeping back to giving up. That was why I represented to him the letting out of the little balls as a skillful action which only I could accomplish, and raised his doubt as to his ability to do the same. I therefore took him through his narcissism and self-esteem, attempting at the same time to clear up, at least superficially, the anxiety which compelled him to keep back his bowel movements, and did all I could to make him feel annoyed at not being able to "give up". That I succeeded in displacing the narcissistic cathexis of his wish to "keep back" to the act of "giving up" was shown by the quick success that was achieved with his symptom. I succeeded, through this displacement of the narcissistic cathexis to the "giving up", in tricking him into deciding to "give up" his constipation at a time when, without this game, his obstinacy and his anxiety would not have allowed him to do so. For since his obstinacy and his anxiety, as was shown in the course of the treatment, were entirely cleared up later, it is plain that the game was no hindrance to the analytic dissolution of the symptom. In this game I had naturally revived, in a disguised form, what would be acceptable to him in the demands of toilet training. I had, as it were, made up to him a part of the toilet training which he had missed before. It was one of the incidental gains of this play that it enabled him, through his deciding himself to shake the wooden beads in and out, to enjoy a symbolic form of satisfaction which had been denied him too early and too quickly. He could enjoy this without coming into conflict with his marked reaction-formations against dirt, and this opened up a way to possibilities of other more sublimated forms of satisfaction.

If we make a brief summary of the progress of the treatment from the theoretical standpoint, we see that from the beginning of the treatment George developed a strong relationship to me, of a kind different from all his other object relationships. He was much interested in me, thought about me, and it was actually the first time he had taken the trouble to win the affection of anyone. This effect was naturally brought about by my behavior, which was quite different from that of all the people who had known him and who had admired him immoderately. The relationship to me became stronger still as I showed him my superiority and thus threatened his self-esteem. Through the appeal to his narcissism, therefore, a particularly good relationship was formed with me, which made it easy for him to identify with me and to incorporate my demands for my sake. But above all, in his relationship to me for the first time he exerted himself to win someone's admiration, and because I had never admired him, but had quite an extraordinary gift for the art of shaking ballies out of my sleeve, he wanted me to admire him, for he said, "Look how well I can do it," and wanted to give me his little sausages, promising me, "I'll make a little sausage for you."

He understood as early as the second hour of the treatment that I was not severe, and he ascertained first of all whether I would allow forbidden words. When he was sure about this, he drew the conclusion that we make clear to every child, that they may tell us everything without fear of being punished. "I'll tell you more about Mary," he had said, showing that he knew that he could tell me everything. Although this good relationship was based on narcissistic satisfaction, that is to say, on the art that he wanted to learn from me, it was at the same time the foundation of a normal object relationship. It made the analytical work very much easier for me, and enabled me in a short time to trace his exaggeratedly strong conscience demands back to their source, to dissolve them, weaken them, and replace them with other more suitable ones.

Hardly was some of his obstinacy transformed into aggression, which was expressed by his attempt to give spankings to Mary and to his mother, to trample on the playthings and so on, when he also gave up his obstinate reticence, talked about anal matters, showed great interest in them, and indulged by means of countless toilet and plasticine games, in the anal gratification that had obviously been entirely denied him in his toilet training. Hand in hand with giving him this satisfaction went a modification of all the severe prohibitions against making things dirty, soiling his pants, and so on. His aggressions increased with the progressive dissolution of his obstinacy, and we see with what pleasure in violence he actively repeated everything he had been made to suffer passively by the nursemaid, how he pressed the toy animals between his thighs, wanted to bite off the nursery school teacher's nose, and so on.

Apart from the possibility of gratification which these games gave him, they also enabled him to free himself through active repetition of much that he had suffered passively. He became freed of anxiety, because he saw that every aggression did not bring in its wake the expected punishment in the form of bodily injury. His family and nurse also permitted him to abreact his long repressed rage, the origin of which he showed clearly in his play with the doll that would not ride on the truck. When, therefore, a part of his obstinate anal refusal to give up his stool was gradually transformed back into aggression and anger, and the guilt feeling lessened through the reduction of the demands and the absence of punishment, then the reappearance during the treatment of all his anxiety about his pee-pee being cut off and his tummy being cut off, gave me the opportunity to interpret to him the origin and cause of these threats and, through the reactions of his family to the acting out of his aggression, to prove to him their unreality. But even he himself had less cause for guilt feeling, since he was now "giving up" willingly what he owed to his educators, namely, his stool. Besides, he was now creating abundant satisfaction for himself on other libido levels, such as on the urethral level, when he stirred his urine around. He comforted himself for his renunciation of the anal satisfaction of "keeping back" his stool by a regression also to the oral level, inasmuch as he played at being a baby and an epicure. He had time now to turn his interest not only to anal objects, but to a knowledge of the difference between the sexes, so that his anxiety that one got female genitals by taking away the penis, was explained and dissolved in connection with his other fears of injury, of being bitten, and so on.

It is interesting to see how during the first short interruption in the treatment George, in the observance of the toilet training, was still very much bound up in his identification with me through the skillful and difficult game of shaking out the wooden beads. For twice he decided on the spot to have a stool, once when he thought that it was particularly hard to pass the little grains of rice through a strainer, and again when he defecated onto the orange seeds. We see thereby that after the separation from me he again refused to give up his stool, a model of his later renewed constipation, which occurred after the departure of the second maid. He did not understand why he was not allowed to come to me, was angry with his mother because he believed that she would not let him come, and kept back his stool; he did so, on the one hand, out of obstinacy, and on the other, he identified me with his stool and would not give up the loved object.

George's behavior after the separation from the second maid had the same basis. He kept back the stool out of obstinacy against his mother, and because he wished thereby to hold fast to the loved object. His ambivalent behavior to me in this phase of the analysis showed plainly that he had transferred two relationships to me. He transferred to me the anger he felt toward his mother, who had taken Lily away, and at the same time sent him away from her, because, as immediately afterwards he was brought to me, he assumed that these separations were connected with me. However, he also transferred to me the attachment that had previously existed to the maid. "You are Lily," he said to me. The conflict between the two relationships is shown particularly clearly in his remark, "I love Aunt Editha and I don't love her. I want to and I don't want to." But the positive relationship that had existed earlier, in which he incorporated my demands, was still present. With the help of this relationship which was free of ambivalence, I succeeded in bringing him out of this conflict, by explaining to him his anger with his mother, and the pain over the loss of the loved object; and by explaining the consequent misunderstanding that had taken place, I let him abreact and work out the pain of separation. George had then repeated in the analysis the conflict which the separation from Lily had brought about, and which had revived his symptom, and through my explanations and interpretation, brought this conflict to a satisfying solution, and his symptom vanished permanently. Even the free acting out of his aggressions, both within and outside of the treatment had no harmful effects on George's development, for after he had convinced himself that he was to be allowed full play without any of the punishments and threats which he had always received before, he reduced his aggressions, without any external pressure, to those of a normal, free and uninhibited little boy.

During the treatment I always strove to diminish George's great narcissism and the exaggerated value he attached to his excretions. My attitude toward him was quite different from that to which he had been hitherto accustomed. I tried to induce the adults in his surroundings to restrict their admiration and spoiling, showing the little boy himself how to find the way to another narcissistic satisfaction, offered by the successful toilet training. But even so, within the compass of this treatment, one cannot be certain that this was completely successful. George certainly had another and much better object relationship than he had before, and his later behavior to his mother and other people plainly showed an increase in his object libido. It must not be overlooked, however, that George's marked narcissism, which would always be sustained by the admiration of strangers who could not help admire this particularly attractive and intelligent child, represented a danger for his later development.

Here I shall add a few supplementary facts from the later life of the little boy, whose development I had the opportunity to observe for many years after his analysis. Both parents learned to understand from the discussions which I had with them about George that they were not quite so free of conflict as they had at first seemed to be. The mother, enthusiastic about the success with the little boy, decided quickly to undergo analysis with me, which was extremely successful. One of the mother's symptoms was an obsessional fear which was not without a connection to the little boy's symptom. This was the content of the obsessional fear: "Something might happen to my little boy while I am away from home." This obsession made the haste with which the mother discharged the nursemaids much more understandable.

George himself, during all the difficulties brought about by the political upheavals of these years, proved himself thoroughly capable of facing them, and reacted to various separations from his parents, to the loss of his country and friends, to readjustment in a foreign country, so unusually well and without any recurrence of his symptom that one could surmise that the analysis he had undergone as a little child had had a protective effect against later traumatic experiences.

OBSERVATION OF A PHOBIA[1]

By ANNELIESE SCHNURMANN (London)

This observation was made of a child who came to the Hampstead Nursery at the age of 7 weeks. It was therefore possible to get a fairly coherent picture of the factors which contributed to her disturbance.

At the age of 2 years, 5 months, Sandy woke up screaming in the early evening shortly after falling asleep. She insisted that there was a dog in her bed and it took a long time to calm her down. From the next day on she showed an intense fear of her bed and a few days later she started being afraid of dogs in the street, getting into a panic whenever she could discern a dog even at a great distance. It was about one month before these difficulties were finally overcome.

Here are the main facts of Sandy's development up to the time of the occurrence of the phobia.

Family History. Sandy's father was killed in a road accident while serving in the army, before Sandy's birth. Her mother held a clerical job with the borough council. Finding this work dull, she first combined it with the activity of an air-raid warden and afterward gave it up altogether to become an ambulance driver. Still later she learned to ride a motorcycle and acted as a dispatch rider. She enjoyed these masculine activities and usually wore some uniform with trousers, but she was also a very devoted mother. She felt particular affection for Sandy, born after her husband's death. She came almost every night to put Sandy to bed and when she was too late from work for that, she at least came to kiss her goodnight and bring her a biscuit or a piece of chocolate.

There were two other children, a girl 7 years older than Sandy and a boy 2 years older. Both were evacuated. The girl died of meningitis when Sandy was 2 years old.

Physical and Intellectual Development. Sandy's physical and intellectual development were normal. She was a daintily built child with ginger hair, greenish-blue eyes and a delicate complexion. People's opinions differed greatly with regard to her looks and attractiveness. Some visitors and new students picked her out at first sight as one of the most attractive and charming children of the nursery, while others found her plain and of unpleasant character.

Instinct Development. When Sandy was 4 weeks old her mother had a breast abscess and Sandy was immediately given the bottle. Mrs. H.

1. Read at Anna Freud's Seminar for workers in Education and Child Guidance, December, 1946.

253

told us that at that time Sandy took to it at once. However, when she came to the nursery 3 weeks later she was found to be a poor eater, and when vegetables were introduced into her diet she became increasingly difficult with her food. Her only pleasure at mealtimes consisted in smearing. Gradually the eating difficulties diminished and when Sandy was about 18 months old they were entirely overcome. Sandy was a very persistent sucker. At 2 months she sucked her fist, by 3 months, mainly her napkins and clothes. This habit she kept up for a long time. During her second year the hem of her dress was always wet from sucking and when she left the nursery at the age of 2 years, 7 months, she still did not go to sleep without a corner of the sheet in her mouth.[2]

Sandy's habit training was easy. She was reliably clean day and night by 2 years, 2 months. After her napkins had been left off during the night and during her afternoon nap, Sandy was occasionally observed to masturbate in bed.

Sandy was very attached to her mother. She had no difficulty in establishing a relationship with me when I became her mother substitute at the beginning of her 2nd year.[3] She was also quite ready to show affection to other workers who took care of her or to the visiting mothers of other children.

At the end of her first year Sandy was the most aggressive child in her group. She had to be put into a playpen by herself to save the others from her attacks which consisted mainly in violent hair-pulling. She showed a peculiar expression during these outbursts. Watching other children of this age in an aggressive act, one gets the impression that they feel happy and relieved in gratifying their instinct; quite often they accompany their attacks with a radiant smile. Sandy's face was tense and hostile, which gave the impression of a tinge of maliciousness. It was probably for this reason that some people disliked her. Sandy hardly ever appeared to be really happy.

Though there can be no doubt that Mrs. H. loved Sandy, there was an element of aggression in her handling of her which brought out an aggressive component in Sandy's response. For instance, when Sandy was about 5 or 6 months old, her mother, while changing her, used to tickle Sandy with her hair. Sandy, whose skin was especially sensitive and who had been ticklish from the age of 3 months, got very excited on those occasions and pulled her mother's hair. Mrs. H. accepted this laughingly as part of the game. At that time Sandy always smiled when playing in this way with her mother. A few months later she started to pull the children's hair and was reproved for doing so. It is possible that it was at this time that she changed the smiling expression with which she had up to then accompanied the hair-pulling, to a hostile one.

Later on, toward the end of Sandy's first year, Mrs. H. started to play a new game with her. When she came to visit Sandy, she approached her only slowly and hesitatingly, leaving her for some time in doubt, as to

2. When the last follow-up visit was made, Sandy was 4 years, 8 months. She was still sucking her sheet.

3. For the organization of family-groups in the Hampstead Nursery cf. A. Freud and D. T. Burlingham *War and Children*, 1943, and *Infants Without Families*, 1944; Allen & Unwin, London, and Internat. Univ. Press, New York.

whether she would really come or not. Sandy reacted with great excitement. Another game was to offer her a piece of chocolate or a biscuit and to withdraw it again before giving it finally to her.

In the beginning of her second year, Sandy started to tease others in the same way that her mother used to tease her. She offered some object to people she was fond of and when they were nearly touching it, she threw it as far as possible in the opposite direction. These teasing games seemed to replace her more direct aggression. When direct outbursts of aggression did occur Sandy got very upset if reprimanded. There was also a marked change in her general behaviour. She became more gentle and affectionate and seemed much happier than before. She also started to make constructive use of toys, which up to then she had been merely throwing about.

At the same time Sandy developed a tendency to turn her aggression against herself. When blamed for pulling another child's hair, she frequently started to pull her own. Once she was observed pulling her hair with one hand and stroking it with the other one. She also played the teasing game with herself and this went so far, that for many weeks she would not take a biscuit or a piece of bread offered to her on a plate, without alternately approaching and withdrawing her hand for several minutes.

At the time of the flying bombs (June, 1944) Sandy was evacuated to the country house.[4] After a difficult initial period, she settled down well there. She returned in October, when she was nearly 2 years old. She had not seen me for 4 months, but recognized me at once and seemed rather embarrassed. She quickly became attached to me again; there seemed to be no difficulties with her mother either, who had visited her there. At that time Sandy appeared relatively stable emotionally.

About 3 months later, Sandy made a relationship with another worker, which reminded us of her earlier teasing games. She started hitting this worker with a defiant, aggressive expression, alternating between suppressed and then open laughter, and demonstrations of affection. Apart from these occurrences which were not very frequent, Sandy did not show any excessive aggressiveness, either in her relationships to adults or to children. She seemed to be very interested in the male workers and tried to attract their attention. Her relationship to her mother and me were good. She got very upset if another child was aggressive toward me in her presence. When told that she could not have or do something she wanted, she quite often replied very sensibly: "All right". Temper tantrums were not very frequent. Sandy started nursery school at this time. She made a good adjustment, becoming deeply absorbed in picture books and Montessori material.

These are the events which seem to have a direct bearing on the formation of the phobia:

In *December, 1944,* when Sandy was 2 years, 1 month old, she became consciously aware of the difference between herself and a boy.

4. The third house of the Hampstead Nursery: "New Barn", Lindsell, Essex for children from 2—10 years. During the time of the flying bombs the children from 5, Netherhall Gardens, were sent there.

Growing up in a nursery she had always had the opportunity to see little boys and girls without their clothes, but up to that time had never, so far as I know, been in any way impressed by the difference between them.

One day a small boy of about 2½ years was brought for his afternoon rest to the group to which Sandy belonged. Before lying down, he used the pot, urinating in a standing position. Sandy stood next to him, watching intently. She had not seen this happen before as the boys in her own group were still in the nappie-stage. A short time after she had made this observation, Sandy asked for her pot and tried to use it holding it up in front of her. When she could not do so she was very dissatisfied; she lifted her frock, showed her genitals, and said something like "bicki" in a demanding voice. "Bicki" was a word she used at that time for desirable things generally. She repeated this several times, becoming more and more urgent in her demand. In the end she nearly cried. The following days she tried again to urinate like a boy, insisting that I should hold the pot for her and getting cross with me because it did not work. She refused to sit down, and though she wanted very much to use the pot, I could finally only persuade her to do so by pushing it from the front in between her legs to the back. I tried to explain to her that only boys could urinate standing up. During the following weeks Sandy showed less open concern in the matter and by the middle of *January* she had entirely given up her attempts to urinate in a standing position. But her interest in the difference of sex remained. When looking at pictures she distinguished carefully between the boys and the girls, and when she met a strange child she referred to it as a boy or girl.

Another important event in Sandy's life occurred in *March*, when her mother had to go to the hospital for an operation. Mrs. H., who up to then had come nearly every day, stayed away for 3 weeks. Sandy occasionally mentioned her with the words, "My mummy sweetie, my mummy chocki, my mummy bicki," remembering the good things her mother had brought her every night. Otherwise Sandy did not appear in any way disturbed. When Mrs. H. came back, she was in very poor health, she walked with great difficulties, leaning on a stick. Sandy greeted her with great affection. Mrs. H. came for 2 evenings. She could not bath Sandy as usual, but she played with her and gave her sweets. Then she left London for convalescence. Whenever during the next days Sandy passed the little room where she had been with her mother on the evening after her return from the hospital, she said, "My mummy in there", and going inside, she touched the armchair where Mrs. H. had been sitting, saying, "My mummy chair". As during her mother's first absence, Sandy did not show any outward signs of distress.

In the beginning of *April* Sandy had another unpleasant experience. While I was bathing her she pushed a piece of soap into her genitals. She was very much upset and frightened at the resulting pain and it took a long time to calm her.

It was in the night from the 13th to the 14th of *April* that Sandy had the nightmare, which marked the beginning of the phobia. From that day I kept daily records from which I am quoting now.

13.4. After being put to bed Sandy was restless and appeared to be upset about something. The nurse on shelter-duty thought that she was frightened of the weight hanging down in front of the shelter door, which she could see moving from her bed.[5] She was taken outside the shelter and shown the moving object on the door. After that she quickly fell asleep. A very short time afterwards she woke up, screaming with terror. She told the nurse a dog was in her bed. Sandy cried for nearly an hour before she fell asleep again.

14.4. When I came to Sandy this morning, she pointed to a crack in the backwall of her bed through which the light from the next shelter was shining and said, "Doggie; doggie sleeping." Then she lifted the mattress, apparently looking for something. During dressing Sandy was obstinate and aggressive and she stayed bad-tempered and difficult all through the day. In the evening, when put to bed with a piece of chocolate which her mother had sent, Sandy seemed at first quite cheerful. Then, as if suddenly remembering something, she sat up, pushed her feet through the net trying to get out of the bed, and cried out in a panic, "Out, out, out, doggie coming". After I had taken her out, she indicated that she would like to lie in one of the big bottom beds. Her own was a small top bed. She said, "Big one bed," and let me put her in. But she got out again after a little while and stayed sitting up with the nurse. Only much later could she be persuaded to go back to bed.

15.4. Sandy's anxiety began to mount as soon as bedtime approached. She said repeatedly, "No bed, doggie coming." She tried putting off going to bed as long as possible until she finally agreed amid tears to lie down in the big bottom bed.

16.4. The second morning after the nightmare Sandy received me barking. She obviously thoroughly enjoyed pretending to be a dog. But when during the same day a little boy played at being a dog, crawling on all fours and barking, Sandy became desperate with fear.

Sandy was still more difficult than on the previous days, unable to bear any "no" from me. Her aggressiveness reached a peak at bathing time, when she started to hit me wildly. After that outburst she seemed to feel guilty, came back and patted me, uttering affectionate sounds. This evening Sandy could not have the big bed she had occupied the previous nights, as the rightful owner had returned from a holiday. We found her another bottom bed, but it was a small one. Sandy was very unhappy, talked of the doggie and asked for the "big one bed".

17.4. When getting ready for her bath Sandy grew anxious again. She repeatedly said, "No bed." Then sitting on the bench in the dressing room with another worker and me standing in front of her, Sandy undertook a thorough inspection of her genitals. She was deeply absorbed in this activity and did not take any notice of our presence. The worker told her that everything was all right there and that all girls looked like that.

A little while later I found Sandy sitting on the pot, drinking from a mug of water. She was saying to herself, "No doggie shelter, no doggie shelter, Sandy water, not doggie water." She repeated these phrases

5. As an air-raid precaution all the children at 5, Netherhall Gardens, slept in the basement which had been converted into a shelter. The beds were arranged in 2–3 tiers. The children in the upper tiers were protected by a net.

innumerable times. But in spite of her efforts to reassure herself she got frightened again as soon as she was in the shelter. No bed was big enough for her and it took some time before she went to sleep.

18.4. On the way to the nursery school some of our children started to play with a strange dog. I explained to them that he might bite if they frightened him. After this little incident all the children, Sandy included, greeted every dog we met with cheerful shouts: "Doggie!" Neither on this nor on the previous days had Sandy shown any fear or even particular interest in the dogs we met in the street. When we had nearly reached the nursery school, Sandy started talking excitedly. First there was a jumble of words: "Doggie, bite, boy, Bobby, mummy, ballie." Then Sandy said quite clearly, and nearly breathless from the longest sentence she ever produced, "Doggie bite naughty boy leg." Immediately afterwards she repeatedly showed her finger, unhurt, saying: "All better."

19.4. Today Sandy refused to play at being a dog. I had encouraged this game after she had started it by herself 2 days after the nightmare. When I wanted to make her play it today by making barking noises, Sandy stopped me and asked me to imitate a cat instead. For the first time she showed fear of a dog in the street. She also talked again about a dog on her way to the nursery school. It was an unintelligible story, the only distinct words in it being doggie and knickers. Sandy again tried to urinate like a boy. To my knowledge this was the first time since her attempts 5 months ago.

... And now Sandy extended the difficult and aggressive behaviour which she had shown since the nightmare to the nursery school. As already mentioned she had made a very good start there 2 months previously, being especially interested in books and Montessori material. From now on she hardly showed any interest in quiet constructive occupations. The only activity she really enjoyed was the handling of hammer, nails and saw. These tools were almost exclusively used by two very aggressive boys. Sandy, like these boys, did not pursue any constructive purpose in her play with the tools. But it gave her intense pleasure to hammer very hard, her face lighting up while she did so. When she could not have the tools, she clung to me, asked to sit on my lap and would not let me leave the room. She cried frequently and tried to provoke people by deliberately doing things which were forbidden.

21.4. The next phase in Sandy's disturbance was marked by her concern about the intactness of her own and other people's bodies. After the encounter with the dog, she had tried to reassure herself by repeating that her finger was "all better". Three days later she came crying out of the bathroom, telling me that she had hurt her feet. She took one slipper off, noticed some fibres from the lining sticking to her sole and said in a disgusted tone, "Dirty." Then she contemplated her big toe with an anxious expression and I had to assure her several times that it was "all better". In bed Sandy was restless and anxiously touched her genitals. She settled down after I had assured her that everything was all right there. Then she touched my ear and hair saying, "Annie ear, Annie hair." I enumerated the parts of my body and of her body and explained that we had all the same things because we were both girls. Sandy listened carefully, said, "All right," and was quiet for a little while; then she suddenly burst out talking, repeating again and again the same sentences, "Lydia ill, Margy ill (two little girls who had been in the sickroom for several days), my Mummy ill, my Mummy come back, my Mummy walkie again;" then in a questioning voice, "Sandy ill?, Annie ill?" and again, "My Mummy back, my Mummy walkie" in between something about "doggie", which I did not understand. I re-assured Sandy about everybody's health and especially impressed upon her the fact that her mother would soon come back and take her for walks as she could now walk very well again.

During this conversation Sandy was lying quietly under her bed-clothes holding my hand. In contrast to the previous evenings she objected only slightly to being left alone and did not make a fuss when I finally went.

22.4. The morning after this talk Sandy received me in a disgruntled mood. She said in a weepy voice, "Bite Annie, bite." I asked, "Where bite?" She lifted her nightie, pointed to her genitals and said, "There bite." Then while going up the shelter stairs Sandy examined my finger and remarked, "Annie all better." (There had been nothing wrong with my finger.) When I was doing her hair Sandy insisted on having a big-ger hair-ribbon.

In the evening Sandy quickly got under the bedclothes saying, "No doggie bed, Sandy bed." Then she became very affectionate, kissed me and repeated several times, "My own Annie." This she followed up with a repetition of our conversation from the previous day, when we had compared the different parts of our bodies. Sandy started with our clothes saying, "My own dressing gown, Annie's own apron," etc. After enumerating several other things we had in common, Sandy pointed to my glasses with the words, "Where my glasses?" She was however easily persuaded that glasses are not an essential part of a person's body.

23.4. Today at bathing time Sandy investigated her navel with an unhappy face. In bed she pointed to her genitals, making worried sounds, and after she had already been covered up, she suddenly cried out, "My legs, my legs," holding both her legs.

24.4. Tonight Sandy extended her worry about her body to her bed. She had just settled down and I was still sitting with her. Sandy had taken hold of my hand and was vigorously sucking her sheet. Sud-denly she started to cry miserably, "My bed, my bed!" I adjusted the sheet and Sandy tried to go to sleep, but every few minutes she started up crying, "My bed." I reassured her about the intactness of all parts of her body and explained again in detail the difference between girls and boys. While I was talking Sandy had become very quiet and did not protest when I left her.

27.4. Sandy showed concern about her bed for 3 or 4 nights. The first night, nothing I did with the bed could satisfy her, but the next evenings she was contented when, upon her request, I arranged the bedclothes neatly. Once she looked anxiously under the mattress, as if afraid the dog might be hidden there.

... It is interesting to consider at this stage Sandy's worry about an imagined damage to her body, in contrast to her lack of concern about real accidents. One day (23.4.) she scratched her foot in my absence and was treated with gentian violet. She did not remark about the incident to me. Another time (29.4.) she was watching a child having a bath and fell into the bathtub. She had a bad fright and trembled all over when we got her out. But after she had been put to bed she talked quite cheerfully about the accident and it was the first evening since the nightmare that she went to sleep without showing any signs of anxiety. It is possible that it was just the lack of any visible damage that was an essential feature of the dreaded "illness". Obvious injuries and accidents did not concern her.

There are some indications that Sandy regarded her imagined injuries in the nightmare as a punishment. After the incident with the dog in the street she commented, "Doggie bite *naughty* boy leg." Another day while she was in her bath she proceeded to soap her face and continued to do so in spite of my prohibition. Suddenly she broke out into desperate screams, "Soap in mouth!" This was pure imagination, but she still made a fuss about it when she was in bed and calmed down only after I shone a light into her mouth, assuring her that there was no soap to be seen. Sandy actually had a sore throat that day and it is possible that she suddenly became aware of it and brought it into connection with the act of putting soap into forbidden places. She may have remembered her former experience with the soap in the genitals.

30.4. Encounters with dogs in the street continued to be unpleasant, though Sandy tried hard to reassure herself. On one occasion she clung tightly to my hand at the sight of a dog, calling out: "Doggie not bite my coat, not bite my hat!" Today Sandy got into a panic when on the way to the nursery school a dog appeared around a corner. Only the dog's head was visible and this at a distance of about 50 yards. Sandy shouted in despair, "Doggie not bite!" She started the day at nursery school in a state of upset, but played later on quite happily with a doll's pram. I asked her whom she had covered with the blankets. She produced a dog. I said, "A doggie." Sandy replied, "No, pussy-cat."

1.5. On the 1st of May, a fortnight after the nightmare, Sandy's mother came back. She had not announced her return previously and her arrival was a surprise for Sandy. The first I saw of mother and daughter, was Sandy on Mrs. H.'s arm, smiling and waving goodbye to me. Mrs. H. looked well and walked without difficulty. While, in the process of getting Sandy ready for her first walk with the mother, I' was adjusting her knickers, Sandy remarked, "My knickers;" then she tried to look under her mother's skirt, asking, "Mummy knickers got?"

Sandy returned very happy from her walk. Her mother bathed her and took her down to the shelter. Sandy let her mother put her into bed without objection, lay down immediately and did not ask for anybody's company.

... With the mother's return Sandy's fear of going to bed had disappeared. Mrs. H. told me that there were never any difficulties. As Sandy spent most of the time with her mother during the next fortnight, I saw very little of her. So I cannot tell whether she had also ceased to worry about her body.

Her fear of dogs still persisted. Then exactly 1 month after the nightmare and a fortnight after the mother's return Sandy overcame this fear as well. When on the way to the nursery school we met a dog who was on a lead. Sandy at first made a withdrawing movement, then she approached the dog hesitatingly. When another dog came into sight, Sandy walked directly toward him and barked.

This was the end of the actual phobia. But the behaviour difficulties that had accompanied it still persisted.

Further Development. After the house at 5, Netherhall Gardens had closed down (June, 1945), Sandy went to live with her mother and came to the nursery school as a day-child. There she was still one of the most difficult children, unable to concentrate and trying hard to provoke the adults in charge.

I left the Hampstead Nursery a few days after Sandy had gone to live with her mother; whenever I came to see her in the nursery school or in her home she was very pleased, but I do not think that she missed me, as she now had her mother. Her attachment to her mother, with whom she shared a bed, grew very intense. Mrs. H. was delighted with Sandy's demonstrations of affection, but she complained about her falling asleep late and waking early in the morning. When Mrs. H. brought her to the nursery school, Sandy's screams could be heard a long time before she reached the nursery. The separation from the mother was a new tragedy every day.

When the Hampstead Nursery closed down altogether in October, 1945, Sandy went to a London County Council Nursery School, where according to her mother she settled down quite well. During this time I visited a tea shop with Sandy and her mother. Sandy started wandering about and whenever she passed a certain woman, seated at a nearby table, she gave her a furtive little slap, half aggressively, half affectionately. The woman was her present nursery school teacher. In her relationship to the teacher she seemed to show her old tendency to alternate between affection and aggression mixed with fear. In the street Sandy approached every dog who was not looking her way, smacking him gently on the back. When the dog turned round, she retreated with a rather frightened expression. There was a certain resemblance between her reaction to the dog and to the nursery school teacher. Mrs. H. told me that Sandy was usually still afraid of dogs, but that she apparently wanted to show off for my benefit.

In the late autumn Mrs. H. married her first husband's brother. They went to live in a small village where Mrs. H. had been born and had grown up and where her parents are still living. During the following months Mrs. H. wrote several letters, telling me about Sandy's progress.

From the beginning she got on very well with her stepfather and his 11-year-old daughter. The latter lives with relatives in a nearby town and comes home during the holidays. Sandy's brother Barrie is now 6 years old. For the first few months after his mother's remarriage he remained with his aunt in another village, where he had been all the war. He came for occasional visits to his mother's home and there, as Mrs. H. put it, Sandy and her brother were fighting like cat and dog. Later on Barrie came home permanently and after some time Mrs. H. wrote that the two children were getting on better.

Mrs. H.'s letters always indicated her genuine feelings of affection for Sandy. She was pleased with her physical development, proud of the clever remarks she made and of her popularity with the whole family and the village people.

In June, 1946, I accepted an invitation to spend a weekend with the family H. I met Sandy at the station, not having seen her since my visit to her in London 7 months previously. She struck me as a healthy-looking 3½-year-old. She did not recognize me and greeted me as "Auntie", seeming to have forgotten all about the nursery.

Mr. H. is a miner, a fairly young, friendly and quiet man. He does not talk much, but the children like being with him when he is working in the garden or looking after the animals. Mrs. H. seems happy and contented. The house is not too clean and certainly not tidy, but there is a warm and homely atmosphere. Mrs. H. is not the type of mother who disturbs her children's activities for fear of a mess. Mrs. H.'s demands with regard to Sandy's behaviour are on the whole reasonable and adequate for Sandy's stage of development. If there is a clash between the wishes of mother and child, Sandy conforms in most cases without difficulties. However, if she wants something very much or is bad-tempered or tired, she flies into a rage, screams, shouts at her mother, and hits her. Mrs. H. does not make serious attempts to check these outbreaks, but gives in to Sandy's wishes.

Sandy speaks with a broad country accent, she talks a lot, has a great vocabulary and facility of expressing herself and enjoys repeating strange and difficult words. She takes an active interest in all the happenings in the home. She runs errands, reports when the chickens have got out of their run, knows about and participates in all the stages of meal preparation. Her favourite activities when she plays by herself are water-play, i. e., amusing herself with running the tap at the sink, and cutting up paper with a large pair of scissors which she handles very skillfully.

For a short period after they moved into the new house Sandy asked her mother to stay with her when she was put to bed. Mrs. H. complied with her wishes and after a month Sandy no longer required her mother's presence. She is sharing her parents' bedroom, while Barrie sleeps in a room by himself.

As Sandy had reacted so strongly to her discovery of the difference between the sexes, we rather expected that she would find it difficult to adjust to life with a brother. I mentioned before that there were violent clashes between the two in the beginning. I do not know what actually happened during the children's first meetings, and whether Sandy showed the jealousy we had anticipated. At present Barrie is extremely jealous of his small sister and Sandy seems to be secure in the feeling that she is the favorite. Mrs. H. shows her preference for Sandy quite openly and in a dispute between the two children always takes Sandy's part, even if this is quite unjustified. Barrie reacts to this situation with uncontrolled aggression directed against his mother, sister and the cat, and also with babyish behaviour, apparently in imitation of Sandy. As far as I could observe, Barrie demonstrates these difficulties when both his mother and Sandy are present. If the two children are left alone together, he seems to assume the rôle of the protective older brother. He is an intelligent child; his teacher is very satisfied with his school work. Sandy reacts to Barrie's often very violent aggression sometimes with crying and withdrawal to the mother for protection, sometimes with aggressions of her own. She certainly does not try to get out of her brother's way to avoid his attacks.

I had the impression that Sandy was being exposed to several situations that might easily arouse the same conflicts which a year ago had led to the development of her phobia.

Her brother's aggression often assumed an overtly sexual character. He attempted to lift her frock and to hit her on the genitals; he also showed off his penis in front of her and on one occasion urinated on her. When he once tried to lift her frock in the street, Sandy said in a matter-of-fact tone, "Nobody wants to see me undressed," but to the other provocations she reacted with crying.

I further observed how freely the castration threat, although in a slightly disguised form, is used in some social milieus. Sandy was indulging in some forbidden activity. Mrs. H. started to sing a song of the "Scissor-man" who comes to naughty children and says "snip-snap, snip-snap". Sandy cheerfully joined into the song. Another time Mrs. H. was leaning out of the window, talking to her son who was playing in front of the house and apparently misbehaving. Mrs. H. called out laughingly that she was going to cut off his behind. Actually I had the impression that these threats were uttered and understood as a joke.

The H.'s have acquired a huge Alsatian dog. Mrs. H. told me that during the first 2 days after the dog had joined the household, Sandy was rather afraid. Later she simply ignored the dog, an attitude which she still maintains.

It was of course not possible to form a definite judgment after a visit of little more than 1 day. My general impression was that Sandy had very satisfactorily developed in every respect. It seemed that she had largely overcome the conflicts that had resulted in the formation of a phobia a year ago.[3]

The foregoing case history deals with the origin, development and overcoming of a phobia. The relatively simple structure of the disturbance and the opportunity for direct observation make the case especially suitable for the study of the factors contributing to the formation of a phobia.

Sandy was a child with a probably healthy emotional disposition. Her sustained need to suck as well as her lack of interest in food during the first 18 months may be connected with the sudden weaning. Her early aggressiveness can be explained partly as a reaction to the mother's aggression and partly as an identification with the mother in whose emotional behaviour, expressions of love and aggression were mixed up with each other. The masochistic tendencies which Sandy showed in the struggle with her aggressive impulses may also have been reinforced by the mother's attitude; and the particular kind of object relationship, in which love, aggression and fear appeared simultaneously, was certainly

6. One year later the family H. came for a visit to London. Sandy's development appeared to be that of a normal 4½-year-old girl. Since then she has started school where she is making very good progress.

a reproduction of the early relationship with the mother. It is interesting that while at first all Sandy's relationships were modelled on this pattern, she later on behaved in this way only with a few people, and finally gave it up altogether. Perhaps this was due to identification with other persons and also to a possible lessening of the mother's aggressiveness after she had concluded a happy remarriage.

The quickness and ease with which Sandy responded to any kind of help offered to her seemed to indicate a fundamentally sound disposition. It is an interesting question why this child developed a phobia which was comparatively more severe than similar disturbances frequently met with in children of this age.

Pre-History of the Illness. At 2 years of age Sandy was an apparently well-adjusted child. One could perhaps assume from her history that she had an intense struggle with her aggressive impulses.

The chance occurrence of the small boy urinating in her presence must have coincided with the beginning of the phallic phase in her own libidinal development. The fact that I was assisting the boy may have given her the idea that I was in some way connected with the boy's achievement. This may have added the jealousy felt on this account to the suddenly awakened penis-envy. However, she did not at once accept the fact that she had no such organ, as very soon afterwards she tried to imitate the boy. After she had found out that the organ necessary for this achievement was missing, she asked me for it in the same way that she would have asked for a sweet, and grumbled as she would have done in that case, when her request was not granted. Her idea that it was within my power to give or withhold the penis was also clearly expressed in her wish that I should hold the pot for her as I had done for the boy, and in her anger toward me when even after I had complied with this demand, her attempts failed. However, after some time she seemed to accept my explanation of the difference between boys and girls, and her subsequent interest in picture books, where she so carefully distinguished between the girls and the boys, can perhaps be regarded as an attempt to deal with this problem in a sublimated form.

Then came a series of traumatic events in Sandy's life, which caused the established adjustment to break down and reactivated the old conflict. For the first time Sandy was separated from her mother, who upon her return was hardly able to walk. Sandy must have felt that something terrible had happened to the mother, that her body had been damaged. The mother's second disappearance after 2 days aggravated the trauma. Sandy gave no evidence in her overt behaviour of being deeply disturbed. Her remarks when passing the room where she had last seen her mother showed some longing and affection, but no great distress.

The unpleasant experience Sandy had with the soap probably strengthened any fears she may have had about injury to the genitals.

The Nightmare. The nightmare occurred about a week after the mother's second absence. We do not know about any event of the previous day that may have been the immediate cause.

In the nightmare—as it became clear in Sandy's subsequent behaviour and remarks—a dog was assaulting Sandy in her bed, injuring her genitals, i. e., biting off her penis. A reconstruction of the single factors which combined to produce this terrifying dream leads to the following conclusions:

The most decisive event in the formation of the nightmare and the subsequent phobia was probably the experience of the injury done to the mother and of her disappearance. Both occurrences reawakened old anxieties. The sight of the damaged mother may have confirmed a fear which Sandy experienced when she compared the small boy's genitals with her own; the fear that one can lose a part of one's body.

The separation from the mother also meant a loss. As at this age the mother is somehow felt to be part of the self, her disappearance and the presumed loss of the penis combined in creating in Sandy an overwhelming sense of frustration and fear.

This accounts for the anxiety-situation out of which the nightmare developed. The actual content of the dream, the dog biting off the penis, must be traced back to other sources.

The discovery of her own bodily shortcomings may have aroused the wish-fantasy—sometimes met with in little girls—to bite off the boy's penis. As shown in the history of Sandy's instinct development, there was a certain amount of oral fixation, which would make it seem probable that Sandy had a similar fantasy. During one of the temper tantrums she developed at the time of the phobia, she actually did bite me.

As a next step, following the wish to attack her playmate in this way, came the fear that the latter might become the aggressor and she herself the victim.

Sandy's masturbation probably also played a part in the formation of her dream. Sexual excitement and physical sensations may have aroused her anxiety when she masturbated. Perhaps there were also aggressive masturbation fantasies, about which she felt guilty. Judging from the mother's later remarks in dealing with her children, one cannot exclude the possibility of an actual castration threat by her.

Sandy's experience when she pushed the piece of soap into her genitals demonstrated to her what she probably feared before, that interference with that part of the body results in injury and pain. Her reaction to my prohibition to soap her face seems to confirm this.

Sandy's fear of damage to her genitals thus had a twofold source: retaliation for her bad wish toward the little boy, and punishment for her masturbation.

It is interesting that she obviously had no clear idea as to whether the supposed damage had already been done or was about to be done. But this fact is not so astonishing if one considers that the thought processes of little children do not conform to the laws of time and logic. As in the unconscious thinking of the adult, opposites do not exclude each other.

The question remains why Sandy chose a dog to represent the aggressor. The people whose aggression she may have feared could have been either the mother, as the possible author of a castration threat, or me as a frustrating person, both of us having perhaps been the objects of sadistic masturbation-fantasies. But according to the existing material it is more likely that the dream was a direct representation, with reversed rôles, of Sandy's wish-fantasy to bite off the boy's penis. The dog would then stand for the little boy.

As Sandy had up to then not shown any special interest in dogs it seems strange that in the dream the dog was invested with great significance. An explanation may be found in the following facts: when the nursery-children were taken out in a group an encounter with a dog was usually met by some kind of emotion on the part of the other children. Sandy, although not showing any excitement, may all the same have been impressed. Playing "doggie" was a favourite game with the toddlers; an identification of dog and child was therefore easy to make. The idea of representing a boy by a dog most probably originated from comparisons between urinating boys and urinating dogs. The fact that 2 days after the nightmare Sandy got into a panic at the sight of a little boy imitating a dog, while the fear of real dogs appeared only several days later, suggests that the dog in the dream was a composite of human being and animal.

The Phobia. The hitherto successfully repressed fears broke through in the nightmare and Sandy was unable to repress them again. She actually made an attempt at a new repression. She "forgot" the dream, and it came back to her with a shock in the evening when she had been in bed for some time. This was the very moment of the outbreak of the phobia. By focussing her fears upon the bed and later upon dogs, she made use of a defence mechanism, which made it possible for her to be free of anxiety on condition that she avoid going to bed and meeting dogs.

As her request to stay up could not be fulfilled, she had to find another way out. She asked to sleep in a big bottom bed instead of her own small one on top. There are several factors which may have caused this wish. First, the idea of the dog was more specifically connected with her own bed, so *any* other bed might be safer. Second, there was no net in front of the bottom bed, Sandy could get out whenever she liked and seek protection near the night nurse. And third, by sleeping in an older child's or adult's bed she was able to identify with this bigger and stronger person and so feel less helpless in a dangerous situation. Possibly she considered the adults generally as "undamaged", and by taking possession of an adult's bed, she felt that all was well with her.

Another defence used by Sandy was the identification with the aggressor. The second morning after the nightmare she received me barking. But this mechanism did not work for long, though I actively encouraged it, and was only restored at the end of the phobia, when Sandy dared to bark at a real dog.

The real dog became the object of the phobia only after the described incident in the street. It is very likely that my suggestion to the other children, that the dog might bite, established for Sandy the connection between the dream dog and the real dog, whereby the fear was shifted on to the latter. Perhaps this incident gave Sandy the image and the words for an up to then only vaguely conceived fantasy. This, together with the newly-aroused emotion in the experience with the real dog, may have caused Sandy's exclamation, "Doggie bite naughty boy leg." The fact that this was the occasion for an intellectual feat—it was an unusually complicated sentence for Sandy—confirms the theory that a strong emotion can further intellectual achievement.

Concern about Body. In this case history the displacement of the supposed injury from the genitals to other parts of the body, to clothes and finally to the bed, can be seen very clearly. One of Sandy's first reactions to the nightmare was a thorough inspection of her genitals (4th day after the nightmare). The reassurance that everything was all right there, was immediately used by Sandy to comfort herself about the imminent danger of going to bed. (Her monologue, "No doggie shelter, Sandy water, no doggie water.")

The incident with the dog produced the idea that the boy's leg had been bitten; possibly this first displacement was connected with the mother's illness, which to Sandy must have appeared as an injury to the legs. Immediately afterwards Sandy displayed her finger with the words, "All better." The next day she was telling a story about doggie and knickers, thus again coming nearer to the original place of the fantasied injury; and when she later appealed to the dog, "Doggie not bite my hat, not bite my coat," she chose well-known penis-symbols for the displacement.

Three days after the encounter with the dog, when the first displacement occurred, Sandy's anxiety about the intactness of her body reached a climax. In quick succession she worried about her feet, her big toe, her genitals. The reassurance given with regard to the latter enabled Sandy to embark on a further investigation of the problem, by enumerating the parts of my body. On being told that she had everything exactly like me, "Because we are both girls," Sandy found herself confronted with the core of her problem. This produced very strong emotion; but on the other hand the lessening of anxiety enabled the whole complex to find access to consciousness and Sandy brought out in one rush the thoughts she had forcibly repressed for a long time. She revealed that she had been upset by the illness of two little girl friends, who because of an infectious disease were still isolated in the sickroom. The fact that she was prohibited to enter the sickroom, and that on one occasion when she followed me there she was turned out rather firmly, must have excited her fantasies about mysterious illnesses. Immediately after the mentioning of the two little girls, she told of her anxiety about her mother. Her mother's illness, her inability to walk, her disappearance, all matters she had never spoken of before, were referred to. She thought that perhaps all girls were ill, and if I was like her, then we were both ill too.

The reassurance given on this point and the promised return of the intact mother quieted her for that night. But the next morning her worry returned; by now her problem having become more conscious, she could indicate the place where the "bite" had occurred. After having expressed her apprehension, she immediately proceeded to reassure herself by stating that my finger was "all better", and by substituting a big hair-ribbon for the missing organ.

In the evening Sandy defended herself against the uprising fear by saying that this was *her* bed, not "doggie bed", and that I was *her* own Annie (thus treating the bed and me as parts of herself); and by initiating the "comparing game" of the previous night. But there was still some doubt left as to whether we really were quite alike—she did not have any glasses.

The fact that Sandy had at one moment clearly realized her problem, talked about it and received reassurance made little difference in her behaviour during the next week. She still worried about various parts of her body, now extending her apprehension to her bed. In the remark, mentioned earlier, she had shown that she regarded her bed in some way as part of herself; the wish for a big bed may also be connected with this idea. At the repeated explanation of the difference between boys and girls her anxiety was very much reduced; this could be taken as an indication that the conflict had lost its strength.

There was, however, no lessening in her fear of dogs. She continued getting into a panic at sight of every dog. The only attempt to deal with this fear was her play with the toy dog, which she called "pussy-cat".[7]

Behaviour Difficulties. It has been seen that along with the phobia Sandy simultaneously developed behaviour difficulties. She became very aggressive, lost interest in and capacity for constructive play, and clung to me and later on to her mother, with an intensity that belonged to an earlier phase of development.

Her aggressive behaviour toward me, which she started on the morning after the nightmare and maintained during the following weeks in varying degrees, can be explained as an expression of her inner tension, but also as a sign of hostility toward me, whom she held in some way responsible for her troubles.

Her provocative behaviour at the nursery school can be attributed to an identification with the two "naughty boys". Sandy's deliberate naughtiness was of the same kind as the behaviour displayed by these boys. She also joined them in their aggressive games; one day I found the three of them in great excitement, chasing and killing a blue-bottle. The identification with the boys presumably served the purpose of making her feel that she was undamaged; in relation to the nightmare it can be understood as an identification with the aggressor.

However, this defence was not very successful, and when its functioning met with obstacles, the aggressiveness changed to a babyish clinging to the adult. Sandy probably feared loss of love in consequence of her aggression. The idea of losing her love object, which she considered as part of herself, was reinforced by her castration anxiety. This and a certain amount of ego-regression due to the emotional upheaval, may have been the cause of her dependent behaviour and her incapacity for constructive activities.

It is interesting that the behaviour difficulties outlasted the phobia for a relatively long time. The sexual stimulation and oversatisfaction which Sandy got by sharing her mother's bed may have contributed to her prolonged unmanageableness.

Overcoming of the Disturbance. With the mother's return the nightly anxieties suddenly vanished, and the fear of dogs was given up within a fortnight.

7. To a question of a member of our seminar, why Sandy in this as well as in a former game wanted to substitute a cat for a dog, Anna Freud replied, that in Sandy's eyes a cat possessed all the pleasant qualities of a dog without the dangerous ones, that for her a cat was a "safe dog".

Sandy's inquiry during the first few minutes of the mother's visit as to whether the latter had any knickers, was answered by Mrs. H. with a very friendly, "Of course, Mummy has knickers." Sandy seemed to take that as an indication that all was well with the mother and also with herself.

It is not possible to say whether the return of the intact mother would itself have been sufficient to put an end to the disturbance, even without our giving any interpretations; or whether the phobia would have disappeared at about the same time without the mother's return. But it seems probable that Sandy could master her castration anxiety and penis-envy more successfully after she had been enabled to gain some insight into her conflict.

The external circumstances of Sandy's further life were favourable for a normal development. It may have been a great frustration to her to have to give up her place in the mother's bed to a man, but she soon established a very good relationship with the stepfather; she had shown a marked interest in men even in the nursery.

It was very fortunate that the brother was taken home only after Sandy had settled down. The fact that she was the favourite of the family may have had its disadvantages, but it certainly helped to reconcile her to being a girl.

The mother's tolerance of her attempts at sublimation, the water- and scissor-play, were also a favourable factor in her development.

Sandy was thus enabled to cope successfully with the presence of a difficult and aggressive brother. She no longer identified herself with the "naughty boy", but chose her mother for a model, while at the same time she stood up quite well to her brother's aggression.

The last follow-up showed a continued satisfactory development.

Conclusions. The conclusions which may be drawn tentatively from this case history can be summed up as follows:

A child with a presumably healthy emotional disposition can acquire a relatively severe neurotic disturbance as the result of a series of unfavourable experiences. These experiences gain traumatic effect and become the cause of a disturbance if they happen at a time when the child's libidinal development has reached a stage which makes the child particularly susceptible to effects of the events in question.

If the disturbance can be dealt with soon after its outbreak by psychological means as well as by the provision of good environmental conditions, it is possible to overcome the neurotic illness in a comparatively short period of time.

It appears that a disturbance of this kind can be dealt with in such a way as not to impede the further progress of instinctual development.

SUBLIMATION AND SEXUALIZATION

A CASE REPORT

By AUGUSTA ALPERT, Ph.D. (New York)

From the psychological no less than from the social point of view, sublimation is the most valuable defense elaborated by the personality against unbridled instinctual gratification. But it has failed sufficiently to engage the attention of psychoanalysts, perhaps because it is the least pathological of the defenses. This gap is even more apparent in psychoanalytic literature on children. Furthermore, the term is as yet loosely defined and may be discussed in the literature under various headings. Thus, Anna Freud's basic book, *The Ego and the Mechanisms of Defence* (4), gives only three sentences to sublimation as such, but in the discussion of other defences, as "altruistic renunciation" and "intellectualization", overlapping with sublimation is implied.

The purpose of this paper is to show how the dynamics of sublimation runs a parallel course with the dynamics of the neurosis and reflects every major conflict. In the analysis of Peter, interference with sublimation by persistent sexualization of ego functions unfolded itself like a slow-motion film. Valuable light was thus shed on sublimation as a developmental process.

Peter was brought to analysis at the age of not quite 11, because he was an uneasy child, with compulsive habits, mild eating and sleeping disturbances, fears at night, dependent and aggressive behavior toward his parents, especially the mother, and achievement much below par. He was diagnosed as a compulsive neurotic with strong sado-masochistic tendencies and well-established fetishism. Though a very intelligent boy of very intelligent and cultured parents, he was an indifferent pupil, with very short attention span both in his school studies and extracurricular activities. His power of concentration was seriously impaired. The patient himself was aware of this problem from the beginning of the analysis. He envied the boys who showed sustained interest in their hobbies and considered himself "different" in this respect.

In the first analytic hour, Peter declared that music was his "most important subject", and science and sculpture his hobbies. But it soon

271

became clear that music was the mother's most important subject for her son, and the storm-center for the mother-son relationship; that the father was the scientist, and the son a frustrated competitor; that an ardent admirer of the mother's was a sculptor, and the patient a gifted but inhibited imitator. Thus the oedipal characters were accounted for in the order of identification.

According to the mother, Peter was judged talented in music by his teachers, but he worked only under duress and with great inhibition. The mother, a concert pianist, supervised the daily practice period, which usually deteriorated into a fight, ostensibly because the mother was critical, but actually provoked by the boy, even when she was encouraging. When he was left to practice alone, he realized that he was utterly incapable of doing so, because music then lost all its meaning and motivation for him. Furthermore, even without his mother there at practice time, he still managed to find in music the stimulus for scenes of violence with the mother. Not until the second half of the analysis, when Peter was able to face his frank incestuous wishes for his mother, could he carry out his oft-repeated threat to drop music. This was then his only way of shaking off what he called his mother's domination. However, within two weeks, he decided independently to shift to another instrument.

This was easier said than done. One instrument after another had to be eliminated because it was invested with some aspect of his mother. When he was down to two instruments, clarinet and cello, he was caught in the typical jam of indecision which characterized all his choices of subjects, hobbies, projects, and to a markedly smaller degree, of other alternatives as well. This taught him that he could not make a free choice as long as he remained emotionally shackled to his mother (on an anal level). He nevertheless did make a choice and the selection of the cello coincided neatly with the weakening of the taboo on manual masturbation. When the analyst underscored the sequence of the two events, the patient added thoughtfully that it must have also interfered with his piano practicing. Further progress in music was made when the analysis revealed that his work suffered from the necessity to achieve immediate success, as in masturbation. The mother's criticism was understood as a reflection on his genital adequacy and forced regressions to anal-sadistic outbursts (the fights). This was facilitated by the mother's participation in toileting until Peter was 12 years old.

To-date, music still suffers from a multiple "contamination" with sexual elements: the cello appeared to him as his mother's body between his legs; his doubts concerning his masculinity are still projected at times on music; normal exhibitionism, which must be an integral part of musical performance, is still inhibited. As Peter naively put it when he told with pleasure of his share in an exhibition of photographs, "I would rather display in public than perform in public!"

Science, to which he referred as his hobby in the first hour, was his favorite subject, but he approached it with a mixture of enthusiasm and anxiety. During the first part of the analysis, interest in science was at its height. "Experiments" were conducted with others at a high pitch of infectious excitement. There was a good deal of mouthing of chemical and biological terms with sexual insinuations, accompanied by seductive giggling. This type of seduction and provocation would fill many an analytic hour and often culminate in a urinary urge. His sexual curiosity also found expression in poring over his father's reference texts, which were peopled with punishing chemicals and disfiguring diseases. These would often keep him awake at night. During this period he would often act out fantasies of being the big chemist far more successful than his father. Notwithstanding poor grades in science, he was convinced that he was "tops" in this subject.

This intense and delusional period came to an abrupt end when he entered a strict high school and consistently received mediocre grades in science. As his work habits improved, his grades rose appreciably, but not so his confidence. He ascribed to the father an exaggerated preëminence in science which, by implication, excluded him. After a fight over a remedial lesson with his father, he broke down during the analytic hour and confessed that he would much rather be a scientist than a musician, but what chance was there! He was enormously impressed to learn that he had made that identical choice in object identification when his frustration as his father's rival for his mother was unbearable. "That's it in a nutshell!" he exclaimed. The soft-pedalling of science came as a reaction to the previous indulgence in it in its sexualized form, and was promoted by the exposure of his "phoney" superiority in the strict high school. The more pressing incestuous wishes for his mother coincided with this period and made any competition with his father as forbidden as though it were the oedipus battle itself.

His productivity in sculpture suffered most of the three "oedipal subjects". What he did do was clearly in the genre of the sculptor interloper, but his identification with the man was more in terms of his ultra-masculine physique and rough manner, in which traits he contrasted sharply against the father and child. For years Peter would dress and act like a roughneck and at the same time indulge in numerous masochistic fantasies, in which he was the victim of a gang or bully. Much analytic work was required before the sculptor emerged from the unconscious as the bully prototype. Peter's love of sports has replaced his love of the bully, but there is still too much contempt for men who do not engage in sports and who are painful reminders of his so recent masochistic past.

The interference with sublimation was by no means limited to this triad of subjects. Quite early in the analysis, Peter asked mournfully, "Why do my projects always flop?" During the course of a school year he "specialized" in mathematics, biology, chemistry, history, mechanics, plane modelling, and photography in quick succession and with the same initial enthusiasm. However brief the life-span of a "specialty", the intensity each time was at white heat. He referred to each as "my mad interest" and gave graphic descriptions of how he would whip himself into an orgastic frenzy by staring at the picture of a plane, for example, and then rush to his work bench while still "hot". In the course of analysis it became clear that this preparatory enthusiasm resembled masturbatory fore-pleasure, which consisted of staring enviously and sensually at the picture of a scantily-clad girl or nude, later admitted as a cover for his mother, until an erection was produced. Furthermore, these "mad interests" were recognized as unconscious parodies of his mother's ebullience, which he envied bitterly and found seductive.

Among his "mad interests" plane-modelling held top place for a while. But the fragility of planes and motors aroused his castration anxiety and prevented an active approach to this hobby. "If only there were two motors," he would sigh. Not only was he afraid to let his planes fly, but as he blushingly admitted, he did not even know what made them fly. Though he was as well posted on technological facts as most boys of his age, his curiosity circumvented the details of motors and related parts, with the result that his planes never could fly. In addition, the aim for quick success, as in masturbation, resulted in slip-shod work. "To make it quick and keep it big," was the patient's version of it. As though there were not enough already to cause this particular project to "flop", he was further handicapped by an intemperate wish to compete with a much more advanced buddy on this project. The masochistic compromise between the wish and the fear of retaliation came out when he thought he would be ready for a motor-model during one April. His friend told Peter that at the rate he (Peter) was going he would hardly be ready before July, but that he himself would get one in June. Peter resented this as a delaying tactic, but bent backward to safeguard his friend's leadership by promising to get his motor in August!

Further light was shed on his displaced castration anxiety in connection with another attempted sublimation. When he received a new and expensive camera, he was impressed by his overt anxiety lest he damage some part inadvertently. This gave rise to a compulsive examination of the camera to make sure it was intact and naturally interfered with its use. He himself recognized it as the same anxiety he felt in connection with planes and motors.

His projects suffered also from displaced ambivalence. He complained of "going crazy" with indecision, of being "pulled as if by a magnet" from one hobby or subject to another. When analysis dealt with one of these, he accused the analyst of "pulling" him away from the other. With characteristic insight, he declared that the subjects felt like rivals contending for his affection. This brought to light a typical fantasy he indulged in after a fight with his mother: mother, father, and he are in court arranging his parents' divorce; the judge asks him to choose between his parents; he switches from one to the other as each pleads with him. (This fantasy antedated the appearance of "Christopher Blake" on Broadway!)

The indecision from which the patient suffered for months mounted unbearably when he entered high school and his curriculum expanded, along with his ambition. As he first felt it, he could not decide whether to "specialize" in the subject he liked best or the one which would bring him the greatest admiration and praise, but the very term "specialization" was unconsciously appropriated from the mother's new specialization studies. The first pair of rival subjects was French and mathematics.

Though he had been looking forward to French, once he began it he could give himself to it only with the utmost resistance. He despised it as a feminine subject, yet envied his mother's superiority in it. His defense against feminine identification was so strong at this time that in his first examination paper he consistently masculinized all feminine nouns and failed the test! He took refuge in mathematics as the subject in which his mother was very poor on account of "an emotional block" and he could "show her up". This was easy enough to do, but his superiority carried no conviction and gave him no satisfaction. Unfortunately, mathematics was also his father's forte. Again and again he would provoke his mother into deflating him and then turn furiously upon her, much as in music. His defeat in mathematics finally came about in a battle fought behind analytic scenes. He became disorderly in class and hostile to his previously loved teacher. At the end of the month his grade went down from 90 to 67 per cent. Painfully he went over the ground with the analyst. He had selected mathematics as his "specialty", in the first place, because the teacher was new; no one liked either the teacher or his subject, so he was the teacher's only and favorite child, without competition (just as at home). His enthusiasm for mathematics flattered the teacher and Peter played on it. "I practically made him!" he said bitterly. When the first rival appeared, he ignored him contemptuously until the rival exceeded Peter by 1 per cent in a test. His confidence was shaken, but not until the teacher casually suggested that Peter ask his rival to show him a certain process, did he throw up the sponge. He became furious with the teacher and decided to punish him by losing interest in him and in his subject. Mathematics has never again recovered its inflated value, since this "betrayal".

French and mathematics represented his mother and father as rivals for his love; but also the struggle within himself between feminine and masculine identification. When this obsessional indecision was at its height, interfering with his sleep and concentration, the patient would amuse himself with the fantasy that the subjects were boxing in Madison Square Garden; he himself was the arena for the match and an audience of classmates, etc., cheered first for one then the other subject. Often he would end the disturbing irresolution by laying out his books and aiming a ball at them. The one hit was chosen for the day!

His painful indecision died down during the summer. When next it made its appearance, it was far less intense. It came up in connection with a valiant fight against an increase in compulsive masturbation, with the onset of puberty. He longed for a hobby as a defense against masturbation, but he could not make up his mind whether it should be planes or music. With desperate frankness, he admitted that he really did not want to give up masturbation. It was a short step from this to the understanding that the indecision was not between two hobbies but between a hobby and masturbation.

Peter's neurosis falls into two periods: (1) the passive identification with the mother, and a sado-masochistic attitude toward the sculptor-interloper, which coincided roughly with the separation of the parents; (2) the oedipus complex proper, with a shifting of identifications toward the normal. This period was attained after 2 years of analysis and after the parents were reunited.

Similarly interest in science was also divided into two periods. During the first period, while the father was away, interest was high and openly expressed in games of rivalry, in which he was the scientist far superior to the father; in highly-libidinized chemistry "experiments" with a homosexual partner; and in searching through his father's texts; all in all, in a generally permissive attitude toward science. During the second period, after the father's return and after his "delusional ideas of grandeur" were put to the test in a high school with strict masculine teachers, interest in science was still keen but furtive; science was regarded with reverence as his father's field, in which he did not stand a chance. An ambivalent, in-between phase, with a wavering attitude toward science, coincided neatly with the transitional phase in the neurosis, when his sexual orientation was torn between masculine and feminine.

During the first and sadomasochistic phase of the neurosis, music was the means by which the patient brought about repeated masochistic frustrations at the hands of the mother, accompanied by analsadistic outbursts. But in the second phase of the neurosis, when the patient was well on the way toward masculine identification, music was privately experienced and enjoyed apart from the mother.

It is as yet impossible to speak of the patient's many interests as true sublimations, nor even to predict their outcome as such. But they are important landmarks in a developmental study of sublimation. The weakest link in Peter's development has been object identification. Just so unstable has been his object choice for purposes of sublimation, as was to be expected on the basis of previous work and writings on this subject (2, 3, 5). Superego formation also suffered from distorted identifications and from a too permissive environment. A weak superego and weak authority figures made prolonged instinctual gratification easy and this in turn colored nearly all ego activities and undermined the executive functions of the ego. Quick and easy gratification, patterned on autoerotic practices, was the patient's expectation for all his undertakings.

Games, an earlier landmark in the development of sublimation, are known to satisfy sexual strivings in a desexualized way (3). In Peter's case, it should be added, *with affect still sexualized*. Thus when Peter played his chemistry games with other children, the pleasure was frankly sexual. Such games during the analytic hour by him and other children are often accompanied by erections in boys and masturbatory tension in little girls. The continuance of such sexually gratifying games into the latency period may well constitute one warning of interference with sublimation.

Theoretical discussions on sublimation accept it as axiomatic that only pregenital strivings are sublimated. Peter's analysis sheds some light on the role of pregenital strivings in the dynamic struggle toward sublimation. Oral, anal and urethral erotism played a conspicuous part in the first science phase. (His remarkable language development was not discussed because conflict free.) But the second phase seemed more under the influence of phallic rivalry with the father. Music, i. e., both piano and cello playing, was under the influence of phallic exhibitionism and genitally tinged incestuous fantasies (with anal-sadism as a pathological by-product in the first phase.) Both exhibitionism and voyeurism found their natural outlet in photography. His sado-masochistic conflicts found their happy resolution in sports. (In a facetious mood, Peter declared that he should be a District Attorney: then he would be endangered enough to make it exciting; yet have the power to make others cower before him!) Of all the pregenital strivings, the phallic has received the least treatment in studies on sublimation. There is an apparent contradiction in the fact that though the genital level of libidinal development has been reached at puberty, only phallic and not genital strivings are sublimated even at this time. It is helpful to make the distinction between genital in the biological sense and in the psychological sense (as Dr. Eidelberg suggested in private conversation), but it does not clear up all the problems. What is needed is a genetic study of sublimation, in relation to other defense mechanisms.

To return to the case under discussion, it should be clear that one major source of interference with Peter's sublimation has been his education. Both home and school were heavily under the influence of the doctrine that repressive discipline was injurious. So they over-corrected the error of the past by undue permissiveness. The result was a prolongation of the "polymorphous" perverted period, without the adequate support for superego formation. Peter, like many children showing this syndrome, covered up his considerable anxiety with a mask of sophistication and pseudo-gaiety. The type of progressive education of which Peter was the product aimed at salvaging the creative powers of children which too often petered out after they entered the conventional schools. Progressive schools did indeed release an abundance of creative energy, but not enough of it was channeled into creative productivity, i. e., sublimation. Too much of it went into its very opposite: instinctual gratification. How to steer a child's development between the Scylla of repressive discipline and the Charybdis of too permissive discipline is the number one problem of education, from the social as well as from the psychological point of view, a problem dealt with by the writer in her paper, "Education as Therapy" (1). But this is put so well by Fenichel, that I shall conclude with his remarks:

"The experiences that interfere with pregenital wishes must be neither too intense nor too sudden and forceful; they must be sufficient to effect a change in the drive without calling forth too strong a reaction. Environmental conditions must be present which aid in the establishment of the sublimation 'substitute' by providing models and suggesting ways out of conflicts." (3)

It is to be hoped that further studies in sublimation will put at the disposal of educators more precise and more detailed findings, which will help in the conservation of human resources.

BIBLIOGRAPHY

1. Alpert, A. "Education as Therapy", *Psa. Quar.*, X, 1941.
2. Bornstein, B. "Zur Psychogenese der Pseudodebilität", *Internat. Zeit. f. Psa.*, XVI, 1930.
3. Fenichel, O. *The Psychoanalytic Theory of Neurosis.* Norton, 1945.
4. Freud, A. *The Ego and the Mechanism of Defence,* Internat. Univ. Press, 1946.
5. Freud, S. *The Ego and the Id,* Hogarth, 1927.

A PSYCHOANALYTIC EVALUATION OF TIC IN PSYCHOPATHOLOGY OF CHILDREN

SYMPTOMATIC AND TIC SYNDROME *

By MARGARET SCHOENBERGER MAHLER, M.D. (New York) [1]

Before we can study "tic" as a psychopathological manifestation we must describe the phenomenon of a tic, and attempt to define and delimit what we mean by this term, from those manifestations which are loosely and interchangeably designated as "tics", "antics", "mannerisms" and "nervous habits". A tic is an involuntary motor automatism. We use the term "tic" to designate those sudden, abrupt and quick repetitious *involuntary* movements of a physiologically interconnected group or groups of muscles. These are movements which have, at the time of their execution, lost any obvious connection with their original purpose, so that their motivation and meaning is no longer self-evident. In common parlance "tics" and habitual autoerotic manipulations are not distinguished from each other. Yet there is always a grain of truth in popular language habits (28). It is often difficult, if not impossible, to draw the line between transient autoerotic habits, repetitious manneristic movements which are devoid of any symbolic meaning, and the true motor automatism, which we call a "tic". In fact, tics in their true, "crystallized" form may be described as but condensations of the more slowly executed "nervous" motor mannerisms and gestures. In children who are fidgety, jittery and restless, in a word, hyperkinetic as small children, their inconstant and flighty nervous habit movements may develop later into swift, repetitious muscular jerks, which they are unable to control because they have become automatic, that is, involuntary. The question then arises: why do the transitory, tic-like habit movements, so frequently found in small children, disappear without residua at school age in most cases, while in others they crystallize into the involuntary motor symptom of .true tics? Recent research on the phenomenon of tics revealed that "motor neurosis" often originates

* From the New York State Psychiatric Institute, New York.
1. Associate in Psychiatry, College of Physicians and Surgeons, Columbia University.

through the interaction of hereditary, or constitutional factors and certain typical environmental attitudes, which we shall discuss later.

The tic as a unit is a rather conspicuous and simple example of neurotic symptom formation with an underlying conflict. In this symptom formation the original, instinctual impulse, censored by the superego, finds its outlet in motility through an unrecognized, condensed ego function, that is, through a quick, more or less involuntary, repetitious gesture or movement. The movement contains elements of discharge gratification and of punishment.

In children symptomatic tics may be observed in the process of crystallization as a component *part* of those disturbances termed *primary or reactive behavior disorders*. In such cases the tic is a sign of an incipient neurosis, of the fact that there is an admixture of neurotic traits in the primary or reactive behavior disorder. In psychoanalytic terms, the fact that the "habit movements" are becoming more and more automatic and involuntary, indicates a degree of internalization of the conflict, that is to say, it marks the consolidation of the superego. From the above it follows that the tic may be one of the symptoms of a psychoneurosis and indeed is a quasi prototype of it.

Clinically and phenomenologically we may describe a *symptomatic tic* as consisting of a rather distinctly patterned and more or less localized and constant single or multiple involuntary twitching. Single or "isolated" tics, as for instance blinking and sniffing, may mark *transient tension phenomena*. But they may also represent a true neurotic symptom, the symbolic expression of a conflict in body language. The tic symptom as such is classified in psychoanalytic literature in the category of a pregenital conversion symptom.

The tic may be part of a *"tic syndrome"*. The tic syndrome belongs to an essentially different psychopathological category from the psychoneurotic tic (36). It is an organ neurosis of the neuromuscular apparatus. It follows the genetic and dynamic rules described by Alexander and Fenichel as characteristic of psychosomatic disease (2), (10). The *tic syndrome,* or "maladie des tics impulsifs" (35), consists of generalized diffuse motor automatisms of the entire striate musculature. The tic patterns appear in intermittent and migratory crops of tics, which develop frequently amidst general muscular restlessness, hyper- and dyskinetic disorders. The tic automatisms in patients with the tic syndrome may involve all parts of the voluntary (striate) muscle system, that is, the musculature of the face, neck, arms, hands, legs, abdominal wall and the trunk. They may involve the muscles of phonation and vocalization, resulting in grunting, barking and yelling tics, which are pathognomonic of the disease, as is the automatic ideomotor emission of obscene utterances, condensed in the so-called coprolalic tics.[2] Different crops or sets of tic patterns may be successively alternated with intermissions of months, weeks or days, particularly in the beginning of the disease. The tic automatisms may inundate the neuromuscular apparatus in such a way that the entire musculature is in paroxysmic motion practically without respite (except when the patient is asleep). Hence the condition is very often mistaken for Sydenham chorea (St. Vitus dance). The personality of this type of tiqueur has very constant and typical traits. It is characterized by a peculiar mixture of high intellectual endowment, emotional immaturity, and proneness to intermittent affectomotor outbursts (temper tantrums) (29, 31, 32).

We wish to emphasize that it is essential to distinguish between those tics which are a sign or symptom of various psychopathological conditions, and as such are only a symptom of these conditions, and the tics which in themselves represent the central and essential disturbance. In the latter case the tic pertains to a characteristic psychosomatic disease of the motor system. If we do not differentiate between the tic as part of the symptom picture of a neurosis or psychosis, on the one hand, and organ neurotic "maladie des tics" on the other hand, we cannot come to uniform and valid conclusions.

Abraham (1), for example, disagreed with the conclusions which Ferenczi put forward in his "Psychoanalytic Observations on Tics" (11). Abraham was inclined to believe that tics could hardly be differentiated from compulsive obsessive acts. Since Abraham based his observations upon only one patient of a certain type, we may readily see how his opinions would differ from those of a number of other psychoanalytic observers, whose conclusions were based on a few patients with different types of tic. As Fenichel expressed it, "the term psychogenic tic covers a continuous series of links from conversion hysteria to catatonia" (9). Gerard (17) to whom we owe a brilliant paper on this subject, also bases her conclusions upon selected cases, "which presented, as *part* of the symptom picture, a *simple tic*" [3] and described only those cases in which "the circumstances at the time of onset were known accurately" This selection restricted Gerard's scope of research to the symptomatic tic. It eliminated from her study, on the one hand, the generalized tics, and on the other, those insidiously developing, migrating tics, both of which are so characteristic of childhood. The present study is based on about 60 cases of tics in children of whom 7 were analyzed and the rest thoroughly studied and followed up, over a period of from 6 months to

---

2. There sometimes occur certain so-called echophenomena of motility, phonation and speech, which are characteristic manifestations (31).

3. Italics of this author.

8 years, as well as several adult cases (one of whom was analyzed by the author).

We propose to classify tics into the following categories:

Symptomatic tics, such as:

(1) Passagère or transient tics, which indicate tension phenomena;

(2) tic as a sign of a primary or reactive behavior disorder on the verge of internalization;

(3) the tic as symptom of a psychoneurosis (anxiety hysteria, conversion hysteria, compulsive obsessive neurosis) or of a psychosis.

In contradistinction to these psychoneurotic, symptomatic tics,

(4) the tic syndrome as an integral part of an impulse or character neurosis;

(5) and finally the tic syndrome as a psychosomatic tic disease (a systemic organ neurosis of the neuromuscular system).

The last two categories of tics have a close relationship.

Most tics of adults which we see in their frozen form, seem to have originated in childhood. Tics which we see in adults are of three kinds. There are those which as irreversible motor automatisms are the frozen traces of a psychoneurotic conflict in body language (conversion hysteria). There are those which represent a condensation and automatization of the compulsive action of an obsessive compulsion neurotic.[4] And finally there are motor automatisms which are the residuals of a generalized tic disease of the "maladie des tics" variety.

Meige and Feindel in their classical monograph on "Tics and Their Treatment" (35)[5] stated that "the tic subject suffers from a disturbance of motility". They also referred to the tiqueur's peculiarities of personality by such general statements as "tic is mental infantilism", and "tiqueurs are big, badly reared children who never learned to bridle their will and actions", etc. etc. Meige and Feindel's statement that patients with tics suffer basically from a disturbance of motility, applies, according to our experience, essentially to the last two categories of tiqueurs, whereas patients with symptomatic tics, according to our experience, do not suffer from a "disturbance of motility". This would be self-evident if our thesis that the symptomatic tic is but *one* symptom of a psycho-neurosis or a psychosis is correct. The tic disease, which we have described as the "tic syndrome", corresponds to the genetic, dynamic, structural, and economic principles of a systemic organ neurotic disease, with particular affinity, as it were, for the peculiarities of the infantile motor organization (29, 31). The tic syndrome, though rare in its full-fledged

4. Ferenczi felt these were "accessory symptoms", demarcated appendages of the personality of the adult tiqueur.
5. Ferenczi (11) based his treatise on tics on this monograph.

form, as "maladie des tics", is, in its milder form, a characteristic and specific psychosomatic disease of the loosely organized personality of the child.

A constitutional and also a predispositional deficiency of the ego in that part of its function which integrates motility, seems to be the effective basis of generalized tic—the tic disease. In psychoanalytic terms the tic syndrome is the result of the ego's failure to integrate the psychomotor system into a hierarchy functioning under the ego's voluntary control. Purposeful, intentional motility should gradually gain uncontested control over the diffuse, impulsive and affect-laden motility—characteristic of the infant and the small child (22, 25). In such directed motility the ego is the central steering system, and its organic basis is the cortico-pyramidal part of the C.N.S. which gradually assumes ascendency over the predominant subcortical psychomotor organization of the early years.

Ferenczi (12) and Landauer (25), as well as Fenichel (8), were the psychoanalytic authors who investigated tics, automatisms and other motor phenomena in relation to the general problem of the development of motility.

The skeletal musculature is the executive organ of self-assertion and of defense. The striate musculature is the executive organ-system for normal and pathological aggression in childhood (14). Whereas for the adult the principal organ of discharge of instinctual tension is the genital, the child's principal means of discharge is action, and thus the musculature has the leading rôle in preserving the libido economic balance of the infantile personality (14, 29, 32). Fenichel in his paper "Über organlibidinöse Begleiterscheinungen der Triebabwehr" expressed the opinion that inhibition of motor expression may cause a partial impediment of the ego's mastery of motility (8). As Fenichel, and recently Felix Deutsch (6) pointed out, every suppression of the motor release of an affect leads to an increase of muscular tension.

The renunciation of instinctual impulsive acts is the essential aim of repression. The child is supposed gradually to repress the motor release of his autoerotic, objecterotic, and particularly his aggressive impulses (15). In a paper, "Tics and Impulsions in Children, a Study of Motility" (29), we described in detail how at the onset of the latency period, the psychomotor apparatus, even of the normal child, is all but overburdened by the need of preventing the objectionable oedipal cravings from being expressed in motility. The task of massive inhibition of motor expression at this period may cause a relative weakening of the motility controlling function of the ego. Ferenczi recognized this phenomenon (11). Many authors have shown, clinically as well as statistically, that the morbidity climax of systemic motor neuroses in children occurs between the ages of 6 to 11 years.

Because the child's motor system has a priority rôle as the executive of affective discharge, and because the child's psychomotor organization is one of a loosely integrated, hierarchic system (consisting of cortico-pyramidal and subcortical parts), one may say that the child's motor system seems to have a special proclivity for becoming:

(a) a preferred system for primary hyper-and dyskinetic behavior disorders and repetitive impulsions in the pre-latency period,

(b) a preferential site of neurotic symptom formation at the school age (Ferenczi, Mahler),

(c) and finally, the organ system of choice in certain cases predisposed to psychosomatic disease (hyperkinetic disease, paracortical motor syndrome [Bender and Schilder], tic disease, hysteric chorea, and hystero-epilepsy).

The musculature is the legitimate discharge organ for surplus tension long after sphincter control is established, and long before the ego's mastery of motility is achieved. Before the massive repression at the age of 5 and 6, and because of the ready response of the subcortical more primitive motility, little children use their expressional and automatic motility in any "normal" situation in which surplus tension has to be released.[6] Repetitious, ritualistic or autoerotic habit movements in little children are so common that hardly a child grows up without having had such transient manifestations.[7] If we were to follow the definition of "tic" proposed by Blatz and Ringland (4), we should find, as they did, that tics occur in nearly 100 per cent of children between 2 and 5 years of age. These differ both phenomenologically and structurally from the crystallized true tics. They are neither so vigorous and quick in their mode, nor so spasmodic, ambitendent and intermittent in their sequence of muscular contractions, as are the true tics. They do not represent in condensed pattern conflicting tendencies (they are ego syntonic) (22, 29). Between such habit movements there may be fluent transitions to the more complex and elaborate yet impetuous actions of little children, which we have described in former papers as impulsions. We have postulated in previous papers (29, 31) that there must be an organized superego plus the trigger effect of a sudden threat or trauma,

6. Their whole body is in motion, and synkinesias are not limited to a few, agonistically selected muscles. Expressional gestural behavior is not confined to the mimetic and facial musculature (22, 24, 26).

7. These habitual manipulations, loosely and falsely called "tic", may be regarded as repetitive discharge phenomena: examples are the habitual wiggling, foot-tapping, sniffing, blinking, frowning and grimacing of little children.

or actual inner conflict in order to produce the crystallization of a true tic. As long as the superego is not solidly differentiated within the child's personality structure, tics are highly reversible semi-automatisms, and may cease if and when the strain is over.

I. Passagère Tics Observed in Statu Nascendi

The passagère, symptomatic tic, when observed in statu nascendi, is likewise susceptible to treatment. Anna Freud, in her book *War and Children* (13) cites such a case in her beautiful description of Patrick, age 3 years and 2 months.

Patrick's case illustrates the fact that under exceptionally trying circumstances and in the face of unusual perplexities, little children may be forced to condense motor actions, particularly gestural behavior, into merely symbolic expressions of the problem and conflict, which formerly they were able to play and act out repetitiously.

During analysis we followed the development of a habitual, spasmodic narrowing of the muscles around the eyes and those of visual accommodation in a little girl, Gloria, when she was 4½ and 5. From the age of 4 the child was analyzed because of a rather severe phobia of wolves. Working herself up into a state of excitement was a characteristic feature of her case.[8] These excitements usually culminated in temper outbursts and scenes or in night terrors. As analysis proceeded, Gloria's excited, diffuse motor manifestations of her anxiety gave way to more quiet, purposeful acting and playing out of her problems which centered around the question of the anatomical difference between her little brother and herself, and around the enigma of her origin. In her case this was an unusually perplexing problem since neither her mother nor her father were her original parents. The perplexities of her situation were first reflected in Gloria's frantic, repetitious play activity and compulsive questioning. After a period of repetitious questioning of her mother, which was distinguished from the usual period of intense curiosity by its frenzy and its intensity, Gloria's frantic activity became reduced. She settled down and tried to find out the answers for herself. She would sit on the window sill and ponder. She would ask, for instance, "Could I see the children who are on the other side of the ocean? . . . Why can't I look into the X's house?" Her little face would reflect the strain, the determined effort to penetrate obstacles in the way of her mental and physical vision. At such times she would contract her eye muscles, narrowing the opening of her eyelids. This tic-like habit, the straining of the accommodation of her eye, was the symbolic expression, her looking inward, her strenuous thinking. From then on, for a while, every time she wanted and could not quite understand or see, she manifested this condensed tic-like gesture.

8. Compare the case of Elmer, 29, p. 438.

Such a pattern of neuromuscular innervation easily could have become a psychoneurotic symbolic tic, a motor automatism, to which the ego resorts as defense under the circumstances described by Gerard (17).[9]

These and similar cases enabled us to observe the formation of the tic, which seemed to have the following genesis: The little child becomes aware of his parents' disapproval of the motor expression (in speech and behavior) by which he has been acting out certain impulses and affective problems. He then tends to suppress or disguise the free expression of these desires. He tries to hide his gestures and actions by automatically speeding up the sequence of motions, and/or by executing the innervations surreptitiously. Thus, acting out may become condensed to a mere symbol of motions, and since such a condensation is no more apt to relieve tension, it also loses its discharge function, and may establish a vicious circle in the child's libido-economic balance. As soon as an organized superego renders the conflict largely independent of the environment, the symbolic motion becomes a true neurotic symptom.[10]

Therefore, if the intensity and duration of such habitual movements in little children is excessive, such tic-like manifestations should concern us inasmuch as they may be the first presenting symptom of:

(a) an incipient neurosis,

(b) or of a so-called tic diathesis, the sign of a constitutional predisposition to motor disturbances (cf. 5).

The question of tic predisposition

We discussed the point that the crystallization of a tic within the matrix of a behavior disorder may mark an incipient neurosis and is frequently the first sign of it. It seems that the persistence of such a symbolic tic, used as defense-innervation whenever anxiety arises, depends upon a hereditary predisposition for tics which has been found in both types of child tiqueurs by many previous observers (5, 35 et al.).[11]

9. We may tentatively suggest that Gloria's well-coordinated, gracious motility may have exempted her from developing motor symptomatology, even if psychoanalysis had not helped her in resolving her conflicts.

10. The movement sequence becomes abrupt, "ambitendent" in its selection of the muscle groups, in order to express in gesture both aspects of the conflict: doing and undoing (cf. Kris, 24). Flexion and extension, opening an orbicular muscle and closing, or narrowing it (eye, mouth, etc.) follow each other rapidly. By relegating the movement pattern to the unconscious strata of the ego and by repressing the ideational representation, or the libidinal cathexis which the motion carried, the tic becomes automatic and thus escapes from the ego's voluntary control (cf. Hartmann, 20).

11. In the histories of even the monosymptomatic tiqueurs we often found other tiqueurs in the ascendent or collateral line. Whether these children (who are

We may definitely state, however, that the constitutional habitus as well as the genesis of tic in our two essential categories of tiqueurs was basically different.

II. THE PSYCHONEUROTIC TIC SYMPTOM

Tic as a conversion symptom

Irma was the only child of German Jewish parents. Her early development was uneventful. She started school in her native country. The teacher commented on her playfulness and lack of serious concentration. The child was 8 years old when reverses entered in her life. Her father was arrested and put into a concentration camp, she and her family were persecuted. She and her mother had to flee from the country to save their own lives, leaving the father behind. During emigration there was another traumatic event in that the mother forgot the keys to her trunks, so that she had to return to the border in order not to lose that modest part of their property they were permitted to take along. Irma overheard somebody cautioning her mother, "If you return to the border, they will keep you there." The child was left with relatives, and although the mother returned, she went through an agony of fear. From that time, she was terribly afraid of losing her mother, especially in the train to their point of embarkation. In still another country in Europe they met further reverses. Then Irma began to show manneristic movements with her feet, and blinking. On her arrival in this country she suffered from *pavor nocturnus;* because of this and the crammed quarters they occupied, the child managed to share her mother's bed. Her mother went to work early in the morning. The child could hardly wait for her return in the evening to tell her the happenings of the day, and could not stop her own questioning and logorrhoeic recounting of her daily experiences. In the morning, before her mother left for her job and while the child was getting ready for school, Irma demanded that her mother comb her long hair and braid it. She was always tempted to tell her mother just a few more things at this time in order to keep her company just a little bit longer. This upset and angered her mother. Sometimes she could not help handling Irma's braids rather roughly, so that scenes and crying were the rule—and the braids literally became the symbol of both the bond and the emotional conflict between the mother and the child. After a long while the father joined them. His return made Irma feel strange at no longer having her mother's undivided attention. She had developed a habit of slowly but repetitiously turning her head as if looking after her mother when the latter stepped out of the house. Later the head-turning became a habit, lost its obvious and actual connection with the original motivation in that it was not performed only on the occasions when someone left, but at any odd time, and the movement was repeated two or three times in a row.

characterized by their imitative, iterative and exhibitionistic traits) merely copied these examples, or whether the same hereditary taint caused the symptom in several members of the same family, is difficult to determine.

Irma's mother always was rather strict with her, yet she could not persuade her daughter to leave her over night until finally, at the age of 12, Irma herself decided to conform to the way of life of her class-mates and to spend part of her summer vacation in a camp. The only obstacle to this plan was her long braids which were her pride and her family's also, and which were the rationalized focus of her dependence on her mother. This dependence, moreover, was pointed out, and she was increasingly teased about it by her aunts and other relatives: who would braid her hair in camp? Hence, in an impulsive mood, Irma decided to have her braids cut off, so as to become independent of her mother's help before going away. After this "heroic" deed Irma went to camp. There she felt very lonesome and depressed,—her menstruation started at this time. When Irma returned, her mother saw with dismay that she shook her head violently. The tic was a head-turning and "braid-hitching" tic,[12] the structure of which was determined by Irma's conflicting emotional tendencies; her wish to bind her mother to her-self, her defense against her dependence, together with many other over-determining factors, such as her decision to cut off the braids, the coin-ciding of the menarche; her masturbatory conflict, her mother as pro-tector against her masturbatory impulses as well as the feared agent of her strict conscience, from which she tried to rid herself.

This symptomatic tic was amenable to psychoanalytic treatment in the manner described by Gerard. In Irma's case the tic was a typical hysteric conversion symptom, the symbolic expression of a conflict in body language.

Tic as a condensed compulsive gesture or action

Herbert was 9 years old when he first came for consultation about a rather long-standing blinking and arm tic. The latter consisted of a two-or-three-times-repeated, rapid, wiping motion of the forearm and hand. Herbert's personality was characterized by traits found in compul-sive individuals. He was meticulous, circumstantial and fussy. He set high standards for himself in terms of achievement, and was very compe-titive with his siblings for the favors of his parents. His habit training had been strict and he was already clean at the age of 16 months. His parents described how early Herbert knew right from wrong, and how he argued his way through early infancy instead of fighting. He could express his aggression in temper tantrums only. Herbert left the analytic treatment before his analysis could have succeeded. However, the structure of his tics was a most instructive example of the condensation of compulsive acts. They symbolized Herbert's psychosexual conflict on an anal-sadistic and masochistic level. Both tics referred to the same topic, namely his struggle between his scoptophilic, aggressive and his exhibitionistic, passive tendencies. The one tic served to show his mother the dirt one could make to spite her and also wiped it away to

---

12. This action represented a combination of Irma's former head-turning tic with another movement, namely a muscular weighing of her lost braids, a loss which she thus repetitiously re-experienced.

prevent her from seeing it. It therefore represented his defiant soiling tendency, as well as his excessively compliant cleanliness, and his great ambivalence.

These two examples illustrate the genetic, dynamic and structural nature of the symptomatic tic. The same principles apply to the symptomatic tic in an anxiety neurosis and also in some cases of child psychosis, in which neurotic defense mechanisms are predominant (34).

THE QUESTION OF "TIC DIATHESIS" AND OF "SOMATIC COMPLIANCE"

In the cases described the tic movements were understood as the symbolic expression of a conflict. If in the course of development or through psychoanalytic treatment the ego succeeded in giving up this method of defense before complete automatization of the involuntary movement patterns rendered the tic irreversible (somatically anchored), the tic was resolved. If not, the tic persisted, demarcated from the ego, and appeared as an accessory symptom, an appendage, as it were, and remained unresolved, even if psychoanalysis of the adult succeeded in curing the psychoneurosis (11). Whereas a certain "tic diathesis" is frequently found in the families of symptomatic tiqueurs (5), it is an entirely *different kind of "organic compliance"* which characterizes individuals suffering from the *tic syndrome,* as we shall describe below. In the initial tics we still may discover some symbolic meaning.[13] In the beginning they may seem to be built according to the psychodynamic principles of the symptomatic tic.[14] But, according to our experience, in many cases in which *multiple* tics long persist or migrating crops of tics pervade the general voluntary muscle system, the ego does not get enough respite to organize the defense mechanisms necessary for the establishment of a systematized psychoneurosis of the hysteric or the compulsive type.

In "Formulations Regarding The Two Principles in Mental Functioning" Freud stated that the infant, as long as he acts according to the pleasure principle, tries to discharge tension immediately and experiences any excitement as "trauma" which is responded to by uncoordinated discharge movements. The overcoming of this state depends on two factors. The first is the physiological capacity for mastering motility. This occurs when the intentional cortico-pyramidal motility gradually

13. Though very often the meaning in these tics is a secondary use of the movement pattern for rationalization.
14. Edith Jacobson remarks (23, p. 343) that in some cases it is hard to define to what extent the symptoms ... should be regarded as psychoneurotic, as psychosomatic, or as a mixture of both.

gains leadership over the subordinate subcortical affectomotility. This results in an exchange of the discharge role of the psychomotor system for the role of the executive system of purposeful actions. The second factor in overcoming immediate muscular discharge of tension is the growing ability of the ego to postpone immediate reaction—because reality requires it—and to accept the interpolation of thinking,—i. e., trial acting—between the impulse and its execution (12, 15). Children who later develop a tic syndrome showed in their histories an impediment in each of the two factors which Freud mentioned as prerequisites for the successful transition from the pleasure to the reality principle.

Two clinical findings of the research on patients with tic syndrome are important in this connection. First, the fact that of 39 patients with syndrome-tic studied, 37 were males and only 2 were girls.[15] Second, that 50 per cent of our boy tiqueurs belonged to the body type which one might call pseudo-Froehlich habitus.[16] They were markedly obese and had feminine distribution of the subcutaneous fat tissue. These two findings pointed in the direction of a constitutional inherent (maturational) deficiency of the kinetic and secondarily the integrating function of the ego (19). The theoretical discussion of these findings follows below.

In children with a tic syndrome the characteristic behavior traits in pre-school age were found to be urgency, impetuousness, drivenness (29) and undirected violence with a lag in sustained effort and persistence. Such children showed an initial temperamental display of enthusiasm—then distractability and readiness to quit in despair, or in fury. A lack of endurance and tenacity, coupled with pseudo-stubborn negativism was another characteristic feature of their personality. The motor automatisms, the multiple migrating and subsequently persistent tics then seemed to have set a vicious circle which caused a secondary developmental weakening of the synthetic function of the ego (cf. 33), so that the multiple persistent tics became a part of a subsequent general "motor neurosis", in which we found the principles of a psychosomatic system or organ neurosis to have become operative (2, 10). The ego's failure to master motility and action became particularly evident at the beginning of the latency period. These children's proneness to affectomotor outbursts, to temper tantrums, at the slightest frustration, betrayed their state of affective tension, particularly their *suppressed*

15. In representatives of symptomatic ties no prevalence of the male child could be elicited.

From the 39 cases all patients with organic (encephalitic) involvement were excluded.

16. Their genitals seemed undersized because of the obesity. This was spurious. Only 6 boys suffered from chryptorchidism at school age.

aggression, and their inability to tolerate frustration. The psychological effect of chronic suppression of aggression led to general and multifocal tension phenomena in the musculature, with restlessness, hyperkinetic or dyskinetic manifestations. When, subsequently, *early multiple tics pervaded* the general voluntary *muscle system* of the child, this marked an *ego defection which* eventually *culminated* in either A) *character neurosis* of the *impulse* neurotic type with *interwoven tic syndrome,* or B) *in a psychosomatic organ neurosis* of the neuromuscular apparatus: *the tic disease ("maladie des tics").*

III. IMPULSE NEUROSIS WITH TIC SYNDROME

We first became aware of the kinship between the clinical picture of impulse neurosis and the "maladie des tics", in the course of the psychoanalysis of a boy patient, Elmer, who showed impulsions and intermittently recurring crops of tics (29). Elmer had suffered from a disturbance which one could best term: impulsions or impulse neurosis. From time to time he displayed multiple tics, at other times impulsive, aggressive and obscene behavior, which seemed volitional, i. e., semi-voluntary. Elmer's impulsive actions and his tics were highly interchangeable, so that we could study the mechanism of his hyperkinetic, impetuous versus tic manifestations like a laboratory experiment. The impression of the close relationship between the two kinds of symptoms was verified by a number of subsequent analyses and long-term psychotherapeutic observation of similar cases.

The close connection between impulsions and motor neurosis was demonstrated in the case of Johnnie, who was 9 when he was admitted to our children's ward. For the past 3 years he had been manifesting a tic formation involving his eyes, shoulders, neck, hands, arms and legs. These symptoms were accompanied by unruliness, unmanageable impudent behavior toward his mother and father and overt, erotic assaultiveness towards his sisters as well as towards other girls.

Fixation at the oral level was evidenced by Johnnie's nursing from the bottle till the age of 3. An attempt to wean him was made at about the age of 14 months, but with the advent of a younger sibling the child rebelled. Consequently he was permitted to go on using the bottle until he was 3. Anal fixation was due to a toilet training begun very early and strictly enforced, "very difficult and prolonged". The toilet training commenced when Johnnie was about seven months old. His mother said, "He was very dirty and difficult to train. It took me about 2 years before I had him broken. I would put him on the toilet and then he would do nothing and then get down and deliberately defecate on the floor in front of me."

From 2½ to 3½ Johnnie began to have severe temper tantrums, and would bang his head against the wall. At the same time he had great fear of thunder and lightning. At 3 he successively contracted whooping cough, chicken pox, measles and mumps. At this time he also developed a squint of the right eye. Following a tenotomy at the age of 4, Johnnie's general hypermotility and restless, fearful and temperamental behavior became worse.

The child grew up in a rigidly religious environment, which from a very early age habitually called on God's justice and punishment for every misdeed.

In spite of Johnnie's violent aggressiveness it was apparent from the very beginning of his social development that he was a poor mixer and that he never liked to play with boys, but only with girls.

At the age of 6 he was enrolled in a parochial school. At the same time he became initiated into sexual play by another boy. He was severely reprimanded and threatened with punishment. All of the religious fears were invoked to subdue this interest. He was subsequently found exposing himself to his sisters. During his 6th year Johnnie was observed to be overtly masturbating. His parents were greatly alarmed. He was told that whenever he did a bad thing, he was nailing Christ on the cross. Johnnie's nervousness reached a peak when he was 6 years of age. He also developed generalized muscular twitchings, which were falsely diagnosed as St. Vitus dance. The parents made the child acutely aware of his condition and frequently threatened him with punishment if he did not stop. From then on he went about provoking girls, lifting up their skirts and exposing himself.

We find in Johnnie's anamnesis several noteworthy features. He showed early rebellion against strict habit training, and precocious "cruel" but patchy superego development. Fixation at the anal level and precocious superego development render the person susceptible to the establishment of an obsessive compulsion neurosis. However, in Johnnie's case, other, more specific etiological factors competed with these fixations. One was the child's strong oral fixation, the other was his impetuous anal and genital exhibitionism. Concomitant with these was his narcissistic overcathexis of the neuromuscular apparatus, resulting in an increased motor urgency.

When we met Johnnie, he presented the picture of a severely disturbed boy. Only at a very superficial evaluation could his symptomatic behavior fall into the category of primary conduct disorder. The dynamics of his symptomatology placed him in the category of impulse neurosis with a mixture of anxiety symptoms and pseudo-compulsive acting-out mechanisms with interspersed tics. He gradually evidenced definitely paranoid traits with abundant use of the mechanism of projection.

Johnnie was destructive, but if attacked by the boys, he did not defend himself by adequate aggression; "If I fight, God will suffer—unless there are 4 to 1 against me." He also expressed a fear of being jailed or otherwise restrained in his freedom of action and began a compulsive preoccupation with locking and unlocking doors, taking and keeping the doctor's key, so as to have possession of the tool with which to incarcerate other people or to set them free.

When Johnnie was asked what he thought was wrong with him, he answered: "I have nerves and I shake my arms and head." He also developed the idea that if his uncle watched his tics constantly, one by one, and scolded him, they would cease. This relative was his favorite uncle and "lots of fun". This external superego and ego extension was the one to whose magic power he wished to turn for help in his predicament.

He also expressed the opinion that his involuntary automatisms might have started "the time they poured water on me... They poured water on my head when they baptized me." He also related in this connection that his mother thought that whenever he did something wrong, he was nailing Christ to the cross. The next association was his liking to lock himself up into the attic room whenever he visited his favorite uncle's house, so that the "uncle would be locked out of the room". In that room where he liked to lock himself, his aunt kept interesting old junk, which Johnnie liked to see and play with, and his uncle was thus prevented from throwing out those things. So, on the one hand, Johnnie wanted his uncle to cure his tics by watching and scolding him, and on the other, he locked himself in to indulge in his autoerotic activities without being disturbed by onlookers. The conflict is clearly discernable between his *exhibitionistic versus scoptophilic tendencies,* his *desire to be watched and scolded,* prevented from being bad, and his *impulse to do bad things* (masturbation etc.) *which might* nail, that is, *painfully immobilize* Christ on the cross. This alternation culminated in his difficulty to bear any motor impulse in abeyance, and finally, in his ambitendent tics.

Elmer and Johnnie used interchangeably provocative erotic aggressive behavior, consisting of intensive peeping and of swearing, bathroom language, grimacing and other exhibitionistic performances, and the condensed symptoms thereof: the tic syndrome. With the former they sought to infuriate, belittle, embarrass and disturb people. With this provocative aggressive behavior they tried to ward off their passive submissive tendencies which were clearly understood from the analytic material. The provocative impulsive behavior was aimed at being attacked and quelled by a father figure. This was evident, f. e. from Elmer's fixation to the traumatic event of his father s return from a long trip, when Elmer was about 5 years old. The father was told that during his absence Elmer had been a bad boy, and particularly that Elmer was constipated. Thereupon the father overpowered Elmer and gave him an enema. During analysis Elmer fantasied and acted out his fear and masochistic expectation of being attacked from the rear. His impulsive sticking his finger into the rectum of his playmates in kindergarten was later exchanged for an inordinate revulsion against the anal masturbation allegedly practiced by his schoolmates The counterpart to the many operations, accidents and body traumata in Elmer's life was his cruelly sadistic fantasies and dreams about mutilated bodies, dismembered extremities cooking in boiling water, blood and murder.

The clinical course of Johnnie's narcissistic disturbance was also characterized by the unpredictable alternation of impulsive and tic-free intermissions of weeks and months, with periods of "unruly" impulse-ridden behavior, with or without multiple tics. During their course we could observe the ego's struggle and its increasing failure in personality integration.

The impulsive, aggressive, erotic behavior was the diffuse, amorphous manifestation of the *same basic affective attitude* which we found *underlay the tic syndrome* of this type and also of the tic syndrome of the organ neurotic type.

Psychoanalysis of tiqueurs with impulse neurotic character formation revealed that these impulse-ridden children did not succeed in erecting ego defenses necessary for systematized psychoneurosis. They did not even succeed in erecting solid psychosomatic barriers, massive and organized enough for psychosomatic organ neurosis. Fenichel pointed out that, "Impulse neurotics tend to react to frustrations with *violence*". The main conflict of the impulse neurotic is one between "a tendency towards violence and the tendency to suppress all aggressiveness through fear of loss of love." In the impulse neurotic tiqueur, it seems, violent oral and phallic aggression is ineffectually prohibited by their patchy superego.

Their ego was continually carried away by affective actions (21) for which Elmer and Johnnie, for instance, felt guilty and expected punishment. They were torn between this guilt feeling and their pent-up erotic, aggressive impulses, which threw them into a chronic state of conflict. The ego's failure to interpolate trial acting between impulse and action, on the one hand, impulse and automatic discharge motility (tics) on the other, had a seriously disorganizing effect upon these patients. They resorted to the abundant use of projection in order to defend themselves, and thus may have proceeded in the direction of psychosis. They were prone to paranoid and depressive moodswings.[17] One of the main difficulties in Elmer's analysis was the handling of his projection mechanism: Not he, but his mother ought to change, or should be analyzed. Not he, but the maid started arguments. Not he, but another pupil was responsible for the teacher's anger. Everybody was mean and unjust to Elmer.

Also, Johnnie's paranoid projection mechanisms were prominent. He could not confine himself for any length of time either to the display of his semi-voluntary grimaces and his logorrhoeic accusations. His mother and sisters were blamed for his misbehavior in school, etc.: "My sisters are making trouble, my mother opens her big mouth, I get blamed for everything, and my father wallops me when he comes home. He has an awful temper."

In a typical psychotherapeutic interview Johnnie tried to destroy toys; he said he "just didn't like them", and began to slam the toy soldiers into the cabinet. He then pounded clay with vigor all over the room. All the while he sang shrilly, and increased the volume whenever conversation was attempted. Finally he sat down and said, "Take my mother's c . . . and throw it away. It's no good." (?) "It has hairs on it." (?) "Can you stop me from getting any?"

17. Fenichel (9, p. 369). Cf. Footnote, p. 28.

Johnnie's struggle against his very marked feminine identification tendencies, his fear of growing up to be an adult man, took the above described frantic, inconsistent form. One week he acted out his conflict by unacceptable conduct in school, swearing at his sisters and mother—and attacking them violently so as to provoke his mother into having to report his behavior to his father. Then Johnnie would receive his beating. Another week a crop of tics prevailed.

His mother was alarmed by the extent of Johnnie's impulsiveness: "It comes on so sudden." Grandmother says she would not allow Johnnie in her house if he were older, for fear "he would pick up a knife." He threw a bolt at his 5-year-old sister and cut her badly on the temple. It bled profusely. Johnnie was remorseful and behaved well for awhile. Then he again wrote "obscene" notes to girls in the class.

Whereas Johnnie bullies and bosses his sisters, he will not even try to join the boys' competitive games. He wants to play with teddybears and dolls, even steals the doll out of his sister's bed after she is asleep at night.

His sexual confusion is shown by his graphic and somewhat provocative description in the presence of his aunt how a woman's stomach "gets big and hard before she has a baby".

IV. ORGAN NEUROSIS — "MALADIE DES TICS"

The vicissitudes of the erotic, aggressive drives, the mode of the ego's defenses and the structure of ego and superego differed in the two types of tic syndrome. The change in the behavior of children with organ neurotic tics at the onset of the latency period was very conspicuous. The impulsive tiqueur continued to be hyperkinetic, obtrusive, violent and destructive, or even antisocial, beyond latency. In the organ neurotic tiqueur, however, at the latency period one usually found that the noisy aggression, hyperkinetic impulsions, the pseudoactivity and demonstrative behavior changed and gave way to an overcompliant, ingratiating affability and submissive passivity with cropping up of tics. The organ neurotic tiqueur's syndrome appeared in a markedly *hypokinetic,* inhibited, often depressed, anxious and submissive personality, which seemed impoverished in emotional modulation and expressional capacity, and which had no free locomotor and athletic pursuits and avoided the competitive games of contemporaries.

As illustration we would refer to the cases of Freddie (31) and Pete (30), and cite the case of 7-year-old Henry.

From the time he was 3 years old Henry's impulsive behavior had changed insidiously into tics. They involved successive crops of automatic movement patterns of his face, neck, trunk and extremities, and the muscles of vocalization, and finally invaded the ideomotor area with coprolalic four letter utterances. Henry, the only child of his parents, was an obese, flabby-looking little boy, awkward and timid, with few spontaneous gestures, and with signs of depression.[18] His intelligence was superior.[19] In pre-latency Henry had displayed entirely opposite behavior picture. He had been an impetuous, demonstrative, outgoing, affectionate, happy and very noisy little child.

Throughout pregnancy Henry's mother had very severe nausea and vomiting; she stayed indoors most of the time and had frequent fainting spells; in the course of one of these she severely hurt her spine and shoulder.[20] Pregnancy, delivery and Henry's earliest infancy were uneventful. However, at 3—4 months he developed a severe sore throat and from that time on vomited "all of his food". This continued until he was 2 years of age. When he was 2½, an A and T was performed, mainly to eliminate the cause of vomiting. That Henry interpreted this operation as a punishment was subsequently shown by his behavior. His mother said, "The removal of his tonsils did not stop the vomiting. He used to raise a scene from then on and vomit." The mother feels that vomiting was used by the patient when he encountered unsatisfactory situations. Toilet training was begun at 7 months and achieved without difficulty. But in the area of anal habit training the mother also infantilized and overprotected the child. Fixation in the anal sphere was indicated by the mother's constant watching over her son's excretory functions. She used suppositories almost daily to "give him the habit of moving his bowels once a day". The patient would sit on the toilet from a half-hour to an hour at a time, and even when he was 7, his mother would accompany him to the toilet and forbid him to flush the water before she had inspected the bowel movement. The boy stated, "Mother always wants to see if I make enough." By means of the same affective attitude which had produced his habitual vomiting—namely a distorted expression of suppressed rebellion—the patient now developed chronic constipation and finally hemorrhoids, which at times resulted in rectal bleeding.[21] This established another vicious circle in the "appersonated" mother-child behavior pattern.

The mother stated that during his first 3 years Henry had a happy, outgoing disposition. He was very affectionate and very emotional. He talked out loud even when playing alone. He always played noisily. When cautioned, he would try to reduce the noise, but promptly forgot and became noisy again. He was alert and full of questions, but was—as far as could be ascertained—never particularly graceful or deft with his body and/or in small muscular coordinations. He was quite *highstrung*. The mother dates the onset of the child's symptoms with her own hospitalization for a perirectal abscess, when Henry was about

18. We may state that whereas the symptom tic is used by the ego to ward off anxiety (Gerard), the impulsions and the tic syndrome (condensations of the violent impulsive actions) serve the purpose of warding off depression and deep narcissistic fear of ego disintegration (26, 41). Cf. Fenichel (9, p. 369).

19. All children with organ neurotic tic syndrome (except those with organic brain damage) had an I. Q. which placed them into the bracket of superior intelligence; the impulsive tiqueur's I. Q. was somewhat lower.

20. We saw conflict about free movement in the environment of practically everyone of this type of tiqueur.

21. The psychodynamics of his constipation and rectal bleeding were reminiscent of principles described by M. Sperling in the case of psychosomatic ulcer formation (38).

4 years old. *The mother and child's interdependence seemed to have
been quite extreme at all times.* During the period in which he vomited
regularly at night, he at first always gave a cry for his mother. His
father hit him frequently and his mother yelled at him occasionally.
At such times Henry would become quite *stubborn* and determined.

The first set of motor symptoms developed at 3 or 4 years and consisted of manneristic movements of his index finger, flinging his arms
about and jumping up and down. These rituals were exchanged for
another set of more condensed tic movements: blinking of the eyes,
twisting of the legs and throwing of the head. Between the different
sets of symptoms there was usually a short period when he was free of
tics. However, as he grew older, each successive crop of tics lasted longer,
and "lately he is practically never free of them". The formerly noisy
and outgoing child had become increasingly shy and timid. "He became
fearful of other children and never fights back, and he has occasional
outbursts of temper tantrums" (29, 32).

His present condition, which we shall describe briefly, became more
severe in connection with the mother's illnesses and a series of accidents.
The mother stated, "His trouble seems to center around me. I ought to
get well and then maybe he will."

The conflict between longing for personal—particularly motor—
freedom versus fear of injury and loss of love, was beautifully expressed
in Henry's stories and fantasies: "Once upon a time there was a boy. He
was going to fall off a cliff but there was a hole near the cliff and he saved
himself. He wanted to know how far it was to the bottom." We see
both the conflictful sexual curiosity and the peeping tendency struggling
with the fear of castration; we also see the fantasy of the danger of
motor freedom.—"There was a big tree which he tried to chop down.
After he chopped it down he pushed it over the cliff and then he was
going to go back home." He is powerfully, aggressively active in his
fantasy.—"In the morning he got up and went to find more trees by the
cliff. On the way there he fell into another hole but he got out." The
very hole which saved him once became a dangerous trap in this version.
—"Then he saw a big tree nearby, so he picked up a big log and threw it
at the tree and both logs fell off the cliff." (Why did he throw them
down?) "So that if he wasn't looking and went near to the cliff, he
wouldn't bang into them." Banging into the log symbolized the obstacle,
the father, in Henry's close relationship with his mother. Thus the
obstacle and not the boy, fell off the cliff.—"The next day the boy went
away to the city and went to the park and started to chop down all the
trees, then he started to play ball on the grass with his father."

Henry had clearly identified himself with a puppy.[22] "The next
day Dick (his fantasy—alter ego) bought a puppy—his mother said he
could—and he went to the park with the puppy and played ball. One
time the boy threw the ball so far the puppy had to go in the pool to get
it." (Would you like a puppy?) "No,—well, I would like one, maybe,
when I got a little bigger. I would have to keep it in my room. Mother
used to sleep in my room. But now she sleeps in the dining room. So
now the puppy could sleep in my room in a little bed. Mother says when

22. In many tiqueurs we found identification with a pet animal.

I am 13, I can have one."—We see how timid and ambivalent Henry became in his relationship with his mother.

Another fantasy: "One night Dick was sleeping when the dog heard a noise, so he told Dick and Dick got up and looked out the window and saw a little parrot. It was singing all night long. Dick finally shot it, so it couldn't sing any more." The sleeping arrangements in Henry's house made the auditory witnessing of the primal scene unavoidable. In his fantasy Henry kills again, in his violence toward the singing parrot.

The conflict between active aggression, motor independence and bodily anxiety is expressed in the following fantasy: "The next day Dick took the dog to the park and threw a ball for Don, the dog. Don had to run very far after it, the ball hit a tree, bounced back and hit Don on the nose. He got the ball and brought it back to Dick who threw it again, and this time, Don, the dog caught the ball right in his mouth. The next day they got up early and they heard a horse. They couldn't see where the noise came from but finally decided the horse was in the barn and someone was trying to shoot him. (Why?) They didn't like him. They were bad men. Dick brought the horse into the living room. The next day they all went to the park together, Mother, Father, Dick and Don, and played ball together. The next day Dick was already 10 years old." (Nearer to 13, when he will be permitted to have a puppy.) Finally the bad boy who ventured to stray away from his mother, is punished: "There was a house, and in the house lived a little boy, two dogs and a cat. The dog and cat went to hunt for food, they saw a little boy sitting in the woods. They went over to him and saw that he was sleeping. They went away, came back there the next night and hunted for the boy but he wasn't there. They looked all over the forest. He fell off the cliff. He got up, he thought it was daytime, but he had his eyes closed and he walked right off the cliff." In this version the boy perished because he had strayed away from home.

(The habitual typical affective attitude of the mother and of the child tiqueur is illustrated in the following example): Henry drew a woman with a dog on a heavy leash. "He likes to run away. The dog stretches the leash when he pulls. He is pulling because he wants to run away. He likes to scare cows off the cliffs. He is a bad dog. He wants to get rid of everybody on the farm. He doesn't like the farmer. *After he gets rid of everybody he can run away.* He does not want to make friends with anybody. He likes to be free and to do everything he likes to do." (What?) "Go up on hills, push rocks off. Once he pushed a rock off and it hit a tree and the tree came out of the ground and fell on him. It just hurt his foot. Just a little bit." He increases the length of the leash in the drawing. "I like dogs very much. My aunt's dog, Sandy, always runs away. He pushes open the door *if it is unlocked.*" Henry's depressed mood gets more prominent.

One of his mother's chief complaints about Henry was, "He cannot stand anything around his *neck*!!" It was obvious and was interpreted to Henry that he, like Sandy, sometimes would like to run away, and do what he pleases. So the dog pulls and pulls at the leash. It was even suggested that this pulling gesture of his neck might have something to do with his feeling of wanting to pull away from his mother: he feels bad about his wish to disobey his mother; thus ever since he was able to talk he has insisted upon knowing where his mother is and what she is doing every minute of the day, and followed her like a shadow.

The form of Henry's oedipal conflict was also characteristic for the boy patient with "maladie des tics": Henry began to draw a house which filled the entire paper except for a narrow margin reserved for the sky. He then added a chimney, a door, windows on two floors, and then drew a man entering the door. He glanced up nervously at the doctor every few minutes. (Who is the man in the door?) "My father. He is going into a haunted house. It's haunted inside. It is his birthday and I want to scare him." He then said the two upstairs rooms are for him and his mother, and the downstairs ones for his father and uncle. He drew lines to indicate how he could gain access to his mother's room, and to escape back to his own room when the father came up to his mother's room looking for him after failing to find him in the uncle's room. He first said that he would have all the windows locked so that his father could not climb up from the outside. "He is scared of me because I like to beat him up. We play football. I tackle him. I dreamed I played football with him, and he chases me, tackles me and then I throw the ball to him. He starts running and I jump on his feet, and he falls down and I grab the ball and make a touchdown."

Henry sleeps on a cot in his mother's room. "I like to sleep in her bed. Sometimes my father sleeps on the cot and I sleep with my mother. He does not care too much. The cot does not feel comfortable to him." His mother reported, "If his father puts his arms around me on a Sunday morning, Henry jumps on top of us and tries to separate us and tells his father to leave me alone."

In the "maladie des tics" patient the passive submissiveness, the eroticized, provocative, aggressive defense attitude, is supplied from two sources: the identification with the mother (a preoedipal mother fixation) and the defense against the passive homosexual claims directed toward the father. This struggle only superficially looks as if it were an intensification of the normal positive oedipus complex.

In the first weeks of Henry's stay in the hospital his actual crop of tic patterns consisted of: a pulling tic of the neck, jerking his head forward, down and sideward, a blinking tic of the eyes, retracting motion of the lips, and a rapid upward thrusting of one or both forearms (with extended wrist and index finger as if pointing toward something, and/or admonishing someone), he said f ... f ... spasmodically while quietly absorbed in some activity (e. g., reading). At times one tic predominated, at other times they alternated rapidly.

We see the difference in the structure of Henry's obscene tic automatism as compared with Elmer's and Johnnie's impulsive obscene verbal assaults and subsequent remorse. In Freddie's (30) and Henry's case, release of the erotic aggressive impulse and defense against it is condensed in the ideomotor symptom. In the impulse-ridden tiqueur the *biphasic* acting out is predominant.

Elmer's and Johnnie's deliberate making faces, cursing at people, provoking them with repetitious teasing, obscene rhymes as well as notes, was the unorganized acting out of erotic aggressive impulses. Such outbursts were followed by anxiety, repentance, guilt feelings and subdued behavior—and finally by the tic automatisms.

All these elements can be detected in a condensed form in Henry's coprolalic tics which were quite marked after he became familiar with his ward-mates' bathroom language. He felt very guilty about his coprolalic tics, and felt them to be ego-alien and overwhelming. He stated, "Some people beat children for saying things like that." "Sometimes I can hear myself saying it but sometimes it sounds so low that I don't even hear myself saying it."

In the interview it became evident how important it was to Henry to be a good boy; also, how much afraid he was of his father. When he talked about the latter, he thrust his hands protectively toward his genitals. He also admitted having been repeatedly hit on his hands by his father. The pointing tic was then interpreted as possibly meaning an admonition to himself when he feels like being bad: "Beware, do not do, or think, or say things that are not nice."

The effect of such direct but obviously correct interpretation concerning this and scores of similar single tic patterns in organ neurotic tiqueurs was often striking and most instructive. It seemed that through bringing the meaning of a special tic pattern to the awareness of the tiqueur, they had to give up the pattern. However, as long as the basic affective attitude, causing the psychosomatic disturbance, was not worked through, the tic pattern was replaced by the use of other groups of muscles and other movement automatisms. By substituting alternate tic patterns (called paratics by Meige and Feindel) the tiqueur continued to express the pathogenic attitudes and ambivalence conflict, which previously he had vented by means of the patterns eliminated by the interpretations. Henry, for example, never again used the pointing and leash-pulling tics after the above interpretations.[23]

THEORETICAL DISCUSSION AND CONCLUSIONS

If our thesis that the tic syndrome is a psychosomatic disease is correct, we cannot expect the syndrome to be only a localized and limited symbolic expression of a specific conflict in body language. It seemed,

---

23. Following the disappearance of his pointing and leash-pulling tic, Henry's predominant tic became a vigorous backward bending of the head with a concomitant rapid, spasmodic opening of the mouth (as if commanded to let his tonsils be inspected) and a sudden violent snapping back of the head and a closing motion of the jaws, a violent oral, aggressive gesture, which had a secondary (rationalized) symbolic meaning, yet the same psychosomatic disturbance at its genetic root! (Cf. 31, p. 20).

however, from the psychoanalysis of such tiqueurs (Freddie, Elmer and Pete) that the "motor neurosis" as such was not entirely free of a certain unconscious meaning. The underlying unconscious fantasies were uniform. The dominant theme was concerned with movement and quiescence, attack and immobilization, paralyzation, falling, etc. Furthermore we were able to analyze in many cases of generalized tic disease the unconscious symbolic meaning of the temporarily predominant "presenting tic" pattern: although the meaning of this tic pattern could thus be retranslated from its body language and by so doing, dissolve the tic symptom, this did not, however, resolve the disease unless the basic affective attitude was also analyzed and worked through. Therefore it would seem that the psychomotor neurosis, the tic syndrome, follows the rules of both the hysteric conversion and the psychosomatic organ neurotic disease.

Alexander states that the conversion symptom is a symbolic substitute for an unbearable emotion, a kind of physical abreaction or equivalent of an unconscious emotional tension—it is "a symbolic expression of a well-defined emotional content... an attempt at relief." In contradistinction: the psychosomatic disease (which Alexander confines to the vegetative organs) "... is not an attempt to express an emotion but is the *physiological accompaniment* of constant or periodically recurring emotional states." [24]

We believe that the generalized tics (and perhaps several other "motor neuroses") represent two things. They are an attempted drainage of a chronic state of emotional tension and utilize for this purpose certain variable but well-defined symbolic expressions. But they are also the physiological accompaniment of a chronic affective attitude. The tic syndrome is the result of specific emotional constellations. Furthermore the organ neurotic and the impulse neurotic tiqueur were found to be suffering from both an innate (maturational) as well as developmental ego defection revealed in the area of their motility integrating function. We described the tiqueur as impetuous, hyperkinetic, oversensitive and intrinsically endowed with an increased "motor urgency". We found furthermore that there were typical and specific environmental influences which acted on the characteristics of these children to shape them "by the blocking of certain reactions to gratifications and frustrations and by the favoring of others." [25]

The tic syndrome (the dyskinetic disturbance of the neuromuscular

24. Cf. 2.
25. Cf. Fenichel, 10, p. 287.

apparatus) is the pathophysiological concomitant of a chronic state of affective tension; whereas the transiently predominant "presenting" tic patterns were an expression—an attempted drainage, of the emotional tension with a (secondary?) symbolic meaning (2, 10, 36).

By examining our material both in cross-section and longitudinally, we found strikingly constant factors and constellations:

(1) In these cases there was a predominance of male children (a ratio of 9:1).

(2) The children showed a constitutional increase of motor urgency. (Compare the pre-tic behavior previously described).

(3) Fifty per cent of boy tiqueurs presented a pseudo-Froehlich habitus, known as prototypes of passive submissiveness and suppressed hostility (David M. Levy).

(4 a) There was a high incidence of an accumulation of sicknesses which restricted motor freedom during the exercising period of locomotion and which restricted "performance motor"-independence (especially in the impulse neurotic tic syndrome), and/or

(4 b) The children showed a tendency toward accidents, they were "motility conscious" and a conflict about even indirect restriction of locomotor freedom was prominent in group 5 of the tiqueurs.

(5) The children occupied a position of abnormally increased importance in the family setting. (In about 90 per cent of our cases).

(6) There was a prolonged appersonation by and of the mother: a kind of emotional symbiosis between mother and son was marked by reactive overprotection, pampering, and infantilization, particularly in group 5 (cf. Spitz).

(7) The mothers of such patients showed an intolerance of "phallic aggression", coupled with markedly high standards of intellectual achievement.

(8) Both at the onset of the disease and during the course of it, an acute masturbation conflict was frequently a cardinal problem (11).

ad (1)

We believe that the overwhelming predominance of boys is due to the fact that in the male sex the biological function of the neuromuscular apparatus as the organ of erotic, aggressive attack, and as the weapon for self-protection is prominent. The narcissistic importance and functionality of an organ—according to Freud—renders it proportionately susceptible to becoming the site of the neurotic conflict solution (16).

ad (2)

We have described the pre-tic behavior disorder of our patients which was characterized by increased emotionality, especially aggression, and "motor urgency". These characteristics made repression and reaction-formation at the onset of latency difficult.

ad (3)

It is not easy to determine how far the pseudo-Froehlich habitus, which we found in 50 per cent of our boy tiqueurs before puberty,[26] was a primary factor of the psychosomatic tic disease or a result of it. The pseudo-Froehlich habitus of our tiqueurs was found to be spurious since the essential feature of the Froehlich habitus, true hypogenitalism (undersized organs), was not present. The obesity of the organ neurotic tiqueur may very well be the result of overeating, coupled with his characteristic hypomotility. The feminine distribution of the fat tissue, however, marks perhaps a primary endocrine inclination towards passivity.[27] (Compare also discussion of points 6 and 7).

The unconscious fantasies which we analyzed in two of our obese boy tiqueurs (Freddie and Elmer) led us to believe that their obesity represented or was the result of their wanting to have babies, to be pregnant. Elmer, for instance, maintained the theory of oral impregnation long after other children give it up. He ate ravenously, loved little children and was exultant when his white rat had a litter. His affection was boundless and he kissed and hugged the animal.[28]

ad (4a)

There was a high incidence of cumulation of childhood diseases at the period of learning to master the independent motility function which interfered with the function (particularly in the group of impulse-ridden tiqueur). It seems that the concurrence of motility restriction plus painful and uncomfortable bodily sensations (sickness) increased the amorphous aggressive drive of the candidates for character neurosis with tic syndrome, and had a particularly disorganizing effect on the child's personality.[29]

26. Previous authors, unfamiliar with child tiqueurs of this type, have stated that an asthenic habitus was characteristic of the tiqueur.

27. The feminine distribution of the subcutaneous fat tissue may also signify a psychosomatic correlate of the feminine identification tendencies of the tiqueur, described in this paper.

28. Elmer showed a violent reaction when he had to give up the rat as he was found to be allergic to the rat fur.

29. Cf. 18; also 29, pp. 439, 641.

ad (4b)

Other tiqueurs, especially those of the hypokinetic group, from early age on were prohibited from crying, shouting, running, hammering or playing with abandon, because of overconcern for some member of the family or a neighbor. "More pathogenic still was the indirect and subtle restriction" (32), through the mother's emotional attitude towards the son's motor independence. (E. g., constant admonition about all the risks connected with freedom of activity, watching over every move, etc.). As mentioned above, we found a history of repeated accidents in the family of everyone of these tiqueurs.[30]

ad (5)

We said that 90 per cent of our tiqueurs occupied an inordinately important or exceptional position within the family group. This position became theirs either because they were only children; or "the baby" sometimes of old parents; or they were the first living child (in 6 cases, after miscarriages, death of older siblings or habitual abortions); or they were "only sons" among several sisters.

ad (6) and (7)

The combined effects of their position and their mothers' neuroses resulted in an unusually strong interlocking of pathogenic and pathognomonic affective attitudes between these sons and their mothers—an emotional interdependence which made these children peculiarly susceptible to psychosomatic disease.[31] The mothers of these impulse-ridden tiqueurs were overprotective, vindictive and extremely intolerant of any manifestation of phallic aggression or exhibitionistic tendencies in their sons. The fathers usually were punitive, strict and perfectionistic. A severe masturbation threat was frequently found to have had a trigger effect in touching off the tic syndrome in this group.

In several papers we described the reactive and seductive overprotective attitude (appersonation) which is characteristic of the mothers of organ neurotic tiqueurs. Pampering, coupled with intolerance of the child's activity and aggression, frustrated any step towards their son's

---

30. Or else there was an acute conflict about free movement or some motility restricting ailment and, in one case, also epilepsy (30).

31. Cf. 38, 39.

independence. In the *hypokinetic* group of tic syndrome patients we found that separation from the mother—amounting to not more than a gradual psychobiological separation tendency on the part of the child —was felt as a threat and reciprocated by threats, on the one hand, and increased oversolicitude on the other.

The organization of the kinetic function of the ego, particularly that of locomotion, presents for the 2-3-year-old the first serious step toward his individual, autonomous and independent development, *away* from the mother. This part of progressive personality development, *away from the mother*, was impaired in the tic children by the endogenous and exogenous factors described. The children became disarmed, helpless and anxious, they were afraid not only to show aggression, but to move about freely lest they lose their mother's love, or hurt themselves. In these children suppressed aggression, and particularly curtailment of adequate motor outlets in the formative phase of independent ego development, led to a state of *being dammed up* as early as their third and fourth years. This *state of being dammed up* is comparable to the condition of adult candidates for organ neurosis, whom Fenichel described as having "the disturbed chemistry of the unsatisfied person" (10).

This inhibition of motor expression led to a partial impediment of the ego's mastery of motility (8). Children with tic disease showed a muscular hypertension, or dyskinetic diffuse innervations (general muscular restlessness, poor coordination, etc.) of their neuromuscular apparatus, which was the physiological concomitant, the equivalent countercathexis of their affective tension. These multifocal, muscular sensations finally found an outlet in the automatic motor symptoms, the multiple tics. The resulting *hypomotility,* the inhibition of the kinetic function par excellence, was the outcome of a secondary emotional armor-plating (Panzerung) of the ego via the narcissistically libidinized organ system. This system had regressively again become an organ of automatic (subcortical) affective discharge.

From the analysis of a number of cases with a tic syndrome (groups 4 and 5) we found that as the semi-voluntary (ego syntonic) impulsions were completely or partially replaced by their condensed involuntary derivatives, the tics, these children constantly had to bear the experience of being overpowered by ego-alien, unpredictable forces.[32] In an attempt to counteract these compelling, muscular sensations (felt as multilocular

32. The muscular tension was felt and described as a kind of erection, reminiscent of the feeling of a tumescent penis. The children felt self-conscious and guilty about them.

tenseness) a particularly strong narcissistic countercathexis of the entire musculature (and also of the entire body) was set up. The neuromuscular system was compelled to revert (regress) to its role as discharge organ, and thus became the organ of the *psychosomatic "motor neurosis"* (16).[33] The erotization of the body made these patients susceptible to hypochondria (cf. Ferenczi, et al).

ad (8)

The tics symbolized the child's own inner experience of being overwhelmed by the impulse (tumescence) originally brought about by working himself up to a peak of instinctual excitement (masturbation), and at the same time it was a defensive innervation against it. In concomitant behavior the tiqueur tries to reproject an internalized conflict into the outside world by accusing people or forces in the environment. The rhythmic, paroxysmic nature, and (at least in the beginning) the obvious drive toward a climax of the tic syndrome (and not only the tic symptom) showed it to be a masturbation equivalent.[34]

SUMMARY OF PSYCHOANALYTIC FINDINGS IN REGARD TO THE DIAGNOSIS AND PROGNOSIS OF "TIC"

Diagnosis

Diagnosis as to which of the described categories of tics a case belongs in, needs only a relatively short period of psychoanalytic observation. We must, however, expect overlapping in "tics" as in any other area of the psychopathology of childhood. We have seen some psychosomatic cases start with single tics—they sometimes, though rarely, end with one or two strictly localized residual tics (31, 33). The psychoneurotic tic often shows some spreading and sometimes concomitant general mus-

---

33. If the massive psychosomatic "armor-plating" was ineffectual, *psychotic disorganization of the ego* occurred after puberty.

34. H. B., a 19-year-old impulsive tiqueur describes her tic paroxysm as follows: "If I am not in it (the tic paroxysm), it is like working myself into it, like an automobile which gets momentum going down the hill. This is more a habit now. I can stop it but then I do it out of spite when I get that pent up feeling ... I must have a spiteful streak in me ... I cut off my nose to spite my face. Sometimes I am so wound up that I just keep going. Any irritating thought that passes through my mind causes those 'spasmodic outbursts'.... I pick those words up ... I get my mother and brother very nervous with those f... f... sh... sh...." In contrast, the "inhibited organ neurotic tiqueur" describes his syndrome in the following way: "I always feel it (the sensation of muscular tension) coming on and I try with all my might not to move, but then it moves anyway."

cular restlessness in the beginning. However, in the course of psycho-analysis and/or prolonged clinical observation the genetic, dynamic and prognostic differences become evident.

Treatment

We would add one more point of contrast between the organ neurotic tiqueur and the impulsive tiqueur in regard to their respective psychoanalytic treatment. The patient with the tic disease has, in our experience, been most rigid and resistive to giving up his defensive armor-plating. Children with the tic syndrome (group 5) eventually arrive at a stage when they dread any *spontaneous* innervation or move, and thus psychoanalytic treatment is very difficult with them. They not only lack spontaneity and initiative. They try to adopt the general attitude of defending themselves by overcompliance; a conformity which literally waits for and imitates [35] every move of persons in their environment (including the psychoanalyst), in ideational as well as in action fields. They have complied with their mother's wish for their remaining vegetative creatures, with no will and intention of their own and resist changing this defensive attitude. The impulsive tiqueur, on the other hand, like the delinquent, is artful in evading therapeutic interference by "acting out" and projection mechanisms.

Prognosis

We were surprised to find in a follow-up study that the prognosis of the tiqueur with consolidated organ neurotic motor syndrome was relatively favorable compared with that of the impulse-ridden tiqueur.[36] The organ neurotic tiqueur with the defensive armor-plating of his ego was better able to withstand the potentially disorganizing effect of the psychophysiological upheaval of puberty than either the impulse-ridden child tiqueur or the patient with the tic disease, whose defenses had been broken down through ineffective deep psychotherapy. This was especially true when there had been a one-sided release of aggression

35. That gives then the impression of imitativeness in these children. That is, however, actually a mechanical, a pathological imitation phenomenon, which can, if it is cathected with the repressed affect quantities, result in echophenomena, echolalia, echokinesia, and palilalia. This differs also from the psychoneurotic *and* the impulsive tiqueur, both of whom are characterized by their gestural imitativeness, their inclination and talent for play-acting, their dramatic creative imitation (29, p. 440).

36. It seems that the organ neurotic tiqueur's armor-plating has a similar bracing effect against psychotic disorganization of the ego, as have some forms of obsessive compulsion mechanisms against schizophrenic personality disintegration.

and a "liberation" of erotic drives through symbolic interpretation without concomitant strengthening of the ego's synthetic faculties (cf. 33, 34, 35).

BIBLIOGRAPHY

1. Abraham, K. "Contribution to a Discussion of the Tic", *Selected Papers,* Hogarth, 1921.

2. Alexander, F. "Fundamental Concepts on Psychosomatic Research", *Psychosom. Med.,* V, 1943.

3. Bergmann, T. "Observations of Children's Reactions to Motor Restraint", *Nerv. Child,* IV, 1944-45.

4. Blatz, W. E. and Ringland, M. C. *The Study of Tics in Pre-School Children,* Univ. Toronto Press, 1935.

5. Boenheim, C. "Ueber den Tic im Kindesalter", *Klin. Wchschrift.,* 9, 1930, 2005-11.

6. Deutsch, F. "On Postural Behavior", *Psa. Quar.,* XVI, 1947.

7. Elkisch, P. "A Case of Child Tiqueur", *Am. J. Psychotherapy,* I, 1947.

8. Fenichel, O. "Ueber organlibidinoese Begleiterscheinungen der Triebabwehr", *Internat. Zeit. f. Psa.,* XIV, 1928.

9. Fenichel, O. *The Psychoanalytic Theory of Neurosis,* Norton, 1945.

10. Fenichel, O. "The Nature and Classification of the So-Called Psychosomatic Phenomena", *Psa. Quar.,* XIV, 1945, 287-312.

11. Ferenczi, S. "Psychoanalytic Observations on Tics", *Further Contributions to the Theory and Technique of Psychoanalysis,* Hogarth, 1921.

12. Ferenczi, S. "Denken und Muskelinnervation", *Internat. Zeit. f Psa.,* VI, 1919.

13. Freud, A. and Burlingham, D. T. *War and Children,* Allen & Unwin, and Internat. Univ. Press, 1943.

14. Freud, S. *Three Contributions to the Theory of Sex,* Nerv. Ment. Dis. Mon., 1910.

15. Freud, S. "Formulations Regarding the Two Principles in Mental Functioning", *Coll. Papers,* IV.

16. Freud, S. "Psychogenic Visual Disturbance According to Psychoanalytical Conceptions", *ibid.,* II.

17. Gerard, M. W. "The Psychogenic Tic in Ego Development", *this Annual*, II, 1946.

18. Greenacre, P. "Infant Reactions to Restraint: Problems in the Fate of Infantile Aggression", *Am. J. Orthopsychiat.*, XIV, 1944.

19. Hartmann, H., Kris, E. and Loewenstein, R. "Comments on the Formation of Psychic Structure", *this Annual*, II, 1946.

20. Hartmann, H. "Ich-Psychologie und Anpassungsproblem", *Internat. Zeit. f. d. gesamte Neur. und Psychol.*, 78, 1922.

21. Hartmann, H. "On Rational and Irrational Action", *Psa. and the Social Sciences*, I, Internat. Univ. Press, 1947.

22. Homburger, A. "Ueber die Entwicklung der menschlichen Motorik", *Zeit. f. d. gesamte Neur. und Psychol.*, 78, 1922.

23. Jacobson, E. "A Case of Sterility", *Psa. Quart.*, XV, 1946.

24. Kris, E. "Laughter as an Expressive Process", *Internat. J. Psa.*, XXI, 1940.

25. Landauer, K. "Die kindliche Bewegungsunruhe. Das Schicksal der den Stammganglien unterstehenden triebhaften Bewegungen", *Internat. Zeit. f. Psa.*, XII, 1926.

26. Landauer, K. "Automatismen, Zwangsneurose und Paranoia", *ibid.*, XIII, 1927.

27. Levy, D. M. "On the Problem of Movement Restraint. Tics, Stereotyped Movements, Hyperactivity", *Am. J. Orthopsychiat.*, XIV, 1944.

28. Mahler, M. S. "Introductory Remarks" to the Symposium on "Tics in Children", *Nerv. Child*, IV, 1944-45.

29. Mahler, M. S. "Tics and Impulsions in Children: A Study of Motility", *Psa. Quar.*, XIII, 1944.

30. Mahler, M. S. and Gross, I. "Psychotherapeutic Study of a Typical Case with Tic Syndrome", *Nerv. Child*, IV, 1944-45.

31. Mahler, M. S. and Rangell, L. "A Psychosomatic Study of Maladie des Tics", *Psa. Quar.*, XVII, 1943.

32. Mahler, M. S., Luke, J. and Daltroff, W. "Tic Syndrome in Children", *Am. J. Orthopsychiat.*, XV, 1945.

33. Mahler, M. S. and Luke, J. "Outcome of the Tic Syndrome", *J. Nerv. Ment. Dis.*, 103, 1946.

34. Mahler, M. S., Ross, J. R. and De Fries, Z. "On Psychosis in Children", *Am. J. Orthopsychiat.*, in press.

35. Meige and Feindel, *Tics and Their Treatment*, Wm. Wood, 1907.

36. Pacella, B. L. "Physiologic and Differential Diagnostic Considerations of Tic Manifestations in Children", *Nerv. Child*, IV, 1944-45.

37. Ritvo, S. "Survey of the Recent Literature on Tics in Children", *ibid.*, IV, 1944-45.

38. Sperling, M. "Psychoanalysis of Ulcerative Colitis in Children", *Psa. Quar.*, XV, 1946.

39. Spitz, R. A. "Somatic Concomitants of Emotional Vicissitudes in Infancy", paper read at the Annual Meeting of the Assoc. for Psychosom. Research, Atlantic City, New Jersey, May, 1948.

40. Wilder, J. "Tic convulsif as a Psychosomatic Problem", *Nerv. Child*, V, 1946.

41. Wilder, J. and Silbermann, I. *Abhandl. a. d. ges. Neurologie*, Heft 43, Karger, Berlin, 1927.

THE PSYCHOANALYSIS OF A PSYCHOTIC CHILD [1]

By ELISABETH R. GELEERD, M.D. (New York)

A brief description of this child has been given under Case B in the paper, "A Contribution to the Problem of Psychoses in Childhood" (3). In the present paper an attempt will be made to give a more detailed description of this child and the course of his analysis of 2½ years' duration. The analysis was not carried to completion.

Allen was brought to the Southard School when he was 7½ years of age. The reason for referral was the boy's acutely disturbed behavior while at summer camp. The report from the camp described him as highly excitable and having outstanding anal and sexual habits. He was supposed to have grabbed the penises of other boys when they went swimming or were undressing, or he would chase the other children excitedly with feces on a stick. The camp director had felt that the only way to quiet him down was to remove him from the group. He had been sent to live with a young couple, and when alone with them he had resumed his earlier charming but very dependent behavior. They observed, however, his sex play with the dog.

Further investigation revealed that this disturbed behavior was not an isolated episode. In the year preceding the camp experience Allen had been admitted to the first grade of school. The teacher had remarked on his keen intelligence and his rich imagination but found him hard to manage in a group. He would never obey any of the rules. Instead he would get up out of his seat and walk through the classroom as soon as the teacher paid no attention to him. Often he would go to the lavatory to get cups of water, which he would throw at the children. He was also keenly interested in the excretory functions of the other children. The teacher had to keep him out of the bathroom when others were there. The only occasion when he really got along was when the whole class participated in fantasy games of his creation.

Allen's career in kindergarten had not been much better. The report was that he had been uncontrollable, never obeyed, and played little with the other children. He had been apt to shove them around and to throw spit-balls at them.

The home situation also revealed Allen's disturbed behavior. He was the second child of well-to-do, neurotic parents. His birth occurred during the depression, and this fact probably plays a part in the dynamics

---

1. Treatment was carried out in The Southard School, Topeka, Kansas.

of his mental disturbance. His brother, two years his senior, had definitely been a wanted child and had received a great deal of attention. Unfortunately, due to some business difficulties, the father was depressed at this time and became much more dependent upon the mother. One gained the impression that there was really no room for Allen in the emotional pattern of the family. The mother described him as a rather quiet baby, and an exceptionally bad eater. Breast-feeding was never attempted, and the mother had insisted that the child empty his bottle at every feeding. Often it took her more than one hour to achieve this.

Allen's toilet training was started at 2 months. He partially stopped soiling at 1 year and wetting at 3 years, although complete control in either was not achieved until late in his analysis. The toilet training was carried out in a manner similar to his feeding. He was forced to sit on the toilet as soon as he could sit up and had to sit there until he performed. During those sieges on the toilet he developed the habit of reaching into the water of the toilet bowl and moving the water back and forth with his hands. This play developed into a tic-like habit. When he grew up it was noticeable whenever he became excited. People remarked about the way Allen waved his hands. The mother had been accustomed to taking the older boy out every morning while Allen was left on the toilet. She later described with regret how the little one had sat there with a terribly forlorn expression on his face.

Between 2½ and 3 years of age he developed a great interest in feces. He would say to his brother, "Eat grunt." He spent most of his time in the dog kennel, playing with the dog's feces and his own. He also became more and more destructive. To break him of these "bad habits" the mother engaged a Prussian nurse, Rhea, who was recommended because in addition to her love of children she was a great disciplinarian. This woman took over the entire care of the child. As she was highly possessive, she kept him away from other children because "they were too dirty." She held lengthy sessions with the boy, telling him that he was the only one in the whole world whom she loved, and he had to reciprocate. On the other hand, she treated his "naughtiness" with extreme severity. She would put Tabasco Sauce on his fingers because he sucked his thumb and would tie him to the radiator when he wet his pants. She thus succeeded in suppressing much of his apparent behavior. Rhea also used efficient techniques for making Allen go to sleep at night. She told him that if he would not be quiet and close his eyes right away Jack Frost would get him. To make this more dramatic, she sometimes went out on the balcony to imitate the moaning voice of Jack Frost, who was coming to get little Allen. Later, in his analysis, Allen told how he would hide under the blankets for fear Jack Frost would come after him.

Another technique instigated by Rhea and carried out by the family was the following: Whenever Allen was mischievous Rhea would say, "Wait until your father comes home and spanks you." Actually, every night when the father returned he was met by Rhea and the mother, with an account of all the misdemeanors that had been committed during the day, and the father took the child over his knee and spanked him severely. Allen remembered in his analysis how he had dreaded his father's home-coming because of these spankings. However, the family was greatly pleased with the progress he made under Rhea's care and discipline, and they found it hard to believe the reports from the camp.

As a result of the camp experience Allen was taken to a well-known child psychiatrist, who promptly referred him to the Southard School.

Unfortunately the writer never had a chance to receive a more detailed account of Allen's childhood. One of the great drawbacks in the analysis of a child away from home is the almost complete sterility as to detailed data of the child's past life. The parents only visited the child a few times a year, first because of the great distance; second, because it was felt by the school authorities that frequent visits of the family were only upsetting to this particular child.[2] At first the usual recommendation of frequent visits had been made. Soon, however, it was noticed that each visit brought great disturbances in Allen's behavior and he seemed to become more upset, more uncontrollable, and more infantile. Therefore for the first two years of analysis the visits were kept at a minimum.

On the occasion when the parents visited, the writer always received the same stereotyped story of the events in the child's life. The author at times wondered about the factual accuracy of their account. It is generally experienced in child analysis that with the progress of the analysis the parents, especially the mother, will remember many fine points pertaining to the child's life. In Allen's case one had to do entirely without these.

When Allen was first admitted to the Southard School the consensus of opinion was that he was one of the most charming and intelligent little boys we had ever met. He went out of his way to win every new person, especially the women. He would come up to them, immediately establish a very close physical contact, and start paying the most lavish compliments about their appearance, such as, "What a beautiful texture," pointing to some one's dress; "What a lovely necklace you are wearing," etc., unconsciously almost knowing what would please the owner of these beauties most. The women were enchanted by his intelligent remarks and his skilful flattery. However, after a short while it became apparent that the relationships he established were only tenable under a definite set of circumstances—namely, when Allen was alone with one person who gave him her undivided attention (3). Whenever this attention was withdrawn, either to attend to some necessary business or when another person, especially another child, was around, Allen would either wander off or—particularly when another child caused the interference—go into a severe temper tantrum. He would begin by just being furious but soon his language would become more and more abusive, his facial expression would change completely, his eyes would roll in their sockets, he would start kicking, hitting, and spitting, and attack the adult as well as the child who he thought had hurt him, and this outburst would become increasingly violent. When attempts were

2. This procedure differs from the methods usually applied. Due to the nature of Allen's disturbance, an exception had to be made. See below.

made to stop these tantrums in the usual way, by telling him that he was wrong, that he should be quiet, that he should not use such language, that he should not destroy property, that he would be removed from the room if this behavior continued, etc., the tantrum only got worse. However, it was found that when another person with whom he had a good relationship, preferably not the one who was connected with the tantrum, came on the scene and would put her arms around him and treat him like a young child, holding him on her lap, talking soothingly to him in a loving way, he would soon quiet down and start to cry, and, sobbing, would tell her how everybody was against him, enumerating incidents where he had felt people had slighted him, mistreated him, or taken his possessions away. Included in those accusations were many incidents of the past, of a similar nature, which had in fact been true. But the way he described these gave the impression that they were the most severe injuries that could have been inflicted (3).

The temper tantrums were not only apparent when he had to share the attention of a beloved adult with another individual, but also when he had to learn in school. He refused to do any work, and an ordinary amount of persuasion was again met with a severe temper outburst. On the other hand, during his school hours he would indulge in mischief; i. e., he and another little boy would climb out of the window during class, onto the roof, regardless of the danger of the situation. On one occasion he went to the bathroom, urinated into a paper cup, and threw the urine over the teacher. At other times he would lock himself in the bathroom and react with a severe tantrum when the door was forced open.

The teachers, whose methods were progressive, used to encourage the children to develop their fantasies. They were surprised to find that when Allen was telling stories or when he fantasied to pictures he drew, he himself would become part of his production and talk for the various persons or animals in the fantasies. Invariably the story would end in a fight between a stronger and a weaker animal and soon Allen took over the part of the weaker animal, who would behave the way the patient did in his tantrums. Gradually the story seemed to take on more and more reality for him, and the patient attacked the environment physically.

Allen was a bad eater. With the let-up of the ordinary pressure to eat, he actually did not take more than a glass of milk and some cookies daily. Also, he generally had to be removed from the table because of unacceptable behavior.

He was unable to dress or undress himself, and when left alone he was frequently found sitting on his bed just daydreaming.

He was extremely dirty and sloppy, his shirt-tail was usually out, his shoes untied; often he would wear different socks or different shoes on each foot; the fly of his pants was generally open, and he often smelled of feces and urine. He would pick his nose constantly and smear the secretion all over himself, other people or furniture. As a result he had many nasal infections, which in turn made him more anxious and therefore more uncontrolled. All medical intervention was met with severe temper outbursts. Sometimes he would defecate on the bathroom floor or in the bath tub and smear feces all over. Frequently he would soil his pants. He readily participated in any sex and anal play that was going on.

Out-of-doors he could spot any car a block away and identify the make, year, and model. Most of the time he himself played that he was a car and made all the accompanying noises. He would never forget to shift gears when he went up a hill or a staircase.

In the manual workshops Allen would grab the most dangerous tools, handle them very unskillfully, thus causing great damage to the objects and being a severe menace to himself as well as to others present.

Every possible opportunity to be mischievous or indulge in dangerous, destructive or dirty behavior was taken by the boy, and it seemed that he was more and more overcome by it. It was striking to observe how his facial expression then changed, it became impossible to stop him, and the final result was a temper tantrum.

Over a period of three to four weeks it was observed that his temper outbursts and mischievous behavior invariably occurred when Allen was a member of a group. It was therefore made a definite procedure to set up a regime which provided for his always being alone with an adult whom he liked and trusted; and the number of adults to be with him was made as small as possible. He was taught by one or two maternal women teachers. During hours when there was no class, he was removed from the group and was in the company of an adult. He also took his meals apart from the other children.

Description of the Analysis

Already in the first session of his analytic treatment Allen showed the same disturbed behavior. He started out with lavish compliments about the analyst's appearance. This lasted until he found a bottle of glue on her desk.. He then could not stop until he had emptied all of the contents over a chair. There was no way of dissuading him. He laughed in a curious fashion, which might be called sexually excited, at the same time looking out of the corner of his eye at the analyst, seemingly wanting to be stopped, in order to defy her.

In one of the early sessions he started to draw pictures of a big shark pursuing a smaller one. The smaller shark was supposed to shout, "Stop it! Stop it!" Allen shouted this. He walked back and forth with the pencil in his hands, skillfully drawing the bottom of the sea. "Do you see the shark? He has big teeth." At this time the walking back and forth became more precipitous, he waved his hands more and more. He then shouted at the big shark, "Go away! You stop it! Get out!" He started spitting at the analyst and in a very short while one of his severe temper outbursts had developed. For him the analyst had become the big shark who pursued him, the baby shark. He threw articles around, especially possessions of the analyst's, such as her pocket book, scattering the contents all over the floor. She was able to quiet him down by putting her arm around him, telling him that she was not a shark and had no intention of hurting him, and that she loved him very much. He responded gradually to this.

His behavior was always highly provocative. In general he would break all restrictions such as have to be made in an office. He was asked not to use the telephone. Thus he would always telephone to somebody, and he loved to listen in on conversations which were carried on a double line, and shout dirty remarks into the phone. When an attempt was made to stop him, more temper outbursts would follow. Before the analyst was completely prepared for his behavior, he had torn up papers, opened all the closets, dirtied and destroyed the things that were in them, and had smeared rouge and lipstick over her, himself, and the furniture. He often went into the bathroom, played with water, and threw it at whomever came near.

He would walk into other offices where either treatments or classes were going on. As a whole he seemed to be overcome by his impulses but always with a strong provocative element. He would often beg the analyst to hit him, to spank him on his buttocks, and would become very furious at her when she refused. On one such occasion when she explained to him that she would never hit him and did not believe in hitting children and wondered why he wanted to be hit and hurt by her, he answered, "You have to hit me when I tell you because I have to have control over you." This statement of the patient's suddenly made much of his behavior clear. All the years that Rhea had been in the home the outstanding feature of Allen's relationship to his environment was that the boy was naughty and Rhea punished him, and his father spanked him at night. In the Southard School he tried to repeat this behavior in a desire to be punished not only because he acted out certain unconscious fantasies but also to re-establish the lost world of home.[3] To provoke punishment also meant to control the punishment, and thus he could alleviate its painful effect. Another meaning of the desire for control was that to behave well, to submit to a request, to him implied that some one else had control over him, which was too frightening. This also explained his problem in being taught: to learn something new meant that the teacher knew more than he did, and thus by virtue of her superior knowledge could control him. He only participated in a game with other children when he had made up the game and was the accepted leader, because he then felt in control. Not to be in control was connected with fantasies which were too frightening.

In many ways Allen behaved like a young infant. He needed the undivided love and attention of one adult and was unable to share this person with someone else. He could not tolerate a situation where he did not feel in complete control. He had to be omnipotent. The need to control the beloved object is necessary in the case of utmost dependence. The dependent individual feels that his security is threatened when the love object is not completely and at all times at his disposal. Freud (2) explains this fantasy of omnipotence as a consequence of the state of primary narcissism where all libido is invested in the ego,[4] as far as it is developed. Much of Allen's behavior could be explained if one assumed that partially he had not developed beyond this state of

3. Suggestion of Dr. Marianne Kris.
4. Better said, "self". See Hartmann, Kris, Loewenstein, *this Annual*.

early infancy. But Allen had suffered many rejections by his mother from early babyhood, since she had always spent more time with his brother. He needed to control his love object not only because of the fantasy of omnipotence but also because he could no longer stand having a rival take his place.

As has been mentioned, it had been decided to work out a regime whereby Allen spent his whole day away from the group. The adult in whose company he was played as much as possible the role of an indulgent and permissive mother figure. This was necessary for practical reasons, such as to protect the boy and others as much as possible from his outbursts of rage; but also the analyst hoped that by reinstating a situation which in some ways resembled the early mother-infant relationship, he might be able gradually to grow out of this stage. In addition she expected that the interpretation of unconscious mechanisms and fantasies would bring about further growth and maturation.

At the same time it became apparent to the analyst that this analysis could not be conducted in the usual way. The production of fantasies and their further elaboration is usually felt to be a useful tool for the understanding of the unconscious mind of the patient. All of Allen's fantasies ended in the destruction of one person or animal. These fantasies of killing, destroying, or devouring generally were accompanied by a more or less severe outburst of temper on the part of the child. The analyst gained the impression that the temper outbursts occurred when the fantasy to him became reality. He identified with the victim and in the tantrum defended himself against the attacker. She therefore decided on a variation of the usual technique. Whenever a fantasy became frightening the analyst would say something like: "It isn't so. The Mama shark and the baby shark are going out together and are having a lovely time." Train and car wrecks did not occur any more. Burglars did not get into the houses, guns did not shoot at people, etc. The result of this was striking. In the first hour that this procedure was attempted the patient climbed onto the analyst's lap, nestled in her arms and said, "I want my Mommie." It is possible that he had understood and had interpreted correctly her attitude of a kind and reassuring mother figure. He expressed desires to see his mother and his brother, and started to remember some pleasant events of his home life. But very soon frightening and more disappointing memories, such as those which indicated defeat in the competition with his brother, came to his mind.

Also, as soon as the analyst had discovered that having many articles around the room was an invitation to provoke him, she took measures before seeing Allen. She emptied her office of all personal items, locked all the closets and removed the keys. This protected her property as well as served a necessary therapeutic purpose because it prevented Allen from getting over-excited through all the mischief he could get into and the subsequent temper tantrums.

From now on a period developed in the analysis where the patient would lie in the analyst's lap, would suck on her dress or her arms, and she would tell him stories. The trend of the stories which she made up was what she thought might be a wish fulfillment of Allen's. Very soon afterwards they became a combined fantasy of both the analyst and the patient's. The central figures here were two playful puppy dogs, Puppy and Peppy, who were owned by a lady called the mistress. They were bubbling over with gayety, always getting into mischief. Their naughtiness was generally directed at the maid, and their playful acts consisted mainly in making the maid drop food, or in upsetting her pails of water. Allen had talked about his brother as a rival as well as some one with whom he got into mischief, such as playing April Fool jokes on his mother and nurse. The analyst felt that she could introduce these themes as part of the Puppy and Peppy story; also because from the start he had perpetuated this kind of behavior in his relationships with little boys in the school. The envy had been expressed by his temper outbursts when he felt that another child was preferred. His ready participation together with another little boy in naughty and destructive games and dirty acts seemed to reflect the other side of the relationship to his brother. Thereupon Puppy and Peppy had been created.

During the first 16 to 18 months of the analysis the sessions seemed almost completely chaotic. A few examples will illustrate this:

One session began with Allen's announcement that there was a war between Russia, China, America and the South. Two army trucks were introduced, each having three cannons. A little shooting followed but suddenly he interrupted to tell the analyst, "I'll give you eight cents because you once gave me ten cents." He then continued, "You are Ellis Robbins, but I will eat you. I will eat everything but leave you your ears, your penis and your behind." At this point he attempted to look under her skirt and talked about the enormous penis that his Daddy had. So had Mr. Geleerd. After a little struggle in which a severe temper outburst had been prevented, he said, "Mr. Geleerd is sitting in an air ship and he has a radiant light." He then started spitting at the analyst and said, "We are two dogs who are fighting. Let's eat each other." He then grabbed the telephone, spat into it, said "shit" into it, and started beating the analyst's face. When asked why he did this, he said, "Because you beat me. Don't you dare touch me." At this point the analyst tried to reassure him in the usual fashion, and after he had quieted down she explained to him that she knew very well that he had actually started the beating, that now he was afraid of her retaliation and therefore accused her of beating him. Thus she made him aware of his projection after she had quieted him down.

In another session Allen came in and said that his friend, Jackie, had urinated in a paper bag. As usual he was very keen on observing all the misdemeanors of other children and showed very clearly how he knew intellectually what was right and what was wrong. Then he started a conversation about a bowel movement which could not be flushed. He told how another boy had done a bowel movement on the bathroom floor. (It had been reported to the analyst that the child who had actually done this must have been Allen.) He then invited the analyst to come to the bathroom to show her and to see whether there was more bowel movement there. In the meantime he started pulling on the analyst's dress, tried to put it in his mouth, and then started tearing it. When she attempted to prevent this, he said, "I'll smear you all with bowel movement. You stink and I'll make you pay by doing a million bowel movements on the floor." Then he announced that he was never coming back, called her "stinky", sat down squatting, grunted, and said, "I am doing you," meaning that the analyst was a piece of bowel movement which was coming out of his body. Subsequently, in his play this piece of bowel movement had to be flushed.

In the next hour he saw a little old Ford car outside of the window. He became terribly excited and said, "It is Grandpa's car. It is a stinky, rotten little BM, Grandpa Grunt." He started drawing a little car with two exhaust pipes. While drawing he turned to the analyst and said, "Why do women have no Adam's apple? I'm a plane and I come to crash into you." He turned into a python which came to eat Mr. Geleerd, then the python came to kill the analyst, but she shot the python and took Mr. Geleerd out of its stomach. Allen had been leaning very close to the analyst. It seemed that his thoughts about the shooting and killing made it so real to him that only a close physical contact could reassure him sufficiently. He took the analyst's crayons when he left and shouted at her, "Don't you dare!"

In another session he was a bride dressed up in a long dress. Suddenly in the fantasy a man disappeared from the jail, apparently supposed to come to wreck the wedding party, but before this happened the man drove out of the jail very fast and crashed into a telephone pole. The police came after the man but instead chased a fox. The fox was put into a tub with grease. Allen then shouted at the analyst, "You are Grandpa's wife." He picked up a doll and said, "The doll does wee-wee over your face." After this the fantasies shifted completely. There was a girl on a ship which hit a mine. The girl was eaten by a swordfish, but suddenly she found herself on an island. There was a big flood. Everybody was drowned. Allen suddenly shouted at the analyst, "Pick up that pencil," and tried to push her into a closet and lock her in.

In one of the next sessions Allen played out a fantasy in which he and the analyst were in a boat. There were high waves, they were almost drowned, when a ship with robbers approached. The analyst suggested that they hide from the robbers and perhaps they could make friends with them. Allen took up the suggestion and continued the fantasy so that they could finish their boat ride. Then, however, he introduced the analyst's husband, who chased her, and she chased him. Allen suddenly noticed the fan and said, "Oh, the fan falls on you and cuts you into pieces. It falls on your fanny and it is being ground." When the analyst told him that the fan was fixed firmly, Allen came over and sat down in her lap.

On another occasion while he was sitting in the analyst's lap chatting about airplanes and cars, a ray of sunlight came into the room and was then covered by a passing cloud. At this moment he stopped talking, said that he could not go on at this point because he had to be a statue, otherwise the witches would come to take him and eat him. He watched the moving shadow and said, "Look, the cars are going backward and forward." Then he quickly made an alligator out of clay: "No, it's a rhinoceros; it comes to eat you. No, it's asleep. He loses his teeth and then he is dead. Do you hear Grandpa's car outside? Grandpa is asleep. He is snoring." Allen made a snoring noise.

Although the patient did not give the impression that he was hallucinating, it seemed as if frequently a fantasy for him became a reality. This always occurred when fantasies became too dangerous, whether represented by people or by a drawing; even on a drawing, to him they became the actual attackers. For instance, he would tell a story and draw a picture of how a snake would swallow a frog, therefore have green spit; or the frog jumped down the throat of the snake, who bit off a leg of the frog's. "You see, the blood. Rhea is afraid of mice. They jump in her fanny hole. Look. There are rats and mice." At the end of the hour he refused to go, grabbed all the candy the analyst kept in the office. He spat all over her, came back, sat in her lap, laughed loudly, and said, "You broke my neck."

Although many fantasies were quite clear in their symbolic meaning, the analyst refrained from interpretation of this meaning. At this period it was felt that the child first of all needed help against the seemingly overwhelming onslaught of fantasies. This was given by constant reassurance and an extremely loving and tolerant attitude, and where possible a correction of his faulty interpretation of reality.

After the change in handling Allen's treatment sessions the content consisted of four elements: 1) The patient continued to bring his fantasies, but they could be transformed into less frightening ones. 2) He became more loving toward the analyst, but also smeared her and dirtied her much more frequently, which she allowed him to the extent that she could tolerate it. 3) The story about Puppy and Peppy was continued. The dog which seemed identified with the patient, was definitely in a much more favorable and beloved position than the other. 4) Many incidents that happened in his life were discussed and could be understood in the analytic session in terms of having to have control. Allen had to have control not only to be the boss but also to save himself from being hurt. This was also clear in his temper outbursts. These were explained to him as efforts to defend himself against a fantasied attacker when he felt that he had lost control of the situation.

Allen's ambivalence toward and fear of the analyst were striking. One day he had been outside and his socks were very wet. The analyst suggested taking them off and drying them. Because he could not undress himself and seemed so helpless, she wanted to take his shoes and socks off for him. He immediately started to hit her, but when she reassured him that she had no intention of hurting him or doing anything mean to him, he put his arms around her and licked her with his tongue. This ambivalence was always marked. He would alternate his behavior of loving and hugging with hitting, kicking or punching. He would try to put his teeth into her dress and tear it or find one of her possessions and attempt either to destroy it or to throw it out of the window, etc.

Allen's birthday was approaching. The patient mentioned a date for his birthday which was incorrect. For a long time the analyst could not find out why he changed it to this particular date. However, accidentally she found that the date he gave was actually his brother's birthday. The analyst had promised to take him out on his birthday and Allen suggested that they take a room in the biggest hotel in town. Then he thought that Mr. Geleerd might come there, too, but Allen would kill him right away. There should be a birthday cake and all the children would be jealous about the cake. "I want you to eat all the children you have in analysis and I can have all their hours." His sibling rivalry and his positive oedipal wishes were emerging in the transference.

After about nine months of treatment Allen played fantasy games, the details of which reminded the analyst of his temper tantrums. For instance, he would order the analyst in his usual fashion, "Put your foot on my behind or I'll kill you." After many explanations that the analyst did not intend to do so, he would proceed to lie down on the floor, attempt to put her foot on his buttocks, and then shout, "Stop kicking me." After a while a fantasy game was built around this. Allen was Dickter Higgins (this was a slight modification of Dr. Mary O'Neil Hawkins). Dickter Higgins was speeding along the highway and the police came after him. However, when the police dragged Dickter Higgins into jail, the jail caved in on top of the police, who were killed. Allen danced excitedly at the death of the police, and it seemed to the analyst that this fantasy was related to the temper tantrums; that is, the attacker who was coming to punish was definitely conquered. The significance of this fantasy became clearer after the patient had volunteered that his father was Police Commissioner in his home town and thus was identified with the police in the fantasy. The fantasied attacker and the defense against the attacker seemed definitely related to his oedipal fantasy.

These oedipal fantasies became more marked. He made plans for going on a train trip with the analyst. He and she would share a room on a train. He hugged her a great deal and moved his mouth all over her body, as though he were eating her and gobbling her all up. Then he said, "I love you and I want to kill you."

There were many fantasies which in a more or less veiled way dealt with the analyst's relationships to men. For instance, she was riding along the highway in her car and a man would ask her for a ride. She would refuse the man angrily but the man would then steal her cigarette lighter. At this moment Allen would pretend that he was smoking a cigarette, leaving no doubt as to who the man was. The man would ultimately steal the dashboard and the throttle of her car. In the end the man was shot.

In another fantasy the analyst was put in jail and had to pay a large fine. She would have handcuffs on and her neck would be tied. A bank would give her the money to pay the fine. The jailor would be a disguised thief. But her husband (played by the patient) would come after the thief and save the analyst. At this time Allen reported a dream in which his mother was in jail and the patient had bailed her out. This dream showed how closely his feelings for his mother and for the analyst were related.

In his daily life as well as in the analysis, he showed clearly that one of the defense mechanisms he used was denial. Apparently related to his denial was a nightmare in which he could not do anything: he could not make a drawing; he could not fix a toy motor car, etc. The associations showed that he compared his productions with the work of others. Also, it had been known all along to the analyst that he hardly ever participated in anything or accomplished anything. Whenever he started a drawing or a poem or school work he became very unhappy and irritated. The pencil was not right, the paper was dirty. He would immediately destroy whatever he had done and subsequently become more and more tearful and enraged. When the analyst discussed this with him, and explained that his lack of performance and participation were due to his desire to do better than any one else, he became furious and ended in his usual fashion, saying, "This is not true. Cut it out. You are a bastard," and ran out. However, he was persuaded to come back and said, "Tell me a story." The analyst made up a story which on the patient's command had to deal with Dickter Higgins. Dickter Higgins had a nightmare and the director of a hotel persuaded him to go to a doctor who knew about problems. The patient, who had taken over the role of Dickter Higgins, walked out sneering that he had no problems and everything was wonderful with him. At this moment he stumbled on the floor, indicating by the parapraxis that he unconsciously knew better.

In connection with the nightmare, his envy and jealousy were discussed. In addition to the fact that they stemmed from his sibling rivalry, they were determined by his relationship to men. His fear of not being able to compete with them and his desire to outshine them, combined with the knowledge that he was only a little boy, paralyzed his productiveness completely. He could not compete with the older and stronger men for realistic reasons as well as out of fear. In one of his rare conversations about his home life, Allen sadly reported how his brother was so smart in school and had saved up so much money.

Allen had always shown his possessiveness of the analyst. He was inquisitive about what the other children discussed with her, and whenever he supposed that an article in the office belonged to them, or was made by them he would proceed to destroy it. He himself, in the common fantasy about the mistress with the two puppies, brought out that Puppy and Peppy disliked the mistress's husband "because they wanted her for themselves".

The patient would now say much more frequently, "Do this," or "Do that or I'm going to kill you." The order would either be that the analyst should say, "I kiss your ass," or "I'll spank your ass," or some nonsense word. When asked why he wanted this, he answered as usual, "Because I have to have control over you." In the middle of a peaceful game he would say, "I'm going to kill you." At the time of these discussions and fantasies he became more difficult to manage than he had been since the analyst changed her technique. He became dirtier, picked his nose more, was more obstinate, and teased the analyst more by taking away her possessions. He developed a great interest in people's ears. He played with their ears, kissed them or pulled them, and often said, "Kiss my ear or I'll kill you." He played with his penis, as he put it, "to make it long and stiff". At the time when he brought this information he definitely showed more patience in making certain drawings or objects of art and would always comment that the others would be envious of this production. It was possible to discuss with him his competitiveness about his abilities as well as about the length and size of his penis. The analyst also reminded him of his fears and worries lest his penis be smaller than his father's, his brother's, Mr. Geleerd's, and many other boys'.

At this period of analysis, he hugged the analyst much more, held her tight, pretended to eat her, saying, "I love you and I want to kill you." He now complained that one of his companions, a young man, always wanted his own way and wanted the patient to do everything he said, and the patient definitely refused to do so. He became more unmanageable in the treatment than he had been in a long time, left earlier, came later, because, he said "Nobody can boss me around." He swore at the analyst that she "stank," was a "stinky pants", "a skunk". Again he threatened to kill her, eat her; at the same time he kissed her knee and said, "You are only hired here also, you are not the boss. Dr. B. can fire you." He also stated that he was going to kill the analyst because then he could take her money away. In the same session he played that he was an ogre who came after the analyst. However, she closed the door in his face. He opened the door with a pick axe, she grabbed the pick axe and killed him with it. In this hour the patient acted this fantasy game and dramatized it in such a fashion that it was again highly suggestive of his temper tantrums. When this was explained to him, he kissed the analyst's ear.

One day when he touched the analyst's ear again he explained, "This is your penis." He proceeded to push two little motor cars against each other so that "all soldiers are dead". In the next fantasy game he was a little boy who was put in prison by a policeman. However, the mother came to help him and put the policeman in handcuffs. The analyst here interpreted that the policeman represented Allen's father and that the men he was afraid of were his mother's husband and the analyst's husband. His answer was that this was a big lie. However, reminded of the instances when he was afraid of being attacked and pursued by men in his fantasies, he said, "I want to beat you. Mr. Geleerd beats you, too." He demanded water and called it urine, became more and more excited and attempted to reach under the analyst's skirt. When it was interpreted to him that he here wanted to act as if he were her husband, he said, "I'm Joe Brown and I come to kill you. My Daddy will kill you when he comes."

His threat to kill and his need to have control could be explained to him as stemming from his conception of sexual intercourse, in which, according to him, one person is killed by the other. The patient was identified with the attacker. He also had brought out that the woman of his desire belonged to another man, his father or Mr. Geleerd, and he had worried lest his penis was smaller than theirs and he therefore could not compete with them. This husband would take revenge on him and kill him and probably castrate him. (The castration, however, was only indicated indirectly in the fantasies.) Thus his provocative behavior had to bring about the displeasure and therefore in the last instance a corporal punishment to him from a father figure, leading to castration and death. This situation was dramatized in the temper tantrum where he defended himself against this "attacker". On another level the temper tantrum demonstrated his conception of the sexual act as an aggressive performance, the attacker and the victim being the sexual partners. The need for control could be understood to be essential to ward off the punishment of the competitor as well as the danger from the sexual assault.

The boy was highly intolerant of any physical illness. Illness to him seemed to bring nearer the realization of his most intense fears. These fears could now be partially related to the positive oedipal fantasies. Illness always was accompanied by an increase in frightening fantasies and a decrease of organized behavior; and thus an increase in tantrums. Therefore it was difficult for the attending physician to come near him, and simple medical procedures could only be carried out when several strong adults restrained Allen physically. His behavior then was similar to that of a person who was being physically attacked and defending himself. This behavior when he was ill was also interpreted to him as a fear and proof of being attacked.

After these interpretations were made the analytic sessions seemed less chaotic for a while, but soon again they became more disorganized. There was a mixture of two predominantly aggressive and anal fantasies, and castration here was definitely verbalized. He told a confused story of how Puppy and Peppy threw food at the mistress and spilled so much water in the bathroom that it trickled through the bathroom floor on to the dining room table. At this point Allen hit the analyst hard on her ear, threw all the toy soldiers on the floor and at the analyst. He shouted that she was a bastard, he hit her and spat at her. He asked her to kill him, said he would kill her, told a confused story of how a king put a sword in the patient's behind so that it came out at the mouth. He talked about sewers, smells, bowel movements. He threatened to cut off the analyst's breasts, behind, and penis, he ordered her to sit perfectly still or he would murder her, called her a "fucking female" and told her that horse fuck is the same as horse shit. He ordered her to say "Fuck". When she refused, he said that he had power and therefore she should do it. When she still refused, he spat at her because she said such bad words.

In the subsequent hours he wanted to cut off the analyst's ear and tried to bite her because she "snarled" at him. He kicked and spat at her now much more in an apparently defensive action. There was much talk about differences between males and females. As he put it, "Females have a different penis from males."

It could be explained that apparently he thought women want to castrate men and men have to prevent this by castrating women. This interpretation also brought in an additional explanation of his defensive actions in the temper tantrums. He answered this by saying that he was very much afraid at night because ghosts would come and get him. However, this could be prevented by acting as if one were a statue. He volunteered that he therefore often sat completely still in the daytime, in order to mislead the ghosts. The analyst wondered here whether one of the reasons why the patient did not dress himself in the morning was to mislead the ghosts, as well as to be a baby. The ghosts probably stood for the castrating women.

The following sessions gave a partial lead to his soiling. The patient fantasied that he was a salesman who sells picture frames, and had a Model T Ford which held only two gallons. The analyst had a Packard which held one hundred and twenty gallons. They went out in the car. The patient said, "A ghost comes to kill your mother and the ghost telephones for the cops." The patient was the ghost and the analyst had to catch the ghost with a rope. They suddenly found the analyst's mother bleeding, and an ambulance arrived. The ghost still came after them in the car. They tried to get rid of the ghost but he wore a safety belt and won out. The patient then called up the home base to get money, planes, tanks and men because the Germans were dropping bombs. The analyst had to destroy the Germans and lasso them. The patient made many noises in this game, just as when he pretended to be a car, and at the same time he made a slight bowel movement in his pants. At this point it could be interpreted to him that the noises of the car, imitated constantly, were connected with his toilet activities. After repeated interpretation of the connection between his interest in cars and the toilet, there was a definite decrease in the soiling. (Later on in the analysis it became evident that the soiling also seemed to be related to his homosexuality.)

In a more confidential mood Allen said there was nobody in the world who loved him but the analyst and then added, "If Rhea knew you, she would hate you because you love me." He was able at this point to discuss Rhea's possessiveness toward him and the conflict this had created in him in regard to his feelings for his mother. He volunteered that his Daddy had an enormous penis and admitted that he tried to watch the penises of many of the men around him, but immediately this conversation about his real feelings and observations changed. Probably he suppressed some thought about the analyst's husband's penis when he said, "Oh, there goes Mr. Geleerd in a radiant airship."

The next hour was a highly dramatic one, and apparently a turning point in Allen's analysis. In a game the table had to be set in a very orderly fashion. There had to be water on the table, but the patient insisted it was wee-wee. He talked about the cow that squirted milk and wee-wee and when asked more about it Allen revealed that to him the udder was a penis, and he was quite confused about the "milk bags" and the bladder. He then said, "You have to order five hundred penises, they have to be rubbed in snow because this is going to be medicine for the Germans because they all have to be killed." He turned to the analyst and said, "Do you like to eat real old-fashioned crab?" There was no doubt but that he meant the vulgar expression for feces. When the analyst reminded him that Rhea was a German, he became very much excited and pretended that he and the analyst had to eat all the food on the table, which was, namely, penises, urine, and bowel movement. Allen tried to take something away from the analyst and acted as if he were dead. The interpretation was given him that the relationship between Rhea and himself consisted of a mutual eating of many dirty things and that the

penis was also bowel movement. This to him was another conception
of sexual intercourse. From eating this dirty substance death results.
The patient left the session in a more composed fashion than he had
ever before. It seemed that this fantasy had a double meaning. On one
level he brought to consciousness a sexual fantasy of oral-anal content
which leads to death. On another level he killed Rhea who had stimulated his sexual fantasies so intensely. It was reported to the analyst that
from this moment on his eating difficulty gradually subsided and he
became a healthy eater, who made up for the deficit in his weight.
However, not the entire eating disturbance was removed. Many years
later he suffered from a tendency to overeat.

The analyst had the impression that there was some diminution of
temper tantrums in and outside of the analysis, but it seemed hard to
determine whether the environment had become more deft at anticipating the circumstances which led to the outbursts of rage or that
this was a result of the analytic work. Allen still looked terribly messy,
smelled bad, and refused to learn. The analytic sessions continued to be
chaotic. When new themes crystallized the chaos increased. He became
preoccupied with various birth theories, such as impregnation through
the mouth or through operation. The baby grows in the penis, in the
udder of the cow or the breast of the woman. He also showed his confusion about the elimination of milk and urine. Birth takes place
through operation or from the rectum, penis, or breast. He brought
these fantasies while alternately wounding himself and attacking the
analyst. He had also started to handle his genital more and told excitedly many tales of "what other boys did", yet the staff observed that
Allen now participated in and instigated more sexual games with other
boys. He had started to pick on the smaller boys and was highly critical
about some of their unpleasant habits. The analyst felt that this might
be a displacement of his feelings of disapproval about his own sexual
indulgence, although consciously he only showed excitement and many
fears of being hurt or killed. The patient now asked whether the analyst
could cure him of dreaming. He dreamt that he was with her in the
chicken coop, and he and the chickens were afraid. (Chicken dung
played a great rôle for him.) The analyst interpreted to him his fear of
her because she discussed sexual subjects, and showed him the projection of his own sexual fantasies on to her.

Toward the end of the second year of analysis the patient had improved considerably. He soiled and wet himself less often, he became
relatively neater in appearance, the tantrums diminished, and he began to
catch up with his school work. The analyst and the staff of the Southard
School concluded that this child, who was so dependent emotionally on
adults, could not survive in the school set-up where a constancy of
parental figures was difficult to achieve. Because his behavior was not
as disruptive as previously, it was decided to try him out in a boarding
home. This boarding home was carefully selected in order to find the
optimum milieu. The family was prepared to indulge the child according to his needs and was able to tolerate the outstanding demandingness
and dependence which was so out of proportion for a boy of Allen's age.
They also agreed to exert a minimum of discipline and to set compara-

tively low standards for behavior. In addition, there was no competition with other children. The child responded quite well to this set-up. The boarding mother telephoned to the analyst daily to report on the boy's behavior and to ask advice as to how to meet the complicated situations which arose. When the problems became multifold the analyst arranged for an interview with her.

The boarding mother had to dress Allen in the morning. He would dawdle over but finish a lavish breakfast which the boarding mother cooked for him herself. He would follow her around like a little dog, either talking to her in the way he usually talked to women—admiring them greatly—or at times he would test her out on her ideas about what he learned in his analysis. He would ask her whether she had a penis and would be very eager to watch her dress and undress, or to cuddle up in bed with her. The analyst used all the information thus obtained and in the analysis of the child discussed and interpreted it to him. It appeared to her that Allen was testing out whether the freedom which the analyst had permitted him to talk about his sexual fantasies could also be expected from his boarding mother, and whether she would approve of this. To the analyst it seemed that here was a repetition of the earlier conflict between the feelings of love and loyalty toward his mother and the nurse, Rhea. On another plane this conflict also repeated itself in his feelings toward his own home and the boarding home; e. g., Allen had announced to his boarding mother that after his parents died he and his brother would come to live with her and her family for good. The child seemed to feel happier in his boarding home than he had in his own home. The analyst also used this opportunity to discuss with him his ambivalent feelings toward his family.

During the following summer vacation Allen started to play with the children in the neighborhood of his boarding home. There were two or three boys his age, and Allen became a definite member of their gang. They climbed trees, went on bicycle rides, and were taken on picnics or trips by the various parents. Because he had been learning more and more and had begun to play with children his own age, it was decided to try him out in public school. This involved a close cooperation with the public school in addition to that with the boarding home. A visiting teacher from the Southard School kept in regular contact with the public school teacher, and with extra tutoring it was possible to keep Allen in school. He did well there, but at times when he became worried about his school work, or when the analytic work disturbed him, his behavior in class became disruptive and strange.

At one such period he brought a series of fantasies in his analytic sessions which seemed to be related to his homosexuality and castration fantasies. Unfortunately the fantasies were never brought clearly enough to interpret them thoroughly.

Numbers, great sums of money, hoards in dungeons, and robbers came to the foreground; also the element of selling and buying, stealing, exchanging, and losing money. In the many battles against robbers and ghosts the "mistress", the analyst, or the patient, dressed up as a woman, either alone or with the help of a male figure, won out. In a fantasy game an old man wanted to take a picture of Puppy, the dog. However, the mistress, with Puppy's help, upset his camera. The old man behaved in a bizarre way, such as actually displayed by the patient in his tantrums. Now a man on a motor cycle came. Allen made the typical noise, just as when he pretended he was a car. This man was the husband of the mistress or analyst and crashed into the old man. After this Puppy and the man went up in an airplane and did many stunts. At this point the patient actually started to soil his pants and ran to the bathroom. The analyst pointed out the similarity between the crazy behavior of the old man in this fantasy and the patient's mad spells, and drew attention to the fact of the soiling.

In the subsequent fantasies there were always male figures who attacked each other by biting, strangling or shooting. Allen's behavior outside of the analysis became more provocative and aggressive to men, and he did less well in school. The fantasies seemed related to the patient's homosexuality but it was not possible to discuss this with him. He suddenly introduced a different angle: the women emerged as punishing figures, or two women crashed into each other. In another fantasy he became a Jap who threatened the analyst, "I kill you if you don't give me your book." He took the book away and she had to get it back, while the patient laughed in his customary excited and provocative fashion, shouting "Go away!"

At the same time his interest in accidents and hurts was increased and frequently he dressed up in girls' clothes, or he would bandage himself up and not remove the bandage for the rest of the day. He was very much interested in World War II and was sure that all the people in England had lost all their possessions. He was preoccupied with attacks from stronger persons or countries on weaker ones, compulsively wondering how the weaker could outsmart the stronger to overcome his own fears of being hurt: e. g., what does a soldier do when his gun is unloaded? Would a soldier kill a baby? etc., etc. Sessions with such questions alternated with sessions where he attacked the analyst from behind, or where games of attacks were played. He subsequently brought fantasy games which dealt with hospitals where nurses performed surgery on patients in a very cruel, painful way.

But the well of fantasies which had seemed inexhaustible and too forceful in the first period of the analysis dried up completely, and from now on only everyday events could be discussed. After he brought the nurse fantasies, he was no longer able to let the fantasies come to consciousness, but suppressed them completely.

When he had had 2½ years of analysis Allen remarked to his boarding mother, "I think I have outgrown Doc." Although the analyst doubted this, she felt that the child was well enough to return to his own family. His brother was going to leave home for boarding school, which would give Allen a chance to become an only child in his own family temporarily.

When a child's behavior is fairly adequate to his age, the question that must be very carefully considered is whether the child who was in analysis away from home should return home, especially if this means an interruption of the analysis. Allen's parents had for a long time been eager to have him live with them. They were afraid of losing him when he seemed to be so happy in his boarding home. Because the analysis had come to a standstill and the home situation seemed more favorable than before, it was decided to try him out at home. It was explained to the parents that the analysis was not finished, but that its continuation should depend upon the child's adjustment.

The analyst visited Allen and his family after two years. He had developed into a handsome, perfectly behaved young boy of 12, who was apparently happy at home and often went hunting with his father. He was very competitive with his brother. He had stayed in school but had only just managed to make the grade. He had had the good fortune of repeatedly having an understanding teacher, who discovered that it was necessary to have Allen sit in the front row in order to hold his attention. The outstanding feature, to the analyst, was the child's superficiality. In no way did he remind her of the highly imaginative little boy she had known. However, there were no tantrums, he was not much sloppier than other boys of his age, and he could handle dangerous tools and weapons well.

The analyst suggested that his analysis be continued because Allen's adjustment in school was not good, but the child rejected the idea completely.

Two years later the analyst wrote to the family, inquiring about the boy's adjustment, and the answer was favorable. He had since been entered in a boarding school and had passed his grades. After receiving this letter, the analyst decided to publish the case.

After another two years (Spring, 1948) an appointment was made by Allen's mother, who reported that the boy had been put back in school, that he did not work, that he got into trouble with several teachers, and that she had decided to take him out of the boarding school and wanted to continue the analysis. A report from the school revealed that Allen was not liked in school by either teachers or the boys. The latter regarded him as a sissy. He never participated in any sports or social activities, showed no sense of responsibility as far as his work was concerned, and his only real interest was in cars. Apparently a boarding school set-up did not provide an optimal milieu for a boy like Allen.

A psychological report revealed that "the differential diagnosis would seem to be between a severe compulsive neurotic and schizophrenia". As long as Allen's homosexuality and castration fears are not fully analyzed his adjustment will perhaps be unsatisfactory. The boy may be too sick ever to make a good adjustment. Observation over a period of many years will be necessary to determine whether analytic treatment of a child as disturbed as Allen can produce a cure. The degree of improvement, however, in spite of the difficulties which have arisen now, justifies the attempt.

Discussion

In the paper "A Contribution to the Problem of Psychoses in Childhood" (3), the author has discussed why she considers a disturbance of behavior such as Allen's psychotic. The extreme dependence on one person, the intolerance to stand any, even a temporary, interruption in this relationship, the poor hold on reality, the inability to control an impulse, the degree of anxiety as expressed by the great number of severe outbursts of rage, warrant this diagnosis. The treatment of the child had to be adapted to this symptomatology.

A non-psychotic child is, in analysis, consistently made aware of his behavior and the feelings that motivate it. Thus the child's defense mechanisms are analyzed. Simultaneously, all productions of the child's fantasy life are encouraged so that the analysis of the defenses can then lead to the analysis of the unconscious fantasy against which the defense was erected. Other behavior patterns can be analyzed as direct acting out of certain unconscious fantasies. To carry out this procedure the child analyst has to combine the rôle of analyst with that of a befriending, permissive adult. However, as a representative of the child's world of adults the child analyst cannot be all permissive but has to hold the child to certain standards of behavior as demanded by the culture for a child of his age.

In Allen's case the therapeutic procedure had to be modified. The analyst could not remain a friendly but consistent or, at times, even a firm adult. Allen's reactions were those of a much younger child. In many ways he behaved like a baby and usually he did not act more mature than a 2-year-old. (In contrast to this retardation in emotional maturity were certain ego functions, like his intellectual grasp and motor coordination, which had developed more or less normally. Others, however, like reality testing, had developed poorly.) With Allen the analyst had to become an all-loving, indulging, soothing mother figure, who removes as much as possible obstacles from the child's environment. This removal of obstacles generally consisted of anticipating causes for his outbursts of temper so that these might be avoided. The soothing, reassuring attitude also was applied as far as the production of fantasies was concerned. For Allen a seemingly harmless fantasy immediately became frightening. The amount of anxiety produced by these fantasies was so great that we must assume that the boy lost his ability to test reality and the fantasy had become reality for him. In this respect Allen differed fundamentally from the neurotic child, who although engrossed in fantasy play, always is aware of the fact that he is playing and that it is only a make-believe game. Nor could Allen sustain a fantasy for a long time. When the fantasy did not produce a temper tantrum, another fantasy with completely different content, and generally from a different libidinal level, took its place. This may have been an attempt to ward off the anxiety produced by the fantasy. But the new fantasy was again equally or more frightening and another one had to take its place, etc., etc. Hence the chaotic picture of the analytic sessions. The analyst, therefore, actively participated in the production of fantasies and consistently modified the content so that the fantasies did not become frightening. This kind of participation does not occur in the analysis of less disturbed children. On the contrary, usually the attempt is made to let the child alone unfold his fantasies in order to understand them fully and to analyze them. The participation of the analyst may serve just to make this possible.

In Allen's case the analyst hoped to strengthen his hold on reality by constantly offering him a world of reassurance and friendliness as a contrast to his fantasy world. At the same time she analyzed Allen wherever it was possible. She showed him his mechanisms of projection and denial. She also pointed out that his outbursts of rage were connected with his fears and anxiety. Subsequently she could bring to consciousness his reaction to and his identification with the partners in sexual intercourse. Of great significance was the analysis of the oral and anal components of these fantasies. Whether this was a fixation at these levels or a regression could not be determined. However, after these fantasies had been brought to consciousness Allen's emotional maturation could proceed. It had been possible in the treatment of the child to find a balance between the suppression of his fantasies and still to allow sufficient production in order to analyze the unconscious meaning of the primal scene.

At the same time Allen's daily life outside the analytic sessions was completely regulated. This also is a deviation from the analysis of a neurotic child. In general the analyst wants to analyze the child in its own environment and to refrain from interference. This enables him to obtain as clear a picture as possible of the relationships in the family and to analyze the child's reactions to the members of the family. Although this does not necessarily hold true for all children of this type of symptomatology, the author does not believe that Allen could have been analyzed successfully in his home environment. In the school, and later on in his boarding home, a set-up was created which aimed at satisfying Allen's emotional need to be treated like a young child. The regime of indulgence, reassurance, avoidance of competition, avoidance of situations which might provoke fantasies of a dangerous content, and a minimum of discipline, was carried out in the school as well as in the boarding home.

The analysis of the primal scene, especially the uncovering of the oral and anal components, combined with the environmental therapy, produced a change in Allen. The psychotic behavior disappeared and Allen matured emotionally to a level much closer to his age. In his daily life as well as in the analysis he presented the picture of a neurotically disturbed latency child. Now neither the analyst nor the environment needed to indulge him any more.

When Allen had improved this much, regular and frequent visits of the parents were encouraged. Earlier in the treatment these visits had seemed contraindicated. In less sick children visits of the parents are encouraged in spite of temporary setbacks due to these visits (1). Experience has taught that visits prevent the child from feeling rejected by the parents and strengthen his feelings of security. In Allen's case the visits had only provoked his fears and anxieties and had awakened the memories of rejection with which he could not cope.

In the sessions the fantasies no longer had to be modified. As a matter of fact, Allen suppressed and repressed so intensely that it was not possible to interpret to him homosexual fantasies and the fear of castration and death connected with those fantasies. It seemed that when Allen was bringing to consciousness the fantasies of castration by women which were linked up with his sexual fantasies centering around homosexuality, he could not tolerate the anxiety connected with them. At this point the analysis dried up. Whereas in the past the repression only seemed a partial one, in the latter part of the analysis the defense mechanisms of denial and projection were used considerably less and repression took their place.

The dynamics of the treatment procedure may be speculated upon briefly. In her previous paper (3) the author suggested that the disturbance had taken place early in the development of the child. Normally the child learns to be left by the mother or nurse by erecting within himself the image of the mother. This process seems to be essential for the ego and superego development and must be closely related to the processes of identification and introjection, and is instrumental in the development of the relationship to reality. The psychotic child has not at all or only partially, been able to do so and therefore cannot tolerate being separated in any form from his love objects, without withdrawing from reality into a world of fantasy of omnipotence. The fantasy of omnipotence is an expression of the early developmental level where the arrest was made. In Allen's case there had been a fixation on or a regression to the oral and anal levels of libidinal development, simultaneously. (This relation between arrested ego development and libidinal development should be determined by further research.) This arrest of a great part of the ego functions, except for those mentioned above which had matured normally, explained the dependence on his love objects, the poor reality testing, as well as the inability to handle his impulses. The oral and anal fixations explained many of his unacceptable habits. In the author's opinion the arrested ego development accounted for the severity of the child's mental disturbance.

BIBLIOGRAPHY

1. Freud, A. and Burlingham, D. T. *War and Children*, Allen & Unwin, and Internat. Univ. Press, 1943.
2. Freud, S. "On Narcissism: An Introduction", *Coll. Papers*, IV.
3. Geleerd, E. "A Contribution to the Problem of Psychoses in Childhood", *this Annual*, II, 1946.

UNUSUAL SENSITIVITIES IN VERY YOUNG CHILDREN

By PAUL BERGMAN, Ph.D. and SIBYLLE K. ESCALONA, Ph.D. (Topeka) [1]

I. *Introduction*

It was several years ago that the authors were first struck by the observations to be reported here. Some very young children possessed unusual sensitivities manifesting themselves in several, if not in all, sensory modalities (visual, auditory, tactile, etc.). Colors, bright lights, noises, unusual sounds, qualities of material, experiences of equilibrium, of taste, of smell, of temperature, seemed to have an extraordinarily intensive impact upon these children at a very early age. They were "sensitive" in both meanings of the word: easily hurt, and easily stimulated to enjoyment. Variations in sensory impression that made no difference to the average child made a great deal of difference to these children. They were also characterized by a certain precocity, though this was very unevenly distributed among the diverse functions of their personality. The first impression which some of their reactions and abilities gave was that of unusual giftedness such as might be observed in the budding of a genius. Further observation, however, suggested comparison with individuals suffering from a traumatic neurosis, or a psychosis, and even with feebleminded children. Closer study and follow-up then made it appear that childhood psychosis was the fate of these children, though we are not sure yet that all children of the type to be described eventually develop a clear psychotic picture. The present paper is a report of five cases, followed by a discussion of a way in which the relationship between unusual early sensitivities and psychosis might possibly be conceptualized.

As far as we know, cases of this type have not been described in the literature. Closest to them come the cases of "early infantile autism" described by Kanner (6). These "autistic" children are unable to enter meaningful relationships with other human beings, adults or children. They live emotionally in a solipsistic world, except for their queer in-

---

1. From The Menninger Foundation.

terests in some specific intellectual or sensory field. They use language, but not primarily for the purpose of social communication. They may never address themselves to the people with whom they live, while at the same time they may perform amazing feats of memory, e. g., recite by heart scores of poems, or the names of all the presidents. They may show unending fascination with objects and with visual or acoustic stimuli. Only 1 of the more than 30 such children observed by Kanner did not show deep interest in music.[2]

In his paper Kanner does not touch upon the question of general or special sensitivities in the children he describes. The present authors, on the other hand, have been most impressed with the unusual sensitivities in the children under their observation. It is these aspects that will be dealt with in the present discussion. In addition we shall tentatively offer some ideas with the purpose of placing the particular observations into a larger framework of reference. We are not sure that the children described in the present paper belong to the same group as Kanner's autistic children. They might possibly be regarded as a related group of slightly different character. Our children do not quite show the peculiarities of language, the extreme absence of human relationships or the apparent unemotional self-contained intellectuality Kanner describes. Nor is it clear to what extent Kanner's cases possessed unusual early sensitivities.

II. *Case Reports* [3]

The following case reports are not meant to give complete case histories. We will rather restrict ourselves to a bare outline of biographical data and offer in detail only the material pertinent to the special problem of unusual sensitivities.

The cases reported were not all observed in the same manner or under the same conditions.[4] Although we saw all of these children, we did not see the first two until several years after the period with which we are most concerned, namely the first, and to some extent the second, year of life. In these two cases we had to rely on what the parents remembered about the earlier period. We have no reason, however, to cast any special doubts on their statements. The mother

2. Personal communication from the author.

3. We want to express our appreciation to Dr. Mary E. Leitch for her cooperation in collecting this material.

4. However, the Cattell Infant Intelligence Scale, Form A, and the Gesell Developmental Schedules, were administered to all infants seen for psychological examination.

who reported Case 2 impressed us as a skilled and reliable observer. Case 3 was brought to us at the age of 25 months and Case 4 at the age of 28 months. Thus we had the opportunity of comparing the parents' reports of a rather recent past with our own actual impressions. Finally, Case 5 was first seen by us at the age of 2.8 months and then followed up at rather frequent intervals to the present age of 14.3 months. In addition to these five cases we have in recent years seen several others that seemed, at least in some respects, to display similar phenomena. We shall not deal with these here, in order to simplify our task.

Case 1. We saw Stanley when he was 6 years old. The father and mother had their problems; the mother particularly could be called nervous; but there was nothing in them that one does not find in parents of many children in the normal or in the neurotic range. Stanley's sister, who was 2 years younger, was reported to be a healthy and active child.

Stanley was born after an uneventful pregnancy (with the exception of a short time in which a miscarriage seemed to threaten). Labor lasted 18 hours. Instruments were used. Birth weight was 8½ lbs. Stanley was believed to be entirely normal, though when about 1 week old, he began to spit up food continuously. An operation for "Pyloric Stenosis" was performed when he was 3 weeks old. Recovery was rapid. Since that time the child has maintained a healthy appetite. He walked and talked at about 1 year, but he was a strange child from the beginning, and became stranger and more bewildering to his parents as he grew older.

Stanley's sleep was always extremely restless. According to the parents, until the age of 18 months, any noise from a thunderstorm to a conversational tone would awaken him. Then he appeared startled and would scream. But sounds seemed to bother him even in the waking state. Later he learned to enjoy certain types of music, in particular, classical music. The parents say that he never pounded on the piano as other children do, but always just touched it lightly with his fingers. If the parents' memory can be trusted, Stanley used to like his baths, but always screamed when his penis was washed. He used to smell everything and began to talk about his olfactory perceptions as soon as his vocabulary was ready for it. He is still intensely aware of all odors. He smells his own clothing. He loves perfumes and powders. He is aware of his mother's smell when she comes from the kitchen or other places. When he soiled, his own odor made him sick and he gagged.

Case 2. Berta, whom we saw at the age of 7 years, is the youngest of 5 children. Both parents are psychologically and esthetically unusually sensitive individuals. She was, as far as the mother was concerned, an unwanted child, as the marriage came to a crisis at the time. A very severe cold beset the mother during the last 3 months of the pregnancy.

Berta was during her first months almost too "good" a baby, as she was "always asleep". However, during the first weeks she had several pyloric spasms. From the beginning she was bottle-fed and, except for these occasional spasms, there were no feeding problems. Berta seemed to be quite self-sufficient during the first year of her life, in fact she did not seem to care whether she was picked up or left alone. The mother felt that the baby never looked at her or seemed to expect her. Although Berta spoke a few words when less than 1 year old, she stopped all use of language at 15 months and did not speak again until she was 4 years old. (Her later speech characteristically contained both neologisms and expressions of poetic power and beauty.) The child's reactions to sensory stimuli were very much in contrast to her seeming indifference toward people. From early infancy on Berta showed unusually violent reactions to colors and sounds. Often she would wake up and scream when a light was turned on. At the age of 5 months she seemed fascinated to an unusual degree by a bouquet of flowers containing unusual colors. The mother remembers also that at the age of 10 months Berta almost leaped out of her arms when she saw some red flowers. From the age of 10 months until 24 months she would not eat anything of yellow color, e. g., eggs, corn, pudding, and would become furious when something yellow was offered to her. (On the other hand later, between 2½ and 5 years of age, all of her clothes had to be yellow, under no conditions red, and she painted everything in yellow during these years.)

From the beginning Berta seemed to get upset by and angry about loud noises. By the age of 5 months certain kinds of modern, dissonant music would disturb her, while she did not mind other music. She too, like Stanley, always played softly on the piano, never banged it. Later, at the age of 4 years, she would hate certain symphonies because they were "too sad", while she would sit entranced listening to others. She would recognize and identify by name many of these symphonies on hearing a small part.

From very early days on Berta seemed to become absorbed in experiences of touch. While she never could tolerate woolly toys—she still does not want them—velvet would put her into paroxysms of laughter. This response was present at 9 months of age. (At a later age Berta discriminated between related tactile experiences to the extent that when sitting cozily with her mother she would ask to have her cheek patted in one direction, but not in another.)

Berta has in recent years shown a very acute sense of smell, and her mother believes that even as a baby she used to smell her food. The mother believes also that Berta used to be unusually discriminating in regard to the taste of food. In addition she never tolerated any of the usual equilibrium stunts which most babies enjoy, like being swung around, lifted up high, etc. One of the fears which she developed in later years was that of being turned upside down.

Case 3. We saw Stella when she was 25 months old. The parents remembered her early reactions quite well. Our own observations were in harmony with the parents' reports.

Pregnancy and birth had been normal. A small umbilical hernia **was** reduced by repeated applications of adhesive tape. For the first

6 weeks Stella was breast- and bottle-fed. During that time she suffered from colic and cried. At the end of 6 weeks, breast-feeding was discontinued. From then on the child cried very little, but her development did not follow the normal paths. She seemed to live in a world of her own, beyond the reach and influence of her parents. Like Berta, Stella started to talk early, but became mute soon after. When we saw her, she had not yet begun to speak again.

Stella was apparently sensitive to light from an early age on. She used to jerk her head away when sunlight hit her. Her eyes used to squint in bright daylight. Riding in the car at night, she used to blink and duck her head when exposed to lights. (The same was still true at the time of our observation.) It seemed to the parents that Stella "always" had preferred red things.

Stella used to cry when she heard a loud voice or a clap of the hands. She, like the first two children, never banged on the piano, but rather played it very softly. She seemed to enjoy music, to be fascinated by soft musical sounds.

The mother said that Stella "always" used to rock her bed for a time before falling asleep. She enjoyed the rocking provided by the moving automobile so much, that taking her out in the car was a favorite way of quieting her when she was difficult.

Stella used to be very sensitive to cold air. It made her "screw up" her face. Hot weather, on the other hand, seemed also to cause her discomfort. She used to lick cold water and cool things, e. g., metals.

Stella resented being touched at the shoulders, between the legs, and on her face. She never allowed anybody to hold her hand. Until 1 year of age she refused to touch furry or fuzzy toys and since that time has not played with toys at all.

The mother's report stressed also Stella's decided discrimination in regard to taste. She used to gag when certain foods (e. g., spinach, custard, pudding) were given to her. We might mention in this connection again her licking of metals, window glass, the piano and her own hand.

Case 4. Olivia, whom we saw first when she was 28 months old, is the only child of parents both of whom seemed to have many neurotic difficulties. Pregnancy and birth were within normal limits. She had some minor congenital stigmata; two toes grown together and an "odd" facial appearance.

Numerous difficulties occurred very early in Olivia's development. It was hardly possible to establish contact with her and to influence her. She was restless, unhappy, and later fearful and negativistic. This child too showed an interruption of speech development. She had begun to say words when she was 7 months old, then reverted to muteness. At the time of our first observation, she still talked very little, her best being 2-word sentences.

Olivia also showed a number of sensitivities. She used to scream over any noise. At the time of the first examination, however, she had become accustomed to many of the minor noises which previously had

disturbed her. She still startled and got frightened at loud noises. Early
she discriminated between different kinds of music. If she heard music
she did not like, she would cry till it was turned off. She seemed on the
other hand deeply pleased with some selections.

Olivia stood alone and walked at the normal time, but gave this up
shortly thereafter, and at 28 months had not yet recovered these skills.
When the parents attempted to get her to walk by each taking a hand,
she "went to pieces" and was more fearful than usual for a week or two.
Around the age of 8 months there was a period when Olivia had developed the habit of rocking quite vigorously.

Olivia was at all times rather sensitive to odors. She vomited when
smelling certain foods, for example, oranges.

We could not be quite sure whether other sensitivities of Olivia,
those to visual and taste stimuli, both reported by the mother as rather
unusual, really went beyond what one may expect to see in general.

Case 5. Bruce is an illegitimate child. Delivery and condition at
birth were normal. He was breast-fed for 2 weeks. At the age of 2 months
he was separated from his mother and sent by an agency to the home of
an experienced and trusted boarding mother. At the age of 2.6 months,
according to the boarding mother's report, he was sensitive to sudden
noises and cried out in his sleep if the door slammed. He sometimes
acted frightened when she went to the crib to pick him up or turned
him over rather quickly.

We saw Bruce first at the age of 2.8 months. He showed a mild but
definite retardation in most areas of development. He characteristically
gave delayed responses to stimuli. On the other hand he showed excessive
startle reaction to sudden visual stimuli as well as to auditory ones. His
responsiveness to the boarding mother was noticeably more mature and
more spontaneous than to the examiner who was a stranger to Bruce.
Such an observation is rarely made in infants less than 4 months of age
and bespeaks a special precocity in this area of development.

At the age of 5.5 months he would be quickly and violently upset
by light and other stimuli. For example: He was presented with a cup.
He started to approach the cup, bringing his left hand slowly and
cautiously over the edge of the table from under it and then stopped.
When the cup was moved toward him to encourage his picking it up, he
reacted with a violent startle and his face twisted in a peculiarly
tense way.

The boarding mother told us at that time that Bruce had a very
delicate skin and that pressure marks remained visible for a relatively
long time. We were able to verify this observation. His general retardation was again evident at 7.1 months (the I. Q.[5] was 76 at that time),
with wide scatter in the level of different achievements, and with inadequate development in all areas. The observers received the impression
that Bruce was a markedly tense baby who failed to relax even when he

5. Cattell Infant Intelligence Scale, Form A.

fell asleep. Being held in someone's arms he quieted somewhat but never lost his tenseness. His response to people and to objects was of the same quality. Both appeared to be disturbing and threatening to him rather than stimulating positive interest or responses. He appeared to be most comfortable when very little attention was paid to him. His posture at such times suggested withdrawal or, more accurately, protection against outside stimuli. Thus, lying on his back, he characteristically shielded his eyes and a portion of his face by drawing one or both arms upwards or he covered his ears with his hands and closed his eyes. When lying on his stomach he buried his face in his arms and drew his legs under his body. When he was held in such a position as to make such withdrawal impossible and toys were presented or social approaches made, he usually reacted with obvious discomfort and anxiety. This manifested itself by anxious, near-crying facial expressions, often accompanied by moaning and whimpering sounds which developed into sobs if stimulation persisted. In addition, an increased rate of breathing, rhythmic rocking motions, a tight interlacing of hands, and bringing his hands before his eyes occurred when stimuli were presented.

At the time of the next observation (at 8.2 months), Bruce was again seen asleep before the test was started. Even in his sleep his forearm was placed over his eyes as though to shield them though he was in a dark room.

At 9.7 months, for the first time since we had known him, Bruce showed some interest in both people and objects. Yet if he was approached too directly, he showed behavior of much the same sort as was seen before.

Shortly before Bruce was 1 year old, he was given a variety of examinations. EEG and neurological examinations did not detect any abnormality at that time, but medical examination detected a general hemorrhagic tendency of unclear etiology.

Later observations and tests, done about once monthly, the last at 14.3 months of age, showed a generalized mental retardation with the I. Q. again in the 70's. He showed little physical activity and was generally lethargic though not truly relaxed. The protective gestures previously so characteristic of him were noted only on few occasions and occurred in mild forms. But he was comfortable only in close physical proximity to the boarding mother and behaved then almost like an infant a few weeks old. The boarding mother confirmed our impression to the effect that Bruce's dependence on her was increased rather than lessened.

III. *Problems of the Sensorium*

How does the presented case material look from the point of view of the sensorium? To answer this question we would have to know, of course, what the sensorium is like in normal infants and very young children. But no normal population, to our knowledge, has ever been systematically investigated in this respect. We have therefore to admit that our impressions of unusual, even extreme, sensitivity in these children are subjective experiences that have arisen against the background of many, but uncontrolled observations made on other children. Nobody will, however, doubt that human beings differ congenitally from each other in their reactions to sensory stimuli. Future observation may give us the normative data necessary for better understanding and safer evaluation of these phenomena.

If we examine more closely those facts that impressed us as bespeaking unusual sensitivity in the described children, we become aware that they differ from each other in several respects, and can be grouped accordingly. We find that we have observed facts pertaining to many parts of the sensorium, i. e., to visual, to auditive, to tactile, to olfactory, to gustatory, to equilibrium, and to temperature experiences. Some of the children reported on reacted very sensitively to light or colors, to noises and music, to materials that came in contact with their skin, to smells and perfumes, to foods, to rocking and swinging, to cold air or cool objects. Thus, one obvious principle of grouping our observations is furnished by the sensory modality.

Then we find that what impressed us in some observations was the reaction to the intensity or quantity of stimulation, while in other cases the observation is more easily understood as a reaction to quality. Thus if any kind of slight sound seems to awaken a sleeping infant, or arouses a reaction from the waking one, we will consider that he reacts to the intensity of the stimulation, in fact here to a very low intensity. But if certain sounds or combinations of sounds attract a child, while other sounds or combinations of sounds of equal loudness repel him, it seems plausible to consider this a reaction to quality. Other reactions to quantity that we find in our material, are e. g., reactions to light of a certain brightness, reactions to normally imperceptible (or at least not usually reacted to) amounts of odor, reactions to slight disturbances of the equilibrium, to slight impressions on the feeling of temperature. On the other hand, observations pertaining to certain colors, certain materials, specific odors, foods, we can group with reactions to quality. Whether a special fondness of rocking should be grouped with reactions to quality or to quantity may be debatable. With some sensory modalities this distinction does not seem to make much sense. We would not be able to say, e. g., what a reaction to quality would be like in the modality of the sense of temperature.

The reactions to intensity or quantity can be divided into several sub-groups distinguishable without much difficulty. Where a child is found to react to a very slight sound, odor, etc., we might describe the observation with the concept of "lower threshold". The "lower threshold" would be the point on the intensity scale of the minimum stimulus that elicits a sensation or a response. The sensitive child would be expected to have a low "lower threshold", the unsensitive child a high "lower threshold". On the other hand we may group together instances in which the observed children show upset or disturbance because of the too great intensity of the sensory stimulation, for example, too much light, noise, cold air, disturbance of equilibrium, etc. Such observations refer to the "upper threshold", i. e., the maximum stimulus that can be tolerated without eliciting reactions of pain, discomfort, or tendencies of avoidance. While none of the observations in our material pertain to the so-called "difference threshold", that is the smallest difference in intensity between two stimuli that the child perceives or reacts to in a differentiated way, such observations would be very desirable. Future research in this line might, for example, take the form of conditioning experiments with two intensities of the same stimulus that differ only little from each other. If our assumption of unusual sensitivity in the children of the described type is correct, they would—assuming that no other factors interfere—be easier to condition to smaller variations in stimuli than the average child. We would also expect these children to show a low "lower threshold" and a low "upper threshold".

The reactions to quality can also be further grouped. We find in our material several instances of fascination with qualities (colors, sounds, materials, odors, etc.); furthermore, instances of intense dislike of qualities, and finally a few observations that might be interpreted in a manner parallel to the concept of "difference threshold" of intensities, namely small differences in quality that seem sufficient to change the child's emotional reaction from fascination to indifference or dislike, or vice versa.

To convey an impression of these possible groupings we present them in the form of a table using observations from our case material for purposes of illustration. This table should more than anything else remind us of the many data that would be desirable. For not only the blank spaces would need to be filled, in order to achieve a systematic survey of sensitivities, but it has to be remembered also that the illustrations of this table are drawn from several cases, and thus conceal how little we actually know, even in these five cases, of sensitivities of the single child. We would need really to know the actual data concerning the various thresholds for each child.

TABLE I

Data desired for the evaluation of individual sensitivity with illustrations from our material

Modality	A) Quantity			B) Quality		
	1 Low Threshold	2 Upper Threshold	3 Difference Threshold	1 Fascination	2 Dislike	3 Difference
I Visual		Bruce's upset from light		Berta's excitement with red flowers		
II Auditory	Low voices awakening Stanley	Several children's playing the piano softly		Stanley's enjoyment of certain music	Olivia's dislike of certain music	Berta's distinguishing between music she likes and hates
III Tactile				Berta's paroxysm about velvet	Berta's dislike of wool	
IV Olfactory	Stanley's smelling his own clothing			Stanley's love of perfumes	Olivia's vomiting at the smell of certain foods	
V Gustatory					Stella's gagging certain foods	Berta's discrimination in regard to foods
VI Equilibrium		Berta's intolerance of stunts		Stella's enjoyment of rocking		
VII Temperature		Stella's intolerance of cold air				

It is also worth mentioning that this table leaves out all possible complications arising from intersensory experience, i. e., the simultaneous involvement of several sensory spheres, which obviously has its own laws. In addition, it is not impossible to conceive, for example, that the sensitivity within a given modality may vary according to the quality of the stimulus. Infant A may prove to be more sensitive to perfume X than infant B, but less sensitive to perfume Y. It is also entirely hypothetical at this time to assume that individual thresholds remain constant over a long period of time. The value of systematic observations in these areas would be considerable. They might, for example, throw some light on questions pertaining to constitution and to special gifts. One would like to have answers to questions like these: Can there be unequal sensitivity within one sensory modality, e. g., a low "lower intensity threshold", but a high "upper threshold", or a paradoxical lack of reaction to qualities where sensitivity to intensities seems great? Is it possible for one sensory modality alone to show unusual sensitivity? Do certain sensory modalities tend to have similar characteristics in respect to sensitivity, allowing for the assumption of a closer relationship amongst them as against the rest which do not share these characteristics of sensitivity? Is sensitivity essentially the same in all sensory modalities, i. e., is it a general characteristic of the organism?

We cannot answer any of these questions at present. We should like to return to the observations concerning the particular children we have described. To do this, however, we feel obliged to introduce a concept that will allow us to view the phenomena in a more meaningful framework.

IV. The "Protective Barrier Against Stimuli" (Reizschutz)

The concept in reference to which we shall attempt to explain the observed phenomena has been introduced by Freud: the organism's "protective barrier against stimuli" (Reizschutz). It is one of those concepts which, as marginal by-products of his creativity, Freud has given to us. It is a baffling, ambiguous, yet provocative concept, that Freud apparently applied to a variety of related, but not identical phenomena.

A) He described the "protective barrier" as something common to all living organisms, but most easily discernible in the simplest living substances, the vesicles of protoplasm. Such a living vesicle has an outermost layer,

"... and this now operates as a special integument or membrane that keeps off the stimuli, i. e., makes it impossible for the energies of the outer world to act with more than a fragment of their intensity on the layers immediately below ..." (1, p. 30).

B) The "protective barrier" functions also in higher organisms, in connection with the sense organs:

"In highly developed organisms the receptive external layer of what was once a vesicle has long been withdrawn into the depths of the body, but portions of it have been left on the surface immediately beneath the common protective barrier. These portions form the sense organs, which essentially comprise arrangements for the reception of specific stimuli, but also possess special arrangements adapted for a fresh protection against an overwhelming amount of stimulus, and for warding off irresistible kinds of stimuli." (1, p. 31).

C) Freud uses the concept as an aspect of his psychological construct "perceptive apparatus of the mind". ". . . the perceptive apparatus of our mind consists of two layers, of an external protective barrier against stimuli whose task it is to diminish the strength of excitations coming in, and of a surface behind it which receives the stimuli, namely the system Pcpt.—Cs." (3)

D) A function of the ego, apprehending, is also conceived as part of the "protective barrier against stimuli". This becomes of clinical importance when Freud regards the ordinary traumatic neurosis as the result of an extensive rupture of the "barrier":

"What conditions it (i. e., the rupture) is the failure of the mechanism of apprehension to make the proper preparation, including the over-charging of the system first receiving the stimulus . . . We thus find that the apprehensive preparation, together with the over-charging of the receptive systems, represents the last line of defense against stimuli." (1, p. 37).

E) In the last years of his life Freud seems to have been inclined to regard "protection from stimuli" as a function of the ego (possibly its primary function) and to consider the organic protective barrier the phylogenetic and ontogenetic precursor of the human ego.

"One can hardly go wrong in regarding the ego as that part of the id which has been modified by its proximity to the external world and the influence that the latter has had on it, and which serves a purpose of receiving stimuli and protecting the organism from them, like the cortical layer with which a particle of living substance surrounds itself." (4)

"Under the influence of the real external world which surrounds us, one portion of the id has undergone a special development. From what was originally a cortical layer, provided with the organs for receiving stimuli and with the apparatus for protection against excessive stimulation, a special organization has arisen which thenceforward acts as an intermediary between the id and the external world. This region of our mental life has been given the name of *ego*." (5)

After this review of Freud's thought about "protection from stimuli" we wish to examine whether introduction of this concept may be advisable for the better understanding of our material.

Assuming that the data of our cases would all pertain to the neonatal period rather than to a spread of time between birth and approximately the age of 2 or 2½ years, we would not hesitate to relate them unequivocally to the "protective barrier". We are used to assuming that a functioning ego does not exist at the neonatal period, and we generally see what we regard as its first traces—delay in response to stimuli—only at a much later period. We see in our case material, however (particularly clearly in the case of Bruce, whom we could observe contemporaneously, rather than rely on later reports), indications that these children start life with a high degree of sensitivity against which they eventually succeed in building some defenses. Furthermore, we see that some of these defenses start early, in fact, as will be discussed later in some detail, that ego functions set in prematurely, apparently in connection with this defensive purpose. It seems therefore justified to us to tentatively regard the unusual sensitivities as not essentially related to qualities of the ego, but rather to something more primitive, constitutional.

The next question to be decided is whether this primitive, constitutional factor necessarily has to be identified as the "protective barrier against stimuli". Does this concept offer any advantages against the idea of over-excitability of the organism we find in the older literature? A word of caution is in place here. We are moving here in realms of abstraction where we might easily fall victims to semantic confusion, unless we are on our guard. We must keep in mind that no different consequences ensue if we call the same phenomena by two different names. In fact, as the following graphic representation shows, degrees of excitability would necessarily be identical with "protective barriers" of different thickness.

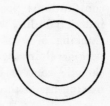

Fig. 1	Fig. 2	Fig. 3
The over-excitable organism, "thin protective barrier".	The normal organism, "normal protective barrier".	The under-excitable organism, "thick protective barrier".

Protective barrier and over-excitability are then really not different modes of explanation, but different linguistic forms for the same explanation. There are several advantages, however, to using the concept of the "protective barrier". It simplifies the task of establishing connections with the phenomena that Freud explained with this concept, mainly the traumatic neurosis and phenomena of compulsive repetition against and "beyond" the pleasure principle. It helps, also, as we hope to show later in this paper, to demonstrate in a simple fashion some interrelationships between constitutional and earliest environmental factors and their consequences for ego formation.

The "protective barrier against stimuli" to us is the conceptualization of all (ideally obtainable) data about the sensitivity or excitability of a newborn infant, whether the stimuli come from outside (sensorium) or inside (organic needs). The advantage of our concept lies in that we can point to phenomena which may eventually supply a measure of something that evidently must be assumed to exist in different quantities. In a similar way, in the past, speculation about intelligence eventually led to measurement of intelligence as defined by certain rules of experiment. Obviously "protection against stimuli" is at present more comparable to a map of yet unexplored territory than to a formula that contains in itself all previously obtained knowledge. We cannot, at this time, even make assumptions about possible differences between protection against outer and inner stimuli.[6] It is a matter that has to be decided by observation, or possibly experimentation, whether infants have the same type of reaction (the same "protective barrier") towards outer and inner stimuli.

It may also be premature to make a choice at this time between two possible conceptualizations of the "protection against stimuli" in the person in whom an ego has become established. One choice would be to follow the idea of Freud's later years that the ego grows in the place, as it were, of the original protective barrier, and it alone protects. The other possible way to look at the data would be to assume that the constitutional protective barrier continues to function throughout the individual's life, while the ego adds to the protection. This would mean thinking of two protective layers, one constitutional, organic, either peripheral in the sensory organs or in the adjoining nervous system (Freud's concept B), or within the central nervous system, but without making use of those higher functions of the organism, which we ascribe

6. Freud at one point wants the protective barrier directed only against outer stimuli: "Towards the outer world there is a barrier against stimuli, and the mass of excitations coming up against it will take effect only on a reduced scale: towards what is within no protection against stimuli is possible..." (1, p. 33).

to the ego and which—through attention, apprehension, symbolization, indirectly also through other functions—would contribute the second protective layer.

What possible observations would make one or the other of these assumptions more advantageous? The decision would have to come from observations of adults or older children. Can we find apparently normal persons, that is to say, persons who can stand a fair amount of frustration, and who show average or better "ego-strength" in relation to id, superego, and the outer world (the three forces with which, according to Freud, the ego has to contend), but who show in some ways that stimuli reach them with unusual intensity? Would, for instance, indications of physiologic disturbance or introspective testimony about the stimulation received suggest to us that the facts can be easier described in terms of two protective barriers? Could just this be the case in individuals of high sensitivity and great gifts who show adequate or superior ego functioning, to take extreme examples, in persons like Goethe, Rubens, Titian? Or what if only sensory stimulations of a certain kind, e. g., loud noises, bright lights, or a cooling off of the body surface, are unusually disturbing, forcing the person to take special precautions and measures of avoidance? Thus a competent contemporary writer is said to be forced to live in the country, and to protect his ears with cottonwool when he has to come near the highways or railroad tracks. Observations of the latter type would, of course, be open to question as to their correct interpretation. One would suspect psychological determination of such sensitivities by experiences in childhood, and by symbolic meaning. But only research can tell eventually what the facts are and what the surviving hypotheses are going to be.

V. *Early Sensitivities and Psychosis*

In this last part of our study we will first present some additional material on our cases that we consider weighty enough to exclude almost any other diagnosis but childhood psychosis (except possibly in one of the five cases, that is not quite clear yet). The rest of the discussion will be devoted to an examination of the possible relationships between unusual early sensitivities and childhood psychosis. The hypothesis will be offered that the infant who is not sufficiently protected from stimuli either because of a "thin protective barrier", or because of the failure of maternal protection, may have to resort for such protection to premature formation of an ego. When this premature ego breaks down, possibly as a consequence of a trauma, the psychotic manifestations are thought to set in.

Stanley and Berta, who were older children, showed at the age at which we observed them unmistakable signs of psychosis. Their behavior and their thought processes were found to be deviant and queer far beyond what can be considered neurotic. The thought content also corroborated the presence of psychosis. Stanley was, for instance, almost exclusively preoccupied with fire and destruction, Berta with toilets and "badness". Neither of these children had with anybody around them any relationship that would stand up under the slightest amount of frustration. They lived almost like strange creatures in the midst of their families.

It was the feeling of all observers (not only of the authors) that Stella and Olivia too could be diagnosed as psychotic children. Our criteria for diagnosing psychosis at the early age of 2 years are, of course, hardly well-established. But here again we had in both cases extremely deviant behavior. Frequently they would not respond in any way when spoken to, called or smiled at.[7] They were beset by many fears, showed extreme negativism, and sometimes outbursts of rage and destructiveness.

All these four children showed spot-like brilliancy and great unevenness in intellectual development, thus differentiating themselves clearly from the feebleminded group. In the case of Bruce, whom we saw last when he was 14.3 months old, we cannot yet offer a diagnosis or prognosis. Our experience and observation of the earliest phases of deviant child development allows us no more than to state our impression that Bruce is a boy significantly deviant from all norms of child development and most likely deviant in a way that will not be compensated for in his later life. We cannot exclude the possibility that he too will turn out to be a psychotic child.

We do not want to give the impression that we regard unusual sensitivities in infants or very young children as a prognostic sign of a developing psychosis. We can definitely state, however, that so far we have seen sensitivities of the described kind and extent only in the most deviant children. Whether children with special gifts without deep personality disturbances would present phenomenologically similar pictures we do not know.[8] The warning may, at any rate, be given not

7. It must at this time remain an open question whether one may attempt to understand the human relationships of our children on the basis of a hypothetical high stimulus value that people would have for them, and against which they would tend to defend themselves.

8. It is attractive to follow the idea of a "thin" protective barrier against stimuli as a possible constitutional fundament of special gifts. To do so would lead to assumptions of this sort: Only the individual liable to suffer from "bad" stimuli in a certain modality would be likely to be able to develop sufficient interest in procuring or producing "good" stimuli. For example, only he who suffers from noise would be likely to become a good musician.

to take such early sensitivities necessarily as signs of an unusually bright future of the child.

It seems possible to us to link in a speculative way the conception of the "thin" protective barrier against stimuli with the development of psychosis in these cases. We may regard an infant as protected from the onslaught of stimuli in two different ways, on the one hand by the constitutional factor of the protective barrier, on the other hand by the mother who both keeps stimuli from him, and provides them in the right dosage. When such protection from over-dosage and provision of the right dosage of stimuli is given, we have the favorable conditions for ego development. Then the ego becomes gradually organized and in turn is able to control the dosage. If we follow this train of thought we are led to make the assumption that disturbances in ego development may occur when either the organic protective barrier or the mother fail in their function, i. e., provide a protection against stimuli which is too little, or too much protection for optimal development. It seems logical to assume that in the event of insufficient protection (because of too "thin" protective barrier, or because the mother fails to be protective, or actively overstimulates the infant), a substitute will be developed for the purpose of protection. This substitute might be the ego, precociously organized for the emergency. Too much protection (too "thick" protective barrier, over-protective, or unstimulating mother), on the other hand, may result in delayed and possibly all-too-delayed ego formation.

The idea of an optimal time for the development of each function is not strange to present psychological thinking. Precocious organization of the ego may therefore be considered equally as deleterious a development as its delayed organization, though in a different way. We wish to discuss here only precocious ego formation and its relation to insufficient barrier against stimuli.[9]

Some of our cases showed at an early period a breakdown of functions. Thus loss of language after a normal or even premature start occurred in the cases of Berta, Stella, Olivia. Earlier acquired motoric skills (sitting, standing, walking) were later lost in the case of Olivia. We will not regard the loss of learned habits of cleanliness, which occurred in several of these cases, as a similar ominous sign, for this particular regression occurs rather frequently in young children. We tend to regard as more weighty signs the indications of failure to master traumatic

9. It may be well to recall here that the concept of the "protective" barrier refers to protection from painful over-excitement. It is not identical with protection of the biological being from damaging influences. A "thick" protective barrier may protect from excitement, but expose to real danger, e. g. when our sense of taste would not warn us against poison.

experiences. For example, Stanley, Berta, and Stella reacted very intensely to routine inoculations. In the case of Berta we can definitely state that in the night after the first diphtheria shot she woke up from sleep with a shriek, and continued to cry for 3 hours in terror: nobody and nothing could calm her, she did not seem to recognize anybody. From that night on this kind of scene repeated itself every night for about a year. In the cases of Stanley and Stella we could not establish when the night terrors had started. However, they were almost as intense as Berta's and lasted also for many months, not unlike those seen in neuroses following a traumatic experience.[10]

It is our impression that there were traces of premature emergence of ego functions to be seen in these cases before their breakdown occurred. For example, we could refer to Bruce's characteristic delay in responding to stimuli, which to the observers had a tentative, inhibited quality. Bruce also distinguished by the age of 2.8 months between his boarding mother—to whom he came only at the age of 2.0 months—and other persons who approached him. Such discriminatory behavior can be regarded as precocious. While it is doubtful to us whether we can distinguish early attention or concentration phenomena in Bruce's defensiveness, we would not hesitate to regard this defensiveness as similar to an ego's attempt to protect the organism from too intensive stimuli through apprehensiveness. We feel that our inability to obtain evidence for precocity of ego functions in the cases we had not been able to observe in early infancy is a real and most regrettable gap in our material and in the structure of this paper, and leaves this part of the paper speculative. The speculation, however, is somewhat supported by observations made on infants who did not have the uninterrupted safety of maternal protection. In such infants, Dr. Escalona and Dr. Leitch observed repeatedly the early occurrence of discriminatory functions, of purposefully directed actions, which resulted temporarily in a relatively high I. Q. on tests. Such early discriminatory behavior may be regarded as evidence of early ego functioning. Thus, while we feel that much further observation will be needed to support the hypothesis of premature ego formation under conditions of insufficiency of the maternal protection or the stimulus barrier, one might nevertheless tentatively regard the material presented as supporting such an assumption. Such a premature ego would be weak, liable to break under stress, and unable to achieve adequate organization later on.

These speculations (if they should prove to be justified) would be in good agreement with Freud's most general formulation of psychosis (2),

10. If these connections should be really valid, a noteworthy relationship between early psychosis and the adult's traumatic neurosis would seem to be suggested.

according to which the essential conflict in psychoses is between the ego and the outer world. Our cases would offer examples for the most primitive type of such conflict, namely, a conflict between an insufficiently protected organism and the stimuli of the outside world.[11] These stimuli set off impulses and excitements within the organism that are overwhelming and destructive through their intensity.

It would be of practical importance to know where the focus of disturbance in these children lies. If our assumption should prove tenable that these children supplement their weak protective barrier against stimuli by a premature ego organization which then breaks and prevents the formation of a mature ego organization, an educational consequence would arise: Parents and others concerned with the welfare of these children would have to protect these children thoroughly from intensive stimulation until such time as the child's ego might be able to take over this function without strain. It would not seem impossible to us that in some cases children with unusual early sensitivities might so be enabled to turn their handicaps to unusual advantages.

After completion of this paper we encountered in the literature the report of an observation similar to our own in a discussion which G. H. J. Pearson gave following a paper of H. M. Little on "The Psychotic Child". Pearson says: "I have noticed, in the two cases with which I have really worked very hard, and a third case with which a friend of mine worked, that these children have a history of having very acute hearing. They are able to hear acutely as babies and are disturbed by noises to a tremendous extent. A little later on they put up a defense against their acuteness of hearing by seeming to be deaf. The two cases of which I spoke later developed an interest in music, which was almost the only interest they had. As a result of these observations, I have wondered whether there is extreme acuteness of hearing in schizophrenic patients, i. e., whether they are able to hear above and below the normal range." *Pennsylvania Med. Journ.*, Vol. 51, November, 1947, p. 178.

Summary

We report in this paper a number of observations in children who very early in life, possibly from birth, showed unusual sensitivities. The general development of these children deviated greatly from normal

11. Such conflict may even result in the organism's death, if we can trust a news item published in the *Topeka State Journal, August 13, 1947*: *Dies of Fright. Philadelphia, August 13 (AP)*—Two-year-old Nancy Lee Pollock, whose mother said the child was deathly afraid of "anything that sounded like thunder", collapsed and died in her crib as a drum and bugle band practiced nearby, Detective Albert Helvitson reported. Mrs. Elba Pollock, who came from her home in Stockton, California, to visit a sister said Nancy Lee awoke screaming Tuesday night and then fell limp in her bed.

lines; 4 of 5 described cases could be diagnosed as childhood psychoses. We attempt to understand the observed phenomena with the aid of Freud's concept of the "protective barrier against stimuli" (Reizschutz). An organism insufficiently protected against stimuli by a "thin" barrier may need to precociously develop some ego functions. These ego rudiments appear to break down under the impact of early traumata. The paper indicates a number of questions that might be answered by future research.

BIBLIOGRAPHY

1. Freud, S. *Beyond the Pleasure Principle,* Hogarth, 1922.
2. Freud, S. "Neurosis and Psychosis", *Coll. Papers,* II, 250-254.
3. Freud, S. "Notes upon the 'Mystic Writing Pad'", *Intern. J. Psa.,* XXI, 1940, 472.
4. Freud, S. *New Introductory Lectures,* Norton, 1933, 106.
5. Freud, S. "An Outline of Psychoanalysis", *Internat. J. Psa.,* XXI, 1940, 29.
6. Kanner, L. "Early Infantile Autism", *J. Pediat.,* 1944, 211-217.

PHYSICAL SYMPTOMS IN EMOTIONALLY
DISTURBED CHILDREN [1]

By BRUNO BETTELHEIM, Ph.D. and EMMY SYLVESTER, M.D., Ph.D.   (Chicago) [2]

I

In the course of psychotherapy, symptoms may disappear without ever having become the specific object of the analytic process. They become unnecessary when the patient grows less anxious with his increasing ability to communicate and therefore acquires more adequate forms of expression. On the other hand, the redistribution of tension which takes place during therapy often makes it necessary for the patient to form new symptoms before he has arrived at ego-acceptable means of integrating his instinctual impulses. These processes were observed during the treatment of emotionally disturbed children living in the therapeutic milieu of the Orthogenic School and the following paper is a preliminary report on the fluctuations of their somatic symptoms during the process of personality integration.

For some children, life in a therapeutic environment made it possible to convert autoplastic mechanisms into outwardly directed activity. In others, personality growth in terms of a greater ability to internalize tension led to the emergence of autoplastic symptoms which had never appeared before. Such changes generally occurred during the process of personality integration, but they appeared much more readily in children who lived in a setting which was therapeutic in its totality.

Delusional preoccupations of various kinds were given up relatively soon. Psychosomatic manifestations of long standing — such as allergies, neuro-dermatitis, ocular-motor disturbances, mucous colitis and other disorders of the digestive tract—also disappeared spontaneously. Six of the eight children who wore glasses at the time of enrollment could dispense with them within their first 3 months at the school. These children were actually slightly myopic or astigmatic, but their visual dysfunction had been out of proportion to the visual defects. The visual defect of one

1. This study was financed in part by the Sonia Shankman Foundation of Chicago.
2. From the Orthogenic School, University of Chicago, Chicago, Illinois.

child improved measurably as soon as his total adjustment made the magic protection of glasses unnecessary. Another child could afford to see clearly when he overcame the fear of exposing his face without the safety of his spectacles.

An example may illustrate this dissolution of the magic investment of parts of the body and of physical props. A 9-year-old boy had been obsessed by a delusional system which involved his whole body and particularly his legs. Psychiatric investigation which preceded his enrollment at the school for many months, had shown that the boy invested his leg with delusional powers of attack and control. In a picture which he drew of himself, he wore gadgets to give him speed for flight and strength for attack. Around his leg were drawn cast-like structures to which he ascribed controlling functions.

The imminent separation from home precipitated a crisis in his adjustment since he felt unable to master this event by his usual methods. His frustration and rage about the helpless inadequacy found expression in an accident which took place just before he was to enter the school. At that time the boy, who was otherwise agile and well-coordinated, fell off a tree and broke his leg. This sudden appearance of self-destructive tendencies made further delay in his admission to the school inadvisable and he entered in a cast. The cast helped him to avoid fear of his inability to actively and realistically approach the new adjustment to the school. It also permitted passive mastery in a state of self-inflicted incapacitation. Accordingly, he stressed its magic powers. During the first few days at the institution, he expressed the wish to stay in his cast indefinitely. It was an insulating layer between himself and the new environment, needed as protection against the impact of external forces and also as a means to control his own destructive impulses. After this period of autistic withdrawal, he tried again and again to break the cast in the presence of his counselor and insisted on its immediate renewal in an attempt to control the persons in his environment. This kind of testing became unnecessary after actual investigation of the new environment convinced him that it was not threatening and that it did not yield to his delusional attempts at control. Then he was anxious to have the cast removed permanently, and said, "It was a powerful weapon, but I don't need it anymore." He stated spontaneously that he had broken his leg when climbing out on a branch which he knew would not carry his weight. This insight into the self-inflicted nature of his injury became possible when magic investment of his body was no longer needed. The autoplastic delusional mechanisms for dealing with his fears and hostilities were relinquished after he was sufficiently convinced of his safety and personal adequacy in an environment which he could master in terms of reality.

The acting-out type of child was generally free from psychosomatic symptoms upon enrollment, while organ neurotic or conversion symptoms were regularly observed in inhibited children who, in addition, gave the impression of having "frozen" personalities. In outwardly directed physical activities, their bodies appeared heavily armored, free movements were visibly impeded and their coordination was often incongruous. For such children, the conditions of the therapeutic milieu initiated an unfreezing process. It is true that the greater permissiveness of the total setting was at first a threat to some of the inhibited children. Nevertheless, they gradually derived security from it because permissiveness was consistently maintained in protective as well as gratifying personal contact with staff members. Moreover, inhibited children saw that the acting-out children availed themselves of such freedom without coming to harm or punishment. As a result, they, too, began to prefer manipulation of their external environment to psychosomatic autoplastic symptoms. Autistic methods of mastery, which had often been uncontrollable, slowly changed into deliberate, controllable actions directed toward personal representatives of their external environment. Such activity, to the extent that it involved the adult staff, represented the first steps in establishing interpersonal relationships.

This process was exemplified by a child who suffered from severe anorexia for many years. In infancy he experienced only a minimum of oral gratification because of a severe oral traumatization which had occurred at the beginning of his life. Because of trench mouth, he had been fed with an eye dropper for the first 6 months. Continued rejection by his mother, who handled him sparingly but harshly, added to his constant frustration and forced him to internalize his rage. He developed many other somatic symptoms such as food allergies, poor coordination, and uncontrollable gagging and vomiting. When he entered the school at the age of 7, his personal relationships remained tenuous for a long time. It was only gradually that he attached himself to his counselor to whom he began to show rudiments of a personal relationship. At last he permitted himself to obtain gratification from her and then started to spit at her. Spitting, as an externalized, personally meaningful aggressive activity, thus replaced the autoplastic gagging. Only later did he express his hostile oral fantasies by preparing "poisonous" concoctions in his games. He also played hostile pranks on children and adults, such as surreptitiously mixing salt and pepper in their food, or putting salt in the sugar bowl. The tension which had been dammed up somatically was now discharged interpersonally in attacks on others. After his eating improved, a total process of the unfreezing of his body set in. Spasticity of movement changed to adequate coordination as he worked through his hostility against other children. Smoother coordination permitted him increased and more successful participation in their physical activities and thus improved his relationship to them.

Such processes of redistribution of tension occur vividly when the child lives in an environment which is therapeutic in its totality. There, the interpersonal, physical and intellectual aspects of the child's total life experiences are sufficiently controlled to form a setting which is benign enough to allow for new cathexes. The greater plasticity of the child's organism permits unfreezing of the body armor under conditions which enable him to invest his libidinal energy in interpersonal relationships.

On the other hand, when the child's need for free and flexible expression of tension is interfered with, the result is frequently a deviation of personality development. This is true for infants brought up under conditions which preclude socialization of somatic tension, or for others who through physical handicaps are prevented from adequate discharge of tension in physical activity. Similarly, symptom formation becomes necessary in older children when the pattern of distribution of tension at which they have arrived does not provide them with adequate tools for mastering specific life situations.

For those children who had not yet arrived àt an adequate level of integration so that they could function in their old environment, old somatic symptoms continued to recur when they visited their parents. Such symptoms reappeared either in anticipation of or during the visit, and persisted temporarily after return to the school. Some children seemed to armor themselves against the possibly harmful impact of home experiences. They fell back on their frozen motility, halting speech, disorganized oculomotor coordination, or poor hearing. Others revived their old tics, digestive disorders, or skin eruptions in attempts to channelize hostile impulses. Thus they tried to safeguard themselves against the overwhelming experience of their own explosive behavior through revival of old somatic defenses. Somatic symptoms had the function of maintaining integration despite their feelings of personal inadequacy in meeting the home environment. Once the children were back within the manageable environment of the school, these props became unnecessary and energies temporarily drained in bodily symptoms were again freed for interpersonal action. A few examples may serve to illustrate.

Deafness was among the symptoms presented by one boy and one girl when they entered the school. With the aid of this symptom they had managed to exclude overwhelming sectors of the outside world. Only with such restriction had they' been able to maintain a minimum of integration. At the Orthogenic School interpersonal relationships were for the first time experienced as predictable and consistently non-threatening. Reality then became safe enough to be dealt with actively, and the children's symptom disappeared. Nevertheless, and for as long as their mastery of reality remained conditional, the symptom could be relinquished only at school.

Within the school situation, the children's hearing became fairly adequate although it was still seriously impeded at home, as a somatic defense, protecting their integration in the presence of parents. With this protection they could afford to insist on frequent home visits during this phase of their readjustment.

When the symptom had disintegrated sufficiently for them to also hear well at home, they soon took steps which resulted in temporary restrictions of home visits. At the same time, it became evident that they were not yet fully able to master the home situation without the somatic defense. During a home visit at this time, the boy started a fire under the bed in which his father slept; the girl, for her part, cut and tore her best dresses in anticipation of a visit.

The children were first able to hear their parents when increasing personal adequacy no longer made it necessary for them to deny their conflicts with them. Thus, the active expression of their original hostile impulses against the parents took the place of somatic symptoms, except that their actions were not yet sufficiently integrated. In terms of his oedipal desires, the boy tried to change his home situation in an effort to eliminate the father. The girl was not yet strong enough for aggressive action at home. She could express hostility directly only in the safer setting of the school. Still, she was no longer using her own body, but had turned against the dresses which her mother gave her. (The mother's insistence on her daughter's neatness of dress and appearance had been a source of friction between them.) Her destruction of the dresses was thus an active expression of hostility against the mother.

In both cases, activity meant progress, because the unfreezing of crippling defenses had been initiated. While both actions were still instances of uncontrolled behavior, they were signal steps in the total process of integration. Such drastic changes in the integrative patterns represent critical stages within the therapeutic process. At such times experience must be carefully dosed to safeguard the integrative capacity against undue taxation. Home visits were therefore discontinued for the time being in these and similar instances—a decision which the children accepted with expressions of relief, and without complaint.

Among the presenting symptoms of one 11-year-old boy were asthmatic attacks and recurrent eruptions of urticaria. These disappeared a few months after he entered the school except for their regular recurrence in anticipation of parental visits. Otherwise, the visits had no effect on his behavior during the first year of treatment. He showed no awareness of emotional tension with regard to them and expressed only pleasure at the prospect of meeting his parents. But the time came when his behavior changed in anticipation of parental visits. He became hostile and obstreperous with counselors and therapist, nagged, cheated and became generally restless and uncomfortable, though he felt no conscious anxiety about the visit as yet. The somatic symptoms continued to appear during the visit and to persist for a short time after his return to the school. But he began to notice how his attitude toward other people changed before parental visits although there was still no awareness of anxiety as such. With this recognition, the nature of his physical symptoms changed. First, asthmatic attacks and urticaria became less intense and were replaced by vague physical complaints. Later these, too, were relinquished and he could permit himself conscious apprehensive tension at the prospect of visiting his parents. Finally he began to procrastinate and to find external reasons for not seeing his parents as often as before.

Initially, the conscious experience of anxiety about home visits had been avoided by damming up tension and discharging hostility against them in his somatic symptoms. As a next step, hostility was discharged interpersonally, though in displaced form, through unfriendly actions at school which were directed against the less dangerous persons of the staff. Gradually he became conscious of his hostile feelings toward them and still later reached awareness of the real aim of his aggression, namely his parents. His last defense against such recognition was to avoid visiting them altogether.

II

Observations about the disappearance of psychosomatic symptoms after removal from the pathogenic environment were not unexpected and confirmed the findings of others. Bernfeld states, "It is notable that very frequently asthma improves appreciably, or disappears entirely, when the child is placed in an environment different from the usual family situation." (1)

Relatively unexpected, however, were the observations on the fluctuation of symptoms which suggest that in children, the origin, persistence and dissolution of somatic symptoms result from the integrative tasks to be mastered at the moment. In our experience, somatic symptoms in children proved unrelated to definite personality patterns or specific conflicts. In many instances, early infantile histories gave clues as to why certain children develop skin disorders, others disturbances of the alimentary tract, of speech or vision, of muscles or joints. Equally important as the early choice of organ, were factors in the more recent biography of the child which determined the choice, at a given moment of development, of somatic symptoms or of active manipulation of the environment in efforts to achieve mastery.

Information on infantile experience which may account for somatic symptom formations must be evaluated with caution. Parental reports on the personality development of children are colored by defensive needs of the parents and by the interpersonal context in which information is obtained. The material on earlier experiences which is reconstructed in the course of a child's psychotherapy is determined by the *hic et nunc* of the psychological situation at the particular moment, and the interpersonal setting in which the material is obtained. Therefore, such data have to be substantiated by direct observations in a setting which considers fully the child's needs and interpersonal relation at the moment of observation. These conditions are most closely approximated in a total therapeutic milieu. There, observational conditions exist which differ from those of psychotherapy, where the child continues to live in the pathogenic environment. Certain differences between our observations and those reported by others are explainable only on this basis. For instance, our observations of children with psychosomatic manifestations show comparatively little specific determination of the symptom itself. That is, a child may frequently be forced to attempt mastery by means of somatic symptoms because of the particular nature of the interpersonal constellation in which he finds himself. The choice of symptom, however, will depend on the state of psycho-biological maturation he has reached.

For example, a child may react with rage to the birth of a sibling and attempt to discharge the rage interpersonally by aggressive action against the mother. If the mother responds with restrictive action or retaliates by holding aloof from the child, the tension created by the sibling's presence can no longer be discharged in interpersonal action against her. Separation fear in such a case may force devious discharge of tension and lead to symptoms which are more acceptable than direct action. The specific interpersonal constellation, namely, the child's fear of the loss of love, makes symptom formation imperative. The nature of the symptom, however, will depend on the child's developmental status and on his mother's attitude toward the symptom. A renewed threat of the withdrawal of love will lead to changes of symptom until a solution is found which will permit discharge of tension without jeopardizing the gratification of a child's dependent claims on his mother. The original tendency toward aggressive action against the mother may, for instance, be split into the components of destructiveness and clinging. The first may be diverted into somatic manifestations while the hold on the mother is assured through the latter component.

Two examples may illustrate this analysis. A 3-year-old boy reacted to the birth of a sibling by developing enuresis. When he was forcefully broken of it by punishment and threats, he suffered a long series of colds which finally ended in asthma. The care he received during his illness satisfied his need to cling to his mother. In addition, his hostile tendencies against an intellectually ambitious mother took the form of withholding gratification from her by developing an intellectual inhibition. Another child showed a similar sequence of symptoms, but failed to consolidate his relationship to the mother on the level of somatic disease. He had to go a step further in modifying his original reaction of rage and disappointment. In addition to physical sickness, he took recourse to self-destructive acts in the form of accidents.

In both cases original symptom formation and later symptom change became necessary because of specific interpersonal constellations. The organs chosen for the expression of conflict were determined by the state of the children's psycho-biological maturation at the moment of disturbance. In the one case, the conflicting tendencies of rage and dependency determined the child's relationship to the mother at the birth of the sibling. Since her attitudes prevented the child from mastering his conflict within the interpersonal situation, an accumulation of tension made symptom formation necessary. In the other case, enuresis was a suitable symptom because of the developmental state of the child at the moment of impasse; his mastery of elimination in its biological and interpersonal aspects had been the most significant step in maturation prior to the disrupting event. Moreover, it was suitable interpersonally because it was a symptom with strong hostile connotations and an expression of revolt against maternal control.

Enuresis as an organ-neurotic symptom must be distinguished from enuresis as temporary regression to a previously won level of gratification; such "benign" regressive behavior is seen in many children on such occasions as the birth of a sibling. Within a secure mother-child relationship, the child has relinquished and integrated the hostile component of soiling when he achieves mastery of his eliminative functions. A regressive flare-up of soiling may frequently occur as hostility is aroused in the child. But if the relationship to the mother has been good, and remains so, regression will be temporary and will soon be given up precisely because of its hostile component. When the child finds it necessary to continue his regressive behavior because he cannot integrate the emotions aroused by the birth of the sibling, then wetting is replaced by regressive types of gratification which are free from hostile connotations to the mother. In such instances, the recurrence of thumbsucking is frequently observed.

Qualitatively different, however, from this reversion to old and safe forms of gratification are other kinds of "malignant" regression, which occur where the interpersonal situation between mother and child has been precarious on even the earliest levels of the child's personality development. The conditional gratification of primitive needs, or excessive parental pressure, may not preclude the establishment of toilet control, but they prevent the child from achieving integrated mastery over the physiological and emotional factors involved in these processes. The result is a lowered ability to integrate and this, in turn, makes it impossible for the child to master additional hostile tension. The lack of unconditional gratification makes regressive solutions equally untenable and symptom formation becomes necessary to prevent disintegration.

Parental attacks directed at the symptomatic behavior merely increase the child's frustration and therefore his rage. Even with changes in the child's manifest behavior, the amount of tension increases. He therefore continues to make use of somatic symptoms in solving the economic task of storing or discharging tensions which cannot be integrated on the interpersonal level.

In summary at this point, it may be said that somatic discharge of emotional tension is conditioned by the following factors:

1. A critical life situation which requires new forms of mastery.
2. Circumstances which prevent interpersonal mastery of a conflict and force autoplastic solution.

The consequences of these factors may either be a change of personality to the degree that mastery of the situation becomes possible without conflict, or

3. An attempted solution of the conflict by means of a somatic symptom.

The choice of organ used for somatic discharge will depend on:

4. The state of psycho-biological maturation reached at the moment of crisis.
5. The suitability of an organ for discharging or storing tensions.
6. The interpersonal attitudes of significant figures toward a particular form of somatic expression.

Where these attitudes prevent the establishment of security, a more suitable organ has to be selected.

These steps may be demonstrated by the development of the boy whose outstanding symptom was severe anorexia.

1. A severe mouth infection which occurred immediately after birth and prevented any sucking constituted the specific trauma and maternal attitudes perpetuated his frustration. The mother's rejection of the baby made feeding a particularly unpleasant experience, against which he rebelled by spitting and kicking.

2. He was deprived of any self-regulation in rate and rhythm of gratification when the mother started to feed him by force. Her unconscious realization of the hostility implied in his resistance served to increase her own anxiety. This she was able to rationalize as concern over his insufficient weight-gain. Justified by her concern she began to restrain him, and as she succeeded in suppressing his spitting and kicking, the baby was forced to abandon all autonomy in the discharge of tension.

3. Somatization of tension became necessary for the boy because he found it impossible to discharge it interpersonally by actively modifying his contact with the mother. He lacked the essential basis for developing extroverted contact with reality because he had been overpowered in his tendencies toward autonomous self-regulation in feeding.

4. Psycho-biological immaturity at the moment of traumatization ruled out any regressive solution through gratification on a more primitive level of libido organization.

5. Tension found an outlet in the modification of peristalsis, when the mother's restraint of his kicking blocked any release in motor action. Smooth musculature was used to discharge tension in the "uncontrollable gagging and vomiting" which he now developed.

6. The reversal of peristalsis proved out of reach of either voluntary or external control. Therefore, it became a valuable symptom since it protected the child from overwhelming parental interference and later ideational elaboration of his primitive hostility. Gagging and vomiting was thus finally established as the preferred avenue for the discharge of tension.

As with many other severely traumatized children, but unlike the usual neurotically disturbed child, this boy developed none of the symptoms which belonged to later levels of libido organization. Through the organ symptom of gagging and vomiting he was able to maintain his libidinal balance both economically and dynamically. He was adequately protected from an excess accumulation of inner tension, and his need for dependent gratification and angry control over the environment were also gratified, since his mother was being made to devote her whole life to him. Education in cleanliness, for instance, proceeded without any new symptom formation.

These and similar observations suggest that the early development of organ symptoms influences the later structuralization of personality. An impoverished personality is the common result where somatization of tension became necessary in the early stages of development. How severe the traumatization will be is determined by the rigidity and exclusiveness of the early patterns established for the discharge of tension. In such individuals growth phenomena do not result in more mature personality configurations. Instead, new tasks of mastery lead to a revival of powerful old cathexes and new conflicts tend to be channelized into the already established somatic symptom.

III

The somatization of tension assumed different significance for a group of acting-out children who had all been free of somatic manifestations upon enrollment. One of their general characteristics was an inability to withstand tension. This expressed itself in hyperactivity, destructiveness or delinquent actions. The group was further characterized by the fact that their past life had failed to provide the experience of consistency. Initially, treatment consisted in offering them personal contact in its simplest form so that they might learn to respond to the integrative appeal which results from consistently benign dealings with protecting adults. Their first reaction to these rudimentary interpersonal relationships was usually an extreme fear of separation and abandonment, in line with their limited capacity to maintain emotional attachments. Once they could recognize that a counsellor cared for them they also came to fear disapproval of those actions which they were still unable to control. This awareness of tension phenomena in contact with others introduced growth, but it also increased the immediate task, often beyond their capacity for mastery. They were now no longer as ready to discharge tension immediately through acting out, but were still unable to integrate it in their interpersonal relationships.

At this stage of development, they began to use the body and the physical functions as a means of maintaining contact. Like much younger children, they would react to all disappointing experiences by running to the counsellor and saying, "I hurt." Such physical complaints appeared in children suffering from organ neuroses as a stage in the resolution of their symptoms. In the acting-out children, the process of integration often began with vague physical complaints and was followed by the development of specific somatic symptoms as a next step in integration. In this manner, they used their bodies and their physical functions to store or discharge tension in a way that safeguarded their self-set emotional commitments to others.

A group of acting-out children whose need for immediate discharge of tension through motility had led to frequent truancies, may demonstrate this point. Running away episodes usually persisted for considerable lengths of time after admission to the school.

The symptom was never attacked as such, but in many instances the critical situations occurring during truancy were useful in providing the child with tangible evidence of the protective function of the school. For this reason the counselor accompanied the child whenever possible. The counselor's presence meant security against dangers of the outer world and this security, offered at a moment when he needed it most, became the basis for the child's relationship to the counselor. During the early stages of adjustment, the counselor took no direct exception to running away but at the same time made no attempt to minimize the real dangers or the subjective anxiety experienced by the child. In any event, the counselors were always quite explicit in offering tangible, unrestricted and unconditional gratification of all physical needs such as food, shelter, warmth, clothing, baths and company.

The children's wish to stay arose spontaneously, as isolated factors in the school—the group, a teacher, certain toys, or in other instances the total atmosphere of shelter and gratification—became acceptable and therefore desirable. This did not mean that running away ceased; the factors enumerated merely created sufficient motivation to make truancy a matter of conflict and the children began to look about for less troublesome ways of avoiding and solving their tension conflicts. The actual resolution of conflicts occurred only much later, after significant changes had been achieved in their personalities.

The growth of conflict in connection with running away meant progress. Before the children could deal with this conflict in an integrated fashion they had first to experiment with old mechanisms of mastery at their disposal. During this period of experimentation, changes in behavior were observed which preceded and initiated the solution of the essential integrative task. The critical event in this process appeared when the child became able to internalize tension in physical symptoms, when he became able to store tension in preference to immediate discharge through action.

Some children attempted to master the conflict of truancy by phobic avoidance of any temptation. They clung to the school grounds and refused to go on walks, they showed anxiety about the free coming and going of others. They hugged the walls and preferred to sit in sheltered corners or under the table. Others found ways to relinquish their symptoms in compromise situations. Immediate discharge of tension through motor activity was still necessary for them, but they managed to satisfy this need through activities within the school curriculum.

One boy whose fear of classroom learning had forced him to run away before every school session, began a vigorous use of the swings on the school playground before class began. In this way he managed a primitive discharge of tension which permitted him to cope with the school situation with less anxiety. The old pattern was maintained but he got by without manifest conflict since the impulse was now satisfied in socially acceptable form.

The pattern of dealing with fearful situations through physical flight appeared in modified form in the reaction of an 8-year-old girl to the arrival of a new child in her group. She made no attempt at the solitary and wild bouts of running which had previously characterized her behavior. Instead, she planned an organized exodus: she engaged the help of another girl, packed her belongings and carried them to a hiding place in several trips. After an hour she returned to the school and spoke freely of her intentions to the counselor, thus making sure that she would not have to carry out her plans.

The conscious wish to give up running away led some children to seek magic solutions as a first attempt at mastery. This was in line with both their essential helplessness and those magic ideas, with which they had previously attempted to master difficult situations.

Some children made attempts to stay put through the magical use of toys or pets, which were regarded as representations of themselves. One of the children tied his arm to his teddy bear and fastened the animal to the post of his bed. Another child asked one of the authors to take care of his favorite toy animal. When this request was denied, he asked quite dejectedly: "How can I run away if nobody takes care of teddy while I am gone?" Others used real animals in similar ways. They claimed they were remaining at school only because their fish or turtles would otherwise die of starvation. Children often disposed of their clothes, especially their shoes, in attempts to suppress the impulse to run away. This impulse they could not yet master, but they could control the external covers of their person and the executive organs of flight. Such control they substituted for the mastery of the impulse. They walked about in the nude, and refused to get dressed. Before running away had become a matter of conflict, they had always been fully dressed, often in more protective layers of clothing than the weather required; they had often insisted on going to bed fully or partly dressed to be ready for flight at the first sign of tension or danger. Now they sought to be rid of their shoes in an effort to forestall running away. One child threw his shoes over a fence, another out of the window, while still others managed to ruin them completely immediately after they were received so that they could not be worn. One boy would wear only bedroom slippers, even on walks with his counselor. In a dramatic demonstration of his attempt to stay put, he shuffled along slowly as if he were unable to lift his feet. In some instances the somatization of tension occurred within the attempt at magic control of impulse; slight accidents to legs or feet were frequently observed which led to real incapacitation and prevented running away. Symptoms such as neuro-dermatitis were observed in three cases. In two others, a contraction of athlete's foot persisted for months although it cleared up within a short time in all other children who acquired it at the school. Recurrence of the infection ceased only when the impulse to run away was adequately mastered.

One 8-year-old girl showed a general tendency to react by skin manifestations. (She also voiced many complaints about the dark color of her skin.) Her masturbatory activity took the form of scratching and she was very sensitive to any tactile contact. At the outset she ran away very frequently. Later her truancies became less diffuse and she showed preference for a stable in the vicinity of the school. At this time she developed the wish to curb her running away without yet having the strength to relinquish it. She began to suffer skin eruptions after each of her impulsive visits to the stable, and finally claimed it was the itching which prevented her from returning there and helped her to stay at school. (It should be mentioned that she developed no skin manifestations on subsequent visits since, after her general progress, a trip to the stables no longer symbolized flight.)

Much later, when her sustained reality adaptation, her good interpersonal relationships, and her improved learning capacity gave indication of a growing integration, she again developed skin manifestations as part of her reaction to the departure of her favorite counselor. At first, the child had a short recurrence of the confused hyperactivity she had shown on entering the school. This excitement soon subsided and was followed by skin symptoms, which were resolved when her reaction to the loss took the form of mourning. She experienced sadness and could tolerate it because she was now able to communicate her emotional experiences to a substitute for the lost counselor. In this instance tension was stored and internalized in the skin symptom and resolved into an adequately communicated interpersonal reaction—which was in marked contrast to the magic way in which her neuro-dermatitis had prevented her from running to the stable.

Such instances of somatization of tension were observed quite frequently. They seemed to mark a turning point in the total integrative structure of the child's personality. Tension which had previously found immediate discharge in acting out came to be stored temporarily in physical symptoms. This tension was finally invested interpersonally in relationships to those whom the children had learned to trust through a frequently long drawn-out period of testing.

Physical toughness, lack of fatigue and an adequate restoration of physical energy characterized the children so long as they functioned on the touch-and-go principle of running away at the slightest provocation. Their health seemed indestructible. While they roamed the streets at night, they got little sleep, ate irregularly and slept in the open, exposed to all the vagaries of the weather. During the runaway period at school they remained spirited and full of vigor, although they always looked harassed, disorganized, and dishevelled and much older than they actually were. When they began to wish to stay put at the school, a delay in the discharge of tension became necessary. Then they began to feel tired and spent many hours resting on their beds. Their expressions became worried and their sleep restless. Nevertheless, they looked more put together, better organized, more childlike, and much younger than before.

They began to complain of physical discomforts, of vague pains in joints and extremities, of headaches, and stomach aches, and eye-strain. Some of them started the habit of picking, biting, or tearing their finger-nails. These manifestations were vague and fleeting. The children were unable to describe them verbally, but they began to seek out the school nurse and went to her room many times during the day. The attention they requested from her was of the most primitive, non-verbal and tangible kind—often without direct connection to the ache they were feeling.

They sought this kind of contact despite the fact that they had achieved far more explicit forms of verbal communication with their counselors. This indefinable stage of vague physical discomfort varied in length. It was not interfered with by persuasion, specific medication, therapy, or encouragement to activity. Comfort and gratification were given in the form and extent which the children themselves could indicate. This permitted them to proceed with the task of internalizing tension at their own rate of speed and thus helped them to integrate the new experience.

Vague worries often accompanied this phase of malaise. They were rationalized by the children as being due to a variety of reasons such as "bad dreams", past misdemeanors, other children's attitudes, or fears about members of their families. Gradually the uneasiness took more definite form. It assumed specific contents determined by the biography of the particular child. Their worries then became communicable to others in psychotherapy, or in relationships to counselors or children, and in this way made the experiences accessible to modification. Then it became obvious that physical symptoms in these children were an important step in personality growth, that a tolerance for tension had to be established before they could proceed from random explosive discharge to mastery of reality. A final example may illustrate.

The running away episodes of a severely disturbed 10-year-old boy had decreased in explosiveness and frequency during the first 2 years of his stay at the school. Critical events, however, such as the arrival of new children at the school or the vacation of his favorite counselor, still led to abortive forms of flight. Finally he became able to stay put during the vacation of his counselor. This turning-point was well expressed in the routine psychiatric interview which he had at that time: he sucked his thumb, asked for a present from the psychiatrist, "something we can do together", and complained about intense hunger. "I had a big breakfast, but my appetite is different these last days." He looked at the candy, ate none, but said, "I like to eat, until I feel good and full, then I wait until I'm a little hungry and then I eat again, that's all I'll do." He also appeared quite listless, spoke in a low voice and said he felt tired, though he had slept all night. He felt that the radiator noises may have disturbed him, that they reminded him of the noise of a Diesel engine. Then he elaborated an incident, which occurred when he was only a little boy. During a vacation with his mother, whose attitude toward men had been a source of threatening danger to him, he had been separated from his grandparents, who were the protecting parental figures of his childhood. While awaiting their arrival at the resort, he had watched a wrecking barge with his mother. He had felt threatened and unprotected at that time, but now he felt able to wait for his counselor's return. Then, the loss of contact with a main protective agent had left him defenseless against outer and inner dangers, while now he felt able to cope with them. Communication of this separation fear at the moment of re-experience meant insight. It was progress in integration—made possible because he had become able to master fearful tension by internalization (with the help of somatic malaise) rather than by immediate discharge. He was now able to libidinize interpersonal relationships that had proved valuable to him even in the absence of the person to whom he was most attached.

In summary, it may be said that the purpose of this paper is to show that the appearance and disappearance of physical symptoms in emotionally disturbed children represent characteristic steps in the integrative process of their emotional readjustment.

BIBLIOGRAPHY

1. Bernfeld, S. "Psychogenic Factors in Bronchial Asthma", *Psychosom. Med. Mon.*, No. 4, p. 90.

PSYCHOANALYTIC ASPECTS OF SCHOOL PROBLEMS

By EMANUEL KLEIN, M.D. (New York)

School experiences are the first important experiences outside the family circle that involve a systematic separation from the home and where the child is confronted with the need to adjust to strange children and adults, and at the same time to perform tasks from which escape is difficult. The attitudes to the teacher, the classmates and the schoolwork are an important bridge between early attitudes to the parents, the siblings and the self, and their later expression in adult life. The component instinctual drives, sado-masochistic trends, scoptophilic and exhibitionistic impulses, oral and anal strivings, and narcissistic attitudes play basic roles in the learning process and its impairment.

School problems have been studied chiefly by child analysts. They are a relatively neglected area in the analysis of adults. The purpose of this paper is to review and comment on some of the analytic aspects of school problems, particularly on the vicissitudes of the learning process and to call attention to them in the analysis of adults. The content of the paper is based on a number of child and adult analyses and on briefer clinic treatment of a large number of children.

The good teacher relies on the sublimated energy from the pupil's component instinctual drives. She tries to direct, stimulate and gratify the pupil's curiosity and his wish to learn and to know. She tries to present to him an educational situation that will challenge his wish to mastery, yet allow for its gratification. She hopes to so regulate the pace of his work that it will not be so easy as to bore him, nor yet so complex that he experiences too much failure, and becomes overwhelmed by frustration. She depends on his wish to please his parents and his teacher, and on his own desire to achieve as well as he can, rather than on his fear of their displeasure or punishment, yet she hopes that both the rewards of success and the fear of failure will spur him on to effort and achievement. In the less neurotic or so-called normal child she can to a considerable degree rely on these factors much of the time. The teacher's task, an impossible one, Freud has called it, becomes yet more impossible when because of fixation or regression the child's sublimations are unstable or feeble.

Many school problems arise out of inhibition or restriction of function. In *The Problem of Anxiety* (13, pp. 16-17) Freud says,

"... the ego function of an organ is impaired whenever its erogeneity, its sexual significance is increased ... The ego renounces those functions proper to it in order not to have to undertake a fresh effort of repression, *in order to avoid a conflict with the id.*

Other inhibitions evidently subserve a desire for self-punishment ... The ego dares not do certain things because they would bring an advantage which the strict superego has forbidden ...

The more general inhibitions of the ego follow a simple mechanism of another character. When the ego is occupied with a psychic task of special difficulty ... as by the necessity for holding constantly mounting sexual fantasies in check, it becomes so impoverished with respect to the energy available to it, that it is driven to restrict its expenditure in many places at the same time."

The insight contained in this short quotation is the base on which rests much of the analytic work that has been done on school problems.

Anna Freud (12) has differentiated between an inhibition and a restriction of the ego. In the latter the ego turns away from a task which it can perform in order to avoid pain or disappointment; narcissistic mortification that arises when one's achievement is inferior to that of another. Even when the teacher does not rely on competition between the pupils, and encourages each one to go at his own pace, some of the children react badly to the comparison they themselves make between their work and the work of those who excel them. They try to avoid doing any of the work at which they are at a relative disadvantage to the most superior ones. Such a child will often work diligently and with great pleasure at a task until he becomes or is made aware of the fact that someone else is doing it better. Then he becomes disinterested, tries to withdraw from the work and seeks new areas of endeavor. Some of these children learn well if they are tutored privately and are spared the distress of comparison of their work with other pupils. When the mechanism is very severe however, the child will be disagreeably affected even by the comparison of its work with that of the tutor, and the tutoring will fail until it is combined with the treatment of the child.

As Anna Freud has brought out, the narcissistic hurt that the child receives is linked to an earlier narcissistic wound which occurred when the boy compared his genital with the larger one of his father which he envied, or it occurs when he is reminded of the hopeless rivalry of the oedipus phase; or when the girl is reminded of the genital difference between the sexes. Bright narcissistic children often get a great deal of gratification in grammar school, where they easily excel their rivals but as the work becomes more difficult at higher educational levels and they meet severe competition from other bright pupils, they encounter the unhappy comparison and begin to withdraw from it. In the more rigid schools where there is little choice of activity these problems come to light much earlier than in schools where the pupil can shift his sphere of interest and substitute achievement in one sphere for failure in another.

Another factor often encountered in the bright pupil's narcissistic maintenance of his status is his need to succeed without effort or study.

An intelligent 17-year-old boy who was not getting the grades in high school that he needed in order to get into a good college, felt that almost anyone could get good marks if he studied hard. He left his studying to the last minute, relying on his ability to cover the whole subject in a brief period of cramming. When he got a B where he hoped for an A, he always consoled himself that he had hardly touched a book all term, so that his B was really a great achievement. He insisted that if he had only studied a little he would surely have gotten all As. He felt contempt for the pupils who studied regularly and got high grades. They were only dullards who worked hard, he said scornfully.

Many of these narcissistic pupils have a considerable verbal ability, can talk and write well and do good work in English, in literature and related subjects and meet their greatest difficulty in mathematics and the sciences where sustained effort and concentration on details is more necessary. The difficulties in the sciences as well as the talents in the more verbal studies often stimulate ambitions to become a writer, often considered an occupation where hard work is not necessary, where one does not have a boss, and where one depends only on inspiration and the effortless outpouring of imagination to gain quick success and glory. Some of these pupils study hardly at all, yet in the face of considerable failure sustain their narcissistic status with the consoling thought that they could have gotten the best grades if they had cared to apply themselves.

A bright 14-year-old boy who was failing all his subjects in high school, reassured himself with the thought that he borrowed from the library books by Freud, Marx and Schopenhauer, whose content was so much harder than anything the others studied at school.

It is characteristic for the narcissistic pupil, who withdraws from the subject in which he does poorly, to minimize the importance of or to ridicule the subjects from which he withdraws. An extension of this attitude often leads to posing, to clownish behavior and to various affectations of superiority. Since many of these pupils aspire to be writers and poets, their affectations of manner and dress often follow traditional conceptions of how a writer looks and acts.

The need to succeed without studying is often associated with the need to prove that one is fortune's favorite child, and with the related need to succeed through charm rather than through effort. Oral factors are prominent and there may be an oral optimism, an expectation or a demand that life should always bring effortless rewards. At other times there is a constant expectation of disappointment, with a resentful pessimistic anticipation of grievance. The persistent narcissism is a denial of the narcissistic blows of the oedipal phase and is a regression to an earlier narcissistic state before these blows were inflicted. Frequently the narcissism has been inflated by the exaggerated praise of the parents and relatives. It is common in bright children who are brought up too exclusively in the company of adults, particularly adoring aunts, grandmothers or doting mothers. Yet it also occurs in children to whom fate has been very harsh, who have learned to use charm or intellect to ward off its blows. Attractive children particularly are prone to depend on it.

The inability to endure relative failure with subsequent restriction of ego activity is not due to narcissistic factors alone. An important element not emphasized in the literature is failure as the source of castration anxiety. As the sexual significance of failure is increased, so is its tendency to produce anxiety. As the child gets older and his incest fantasy and castration fear become unconscious, the guilt and fear become represented in consciousness as a fear that the masturbation has caused a self-inflicted injury to the genital, to the body as a whole, and to the brain or mind. School failure becomes to the pupil the confirmation and tangible evidence that he has actually injured his mind by masturbation. The guilt about the school failure becomes linked with the guilt about the sexual activity. Shame about school failure, with an exaggerated dread of teasing by others, is linked with shame about the inability to control sexual impulses, and fear that the others will learn about the sexual activity by observing in him evidence of the harm done by masturbating. The guilt feelings gain expression as inadequacy or inferiority feelings, which lead to an expectation of further failure. This painful prospect leads to a postponement or avoidance of work which of course helps bring about the anticipated failure. We see this mechanism to some extent at the start of school life in children with delayed latency, but it occurs most often and most sharply in adolescence, when the withdrawal from work is fostered by the struggle to master the instincts. It is to this period that we must apply Freud's previously quoted statement: "When the ego is occupied with a psychic task of special difficulty, as by the necessity for holding constantly mounting sexual fantasies in check, it becomes so impoverished with respect to the energy available to it that it is driven to restrict its expenditure in many places at the same time." (13)

The unstable neurotic balance of the adolescent may be maintained until some precipitating experience or series of experiences occur following which school failure develops. These precipitating experiences may be divided into stimulative or seductive experiences which intensify the id urges, or punishment or threatening experiences which intensify castration fear. The traumatic effect depends in part on whether the experience is homosexual or heterosexual, within or outside the family, with an adult or a companion; in each case, the first possibility is usually the more traumatic. Of the homosexual experiences, simultaneous or mutual masturbation is the most common. It can cause a marked upsurge of guilt feeling that previously could be mastered by the ego, as long as the masturbation had been solitary. An attempted homosexual seduction by an adult, often in a movie or a public toilet, is a common precipitating factor. In more severe cases, the ordinary stimulations of everyday life may be the precipitating factors, with the pupil overreacting to the sexual stories of classmates, their obscene language and pictures, and other ordinary encounters in the school toilet rooms.

A 14-year-old boy who was struggling with his masturbation guilt and his mounting sexual fantasies continued to do well at school until he spent an evening studying with an older boy. At the end of the evening the older boy suggested they both relax by masturbation. At first they masturbated simultaneously, and then the older boy touched the younger boy's genital. Following this incident, acute school difficulties began.

Within the home, attempted seduction by an older sibling often is the stimulating factor that upsets the precarious balance. This most commonly consists of sexual advances made to an adolescent girl by an older brother. Or we see the other side of the picture, in which overwhelming guilt develops in an adolescent boy who has yielded to a sexual impulse toward a younger sister. In children from the most depressed areas of our culture one encounters children who have had advances made to them by the father. Usually this takes place when the father is alcoholic. Sometimes it occurs when the mother is ill and the father has not been able to have sexual relations with her for some time. In several cases the sexual advances were made by the mother at the onset of a psychosis.

The marriage of an older sibling, particularly if she has been a mother-substitute, can lead to a great stimulation of the sexual fantasies with the upsurge of incest guilt. This becomes still more significant when because of the housing shortage the newly-married couple remain in the parents' home. All the complex emotions of the original oedipal experience can then be re-experienced by the adolescent. Of course in many of these cases, compliance on the part of the seduced adolescent plays a role, but this should not lead one to deny the phenomenon of seduction with its important quantitative role.

A harsh teacher generates current reality fear, mobilizes old castration fear, and in this way aggravates the masturbation guilt. (In a 14-year-old boy's dream the harsh teacher asked him not about his school work but about his dirty hands.) In the same way threats and punishment by the parents, or encounters with threatening companions are unconsciously perceived as castration threats and heighten the masturbation guilt. Illness works in two ways. On the one hand it is unconsciously perceived as a punishment, while staying at home makes it harder for the pupil to keep up with the class when he returns. Dental extraction in particular may mobilize castration fear and guilt during adolescence.

The child does his school work not only to gratify himself but also to please his parents, to gain their approval and avoid their punishment. When the child despairs of gaining the parents' approval he may withdraw from the struggle. He may have found the parent too hard to please, and found that no matter what effort he puts forward he will meet with criticism, because the work still falls short of the parents' expectation, or because it is unfavorably compared with that of a sibling, or because the parents' stern superego makes them take good work for granted and to look for imperfections to criticize. When the parents have exaggerated ambitions for and expectations of the child, to fulfill their own narcissistic needs, and are unable to accept his limitations, his reactions to school failure may become of overwhelming intensity, with the development of acute school dread, in which the teacher, the school, and then any school becomes akin to a castrating, or orally feared phobic object (26).

The child whose parent takes good achievement for granted may turn against himself the resentment their attitude generated in him, with the development of feelings that he is unworthy of their approval. This can lead to hard work as an act of atonement, or refusal to work so that he gains the criticism that his inner feeling of badness makes him think he deserves. To the extent that the wish for punishment becomes sexualized into masochism, the child's work failure becomes progressively more difficult to modify (22). In cases where the child incorporated the parents' harsh superego, the child is too acutely aware of any shortcomings of his work. This criticism from an overly harsh superego can also lead to a restriction of the ego and abandoning of one activity after another. Though it is usually associated with narcissistic factors of the kind previously described, the writer believes it is of value to separate the specifically moral aspect of the superego reproach to the ego for its relative failure as a cause of ego restriction, from the narcissistic mortification as a cause of such restriction. In the ego restriction to avoid narcissistic hurt, the ego withdraws from the task to avoid the displeasure, or, as Anna Freud calls it, the pain (Unlust) of relative failure. In ego restriction from superego harshness, the ego withdraws to avoid the shame induced by the imperfect performance. The superego, speaking with the voice once spoken by the critical parent, raises the question of morality and says, "You should be able to do better," and asks "Why can't you?" but does not accept any explanation or excuse.

This mechanism was prominent in a 40-year-old business man with an obsessional character, harshly critical toward himself and others, and with a strong sense of duty. He described how his mother always said "Why can't you do as well?" whenever she heard of a child who excelled, particularly in school work. He was often compared to a girl cousin who was said to be a model child, who never crossed her parents, who played the piano well, and got excellent grades at school. The patient's good work was never praised, not even when he skipped a grade at school, because that was what he should do and therefore no special comment was needed. He remembered how astonished he was when his mother arranged a surprise party for his twenty-first birthday. It was the first time she had shown such indulgent weakness. As a constant spur she used the shame and disgrace of failure. There were many ways that he could disgrace himself and the family, by failing at school, by making a faux pas while visiting, or by associating with an unworthy companion. Before he went to visit relatives his mother would enumerate the ways he might disgrace her, by being noisy, interrupting adult conversations, or appearing to be impatient for the meal served. As he put it, "There was always the moralizing lecture, the possibility of disgrace." She particularly stressed learning, saying that it makes one superior; and what one learns one always has: it cannot be taken away.

The first kindergarten experiences were very distressing and he had to be withdrawn. The fear of the teacher and pupils was very great; he thought of them as sadistic objects. In grammar school he did well and was skipped in the 3rd and 5th grades. At graduation he received an honorable mention but did not win any first prize, and felt horribly ashamed. He kept comparing himself to others, asking himself, "How do I stack up with them? I'm not doing as well as they are." There was constant self-flagellation, with, "Why can't I do as well, I should be able to." He had been eager to get a camera and finally got one when he was 14. The first roll of film turned out badly and he never used the camera again. The same was true of his skating, playing the piano, making a radio, taking an art course.

He entered a high school with high scholastic standards. Here there were many bright boys. He got through the first term, but in the second he began to fail. He could not do his written homework because he was so dissatisfied with what he produced. At the end of the second term he did not return to school to discover how he had done on his final examinations.

He fled from school into the family business and poured all of his energy into it. He managed it successfully for many years, but always under enormous tension, with the dread of failure and disgrace ever before him. He was harshly critical of any mistake he had made in the past, of the smallest error in judgment. Each year when his firm had to turn out new styles he was in a panic. When he would finally solve the problems involved he felt no pride of achievement; he got narcissistic pleasure only from his sternness with himself. When people praised him for what he did he felt embarrassed. What he had done was so obvious. Besides, when things went well, it was an accident and could not last. His strong sense of duty to his family and his sense of reality kept him from fleeing from the business, as he had from so many other activities. When he heard of the success of a rival or encountered limiting factors in production or in sales, depending on the state of the business cycle, there was always a return of the old self-reproaching voice, "Why can't I do as well? I should be able to!" This self-admonition did not lead to a realistic examination of what he could or could not do, a weighing of the alternatives and a choice of the best one, but had rather a paralyzing effect. During the war, and at other times when demand for his product was great he blamed himself for not being able to produce more; when times were bad he blamed himself because the sales were poor. The superego reproach was not placated by large profits or reality considerations. There was always a moral as well as a narcissistic problem.

In contrast to the withdrawal due to the wish to avoid narcissistic hurt, where the pupil generally minimizes or denies the value of the subject from which he is withdrawing, in withdrawal due to superego reproach the activity from which the person withdraws retains its value in his eyes. When the narcissistic pupil withdraws from school he says that school is stupid, the teachers are ignorant and one can learn much more by oneself or from "life". When this patient withdrew from school, far from minimizing the importance of formal education, he magnified it. He felt a deep sense of inferiority, mingled with envy and unconscious hostility toward those who were well educated. His stern superego did not allow him to forget his withdrawals. When he withdrew from an art class in adult life, because of his dissatisfaction with his work, his conscience reminded him of the long series of past withdrawals. In the first type the difficulty is handled by withdrawal and denial, in this type by withdrawal and continued self-reproach. Of course fusions of both mechanisms are common.

Special problems arise out of the difference in intelligence of the parents (32, 36); some are manifest early in school life, others much later, in college or professional school. If the father is more intelligent the boy may despair of equalling him and may turn away from learning generally, or from the father's special interest or occupation. Related to this type of withdrawal is the fear of competing with the father, with its reactivation of the fears of the oedipal phase. In these two phenomena we see again castration fear and the wish to avoid narcissistic hurt. Sometimes the stress is on the fear of excelling the father and thus arousing his jealousy. This may gain expression in relation to other pupils and then cause the pupil to withdraw from subjects in which he is skillful, or lead him to avoid reaching the head of the class.

Freud has generalized this whole series of withdrawals into what he called "retiring in favor of someone else". In "The Psychogenesis of a Case of Homosexuality in a Woman" (14) he offers this mechanism as one of the reasons why the girl became homosexual; she retired from the attention of men in favor of her mother, to remove one cause of her mother's hostility to her. In a footnote Freud lists three other instances of such retirement or renunciation; a case of twin brothers, one of whom retired into homosexuality apparently to avoid the narcissistic hurt of competing with the other who was so actively successful with women; in a young artist who fled from both women and work out of castration fear, and a younger more gifted brother who gave up his musical studies in favor of the older admired one, probably out of mixed castration fear and narcissistic hurt. The case of Dr. Schreber is probably another example of such retirement (15). It will be recalled that Dr. Schreber became ill twice, the first time when he was a candidate for election to the Reichstag, the second after he was notified of his prospective appointment as Senatspräsident. The fear aroused in him by the promotion led him to renounce his work and his masculinity and brought his passive strivings to the foreground.

In a case studied by the writer there were many oscillations between the wish to excel the father and fears of excelling him. As a small boy he began playing his father's instrument, the violin. He would not practise and did poorly until he overcame his father's and music teacher's urgings, and switched to a larger instrument, the cello. He then did very well for a couple of years, switched back to the violin and continued to do quite well until he was in danger of excelling his father, at which he again developed inhibition and reluctance to play.

Learning is generally perceived as masculine. This may stimulate the girl's wish to amass knowledge as a sublimated expression of her masculine striving, or it may cause her to withdraw from it at some point because it conflicts with her feminine strivings. Usually we see many oscillations between these urges. At the beginning of school life, under the spur of her masculine urges we find little girls often do well at school. In adolescence with its upsurge of feminine strivings, some girls lose interest in their studies or become inhibited in them, pouring out their energy in more directly feminine interests. In others, this tendency to retreat from learning occurs during the college years or after.

One woman patient showed these oscillations to a marked degree. She had strong masculine strivings, was interested in intellectual matters, and had considerable skills in music and in sports. She tended to attract weak passive men though she longed for the stronger, successful kind. When she observed the unfortunate social results of beating her male companions at tennis or golf, she withdrew not only from these games but, in her zeal to be less competitive, less efficient, and more feminine, she also withdrew from playing the piano and discussing serious topics.

Social factors that equate ignorance, helplessness, delicate health and timidity with femininity play a large role in creating this conflict between intelligence and femininity. They operate through the parents as well as through subsequent love objects.

Where the mother is the more intelligent parent, learning may seem to be feminine and may result in conflict in the boy. This conflict may be heightened if there are bright sisters or female cousins, or bright classmates. Excelling at school is then often regarded as a sign of being a sissy. As one patient said, "None of the regular guys studied or got good marks. The fellows who studied were the skinny kids with big glasses, the sissies." This trend is further augmented by the fact that learning does require a certain degree of passivity toward the teacher. It is thought to be feminine to be good in the classroom and listen to the teacher. Proof of one's masculinity demands a certain amount of defiance or behavior disorder. Prowess at sport is often contrasted with scholastic achievement. An extension of this is the contrast between masculine activities like business or making money and feminine interests like scholarship, particularly since the latter is not very remunerative. Almost any activity is perceived as masculine if one can make money at it. A sudden changed social situation can convert college professors, usually thought of as not masculine as compared to business men, into very male figures when they work at nuclear physics and atom-splitting. The culmination of the contemptuous masculine attitude to learning is found in the fascist remark, "When I hear the word culture I reach for a gun."

This conflict between a masculine business career and the feminine turning to a cultural pursuit reaches a peak when the cultural ambition is in one of the arts. The common situation, where the father works hard at his business while the mother cultivates her interest in the arts, furthers the concept of the artistic career as feminine, and heightens the conflict in the boy between his masculinity and his talent. Part of the talent itself in such cases is probably based on an identification with the mother. Fear of the father, hostility to him, fear of competing with him, a compensatory contempt for him, a wish to excel in a field in which the father is ignorant and inferior, as well as the son's artistic talents, turn the son to the arts rather than to the father's business. The unconscious feminine significance of the artistic work or its masculine equation with father's fertilizing act may act as a source of conflict and work inhibition. The whole problem is greatly heightened where the artistic talent is very slender.

The commonest flight into the arts by those with very slender talent is into writing where self-deception about the possibility of translation of a small potential talent into actual achievement can be maintained for the longest period of time, and where the need for formal training is less evident or less necessary.

Pseudo-stupidity of emotional origin can reach great proportions and may result in such a general inhibition of the intellectual functions as to cause a child to act like a mental defective. In 1908 Freud (16), discussing the connection between suppression of sexual curiosity and intellectual inhibition, said, "I think the undoubted fact of the intellectual inferiority of so many women can be traced to that inhibition of thought necessitated by sexual suppression." Later (19) he suggested the motive or gain one may get from an assumption of stupidity or innocence. "From my psychoanalysis of neurotics I know that the so-called naiveté of young people and children is often only a mask assumed so as to enable them to say or do something improper without embarrassment." Jones (24) further elaborated: "The motive actuating the behavior of these children is to delude their elders into regarding them as being too young to understand and into therefore ignoring their presence... Another allied motive lies in the freedom the child thereby wins in doing and saying things that otherwise would not be permissible." In a recent paper Mahler (34) further emphasized pseudo-imbecility as a means of participating in the sex life of adults.

Abraham (1) traced the connection between eating and the imbibing of knowledge. He showed that curiosity and the pleasure in observing receives important reinforcements from oral sources. Since then many papers have dealt with the connection between intellectual inhibition and oral factors (4, 8, 9, 21, 38, 39, 40). At the beginning of school life, the most conspicuous manifestion of intellectual inhibition is in reading difficulty. It is obvious that since reading plays so large a role in the acquisition of knowledge, difficulties in this basic activity lead to severe impairment in learning other subjects. Glover (21) points out the oral character of reading, and refers in particular to reading in bed as the ingestion of a "nightcap", a last feeding before going to sleep. Strachey (41) elaborated the concept that reading "is a way of eating another's words..." He differentiates between light easy reading which is like drinking or sucking and reading of difficult works which we must get our teeth into and chew up. He distinguishes between two kinds of attitudes in reading, corresponding to the two stages in the oral phase, "...a preambivalent one where everything seems to go smoothly and easily, and an ambivalent one where difficulties arise at every step." The inhibitions and difficulties of reading "...chiefly arise where gratifications belonging to the second oral phase are predominant in reading and where the reader's attitude is thus essentially ambivalent. If in such a situation the sublimation is unstable or incomplete there will be immediate tendency to the release of a number of sadistic and destructive impulses. Each word is then felt as an enemy that is being bitten up, and further for that very reason as an enemy that may in turn be threatening and dangerous to the reader." Strachey further elaborates that the object that is eaten while reading is feces and that reading is an act of coprophagy. He then links this idea with Melanie Klein's findings about the child's wish to force his way into the mother's body and devour the feces, penis, and children he imagines are to be found there (27, 28, 29).

As noted above, Strachey differentiated between light easy reading matter which can be sucked in, and difficult works, which must be chewed. However, when the child first begins to read, all reading matter is difficult as compared to the effortless flow of words into him that he enjoyed when his parents read to him. He now must shift from the first oral stage to the second. It is only later, when he has learned to read well, that he can again find the first oral pleasure in effortless reading. Difficulty in learning to read is often a rebellion against this shift from being read to and corresponds to difficulties in being weaned. A child with strong passive oral wishes will shrink from this change. In boys this goes with a strong oral attachment to the mother, or with the development of passive homosexual feelings to the father. Being read to then represents being at mother's breast, or at a different phase the fulfillment of fellatio wishes toward father.

Another factor involved is oral impatience. When the child first begins to read he must put forth great effort to get only a little content. When his parents read to him there was a rich flow of material. He heard many words that he understood fully but which he would not be able to read for a long time. When he begins to read, the reading content is much simpler and less satisfying. The orally fixated child is impatient. He finds it hard to put forward such great effort to a task that yields so little, compared to what he got so easily from his parents.

If he gets past his initial problem he may become a very rapid reader whose eye ranges quickly over the page and in a single glance absorbs entire sentences in a very satisfying stream. If his initial difficulties are too great, he may continue to avoid reading, and later turn to comics, with their minimum of reading matter, to movies, the radio and the picture newspaper. In this connection we must remember that children are often read to while they are in bed, the parent close beside them, and before the goodnight kiss and the love-making that may accompany it. Reading as a nightcap is frequently a continuation of this process and is a repetition of the goodnight story that the parents read before the child fell asleep. Reading on the toilet also has this association of reading when one is sexually stimulated (but on a regressed level) as one was stimulated by the close presence of the parent when reading the goodnight story, as well as by the need to replace orally by reading what one is losing anally. Another factor in toilet reading is the wish to be unaware of the pleasure one is experiencing while defecating; a similar wish also leads to reading while eating or masturbating.

One large group of boys who have reading difficulties especially in the first few years of reading are passive boys, with strong oral dependent traits, closely attached to the mother, with fear of a stern father. As they approach the genital stage, the castration anxiety is too great, there is regression and reinforcement of the oral traits, renunciation of masculinity, development of passive homosexual wishes on an oral basis. These boys tend to withdraw from boys' athletic games and street fights, they insist on being dressed to a late age, are clumsy in tying their shoelaces. They clung strongly to breast or bottle, resisted the first weaning and all subsequent weaning processes, like the shift from being dressed to dressing, from being washed to washing themselves, and combing their hair. They are fearful of the first school experience and resist leaving the mother. If the first teacher is very gentle, they may adjust to school after a little while but on encountering the first stern teacher they develop a great fear of the teacher, the school and the school work. If matters are less extreme they may gradually accept the school activity, learn some of the school arithmetic but develop the difficulty in reading, especially if the mother's reading to them has represented an important substitute for giving up the breast. In these patients the female genital is reacted to, as though it were a breast, with a hidden penis from which nourishment can be gotten, with a consequent predeliction for cunnilingus (5). In the case of the girl where passivity normally plays so large a role in personality development, retention of passive attitudes is much less likely to be a disruptive influence. In this connection it is interesting to note that reading difficulties are four times as common in boys as in girls.

In boys who are closely tied to a harsh, critical mother who weaned them early with frustration of the nursing period, there tends to develop a strong fixation on the second oral-sadistic level. There are unconscious oral-sadistic fantasies toward the mother, as well as oral dependent strivings. These are often accompanied by fears of being eaten by the witch, frequent occurrence of cat phobia, greatly reinforced fear of the dentist. Castration fear by the father takes an oral form as a dread of being eaten, as does the passive sexual feeling to father. (One of my patients with obesity and a learning disability had a dream in which he freely and willingly handed over his hip bone or pelvis to a huge vague shadowy figure who devoured it. There was no anxiety in the dream, rather a safe secure feeling.) In these children sibling rivalry assumes oral forms, with fears that the kidnappers who might make off with the sibling, would dismember and eat him. The shift from the passive dependent forms of absorbing knowledge, being talked to or read to, to the more active form involved in learning to read for oneself arouses the oral fears. The content of the reading, with its stress on animal stories, also activates the oral fears as do fairy tales like *Hansel and Gretel*. In these patients the vagina is conceived of not primarily as an organ with a hidden breast-penis, but as the mouth with teeth, the vagina dentata. Jones (25) speaks of the girl's attitude to the vagina, "felt like the mouth to be evil and dangerous." Lorand (33) elaborates the way in which the equating of the vagina with the devouring mouth leads to an inhibition of the vaginal orgasm in women. A similar connection between the eye and curiosity, behind which are strong oral forerunners and reinforcements, can lead to an inhibition of the ability to learn to read (25).

One female patient of 25 brought out these relationships in a striking way. At the age of 2 she ran toward a window sill and drove her tooth deeply into her lip. This interfered with her eating habits and caused her once again to be fed chiefly on fluids. Throughout her life she had eating difficulties associated with distress, especially irritable depression which she often developed. At such times she had difficulty in swallowing solid foods. They became too dry and required endless chewing and she reverted to liquids and semi-solids, with weight loss on such occasions. There was a very strong oral attachment to the mother, fostered by the mother's seductive fondling. Throughout her life there was an oral relation to love objects, a tenacious clinging, with violent jealousy of absent loved ones, a great intolerance of being alone, an exasperated irritation and quick depression at missing anything, or at the threat of missing anything, with intense oral envy of others. In childhood there were homosexual experiences based on the wish to duplicate the relationship to the mother. Her oedipal relationship to her father was grafted on her intense oral dependence on her mother and her great pleasure at the dinner table was to sit and drink in his words, while he held forth on every subject. Reading difficulty began at the beginning of school, and continued in this intelligent girl throughout her life. She read slowly and painfully, having to say each word to herself before she could go on to the next. There was a striking parallel between the slow reading and the slow eating with its need for protracted chewing. She loved to be told things rather than to read about them, and depended on men to keep her informed about current events in which she shared her mother's very lively interest. During her analysis she would ask questions, in an attempt to seduce the analyst to repeat the dinner table delight of the effortless imbibing of knowledge, and often felt sad and rejected when he was silent, like the patient described by Lewin (31). Any question that was answered led to another requiring a more extensive answer. When the analyst explained something to her, her face had a relaxed receptive expression as she drank in the words.

Orgasm was exclusively clitoral at the onset, and was at its maximum in petting when the vagina was covered by clothes, and only the hand was used. Undressing and going to bed with a partner immediately diminished the sexual desire which could be aroused at a lesser level by clitoral manipulation. Sexual curiosity was intense but had to be gratified passively by her being told the facts. There was great fear of her oral-sadism and hostility; and envy, though intensely expressed, was strongly denied. There was a frequent inability to eat eggs because living things come from them, but a marked repression of any memory of sibling rivalry with a younger brother. The reading difficulty was based on both the persistence of passive oral strivings of the first oral stage, plus attempted repression of the strong oral-sadistic impulses.

The sublimation of factors from the anal zone plays a large role in the acquisition of knowledge (7, 31). In "The Predisposition to Obsessional Neurosis" (17) Freud said, "The desire for knowledge in particular often gives one the impression that it can actually take the place of sadism in the mechanism of the obsessional neurosis. After all it is at bottom an off-shoot, sublimated and raised to the intellectual sphere, of the possessive instinct, and its rejection, in the form of doubt, bulks largely in the picture of the obsessional neurosis."

Sublimated anal-sadistic factors are involved in learning and knowledge not only as an expression of sadism, as a form of mastery of the world, and as a means of accumulating facts and knowledge instead of more concrete acquisitions. Learning is also the defense against the aggressive and sadistic impulse. The child pleases his parents and denies his hostility to them by learning for their sake. The sadistic aspect of the learning is further defended against when one learns in order to help others, with such ambitions as those of becoming a nurse, a doctor, a teacher or a preacher. In these ambitions we see again the double role of the ambition as a sublimation of sadism and as a defense against it: the doctor who helps the sick, and the doctor who operates on people and forces them to take disagreeable medicine; the teacher who helps others to learn, and the teacher who punishes, scolds and criticizes; the preacher who teaches people to do the right thing, and the one who castigates them for their wrong-doing.

A 45-year-old man with strongly developed anal-sadistic drives and strong defenses against them remembered that when he was 5 years old and his mother was in the hospital for an operation, he had hoped that she would die. He was overcome with guilt that his bad wish might come true, and resolved to become a doctor who would keep people from dying from such a sickness as his mother had. His mother put great stress on good grades and to please her and deny his aggressive feelings against her he studied hard and got almost perfect grades from grammar school through college. His hard work at school was both a displacement of his sadism from his mother to a desire for knowledge and an affirmation that he was a loving son. He pleased his mother with his meticulous neatness, yet on occasion he smeared himself with feces during masturbation. In this patient there was seen particularly the contribution of the anal impulses to the tenacity and persistence of the learner, to an orderly arrangement of the acquired knowledge and to their role in the capacity for dealing with the abstract.

A breakdown of the sublimations due to quantitative changes of the strength of the anal-sadistic impulses or in the capacity to cope with them, leads to an impairment of the learning process. In this patient an acute impairment of his excellent capacity to learn was accompanied by a flare-up of fecal smearing in masturbation. Obsessive doubt in particular can lead to a slowing up or complete breakdown of the learning process. The reader may doubt that he has actually read the material, or can doubt its contents, leading to a repetitive looking backwards, and to many devices to cope with the doubt. In some individuals subjects that are less exact like history or the social sciences may offer particular difficulties and there may be a preference for mathematics with its exactness.

A 22-year-old woman with a well-developed obsessional neurosis had as a prominent symptom the tendency to doubt and the wish to master the doubt through exact knowledge. In history she had great distress from the disagreements between different textbooks and she plagued her teachers with her demands for more exact definitions of terms like democracy, republic, freedom, and liberty, in particular words that involved the problem of the relation of authority to self-expression or the conflict between the impulse and its inhibitors. She loved the exactness of mathematics and did very well in this subject.

Yet the converse may be true, as in the case of the 45-year old man previously mentioned, who turned from his ambition to be a surgeon, and from sciences, which were too aggressive, to sociology, history, ethics and religious studies which served him better as defenses against aggressive impulses.

Well-sublimated obsessional characters are often excellent mathematicians, but here too dangers lurk which can cause a breakdown. The numbers often acquire or re-acquire special meanings. They can become magical, strong or weak, destructive or good, castrated or entire, male or female (2, 11, 23).

One patient who was usually good at mathematics spent much time in obsessive counting of such things as the cigarettes in her cigarette case. At one time she had stolen a good deal, aggressively taking love that she felt was denied her, and symbolically destroying the one whom she robbed, to make up for her deprivation and castration. The stealing was followed by an obsessional neurosis in which she counted to prove that nothing was missing, she had not robbed or destroyed anyone. If something was missing in the objects she counted, it had disappeared magically through a kind of "poltergeist", and not because of her action; and therefore the things that previously had been missing because she had stolen them had really disappeared magically years ago. This sometimes led to repeated adding of a column of figures, which never came out right.

In some patients we see a combination of good mathematical ability in the higher forms of mathematics, combined with the tendency to make so-called careless mistakes in arithmetic because of the retention by some numbers or combinations of numbers of their magical quality. Sometimes the bad numbers can be avoided by special devices; for example, 6 and 7 then make not 13, but 10 and 3; if one must add 6 and 7 and 9, the thought process is: 6 and 7 is 10 and 3; 10 and 3 plus 9, is 10 and 12, or 22.

Curiosity (3, 16) is of course the component instinctual drive that supplies a large proportion of the energy for the learning process. Curiosity itself is built up on and strongly reinforced by oral factors. Chadwick

(9), Schmidt (39, 40) and Abraham (1) especially emphasized these connections. Fenichel (10) particularly elaborated the oral aspects of seeing as a form of incorporation by way of the eye. The child wants to look at an object in order to feel along with him, to share in his emotion. At the same time oral-sadistic impulses are linked with the scoptophilia. The child wants to see something in order to destroy it, or to gain reassurance that it is not destroyed. On these oral factors as a base there develop the anal factors in the acquisition of knowledge, and on them in turn the genital factors. The sexual curiosity, directed to primal scenes, anatomical differences and the birth of siblings, becomes sublimated into curiosity as a motive force for learning. The repression of the sexual curiosity is fostered both by influences from the genital phase, and by its oral-sadistic component (6, 20). Too massive a repression can lead to a total inhibition of learning or more commonly localized forms. In the early grades it most often involves reading (7); in adolescence it usually involves sciences in general or the biological sciences in particular. Reading difficulties can be accompanied by an intense and persistent curiosity that requires the participation of the adult. The adult must tell the child about it; the child cannot read or find it out for himself. In a number of cases this attitude occurred in boys who were caught and severely threatened or punished for their efforts to gratify their curiosity about sexual difference.

A reversal of this attitude occurs in children who have no curiosity about the assigned lesson, but are very curious about other parts of the book, or who show no interest in the schoolbook but only in other books. Besides the defiance that is involved, there is the disbelief that the knowledge the adult is willing to share, is worth gaining. The child feels that the sexual part is sure to be censored out of it. Only the not yet permitted knowledge is interesting, or the curiosity can only be gratified surreptitiously, by stealth.

Reading difficulties may occur when over-stimulating sexual knowledge has been too freely available. This is seen especially in boys from homes where primal scene material was often displayed before the child. One adult who had had reading and other school difficulties had often been in bed with his parents while they had sexual relations until his fifth year. In a number of boys whose mothers had been prostitutes the denial of the curiosity was an undoing of this oppressive knowledge (42).

The shape, appearance and sound of the letters often play a role in reading, writing, and spelling difficulties (6, 30, 35), in that they may stimulate oral, anal, urinary or genital fantasies.

As was stated above, the inhibition of sexual curiosity often shows itself in adolescence and in later life in science in general, or in biology in particular. As opposed to the situation in reading difficulties which are more common in boys, inhibitions in biology and in the sciences are more common in women.

An adolescent girl of 14 suffered acute anxiety in her biology class, which she ascribed to the fact that she could not understand the classwork or the textbook. She dreaded being called on, began to cut class, and then as the anxiety became more diffuse began to have difficulty in mathematics, in the foreign language and finally in all her subjects. Such words in the textbook as "organ" and "function" were very distressing, as was the knowledge that the subject dealt with the sex life of plants and animals.

The degree to which scientific knowledge, where it bears on sex can be repressed, was strikingly illustrated in a brilliant woman writer who after graduation from college still believed that babies were born through the navel.

A man of 35 who wrote for the theatre and radio, had done extremely well in grammar school but could never master the science subjects in high school or college. Though married for 12 years he could not decide if women urinated through the vagina or the anus.

A man of 30 who had done poorly in science in high school and failed the sciences in college, maintained his ignorance of the female genital although he had been married for 8 years and was the father of a girl of 7. He did not know the position or direction of his wife's genital and had recurrent difficulty in finding it.

A bright adolescent boy of 14 found biology very boring. At first he read the lesson several times without being able to understand it, later he avoided reading it. At the same time he was preoccupied with the problem of world creation and the creation of the universe.

The first conscious sexual fantasy involving an adult not infrequently centers around a teacher, when, in adolescence, the return of the repressed oedipal strivings often seek expression. The detailed exploration of these fantasies sometimes is the most direct path to the earlier oedipal fantasies.

The same is true of the nature of the fear aroused by the school situation. The school fears tell us a good deal about the libidinal wishes and the earlier feared punishment. It is convenient to divide the school fears into fear of the teacher, of the pupils, and of the school work (26). The fear of the teacher is most often a continuation of the castration fear of the father. Sometimes oral elements play a large or predominant role. Fear of the other pupils also has as a strong component the displaced castration fear of the father. The struggle over the unconscious homosexual wish is often prominent in the fear of attack by the aggressive boys. Along with this there is often found in adolescents a fear of the obscene language of the boys which stimulates the unconscious homosexual wish. This problem often gains expression in fear of the school toilet. Here castration fear, fear of ridicule by genital comparison, and fear of homosexual stimulation intertwine. A similar situation is seen in fear of gymnasium participation. The passive boy who has avoided athletic competition with other boys is afraid of his awkwardness in the gymnasium. The feeling is heightened if there is bodily inferiority as in the child who is unusually thin, obese, tall or short. Behind this is found again the fear of genital inferiority and of stimulation of unconscious homosexuality.

BIBLIOGRAPHY

1. Abraham, K. "The Influence of Oral Erotism on Character Formation", *Selected Papers*, Hogarth, 1927.

2. Abraham, K. "Contributions to the Theory of the Anal Character", *ibid.*

3. Bartemeier, L. "A Counting Compulsion", *Internat. J. Psa.*, XXII, 1941.

4. Bergler, E. "Zur Problematik der Pseudodebilitaet", *Internat. Zeit. f. Psa.*, XVIII, 1932.

5. Bergler, E. and Eidelberg, L. "Der Mamakomplex des Mannes", *ibid.*, XIX, 1933.

6. Blanchard, P. "Reading Disabilities in Relation to Difficulties of Personality and Emotional Development", *Ment. Hygiene*, XX, 1936.

7. Blanchard, P. "Psychoanalytic Contributions to the Problem of Reading Disabilities", *this Annual*, II, 1946.

8. Bornstein, B. "Zur Psychogenese der Pseudodebilitaet", *Internat. Zeit. f. Psa.*, XVI, 1930.

9. Chadwick, M. "Über die Wurzeln der Wissbegierde", *ibid.*, XI, 1925.

10. Fenichel, O. "The Scoptophilic Instinct and Identification", *Internat. J. Psa.*, XVIII, 1937.

11. Ferenczi, S. "The Compulsion to Symmetrical Touching", *Further Contributions to the Theory and Technique of Psa.*, Boni & Liveright, 1927.

12. Freud, A. "The Ego and the Mechanisms of Defence", Internat. Univ. Press., 1946.

13. Freud, S. *The Problem of Anxiety*, Norton, 1936.

14. Freud, S. "The Psychogenesis of a Case of Homosexuality in a Woman", *Coll. Papers*, II.

15. Freud, S. "Psychoanalytic Notes upon an Autobiographical Account of a Case of Paranoia", *ibid.*, III.

16. Freud, S. " 'Civilized' Sexual Morality and Modern Nervousness", *ibid.*, II.

17. Freud, S. "The Predisposition to Obsessional Neurosis", *ibid.*, II.

18. Freud, S. "A Child is Being Beaten", *ibid.*, II.

19. Freud, S. *On the Psychopathology of Everyday Life*, in *Basic Writings of Sigmund Freud*, ed. A. A. Brill, Modern Library, 1938.

20. Freud, S. *Three Contributions to the Theory of Sex, ibid.*

21. Glover, E. "Notes on Oral Character Formation", *Internat. J. Psa.*, VI, 1925.

22. Jacobson, E. "Lernstoerungen bein Kinde durch Masochistische Mechanismen", *Internat. Zeit. f. Psa.*, XVIII, 1932.

23. Jefferys, H. "The Unconscious Significance of Numbers", *Internat. J. Psa.*, XVII, 1936.

24. Jones, E. "Simulated Foolishness in Hysteria", *Papers on Psa.*, Wood & Co., 1913.

25. Jones, E. "Early Female Sexuality", *ibid.*

26. Klein, E. "The Reluctance to Go to School", *this Annual*, I, 1945.

27. Klein, M. "Zur Frühanalyse", *Imago*, IX, 1923.

28. Klein, M. "The Role of the School in the Libidinal Development of the Child", *Internat. J. Psa.*, V, 1924.

29. Klein, M. "A Contribution to the Theory of Intellectual Inhibition", *ibid.*, XII, 1931.

30. Landauer, K. "Zur Theorie der Dummheit", *Zeit. f. Psa. Paedogogik*, IV, 1930.

31. Lewin, B. D. "Some Observations on Knowledge, Belief, and the Impulse to Know", *Internat. J. Psa.*, XX, 1939.

32. Liss, E. "The Failing Student", *Am. J. Orthopsychiat.*, XI, 1941.

33. Lorand, S. "Contribution to the Problem of Vaginal Orgasm", *Internat. J. Psa.*, XX, 1939.

34. Mahler Schoenberger, M. "Pseudo-imbecility", *Psa. Quar.*, XI, 1942.

35. Menninger, K. A. "Letters of the Alphabet in Psychoanalytic Formation", *Internat. J. Psa.*, V, 1925.

36. Oberndorf, C. P. "The Feeling of Stupidity", *ibid.*, XX, 1939.

37. Pearson, G. H. J. and English, O. S. *Common Neuroses of Children and Adults*, Norton, 1937.

38. Schmideberg, M. "Intellectual Inhibition and Disturbances in Eating", *Internat. J. Psa.*, XIX, 1938.

39. Schmidt, V. "Die Bedeutung des Brustsaugens und Fingerlutschens fuer die Psychische Entwicklung des Kindes", *Imago*, XII, 1926.

40. Schmidt, V. "Die Entwicklung des Wissenstriebes bei einem Kind", *Imago*, XVI, 1930.

41. Strachey, J. "Some Unconscious Factors in Reading", *Internat. J. Psa.*, XI, 1930.

42. Sylvester, E. and Kunst, M. S. "Psychodynamic Aspects of the Reading Problem", *Am. J. Orthopsychiat.*, XIII, 1943.

ANALYSIS OF A CASE OF RECURRENT ULCER
OF THE LEG [1]

By MELITTA SPERLING, M.D. (New York) [2]

Barbara, at 7½ years of age, became ill of ulcerative colitis. She had been under psychoanalytic treatment for 1 year during which period the analysis brought to light Barbara's jealousy of her brother Jim (4 years younger than she), her hostility toward him, resentment and anger toward the mother, the mother's ambivalent attitude, and the unconscious rapport between Barbara and her mother (20). The symptom of ulcerative colitis disappeared under treatment but Barbara then produced a new symptom—an ulcer of the leg. The subsequent material covers 2 years of treatment, begun when Barbara was 8½ years of age.

I

The ulcer of the leg began with a purplish red swelling of the ankle, which opened after a few days, secreting a bloody fluid and then becoming necrotic. The patient ran a fever which was treated with penicillin. Wet compresses were applied locally. The attending physician advised hospitalization because Barbara's lack of cooperation (she had to be forced to allow him to examine her leg) made it impossible for him to treat her. He could not establish a diagnosis of the ulcer.

Barbara was not hospitalized; at this point, her conflict was presented to her as one in which she would either get well and go to school, thereby relinquishing her mother, or remain sick and maintain her hold on her mother like a helpless, dependent baby. In this way she would be taking the mother away from her brother. The ulcer cleared in a very short time without hospitalization or medical treatment and Barbara was able to return to school and participate in all activities.

The mother, however, was constantly worried, anticipating some disaster. She observed that Barbara would run freely on the street with her friends, but in the mother's presence she would limp and drag her foot. The mother suspected that Barbara was making use of her leg as a worrying device. (One episode impressed her dramatically.)

1. Read before the American Psychoanalytic Association, New York, May, 1947.
2. From the Child Psychiatric Clinic, Pediatric Department, Jewish Hospital of Brooklyn, New York.

During this period, Barbara was under pressure at school where she had to make up two terms of work which she had missed. There was mounting tension between Barbara and her mother; when the mother insisted one day that Barbara stay home because of a cold, she flew into a rage, accused her mother of wanting her to be sick and threatened to "get even" with her. She refused to eat, but instead forced her mother to look on while she would take one bite and crumble the rest of her food. If her mother attempted to leave the room, Barbara held on to her or ran after her. She threatened an ulcerative colitis attack, and screamed that she would make her mother empty the bedpan for her. Although Barbara was up all that night with the bedpan at her side, she was able to produce neither bloody diarrhea nor any of the other colitis symptoms. But she did produce a new ulcer on the same leg.

The consulting surgeon suspected an underlying osteomylitis and hospitalized her. In the hospital she ran a high fever for which she got penicillin injections regularly, but with no apparent effect on tempera-ture or ulcer. The bacteriological findings were negative—x-rays did not reveal any bone pathology. No diagnosis could be established and there-fore no specific treatment could be given. The ulcers were treated locally with boric acid. At the onset of the leg ulcer, the full meaning of the symptom was obviously not apparent to me, and I had interpreted only one of its causative factors to Barbara.

I saw her regularly in the ward during the 6 weeks of hospitaliza-tion, and in this period interpreted to her that this leg ulcer, like the colitis before it, was a new way of destroying her brother Jim, and con-sequently herself. Barbara became disturbed at this and pleaded, "Don't let me do it".

Barbara was much more rational in behavior than she had been formerly, when hospitalized for the ulcerative colitis, but she was still fearful about showing her leg to the doctors. Her attitude toward me may well be described by her remark, "Little Barbara doesn't have much to do with this now—she only started it." (During our sessions, we spoke of her unconscious impulses as "Little Barbara".) The ulcer was clearing, but because of its size, grafting was suggested, which Barbara accepted when she was told it would shorten her stay in the hospital. The skin for grafting was taken from her abdomen.

When Barbara had been home for a week, her mother, greatly agi-tated, came to see me, accusing herself of having made Barbara sick again. On entering the child's room she had found her masturbating. Seeing that Barbara was flushed and perspired, and was moving about restlessly under her covers, as she had been on other such occasions, the mother cautioned Barbara against masturbating. She warned her that the ex-citement and perspiration especially in her present condition, would retard the healing of the wound on her abdomen, and that her leg would be made worse. The next day Barbara's leg began to swell and her temperature rose.

Barbara was again hospitalized on advice of the surgeon. This time she was placed on the Surgical Service and upon direction from the Chief Surgeon, who was antagonistic to psychiatric treatment, Barbara was put through the entire series of examinations for ulcerative colitis, which had been performed several times during earlier phases of her illness on the pediatric service. X-ray and rectoscopic examination revealed the typical findings of residues of a chronic ulcerative colitis. All bacteriological findings again proved negative. No diagnosis of the condition of her leg could be established. The dermatological description of the ulcer was, "Not typical for any specific type of infection. This type or similar ulcers not infrequently seen in association with colitis in adults." This apparently prompted the chief surgeon to put Barbara on a "colitis diet", to urge an iliostomy, and to declare psychiatric treatment contraindicated. This was opposed by the chief pediatrician, who knew Barbara from her previous hospitalizations for ulcerative colitis, and felt that she had responded remarkably to psychiatric treatment. She again received penicillin injections without any apparent effect on temperature or ulcer. She also had some x-ray radiations.

Barbara resented intensely her stay on the Surgical Service and feared that if she were not left alone she would "get sick all over again". Her resentment was also directed toward me because she felt that I should have protected her from all this. I finally succeeded in convincing the surgeon in charge that the ulcerations of her leg were psychosomatic in nature. The diet and all the treatment, except the penicillin injections, were now discontinued and Barbara was left to my care.

Analysis of her negative transference had to be carried on in the ward. I had to show her that she was now ready to destroy herself out of frustration, fury, and disappointment in me. She told me that she had felt that I, too, no longer cared—had deserted her—and that, being all alone, she hadn't felt like fighting Little Barbara (her own sadistic, destructive impulses). We made a deal. I would take her out of the hospital regardless of the surgeon's opinion or permission if she were willing to help both herself and me by fighting Little Barbara rather than me and the doctors. I also pointed out to her that if I took her out of the hospital she would have to accept the responsibility for her symptoms herself. Barbara was very optimistic, saying, "You'll see for yourself soon."

The effect of this discussion with Barbara was striking. When I had spoken to the treating surgeon, he thought it unwise to take her out of the hospital for several weeks. When I saw him two days later (after my discussion with Barbara) he was amazed by the visible improvement in her leg and the change in her entire condition, although nothing had changed in the treatment. Her temperature had dropped almost immediately after my talk with her, and the ulcer was healing rapidly.

I now took Barbara out of the hospital with the consent of the surgeon, who, however, did not seem convinced that Barbara would be able to stay out of the hospital for any length of time. Since she still had a temperature of about 101° to 102°, he advised that penicillin injections be continued.

This suggestion could not be carried out since it was difficult to find a physician who was willing to take charge of the case. One doctor, who was willing to treat her, first wanted to acquaint himself with her hospital record. However, within several days Barbara's temperature dropped without the use of medication. Her ulcer also was practically healed and there was apparently no further need for any medical treatment.

II

Occasionally Barbara would have a sudden rise in temperature for no obvious reason. The mother reported she had observed that on several occasions there was a marked rise in Barbara's temperature after they had quarrelled. I had also been aware that the rise in Barbara's temperature seemed to coincide with the emotional upheavals between mother and child.[3] I advised the mother to adopt a more casual attitude toward it, than she generally had, and I interpreted to Barbara that her rise in temperature was an expression of anger toward her mother. However, elevated temperatures soon disappeared.

An episode illustrating the mother's sober handling of Barbara's tendency to produce an elevated temperature is the following: the day her father returned to work after a two-week vacation, when he had devoted a great deal of time to Barbara, she complained of chills, fatigue and moodiness. She requested her mother to take her temperature and although it was found to be rather high (103°) the mother in a reassuring way made light of it. The next day the spell was over and Barbara was well again.

Barbara took care of her leg herself and insisted on walking after she bandaged it. She had good bowel control, but when she was very angry she would run to the bathroom, expecting her mother to come in and wipe her. Although she and her mother were more agreeable, there were still numerous quarrels, especially about Jim, of whom Barbara was openly resentful.

Barbara now began to show signs of anxiety. Often she was afraid of falling asleep. In speaking of it to me, she was able to analyze this fear herself. "Little Barbara" she said, "really wants Jim to die during the night and is then afraid it will be her."

One day after a quarrel with her mother, she fell while playing ball. She was very upset and implored her mother not to scold. Barbara's interpretation of the accident was that it was really not an accident but that "Little Barbara did not want her to be well, play ball, and do what other children do. Little Barbara is around again," she said, "because Mother nags and scolds me all the time and I had a quarrel with her just before I fell."

Barbara was still wearing a big bandage over her abdomen where she had a scar with a few scabs from the grafting. When I suggested that she take this bandage off, she said, "You don't know Little Barbara. She'll want to scratch." So I suggested that she leave the bandage off during the day and put it on at night. A few days later, Barbara's mother, very much disturbed, called to inform me that Barbara had

3. I had encountered a similar experience in the case of Robert, about whom I reported in the study of ulcerative colitis.

developed a sore on her abdomen. When I saw Barbara she showed me the sore, which had evidently resulted from scratching and pulling off scabs. It was not very extended but rather deep and it exuded a secretion. She said, "You see what she can do." She had achieved her purpose: to prove to me again how dangerous "Little Barbara" was and that it was therefore safer to have this sore covered. She did this by applying some powder and gauze and the sore healed up very quickly.

Several days later the mother reported that Barbara had awakened in the night crying, and asked to be taken to the bathroom. She feared something would happen to her stomach (meaning abdomen). The mother felt that the child's disturbance was related to the bandage on her abdomen. Whereas, formerly she would coerce Barbara to take it off, she said nothing to her about it, but merely listened to her complaints in the bathroom until Barbara said, "Now I feel better," and permitted her mother to go to bed.

Barbara spontaneously told me about the bad night. She told me she could not fall asleep because she was afraid of what "Little Barbara" would do to her stomach and that it was "not the scratching but something else". When she fell asleep that night she had a nightmare in which she found herself at the hospital. We discussed why she should be so scared of Little Barbara at this point. We knew that whenever this was the case it was because she was angry at somebody—usually her mother or her brother, or both. Barbara said, "I have to tell you something. You know, it's about the dog; not that my mother wants to give it away, but she doesn't let me take it out in the yard. And what good is a dog if you don't feel it's yours and can't do whatever you want with it?"

Several weeks before, Barbara got a sudden urge to have a dog and persuaded her mother to get her one the very same day. (It may be interesting to know that one of Barbara's severe attacks of ulcerative colitis more than a year ago had occurred after her mother, who disliked dogs, had disposed of her dog.)

In discussing the urgency of her wish for a dog, we came to understand that the dog represented a penis symbol to her. In one of the preceding sessions Barbara had brought out her belief that she (like all girls) was really born with a penis and that her mother, punishing her in anger for her masturbation, had taken her penis away. She also related to me her feelings about the threats her mother had made about masturbation. Mother had told her that "it would get rotten and foul, and fall off." What would fall off she didn't know. We also came to understand that the leg represented both Jim's and her penis and at the same time Jim himself (pars pro toto). Thus her fear of the surgeon revealed itself as a castration fear, namely, that he, as executor of her mother's castration threats, would cout off her leg-penis. This was something she dreaded and wished for at the same time, the idea being "to get it over with". As she later remarked, "It seems Little Barbara won't rest until I have my leg cut off."

At the end of this session Barbara was resentful and angry with me. She blamed me for insisting upon bringing up such material and said, "Little Barbara is angry at you because you found out about her secrets."

As a reaction to this session Barbara suddenly wanted a dog so badly and insisted that her mother give it to her immediately. To Barbara, obtaining the dog meant getting her mother to return the penis she had taken away from her. When this was interpreted to her, she asked, "Is it bad if I think of my dog as my penis?" Significantly enough, her interest in the dog diminished so markedly after this interpretation that her mother one day remarked: "It seems that Barbara doesn't care for the dog at all any more. I can't understand that; she wanted it so badly." [4]

Another incident her mother mentioned is also illustrative of her castration fear. One night, in her sleep, Barbara called out, "Nurse!" (She did this occasionally when her sleep was disturbed.) When her mother came to the bed, she observed Barbara, half asleep, touching and moving her leg. She then smiled, as if reassured that it was still there.

In discussing her nightmare, she realized she had feared she would have to tear open the healing wound on her abdomen. Barbara had not believed her mother when, upon my suggestion, the mother had retracted the masturbation threats. "This," Barbara said, "she only told me so that I shouldn't be upset, but she didn't mean it." The grafting apparently had supported Barbara's belief that the penis could be taken away and the operation had been conceived of as a punishment for her sadistic impulses, namely, ripping off the penis and also her mother's belly (the baby inside). This was also expressed in her remark, "Little Barbara was glad that I was cut on my stomach."

When we discussed why she distrusted her mother so, she asked, "Do you think this was so even before Jim was born?"

"Perhaps," I said, "but I am sure that Jim's birth had a lot to do with it."

"Yes," she said, "she took my penis away and gave it to Jim."

I was startled by this remark, made very casually. I collected myself quickly and said, "I see. And so this is why you are trying to get it back from him at all costs."

After a while, she asked, "Why should Little Barbara insist upon being a baby?" I suggested, "Maybe that's how she thinks she's forcing mother to attend to her, and in that way she takes Jim's place."

Speaking about Jim and the consideration her mother expected her to show to him, she remembered an incident. When Jim was very little, he had got caught between two dressers as she was watching over him. She got frightened and had to call her father to rescue him because she could not pull him out. She remembered the beating she received for it from her mother. "You know," Barbara said, "I think maybe it's not

4. One of my patients, suffering from a severe depression with psychosomatic manifestations, recalled how, as a little girl of five, she used to hold her dog close to her body, pretending it was her penis. Whenever she did that she was afraid of being caught by her mother, who she feared would punish her severely. This patient had two brothers. She was extremely jealous of the one 3 years her junior. During her analysis she developed pain and swelling in her ankle and she wore a bandage. Whenever her penis envy and her jealousy of her younger brother, which she had unconsciously displaced onto her younger son, were discussed, she registered her feelings in her ankle. At such times she would have the sensation that her leg was expanding and was throbbing (erection). After this had been analyzed her leg symptom disappeared and she discarded the bandage.

even the penis Little Barbara wants and thinks mother took away from her and gave to Jim. Maybe it's the breast or love, or something she took away from me and gave to him." She recalled that during her last hospitalization, when I was present at meal time, she had refused to eat and had taken only ice cream and milk; and that she whispered to me, "You know, babies drink only milk." [5]

III

Material brought out by the mother indicated that, although Barbara's feelings about her were exaggerated, there was some basis in the disturbed relationship of the parents. The mother revealed that her marriage was unhappy and sexually frustrating. She had married her husband, for whom she did not really care, only because her mother thought that he would be the right man for her. The husband was a rather sadistic fellow, she claimed, who showed little concern for her. He made sexual overtures to her, in the most unpredictable way—while visiting at her mother's or at her friend's. He would pull her away and force her to have sexual intercourse. As a matter of fact, she was frigid and never submitted to intercourse unless she was coerced. Barbara's concept of sexual intercourse, as a struggle between man and wife, can more readily be understood since we know that she had been a witness to such scenes. Some of her remarks bear this out: "She doesn't want to sleep with him", and "She kicks him".

The mother never slept in the same room with her husband. Before Jim's birth she had slept with Barbara, who resented it greatly when her mother began to sleep with Jim and put her into a room with her father. The mother recalled how infuriated she had been with Barbara's behavior, then 4 years old.

She related the following episode which illustrates Barbara's awareness of the relationship between her parents. One day when she was out shopping with Barbara, the butcher jokingly asked: "Do your mother and father fight?" And Barbara said, "Oh, yes, and my mother spits in his face," for which the mother gave her a terrific beating.

According to the mother, Barbara had always avoided any physical contact with her and antagonized her by preferring the grandmother, and even strangers, to her. At that time (age 4) she developed a facial tic that persisted until she became ill with ulcerative colitis; it reappeared as an intermediate symptom during the analysis and the dissolution of her ulcerative colitis. Her knuckle-cracking as well as picking

---

5. I cannot resist relating a little episode that reflects Barbara's fine analytic understanding. One day on entering the playroom she noticed a "piece of art" that another little patient had left. It showed two clay figures, one larger and one smaller, tied together on a clay boat. Barbara asked me what it was. "Well," I said, "You know we can't discuss what other patients do here." "Let me guess," she said, "This is a man and a little boy." "How can you tell," I asked her. "Don't you see what a big penis he has," and she pointed to the tall hat with a feather on the larger figure. "And he has one, too," she said, pointing to the smaller figure that was also wearing a similar hat. After a moment of thought, she said, "I was much worse off than he, because Little Barbara was mad at both of them" (mother and father). This little boy at least has his father with him.

and pulling at her skin also originated at that time. These were all manifestations of strongly repressed anger (rage). Barbara could not afford to go into fits of temper, because her mother would not tolerate them. She therefore had to repress and convert her sadistic impulses into symptoms. "I wouldn't let her grow up to be like one of my husband's family," her mother once said to me.

After the father's induction into the navy, Barbara, who was then 7½, was left alone in her room, while her mother continued to sleep with Jim. It was then that Barbara became ill with ulcerative colitis. Only after the mother caught herself becoming sexually excited on many occasions while sleeping with Jim did she sense the nature of her strong attachment for him. Preceding her husband's discharge from the navy, she decided to move Jim out of her bed and have him share Barbara's bedroom.[6]

As the mother brought this material, there was considerable improvement in her relationship with Barbara. Barbara, in turn, began to speak of things which, she explained, she had hitherto hesitated to reveal because she thought I might laugh at her, as her mother was prone to do. In her daydreams she saw herself as a dancer or an actress admired by others. Actually, she felt she would never be able to expose her abdomen and leg because of the scars, which were horrible to her. Her feeling changed markedly, however, when she recognized the association with masturbation.

She tought she would never be able to achieve any of her wishes in reality. I told her that it was "Little Barbara" who did not want her to achieve anything, but that by exercising her foot, she would be able to do anything she wished—dance or jump. She understood me. Soon her mother reported that Barbara was very persistent in training her foot. One day Barbara came in beaming, "You know, I won a contest in jumping rope today. I can jump rope and skate now just as well as any other girl on the block."

She also began to talk about her concrete difficulties. The prospect of school worried her. My suggestion that she get a tutor to help her

6. In relating this, she expressed anxiety at losing Jim's affection due to the necessity of devoting so much attention to Barbara. At least she had possessed Jim, had been sure of his love. But could she be sure of receiving Barbara's love? It seemed very important to her to feel that there was somebody who loved her and was completely dependent on her. She questioned her ability to experience deep feeling. She had become anxious about it when her father was seriously ill. She told me that she felt "like a heel" when everyone, even strangers, cried at the thought of his death while she could not shed a tear, nor feel anything at all. When others told her not to "take it too hard," she felt like a monster. Also, when Barbara was so ill, it was feared she might die, she stayed at her post "like a soldier" but apparently without feeling. When I interpreted that she was thereby over-reacting to her intense feeling, and fear of being swept away by these feelings should they come to consciousness, she opened up and told me she had been called "a cry baby" as a child. Now, she can cry only when alone, and usually for no tangible reason. It was possible to show her that she had projected onto Barbara her own fear of loss of control and that Barbara, through her display of uncontrolled behavior and masturbation, represented a threat to the mother's own balance. She also spoke of a fear of insanity, again projected onto Barbara. To rationalize her fear about Barbara, she gave the case of a girl she knew who had displayed peculiar behavior, and no one but she had suspected the girl insane. Now this girl is in a mental institution.

with math and spelling before returning to school was accepted by her and carried out by the mother.

IV

When the time for my vacation approached, both Barbara and her mother seemed worried about it. It was possible to help the mother understand that her feelings of insecurity, her fear that everything would go wrong, were a reaction to my leaving and that she, like Barbara, felt that I was deserting. Barbara's reaction expressed itself in physical symptoms. A few days before my departure she lost her appetite, felt tired and worried. The extent of her dependence on me was expressed by her need to see me the day I was leaving, as if to halt my departure. Barbara declared that not only was I leaving her but that she would have to put up with a tutor whom she did not like. She was apprehensive about going back to school before I returned. It was now exactly 2 months since Barbara had left the hospital.

Barbara did not write to me as she had promised. The mother, however, wrote to inform me that Barbara had been quite sick, but that the insight she had gained from me enabled her to handle the child. On my return, I learned that Barbara had complained of pain in the wrists and shoulders, so severe as to make her cry. She was not put to bed in spite of pain, fatigue and listlessness. In a sympathetic way the mother made light of it all—even took Barbara out thus avoiding any acknowledgment of illness. For several days Barbara had a series of aches—a severe pain in the knee, swelling of the ankle (where the ulcer had formerly appeared), and swelling and pain in the knuckles.[7]

Although the mother was upset, she managed to carry out the technique of reassurance without treating Barbara as sick. She was able to dissuade Barbara from using the bandage or wintergreen when her leg swelled, pointing out that there was apparently no value in it since the other pains and swellings had disappeared without treatment.

Two startling episodes of this period illustrate the degree of insight which the mother had achieved and the security which she felt in taking responsibility: When Barbara was still feeling so weak and tired that she could hardly walk, the mother took her to a movie, against the advice of relatives. On coming out of the movie, Barbara appeared energetic and completely well. On the day she had the swelling on her ankle, and ran a high temperature (105°), at Barbara's request her mother took her out on the bicycle she had received as compensation for the dog which had been stolen.[8]

7. These symptoms had appeared once before, during one of her attacks of ulcerative colitis. At that time a tentative diagnosis of rheumatic fever had been made. However, as all examinations for rheumatic fever had been negative (Barbara was then in the hospital), this diagnosis was dropped.

8. At a clinical conference at our hospital where I presented both the child and the mother to our pediatric staff, the mother explained to the staff that she had been able to handle these situations in the way described because she had convinced herself that I had put her on the right track and because she had been determined to prove to me that she was able to pull Barbara through without breaking down herself.

That Barbara was aware of the use she had made of her symptoms may be seen in her reaction to an accident in which her brother Jim fell and hurt his eye so that it became blackened and swollen. The mother was very worried about it, at which Barbara remarked: "You're too upset about it. He isn't going to die. You wouldn't worry about me like that." The mother, realizing that Barbara was jealous of the attention her brother was getting, explained that she was only doing for him what she would do for Barbara—taking him to the doctor to make sure that nothing serious had happened. Barbara's reply to this was, "So it wouldn't pay for me to have a black eye."

Barbara kept herself and her mother in suspense about going back to school. She decided, of her own accord, to return at the beginning of the term. The mother reported a very interesting incident which showed her understanding of Barbara and her ability to handle the situation successfully. On the first day of school the mother expected that Barbara would refuse to eat her lunch, because of excitement. However, contrary to her expectation, Barbara came home quite cheerfully asking for lunch. When the mother put the meal on the table Barbara asked to be fed. This the mother did not refuse! She started to feed her with a spoon, remarking pleasantly, "So you think that now you are going to school you are not my little girl anymore and that I won't care for you." Barbara began to laugh and said, "I can eat by myself."

V

When I saw Barbara she did not speak very much about having been sick while I was away. She was very casual about it, saying, "You know Little Barbara. You did leave her, didn't you? But," she added, "I showed her that I am Big Barbara after all, and she really doesn't bother me much."

She looked very well, told me how active she had been, and that she could now roller-skate as well as any child on her street. School still presented a difficult situation but Barbara seemed to feel confident that she would be able to cope with it since she had a tutor to help with her work. "It helps that Jim is going to school too," she said, implying he was not left at home with her mother anymore.

Barbara spoke about the stolen dog and expressed the feeling that he had "left" her,—that he had run away from her. Apparently the dog's disappearance had upset her, and she had therefore sustained a double loss, the analyst and the dog; this may have contributed in bringing on the symptoms previously described.

Barbara's readiness to react with specific physical symptoms to specific emotional stimuli may further be illustrated. For some time the mother had noted a change in Barbara's attitude toward her. In general, the relationship between them had again become tense. The mother herself told me she could not look straight at Barbara because she felt like "bashing her head in". She understood how Barbara felt and why she, in turn, could not look at her mother. The mother thought that Barbara was angry with her because she was giving more attention to Jim, who was then ill with the mumps.

One day, when the mother had scolded Jim and given him a spanking, Barbara said, "You wouldn't dare to beat me up." The mother said, "If you deserved it, I certainly would." Although she realized that Barbara was challenging her, she fell for Barbara's provocation and spanked her on the buttocks. Several days later Barbara complained that she could not sit, and upon examination the mother found that Barbara had a lump about the size of a fist on her buttock and that it was sensitive to touch. I advised the mother to apply a wet compress to the swelling and to minimize the importance of it to the child.

Barbara was very pleased to have the compress applied, and the next day the lump had gone down considerably, to about the size of a walnut.

When I saw Barbara, she showed me the "bump", in a casual manner, telling me that it had been much bigger, but had gone down. She did not attribute the improvement to the epsom salt compress but said, "It's because I caught Little Barbara in time." In discussing what was upsetting her she referred to her brother's mumps and also to the fact that she was not getting along too well with her mother. She expressed a fear that Little Barbara wanted to get her back to the hospital. In this connection we began to discuss masturbation. Barbara said that she had not been masturbating, adding, "When you speak about these things to me, you look like a witch."

The mother, however, told me that some time before, on entering Barbara's bedroom she had found her masturbating. Barbara seemed very frightened when caught and looked very guilty. The mother had made no threats on this occasion. But she remembered that when Barbara had complained of Jim's thumb-sucking, she had told Barbara she would rather see him do that than "something else". Barbara had apparently understood what she meant. The mother added that she watched Barbara a great deal, to observe whether she was masturbating. She apparently did not realize that Barbara sensed this, and that by her provocative behavior she was trying to find out whether her mother wanted to punish (castrate) her, or whether Barbara could trust her. Significant in this connection is the following: one day, Barbara asked her mother, "Who are you really?" Once before, Barbara had said to her mother, "You are like two people; only one is my mother." That night her mother overheard her saying, in her sleep (Barbara frequently talked in her sleep) again and again, in a pleading voice, "Please, mother, don't!"

This change in the quality of the relationship between Barbara and her mother, we came to understand as an expression of intense accumulated resentment in both. When Barbara's maternal grandfather died, she was permitted to sleep at her grandmother's house, assuming the role of guardian. She felt very important and enjoyed the experience. After a few days, however, her mother felt that Barbara was being indulged and would not allow her to sleep there. Barbara apparently felt this was a demotion from a position of responsibility. Although denying to me and to herself that she had been hurt, she told her mother that I had pointed out this was really the cause for her anger.

The mother complained she was overwhelmed by Barbara, and that both were slipping. At this point, I interpreted to her that in this incident of Barbara and her grandmother, she had been acting out her jealousy of her own mother as well as of Barbara. It was difficult at first for her to accept this. However, on reflection, she confirmed this interpretation by telling me that on entering her mother's bedroom and seeing her mother and Barbara in bed together, she "saw red". She expressed strong resentment toward her mother for having rejected and neglected her. She was able to recognize how frustrated she felt by Barbara, who instead of rewarding her mother (who had done so much for her), gave her love to the grandmother. She also realized that this was the very same feeling she had had when Barbara, as a very young child, showed preference for her grandmother. She suddenly understood Barbara's reacting with rage to a telephone conversation she had with a niece of whom she was very fond but of whom Barbara had always been very jealous.

VI

For years, Barbara had not gone to a dentist. She had a great number of cavities that needed treatment but was terrified of the dentist. We were able to analyze her fears as a projection of her own sadistic impulses, colored by sexual fears. This helped Barbara to accept dental treatment, even to the extent of going to the dentist's office by herself. She had an abscessed tooth which had to be extracted. Her reaction to this was traumatic, and revived intense resentment of her imagined castration, as well as her own sadistic castrative wishes. After analysis of this material, Barbara asked me to show her the "baby book" (a book with pictures of pregnant women, the birth process and the fetus), thus confirming that castration and giving birth, penis and baby, were interchangeable concepts to her. This material seems to be so revealing that I should like to report it in even greater detail:

Barbara had been disturbed for a few days after the extraction; she got up at night, asked to have the lights put on, and went to the bathroom. She spoke of her annoyance with her brother Jim, whose thumbsucking upset her and disturbed her sleep. Although Jim had always been a severe thumbsucker, significantly enough it was only at this point that it had begun to disturb Barbara. While she was talking to me about it, her own finger went into her mouth. When I drew her attention to this, she laughed and said, "I have one, too;" she had immediately made the association between finger and penis.

I said, "It seems that Little Barbara would also like to suck." She looked at me and answered, "But not the thumb. I have a funny idea. I think . . ." and she hesitated. "I think she would really like to suck a penis. You know," she went on, "the other day my father got very angry when I walked into the bathroom and he was just making. Since Sunday I have a stomach ache and have been running to the bathroom very often. I'm getting a stomach ache right now."

While discussing what had happened recently to make "Little Barbara" want to have a penis so badly again, she thought for a while and then said, "Do you know that I went to the dentist and had a tooth pulled out?" And she asked, "Can Little Barbara bring on an abscess of a tooth?"

In explaining her question she told me of her surprise at the sudden disappearance of the swelling, almost as soon as the tooth had been pulled. As mentioned before, we had discussed her fear of the dentist and understood it to be castration fear, closely related to her own sadistic castrative impulses (toward Jim). Now she remembered a nightmare she had had the night before:

"I, mother, father and Jim were walking on the street. I wanted to get on the trolley and broke my ankle (the one that had the ulcer). I had to go to the hospital and my leg had to be cut off. I had crutches and I couldn't walk. Jim was teasing me. I spit out all the food that I took in."

"Do you remember that Little Barbara thought the doctors would cut off my leg?" she asked me. "She didn't even want me to show it to you. She didn't trust you. She was glad that I was cut on my stomach" (the grafting).

"Why should she have felt like that?" I asked. "Are you still afraid of the things that will happen to you when you play with yourself?"

"Since you told me that nothing could happen to me," she said, "I'm not even doing it anymore."

She went on to tell me that when Jim was very little, 2 or 3 years of age, she would masturbate in his presence and ask him to do it too. "But he couldn't see anything in it." She used to think of what married people do. The thought of kissing was very exciting to her.

She summed up her dream with the following remark: "It seems Little Barbara won't rest until I have my leg cut off. Do I just want Jim's penis," she asked, "or any old boy's?" She answered herself, "Mother didn't give my penis to any old boy, but to Jim."

Several weeks later Barbara herself was able to interpret the connection between her disturbance and the dentist. She told me that she had received a note from him informing her that he was back from his vacation and could resume treatment. In a very dramatic session that day, Barbara revealed her most secret masturbation fantasy.[9] She was actually trembling with excitement and at one point, in fixing the collar of my blouse, she got panicky and could not speak for a while. She then told me she had had an impulse to choke me when her hand was close to my neck. But now she was not afraid of Little Barbara any more and could tell me everything. And she really poured forth! She travelled all through her analysis and reminded me of a dream she had told me in the very beginning of our association. In this dream she had asked first me, and then her mother, to explain something about soldiers and sailors. (Her father had been a sailor at that time.) But neither her mother nor I would help her. She vomited and had to go to the hospital.

9. It was dramatically brought out to me by Barbara, how essential it is to analyze the oedipal conflict in a patient, as deeply as possible, whether the patient is a child or an adult.

She indicated that had we understood this dream, it might not have been necessary for her to be so sick. We could understand now that this dream, as well as the nightmare in which she had her leg amputated and spit out all the food, dealt with her oedipal wishes orally expressed.[10]

Her masturbation fantasy was also an oral one: There are two boys and each shows her his penis, which she kisses. She asked me again whether it was possible to have a baby in that way, saying, "But a little boy can't do it anyway." Her question, "Whose penis do I really want?", she could now understand to mean not only Jim's penis, which she thought her mother had taken away from her and given to him, but also her father's penis (baby), which he gave to her mother and not to her. Barbara understood that spitting and vomiting meant the undoing of the incestuous impregnation and that it also meant childbirth. At the end of this session, Barbara said, "We did some cleaning today."

The effect of this catharsis was amazing. When Barbara came out of my office, after this session, she hugged her mother, telling her that she loved her and that she was so happy she did not know what to do. This demonstrative behavior was unusual for Barbara. That night she ate ravenously.

The striking change that took place in Barbara's personality with the working through of this material can best be evaluated in the light of Barbara's remark to her mother: "I will not go to the hospital this winter and not next winter. I won't go at all. You know when I will go to the hospital again—when I have a baby." This was the first time that Barbara openly expressed her willingness to be a girl, a woman, a mother. She had always said, "I will never get married or have any children." In school, too, she was able to establish a very good relationship with the children and the teacher, and was chosen president of the class. This pleased her greatly.

The mother's feeling for Barbara may be seen from her own statement: "She is openly affectionate to me. It is remarkable how well she is able to analyze her sudden changes of mood and to overcome them just as quickly. I should never have believed that such a change was possible, or have I changed, too? I couldn't wish for Barbara to be any better, physically and in every other respect. The other day, when I got excited, Barbara said, 'All right, take it easy; we don't have to fight.'"

One day, Barbara, who had become quite friendly with boys and enjoyed the attention they were giving her, told her mother a dirty joke. When Barbara's little friend came in and learned that Barbara had told this joke to her mother, the friend blushed. At this, Barbara said, "Oh, I can say these things to my mother. You can trust her; she understands."

SUMMARY AND CONCLUSIONS

In examining the causative factors in Barbara's illness, I feel that the relationship with her mother was of primary importance. In her

---

10. Vomiting with severe anorexia and abdominal pain had been an outstanding symptom of her colitis.

case, and this is probably typical, there existed an unconscious rapport between Barbara and her mother. Barbara reacted to her mother's unconscious hostility, characterized by ambivalence and, at times, open sadistic attitudes, with an increase of sadism and narcissism, accompanied by an unconscious obedience, almost as though she *had to do* what she felt her mother unconsciously wanted her to do. "All right, you want me to be sick; I'll be sick but you'll be sorry," Barbara once actually said to her mother preceding the onset of the leg ulcer. One day when her mother admonished her to be careful and not to fall on crossing the slippery street, Barbara's reaction was, "Please don't tell me this or I'll have to fall." Her mother's mention of the possibility of falling was to Barbara a suggestion or, rather, a command to fall. She was reacting to her mother's unconscious wish that she fall and not to the counter cathexis in the form of a concern about her falling.

Thus, in unconscious obedience, she also fulfilled her mother's castration threats, namely, that "It would get rotten, foul, and fall off," or as Barbara expressed it, "Little Barbara won't rest until I have my leg cut off." When the mother found Barbara masturbating, following the recurrence of the leg ulcer, the mother had not only repeated the masturbation threats but specifically said, "It will make your leg worse; it won't let it heal." To Barbara this meant that her leg would have to come off; thus the threat precipitated the last recurrence of the ulcer.

The choice of the leg as a representation of the penis in the unconscious is a rather common phenomenon in neurotic women, especially those with exhibitionistic tendencies. This was true of Barbara, who had very strong exhibitionistic feelings about her legs, manifested in her desire to be admired as a dancer, and in her extreme feelings of frustration that she would not be able to exhibit her leg because of the scars.

Other unconscious forces motivating Barbara may be seen in her resentment toward her mother and her jealousy and envy of her brother. Barbara's emotional development had been severely affected by the mother's neurotic need to fight her own undesirable impulses (including her hatred of her husband and his family), by projecting them onto Barbara. According to the mother, Barbara "never smiled and always used to shy away" from her. This very unsatisfactory relationship was shattered almost beyond repair by the birth of Barbara's brother Jim, when Barbara was about 4 years of age. Barbara reacted to this with manifestly neurotic symptoms, such as facial tics, knuckle-cracking, picking at her nails and skin. However, she still had her father, with whom she now shared the bedroom while her mother took Jim into her room. The fact that this happened at the height of the oedipal conflict only increased Barbara's difficulties, namely, through an over-exposure to her father, which evoked wishes and expectations that could not be fulfilled. After her father's induction into the navy, she felt completely deserted and soon after developed the first signs of ulcerative colitis.

In the organic symptoms, the extraordinary degree of repressed sadism was turned masochistically toward her own self. The pronounced narcissism made it difficult for her to tolarate any psychic tension for any length of time. Since to feel an impulse meant to act it out immediately, Barbara could not afford to be conscious of her sadistic impulses but had to release them in physical symptoms.

When, through analysis, the sadism contained in the symptoms of ulcerative colitis was released, Barbara for the first time in her life experienced and exhibited signs of severe anxiety. This anxiety is in proportion to the severer sadism of such a patient, and quantitatively different from similar occurrences in conversion hysteria. It was at this phase of her analysis that she changed from the symptom of ulcerative colitis to the symptom of ulcer of the leg. This was a definite indication that Barbara, at this point, was not yet able to tolerate her sadistic impulses, but had to act them out immediately in physical symptoms. "If I feel like doing something terrible to Jim or my mother, isn't it better I do it to myself?" she once asked me in a state of severe anxiety preceding the onset of the ulcer of her leg.

The guilt feeling and anxiety of the mother provided Barbara with sadistic satisfaction; "I am sick but it is your fault," and provided her with the justification for releasing sadism toward her mother. It was, therefore, essential to treat the mother simultaneously in order to deprive Barbara of this gain which made her illness worthwhile.

Barbara's wish for a penis and her reactive castrative tendencies would appear to be the manifestations of the phallic phase. Closer analysis, however, revealed them to be of a pregenital nature both in regard to the object and to the mechanism applied in securing this object. To Barbara, in her own words, the penis stood for the "breast", "love", or "something" that mother took away from her and gave to the brother. It was something essential to life, as is the breast or mother's love to an infant. The means for regaining it were also infantile, namely, biting, scratching, clawing. These are expressions of oral sadism and perhaps of an even earlier sadistic phase preceding the development of teeth and characterized by scratching as the first sadistic activity of the child.

In the ulcerative colitis the orally incorporated object (breast, baby—Jim, penis) had been eliminated through hemorrhagic transudation and ulceration of the mucous membrane of the colon. After this had been made conscious to her she changed the locus of elimination from the colon to the leg, while the mode remained the same, namely, hemorrhagic transudation and ulceration of the skin. The minor ulcerations that Barbara had on her thigh or her abdomen (where the skin for the graft had been taken) were of a completely different nature. They were the result of scratching and represented means of acquiring the object by ripping it off or clawing it. The hemorrhagic transudation and ulceration of both the mucous membrane of the colon or of the skin on the leg, however, were expressions of restitution and elimination of the sadistically incorporated object, which, on different levels, was either the breasts, the baby (Jim), or the penis.

The element of somatic compliance that is always present in conversion, whether hysterical or pregenital, showed itself in Barbara's case in the readiness to form a serous-hemorrhagic transudate into the mucous membrane and skin with necrosis. Psychogenic skin ulcers beginning with inflammation and ending with necrosis have been observed by Werther, Stern, Bunnemann, and others. The psychogenic nature was established beyond a doubt. They could be produced and cured by suggestion. The association of ulcerative colitis with swelling of the joints has been observed by Cullinan, Sullivan, and others. Skin lesions in association with ulcerative colitis have been observed by Bargen (2). Barbara, however, is the first child in whom it was possible to study these phenomena psychoanalytically for almost 3 years.

BIBLIOGRAPHY

1. Abraham, K. "A Short Study of the Development of the Libido", and "The First Pregenital Stage of the Libido", Selected Papers, Hogarth, 1927.
2. Bargen, J. A. The Management of Colitis, Nat. Med. Book Co., 1935, 62–69.
3. Barinbaum, M. "Eine vorläufige Mitteilung über die Bedeutung der Freudschen Psychoanalyse für die Dermatologie", Dermat. Wchnschr., 95, 1932, 1060–1067.
4. Bolten, G. C. "Vom 'hysterischen Oedem' ", Deutsche Ztschr. f. Nervenh., 73, 1922, 319–328.
5. Bunnemann, O. "Über psychogene Dermatosen. Eine biologische Studie, zugleich ein Beitrag zur Symptomatologie der Hysterie", Ztschr. f. d. ges. Neurol. u. Psychiat., 78, 1922, 115–152.
6. Cullinan, E. R. "Ulcerative Colitis: Clinic Aspects", Brit. Med. J., II, 1938, 1351–1356.
7. Doswald, D. D. und Kreibich, K. "Zur Frage der posthypnotischen Hautphänomene", Monatshefte f. prakt. Dermat. 43, 1906, 634–640.

8. Dunbar, F. *Emotion and Bodily Changes.* Columbia Univ. Press, 1938.

9. Fenichel, O. *The Psychoanalytic Theory of Neurosis,* Norton, 1945.

10. Freud, A. Introduction to Technique of Child Analysis, *Imago,* 1946.

11. Freud, S. "Three Contributions to the Theory of Sex", *Basic Writings of Sigmund Freud,* ed. A. A. Brill, Modern Library, 1938.

12. Heilig, R., und Hoff, H. "Über psychogene Entstehung des Herpes Labialis", *Med. Klin.,* 24, 1928, 1472.

13. Heller, F., und Schultz, J. H. "Über einen Fall von hypnotisch erzeugter Blasenbildung", *München. Med. Wchnschr.* 56, 1909, 2112.

14. Hug-Hellmuth, H. von. *A Study of the Mental Life of the Child,* Nerv. Ment. Dis. Mon., 29, 1919.

15. Mayr, J. K. "Psychogenese von Hautkrankheiten", *Zentralbl. f. Haut- u. Geschlechtskr.,* 23, 1927, 1–22.

16. O'Donovan, W. J. *Dermatological Neuroses,* Kegan Paul, Trench Trubner, 1927.

17. Sack, W. T. "Die Haut als Ausdrucksorgan", *Arch. f. Dermat. u. Syph.* 151, 1926, 200–206 (14. Kongr. d. Deutsch. Dermatol. Ges., 1925).

18. Schilder, P. "Remarks on the Psychophysiology of the Skin", *Psa. Rev.,* XXIII, 1936.

19. Schindler, R. *Nervensystem und spontane Blutungen. Mit besonderer Berücksichtigung der hysterischen Ecchymosen und der Systematik der hämorrhagischen Diathesen,* Karger, 1927, 68 pp. (Abhandl. a. d. Neurol. Psychiat., Psychol. u. ihren Grenzgeb. Heft 1942).

20. Sperling, M. "Psychoanalytic Study of Ulcerative Colitis in Children", *Psa. Quar.,* XV, 1946.

21. Stern, F. "Zur Frage der psychogenen Dermatosen", *Ztschr. f. d. ges. Neurol. u. Psychiat.,* 79, 1922, 218–253.

22. Sullivan, A. J. "Ulcerative Colitis of Psychogenic Origin. A Report of Six Cases", *Yale J. Biol. Med.,* IV, 1932, 779–796.

23. Szollosy, L. von. "Ein Fall von multipler neurotischer Hautgangrän in ihrer Beziehung zur Hypnose", *München. Med. Wchnschr.,* 54, 1907, 1034–5.

24. Werther, J. "Über hysterische Hautnekrose mit erythematosem und exsudativem Vorstadium", *Dermat. Ztschr.* 18, 1911, 341–348.

25. Werther, J. "Die psychogenen Dermatosen", *Ztschr. f. ärztl. Fortbild.,* 26, 1929, 341–346.

METHODS USED IN THE EDUCATION
OF MOTHERS

A Contribution to the Handling and Treatment of Developmental Difficulties in Children Under Five Years of Age

By LYDIA JACOBS (London) [1]

In recent years increasing attention has been paid to the importance of educating mothers of young children. Two aspects of such work have been described: Education of parents in a general way as a prophylactic measure, and work with individual mothers who ask for assistance in dealing with a developmental phase in an individual child. Fries (3) has emphasised the former aspect. Ruben and Thomas (4) have described work with individual mothers referred to them for a particular difficulty. During the last 2 years the writer has had the opportunity of working with individual mothers of infants and young children who have been referred to her because of some difficulty in development. The mothers have been interviewed either in the local Maternity and Child Welfare Clinic which the writer attends each week, or in the Child Guidance Clinic of which she is a member of the staff.

The general aim of interviews with these mothers has been to give them knowledge on which to base a change in their handling of the child, in such a way that the child can take a step forward in ego development. In some cases no more is required of the mother than a change in the handling of a particular situation, while in other cases much more has been required, as for instance, the interpretation of unconscious conflicts in order to bring about a change in the structure of the child's personality. In these cases the mother is fulfilling the role of the therapist. The mothers attend either of the Clinics for an hour without the child and are seen at weekly or fortnightly intervals. Certain theoretical questions arise from work of this kind which it is the object of this article to discuss:

I. What is the content of interviews of this kind? What methods are used by the worker to achieve her aim?

1. From the West Sussex Child Guidance Service.

II. What are the dynamic factors which appear to make possible this method of treating children at this early age through treatment of their parents, and not, on the whole, in the latency period?

III. What are the limitations of this method with reference to the cases that cannot be dealt with in this way?

I. *The content of the interviews and the methods used*

The content of the interviews and the methods used vary according to the problem for which the mother has sought help, and to the mother's personality. Examples will be given of three different types of cases:

a) Feeding difficulties, the problem for which the largest number of children were referred;

b) A night fear in a 2½-year-old boy, a typical developmental difficulty, handled adequately by a stable mother;

c) A more complex behaviour disorder in a 3½-year-old girl handled by a less stable mother.

a) Feeding difficulties.

In the majority of cases the children referred with feeding difficulties were between 10 and 24 months of age and the difficulties were mainly associated with the conflicts of the anal phase of libido development. Interviews with individual mothers of these children have proceeded along very similar lines and the method used in the successful cases can be summarised in the following way:

The feeding difficulties were all of short duration, matters of only months or weeks. Similar situations were described; the child just isn't interested; the mother has tried everything, starting with cajoling and coaxing and ending with an intense battle, the child eating less than ever, the mother's anxiety mounting. The mother then, on someone's advice, has tried what she calls "ignoring the child"; her attempts at this she admits to be half-hearted because she is too worried that the child will starve. She arrives at the Clinic wanting an explanation, and, as many mothers have put it, "ready to try anything". Having appreciated the extent of the mother's anxiety and gained a full picture of the situation, it is often possible to give the following information in the first interview. One can tell the mother that feeding difficulties often occur in relation to training in cleanliness (1). This relationship can be described in detail; how the child transfers his attitude from feces to food, and that this is the result of the necessary reaction-formation against the child's pleasure in dirt. The particular difficulty can then be discussed from this angle. Each of the mothers brought further information and confirmation of their children's disgust for gravy or mashed-up foods, and intense and sudden dislike of sticky hands. Discussion then centres around why this phase has persisted and now become a real problem; this involves consideration of the mother-child relationship and how the child, finding his temporary lack of interest in food provokes a great deal of response, uses the feeding situation in order to express his conflict with his mother, and vice versa.

Following discussion on these lines the mother is asked what she feels should be done to alter the situation. At this stage she is liable to ask the worker for advice, and it seems important to withhold any definite advice and leave it to the mother to work out the details for herself. It is often necessary to explain this to the mother telling her that one can only discuss methods of dealing with the problem in theory. It often happens that the mothers prescribe the right methods themselves. Following their comments one can suggest that the child should be treated like a distinguished guest; his likes and dislikes accepted, no comments made on how, or in what order, he eats, etc. The object should be for the mother to remove herself from the situation altogether so that the child's own instinct to eat can be unimpaired by other instincts, as for instance aggression against the mother. Certain difficulties have to be pointed out here, for instance that the result will not be evident for perhaps a week or longer; that the child, if left to his own devices, may use his fingers and this may be difficult to tolerate. Finally, the mother should be prepared for a good deal of worry during the initial period, and be told that she can have further discussions if she does not wish to tackle the experiment yet.

The content of four interviews with Mrs. W. will illustrate some of the above points, her problem being typical of the mothers of this group of children. N., now 12 months, has been "right off his food" for eight weeks. Until eight weeks ago he had been a good eater and Mrs. W. had been proud of his all-round development. A few days before he began to refuse his food Mrs. W. had bought him an anti-splash pot to which he had strongly objected, "going stiff" each time she had tried to force him to use it. Since then she had been engaged in battle with him over his potting and feeding. Meals, she said, were a nightmare; N. spat his food out, "went stiff" and finally vomited as she tried to force it down. Often he swept his arms around knocking the food onto the floor. As she put it, "I feel so defeated and stupid." This feeling was enhanced by the attitude of her 5-year-old boy who sat watching the battle, fascinated, until his meal got cold and he had to be coaxed; in the end she found herself too distracted to enjoy her own meal.

The anti-splash pot was the key to this problem. Mrs. W., a vital, attractive woman from a middle-class family, admitted that she is "a terribly fussy person"; very house-proud, and known to all her friends as extremely fastidious. She welcomed the anti-splash pot as "a wonderful idea" because occasionally with the other pot some urine went on the carpet. No doubt her introduction of this pot to N. was accompanied by remarks about being "nice and clean" and "good". Her description of the feeding and potting were accompanied throughout the first interview by semi-humourous remarks about how it all disgusted her.

At the end of the first interview Mrs. W. was given an impression of the change in the mother-child relationship which takes place toward the end of the first year. The divergence between the child's and the adult's attitude to dirt was particularly stressed. This led to further observations of how N. could not stand sticky hands in the last few weeks, and his special dislike of mashed foods or gravy, while at the same time he appeared unconcerned about wetting and soiling and had to have his hands held down at meals to stop him from plunging them into his milk and vegetables. Mrs. W.'s interest was aroused and she immediately began to wonder how she could change the situation. She realised that she would have to stop forcing N. to eat and allow him to experiment with his fingers; she thought the new pot would have to be abandoned. Discussion of how especially difficult this would be for someone like Mrs. W., who was so particularly sensitive to messes, was encouraged.

A week later Mrs. W. arrived laughing and saying how dreadful the mess was and that she was the last person who should be expected to stand it! She described the week's events dramatically; how N. ate nothing the first day and swept the food on the floor looking at Mrs. W. at the same time; clearly, she thought, to see what she would do. She was proud to report that she had restrained her feelings, and that this did not occur again. By the end of the week N. had started to ask for certain foods to which in the past he had shown total indifference. She had taken care not to mash the food and to avoid gravy, and where possible he was helping himself. Mrs. W.'s main feeling was, "It's a relief to be doing something about it," and it was wonderful to get on with her own dinner. Her older son was so astonished by her changed attitude that he commented all the time, and finally arrangements were made for N. and Mrs. W. to have their dinner at another time.

The old pot was reinstituted, but now N. had to be forced to sit on it, in the course of which he bit Mrs. W. She took this as an example of her wrong handling and decided herself that it was useless to proceed with potting until their relationship improved. She quickly understood that she should really wait until N. could sit and stand up on his own. During this interview there was discussion about disgust as a reaction-formation against the pleasure in dirt. On the basis of Mrs. W.'s inquiries about the inconsistencies in N.'s attitude to dirt it was explained how this attitude gets transferred to food.

During the next interviews Mrs. W. described N.'s positive interest in food and his pleasure in handling it. She mentioned how she used to wipe his mouth after every rejected spoonful. She felt she no longer had cause to worry, and she gave many examples of general improvement in their relationship. Her attitude to the feeding and habit training now betrayed an interesting mixture of intense pleasure and disgust; she told, smilingly, and with evident pleasure, of how N. soiled his cot. She said in many ways it thrilled her to watch him playing with his food. She emphasised how surprised her friends and relatives were that she could stand the new feeding method, and she seemed to be enjoying the situation enormously. It appeared necessary to encourage her to continue with the training to cleanliness, since her apparent enjoyment of N.'s messes was preventing her from showing him her preference for clean nappies.

This case has been described in some detail since it illustrates the close relationship between strict habit training, and feeding difficulties, so typical in the histories of feeding problems in children of this age. It also indicates the nature of the mother's reaction-formation and its effect on the handling of these situations, which resulted in the problem for which she came for assistance.

b) The handling of a night fear in a 2½-year-old boy.

J.'s mother was able to use the knowledge she obtained in a very skillful manner to analyse her boy's night fear. This was achieved in fortnightly interviews over a period of months. Mrs. L. was a rather serious and intelligent woman with an only child in whom she vested all her interest since, although she lived with her husband, the marriage was not satisfactory. Mrs. L. had been in the habit of offering constant reassurance to the boy, and comforting him at night. When she had learned that reassurance could not allay the fear, she set herself the task of finding out its real nature. In stages J. told her that he was afraid of a lady who had no arms and who was coming to bite his hands off. A few weeks later Mrs. L. had a discussion with J. in the evening about how they got angry with each other that morning when J. remarked that the lady was not his Mummy but "Tiggy's" Mummy (Tiggy being his nickname), she had arms and legs, she was very angry and going to bite him. Further encouragement to verbalise his aggression against his parents led to a change in the fantasy; he told of what he called another lady who was going to bite Mummy and Daddy.

At this period J. became more aggressive and quite often actually bit Mrs. L. He talked about his "Little John" (his name for his genital) comparing it to his father's, and constantly inquired whether Mrs. L. had one too, and could not be convinced that her genitals were different. One day in the bath he inquired whether Mrs. L. had a penis, and pushed his penis in between his legs saying his was gone now, too. Mrs. L. asked him whether he thought she had had one, and he said she had but it was cut off. Following this conversation no more was heard of the "Lady". In the course of discussion of this fantasy Mrs. L. gained considerable understanding and was able to interpret the "Lady" in terms of J.'s castration anxiety.

One day Mrs. L. reported, "A perfectly dreadful thing has happened." J. had been angry and had hit her face; his thumb had gone into her mouth by mistake, and she had bitten him, by mistake. This was apparently a traumatic situation for both of them. J. ran around howling "Mummy *did* bite me." For several nights after he again complained of the lady coming to bite him, but he didn't have to search the room to find her, and Mrs. L. did not think his fear was as genuine as it had been before. In the same interview Mrs. L. remembered that the night fear began on the evening of a day when he commented on a china ornament of a lady without arms and legs which he had seen before in a friend's house.

In following interviews it became clear that J. was "playing up his fears." He did not seem afraid at night any longer, but when he was put to bed he would say, "I'll cry if you don't tell me two stories," and seemed to try to produce an interesting fantasy for his mother. One night

he simulated a fear of the rain, saying that the rain drops would hurt
his cheeks.

At the same time it seemed that Mrs. L. was becoming more interested in recovering the child's fantasies than in helping him to modify
his instinctive urges. She allowed J. to become very excited in the
evenings, to the extent of giving him a saw to take to bed so he could saw
his cot; she felt he needed some consolation for the separation from her.
She failed to discourage him from coming to the living room in the late
evening to satisfy his curiosity, and had great difficulty in getting him
back to bed. Mrs. L. found it hard to understand that some instinctive
desires can never be fully gratified, particularly oedipal wishes, and that
modification of them has to take place. This difficulty was probably
associated with her own conflicts and her dissatisfaction with her
husband.

Following Mrs. L.'s understanding of the need for education she
reported that J. seemed happier altogether and the trouble at night had
completely stopped. Follow-up interviews showed that J. was developing
very satisfactorily, and Mrs. L. brought interesting material regarding his
masturbation fantasies, particularly his oedipal wishes. She remained
rather over-interested.

c) The handling of a behaviour disorder in a 3½-year-old girl.

S. was referred to the clinic because of negative and inhibited behaviour, severe constipation and feeding difficulties. In a brief initial
interview with the worker the child was unable to separate from her
mother or to speak or play. Mrs. B. was a pale, delicate looking little
woman in the early thirties, shy and short-sighted. She wore a scarlet
coat, spoke in a brusque manner and appeared to react to anxiety by an
aggressive attitude. In contrast to the other mothers discussed, she
struck one immediately as a hysterical type. She lived in a working class
community with her husband, a labourer, and a boy of 3 months. A girl
had been born when S. was 20 months and had died of pneumonia
6 months later.

At the onset of treatment Mrs. B.'s attitude to S. was quite rigid.
She accused the child of disobedience and lying, and of having no love
for anyone. She recognised an element of defiance in her refusal to
complete a meal. Her main feeling about the constipation was that of
intense interest and worry. She clearly took pleasure in describing the
child's bowel movements in minute detail. She gave her a laxative
daily and devoted a great deal of thought to her medication. One had
the impression that this preoccupation with the child's bowels represented the strength of her own anal interests.

Mrs. B. established a strong positive relationship with the worker
in the first interview and attended the clinic punctually ten times over
a period of 5 months. In the second interview the feeding difficulty was
discussed with Mrs. B., since she already appeared to have some insight
into this; she changed her handling of it with good results and the
question was not discussed again until the fifth month when S. appeared
to be overeating for a short period. Mrs. B.'s success with the eating
encouraged her, and she was able to report and understand S.'s comment

to a neighbour, "Mummy doesn't make me eat now, so I don't eat anything."

S.'s "lies" were also discussed at this stage, and Mrs. B. began to express her guilt when it was pointed out to her that small children are entitled to fantasies, and some confusion with reality. She felt she had always been too strict and described how she restricted S. in almost every field of her activity. It was suggested to Mrs. B. that perhaps she had to be so strict because she worried a lot about something, maybe she feared that S. would not grow up right. Mrs. B. then told how she had contracted infantile paralysis at 10 months, as a result of which her right arm was slightly withered. She said it had been a cloud over all of her childhood, mainly because it prevented her from being able to stand on her hands, as the boys did. She also never understood the cause of it; one idea was that her mother had damaged her arm by lifting her up. As soon as she married she consulted doctors about the possibilities of transmitting the deformity to her children. Although she was reassured, she still believed that S. might have been affected, and that idea had made her so worried and angry if S. climbed or was active. It was clear that Mrs. B. still believed that she was actively infected; she expressed great surprise when told the nature of the illness. Throughout the first interviews Mrs. B. constantly asked for advice about the constipation. Each time she was told that it would be necessary to understand more about S., and that the worker was not worried about the constipation.

After three interviews Mrs. B. brought material about S.'s fantasies. She had now become interested in them and was encouraging them. They contained indications of S.'s hostility to the baby and of her sexual curiosity. Questions of ambivalence were discussed with Mrs. B., as well as the giving of sexual information, so far denied to S. Mrs. B. raised the subject with S., of how babies come, understood the child's initial denial of interest, and finally managed to discuss the matter satisfactorily. At this stage Mrs. B. was finding S. easier to handle; she was less negative and the relationship between them had already changed. S.'s next fantasies were about people getting hurt, and in particular having their ears cut off. She was found one day examining her genitals and comparing them with the baby's, remarking that she had a "Tiggy" like baby. Mrs. B. handled this very well, telling S. that she did not have a "Tiggy" like the baby, but that she would be able to have babies when she grew up. She had appreciated S.'s wish to be a boy.

At this stage Mrs. B. reported a change in S.'s cooperative behaviour. S. suddenly became overtly aggressive against Mrs. B., and seemed to do "everything to annoy". Included in this was constant eating of sand which Mrs. B. told her would produce a lump in her tummy! She told Mrs. B. that she had swallowed a hair slide, which it seemed was probably a fantasy. During this fortnight her fantasies were largely concerned with an imaginary boy whose name was the same as the baby's. When Mrs. B. asked her to do something she refused and shouted the commands at the boy. Sometimes the boy was her imaginary baby, toward whom she was extremely dominating. It seemed that S.'s hostility to Mrs. B. could be understood in terms of her wish for a penis, which she felt Mrs. B. had denied to her. It seemed doubtful whether Mrs. B. could succeed with an interpretation of this kind on account of her own penis envy. However, she appeared to understand the explanation of S.'s hostility in these terms. She gave the interpretation to S., and returned the following fortnight to report that their good relationship had been reestablished.

Mrs. B. in a later interview reported the following conversation about the baby girl who had died, and whom she had never before discussed with S. Mrs. B. had raised the subject herself.

S.: "God took her away."

Mrs. B.: "Why?"

S.: "Because His Mother told Him to."

Mrs. B.: "Why did she?"

S.: "She told God L. mustn't stay anymore in the house with that little girl."

Mrs. B.: "Perhaps the little girl didn't love her much."

S., promptly: "Yes, the little girl loved her but Mummy didn't love her."

Mrs. B. understood this as a projection on S.'s part.

During this interview Mrs. B. told of the change in S.'s relationship to her father. She had mentioned in the first interview how S. would not allow her father to kiss her, and how angry she became if Mr. and Mrs. B. were affectionate to each other. In the past weeks S. had become affectionate to her father, and very often told Mrs. B. that when she grew up she would have a Daddy of her own but she would want *her* Daddy as well.

At this stage Mrs. B. again referred to the constipation. The previous fortnight she had pressed the worker for advice on medication. She said she had not given S. any medicine for 5 weeks now, and that S. had movements only about once a week. She was still worried about it, but since the worker was not concerned as to whether S. had laxatives or not, Mrs. B. thought she might as well stop giving them. Later in the same interview Mrs. B. described the baby's death in detail, expressing intense feelings of guilt about it. Although the death certificate stated that the baby died of bronchial pneumonia Mrs. B. said she had always believed the death was caused by a fit. A few days after the death she had asked a nurse the cause of fits and been told that it was over-feeding and constipation. She was certain the baby had not been over-fed, so she concluded that the cause of death must have been constipation. From this, Mrs. B. went on to discuss her infantile paralysis. She said she had felt quite different about it since she had last discussed it at the clinic. She no longer believed she was still infected, and at the same time she had lost her self-conscious feeling about it. She had been so conscious of her arm that she had told her in-laws she was left-handed in order that they should not know. She felt intensely embarrassed when meeting strangers lest they find out.

Following this interview Mrs. B. seemed to lose her worry about the constipation. She gave no more laxatives, and said that sometimes she even forgot to inquire into the details of S.'s bowel movements. During the week before the interview she had taken some notice and found that S. had been having a movement every day. It seemed that Mrs. B.'s fantasies about her illness had been associated with having fits, and that really both were caused by constipation. From Mrs. B.'s remarks one could infer that her upbringing had been strict and one could guess that her illness at ten months may have resulted in a breakdown of habit training with a consequent intensification of her anal interests during the following months.

At the end of the 5 months of treatment the relationship between Mrs. B. and S. appeared to have been established on a satisfactory basis. S. had become active and increasingly independent, and able to hold her own with other children. The worker had another interview with S. at the completion of treatment. She was then a friendly, active child, able to separate from her mother without difficulty, and to talk and play throughout the interview. One could imagine her entering school in a few months without difficulty. Mrs. B. continued to attend at monthly, and then bi-monthly periods for follow-up interviews. She reported that improvement was sustained, and became interested in discussing the upbringing of the baby with whom she wanted to avoid the mistakes she had made with S.

The most important factor in this case was the mother's ability to form a good relationship with the worker. Her personality was more unstable than the other mothers so far referred to, but it appeared that her positive transference compensated for this, or may even have been enhanced by her somewhat hysterical make-up. There was a strong element of identification indicated by the ease with which she took over the worker's attitude from the beginning, in spite of the totally different attitude with which she came to the clinic. This was also shown by her remark that she did not have to worry about the constipation if the worker did not worry.

From this case, and from work with other mothers with this type of disturbance one can conclude that an unstable mother does not in itself make work of this kind impossible. The limits appear to be set by the type of the mother's disturbance. This will be discussed below.

Another factor appears to be the relative superficiality of the child's disturbance, although the picture gained at first indicated a more severe disturbance, with the possible establishment of a neurotic conflict. Because of this, during the first weeks the worker had in mind the need for direct therapy with the child. It seems however that the child's main conflicts were still between her own instinctive demands and a prohibiting environment. Had this not been the case it seems unlikely that the child would have changed in so short a time, or responded to the methods described above.

It may be noted that the methods used in the three cases described have certain factors in common, although the fields of discussion varied. The most important factor appears to be the establishment of a positive relationship without which work of this kind cannot be undertaken; therefore the achievement of this in the first interview is the writer's first aim in work with these mothers. Where there are indications for a negative transference an attempt is made to counteract it by means other than interpretation, since it seems that transference interpretations are to be avoided in work of this kind. In the case of Mrs. W., the establishment of a positive relationship was made easier by her real and genuine wish for help. Mrs. L., being a rather isolated person, grasped the opportunity for a contact. In addition, she had a real interest in child psychology and her intellectual interest was aroused. The nature of Mrs. B.'s relationship with the worker has already been referred to. A more detailed consideration of the dynamics of relationship would not be appropriate in this paper.

Another common factor is that although in each case the mothers, naturally, indicated their personal problems, no attempt was made to deal with them as such. It seems important that no such attempt should be made in interviews of this nature, since experience shows that one is liable to meet a resistance which may disturb the positive relationship; in addition the mother has not consulted the Clinic about her problems. Where a mother shows definite neurotic traits, and a wish for psychological treatment, the worker can refer her to an adult out-patient clinic. Mrs. L. was not, therefore, encouraged to discuss her marital relationship, and care was taken not to press Mrs. B. to reveal her deeper fantasies concerning her illness. It seems that one can refer to the mother's problems only in so far as they have a direct and conscious bearing on the child's. This does not exclude the use of knowledge of the mother's unconscious conflicts in the ways implied in the case material, as for instance, in the discussions about dirt with Mrs. W. This question will be referred to again.

II. *A consideration of the dynamic factors which appear to make possible the treatment of children through their parents at this early age and not, on the whole, in the latency period*

There appear to be certain inherent factors which account for the possibility of doing work such as that described with mothers of under-fives. Some of these factors lie within the child and some within the mother. It will be noted that the problems for which the under-fives were referred were the result of the wrong handling of situations occurring in a developmental phase. As we know, the child's personality is still incomplete; his conflicts are still between the instincts and the environment rather than between the instincts and an internalised superego, as is usually the case with children in latency who are seen in Child Guidance Clinics. For this reason the under-five is still very responsive to the mother's handling. This responsiveness impresses anyone accustomed to working with parents of older children. This is illustrated interestingly in cases where the most superficial problems of the child have

responded to a change in the mother's handling, but the neurotic conflicts have remained; the indication is that these conflicts are dependent
on an inner change for their solution.

The second factor within the child is also related to the incom-
pleteness of the personality, which makes it possible for the mother to
observe the child's unconscious before the defense mechanisms are fully
established. This appears to be the main reason why the mother is able
to accept the information. Few mothers attending the clinic will long
deny observations of aggressive wishes and pleasures in dirt in their
2-year-olds. Six years later, the mothers of these same children, now
perhaps very clean and inhibited 8-year-olds, will stoutly deny the existence of aggressive instincts. One would seldom venture to explain the
oedipal wishes, or castration fears, to the mother of a latency child, since
these conflicts have undergone repression and the mother would find
no confirmation of the information she is given and therefore would
not gain the conviction necessary to use the information effectively.
It appears that it is mainly the conviction that mothers of under-fives
can gain by their own observations which results in a real understanding
of their child's unconscious. In the case of Mrs. B. this was very evident;
as soon as her attitude made it possible for S. to verbalise her fantasies,
she brought confirmation of the child's sexual curiosity, penis envy,
and aggressive wishes. Similarly, in the case of Mrs. L., as soon as she
ceased to reassure J., she could find a meaning for his fear in terms of
his unconscious conflicts. One could not have expected either of these
mothers, particularly Mrs. B., to accept the theory, without the knowledge that such confirmation would occur.

The most important factor within the mother seems to lie in the
difference in the relationship between the mother and an under-five
and the mother and an older child. The young child, it seems, is still
regarded by the mother as part of her own body, and when she comes
to the clinic saying that something has gone wrong, it almost seems she
is saying something has gone wrong with her. Perhaps as a result of
this she assumes from the onset that she has handled the child wrongly
and very often says so. She would not think of suggesting that the child
attend the clinic instead of her; in contrast to the mothers of older
children who often ask whether the children could attend on their own
for treatment, instead of coming themselves. The mother of an older
child no longer regards the child as part of herself, but as a separate
object to whom she has transferred her own conflicts and toward whom
she has an established pattern of behaviour. One is familiar with cases
where the mother's description of the child's personality represents a
description of her own problems, or she may describe the child in

exactly the same manner in which she describes her early love objects. Projections of this kind occur less frequently with the mother of an under-five and seldom prove a barrier to work with the mother. One could observe that Mrs. B.'s initial description of S. represented a description of her relationship with her own mother, and had she not come for treatment it seems likely that such a relationship would have been fully established, and made work with Mrs. B. extremely difficult at a later stage.

III. *The limitations of educational work with reference to the cases that could not be dealt with in this way*

A small number of cases were seen which could not be treated by the methods here described, either because the child already had a neurotic conflict, referred to above, or because of the mother's personality. As has been implied, the mother's unconscious conflicts create the limit of her capacity to change her handling of the child. This was most apparent in cases such as those of Mrs. L. and Mrs. B. where something more was required than the changed handling of a particular situation.

There was only one case amongst a group of feeding difficulties in children under 2½ which could not be dealt with because of the mother's conflicts. This was the case of a 1-year-old girl whose mother was still feeding her with food put through a sieve. The mother was unable to alter her handling of the situation, reported continued failure to eat for 3 weeks, and failed to keep further appointments. In the last interview the mother mentioned that her 5-year-old boy also had a severe feeding difficulty; and that she herself could not eat as a child, and restricted herself to a very small number of foods at the present time. The nature of the mother's disturbance could not be investigated, but it could be assumed that her inability to alter the feeding situation was associated with her own unconscious fantasies which underlay her own feeding disturbances.

A small group of mothers who seemed unable to change or to apply information they were given were those who had already established a sado-masochistic relationship with their children.

A typical case was that of Mrs. X. and her son R., who was unable to separate from his mother. He was chronically constipated, and inhibited in all his activities. He had long fair hair kept in place with a slide, and looked more like a girl than a boy. Mrs. X. was superficially friendly and cooperative. She always carried out recommendations in such a way as to insure their failure.

In her relationship to R. Mrs. X. was nagging and demanding; she said she had wanted a girl. Although she recognised his fear of animals, she hung a picture of an open-mouthed crocodile over his bed. She complained that he was sometimes cheeky and dominating, for instance, when he imitated his father and addressed her in terms of endearment.

Mrs. X. lived with her mother and husband, complaining bitterly of her mother's presence but rationalising as soon as any suggestion to change the situation was made. Mr. X. spent most of the evenings at meetings since he could not tolerate the friction between Mrs. X. and his mother-in-law. Mrs. X. brought to the clinic the same ambivalent attitude that she displayed toward her mother and R. Her attitude to the worker was always friendly and rather dependent, but it was accompanied by repeated failures to keep appointments, and what seemed a determination to prove the clinic advice wrong.

It was finally necessary to take R. himself into treatment and to attempt no more than to maintain Mrs. X.'s cooperation for his regular attendance. This minimum of cooperation was difficult to achieve since Mrs. X. frequently kept R. away from school on account of colds, maintaining that he could therefore not attend the clinic either.

The following is an example of a mother whose unconscious castration wishes made it impossible for her to interpret her 5-year- old girl's penis envy. Mrs. H. was a seemingly stable personality who, over a period of 4 months in weekly interviews, succeeded in changing her handling of certain situations, and transforming a mutually hostile relationship between herself and T. into a happy and satisfactory one. She had also achieved remarkable understanding of T.'s marked obsessional traits. T. then began to show interest in the difference between the sexes based on her observations of her 1-year-old brother. When she asked Mrs. H. why she was a girl and he a boy, Mrs. H. explained that she already had a girl and wanted a boy, thus confirming T.'s fears. On another occasion T. commented on her chest, and asked Mrs. H. if she had spots there too. Mrs. H. replied, "You will have bumps there when you grow up, like me—we are funny, aren't we? but H. is funnier, isn't he?" T. is reported to have changed the subject immediately following Mrs. H.'s remarks. When T. expressed her wish to have babies Mrs. H. found it difficult to accept this as the usual wish of a girl as a compensation for not having a penis.

Mrs. H. betrayed her castration wishes in other contexts. She described in detail how she had explained circumcision to T. when the baby was circumcised at five months. She wondered at the time what T. would think about it, since she had observed how T. did everything to her teddy that was done to the baby. She was fascinated by the idea of T. trying to circumcise the teddy. It was striking that Mrs. H. found it necessary to explain circumcision to T. at this time, when she had been unable to explain the facts of reproduction to her, or to satisfy her sexual curiosity.

Mrs. H. spent most of another interview telling with great interest of two observations she had made of the baby's activities. The first was how he screamed when he saw her finger bandaged, the second was a description of his anxiety when he saw a rag draped around a dripping tap. Later Mrs. H. told of some incidents from her own childhood. The most wonderful moment of her life, she said, was when her school report stated, "She is following in her brother's footsteps."

In this case therapy was finally recommended for the child, partly because of the nature of her disturbance, but also because the mother's unconscious conflicts would prevent her from proceeding further with interpretations satisfactorily.

These cases which could not be treated by the methods described represented about 16 per cent of the under-fives referred to the worker at the two clinics. The results of the cases which could be treated by these methods can be regarded as very satisfactory compared with other results of treatment in the Child Guidance Service. In addition, satisfactory results were achieved in comparatively few interviews. The criteria adopted for satisfactory results were that the problem for which the mother came responded to a change in the mother's handling, and that the mother gained sufficient insight and knowledge to enable her to handle the next developmental phase independently. There may be a tendency for the worker to continue interviews after the disappearance of the original. problem; this does not seem desirable since the mother is inclined to become overinterested (as in the case of Mrs. L.), or to regard herself, or her child, as a "problem". Interviews with mothers in groups of 6 to 8, held at fortnightly, or monthly, intervals, serve the purpose of follow-ups, without creating these difficulties.

Educational work with mothers of young children has been an important part of the program of the West Sussex Child Guidance Service (2). In the last year, as a result of lectures, some mothers of young children have spontaneously formed small groups in the villages and asked a clinic worker to discuss child development with them at regular intervals. Group work of this kind, as well as the individual interviews described in this article, offer the worker a unique opportunity, since one can almost say for the reasons implied above, knowledge of unconscious mechanisms is more accessible to mothers of children under 5 than to any other section of the community, excluding those who have had a personal analysis.

BIBLIOGRAPHY

1. Freud, A. "The Psychoanalytic Study of Infantile Feeding Disturbances", *this Annual,* II, 1946.
2. Friedlander, K. "Psychoanalytic Orientation in Child Guidance work in Great Britain", *ibid.,* II, 1946.
3. Fries, M. "The Child's Ego and the Training of Adults in the Environment", *ibid.,* II, 1946.
4. Thomas, R. and Ruben, M. "Home Training of Instincts and Emotions", *Health Ed. J.,* London, 1947.

NEUROSIS AND HOME BACKGROUND

A Preliminary Report

By **KATE FRIEDLANDER, M.D., D. P. M.** (London)

Some years ago, when examining the environmental factors that cause antisocial behaviour I tentatively put forward the view that the gross disturbances in the early home background of delinquent children are not met with in the histories of our adult neurotic patients (2). At that time I had at my disposal the hihgly selected case material of my own patients and of published case histories.

Examination of cases observed over the last 2 years at a child guidance clinic[1] showed as a whole striking differences in the home background of neurotic as compared with that of antisocial children. The diagnosis of antisocial behaviour is not made only on the basis of manifest delinquency, but whenever there are signs of an antisocial character formation. In such cases there is a history of unmanageableness at home, and—if the child is old enough—at school, of running away, destructiveness, lying, and very often pilfering in the home.

Out of 34 cases of *antisocial* children, the child had in 12 instances been separated from the mother before the age of 5, and grown up either in institutions or in unsuitable foster-homes, with a frequent change of the adults in charge of them. In another 12 cases there were other gross disturbances of the early family setting: some of the children lived with the mother alone, either because of their illegitimacy or because the father deserted them before they were 5 years old. In some cases they were separated from their mothers after that age, and in 2 cases the mothers were borderline psychotics. Only in 10 cases were the children living at home with both their parents, and in 2 cases only were these homes stable. In both these 2 cases, delinquent behaviour appeared for the first time at puberty and could be regarded as a passing phase.

Among the *neurotic* children were included those who were suf-

1. The Horsham Child Guidance Clinic, West Sussex Child Guidance Service.

fering from anxiety hysteria, obsessional neurosis, neurotic character disturbances, neurotic learning inhibitions and primary behaviour disorders in which neurotic traits governed the picture.

Of 33 neurotic children between the ages of 5 and 14, in 32 cases there was no interruption of the mother-child relationship either before or after the fifth year, and in all these cases the home was stable. In one case the child was illegitimate, but was adopted by the maternal grandmother at the age of 3 weeks and thereafter lived with the grandparents as their own child in a stable home.

It is not easy to define what is meant by a stable home, and it therefore seems necessary to state some of the factors which may be regarded as pertinent. In this series of cases, with one exception, there had been no separation between the parents save for those necessitated by the war, when some of the fathers were in the fighting forces. In 4 cases only could we find a definite disturbance in the parental relationship, whilst in 22 cases, all of whom we had under treatment for more than 6 months, the interparental contact was exceptionally good. In all but 4 cases, both parents were interested in the education of their children and very concerned about their physical and mental wellbeing. Weekends were spent together with the children and holidays were shared by the whole family. In all but 3 cases the families had lived in the same place for many years, some in a small town, some in the rural district of the county. The group is composed of working class, lower and upper middle class families.

The attitude of the parents of neurotic children to the clinic is rather typical. With a few exceptions, the mothers are eager to supply us with the facts we wish to know and are glad if we propose treatment. In all but two cases we were able in time to gain the cooperation of the mother, and, where we wished, of the father as well. Fathers often expressed their desire to come to the clinic before we proposed it. There were no difficulties in follow-up studies of the cases, as the parents were only too willing to give us information about the child's progress, and were glad about our interest; and in a number of instances the mother herself expressed the wish to be allowed to keep in contact with the clinic after treatment was concluded.

As is usual in the population of this district, the role of the parents within the family is rather autocratic.

As has been shown, the stability of the home background amongst the group of neurotic children was very well marked, and in sharp contrast to that of the antisocial group. There was no opportunity to examine a group of normal children from the same environment regarding their home background, but it is interesting that the home background of children with primary behaviour disorders does not show this high percentage of stable homes. Out of 48 cases, in 33 there was a stable home background and an uninterrupted mother-child relationship, whilst in 11 the mother-child relationship was interrupted before the fifth year with the children living away from home, and in the remaining 4 cases there were other gross disturbances of the early home background.[2]

	Neurotic Disturbances	Antisocial Conduct	Primary Behaviour Disorders
Uninterrupted mother-child relationship; living at home with both parents	32	10	33
Interrupted mother-child relationship; not living at home		12	11
Other gross disturbances in early family-setting	1	12	4
	33	34	48

It is realised that child guidance material is still selected material and does not represent a fair sample of disturbed children in the community. As the sources of referral are slightly different in the case of antisocial and neurotic children, the latter being referred in agreement with the parents whilst the former may be referred by the Court, this may influence our figures to a certain extent. On the other hand, more than half of both neurotic and antisocial children are referred at the request of the schools and the Maternity and Child Welfare Centre, and not directly by the parents or the Court.

These findings confirm some of the analytical views on the causation of neurotic illness. The conflict with the environment will only lead to an internal or neurotic conflict if the superego has already taken

2. The figures attained from the other 2 clinics belonging to the same service were similar. They are not included because the individual cases have not yet been sufficiently scrutinised.

over the external demands and if the ego is strong enough to keep instinctive urges away from direct gratification. The stable home with its intense intra-family relationships and its high moral standards offers the best medium for a strong ego development and a superego which may be severe.

Why have these children, growing up in apparently satisfactory homes, nevertheless become neurotic?

In recent years there has been a tendency to attribute the appearance of neurotic illness to single environmental factors, first and foremost to the mother's attitude towards the child. Such terms as "rejection", "over-protection", "ambivalence", are used very freely, and material is produced illustrating the overwhelming importance of one or the other factor for the development of the disturbance. It therefore has seemed of interest to examine cases from the point of view of whether such single factors could be made responsible for the disturbance in a large pro-portion of cases. Our material seemed suitable for such an investigation because the majority of cases had been under treatment for more than 6 months, so that many more factors came to light than is usual in diagnostic investigations. The children have not been under analysis, but were seen once or twice weekly, and in the majority of cases the mothers were seen at the same time. The data are therefore not so complete as those gained in analytical treatment, but more details are available concerning the mother and her conflicts, and fathers and siblings were often seen as well. Child guidance material offers the advantage of a greater number of cases and a better first-hand knowledge of the family background, and more especially of the mothers' attitudes. I need not mention the considerable disadvantages in comparison with analytical material.

When studying the influence of the mother's attitude on the origin of the child's disturbance, we must be careful to distinguish between her attitude towards the child during the first 3 or 4 years of life and that which she displays when she brings the child to a clinic after the dis-turbance has already been established for some time. This latter atti-tude may be a reaction to the child's disturbance, and though it may be unsatisfactory, it may be very different from the mother's attitude before the disturbance became manifest. Often the primary attitude can be ascertained only after a long period of treatment of both mother and child. In general, the relationship of the mother to the child is dif-ferent during the first 5 years from what it is later. We are more likely to see the originally disturbing influences at work during early child-hood; toward children of the latency period, there may have set in transference reactions and identifications, on the part of the mother, which were not present during the first years, at the time when the roots for the disturbance were laid.

It is also important to bear in mind that every mother is to a certain extent ambivalent toward her child, and that at times she may show a certain degree of overprotection and even of rejection. In order to prove that one or the other attitude stands in causal relation to the disturbance, it must be shown at what stage of development and in which way normal development was interfered with by a specific attitude on the part of the mother.

The material was examined at first from the point of view of ascertaining whether, had all the factors about the intra-family relationships and more especially about the mother's attitude been known, the neurotic development could have been predicted. Or, in other words: were there cases where a child of normal endowment could not have passed through the early phases of instinctual maturation without fixations on the pregenital levels and subsequent disturbance at the oedipal level?

In the light of our present-day psychoanalytic knowledge of child development it seems likely that this was so in 6 out of the 33 cases.

The clearest example, and, I believe, a very typical one is that of Ronald.[3] He was an only child and 4½ years of age when we first saw him. He was sent to us on account of his inability to separate from his mother, his fears of the dark and of loud noises, his bedwetting and constipation, his baby talk and his generally immature behaviour.

Ronald was the child of middle class parents, the father being a teacher in an elementary school. The family lived in a small house, with the maternal grandmother. Mrs. X. had married at the age of 29 not for love but because she wanted to separate from her mother. Her father had died 5 years earlier and she had been suffering from digestive troubles for some years after his death. There was an older brother whom Mrs. X. disliked. A few months after Mrs. X.'s marriage, her mother came to stay with her, at Mrs. X.'s suggestion, and has lived with her without interruption for the last 10 years. Mr. X. spends a lot of his free time in committees and boys' clubs because he cannot stand the constant bickering between the two women. He did not openly tell us, but implied, that his wife and his mother-in-law treated him like a little boy, constantly reprimanding him for disturbing the order in the house and in the garden. He gave us a vivid description of how, when Ronald goes into the garden, the two women follow him to see what he is doing and how they clean him up the moment he gets dirty. They also interfere when the father wishes to take Ronald out with him. It was due to the father's own passive attitude that he was unable to change the situa-

3. This case is referred to by L. Jacobs, *this Volume,* p. 420.

tion; although he complained to us he never tried to discuss his dissatisfaction openly with his wife, but always gave way. Superficially Mr. X. appeared active and rather aggressive, but this attitude was a defence against his passive feminine tendencies which he constantly satisfied in the home situation. From 1940 to 1945 Mr. X. was in the R.A.F., but not abroad, so that for the first years of Ronald's life he was only at home for weekends and when on leave.

Mrs. X. had a number of hysterical symptoms during her pregnancy but against her expectations the birth was normal and she was able to breast-feed Ronald for 5 months. She had wanted a girl, a wish which she admitted only once and then immediately denied. Her description of the boy was that of a miserable child who constantly suffered from ill-health and who was so delicate that she was doubtful whether she would be able to bring him to the clinic in 2 days' time, because he might get ill meanwhile. According to her he has been constipated since he was 6 months old, and ever since then she has had a struggle to get him on the pot although he never dirtied or soiled himself. When he was 4 she still potted him 3 times a day. He has always had purgatives, in the form of suppositories or paraffin. When he was 15 months old the mother observed that his feet were turned in. Sunray treatment was advised and he had 11 sittings, although he was terrified by the dark glasses and screamed during all of the time. When he was 2 years of age he had ulcers on his penis for which he had treatment. He has frequent colds and 2 months before he came to the clinic he had been in the hospital for a week because he had complained about a pain in his tummy. He was found physically healthy and after the first day not troublesome. He shares his parents' bedroom. The mother rationalises this on the basis that she has to have her mother living with her. Ronald has never stopped bedwetting except for the time he was in the hospital; but he was unable to get out of his own cot by himself because the side was fastened at night.

Ronald was a very healthy-looking, lively child, rather tall for his age; when first seen in the waiting room he looked like a girl. He had long fair hair with a slide in it and a cheque beret sat at an angle. Although it was fairly warm weather, he was clothed in so many woollies that it was difficult for him to move.

This boy was seen at weekly interviews for over a year, with interruptions owing to illness and the mother's uncooperative attitude. The mother was seen fortnightly, with interruptions, during the same time, with the purpose of maintaining contact and gaining some cooperation. It had not seemed possible to attempt to change her sado-masochistic character disturbance in weekly interviews.

Mrs. X. was small, very neatly dressed, very feminine in appearance and demeanour, with an artificial smile on her face. She talked in a low voice and was never openly aggressive but nevertheless constantly trying to pick a quarrel. It irritated her when she was told that the boy was healthy physically and she drew attention to his constipation as a sign of ill-health. This cleared up very quickly when she was able to allow him to use the lavatory by himself. It appeared that the boy had shown all along signs of normal behaviour, such as a desire for boyish toys and boyish activities. But his desire to hammer, for instance, impressed the mother as naughty behaviour, and she proudly said that she had taught him to knit instead. After some time she agreed to send him to a nursery where he found outlets for his activity. She reacted with irritation and annoyance when Ronald, imitating his father, called her "sweet" and "pet".

Although Mrs X. was able to adapt her attitude to a certain extent to the knowledge she gained of the boy's conflicts, she was never able to cooperate fully and to accept that the boy could change under treatment. She would tell at the end of an interview when she was about to leave that Ronald had not wet his bed for a fortnight, adding with a sweet smile that this must be because of the orange juice he was taking. When we offered to see the boy twice weekly instead of once she kept away for a fortnight. From the beginning she was annoyed that he separated from her so easily in the clinic and once really verbalised her fear by saying that she would not allow the boy to be taken away from her altogether. But, toward the end of treatment, she herself had the plan of sending him to a boarding school, because she was afraid that the father might spoil him. At that time we had succeeded in gaining the father's cooperation so that he allowed the boy to help him with his carpentry.

Despite the uncooperative attitude of the mother, the boy responded well to treatment. His castration fears, expressed in the beginning in oral aggressive and anal sadistic fantasies could be relieved; this allowed him to express his sexual curiosity and genital fantasies. The analysis of his passive tendencies, expressed in urethral fantasies, led to the cessation of his bedwetting. His sado-masochistic relationship to the therapist was in time linked up with his attitude to his mother. At the end of treatment, he impressed his teachers and other people who came in contact with him as very boyish and active, and he adjusted well to school which he started some months before treatment was given up. (He had an I.Q. of 105.) The analysis of his infantile neurosis may allow normal development during the latency period but whether it will prevent a more serious breakdown at or after puberty is doubtful as no change could be effected in the mother's attitude and the home environment in general. It is this family constellation which we often find in the histories of passive and homosexual men patients.

When mother and child came to the clinic there was already a well-established sado-masochistic relationship between them. The most impressive factor which emerged from the history was the free expression of the mother's castrating tendencies from the beginning of life onward, most pronounced toward the phallic desires in the oedipal phase. Her behaviour during the child's training to cleanliness was apt to cause a fixation-point at that level. Her constant attention to the excretory functions, the administration of suppositories, and so on, increased anal pleasures and passive tendencies. The expression of his oedipal desires was repressed and both mother and grandmother verbalised castration threats. At the same time he continued to share the parents' bedroom and was often taken into the mother's bed in the morning on condition that he took off his wet pyjama trousers. This stimulation naturally increased his castration anxiety.

The mother had centered all her emotion around this little boy, in whose company she was from morning to night and who was more important and nearer to her than her husband. During treatment, when we succeeded in centering her attention on her relationship to her mother and in discussing her hostility to her, her relationship to the boy became more normal for a time and she could enjoy his changing attitude. She then sided with him against her own mother.

The neurotic development of this boy was not a result of the mother's hostility or of her identification of him with her older brother. It is true that on the basis of her penis envy she expressed against the boy the same castrating tendencies which she probably had against the older brother and with more effect. But her positive relationship to her son was as strong as the negative attitude and it was the sado-masochistic quality of the relationship which led to the outcome. Had the mother been only hostile and castrating, the chances are that the boy's object relationships and ego development would have been much more severely disturbed and that instead of a neurosis we might have found an anti-social character disturbance (3).

The fact that the boy responded so well to treatment although the intra-family relationships did not change very much gives us some indication that the disturbed development is more the result of environmental factors than of innate tendencies. In accordance with the knowledge we possess about the maturation of instinctive drives, this environment was apt to cause fixation-points and disturbed oedipal development. An immediate repression of oedipal desires and an identification with the mother with subsequent passive tendencies seemed unavoidable and the bedwetting was the symptom which resulted.

This family constellation is by no means rare and we have seen a number of cases of the kind, with a similar outcome in the child. Pure sado-masochistic relationships are even more common than this strong expression of castrating tendencies.

In this case, therefore, the personality of the mother and the intra-family relationships made it possible to predict that a boy, especially if he were the only child, would develop a neurosis. The intimacy of the mother-child relationship and the strong positive bond on the part of both parents to the child allowed a strong ego and superego development, without which another disturbance, but a neurotic one, would have resulted. Although it was the whole family constellation which contributed to this outcome, in the end it was the personality of the mother which shaped this family. It was because of her sado-masochistic relationship to her own mother that she allowed her to live in her house and to restrict the boy, and because of her personality that she had chosen a passive husband who allowed himself to be dominated by her. It was not one single factor in the mother's attitude, for instance the hostility to the child, which dominated the picture, but the complicated sado-masochistic relationships which she established with every member of the family.

In none of the other 6 cases was the damaging nature of the environment so clear, and the case described was the only one where the disturbance could be ascribed rather to the environment than to the innate tendencies. In all the other cases it appeared as if something in the child responded rather quickly to negative environmental influences.

The following case could easily have been classed under the heading of a "rejecting mother" had it not been possible to unravel the history during the child's treatment, which lasted over a year but could not be completed.

Mary was a girl of 6, who was referred to us by the health visitor. She had had an eating disturbance from the age of 10 months, and when we first saw her she was underfed, tiny for her age, with very small wrists and blue rings under her eyes. When the mother came to the clinic for the first time she had to bring with her her other child, a baby of 1 year, whom she held on her lap and with whom she was so intensely occupied that it was difficult to establish any contact with her. She expressed an attitude of defeatism. She had come because she had tried everything else and one more thing would not matter. She did not believe we could help her, and it did not matter very much to her, one way or the other. She would not have bothered had she not been sent. She gives Mary her food, and if Mary does not eat it, it is just too bad. She was obviously happy with her baby, and it seemed that she completely rejected the older child.

This attitude on the mother's part was sustained for the first few months of treatment. She talked disparagingly to the child about the clinic, she refused to come, and during home visits only gave the barest information when pressed for it. It was not possible to get a clear picture of the intra-family relationships, except that Mary was on better terms with her father than with her mother, and that he often gave her her bath and put her to bed. We did not succeed at this stage in getting any details of early development, except for the fact that Mary was already clean between the ages of 1 and 2, walked and talked normally, and "never ate".

During treatment it could be seen that the function of eating had become invested with all the unresolved conflicts of the child's instinctive development, and oral, anal and genital fantasies disturbed her attitude to food. There was fear of being poisoned by food, an identification of food with dirt, and oedipal fantasies about oral conception. When the child became conscious of her disgust for food because it reminded her of dirt, she began to eat. A few days later the mother was seen again. Her attitude had changed during these few days from one of complete non-cooperation to one of great friendliness and a desire to help and to accept help.

We were now able to explain the reason for the mother's apparent rejection of the child. Before her marriage the mother had been a children's nurse, and had been very successful in her handling of children, especially little ones. In all her experience she had never met a child as difficult as Mary was, and she had therefore had a feeling of failure ever since the child was about 3 years of age and none of her methods had succeeded. She defended herself against this unpleasant realisation by pretending to herself that she did not mind. This overt "rejection" of the child was therefore an attitude developed as a response to the child's disturbance.

The mother's changed attitude now made it possible to obtain some details about the occurrences during the first year of life which might be responsible for the type and severity of the disturbance. The mother had been engaged for 10 years before she and her fiancé were able to marry and live in a house of their own. She wanted children very much and was happy during her pregnancy. After the confinement she had a depressive phase lasting for about 6 months. This was later on confirmed by her husband. She was unhappy, cried a lot, could not do her housework properly, and was not as fond of the child as she had expected to be. Probably in response to this the child did not suck well, and this increased her feelings of guilt. She got better when the baby was weaned at the age of 6 months. When Mary was 10 months old the father was called up for war service. The mother was afraid he would have to go abroad very soon, and was again very unhappy. This event coincided with the beginning of the training for cleanliness and the onset of the severe eating disturbance. In a very typical way the child was very clean at an early age but the feeding difficulty grew worse.

The mother's emotional withdrawal during the child's first year of life caused a disturbance in the establishment of-the early oral object-relationship. The child's present attitude toward the mother was a mixture of insatiable oral demands, and hostility and withdrawal aroused by the unavoidable frustrations. The mother tried very hard to satisfy these demands, and felt guilty because she was unable to establish a positive relationship and hurt when she found that the girl responded much better to the father. It was only at this stage that we learned that Mary had been given the whole family's sweet rations for years.

It was interesting to observe how quickly this mother changed her attitude when the child started eating. She developed an amazing insight into the child's demands and hostility, and became able to endure it without reverting to her defence mechanism of not caring. She understood the difficulties which the child presented whilst her therapist was on holidays, and was able to reassure her. She became aware of the child's jealousy toward her younger sister which was expressed on an oral level, and realised that she had handled the baby better and more leniently during cleanliness training.

Owing to the disturbance in object-relationship during the first year, frustrations by the mother during the training for cleanliness increased the child's fear of and hostility toward the mother, which was expressed in the feeding difficulty. The relationship to the therapist was first established on the basis of the satisfaction of oral demands.

It is important to realise that the rejection which seemed so obvious in the beginning was not the cause but the effect of the child's disturbance; it seems misleading to use the term "rejection" for the mother's attitude during her depressive phase, although the child may have felt it to be such. This term should be reserved for those cases where it is a consistent attitude directed against the child, an attitude which usually expresses itself in a complete lack of interest in the child's need and behaviour except when the child is disturbing. It is an attitude more common in parents of antisocial than of neurotic children.

According to our knowledge of a disturbance in the mother-child relationship during the first year (1, 6,), there is some justification for the thesis that in this case a disturbed development was likely to occur. That the disturbance is a neurosis and not a distorted ego and superego development is probably attributable to the strong positive emotion which the mother showed toward her child as soon as her mental equilibrium was regained, to the child's positive relationship to the father and to the general stability of the home and the intra-family relationships.

It is open to doubt whether a child with different innate endowments might not have been able to go through the same experiences with less far-reaching disturbances. Such questions can be solved only by follow-up studies of babies going through similar experiences during the first year of life.

In the other 4 cases of this group the constellations were equally complicated and they could not be attributed to single factors.

In the remaining 27 cases, the home environment, the personality of the parents and the intra-family relationships were such that in each case the chances of normal development seemed to be good, and in the majority of cases there were mentally healthy brothers and sisters. In most cases it was possible to unravel the genesis of the neurotic disturbance, and it could be seen very clearly that conflicts arising in the child —the usual conflicts of early development—were enhanced by environmental factors, which had led to the abnormal outcome. In all these cases, Freud's assumption of two series of factors, inherited and accidental, which together are responsible for the disposition to neurotic illness, could only be confirmed. In all these cases the conflict constellations were complicated and were not governed by one single personality factor in the mother.

It would lead us too far from the purpose of this paper to give case histories in detail. I shall therefore give examples from 2 case histories, illustrating a similar conflict situation, without giving the full particulars.

A girl, Maureen, came for treatment at the age of 9½ on account of a neurotic learning inhibition and character difficulties which had existed from the age of 3 or 4. She was always dissatisfied, always wanted more than she could get, and frequently staged scenes involving the whole family. In school she had difficulties in her contact with other children toward whom she was aggressive, and could not learn although she had an I.Q. of 137. Her learning inhibition was caused by her unresolved penis envy, and her character difficulties appeared to be the outcome of her sado-masochistic relationship with her mother. She had a sister, 6 years younger, of whom she was unconsciously intensely jealous.

According to her mother she had been a beautiful and forward baby, talked very early, and seemed to justify the high hopes which her very intelligent parents had invested in her. This changed when she was about 2½ years old, during a holiday at the seaside where she had occasion to see naked boys. Shortly after that time she became aggressive toward her mother, who responded with a masochistic attitude. Her character difficulties became pronounced when she was between the ages of 4 and 5.

During treatment it became clear that the girl's dissatisfaction and learning inhibition were the results of her inability to sublimate her penis envy. Being a girl for her meant being damaged, and her attempt to identify with men failed on account of her guilt feeling—she believed unconsciously that it was because of her masturbation that she was not a boy. Attempts at tomboyishness ended in her hurting herself. She regressed to the pregenital mother relationship and found satisfaction in sado-masochistic strivings. This sado-masochistic relationship was the direct outcome of her conflict: she reproached her mother constantly for not giving her what she wanted and thereby provoked being hurt by her.

The analysis of these fantasies and their connection with her inability to learn led to an almost immediate and successful attempt to sublimate her penis envy in an interest for geometry, and this in time led to an increase of interest in school subjects generally.

The main conflict in this case was the girl's unresolved penis envy and her subsequent sado-masochistic relationship with her mother. To this the mother responded, probably on the basis of the same unconscious conflict. As far as could be ascertained there were in the environment no outstanding accidental events which could have stimulated the girl's penis envy to that degree. There was no older or younger brother. The parents, both secondary school teachers, had a very good relationship with one another and had both wanted to have a girl as their first child. The mother gave up work after the girl's birth and was very satisfied with her life at home. But it was obvious that she had no understanding of the child's conflict when it first appeared and was therefore unable to help her. She did, however, encourage the child's achievements in every respect. She was very upset by the child's lack of interest in school and in any activity, but this was a long time after the disturbance had been established. She allowed herself to be provoked by Maureen's aggressions and responded with a sado-masochistic attitude, and this may have led to the fixation of this attitude in the child. It is interesting to note that the younger child is developing very differently. At the end of our period of observation she was 4 years of age and had never presented any behaviour disorders. She had begun to learn to read and write with the greatest interest. The achievements of the younger sister enhanced Maureen's conflicts but did not cause them. Every manifestation of the younger girl's cleverness increased her feeling of failure, and she used this situation in order to exhibit her defect.

NEUROSIS AND HOME BACKGROUND

The original conflict which proved to be the basis for the disturbance developed without undue stimulation by the environment. Once this conflict was active environmental factors tended to increase it, for instance, the mother's ambitions and her sado-masochistic response.

The mother reacted well to explanations given her about the child's inexplicable behaviour. As soon as she understood it as a defence mechanism she was able to control her own emotions, and in time Maureen's negativistic attitude no longer aroused her sado-masochistic reactions. Although her personality structure made her respond so easily to the child's provocation there was no need for her to support the pathological relationship.

From all the factors known in this case there appears to be no reason why the child should not have grown up without neurotic disturbance; on the other hand it is easy to see how the mother's lack of understanding of the child's conflicts and her reaction to the child's provocation made it easier for the neurotic conflict to remain unresolved. The fact that the young child seems to be growing up quite normally in a very similar environment substantiates this point.

When this mother was seen for the first time her own sado-masochistic relationship to the child was very pronounced, much more so than later when Maureen had already changed. Recently such mothers have often been called "ambivalent", and the child's disturbance is then ascribed to the unconscious hostility of the mother. By emphasizing one aspect of a sado-masochistic relationship, namely the ambivalence of feelings which is characteristic of the anal organisation, one does not give a true picture of the inner psychic situation and of the dynamics of the relationship. Positive feelings are as strong as negative ones, and the damage is caused by the pleasure which the child derives from quarrel situations, which tends to lead to a fixation on that level. A sado-masochistic mother never rejects her child, but tends to keep him for too long a time in much too intimate a relationship.

It was possible to study environmental factors more closely in another girl with similar conflicts.

Sylvia was brought to the clinic as early as the age of 5. Both parents were stable working class people; the mother a particularly kind and understanding woman who had been most patient in dealing with the child's obsessional behaviour. A brother was born when the girl was 4 years old.

Sylvia has had obsessional symptoms from an early time. She had been very sensitive to changes in routine even at the age of 1. During her 2nd year she became overclean, although the training for cleanliness was not strict. She had bed rituals between the ages of 2 and 3, and presented constant difficulties over dressing and undressing. She never showed any overt aggression or destructiveness, and did not attempt any task before she was certain that she would achieve it to perfection. She had innumerable food fads and rituals at mealtimes. She became more difficult after the brother's birth, for which she had not been prepared, but did not express any hostility to him. There are reasons for believing that the time after the brother's birth was traumatic for her. The baby cried incessantly and was taken to the hospital for a few days when 3 months old. During this time Sylvia was rather neglected.

Amongst the unresolved conflicts underlying the obsessional symptoms, her penis envy aroused the strongest aggressions, expression of which she feared. During the first interview she verbalised the fantasy that her brother would soon turn into a girl, and that she also, once upon a time, had been a boy. She was over-ambitious at school, which she had just started, and owing to her high abilities she made excellent progress and was with children much older than she.

In regard to causal factors in this case, the early appearance of obsessional tendencies is rather startling. Training for cleanliness was begun at the age of 14 months, and we have no reason to disregard the mother's contention that it was easily achieved without strictness on her part. The mother herself drew attention to the fact that she found the little boy's pleasure in dirt more normal than Sylvia's cleanliness at the same age.

There are personality traits in the mother which are similar to those in the child, so that a strengthening of these tendencies may have occurred unconsciously. Mrs. B. was very ambitious herself. She therefore identified herself with the child in her perfectionism. But, at the same time, the mother did not regard this as a normal behaviour, and she herself was not obsessional.

Of more importance probably is the identity between the mother's and the child's unresolved penis envy. During treatment the mother understood Sylvia's envy concerning the little brother, and began to encourage the child's questions as to the difference in sex. Although she had a remarkable gift for interpreting correctly the girl's disguised questions and allusions, her explanations always implied her own belief that boys are better than girls. She could deal much better with the child's unconscious aggressive tendencies, and succeeded in making them conscious to her; and she was very tolerant toward the child's expressions of hostility toward herself.

The traumatic events of the brother's birth and the subsequent increase in conflicts occurred at a time when the disturbance had already been established. The mother handled Sylvia throughout with infinite patience and a realisation that the child was disturbed, but until she came to the clinic had no insight at all into the nature of the child's conflicts.

In this case inherent tendencies were strengthened by environmental attitudes and by accidental factors such as the birth of a younger brother. But it would seem that the intra-family relationships and the personalities of the parents were such that another child might have escaped a neurotic disturbance of like severity.

From the investigation of this group of 33 neurotic children and their families some preliminary conclusions can be drawn.

1) In none of the cases did the disturbance appear to depend on one single personality factor in the mother, but rather on the complicated

interplay between the conflicts arising in the child on the basis of the impossibility of satisfying its primitive instinctive urges and the reaction of the environment to these drives. The early environment is represented by the mother, and personality deviations may make normal development impossible. The outcome may be a neurosis, if the family unit is preserved.

2) In 6 out of the 33 cases, that is, in 18 per cent, the environmental constellation was such that the development of a neurotic disturbance might have been predicted.

3) In 27 cases, that is, in 82 per cent, neurotic development could not have been predicted. The analysis of the factors liable to have caused the disturbance leads to the assumption that the child responded very quickly and easily to adverse environmental conditions, which were well within normal limits.

4) In considering the question how neurotic development could have been prevented in these 27 cases it may be suggested that special management when the conflicts caused behaviour difficulties at first, in the phase of the infantile neurosis, may be effective. There are children whose innate tendencies make them more sensitive to conflict situations so that they are unable to work through them without help.

In view of the positive results of work with mothers of children under 5 years of age (4, 5, 7), it might be possible to prevent the fixation of these conflicts and their further unconscious elaboration if the mother were able to understand the child's emotions, to interpret them to him and help him verbalise them. This might lead to a strengthening of the ego and to a reduction of the severity of the superego in formation, so that the conflicts could be resolved.

There are many ways in which this knowledge could be transmitted to mothers, and many such attempts are already being made. The most important need is for a sufficient number of specially trained workers who could undertake this task either in individual or in group work with mothers.

BIBLIOGRAPHY

1. Freud, A. and Burlingham, D. T. *Infants Without Families*, Allen & Unwin, and Internat. Univ. Press, 1944.
2. Friedlander, K. "Formation of the Antisocial Character", *this Annual*, I, 1945.

3. Friedlander, K. "Latent Delinquency and Ego Development", *Searchlights in Delinquency*, ed. K. R. Eissler, Internat. Univ. Press, 1948.

4. Fries, M. "The Child's Ego Development and the Training of Adults in his Environment", *this Annual*, II, 1946.

5. Jacobs, L. "Methods Used in the Education of Mothers. A Contribution to the Handling and Treatment of Developmental Difficulties in Children Under 5 Years of Age," *this Volume*.

6. Spitz, R. "Anaclitic Depression", *this Annual*, II, 1946.

7. Thomas, R. and Ruben, M. "Home Training of Instincts and Emotions", *Health Ed.*, London, 1947.

SOME REMARKS ON THE PSYCHIC STRUCTURE AND SOCIAL CARE OF A CERTAIN TYPE OF FEMALE JUVENILE DELINQUENTS [1]

By AUGUST AICHHORN (Vienna)

A considerable number of girls, prospective or already active as prostitutes, were taken into custody by the Vienna police between March 1, 1946 and February 28, 1947. They had come to the attention of the police during raids on taverns, night clubs or music halls. Of these girls, as many as 1,916, ranging in age from 12 to 18 years, were held in police custody; I here give their age breakdown:

107[2]	....	12 to 14 years old
646	....	14 to 16 years old
1163	....	16 to 18 years old.

At the same time a number of similar cases were handled by the Vienna Municipal Board for the Care of Youth (*Wiener Staedtisches Jugendamt*).[3]

After the first World War, when the Municipal Board had been faced with the same problem, I had asked myself two questions:

---

1. Presented at the Congress of the *Union Internationale de Protection de l'Enfance,* for the study of problems of neglected juveniles after the war, April 29 to May 2, 1947, Geneva.

2. These figures are taken from statistics put at my disposal by Mrs. A. Grün, director of the social agency of the Vienna Police Department.

3. The statistics of the latter office do not separate cases taken over from the police from those referred by other sources. Consequently I do not quote its figures, as duplication would be inevitable. However, making a careful estimate, I may say that more than 2,000 of such girls became the responsibility of the Municipal Board.

(1) "What are the psychological determinants responsible for the tendency in young girls towards prostitution and for their actually becoming prostitutes?"

(2) "What measures are advisable in order to deal with this type of delinquent girls?"

I shall discuss the first question at some length: Experiences I was able to gather over a period of many years and at hand of a large number of cases [4] led me to assume with increasing certainty that a specific instinctual constellation must be one of the determinant factors, but that environment and destitution can only be concomitant factors.

From the outset it was clear that it was not strong, indomitable "femininity" which was responsible for a girl's being either inclined or, in certain cases, compelled to become a prostitute. For the prostitute is, without exception, sexually active and aggressive. In her wooing she comes close to the way a man is supposed to behave in normal sexual life. Her instinctual structure must, therefore, be one that deviates from normal sexual development.

In the psychoanalytic treatment of women engaged in professions or business one frequently uncovers the wishful fantasies to lead the life of a prostitute. Corresponding to actual information about the life of prostitutes, the contents of such fantasies range from the reality-adequate to the grotesquely distorted. Analysis regularly reveals that these women have in common the same infantile libidinal attachments, the same instinctual fixations and the same etiological factors. These I shall not discuss any further. Thus we find here a corrolation between a group of delinquent girls and a group of neurotic women which differ inasmuch as the former act out what the latter fantasy. Therefore the assumption is probable that the same infantile instinctual fixations as well as instinctual constellations operate in both groups. This becomes all the more probable if one observes that a considerable number of juvenile prostitutes in vocational guidance interviews express their preference for those very professions in which the above mentioned neurotic women mostly are engaged.

4. In the Settlement for Social Care and Training (Fuersorge-Erziehungsanstalt), established at that time at Oberhollabrunn by the City of Vienna, and later in the Child and Youth Guidance Clinics of the Vienna Municipal Board for the Care of Youth.

If this hypothesis is correct, it is obvious that a certain infantile instinctual fixation may lead either to prostitution or to a neurosis moulding the choice of a specific profession, or to the choice of a specific profession without accompanying neurotic illness.

Thus, in order to answer our first question, we have to investigate, a) whether identical infantile instinctual fixations are really evident in juvenile prostitutes and in a certain type of neurotic women; b) under what conditions a certain infantile instinctual fixation will lead not to neurosis, but to prostitution or the danger of promiscuity.

One preliminary task, important for our investigation, has been accomplished. From psychoanalytic treatment we have become familiar with the origin and types of infantile instinctual constellations such as the unresolved, repressed, libidinal attachment to the father, which in consciousness is often reversed into the opposite, the narcissistic component, and the latent homosexuality. We also know that the frigidity of these women is not identical with the frigidity of hysterical women.

Let us interrupt here for some general considerations, and return to our problem later.

Let us formulate our question in different terms: the instinctual demands pressing up from the unconscious enforce the same instinctual constellation and the same infantile fixations in both juvenile prostitutes and the neurotic women mentioned above. The difference in development of the two types can therefore originate only in differences of the way in which the superego copes with instinctual demands in each instance. The question is now, "What are the disturbances in this formation of the superego that permit the development of prostitution?"

To solve this problem it would be necessary to institutionalize a number of delinquent girls under appropriate social care and guidance. Under such conditions the inmates could be subjected to a scrutinizing psychological investigation.

The period after the first World War did not favor such an enterprise. At that time it was even doubted that the uncovering of the psychological etiology of delinquency would yield significant results which could be used in the practical dealings with juveniles. Research in delinquency which had been based on statistical methods had indeed discovered little of importance. The application of Freud's dynamic concepts was hardly known and far from being recognized. Research in delinquency on a psychoanalytic basis was initiated by the author. Since then conditions have changed profoundly and a project as outlined above is being conducted.[5]

Two hundred and fifty juvenile prostitutes were chosen at random and after a preliminary examination were divided into groups according to their behavior prior to their referral.[6] Even this initial screening yielded significant information.

Seventeen girls (6.8 per cent) had *apparently* attained the stage of sexual development of adult women. They had sexual partners to whom they had been faithful for a considerable length of time, regardless of whether or not the partners had been accepted by the girls' environment. The girls' attitude toward their work was normal; they showed no signs of delinquency, even if, as it had happened in a number of cases, they had got into conflict with their environment. Their capacity to respond to pedagogical guidance appeared rather limited as was their ability to sublimate their drives, i. e., their ability to substitute aims of high social value for those of direct and primitive instinctual gratification.

Nineteen girls (7.6 per cent) showed such impairment of intellect that re-education could hardly be thought of.

Three girls (1.2 per cent) were in a state of psychotic delinquency.

Before I continue to discuss the grouping of the girls, a few explanatory remarks seem appropriate.

In contrast to the assertions of other schools of psychology, psychoanalysis has discovered that puberty is not the beginning of sexual life, but only one, albeit most significant, phase of development in which a previous one, of early childhood, is revived though under different circumstances. The most important of these new factors are: biologically, the physical sexual maturity, and psychologically, the fact that the resurging infantile sexuality is confronted by an ego no longer infantile. Correlated to the physical sexual maturity, the genital drives gain pre-

5. It has been made possible to examine psychologically delinquent girls and juvenile prostitutes between 14 and 18 years of age who had been placed in remand homes, thanks to the co-operation of the City Councillor Dr. F. Freund who is also head of the Vienna Municipal Board for the Care of Youth.

6. This work has been done by one of my coworkers, Mrs. R. Dworschak, child guidance councillor on the Municipal Board.

dominance over those drives that were powerful in the earlier period of development, were of an entirely different nature and have entirely different aims. The undeveloped, yielding ego of early infancy has been consolidated, and consequently has become capable of adjusting itself to the desires of the id, and the demands of the superego.

Puberty, the period in which sexual maturity is attained is preceded by pre-puberty, the time during which physical sexual maturity is in the making and the ego is after years of quiescence, again harassed by instinctual impulses. Physiological processes intensify the instinctual drives and barriers erected in previous years are broken through. However, what occurs in pre-puberty is only a *quantitative* intensification of instinctual impulses, and it is during this period, far more than during puberty, that the phases of early childhood are reactivated. Conflicts which were believed settled long since, may re-emerge, frequently in grossly distorted form. The behavior during pre-puberty is characteristic and significantly different from that of the pubescent.

In puberty there occurs in addition to the quantitative intensification, a *qualitative* change of instinctual impulses. Its most conspicuous manifestation in the psychological sphere are changes in object-representation and in emotional and instinctual aims. Great vascillations in the psychic equilibrium are conspicuous as well as sudden conflicts based on irreconcilable extremes.

Puberty is also the period of inner emancipation from the parents, which not only enables the adult to make the transition from allegiance to the family to that to the larger social community, but also gives him the strength to establish lasting, satisfactory emotional attachments to a sex partner.

Now let us take up again the problem of the grouping:

Of 250 girls, 39 (15.6 per cent) have been classified above. The remaining 211 show such typical behavior patterns that their division into two groups offers no difficulties. The conduct of 92 girls (36.8 per cent) corresponds to the exaggerated, distorted behavior observable in pre-puberty. They are shameless in conduct and language and make themselves a public nuisance by their conspicuous manners in streets and public places; they gather in front of dance halls of the Allied soldiers, provoke young men to "pick them up" and also very easily make friends with one another. Frequently their attachment to an older girl friend is so strong and conspicuous as to convey to their anxious parents the impression that their daughter has merely been "seduced into participation" by her "wicked" friend. (Dressing up as "sisters" is very popular.) Their craving for pleasure is excessive; their loitering in the streets often degenerates into vagrancy.

Apart from their sexual experiences they are immature, they have not yet attained a reality-adequate attitude toward work, and are lazy and mendacious. Their sexual impulses comprise all conceivable kinds of sexual experiences, including sexual intercourse itself, in which they mostly remain unsatisfied. As in every other respect they act out excessively their likes and dislikes, and refrain as little from physical violence among themselves as from lesbian relationships.

The lower their intelligence, the cruder their behavior. None of the girls in this group is of higher than average intelligence. Fifty-two girls (20.8 per cent) show normal intelligence, and 40 (16.0 per cent), subnormal intelligence. The latter group could be further broken down into even lower categories. The lower the level of intelligence, the more reckless and inaccessible to influence the girl becomes.

The behavior of the other group of 119 girls (47.6 per cent) can best be paralleled to the phase of puberty. However, this must not be understood to mean that these girls are going in a normal way through puberty which period even without the bearing of particular psychopathology inclines toward tempestuosity. In them, all the characteristics of puberty appear crass, as it were, and one gains the impression that their state is not one of transition from one phase of development into another, but rather, their development appears arrested in the phase of puberty.

A difficult family situation such as a brutal father, a frivolous mother, the presence of a stepfather, or a stepmother has in all cases a particularly unfavorable effect, because of the incestuous attachment of the girls to their fathers. Conflicts drive the girls from their homes. They feel lonely, abandoned, and, if they find a partner, they drift into attachments which they themselves can no longer control. In most cases such attachments lead to a relationship of marked dependency. In this group we find girls who disappear for weeks from their environment, and secretly live with an Allied soldier. Their subsequent evaluation of the man is characteristic. Again and again, one hears the statement: "He was so good to me." In all these girls the narcissistic component is conspicuous.

Of the 119 girls, 82 (32.8 per cent) are of average or above average intelligence; 20 (8.0 per cent) are below average; 17 (6.8 per cent) must be considered as a separate group: they are in their puberty, but nevertheless show a greater degree of sexual repression than the rest, and further they come to attention mainly by thievery.

The following is a summary of the grouping:

I. Apparently adult 17   6.8%

II. In puberty 119   47.6%

    a) normal intelligence 82   32.8%
    b) subnormal intelligence 20   8.0%
    c) other defects 17   6.8%

III. In pre-puberty 92   36.8%

    a) normal intelligence 52   20.8%
    b) subnormal intelligence 40   16.0%

IV. Feeble-minded 19   7.6%

V. Latent psychosis 3   1.2%

Before the question can be answered as to what kind of care and treatment these girls are to be given, it is important to know some further details about them.

The girls described in Group I, the apparently adult, come to the attention of social agencies for a variety of reasons: because of family quarrels, vagrancy, or lack of identification papers; and less frequently because of delinquency per se. They, as well as the girls of Group II (puberty) suffer from an irrepressible need to cling to others. In some of them this need is more or less distinctly recognizable, others apparently ward it off and hide it behind aggressive behavior. If, however, this need is recognized and the right approach is used, it hardly makes any difference whether the object of their attachment be a woman or a man. Why this is so, is easily understandable: in the first instance the transference takes place on a homosexual basis, in the second it is based on the attachment to the father. The girls run away from their homes if their cravings for "clinging to" are not offered opportunities of satisfaction and they consequently are subjected to serious disappointments. In the girls who are in their puberty[7] the need to cling has not yet become fixed onto a specific object, and with proper understanding they can quickly be compensated for the loss of the partner whom they had found outside of their homes. In many cases the infantile fixations are markedly repressed. These girls need an atmosphere of particularly great warmth.

7. The concept of puberty refers here to its psychological connotation.

The sublimation of the narcissistic component, i. e., its displacement onto socially acceptable achievements is more easily attained by the girls who are both talented and pretty than by those who are talented but less attractive. In the latter a certain amount of suspiciousness must be overcome first. The less intelligent girls appear more in danger than the rest on account of their lower capacity for judgment. They are also' more exposed to the danger of flight by running away than the girls of Group I.

Group III, the girls of pre-puberal age, comprises those who are most difficult to guide. In them the capacity for social empathy or the need for community with others is still on an exceedingly primitive level. Consequently they associate with others exclusively for the sake of satisfying primitive sexual needs or for the purpose of achieving specific aims. They make themselves conspicuous by their talk, by bragging with actual or fictional sexual experiences. They are very touchy, inclined to react with immediate defiance, are quite erratic, and will often run away from the institution for no obvious reason. The lower their intelligence, the grosser their symptoms.

Here I shall answer the second question previously asked: "What measures are advisable in order to deal with this type of delinquent girls?"

Help, treatment, and cure are impossible without the establishment of institutions adapted to the particular needs of each group.

1. Girls of Group I can be placed in any home in which their reality situation is considered and accepted, and the girls are permitted to continue their relationships to their sex partners, albeit to a limited extent. It even might be considered to place these girls in a home for non-delinquent girls. Under no circumstances must they be put together with really delinquent girls, because the latter would be unable to understand the reasons for the relative freedom granted to the former. Although the extent to which the girls belonging to Group I can be influenced by educational means is limited they need guidance. The worker responsible for them must know the severe degrees of dependency which results from incestuous father fixations, and further must be able to initiate the severance of the libidinal ties from objects of early childhood.

2. Regardless of differences in intellectual endowment the girls of Group II may be housed together in one home which, however, must be strictly separated from others. In such a Home the girls can as a rule be

guided with comparative ease provided that pedagogically well-trained workers are available. Differentiations in treatment will have to correspond to the selections of sublimating activities. In smaller Homes with women teachers it is advisabe to have a male superintendent. In larger Homes it is advisable to have both women and men as educators, the latter in smaller numbers, e. g., as instructors and special teachers.

In these Homes, an exclusively educational approach will prove inadequate; training of the educators in psychoanalysis will be indispensible.

3. The girls of Group III (pre-puberty) present the most difficult problem of rehabilitation. The normally intelligent girls must be separated from those of subnormal intelligence; and both groups must be confined to closed institutions.

The closed institution for the normally intelligent girls must offer opportunities for occupational training. Within a simple setting, systematic retraining based on well defined goals must foster a development towards maturity. This can be achieved by consistent dispensation of rewards and pleasure premiums for each step forward.

Overt perversions are to be treated by psychotherapy. A psychotherapist will also have to be consulted in Homes for girls of Groups I and II, in instances of manifest neurosis or of severely neurotic delinquency.

In closed Homes for girls of subnormal intelligence the requirements of vocational training will be kept on a lower level. In many cases, training will be restricted to agricultural or domestic work. However, these institutions also need highly qualified educators.

Future research will clarify the details concerning therapeutic measures.

4. Feeble-minded girls whose intellect is as badly impaired as that of the 19 girls in Group IV, can hardly be re-educated. Such girls have to be segregated in a special institution, and merely protected from becoming incurable delinquents.

5. Girls with latent psychosis, like those in Group V, must be placed in an institution under supervision of a medical specialist. I shall deal in another report with questions of the required set-up.

At this point the reader will probably ask why I report about this work at a time when I have done hardly more than pointed out a problem and formulated a hypothesis.

Agencies which aim at the care of youth endangered in its moral and ethical development face today a task which scarcely can be accomplished unless new and effective ways of coping with the emergency are found. A considerable part of these agencies' responsibility concerns girls manifestly or latently delinquent whose number skyrockets during the present postwar period. Even now, at the beginning of this my work which I am planning with the co-operation of my coworkers, it has become obvious that our preliminary grouping, our hypotheses regarding the girls' psychological situation, our suggestions regarding their education, the desirable qualifications of educators and the organization of the Homes will contribute to finding solutions of those problems that confront agencies and social workers.

Consequently we are not merely entitled, but rather obligated to publish our preliminary results.

RIOTS

Observation in a Home for Delinquent Girls

By RUTH S. EISSLER, M.D. (New York)

During the three years of my work as consulting psychiatrist to a Home for delinquent girls, I had opportunity to observe certain typical reactions on the part of the individual and the group. The majority of these girls were white Protestants, ranging in age from 12–18 years, whose delinquency consisted in the main of sexual promiscuity, petty larceny, and running away from home. Only a few of these girls were involved in any serious criminal activities. Most of them came from families of the lowest income groups, many from broken homes or completely deteriorated backgrounds. A certain percentage were adopted children, others had stepfathers or stepmothers. Scarcely any child came from a stable family environment. Even though every girl showed her own individual reaction pattern, based on her life history, nevertheless, there were certain reactions, typical of all of them, which under certain specific circumstances were predictable. Thus, for instance, if a girl had not had sexual intercourse prior to her commitment, it was predictable that she would run away some time later in order to obtain this experience. No bars were too thick, no doors too well protected to prevent her breaking out. By the time she had returned, which she generally did, she had invariably had the necessary experience. I say necessary, because this experience actually was a necessity for her status in the group; by it she proved herself heterosexual and thereby could ward off any suspicion of homosexuality.

Running away, which had played a role in the history of every girl committed to the Home, was one of the most ferquent reactions and was typical of both the individual and the group. It always occurred when tension accumulated whether the stimulus was internal or came from the environment. But it seemed that an individual escape usually signified an inner conflict of that individual, whereas the mass escape was precipitated by events that reflected dissension or tension among the supervising staff. Where the conflict was primarily one between an individual girl and her surroundings, defiance or temper tantrums were the rule.

The most interesting and complex reaction that occurred was the riot. At first view it seemed neither to be predictable nor to have any definite psychological structure, but occurred rather like an electrical storm. Gradually it became evident that this mass reaction had a very definite psychological structure and followed a quite specific psychological pattern.

I should like to give a brief description of this institution and how it was run, since its policies possibly had a bearing on the particular structure of the mass reaction we observed, even though some elements of that reaction might well be common to and typical of all riot situations.

The building was a barren, old, brick house, situated in one of the worst districts of the city, a deteriorated and over-populated colored section. Delinquency ran high in this area. The doors of the institution were locked, the windows protected by iron bars. The number of resident girls varied between 50 and 65. Although the majority were white and Protestant, there were a few Catholic and Jewish girls. Only occasionally was a colored girl committed. They were divided into 3 groups, for convenience of management only, and with no regard for the age or psychological needs of the individual. They slept in separate rooms, furnished with only the bare necessities of a cot and sometimes a chair. The rooms were without heat, and light had been installed only a short time before I came to the institution. Each group had its own living room, but all 3 groups ate in a common dining room. The institution's school, which the girls attended, was part of the public school system. The staff of the home consisted mainly of untrained personnel whose only qualification was their years of experience in the institution, which in several cases amounted to about 25. Each department had a housemother. The work about the house was done by the girls and was considered the chief educational project since it was supposed to train the children for their future role as housewives. They were almost completely isolated from the rest of the world: no newspapers were permitted, letters were censored, visitors were permitted only once a month, outings were kept at a minimum. Nor did they have any privacy, but were constantly under observation and did not even have a locker or box in which they could lock their most cherished possessions in order to guard them from the others. Aside from the contact with their own housemother, the contact with other members of the staff or with girls in other departments was discouraged. They had neither understanding of nor voice in the policies of the institution, but, on the contrary, were kept in ignorance of everything that went on in the Home on principle. When the assistant superintendent left the Home after 25 years of service, the children were not informed. They were almost completely separated from the life of the adult world around them. This adult environment consisted only of women: few men ever entered the building. The children were kept under strict discipline, with rigid routines and a rigidly planned schedule. Punishment consisted in deprivation of small privileges, such as an occasional visit to the movies or a visit home, and solitary confinement for hours or days.

Shortly before I became the consulting psychiatrist, a new superintendent had been appointed who began to change some aspects of the institution, mainly by bringing in a few professionally trained people (a social worker and some recreational workers), and by introducing a planned recreational program. In the course of the following years the setup changed to a certain extent, but unfortunately many of the intended and proposed changes, although vitally necessary, could not be realized. In part this failure stemmed from some of the basic resistances to effective procedures in the problem of delinquency as a whole. This aspect forms the subject of another paper and can only be mentioned in passing here. In part the failure was also due to the wartime situation which made it almost impossible to find adequate personnel.

However, it is important to mention that riots occurred only during the first period, the period of transition from the very rigid discipline to a more liberal attitude. Later we found methods of channelling these mass reactions into organized ways of expression which were socially more acceptable.

From this sketch of the institution's organization, it is obvious that there was no opportunity for individualized reactions, which, if they did occur, were promptly suppressed by disciplinary measures. Therefore the child who was committed to the institution found herself in a threefold conflict: 1) She had to cope with her own impulses, 2) she had to comply with the demands of an adult world in which she had no share, and 3) she had to make and safeguard a position for herself with the other girls of her group.

The latter task was most important, since otherwise she was left completely isolated without any support in the first two conflict situations. Also her hope of any libidinal gratification depended on this group. However, these very libidinal strivings toward the other girls represented at the same time a tremendous danger. Through insight gained by individual psychotherapeutic interviews with members of this group and through analysis of similar cases, it became evident that the delinquency of these adolescent girls represents essentially a defense against their homosexual impulses directed toward their mothers, but, simultaneously, it serves as revenge for the imagined or real rejection by their mothers. Whether this homosexual attachment is based on guilt feelings stemming from the oedipal situation, or is a regression to the pre-oedipal phase because the relationship to their fathers was either too tenuous or too traumatic, could not be definitely evaluated. Only psychoanalysis of a series of cases of this type would furnish an answer. Unfortunately such cases very rarely remain under analysis for a period long enough to reach these deep layers of material. Usually the patient's environment interferes, for reasons closely connected with the problem of delinquency, and brings treatment to an end before this stage can be reached.

These delinquent girls, locked in and isolated from the rest of the world, were unable to apply their previous defenses against their homosexual impulses. They were constantly in danger of being overwhelmed by and becoming conscious of their homosexual desires and strivings. Therefore it is understandable that whenever their desire was very close to consciousness, or at the point of being actively satisfied, they were on the verge of panic and either reacted with acts of aggression or attempts to escape. Such occasions arose, for instance, whenever they felt unjustly treated or had any grievances against the staff. The natural reaction would be to turn for consolation and libidinal "repair" to other group members, but then the homosexual danger would become acute. Apparently the only acceptable way to satisfy these desires, at least in some cases, was by the care and protection of a younger member of the group, and the younger, smaller, and more infantile such a group member was, the more easily the other girls could assume this protective role. One of the riots, which will be discussed later, started in connection with such a youngster, who in addition was mentally retarded.

If we now realize that the main conflict in such a setup centered around the girls' homosexual strivings, it will not be surprising that the strongest group reactions took place whenever one of the girls revealed herself as being overtly homosexual, or was discovered or merely rumored to be a pervert, no matter of what kind of perversion she might have been accused. However, this factor by itself was not sufficient to set off a riot. It only procured the necessary victim, the scapegoat.

Everyone who has worked in an institution of the kind described, soon becomes very sensitive to mounting tension among the inmates. Whatever physical evidence it is that conveys the impression, whether it be a threatening silence, the expression on the faces, conversation by whispering, the guarded look of staff members and girls, or defiance in physical posture, it is so unmistakably noticeable, that it was usually easy to predict the possibility of some kind of outburst. The most urgent problem was to investigate the causes for this accumulation of tension in order to be able to neutralize it. We found that whenever the equilibrium among the group of adults was labile, either because of changes in personnel or because of dissension within that group, although the children were not taken into their confidence, they reacted with rising tension. Apparently their own insecurity was so great, their narcissistic needs so strong, that any change in the atmosphere of the adult world which surrounded them constituted an immediate danger and produced anxiety. The delinquent even more than the normal or the neurotic child reacts almost reflexively to any change in his environment, be it physical or emotional, and frequently one receives the impression that the reaction is but a distorted reflection of the adult's attitude. What seems to be incomprehensible, irrational behavior on the child's part, at closer investigation reveals itself as a mirror image of the grown-up's irrational behavior, an image produced by one of those mirrors which distort the original object. Inevitably this increasing tension of the children was then felt by the staff members who, expecting a violent outbreak of some kind, became frightened and expressed their anxiety in greater irritability and severity. It can easily be seen that this situation formed a vicious circle which lasted until the tension reached its peak and some outlet presented itself. The outlet usually found was in a riot against the above-mentioned scapegoat.

It is a justifiable question to ask why the riot was not directed against the adult world, the staff, but against a group member.

I shall now describe the two riots that took place shortly after I became connected with the institution.

They occurred during the period of change and discharge of personnel. The older staff members felt insecure about their positions and very hostile against the new professional members who tried to lessen the rigidity of discipline and routine. Aside from the fear of loosing their jobs, they were afraid of the girls, except when their initiative was suppressed and they were held down. Possibly they expected retaliation from them. They did not believe in showing the children more warmth or giving them more freedom. The children, in their turn, although forming a closer relation to the recently introduced members of the staff, were puzzled and upset by the departure of their old guardians against whom they had felt mainly antagonistic.

As it happened, one of the professional staff members who had been a particular favorite of the group left of her own accord in order to get married. She was especially loved by June, a tall, voluptuous 17-year-old girl, who was either known to be or suspected by the girls of being overtly homosexual. June was one of the girls who was quite undisciplined, seeking for extra privileges, and inclined to very demonstrative behavior. However, although she did not get along very well with the other girls, their hostility so far had taken no active form. But very soon after the beloved counselor left, June ran away and succeeded in making a dramatic scene with her mother (a direct reaction to the loss of her love object). She returned to the institution willingly and was not too severely punished for her misdemeanor. But in the meantime the group tension had mounted excessively and suddenly there was a violent riot against June, who was knocked down and beaten by the other girls and accused of homosexual acts.

The second riot occurred during the same period of change in personnel, somewhat later than the one just described. It was this second riot to which I referred in connection with the tendency of the girls to care for and to protect younger members of the group. At that time a 12-year-old girl was committed to the institution. She was physically attractive and very small, in appearance rather like an 8-year-old; emotionally and mentally she was on an even younger level. She was enthusiastically accepted by the other girls, who felt very protective toward her and rightly felt that she did not belong in such an institution. They took care of her tenderly, pampered her, and were not at all aware of the influence which she gradually exerted over the group. As is frequently the case with these mentally retarded children, she had a certain shrewdness and used it to create antagonism among the girls who competed for her favors. Another girl was committed who was reputed to be a pervert; she was accused of sexual activities with babies and animals, especially cats. The source of this information remained unknown, but apparently some one of them had been with her in the Juvenile Detention Home and then carried this rumor to the institution. But not this rumor alone: suddenly the belief was whispered that the unfortunate girl had a tail and actually looked like a cat. After she had been in the institution for just a few days a riot started up crystallizing around the accusation that she had attacked the little protégée of the group. This riot began in a very peculiar way, however. The said "catgirl" was taking a bath, and the other girls at first tried to peep into the bathroom to verify their belief of her physical monstrosity. At first they teased and tormented her with their voyeuristic activities, trying to look through the transom, opening the door, and trying to snatch off the garments which she put on to protect herself. Then, whether disappointed in their expectations or for other precipitating reasons, they went on to violent physical attacks. It was difficult for the housemother and other staff members to intervene and rescue the victim. It must be added that this scapegoat was a psychotic girl who was quite withdrawn, almost stuporous, and who later was sent to a mental institution.

One of the most interesting features of this riot was the evidently infantile level on which it took place, i. e., the voyeuristic element, and the fantasy of the victim's bodily difference, the tail. Quite obviously, aside from the phallic meaning of the tail, she must have representad the devil to them, the devil who attacks little childen. Furthermore, it became evident that this specific type of riot occurred on account of the youngest and most infantile member of the group and that the intellectual and emotional level of all sank to the level of this mentally retarded child.

Before trying to connect these examples of group reaction, I should like to add another observation which shows the previous riot situation transformed into a socially more acceptable mass reaction.

I mentioned before that one of the most immediate tasks which faced me was the prevention of these riots. None of the obvious approaches to this problem could be used because of lack of time. It was not possible to use individual psychotherapy with the girls. The changes of personnel were unavoidable—the physical improvements of the institution could only be gradual. And finally, the necessary education of the staff could not occur over night. We therefore had to hit upon an emergency measure. Accordingly when tension again accumulated to such a degree that some violent reaction could be expected, we suggested an immediate mass meeting with the girls and only the superintendent present. It worked exceedingly well. Although it was a stormy session, the voice of reason, namely the superintendent's, was heard and finally accepted. The girls calmed down. These meetings were repeated a few times whenever there was noticeable accumulation of tension, and before it had reached the peak of a riot situation. We stressed the importance of only the superintendent being present because we aimed to make the superintendent the center of the girls' emotional life. It would lead too far away from the subject of this paper to discuss the necessity of such an emotional point of gravitation in an institution for delinquents, but it should be said that the success of our endeavors hinged on this, and that whatever we achieved during the unfortunately brief period of rehabilitation of the institution was due to this factor.

After several of these meetings had been called by the superintendent, and the riots had been successfully prevented for some time, an incident occurred which had not been foreseen by any of us and which greatly surprised us.

It was during the holiday period between Thanksgiving and Christmas; a period which per se had always been full of strong reactions and difficulties because of visits home, jealousy, increased shortage of personnel, etc. This year, however, certain changes had to be made in the living arrangements at the institution just at this period. These changes deprived one of the departments of its larger living room and also put the girls under greater strain since they had to move their things and do additional housework. The main factor, however, was that the beneficiary of these changes was the superintendent, who needed a more satisfactory office. A great mistake was made in not discussing these changes beforehand and not letting the girls voice their opinions, which probably could have been easily adjusted to the realistic necessity of this move. At first no noticeable reaction occurred; however, on the basis of previous experiences, we expected a delayed reaction. After a few days had passed the tension rose so quickly and so high that all the staff members became afraid. Even the superintendent, who avoided any group discussion of the matter felt so uneasy and was so wary of a possible outbreak of violence that she did not dare to undress at night. Yet she did not call a mass meeting. And now, when the tension actually reached the boiling point—the girls, instead of rioting, took the matter into their own hands, called a mass meeting, and insisted on the superintendent's presence. It was the first time that, instead of rioting, they took the initiative toward an organized, socially acceptable mass procedure. At the same time they forced the adult to play the game according to the rules and to abide by the law she had taught them. This was an unexpected and interesting progress but the more interesting part was what followed. This spontaneous mass meeting actually proceeded true to the structure of the riot. The girls did not attack the superintendent but selected a scapegoat One of the girls in the department was a cardiac case and on the basis of this condition she was exempt from heavy work. However, in spite of her ailment, she sometimes indulged in jitterbugging. This untoward behavior infuriated the other girls. She was not admitted to the meeting, but violently denounced, and her behavior was criticized and verbally attacked to such a degree that it made this meeting the stormiest in the history of the Home. The superintendent finally took the floor and explained to the assembly the reason for the frequently irrational behavior of such an individual who had to endure so many deprivations, and then she asked if she might call the girl and give her a chance to defend herself. This was agreed to and the defendant, first defiantly but soon pleadingly, told them her story of suffering, deprivation and unhappiness, using almost the same words as the superintendent. The reaction of the group was striking. They were moved to tears. One girl after another rose to assure the defendant of her sympathy and to tell about her own experience of loneliness and deprivation. The criminal was forgiven and again accepted into the group. The storm had passed by, but what had actually happened?

I will add here, to complete the picture and to exonerate the superintendent, that she called a staff meeting the next day and, although the children had not come out with their real grievance against her, new decisions about the distribution of housework were made, which eased the children's life considerably. She apparently had understood the meaning of the meeting even though it had not been directly verbalized.

After this first attempt to react in an organized way, the children repeated it whenever they felt the tension accumulate within their group. These mass meetings invariably showed the same structure with the one important addition, namely, that after the violent attack on the scapegoat, one of the former attackers always spontaneously took over the defense of the victim and usually did such a good job that the others calmed down and began to deal quite rationally with the object of their wrath. It was impressive to see how willing they were to behave with justice and fairness. However, in the history of these meetings they never once turned against the superintendent who, after the above-mentioned dramatic spontaneous assembly, kept herself completely in the background. This signifies that the meetings still had essentially the character of a riot; they were always directed against one member of their group who by certain provocations had drawn upon herself the anger of the others, and therefore could be easily used as a scapegoat. The actual cause of their tension, namely the behavior of the adults, was never brought up on these occasions. We never learned the answer to the question whether by skillful leadership the assembly could have been induced to face and verbalize their real feelings about the adult world and their relationship to it. Unfortunately, the ubiquitous unconscious resistance against any possibly effective means to deal with the problems of delinquency showed itself. For it was not long before the maintenance staff, unchecked by those who should have known better, made a mockery of these attempts on the girls' part to make themselves heard in an organized way. They sabotaged their initiative by calling meetings on their own accord, presiding at these meetings, and telling the children what to do and what not to do. Naturally there was no impetus left in the group to continue with what must have meant to them the first step toward an ordered society of their own.

I have tried to present the structure of the riots and the mass meetings which I had opportunity to observe, but the question, why the aggression was not directed against the adult population of the institution, has still not been answered. However, we may be able to find an explanation if we return for a while to my previous statement about the struggle against homosexual impulses, a conflict which appears to be the basis for the delinquency of these adolescent girls and which necessarily was greatly sharpened by the atmosphere of the institution.

The delinquent girl scarcely ever professes guilt feelings for her promiscuity, or if she does, she evokes the impression of giving pure lip service. I think that this impression is correct. Usually such a girl does not feel guilty for her heterosexual activities; on the contrary, she may be quite proud of them. This does not mean, however, that these children do not know feelings of shame and guilt. Strangely enough the one constant complaint voiced by every girl in interviews with the psychiatrist was the complaint about the bad language used by all the other girls. Whatever this may mean, every one of them was deeply concerned about this fact, even though every one of them used "bad language". The overt feelings of guilt were usually expressed in connection with their mothers, in repentance because they caused them so much worry, in fear lest their mothers would not love them any more, and in desire to go home to them and to undo the harm they inflicted upon them, etc. Indeed, the desire and longing for their mothers was exceedingly strong even in those children who, in reality, never had received any kindness or love from their mothers. None of these girls had formed any real object relationship to any male. They changed their male companions quite frequently and casually, and even exchanged them with their girl friends. In only a very few cases could one detect any tender or affectionate feelings for the father. It seemed therefore that in spite of the noisy demonstration of heterosexuality, the relationship to male objects was quite tenuous. On the other hand their need for the affection and love of a mother was excessive, as was shown during the years when the methods for dealing with the children were liberalized. We experienced over and over again that as soon as homosexual impulses came more closely to consciousness the girls would run away. However, they either returned very soon of their own accord or arranged matters in such a way that they could be easily traced and brought back.

Apparently the actual unconscious feelings of guilt were due to their homosexual desires. These desires were absolutely unacceptable to them and they believed them unacceptable to the people of their surroundings as well. Their backgrounds of broken or incompatible marriages had exposed them to an inconsistency of treatment which made their superego formation unstable or defective. They had never received any consistent support against their impulses and were frightened as much of the strength of these impulses as of the uncertainty of the consequences. Therefore any consistency of treatment, any certainty of consequences was welcome, even though the treatment was cruel and sadistic. Dissension or changes in the surrounding adult world increased their anxiety as to their own unconquerable and unacceptable impulses. Changes in personnel could only mean that someone had been punished by being sent away, and they immediately identified themselves with that person on the basis of their guilt feelings and were afraid of having to suffer the same consequences. They were usually able to accept punishment if it was dispensed according to set rules. But any injustice, any favoritism or irrational behavior on the adult's part would shatter the artificially built-up security and the same increase of anxiety would again occur, since they would feel unloved and rejected for the unconscious guilt connected with their homosexual impulses. From this analysis then it is easier to understand why they had to select a scapegoat. By rioting against an overtly homosexual victim they cast their own guilt upon her and by attacking her denied their own homosexual impulses. One might almost think that it was a ritual in which their unacceptable tendencies, personified by the scapegoat, were sacrificed to the irate gods.

That they identified themselves with the scapegoat is shown by their attitude in the mass meetings, which were actually trials of a single victim who was then spontaneously defended by one of the attackers and subsequently again taken into the fold. During the first of these trials the superintendent had opened the way to verbalization of this identification. The readiness with which the whole group started to identify itself with the suffering of the cardiac girl was due to the presence of this adult and was a bid for the same love that she showed in her sympathy and consideration for the attacked girl. And since they were pleading for her love and forgiveness, they were certainly not able to attack the mother image. If they had attacked her, they would have destroyed the source of their security and the object of their longings.

I have only once had the opportunity of learning in an analysis about the psychological consequences which participation in a riot might have for an individual. The analysand in question was not a delinquent, on the contrary, she had a very severe superego and belonged rather to the compulsive neurotic type without manifest symptoms.

She was brought up in Central Europe and was at the beginning of puberty by the end of the First World War. Her father had been gone during the whole period of the war, leaving her mother to manage a rather large family without the support of any male authority. The patient was very much attached to her mother throughout her childhood, almost to the extent of infatuation. At puberty these feelings were transferred to a female teacher with whom the girl was quite consciously in love. Following a period of hunger there were riots in the town in which she lived, and mobs tore through the streets screaming and plundering. One of these riots was directed against a factory for canned goods, the owner of which had been accused of using the genitalia of animals in his products. On her way to school the young girl met the rioting mob, was drawn into it, and found herself in the plant where the products were being thrown out of the windows or destroyed. Completely identified with the mob, the girl grabbed some of these cans and finally, after having become separated from the rioting masses, she ran to school with her loot. There, still in an over-excited and exhilarated emotional state, she put the stolen can on her beloved teacher's desk. The somewhat reserved and puzzled expression on the teacher's face suddenly restored the girl to normalcy. It was like awakening from a dream and she was overwhelmed by feelings of shame and guilt. Even after many years, when she had reached adulthood and had developed into an almost compulsively self-disciplined person, she could not think of the incident without experiencing the same feelings of shame and guilt. This incident, which had proved to her how easily an individual may surrender his inhibitions in a mass situation, led to a complete inability to adjust herself to any group. She could not participate in any group situation even though it might be a perfectly acceptable organization whose goals she might have supported whole-heartedly or whose individual members might even have been her personal friends. There was only one exception to this, namely, if she was the leader and was able to exert a restraining influence on the impulses of the group. The real cause for her shame and guilt was, I think, not the identification with the uncontrolled mob, but the homosexual love for her teacher, and the symbolic sacrifice of the male genitalia represented by the stolen can which was rumored to contain the genitalia of male animals.

At the beginning of this paper I raised the question of the general validity of my observations concerning riots in a Home for delinquent girls. I still hesitate to draw any general conclusions. However, there are certain aspects which, at least, may permit speculations about riots as social phenomena, their social function and unconscious meaning. Participation in the riots described and analyzed above was interpreted as a defense against unsublimated homosexual impulses, which were provoked in response to the insecurity and anxiety arising from feelings of rejection by a parental imago. The riots were directed against a scapegoat who represented the unacceptable homosexual impulses of the group members, and who had to suffer the violence with which these impulses were rejected. Thus, symbolically, the scapegoat and the homosexual strivings were sacrificed to the parental imago.

According to Freud's analysis of mass phenomena in *Group Psychology and the Analysis of the Ego,* the main forces which bind together the individuals in a mass are the projection of the ego ideal on to the leader, the identification with this ego ideal, and the ensuing identification with the other members of the group on the basis of sublimated homosexual impulses. The organization of a group remains intact as long as the feeling of love and acceptance by the leader is preserved. However, when something occurs which shakes the conviction of this feeling the identification with the leader is annulled and the sublimation of the homosexual impulses breaks down. Through the sudden onslaught of homosexual libido the ego of the individual group member is endangered and is overwhelmed by unbearable anxiety; the object relationships to the fellow group members are severed, the group disintegrates rapidly and panic ensues. The individual, isolated and endangered by his own overwhelming impulses tries to save himself by flight, projecting the inner danger indiscriminately onto an external world which does no longer appear to consist of individual objects, but the aspect of which becomes a fusion of vague and terrifying impressions.

If we compare the phenomenon of riot with the one of panic then we cannot avoid the conclusion that riots seem to have an integrating social function at least for their duration. Instead of complete isolation of the individual and disruption of object relations, as occurs in the case of panics, in riots identification of the individual group members with each other takes place on the basis of identical guilt feelings; a common object is found onto which the rejected impulses are projected and which is then sacrificed for the sake of regaining the love of the ego ideal or the parental imago. In this one act—the riot—all three factors, namely, the parental image, the attacking mass and the scapegoat, are riveted together, and one gains the impression that the riot as a social phenomenon resembles in structure a neurotic symptom. There, likewise, superego, ego, and id, compromise in the defense against disintegration. But in contrast to the neurotic symptom, which is an autoplastic solution of a conflict, the riot is an attack launched against an external object. The discharge of aggression by means of an attack against a scapegoat preserves coherence of the group which is on the verge of disintegration. Without the emergence of a riot the individual would be exposed, in a specific situation, to the outbreak of indomitable anxiety, would lose all object ties and be thrown into complete isolation. The riot is an emergency defense against the acute danger of panic.

FEEDING PROBLEMS OF PSYCHOGENIC ORIGIN

A Survey of the Literature

By EDWARD LEHMAN, M.D. (New York) [1]

The psychologic aspects of eating and foods are of great significance. According to English and Pearson (30), the emotional disorders of appetite, ingestion and digestion of food constitute about 24 per cent of all pediatric cases. They state, "Many pediatricians consider that nearly every child has had some more or less marked disturbance in eating by the time he attains 7 years." Escalona (31) wrote, "It would seem that in the case of infants and young children eating behavior may serve as an especially sensitive indicator of general adjustment." Because of the significance of eating and feeding problems, we are surveying the related literature, with some brief discussion of its implications.

DEVELOPMENTAL FACTORS

I. Psychic Significance of Eating. Breast-feeding. Nursing and Weaning. Restoration of Active Role to the Child

Normally, "To be loved is to be fed" (67). Consequently a child's rejection of food may be a reaction to rejection of the mother (25, 72). Such a child feels unconsciously, "Since mother does not love me I need not eat her food." Thus, as Lorand (63) stated, food may become "a vehicle of love and punishment". Food may be refused to tyrannize the surroundings (49), or, according to Alexander (3), to get attention. Frequently, however, a desire for attention is a desire for love. The parent's interest may be enlisted not only by refusing food but, in other cases, by staying fat and refusing to follow a reducing diet (14).

According to Senn and Newill (90) a' child may eat willingly for one person but refuse to accept identical food offered by another. Schmideberg (83) reported a child who believed that whatever the

1. From the Pediatric Service of Dr. Murray H. Bass and the Psychiatric Service of Dr. M. Ralph Kaufman, Mount Sinai Hospital.

mother gave her to eat was "bad" and that what was withheld was "good". This thought resulted from a projection onto the mother and represented the way the child herself unconsciously wished to treat the mother.

For the mother, Middlemore (70) describes breast-feeding as a "delightful experience", and for the baby it must be similar. Even the term "alimentary orgasm" has been used by Rado (76) for the gratification that results from satiation. Today breast-feeding is very frequently neglected (16), often for the convenience of mothers, who thereby express some unconscious rejection of their infants. Too often the physician interferes with breast-feeding without sufficient reason, sometimes right after birth, not even giving the breast a trial. Usually the bottle is a very successful source of nourishment. However, as Selling and Ferraro (88) stated, "No formula has as yet been devised which will enable the bottle to give the love, security, affection and the pride that even an infant seems to be able to gather from the mother's affectionate embrace while he nurses from her." Therefore, at least part of the child's food should if possible be supplied by the breast during most of the first year. This may be complemented at each feeding by any necessary additional nourishment. The bottle, especially if it is the sole source of milk, should be given in a manner that simulates breast-feeding as closely as possible. Too frequently the baby receives the bottle lying down and often the infant must hold its own bottle. The mother or nurse should at least help support the bottle, and the baby should always be held in the same position in her arms as if at the breast (90). Under these circumstances the mother, if capable of loving her child, will convey a sense of her affection by caresses and endearments.

The reaction to change is very important in the earliest eating disorders, which occur during the neonatal period. Just as the function of respiration must be assumed by the pulmonary system within the first few minutes after birth, so the function of maintaining nutrition must be newly undertaken by the alimentary tract within the first few days. A stubborn refusal to nurse occurs sometimes in the newborn, for example, Feldstein (32) reported a "breast and bottle shy" infant. Alexander (3) believes that feeding difficulties at this period may be caused by a resistance to the changed conditions after birth. Gesell and Ilg (50) state that the young infant who feeds poorly, "really seems to prefer sleeping to eating as though he were still in a quasi-fetal state of existence." According to Spock and Huschka (95) "Some infants nurse well from birth while others appear either not to know what it is all about or to actually balk and resist and get angry. Many of the latter group learn to nurse in a few days and do it well. But there is an appreci-

able number who don't." Fries (48) classified new born infants into
3 groups: active, moderately active and quiet. She reported that the
poor feeders are particularly present in either extreme group, that is
among the active or the quiet infants. Middlemore (70) carefully studied
the early course of mutual adaptation by mother and suckling in the
relationship of nursing, and, amongst other disturbing factors, she mentioned roughness and clumsiness of nervous mothers. Escalona (31)
found that no amount of direct teaching changed the nursing behavior
of such a mother, and that the babies on the same day may accept a
formula when offered by someone else but refuse to take it from the
mother.

Norval (73) regarded the sucking response of 50 newborn babies at
the breast as poor in only 4 per cent. However, Ribble (80) stated that
in a group of 600 newborn infants, at least 40 per cent ". . . had to be
taught to suck in the following manner: the mouth was opened by the
nurse or mother, the nipple inserted well inside the mouth cavity, and
the chin of the baby worked rhythmically up and down." Ribble placed
great emphasis on the importance of the right kind of mothering, which,
she stated, ". . . is really a continuance of the closeness of the prenatal
state, and the more clearly it imitates certain of the conditions before
birth the more successful it is in the first week." She advised that the
newborn baby still needs to be carried about at regular intervals because
holding gives him reassurance and the contact with the mother ". . . takes
the place of the physical connection before birth when the child was like
an organ of the mother's body. In addition, mothering includes the
whole gamut of small acts by means of which an emotionally healthy
mother consistently shows her love for her child, thus instinctively stimulating his psychic development. Obviously feeding, bathing and all the
details of physical care come in, but in addition . . . fondling, caressing,
rocking and singing or speaking to the baby."

Discussing the new conditions, to which the infant must adapt right
after birth, Frank (36) stated, that "The frequent pattern of newborn
care, especially in hospitals, is that he is taken away from his mother,
deprived of cuddling and soothing and of opportunity for sucking and
the comfort of breast feeding. He is also prematurely subjected to prolonged fasting after having been continuously nourished during gesta-
tion and is subject to strong emotional provocation, allowed to cry
uncomforted and to undergo prolonged fits of rage or of fear and anxiety.
In consequence, eating, which should be a simple, pleasurable experience, may become an occasion for tension and emotional disturbances
which may be the beginning of frequent feeding problems observed
among pre-school children."

Not only right after birth but thenceforth particularly during the first year, eating disorders are precipitated by change. When new foods are introduced difficulties may occur, at first with liquids such as fruit juices and cod liver oil, later with soft substances such as cereals and prepared vegetables, and still later with "solid" food. Sometimes these foods are started too early, and Gesell and Ilg (50) believe symptoms may result from "awkwardness due to the immaturity of the oral apparatus". Escalona (31) found that approximately one out of twelve infants showed stubborn resistance to solid food, and that this same food might be accepted without difficulty when fed by another fairly relaxed person using proper technique although violently resisted when offered by the mother.

Not only may the effect of change be observed sometimes after the introduction of new foods, but even greater disturbance may be induced by the discontinuance of already established modes of nutrition for, as is well known, weaning, particularly from the breast but also from the bottle, may induce an emotional reaction in a baby (12). The same milk that was taken eagerly from the bottle may be stubbornly rejected when offered in a cup or glass. Grulee (53) stated, "Not infrequently at the time of weaning we encounter very severe cases of anorexia which resist almost all efforts at feeding artificially." Spock and Huschka (95) believe "weaning is life's first major frustrating experience." According to Schmideberg (83) weaning from the breast may be equated by the infant with losing the mother entirely. Melanie Klein (58) believes that the infant may react to weaning with depressive feelings or even beginning melancholia, and she said, "The object which is being mourned is the mother's breast and all that the breast and the milk have come to stand for in the infant's mind: namely love, goodness and security." Freud (45) stated, "For however long a child is fed at his mother's breast, he will always be left with a conviction after he is weaned that his feeding was too short and too little." According to Hill (54), a feeling of deprivation from lack of the breast may result in antagonism to the mother, and he believes that both inadequate and excessively prolonged breast feeding are undesirable.

Various prophylactic measures have been suggested. During the first month, Aldrich (2) presents a bottle to the breast-fed infant so that the baby may "accustom himself to the feel of the rubber nipple and the taste of artificial food before his appetite is formed for breast milk exclusively." In preparation for eventual weaning from the bottle Spock (94) recommends that the infant be offered a sip of milk a day from the cup beginning at 5 months. In my experience the daily administration of only orange juice by cup may not suffice for this training.

If there is resistance to weaning, the issue should not be forced but rather postponed until the child is older and more ready to accept the deprivation. Then the child should be weaned gradually; Spock suggested that during these months of transition it is important ". . . that the mother refrain from urging the cup or withholding the bottle, since this seems to increase his dependence on the bottle and postpone his readiness for weaning." He added that even when the initial progress is good the child is apt to want the supper bottle for several months more. Whenever possible, a similarly gradual process should be followed when weaning from the breast. Similarly, the introduction of new foods into the infant's diet should not be forced. Spock found that apple sauce or mashed banana were more likely to be accepted by the infant as the first solid than cooked cereal.

Since parental activity frequently produces resistance to eating, a restoration of the active role to the child appears logical and in practice has proved very successful. Clara Davis (20) demonstrated the value of "self-selection of food" by permitting newly weaned babies and older institutionalized children to eat whatever they chose from a considerable variety of foods placed before them. Thus the initiative was returned to the children, and without any restrictions they ate any foods in any order, and as much or as little as they desired. Sometimes a child went on a "food jag", for example, eating as many as 10 eggs at a meal, but over a long period of time these children themselves consumed a diet adequate in every respect. Under this regime the meal became a real source of pleasure, eaten because it was desired and enjoyed, not because someone else wanted the child to ingest it. The establishment of such an attitude towards food is the only worthwhile objective in the treatment of anorexia. Davis reported an absence of all feeding difficulties, and she could not detect any other psychogenic problems among her children. This observation suggests the importance of a happy feeding experience in safeguarding a child's mental health.

Judging from his private practice, Sweet (99) also reported that "Healthy children, if allowed to do so, will voluntarily chose an adequate diet from a well supplied family table . . . Children who are allowed to omit food at will do not develop a lasting dislike for it as they do when it is forced on them against their will."

Similarly, in infant feeding Gesell and Ilg (50) advised against "making a fetish of regularity" and recommended a "self-demand schedule". They find that by this regime, which really restores the active role to the baby, the infant is most completely satisfied and that the consequent freedom from frequent frustration "will nourish that sense of security which is essential to mental health". Other authors (101) have had a similar success with the "self-demand" regime of infant feeding.

Self-feeding is also helpful in restoring the active role to the child. Spock and Huschka (95) recommend its early establishment, and Davis (20) employed it as soon as possible. In its first form the child is able to indicate by pointing from which food, among those placed before him, he wishes the next mouthful. There may be a transitional phase of feeding with both adult and child grasping the spoon. The parent with a compulsion to feed her child, is apt to be very late in instituting self-feeding, and even then she still feeds the child the foods which she believes are "good for him", but which he does not eat willingly. An infant is able to eat with his fingers and hand before he can manipulate a spoon, but all early attempts at self-feeding are apt to be messy, and often are discouraged by the parent who is over-fussy about cleanliness. However, a child can learn to do anything only by practice, and early use of the hands probably promotes later manual skill. Self-feeding alone does not guarantee a restoration of the active role to the child, because not only by disregarding the child's wishes in choosing the foods to be placed before him, but also by propaganda, by coaxing, by urging and by other subtle forms of coercion the parent may still be able to control the child's eating. With self-feeding, however, the parent is at least no longer able literally to cram the food down the child's throat.

II. Effects of Emotion on Appetite

A child's mood, whether momentary or more constant, affects the appetite. According to Davis (22) the child may eat less when "un-happy, afraid, angry or excited". Food intake may be diminished when the child's attention is elsewhere than on his meal and therefore it is wise to refrain from arguments and scoldings at the table. The appetite may be poor when anxiety is present or when the child is mourning even a temporary loss of a parent (79), nurse, sibling, playmate or pet. The latter occurs even in animals after the loss of a mate or master (61). Sibling jealousy may be a cause of anorexia. For example, English and Pearson (30) reported a boy who ate poorly between the age of 7 and 12 years due to a constant dread that his mother might have another child. Lowrey (64) reported eating disorders due to early institutional care, and Bakwin (6) noted that infants on hospital wards become disinterested in their food because of emotional deprivation and may even die of "hospitalism" in a state of severe undernutrition. Lurie (65) found that anorexia is more common in broken and unhappy homes, and in almost all of her cases the child was unplanned for and unwanted. Neurotic children are more prone to disorders of appetite along with other difficulties such as temper tantrums (65). Dworkin (28) noted a poor appetite in animals with experimentally induced neurosis. Bruch (15), on the other hand, has noted overeating in one child after an upsetting experience and in another child with a fear of bodily injury. Lowrey (64) noted voraciousness when institutionalized children were first placed in a private foster home.

III. Effects of Parental Attitudes

Disturbed parental attitudes frequently cause disorders of appetite. Fewer problems arise if the mother is merely passive while the child plays the active role in determining the kind and quantity of food ingested. Today, however, a baby usually receives a carefully computed formula and diet, and as noted above, the mother is often very conscious of present precepts concerning infant feeding and feels obliged to follow schedules rigidly in regard to quantity and frequency of feeding. In addition she often is reluctant to see the food and her efforts in its preparation wasted. Consequently she frequently becomes active, forcing the food. Often such efforts merely provoke revolt, and subsequently, anorexia and malnutrition or even a hunger strike. As Spock and Huschka (95) state, "The baby's obstinacy and hostility become aroused and overdeveloped and will tend to persist. He learns to prefer to fight even if he has to go hungry to do it." Sometimes the struggle between parent and child over eating may begin during convalescence from an acute illness when a diminution in a child's appetite frequently occurs (91), or between 1 and 2 years of age when the child's rate of gain in weight is much diminished (74).

In the unconscious food is equated with life, health and growth (81), and especially with love. Feeding becomes a medium through which a mother expresses her love and devotion (91). However, mothers who are incapable of loving their children or who did not desire the children before their birth (65, 81, 95) may develop excessive feelings of guilt and anxiety about the child's nourishment, and therefore devote excessive attention to feeding procedures. As a result, they manage to produce anorexia in the child and thus indirectly express the unconscious death wishes. A mother with "feeding neurosis" (25) really cannot follow a physician's advice to stop forcing food (65). Spock and Huschka (95) have described various other neurotic patterns in such mothers, and Lurie (65) found that they have an aggressive masculine character which is assumed to explain their defective maternal instinct and their adoption of an overactive role in feeding their children. Bruch (15) stated that parental feeling of guilt over the loss of another child sometimes causes a parent to force a child to eat. According to Lippman (61), other unconscious anxieties and conflicts in a mother may be expressed as anxiety about her child's eating.

Excessive parental attempts to force food result sometimes in obesity in the child, at other times in revolt with refusal of food and undernutrition. In the latter instance eating may be equated with subjugation and feeding may become the "representative of all tyrannies" (18). The child may revolt against the quantity of food offered, and it has been found wiser to give miniature portions and allow the privilege of receiving additional servings as desired, so that the child's impulse will be to say "Is that all I get?" instead of "Do I have to eat all that?" (95). As Aldrich (2) stated, "The sight of too much food decreases appetite just as the sight of a little stimulates it." The child's revolt may be against a rigid feeding schedule, enforced for the convenience of the mother or servants, which completely disregards fluctuations of appetite. Even more often the child revolts against being forced to eat foods that are supposed to be "good for him". Frequently resistance is expressed by eating such foods only when fed to him by the mother, whereas the child feeds himself the foods he desires. The ill effect of an over-scientific attitude concerning the feeding of children was described by Lippman (62), "With all our weighing and measuring, and all our rules and regulations as to when, where, what and how much to feed children, we have succeeded in doing just one thing—we have taken their appetites away."

Sometimes the child's resistance against being forced to eat unwelcome food takes the form of dawdling. In severe cases, meals may be so prolonged that little or no interval remains between them, and the child spends most of his day at the table. Between each mouthful, the child talks, plays and looks around indoors or out the window, thereby postponing the intake of the next morsel of food as long as possible. The parent, on the other hand, determined that all food served shall be consumed, may try to accelerate the meal by feeding the child, or may just sit with him, coaxing him to eat, telling him stories or reading to him, in order to prevent the child from leaving the table and the food. Such parental attention is a secondary gain for the child with this neurotic eating patttern, and helps to perpetuate the disorder. Sometimes such a child will ingest only an infinitesimal bite of food at a time. The child when fed by the parent may open his mouth at her command, but by not closing his lips over the spoon he may express a refusal of the food, which, however, is defeated by the mother, who merely "shovels" the food into him. Even after a morsel of food has been introduced into the mouth, dawdling may still continue, for the food may either be held there without chewing, or it may be masticated four or five times longer than necessary, or the prolonged chewing of a single morsel may be interrupted at intervals by intermissions of just holding that piece of food in the mouth. Often the dawdler eats the food he likes as quickly as the average child, but requires an inordinate time to consume the food that is supposed to be "good for him". In the severe cases almost all food is taken exceedingly slowly, but even then something very tempting, for example, a slice of fancy birthday cake, may be rapidly devoured.

Dawdling may begin as a reaction during the first year of life, when, besides the breast and bottle, new foods with strange tastes and consistencies are introduced, and it is perhaps more apt to occur when these foods are started either prematurely or later than usual. Particularly during infancy food may be held in the mouth without swallowing, and and occasionally an impatient parent may continue to push the food into the child's mouth so that the cheeks become distended. The quantity of food eaten is an important factor, as even a normal child may dawdle after reaching satiation. In general, dawdling represents a "slowdown strike" and signifies, "I eat this food against my will." According to Bakwin and Bakwin (7), all types of dawdling are "... most commonly seen in the children of over-authoritative parents. Fearing to resist openly, the dawdling child complies with the parental requests slowly and unwillingly."

Both the forcing of unwelcome food by the parent and also the other psychic factors, yet to be discussed, which produce disorders of eating such as poor, finicky or excessive appetite, may still operate after food is ingested. Then many additional symptoms may result which, however, are not within the scope of this paper. Among these psychogenic disorders are disturbances of swallowing including cardiospasm, nervous vomiting, abdominal pain, diarrhea, constipation, various gastrointestinal neuroses, and, according to Schmideberg (83) and others, certain character disorders.

PATHOLOGICAL FACTORS

I. Anorexia Nervosa and Other Syndromes

The suckling of the mother's breast by the infant has been likened to coitus. This original infantile oral erotism may later in life find expression in various pathologic psychic syndromes involving the ingestion of food. For example, the psychosexual significance of eating is clearly expressed in anorexia nervosa, in which the refusal of food and consequent emaciation may be so extreme that life is endangered. In this disorder a number of different investigators (102) have all reported approximately the same psychic mechanism. There is not only a marked repression of the sex drives but also an inhibition of eating because the individuals unconsciously feel that eating is a sexual act. They have a disgust for food, which therefore is rejected, because eating is equated with intercourse, gratification and impregnation. One may infer that food may be regarded as a penis. Unconscious fantasies of fellatio and cunnilingus may be present, and food may be equated with an impregnating substance, or according to Lorand (63), with a poison. This attitude towards food is partly a consequence of the common sexual theory of children, expressed by Freud (44), that "one has a baby by eating". Sherman and Sherman (92), for example, reported a boy of 7 years who refused food for fear he would become pregnant.

Wulff (103) reported several patients with an unconscious attitude towards food and eating very similar to that present in anorexia nervosa, who had alternate cycles (sometimes coinciding with the phases of the menstrual cycle) of self-starvation and voraciousness. During the phase of excessive eating these patients also had an excessive need for sleep, were disgusted with themselves, and therefore felt depressed. Wulff compared their urges for food and sleep, which were at times irresistible, to drug addictions. I have seen this syndrome in a mother, one of whose children was a marked dawdler at meals.

A refusal of food similar to that which occurs in anorexia nervosa may be due to an actual psychic trauma. English and Pearson (30) recorded a girl of 6 years, who would not willingly eat food of any kind. Her disorder began when she was 4 years old, right after her father, who was a chronic alcoholic and probably mildly psychotic, attempted unsuccessfully to have vaginal intercourse with the child, causing some bleeding and pain. Right afterwards "he committed fellatio—introducing his penis into her mouth where he had an ejaculation". This girl's subsequent refusal of all food until cured by psychotherapy 2 years later, might be compared to anorexia nervosa except that instead of being based upon fantasy it was caused by a real traumatic experience.

Many religious cultists unconsciously regard eating as a sexual act and consequently they attempt to "escape from the fears of the instincts" (18) by fasting. According to Alexander (3), whereas eating signifies gratification, fasting is equated with repentance.

II. Obesity and Bulimia

The unconscious idea that eating results in impregnation and pregnancy may result not only in the extreme emaciation of anorexia nervosa but also in obesity when an infant is greatly desired (102, 25, 81, 60). I have reported a girl of 7 years (60), who held her stools until she had both a marked retention of feces and also at the same time incontinence by overflow (obstipatio paradoxa). This girl had an extremely intense desire for an infant to mother and was unconsciously trying to make a baby by attempting to attain the enlarged abdomen observed by her in various pregnant neighbors. She was permanently cured of her obstipation and encopresis by this interpretation. This girl was moderately overweight because of an excessive intake of food, which too had the unconscious aim of achieving the enlarged abdomen of pregnancy. Thus getting fat by overeating may, as in this case, be due to an unconscious fantasy of oral intercourse and impregnation.

However, bulimia (marked overeating) may indicate merely a demand for love. As Alexander (3) pointed out, to be fed is to be loved, to be taken care of, to be helped, to be maintained in infantile dependence. According to Selling and Ferraro (88) refugee children brought to the United States between 1933 and 1939 gorged themselves until they were shown affection and given a sense of security in their foster homes. Abraham (1) and Alexander (3) stated that overeating may be a substitute gratification. Therefore, the frustrated and unhappy individual finds consolation in the pleasure of eating. As Bruch (15) wrote, such a person regards "food as a comfort, as a means of combating unpleasant circumstances". She also found that "In some cases food seems to be the only source of satisfaction and the longing for it becomes an uncontrolled craving." She added that "Sometimes a feeling of helplessness and smallness makes a child crave more and more food in order to become as big and powerful as the person whom he fears."

III. Zone Displacements

Sterba (98) reported two infants whose eating disorders began just when they started to respond to training for cleanliness by bowel control. An 8½-month-old infant went on a hunger strike refusing to permit any food to pass through her lips, and a 20-month-old child would not chew or swallow any solid food, so that it accumulated in her mouth. In both cases the eating disorder ceased at once when the children were again permitted to soil themselves and were encouraged to cease efforts at bowel control. In these cases there was a displacement from the anal to the oral zone so that the resulting symptom had "the same value as withholding the content of the bowels". In these two cases, according to Sterba (98), "The anal rebellion against giving out becomes at the mouth reversed to a refusal to take in". A somewhat similar process may have been present in a case reported by Schmied (84), and apparently also among other factors in a more complicated case of Pörtl (75); Lurie (65) too observed this phenomenon. Bornstein (13) reported a 2½-year-old child who at one time refused to eat because the food was unconsciously regarded as feces. By this process of displacement "excrement becomes aliment" (38); according to Menninger (69), all food and speech may be equated with feces.

Sterba (98) has also stated, "Behind the mask of orality we find intensive genital wishes, chief among which is an unconscious wish for fellatio. The defense against such wishes is expressed in the form of anorexia, dysphagia, nausea and vomiting." These displacements commonly follow the path "from behind forward" (38) or "from below upward". However, in a minority of instances such a displacement may be from above downward, as in the idea of vagina dentata, which displaces oral characteristics onto the genital zone.

IV. Eating Inhibitions. Phobic Anxiety. Sadism. Masochism

The suppression of one oral activity may cause the inhibition of another. Freud (47) pointed that the repression of thumbsucking may result in disgust for eating and in hysterical vomiting. Sterba (98) stated that the inhibition of oral sadism may lead to the "avoidance of biting and chewing". Schmideberg (83) found that the repression of aggression including biting may produce an inhibition of eating. Frustration may produce an aggressive reaction including the unconscious urge to bite, which, however, may be repressed because of a sense of guilt and the end result may be an eating disorder or a chronic disturbance of the gastrointestinal tract. Alexander (3) stated that the repression of oral character traits also may result in an inhibition of eating.

Various authors including Anna Freud (37) and Moulton (72) have stated that eating may be equated with castrating. Such unconscious oral attitudes are derived from the early infantile period after teeth have begun to erupt. The infant, who then probably has fantasies of eating the breast, may actually bite the nipple. Later a girl with penis envy may have a wish to bite off the father's penis (37). These oral aggressive impulses merge with the preexisting oral erotism to form oral sadism. The latter may be even manifested in adults by biting while making love. As a result of oral sadism the eating of any food may be unconsciously equated with cannibalism (1, 66) and, as has been noted by Schmideberg (83), Fuchs (49), Milner (71) and Lurie (65), particularly with eating the parents. This attitude includes fantasies not only of eating the mother's breast (58, 10) the mother herself and, according to Melanie Klein (59), the mother's body contents, but also the father's genitals. In a case recorded by Kaufman (57) food was equated with the father and eaten compulsively. Malcove (66) stated that food can easily be identified by the child with various persons and that "For the child, eating is literally a cannibalistic procedure, which includes the ante-mortem tortures of cutting and crushing, and in which the table silver supplements the teeth and the hands." De Lee (24) referred to a preg-nant woman "who craved a bite of her husband's arm and actually took it". Sylvester (100) reported a girl of 4 years with marked sibling jealousy and penis envy, which resulted in a strong cannibalistic urge directed at members of her family and particularly at the penis of the males. The inhibition of these unconscious urges resulted in a refusal of food and an inanition comparable to anorexia nervosa.

Moulton (72) stated that in two cases, she observed "a real phobia against the mere taking of food, as eating was associated with anxiety". Alexander (3, 4) has described a definite syndrome which he termed "eating phobia". A young woman, 26 years old, could eat only her mother's food at home. Because of pathological fear she could not eat in a restaurant with a young man friend. Here too one may infer that eating was unconsciously regarded as a sexual act, that under these circumstances food may have been equated with penis and eating with fellatio. In Alexander's patient, eating had an "aggressive castration significance", which means that mastication of food in the presence of her male friend was unconsciously equated by the girl with biting off the man's genitals. Therefore, "her eating phobia was based on the inhibition of oral aggressive tendencies".

Not only does sadism play a role in eating disorders but masochistic traits are also sometimes conspicuous. According to Lurie (65), not eating may be a self-punishment for aggressive feelings towards a frustra-ting mother or, according to Lorand (63), it may be a reversal upon the self of death wishes directed toward such a mother. The patient with anorexia nervosa evinces masochistic tendencies when she chooses to endure the pangs of starvation. Conrad (18), Lorand (63) and Milner (71) believe that not eating may be unconsciously equated with death and may represent an attempt at suicide (sometimes successful in ano-rexia nervosa). According to Conrad (18), "many unconscious suicide wishes lurk under poor eating in hospitals and out.—They don't want me, I don't want them or myself, I don't want life".

The process of eating involves conflicting, antithetical attitudes. It involves active, aggressive, sadistic tendencies, which may be regarded as masculine, and which are expressed chiefly by the use of the teeth. It also involves passive, receptive and masochistic tendencies, which are expressed chiefly by sucking and deglutition, and which because of the incorporative nature may be regarded as feminine.

V. Food Idiosyncrasies

Thus far psychic factors affecting the general appetite have been discussed, but likes and dislikes for individual foods occur frequently. Baldwin (8) found that 56 per cent of the children investigated by him were unreasonably finicky. Out of 82 psychoneurotics, Selling (87) reported that 74 had eccentric eating interests. But the patient and the physician usually explain vagaries in eating by obvious factors such as taste and smell or on the basis of idiosyncrasies of digestion and allergy. In the choice of food, class, cultural, familiar, regional, economic and other factors (78) may be recognized, but often even then the psychologic influences are predominant. For example, love of the mother frequently results in an overestimation of "mother's cooking" (88). A host may serve rare and expensive viands chiefly to impress and flatter his guests.

Suggestion is often a factor (18, 89). The parent's or nurse's attitudes toward specific foods may affect the child. According to Selling (89), a beloved father, "who will not eat fish may in many instances be responsible for a family of children none of whom like that particular article of diet." Dunbar (26) reported an example of "emotional contagion", where an infant would take liver without difficulty when fed by the mother, but not when fed by a great-aunt, who was disgusted by the thought of liver. Similarly Escalona (31) correlated the refusal of orange or tomato juice by young infants with the same dislike for these juices felt by the person who fed them. Duncher (27) studied experimentally the role of social suggestion, and demonstrated that the food preference of one child was influenced by just witnessing the preference of another. Likewise at camp or in a nursery school a child may follow the example of the others and eat things theretofore rejected.

Favorable and unfavorable associations with a food may play a role. According to English and Pearson (30), a frightening occurrence associated with the introduction of a specific food into a child's diet, may thereafter cause the child to refuse that particular food. Selling and Ferraro (88) stated that a person may dislike a food which disagrees with him. They reported a child who became very sick and had to have a stomach wash after drinking milk into which some oxalic acid had been dropped. Thereafter this child had an aversion for milk.

For the average child most foods may be classified into two groups. First there are the foods which the child wishes to eat, which he regards as "good", but which the parents usually feel are "bad" for him. Secondly, there are foods which the child dislikes, which he regards as "bad", but which the mother wishes him to eat because she believes that they are "good" for him. Among foods frequently regarded by the children as "good" are frankfurters, other sausages and delicatessen, pickles, many condiments and relishes, all sorts of sweets and coffee. Many parents either prohibit these foods or severely restrict them, saying they are "bad for the child". Formerly the banana belonged in this group, but its reputation is now greatly improved, possibly due to its use in celiac disease. Among foods usually regarded by the parent as "good for the child" are cooked cereals, cooked vegetables, soft-boiled eggs, custards, other similar desserts and milk. The children, nevertheless, reject many of these foods, calling them "bad". A large role in these attitudes is played by the unconscious associations with particular foods, as described below. However, children try to rationalize their preferences on the basis of taste, while the parents in self-justification cite dietetic precepts. Possibly because of such differences, Mead (68) found that in our culture food is "part of a moral plot": "If you eat enough food good for you, you can eat a little of the food that is good, but not good for you." She stated that this is enforced by the mother or wife; that eating is thereby dramatized as a "conflict", and that the child refuses food to prove his independence and masculinity.

Some foods are regarded as "inedible", and this is because they are equated with excrement, human flesh, the genitals, or have "magical" properties. Pets are not eaten because they are regarded as members of the family, that is, as "human flesh", and this applies to horse meat as this animal is not only a pet, but in phobias it often symbolically represents the father.

Ferenczi (35) wrote, "Many children often suffer from an unconquerable disgust for breakfast. They had rather go to school with empty stomachs, and if compelled to eat they vomit." When this occurs only on school-days, difficulties with the teacher and the scholastic work may be suspected. Another cause for anorexia in the morning may be the common unconscious disgusts for the traditional breakfast foods such as cooked cereals, milk and eggs. Ferenczi (35) analyzed a man who had severe disgust for breakfast dating back to his childhood. When a boy he was aware of the parents' intercourse, and his disgust originated in the unconscious thought that the breakfast was prepared by his mother with hands soiled by coitus. Thus one may infer that the food was equated with the parents' genitals or their secretions. This is an example where food has an unconscious significance not because of its own characteristics but by a fantasy of contamination (a displacement). A similar process is present when food is equated with filth (really with feces) and is rejected with disgust because the kitchen is dirty or the cook is believed to be careless in her personal hygiene. A disgust, perhaps more justified, is aroused in a child who finds in his milk a black particle, which he also equates with dirt (and feces). A similar great disgust is produced when a worm is found in a fruit or salad. In general, such foreign objects cause the food to be equated with the contaminant.

There is very little in the literature about cravings and aversions for specific foods, although textbooks of obstetrics (24, 96) mention the occurrence of this symptom in pregnancy. Hupfer (55) interviewed 40 gravid women, a number of whom were unmarried. She concluded that their cravings and aversions represented the opposite poles of the same psychic complex; that cravings expressed a desire for pregnancy, whereas aversions indicated a rejection of it. She considered that these symptoms might sometimes express the woman's attitude towards the expected infant or towards its father. None of these 40 women were analyzed or studied at any length. Hupfer supported her thesis by citing the infantile sexual theory that conception results from eating some food or from kissing, by pointing out that some of the foods were obvious penis symbols, and by referring to mythology and the ideas of primitive peoples to prove that the other foods were believed to promote fecundity and fruitfulness.

Unconscious attitudes toward the menses may also influence the choice of food. According to Chadwick (17), the menstruating woman "feels a repugnance to usual food and has strange longings for curious articles of diet, often showing a marked preference for meat, especially that which is underdone, which reminds us of the cannibalistic tendencies of the witches, or contrarily, she will be repelled by meat and prefer a vegetarian diet, such as was allowed to the primitive woman at menstruation."

In children most authors have spoken of food "likes" and "dislikes" although the terms, "rejection" and "aversion", have occasionally been employed. Davis (22) stated that the food "jags" observed by her in children "seem akin in character to the cravings that adults often have for particular foods". Fenichel (34) has referred to these attitudes as "food addictions" and "food phobias". He also stated that "Sometimes analysis succeeds in cases of food phobia, in uncovering a forgotten period of morbid craving in childhood for the kind of food subsequently avoided." Usually there has been a certain tendency to minimize these attitudes in children, but sometimes they are so intense that the terms, cravings and aversions, are fully justified. For example, a girl of 8½ years with many phobias had in addition a strong craving for bananas, frankfurters and pickles and an equally intense aversion for blood, liver and all other meats. The latter foods aroused in her a strong feeling of disgust so that their ingestion was always followed by vomiting or abdominal pain. All the foods she craved were unconsciously equated by her with male genitals whereas the foods she rejected were similarly equated with female genitals. Thus her attitudes represented the opposite poles of the same psychic complex, in particular, the reaction to the differences in the sexual organs of men and women (46). Goldman (51) speaks of "eating a penis in order to have one". Bergler (11) noted an association between meat and the idea of the loss of the penis. Benedek (9) had a patient, who avoided meat and later all cooked food due to the unconscious thought, "I do not want to have the body of a woman."

The expression of psychic attitudes by means of food cravings and aversions, may not be very rare in children. I have had another patient, a boy of 10 years, who had an aversion for all women, except the mother, so that he shrank from their touch, and who since his second year of life had refused all meats, poultry and fish except frankfurters and salami. He likewise had a craving not only for sausages but also for bananas and pickles. Because treatment was interrupted conclusions in regard to this boy were not arrived at, but because of the similarity in his choice of foods and that of the girl mentioned above, one may suspect that his cravings and aversions had a similar significance, and this interpretation would fit perfectly this boy's attitude towards the female sex.

Cannibalistic tendencies, which have been discussed under sadism, often play an accessory role in these cases and require interpretation before the child will begin to eat meat. The inhibition of oral aggression appears to be the chief factor in a girl of 7 years, who has aversions for blood, steak, liver, rare meats and soft boiled eggs. She equates the eggs with "guts". This case has not been studied long enough for us to draw final conclusions, but undoubtedly these foods represent the flesh and viscera of the girl's mother and baby sister, whom she has strong but repressed urges to attack by biting.

Probably vegetarianism often results from food aversions. The vegetarians term the eating of any flesh, cannibalism, because they regard all animals as "fellow-creatures". They may rationalize their attitude on an "ethical", "religious", "esthetic", "scientific" or "dietetic" basis (29). Some religious cults have vegetarianism as one of their tenets. In a patient of Goldman (51) vegetarianism was described as a defense against oral aggression or tendencies to cannibalism. Bergler (10) referred to vegetarianism as a defense against the repressed infantile urge to bite the mother's breast, and Fenichel (33) stated that meat or other red foods may be disliked by people with cannibalistic trends. Moulton (72) stated that animal food such as meat, milk and eggs may be revolting because of a fear of animals. However, as Freud (42) pointed out, an animal phobia may sometimes be produced by the projection onto the animal of the child's own repressed impulses to bite the parent and secondly by a fear of similar injury which is expected as a retaliation by the parent, whom the animal symbolically represents. The vegetarianism of children with aversions is, in my experience, often inconsistent: they reject some meats but may eat others and do not claim a philosophic or religious basis for their attitudes.

VI. Food Symbolism

Frequently a symbolic significance may be unconsciously attributed to a particular food. This plays a great role both in ordinary finicky eating and in the less frequent food cravings and aversions of children. According to English and Pearson (30), "Such specific articles, usually by their color, shape, consistency or other physical properties, resemble either bodily excretions or parts of the body and are rejected with disgust, either through a refusal to eat or vomiting after eating them." Melanie Klein (59) states that in small children a food may take on "the significance of their father's penis and their mother's breast and is loved, hated and feared like these. Liquid foods are likened to milk, feces, urine and semen, and solid food to feces and other substances of the body." Undoubtedly Freud (43) referred to this imputation of symbolic significance when he found a "definite sexual meaning" in the observation, ". . . that some neurotic children cannot look at blood and raw meat, that they vomit at the sight of eggs and macaroni."

A search through the available literature reveals many instances where food had symbolic significance. However, some authors have overestimated the importance of the factors of taste and have disregarded the factor of food symbolism, which is largely unconscious. To the uninformed, food symbolisms may seem to have incredible and grotesque characteristics somewhat like dream symbolisms, but like the latter they are a very valuable approach to an understanding of the unconscious.

Among foods that may be equated particularly with the penis, are the banana according to Moulton (72), asparagus mentioned by Fenichel (33), and pears or other pendant objects as recorded by Jelliffe (56). Other foods included in this group, are the frankfurter and the pickle, which are condemned by many parents sometimes because of this unconscious association, but which are eaten eagerly by the children partly because of the prohibition but often also because of the symbolic significance. Sometimes, however, as in an adult mentioned by English and Pearson (30), the association of foods with the penis results not in a craving but in an aversion for the particular foods.

Freud (41) wrote that in dreams the breasts (which are also pendulous) "as well as the larger hemispheres of the female body, are represented by apples, peaches and fruit in general". Such symbolic significance possibly contributes to the general popularity of fruits.

The female genitals may be associated with blood, liver or meats, especially if exuding bloody juice. One may suspect that the rejection of rare meat by many individuals is due to this unconscious association. Sometimes, however, foods equated with blood may be desired because eating them is unconsciously regarded as an oral blood transfusion, conveying life and health. Among edibles that may be equated with blood are meats and other red foods, which include tomato soup (82), beets, beet soup and red wine. Abraham (1) mentioned a patient, who was reminded of milk by the taste of meat, because both were "greasy and sweet". At times this man craved either meat or milk because he equated the meat with the female breast and with its product, milk.

The significance of a fish is naturally ambiguous because owing to its shape it may be regarded by some persons as a penis, but on the other hand because it is a kind of meat it may be associated by others with the female genitals, and this linkage is possibly furthered by the fishy odor usually present in the vagina. Lurie (65) reported that children may refuse fish because of its disgusting appearance and odor. If a prepared food is liquid with floating solids, the latter may be regarded as "fish". Sterba (97), for example, found that one child regarded soup with noodles as "pond water with carp and pike", and Schmideberg (83) made a similar observation.

Among foods equated with feces are spinach according to Bernfeld (5), Fenichel (33) and Schmideberg (82), chocolate mentioned by Kaufman (57), and various "mushy" foods as stated by Moulton (72). In this group too belong the yolk of a hard-boiled egg, which may be unconsciously equated with a scyballum, and also various cooked vegetables and cereals. A brown or dark color may favor this association as in the case of brown cereals and brown bread. Children may eat a vegetable such as string beans when cut in large pieces, but reject the same beans when chopped fine, calling them "mud". Finely chopped foods may also be regarded as baby food. An odorous cheese like Limburger may be disliked because its smell suggests feces. Some persons will not eat overripe fruit, and this applies even to the banana, because any dark spots are unconsciously equated with feces. However, even a cooked white cereal or scrambled eggs may be so identified due to the "mushy" consistency or perhaps due to some resemblance to an infant's stools. Children need not be too consistent in rejecting brown foods, as some youngsters with this tendency may nevertheless like chocolate candy or chocolate pudding, which are regarded as "sweets". A boy of 7 years under my care has apparently never masturbated, but instead he holds his stools a long time in order later to derive a more voluptuous sensation from their evacuation. This boy's psychosexual development is fixated at the anal stage. He had abdominal pain after eating frankfurters, which he regarded not as a penis but as "a long red bowel movement". A few days later he had similar but milder discomfort after eating layer cake with chocolate icing.

Foods sometimes equated with urine are especially the liquids. They include orange juice, pineapple juice, other beverages and at times soup. Fuchs (49), for example, reported a boy of 7 years who compared lemon juice with urine. On the other hand, an increased water intake by an individual with a cleanliness obsession, may be a "cleansing and purification rite" (102). I have observed this phenomenon in a boy of 8 years who was admitted to the hospital with the report that for 5 months he had been drinking increased quantities of water and frequently passing large amounts of urine. This boy never used "dirty" words, frequently washed himself and his clothes, and was trying to cleanse the "insides" of his body.

A feeling of disgust is commonly aroused by slippery or slimy foods, which, according to Moulton (72), may be equated with pus, mucus and semen. Perhaps the most conspicuous example of this type of food is egg white, especially when undercooked. In this group too belong the cooked cereals, which are equated not only with feces but also with mucus, and here also should be mentioned many cooked vegetables, for example, onions and okra. The mucus, unconsciously referred to, may be the secretions of the respiratory tract including the nose and throat, or the secretions of the genital tract, either from the vagina or from the male urethra. In this category are raw oysters, which because they may be equated with semen are popularly supposed to enhance male sexual activity. Fuchs (49) reported a woman of 27 years, who since childhood not only refused gelatin and other similar foods which she equated with semen, but also bananas. After the symbolic significance of these foods was explained to the patient, she was relieved of her aversions.

Candy and desserts are very popular with almost all children, and often to an excessive degree. Moulton (72) suggested that this may be due, at least partly, to the equating of "sweets" with love. Coriat (19) expressed a similar opinion, mentioning the "candy kiss". Moreover, Freud (40) has stated, "In dreams sweet things and sweetmeats stand regularly for caresses or sexual gratification". Additional proof is furnished by the common use of various saccharine words as terms of endearment, for example, "sweet", "sweetheart" and "honey". Abraham (1) suggested that a craving to suck candy may be related to "repressed wishes referring to sucking the male genital".

Milk is the first food of babies, and therefore is closely associated with infancy. Sometimes, as noted by Lurie (65) and Rose (81), after the birth of a baby, sibling jealousy causes an older child to suddenly refuse all foods except milk. Sterba (97), however, notes that older children may often refuse milk just because they equate drinking milk with being a baby. To drink coffee, on the other hand, is to be an adult. Therefore, the addition of some coffee may make milk acceptable to many children. Fenichel (33) suggested that milk may be disliked because of a repressed unconscious wish to regress to the oral nursing stage. Milk may be vomited or rejected with disgust by an older child, particularly when taken from a nursing bottle, because the milk is equated with urine (52) or semen. This is explained by the equating of the nipple with the penis, and this association is furthered by the penis-like appearance and location of the teats of the cow (39, 85). Some children have a disgust only for boiled milk due to the resulting "skin", which probably places the milk then in the category of a slimy food.

Hill (54) reported an alcoholic, who regarded his beverage as "Mother's milk". More commonly, however, as Fenichel (33) stated, alcoholic beverages may be associated with the idea of dissipation.

Foods equated with vomitus may be concoctions prepared from small chunks of meat, potato and possibly vegetables, in some sauce, or sometimes soups with similar ingredients. Such mixtures somewhat resemble the appearance of gastric contents after an ordinary meal. Selling (86) observed that "Most children, until they reach adolescence, dislike mixed food," and he added that "Should the ingredients in the stew be served separately, without gravy, the child will frequently eat them." Not only may cooked vegetables and cereals be equated with feces and mucus but sometimes with vomitus. Undoubtedly these associations are partly responsible for the frequent unpopularity of these foods.

The earliest age at which a symbolic significance may be attributed to particular foods is not precisely established but such attitudes appear early in childhood. For example, I knew a little girl who between 2 and 3 years, happened to witness her father urinating and referred to his penis as his "frankfurter". Conrad (18) wrote, "We cannot understand the food disgusts until we realize that about the time new foods are presented in variety children are being taught their reaction of disgust. The nurse makes faces of disgust at mucus. Many a child finds white of egg forever repulsive because the two come to mind simultaneously. Consistencies, colors and smells get so associated at the time when training in excretory habits is achieved." Freud (47) indicated how early symbolic significance may appear when he stated that, "...sexual symbolism, the representation of the sexual by non-sexual objects and relations reaches back into the years when the child is first learning to master language."

SUMMARY

Psychogenic disorders of feeding may occur almost immediately after birth. During infancy, change, including the introduction of new foods and particularly weaning, may induce an emotional reaction against eating. The appetite of a child is affected by his emotions and by his attitude towards the person who feeds him. Excessive attempts to force food by an oversolicitous, rejecting parent may result in anorexia or dawdling, whereas the "self-selection" of foods by the child and the "self-demand schedule" for the infant minimizes difficulties. The love relationship between the mother and baby finds expression in the act of breast nursing. Later in life, eating may be regarded as a sexual act and its inhibition may result in anorexia nervosa, eating phobias and other syndromes. Marked overeating and obesity may also be caused by psychic factors. Oral sadism, often directed at a parent, may result in anorexia because eating is unconsciously equated with cannibalism. Masochistic attitudes with unconscious attempts at self-punishment and suicide may produce poor eating. The suppression of oral activities, for example thumbsucking, or of oral character traits, may cause an inhibition of eating. A displacement to the oral zone of the phenomena of another zone, particularly the anal, may produce eating disorders. In the attitude toward individual foods suggestion and associations play a role, but a frequent factor may be a symbolic significance unconsciously attributed to particular foods because of their appearance and physical properties. A fantasy of contamination may cause the rejection of food. Various possibilities of food symbolism are enumerated with the aid of the available literature. Unconscious attitudes, sometimes opposite poles of the same psychic complex, may be expressed symbolically by food cravings and aversions. Sometimes aversions may result from repressed cannibalistic tendencies.

BIBLIOGRAPHY

1. Abraham, K. "The First Pregenital Stage of the Libido", *Selected Papers*, Hogarth, 1927.

2. Aldrich, C. A. *Cultivating the Child's Appetite*, Macmillan, 1928.

3. Alexander, F. "Gastrointestinal Neuroses", in Portis, S. A., *Diseases of the Digestive System*, Lea & Febiger, 1941, 206—225.

4. Alexander, F. and Wilson, G. W. "Quantitative Dream Studies", *Psa. Quar.* IV, 1935, 371—407.

5. Dr. B. "Zur Idiosynkrasie gegen Speisen", *Internat. Zeit. f. Psa.* V, 1919, 117.

6. Bakwin, H. "Malnutrition and Mental Disease in Children", *Nerv. Child* III, 1944, 160—161.

7. Bakwin, R. M. and Bakwin, H. "The Psychologic Care of the Preschool Child", *J. Pediat.* XVI, 1940, 89—105.

8. Baldwin, A. L. "An Analysis of Children's Eating Habits", *J. Pediat.* XXV, 1944, 74—78.

9. Benedek, T. "Dominant Ideas and Their Relation to Morbid Cravings", *Internat. J. Psa.* XVII, 1936, 40—56.

10. Bergler, E. "Eight Prerequisites for the Psychoanalytic Treatment of Homosexuality", *Psa. Rev.* XXXI, 1944, 253—286.

11. Bergler, E. "Psychoanalysis of a Case of Agoraphobia", *Psa. Rev.* XXII, 1935, 392—408.

12. Bjerre, P. "Obsessive Symptoms and Their Treatment", *Psa. Rev.* XI, 1924, 1—27.

13. Bornstein, B. "Phobia in a Two-and-a-Half Year Old Child", *Psa. Quar.* IV, 1935, 93—119.

14. Bruch, H. "Food and Emotional Security", *Nerv. Child* III, 1944, 165—173.

15. Bruch, H. "Obesity in Children: Physiologic and Psychologic Aspects of the Food Intake of Obese Children", *Am. J. Dis. Child* 59, 1940, 739—781.

16. Byington, G. M. "Incidence of Breast Feeding in Detroit", *Psychosom. Med.* VII, 1945, 173.

17. Chadwick, M. *The Psychological Effects of Menstruation*, Nerv. Ment. Dis. Pub. Co., 1932, 25, 30, 43.

18. Conrad, A. "The Attitude Toward Food", *Am. J. Orthopsychiat.*, VII, 1937, 360—367.

19. Coriat, I. H. "Sex and Hunger", *Psa. Rev.* VIII, 1921, 375—381.

20. Davis, C. M. "Self-Selection of Diet by Newly Weaned Infants", *Am. J. Dis. Child* 36, 1928, 651–679.

21. Davis, C. M. "Self-Selection of Diets: An Experiment with Infants", *Trained Nurse & Hosp. Rev.* 86, 1931, 629–634.

22. Davis, C. M. "Feeding After the First Years", in Brennemann, J. *Practice of Pediatrics*, Vol. I, W. F. Prior Co., Chap. 30, 1–27.

23. Davis, C. M. "A Practical Application of Some Lessons of the Self-Selection of Diet Study to the Feeding of Children in Hospitals", *Am. J. Dis. Child* 46, 1933, 743–750.

24. De Lee, J. B. *The Principles and Practice of Obstetrics,* ed. IV, W.B. Saunders Co., 1924, 112.

25. Deutsch, F. "Prophylactic Aspects of the Nutrition Problem", *Nerv. Child* III, 1944, 195–215.

26. Dunbar, F. "Effect of the Mother's Emotional Attitude on the Infant", *Psychosom. Med.* VI, 1944, 156–159.

27. Duncher, K. "Experimental Modification of Children's Food Preferences Through Social Suggestion", *J. Abnorm. & Social Psychol.* 33, 1938, 489–507.

28. Dworkin, S. "Conditioning Neuroses in Dog and Cat", *Psychosom. Med.* I, 1939, 388–396.

29. Efron, E. "Heydays for the Vegetarians", *N. Y. Times Magazine,* Apr. 8, 1945, 17, 32.

30. English, O. S. and Pearson, G. H. J. *Common Neuroses of Children and Adults,* Norton, 1937, 82–100.

31. Escalona, S. K. "Feeding Disturbances in Very Young Children", *Amer. J. Orthopsychiat.* XV, 1945, 76–80.

32. Feldstein, G. J. "A Breast and Bottle Shy Infant: Nursing Only When Asleep", *Am. J. Dis. Child* 35, 1928, 103–108.

33. Fenichel, O. *Outline of Clinical Psychoanalysis,* Norton, 1934.

34. Fenichel, O. *The Psychoanalytic Theory of Neurosis,* Norton, 1945.

35. Ferenczi, S. "Disgust for Breakfast", *Further Contributions to the Theory and Technique of Psychoanalysis,* Hogarth, 1926, 326.

36. Frank, L. K. "The Newborn as a Young Mammal with Organic Capacities, Needs and Feeling", *Psychosom. Med.* VII, 1945, 169–171.

37. Freud, A. *The Ego and the Mechanisms of Defence,* 2nd ed. Hogarth, 1942, 52–53.

38. Freud, S. "Character and Anal Erotism", *Coll. Papers,* II, 45–50.

39. Freud, S. "Fragment of an Analysis of a Case of Hysteria", *Coll. Papers,* III, 64–65.

40. Freud, S. "From the History of an Infantile Neurosis", *Coll. Papers*, III, Hogarth, 473—605.

41. Freud, S. *A General Introduction to Psychoanalysis*, Garden City Pub. Co., 1943, 139.

42. Freud, S. *Inhibitions, Symptoms and Anxiety*, Hogarth, 1936.

43. Freud, S. "The Interpretation of Dreams", *Basic Writings of Sigmund Freud*, ed. A. A. Brill, Modern Library, 1938, 523.

44. Freud, S. "On the Sexual Theories of Children", *Coll. Papers* II, 59—75.

45. Freud, S. "An Outline of Psycho-analysis", *Internat. J. Psa.* XXI, 1940, 27—84.

46. Freud, S. "Some Psychological Consequences of the Anatomical Differences Between the Sexes", *Internat. J. Psa.* VIII, 1927, 133—142.

47. Freud, S. "Three Contributions to the Theory of Sex: Infantile Sexuality", ed. A. A. Brill, *Basic Writings of Sigmund Freud*, Modern Library, 1938, 580—603.

48. Fries, M. E. "Psychosomatic Relationships between Mother and Infant", *Psychosom. Med.* VI, 1944, 159—162.

49. Fuchs, E. "Verweigerte Nahrungsaufnahme", *Zeit. f. Psa. Päd.* IV, 1930, 128—133.

50. Gesell, A. and Ilg, F. L. *Feeding Behavior of Infants*, Lippincott, 1937.

51. Goldman, G. S. "A Case of Compulsive Handwashing", *Psa. Quar.* VII, 1938, 96—121.

52. Graber, G. H. "Primal Scene, Play and Destiny", *Psa. Quar.* IV, 1935, 467—475.

53. Grulee, C. G. "Anorexia Nervosa", in Abt, I. A. *Pediatrics*, Vol. III, Saunders, 1924, 363—365.

54. Hill, J. "Infant Feeding and Personality Disorders; A Study of Early Feeding in its Relation to Emotional and Digestive Disorders", *Psychiat. Quar.* XI, 1937, 356—382.

55. Hupfer, S. "Über Schwangerschaftsgelüste", *Internat. Zeit. f. Psa.* XVI, 1930, 105—119.

56. Jelliffe, S. E. "The Sexual Life of the Child", in Abt, I. A. *Pediatrics*, Vol. VII, Saunders, 1925, 796—854.

57. Kaufman, M. R. "A Clinical Note on Social Anxiety", *Psa. Rev.* XXVIII, 1941, 72—77.

58. Klein, M. "Mourning and Its Relation to Manic-Depressive States", *Internat. J. Psa.*, XXI, 1940, 125—153.

59. Klein M. *The Psycho-Analysis of Children*, Hogarth, 1937.

60. Lehman, E. "Psychogenic Incontinence of Feces (Encopresis) in Children", *Am. J. Dis. Child* 68, 1944, 190—199.

61. Lippman, H. S. "Discussion of Lurie", *Am. J. Orthopsychiat.* XI, 1941, 464—466.

62. Lippman, H. S. See Davis (22).

63. Lorand, S. "Anorexia Nervosa: Report of a Case", *Psychosom. Med.* V, 1943, 282—292.

64. Lowrey, L. G. "Personality Distortion and Early Institutional Care", *Am. J. Orthopsychiat.* X, 1940, 576—585.

65. Lurie, O. R. "Psychological Factors Associated with Eating Difficulties in Children", *Am. J. Orthopsychiat.* XI, 1941, 452—467.

66. Malcove, L. "Bodily Mutilation and Learning to Eat", *Psa. Quar.* II, 1933, 557—561.

67. Masserman, J. H. "Psychodynamisms in Anorexia Nervosa and Neurotic Vomiting", *Psa. Quar.* X, 1941, 211—242.

68. Mead, M. "The Problem of Changing Food Habits: With Suggestions for Psychoanalytic Contributions", *Bull. Menninger Clin.* VII, 1943, 57—61.

69. Menninger, W. C. "Characterologic and Symptomatic Expressions Related to the Anal Phase of Psychosexual Development", *Psa. Quar.* XII, 1943, 161—193.

70. Middlemore, M. P. *The Nursing Couple,* Hamish Hamilton Medical Books, 1941.

71. Milner, M. "A Suicidal Symptom in a Child of Three", *Internat. J. Psa.* XXV, 1944, 53—61.

72. Moulton, R. "A Psychosomatic Study of Anorexia Nervosa Including the Use of Vaginal Smears", *Psychosom. Med.,* IV, 1942, 62—74.

73. Norval, M. A. "Sucking Response of Newly Born Babies At Breast", *Am. J. Dis. Child* 71, 1946, 41—44.

74. Platou, R. V. "Johnny Won't Eat", *Bull. Tulane M. Fac.* III, 1944, 41—47.

75. Pörtl, A. "Profound Disturbances in the Nutritional and Excretory Habits of a Four and One Half Year Old Boy", *Psa. Quar.* IV, 1935, 25—36.

76. Rado, S. "The Psychical Effects of Intoxication", *Psa. Rev.* XVIII, 1931, 69—84.

77. Rahman, L., Richardson, M. R. and Ripley, H. S. "Anorexia Nervosa with Psychiatric Observations", *Psychosom. Med.* I, 1939, 335—365.

78. Renner, H. D. *The Origin of Food Habits,* Faber and Faber Ltd., 1944.

79. Ribble, M. A. "Disorganizing Factors of Infant Personality", *Am. J. Psychiat.* 98, 1941, 459–463.

80. Ribble, M. A. *The Rights of Infants: Early Psychological Needs and Their Satisfaction,* Columbia Univ. Press, 1943.

81. Rose, J. A. "Eating Inhibitions in Children in Relation to Anorexia Nervosa", *Psychosom. Med.* V, 1943, 117–124.

82. Schmideberg, M. "Anxiety States", *Psa. Rev.* XXVII, 1940, 439–449.

83. Schmideberg, M. "Psychoneuroses of Childhood: Their Etiology and Treatment", *Brit. J. M. Psychol.* XIII, 1933, 313–327.

84. Schmied, M. "Essstörung und Verstimmung vor dem dritten Lebensjahr", *Zeit. f. Psa. Päd.* X, 1936, 241–250.

85. Seeberg, E. "Analysis of Aggression in a Five Year Old Girl", *Am. J. Orthopsychiat.* XIII, 1943, 53–61.

86. Selling, L. S. "Behavior Problems of Eating", *Am. J. Orthopsychiat.* XVI, 1946, 163–169.

87. Selling, L. S. "The Role of Food in Psychiatry", *Dis. Nerv. Syst.* V, 1944, 365–368.

88. Selling, L. S. and Ferraro, M. A. *The Psychology of Diet and Nutrition,* Norton, 1945.

89. Selling, L. S. "Psychopathology and Nutrition", *Dis. Nerv. Syst.* IV, 1943, 38–42.

90. Senn, M. J. and Newill, P. K. *All About Feeding Children,* Doubleday Doran, 1944.

91. Senn, M. J. "Influence of Psychological Factors on the Nutrition of Children", *Am. J. Pub. Health* XXXV, 1945, 211–215.

92. Sherman, I. C. and Sherman, M. "Birth Phantasy in a Young Child", *Psa. Rev.* XVI, 1929, 408–410.

93. Simsarian, F. P. and McLendon, P. A. "Further Records of the Self-Demand Schedule in Infant Feeding", *J. Pediat.* XXVII, 1945, 109–114.

94. Spock, B. "Avoiding Behavior Problems", *J. Pediat.* XXVII, 1945, 363–382.

95. Spock, B. and Huschka, M. "The Psychological Aspects of Pediatric Practice", in Blumer, G. *Practioners Library of Medicine and Surgery,* Appleton-Century, 1938, XIII, 757–779.

96. Stander, H. J. *Williams' Obstetrics,* ed. 8, Appleton-Century, 1941, 251.

97. Sterba, E. "An Abnormal Child", *Psa. Quar.* V, 1936, 560–600.

98. Sterba, E. "An Important Factor in Eating Disturbances in Child-hood", *Psa. Quar.* X, 1941, 365–372.

99. Sweet, C. "Voluntary Food Habits of Normal Children", *J. Am. Med. Assoc.* 107, 1936, 765–767.

100. Sylvester, E. "Analysis of Psychogenic Anorexia in a Four-year-old", *this Annual*, I, 1945, 167–187.

101. Trainham, G., Pilafian, G. J. and Kraft, R. M. "A Case History of Twins Breast Fed on a Self-Demand Regime", *J. Pediat.* XXVII, 1945, 97–108.

102. Waller, J. V., Kaufman, M. R. and Deutsch, F. "Anorexia Nervosa", *Psychosom. Med.* II, 1940, 3–16.

103. Wulff, M. "Über einen interessanten oralen Symptomenkomplex und seine Beziehung zur Sucht", *Internat. Zeit. f. Psa.* XVIII, 1932, 281–302.

CHILD PSYCHIATRY IN THE 1830'S — THREE LITTLE HOMOCIDAL MONOMANIACS

By BERTRAM D. LEWIN, M.D. (New York)

NOTE: Readers of Dr. Raymond de Saussure's article (this Annual, II, 1946) on Dr. Descuret's handling of neurotic children in 1841, will be interested in these case histories of Esquirol, published in 1838, in his famous book, Maladies mentales *(Paris: J.-B.-Baillière. Vol. I, pp. 384-388). They are to be found in the section entitled* monomanie homicide, *which otherwise contains reports of adult cases that now would be considered paranoias or paranoid schizophrenics.*

In the following observations we shall see two individuals, born with perverse inclinations and a bad character. As the inclinations and character were not corrected by education, at the earliest appearance of the passions, they overthrew the intelligence, misled the reason, and initiated a homocidal monomania.

A little girl was put out to nurse during 13 months, in the country two leagues from Paris. Then she was brought up by her grandmother, a very respectable and religious elderly woman. Some months ago, at the age of 7½ she was brought to Paris to be near her mother and father. The child is sad, does not play, laugh or weep. She persistently sits in a chair, with her arms folded, and if her mother turns her back, the child strikes her. She is being taught to read, sew and knit, but pays little heed to her instruction. Three feet, 8 inches, in height, she has light brown hair, black and alert eyes, and a turned up nose. Her mouth is small, her cheeks full and of good color; her physiognomy is pleasant and sensitive.

Since the age of 4, the child has practiced onanism with boys of 10 to 12 years of age. Her separation from the boys is the cause of her sadness. Unless constantly watched, she engages in the practice by herself. Her mother's care, her religious instruction, and the advice of her physician have not succeeded in triumphing over this disastrous habit. Her mother fell ill of chagrin, and the unfortunate child expressed her regret that her mother did not die, for if her mother had perished, she would have inherited her wearing apparel and had it cut to fit her, and when the clothes were worn out, she would have gone out to get others from men. The only reason she did not kill her mother during the latter's illness was that she was too well guarded. "But," said the mother, "if I should die today, I should come back tomorrow. Our Lord was resurrected." "No," replied the child, "I know very well that when you die you don't come back. Jesus rose because he was God. My little sister and brother did not come back." "But how would you go about killing me?" asked the mother. "If I were in the woods, I would trip you with your skirts and stick a dagger into your breast." "Do you know what a dagger is?" "Yes, a man left a book in which a woman stabs a man in the heart with a dagger." This book had actually been left at their home. "But if you killed me," said the mother, "my belongings would go to your father." "I know that my father would put me in prison, but I want to kill him too." Since then the child has often repeated that she does not love either her mother, her father, or the grandmother who raised her. Some months later, on hearing of a child's being murdered, she said to her mother that if she used a knife to kill her, she would get her clothes bloody, so she would take the precaution of undressing before committing the act, so that she would not be suspected. A week later she said that to avoid getting blood on her clothes, to kill her mother she would use the kind of poison that they sprayed on plants in the country. By way of an experiment, a neighbor put some flour into a glass of wine, telling her it was arsenic, and offered it to the child. The child began to cry out: "I want to give it to my mother, but I won't drink it." She clamped her teeth when they tried to force her to swallow it. Such was the moral state of this little girl at the age of 8, when she was taken before a police court officer, who interrogated her both in the presence and in the absence of her mother. Some months later she was questioned again.

Our learned and respected colleague, Dr. Parent-Duchâtelet, a victim of his zeal for humanity, and too soon taken from science and his friends, has reported this observation in all its details, and followed it with this note: "The little girl was placed in a convent through the efforts of the administration, which paid her board; some months later she developed a pediculous condition and was sent home to her mother, and on her recovery returned to the house in which she had been placed. She left some months later with a depressive illness, which was thought to include symptoms of scurvy. Again admitted to the convent, she was given education of a sort, consisting in manual work, she made her first communion, and left after several years.

"Today in December 1831, the girl, 14 years old, has been apprenticed to a jewel cutter. She is manually skillful, but cannot read or write. Every Sunday she visits her mother and spends the evening with her, and is quite well-behaved, submissive, and never mentions her previous life. But she is always sad and taciturn, never plays or amuses herself. She complains of the rude manner in which she was treated in the convent. Her mother presumes that the onanism continues."

On June 7, 1835, I was consulted about a little girl of 7½, who was of average stature, with white skin and abundant hair, coarse and blonde, with deep blue eyes, and her upper lip somewhat thick, but with no symptoms of scurvy. Her physiognomy gave an impression of slyness; her eyes often were turned to the internal orbital angle, which gave her face, which was somewhat pale besides, a convulsive appearance. Her intelligence was well developed and though a laborer's child she could read and write. She tried to read the title of a book on my desk, while her stepmother gave me the following account; for at first the child would not talk to me at all nor answer my questions. She listened to her mother's story with complete indifference, as if it were about some one else.

"I am my husband's second wife, and at my marriage this little girl was 2 years old. We sent her to her grandparents, who disapproved of their son's marriage, and who often expressed their dissatisfaction before the child. She was 3 when my husband and I visited the grandparents. They made me welcome and were friendly; but the little girl, who demonstrated great pleasure at seeing her father, rejected my caresses and refused to embrace me; nevertheless she returned with us to Paris. Whenever she found an opportunity, she would scratch and hit me, repeating, 'I wish you would die.' When she was 5 years and 3 months old, I was pregnant, and she kicked me in the belly, expressing the same wish. We sent her back to her grandparents, where she stayed for 2 years more. Returning again to us, at the age of 7 years and 4 months, she started again to maltreat me, and she unceasingly repeats that she wishes I would die, as well as her little brother, who is out to nurse, and whom she has never seen. Not a day passes without her striking me. If I stoop in front of the fireplace, she tries to push me into the fire. She strikes me with her fists, and secures scissors, knives, and other implements that are at hand, constantly accompanying her cruelty with the same statement: I want to kill you. Her father has often punished her, though I am opposed to it, but the child has never been willing to abandon her design. Her father once threatened to have her put in prison. 'That will not stop me,' she said, 'from killing my mother and brother.'" After this account, which the child heard calmly, I addressed to her the following questions. She replied without bitterness, or anger, and with calm indifference.

Q. Why do you wish to kill your mamma? A. Because I don't like her.

Q. Why don't you like her? A. I don't know.

Q. Has she mistreated you? A. No.

Q. Is she kind to you? Does she take good care of you? A. Yes.

Q. Why do you strike her? A. So that she will die.

Q. What! You want to kill her? A. Yes, I want her to die.

Q. Could your blows kill her? Aren't you too little? A. Yes, I know I am. You have to suffer to die. I want to make her fall ill so that she will suffer and die, as I am too little to kill her all at once.

Q. When she is dead who will take care of you? A. I don't know.

Q. You will be cared for badly, badly dressed, you unfortunate girl! A. I don't care. I shall kill her. I want her to die.

Q. If you were big enough, would you kill your mother? A. Yes.

Q. And your grandmother? (the young woman's mother, present at the conference). A. No.

Q. And why wouldn't you kill her? A. I don't know.

Q. Do you love your father? A. Yes.

Q. Do you want to kill him? A. No.

Q. Yet he punishes you. A. That doesn't matter. I shan't kill him.

Q. Even if your father scolds and beats you, you love him? A. Yes.

Q. You have a little brother? A. Yes.

Q. Do you love him? A. No.

Q. Do you want him to die? A. Yes.

Q. Do you want to kill him? A. Yes. I asked papa to have him sent back from his nurse so that I may kill him.

Q. Why don't you love your mamma? A. I can't tell you. I want her to die.

Q. Where do you get such horrible ideas? A. My grandfather, my grandmother, and my aunt often said that my mother and my little brother ought to die.

Q. But that is not possible! A. Yes it is. I don't want to talk any more about my plans. I shall keep them for when I grow up.

This conversation lasted for an hour and a half. The sang-froid, calm, and indifference of the child excited in me a most painful feeling.

The little girl's stepmother was young, her physiognomy was gentle, her tone and manners pleasant. She lives in the Jardin des Plantes quarter and enjoys a good reputation, as does her husband. Following my advice, they sent the child to nuns, in the country, where she spent three months. Then her grandparents took her back to their home.

This observation is remarkable in more than one respect: first, because of the fixity of the desire, in a little girl of 8, to destroy her stepmother, who by her own statement had given her no grounds for complaint; second, because of the age in which this deplorable tendency developed. The grandfather and grandmother of this little girl, dissatisfied with their son's marriage, used violent language to express their disapproval, without foreseeing what effect such expressions might produce on a child of 2 or 3 years of age. What a lesson for parents who do not know how they appear, either in their words or in their deeds, in the presence of their children, whose mind and heart they corrupt from earliest infancy.

On June 15, 1834, in the little town of Bellesme, the corpse of a 2-year-old girl was removed from a well. Two days later, another child, 2½-years old, was taken from the same well. A young girl of 11, known throughout the district for her evil habits, never met smaller children without beating them or tormenting them in a thousand cruel ways. She had successively led the 2 children to the well and then pushed them in.

These three obeservations are extremely instructive. Was it not the lack of intellectual and moral development, the vices of these three children's, their upbringing, which deprived them of the discernment necessary to appreciate the horror of the acts they committed? Did not the habit of onanism, contracted at the age of 4, check the development of the first little girl? Did not the careless statements of the grandparents make a profound and fatal impression on the heart and mind of the subject of the second observation? As to the third, nothing corrected the wicked habits contracted as far back as infancy.

Doubtless the modern reader will consider the observations instructive too, not least for the tacit assumptions concerning the responsibility of children to their parents, the good conscience with which they were put out to nurse for years, and finally for the impressive diagnosis of *monomanie homicide.*

CONTENTS OF PREVIOUS VOLUMES

VOLUME I

VOLUME II